THE ITALIAN CINEMA BOOK

THE ITALIAN CINEMA BOOK

edited by PETER BONDANELLA

A BFI book published by Palgrave Macmillan

First published in 2014 by
PALGRAVE MACMILLAN

on behalf of the

BRITISH FILM INSTITUTE
21 Stephen Street, London W1T 1LN
www.bfi.org.uk

There's more to discover about film and television through the BFI. Our world-renowned archive, cinemas, festivals, films, publications and learning resources are here to inspire you.

Palgrave Macmillan in the UK is an imprint of Macmillan Publishers Limited, registered in England, company number 785998, of Houndmills, Basingstoke, Hampshire RG21 6XS. Palgrave Macmillan in the US is a division of St Martin's Press LLC, 175 Fifth Avenue, New York, NY 10010. Palgrave Macmillan is the global academic imprint of the above companies and has companies and representatives throughout the world. Palgrave® and Macmillan® are registered trademarks in the United States, the United Kingdom, Europe and other countries.

Cover image: 8½ (Federico Fellini, 1963), Cineriz di Angelo Rizzoli/Francinex
Designed by couch

Set by Cambrian Typesetters, Camberley, Surrey & couch
Printed in China

This book is printed on paper suitable for recycling and made from fully managed and sustained forest sources. Logging, pulping and manufacturing processes are expected to conform to the environmental regulations of the country of origin.

British Library Cataloguing-in-Publication Data
A catalogue record for this book is available from the British Library
A catalog record for this book is available from the Library of Congress

ISBN 978–1–84457–404–9 (pb)
ISBN 978–1–84457–405–6 (hb)

Contents

Acknowledgments

Naturally, my gratitude goes out to my contributors, all of whom had onerous research projects already underway before they kindly agreed to join this collective endeavour. Without the guidance of Rebecca Barden at BFI/Palgrave Macmillan, and the work of Sophia Contento, Rebecca's associate in charge of photographic illustrations, and my editor, Chantal Latchford, this book would never have been proposed or completed. A note of thanks goes to two graduate students at the University of Warwick, Dominic Holdaway and Mariarita Martino Grisà, whose invitation to speak at Warwick in 2010 shortly after my retirement awakened me from my metaphysical slumber about Italian film history and criticism and ultimately led to this book.

Let me also thank some of my former graduate students, all of whom through almost four decades have taught me a great deal about Italy: Torunn Haaland; Federico Pacchioni; Manuela Gieri; Andrea Ricci; Veronica Pravadelli; Virginia Picchietti; Colleen Ryan; John P. Welle; Joseph Markulin; Guy Raffa; Philip Balma; Lucio Bartolai; Norma Bouchard; Ryan Calabretta-Sajder; Angela Porcarelli; Fabio Benincasa; Nick Albanese; Ermanno Conti; Jon Cavallero; and Cristina Degli-Esposti.

Julia, my long-suffering wife and frequent collaborator, has retained her patience and understanding through what I have promised her is my very last book, and as always, she is my most demanding but also most sympathetic critic.

Notes on Contributors

GIANFRANCO ANGELUCCI is a scriptwriter, director, journalist and past Director of the Fondazione Federico Fellini who also teaches the History of Cinema at the Accademia delle Belle Arti in Carrara, Italy. He is the editor of a number of Fellini's film scripts; the author of two novels (one about Fellini); and co-scriptwriter of Fellini's penultimate film, *Intervista* (1987).

GIORGIO BERTELLINI is Associate Professor in the Departments of Screen Arts & Cultures and Romance Languages and Literatures at the University of Michigan; the author of *Emir Kusturica* and *Italy in Early American Cinema: Race, Landscape, and the Picturesque* (winner of the American Association for Italian Studies Book Award for Film Studies); and editor of *The Cinema of Italy* as well as *Italian Silent Cinema: A Reader*.

PETER BONDANELLA is past President of the American Association for Italian Studies, a member of the European Academy for Sciences and the Arts and Distinguished Professor Emeritus of Comparative Literature, Film Studies and Italian at Indiana University and the author of numerous books and editions, including *A History of Italian Cinema*; *Hollywood Italians: Dagos, Palookas, Romeos, Wise Guys and Sopranos*; *The Films of Roberto Rossellini*; *The Cinema of Federico Fellini*; and *The Eternal City: Roman Images in the Modern World*. He has translated or edited a number of Italian literary classics by Boccaccio, Cellini, Dante, Machiavelli and Vasari.

GUIDO BONSAVER is Professor of Italian Cultural History at Oxford University and a Fellow of Pembroke College. He is the author of *Censorship and Literature in Fascist Italy* (2007) and co-editor of *Culture, Censorhip and the State in 20th-century Italy*, with Robert Gordon. He collaborates with the BBC World Service on Italian cinema.

FLAVIA BRIZIO-SKOV is Professor of Italian at the University of Tennessee where she teaches Modern Literature and Cinema. She is the author of *La scrittura e la memoria: Lalla Romano* and *Antonio Tabucchi: Navigazioni in un universo narrative*; editor of *Reconstructing Societies in the Aftermath of War: Memory, Identity, and Reconciliation*; and *Popular Italian Cinema: Culture and Politics in a Postwar Society*; and has published numerous scholarly articles. She is currently working on a revisionist history of the Western.

GIAN PIERO BRUNETTA is Professor of Film History and Criticism at the University of Padua. Besides numerous books and editions in Italian, including the most comprehensive treatment of Italian cinematic history available, he is the editor of the five-volume *Storia del cinema mondiale* and author of *Guida alla storia del cinema italiano 1903–2003*, recently translated into English as *The History of Italian Cinema 1903–2003*. He was awarded the title of Commendatore della Repubblica Italiana for his contribution to the study of Italian cinema in 1995.

RÉKA BUCKLEY, formerly Senior Lecturer in Film Studies at the University of Portsmouth, is an independent scholar and the author of many articles on Italian film stars, film fandom, glamour, costume and fashion in Italian cinema, and the issues of stardom, audiences, gender, feminine beauty and national identity.

ANGELA DALLE VACCHE is a Professor of Film Studies at the Georgia Institute of Technology. She is the author of *The Body in the Mirror: Shapes of History in Italian Cinema*; *Cinema and Painting: How Art Is Used in Film*; *Diva: Defiance and Passion in Early Italian Cinema*; editor of *The Visual Turn: Classical Film Theory and Art History* as well as *Film, Art, New Media: Museum without Walls?*; and co-editor, with Brian Price, of *Color: The Film Reader*.

GIOVANNA DE LUCA is Associate Professor of Italian at the College of Charleston and the author of *Il punto di vista dell'infanzia nel cinema italiano e francese: rivisioni* and numerous articles on Italian literature and film.

DAVID FORGACS holds the Guido and Mariuccia Zerilli-Marimò Chair in Contemporary Italian Studies at New York University and is the author or editor of numerous works, including *The Antonio Gramsci Reader*; *Italian Cultural Studies*; *Roberto Rossellini, Magician of the Real*; and *Italy's Margins: Social Exclusion and Nation Formation since 1861*.

JEAN A. GILI is Professor Emeritus of the History of the Cinema at the Sorbonne. Besides being very active on a number of major film journals (*Cinéma, Écran, La Révue du cinéma/image et son* and *Positif*), he is the author of numerous books on Italian cinema, including *La Comédie italienne*; *L'Italie de Mussolini et son cinéma*; *Parigi-Roma: 50 anni di coproduzioni italo-francesi*; *Le Cinéma italien*; *Elio Petri & le cinéma Italien*; *Nanni Moretti*; *Francesco Rosi cinéma et pouvoir*; *Paolo et Vittorio Taviani*; *Luigi Comencini*; *Ettore Scola, une pensée graphique*; and *Fellini: Le magicien du réel*.

ROBERT S. C. GORDON is Professor of Modern Italian Culture and Head of the Department of Italian at the University of Cambridge. He is the editor of *The Cambridge Companion to Primo Levi*; co-editor of *Culture, Censorship and the State in 20th-century Italy* with Guido Bonsaver; and author of *Pasolini: Forms of Subjectivity* and *Bicycle Thieves*, as well as DVD and Blu-ray audio commentaries on Pasolini's *Teorema* and De Sica's *Bicycle Thieves*.

STEPHEN GUNDLE is Professor of Film and Television Studies at the University of Warwick and the author of *Death and the Dolce Vita: The Dark Side of Rome in the 1950s*; *Glamour: A History*; *Bellissima: Feminine Beauty and the Idea of Italy*; and *Between Hollywood and Moscow: The Italian Communists and the Challenge of Mass Culture, 1943–91*.

TORUNN HAALAND is Assistant Professor of Italian at Gonzaga University and the author of essays on Italian cinema and culture, as well as the recent *Italian Neorealist Cinema*.

DANIELLE HIPKINS is Senior Lecturer in Italian at the University of Exeter and specialises in feminist theory in relation to the study of Italian cinema, gender representation in post-war Italian cinema and spectatorship. She is the author of numerous essays in these areas as well as *Contemporary Italian Women Writers and Traces of the Fantastic* and co-editor of *War-torn Tales: Representing Gender and World War II in Literature and Film*.

MIKEL J. KOVEN is Senior Lecturer and Course Leader in Film Studies for the Institute of Humanities and Creative Arts at the University of Worcester. He has written extensively on folklore and Italian genre films, including a book entitled *La Dolce Morte: Vernacular Cinema and the Italian 'Giallo' Film*. He is also on the Editorial Board of the *Journal of Italian Cinema and Media Studies*.

MARCIA LANDY is Distinguished Professor of English/Film Studies with a secondary appointment in the French and Italian department at the University of Pittsburgh. Her books include *Fascism in Film: The Italian Commercial Cinema 1931–1943*; *British Genres: Cinema and Society, 1930–1960*; *Film, Politics, and Gramsci*; *The Folklore of Consensus: Theatricality in Italian Cinema*; *Italian Film*; and *Stardom, Italian Style: Screen Performance and Personality in Italian Cinema*.

RÉMI FOURNIER LANZONI is Assistant Professor of Italian at Wake Forest University and the author of *French Cinema: From Its Beginnings to the Present* and *Comedy Italian Style: The Golden Age of Italian Film Comedies*.

FLAVIA LAVIOSA is the founder and editor of the *Journal of Italian Cinema and Media Studies*; Senior Lecturer in Italian Studies and Cinema and Media Studies at Wellesley College; and the editor of *Visions of Struggle in Women's Filmmaking in the Mediterranean*.

GIANCARLO LOMBARDI is Professor of Italian and Comparative Literature at the College of Staten Island and at the CUNY Graduate Center. He is the author of *Rooms with a View: Feminist Diary Fiction*; and co-editor of *Remembering Aldo Moro: The Cultural Legacy of the 1978 Kidnapping and Murder* and *Terrorism, Italian Style: Representations of Political Violence in Contemporary Italian Cinema*.

MILLICENT MARCUS is Professor of Italian and Film Studies and Director of Graduate Studies in the Department of Italian Language and Literature at Yale University. She is the author of numerous books on Italian film, including *Italian Film in the Light of Neorealism*; *Filmmaking by the Book: Italian Cinema and Literary Adaptation*; *After Fellini: National Cinema in the Postmodern Age*; and *Italian Film in the Shadow of Auschwitz*.

GAETANA MARRONE is Professor of Italian at Princeton University, author of *The Gaze and the Labyrinth: The Cinema of Liliana Cavani*; editor of *New Landscapes in Contemporary Italian Cinema*, film issue of *Annali d'Italianistica*; and general editor of the two-volume *Encyclopedia of Italian Literary Studies*. She is currently finishing a book entitled *History, Memory, and Representation: The Films of Francesco Rosi*.

GINO MOLITERNO is Senior Lecturer in Film Studies at the Australian National University. He is the General Editor of the *Historical Dictionary of Italian Cinema* and the *Encyclopedia of Contemporary Italian Culture*.

ÁINE O'HEALY is Professor of Italian and the Director of the Humanities Program at Loyola Marymount University. She is the author of numerous essays on Italian cinema; co-editor of *Transnational Feminism in Film and Media* as well as a special issue of *Feminist Media Studies* titled *Transcultural Mediations and Transnational Politics of Difference*; and co-curator of the Global Cinema Series for Palgrave Macmillan.

ALAN O'LEARY is Associate Professor in Italian at the University of Leeds; the founding editor of the annual film issue of *The Italianist*; the author of *Tragedia all'italiana: Italian Cinema and Italian Terrorisms 1970–2010* and *Fenomenologia del cinepanettone*; and co-editor of *Imagining Terrorism: The Rhetoric and Representation of Political Violence in Italy, 1969–2006* and *Terrorism, Italian Style: Representations of Political Violence in Contemporary Italian Cinema*. With Catherine O'Rawe, he edited the special number of *Italian Studies* on 'Thinking Italian Cinema'.

CATHERINE O'RAWE is Senior Lecturer in Italian at the University of Bristol and the author of *Authorial Echoes: Texuality and Self-plagiarism in the Narrative of Luigi Pirandello*, as well as numerous articles and book chapters on Italian cinema. She has co-edited *The Femme Fatale: Images, Histories, Contexts* and the special number of *Italian Studies* on 'Thinking Italian Cinema' with Alan O'Leary.

LAURA RASCAROLI is Senior Lecturer in Film Studies at University College Cork. She is the author of *The Personal Camera: Subjective Cinema and the Essay Film* and the co-author, with Ewa Mazierska, of *The Cinema of Nanni Moretti: Dreams and Diaries*; *From Moscow to Madrid: Postmodern Cities, European Cinema*; and *Crossing New Europe: Postmodern Travel and the European Road Movie*. She co-edited *Antonioni: Centenary Essays*, with John David Rhodes and *The Cause of Cosmopolitanism: Dispositions, Models, Transformations*, with Patrick O'Donovan. She is General Editor of *Alphaville: Journal of Film and Screen Media*.

JACQUELINE REICH is Professor and Chair of the Department of Communication and Media Studies at Fordham University. She is the author of *Beyond the Latin Lover: Marcello Mastroianni, Masculinity, and Italian Cinema* and co-editor of *Re-viewing Fascism: Italian Cinema, 1922–1942*. She also curates the book series, *New Directions in National Cinemas*, for Indiana University Press.

DANA RENGA is Assistant Professor of Italian and Film at Ohio State University and the editor of *Mafia Movies: A Reader*, and the author of *Unfinished Business: Screening the Italian Mafia in the New Millennium*.

MARK SHIEL is Reader in Film Studies at King's College, London. His research interests are in cinema and the city, Italian neorealism and Hollywood cinema. He is the author of *Italian Neorealism: Rebuilding the Cinematic City* and *Hollywood Cinema and the Real Los Angeles*; co-editor of *Screening the City* and *Cinema and the City*; and has contributed chapters to *Cinematic Rome* and a number of other books. He is presently editing a collection of essays entitled *Architectures of Revolt: The Cinematic City circa 1968*.

PAULINE SMALL is Senior Lecturer in Film at Queen Mary, University of London. She is the author of *Sophia Loren: Moulding the Star* and numerous articles and chapters on diverse aspects of Italian cinema and contemporary Italian film directors.

JON SOLOMON is Robert D. Novak Professor of Western Civilization and Culture, Professor of the Classics and Professor of Cinema at the University of Illinois. He is the author of *The Ancient World in the Cinema* and combines a distinguished career of traditional classical scholarship with a keen interest in the relationship between contemporary film and the classical world.

PIERRE SORLIN is Professor Emeritus at the University of Paris III–Sorbonne Novelle but continues to work as a researcher at the Istituto Parri–Emilia Romagna. He is the author of many books on Italian cinema and the sociology of the cinema including: *Sociologie du cinéma*; *The Film in History: Restaging the Past*; *European Cinemas, European Societies: 1939–1990*; *Italian National Cinema 1896–1996*; *Dreamtelling*; *L'immagine e l'evento*; *I figli di Nadar. Il secolo dell'immagine analogica*; *Persona. Del ritratto in pittura*; and *Gli Italiani al cinema*.

M. THOMAS VAN ORDER is Chair of the Department of Italian at Middlebury College, a specialist in Italian film music and the author of *Listening to Fellini: Music and Meaning in Black and White*.

FABIO VIGHI is Reader at the School of European Languages, Translation and Politics at Cardiff University. He is the author of a number of books, including: *Le ragioni dell'altro. La formazione intellettuale di Pasolini tra saggistica, letteratura e cinema*; *Traumatic Encounters in Italian Film: Locating the Cinematic Unconscious*; *Sexual Difference in European Cinema: The Curse of Enjoyment*; and *Critical Theory and Film: Rethinking Ideology through Film Noir*.

CHRISTOPHER WAGSTAFF is Senior Lecturer of Italian Studies at the University of Reading. He is the author of *Italian Neorealism: An Aesthetic Approach* and *Il Conformista (The Conformist)*, as well as numerous articles on Italian cinema and the film industry there.

JOHN P. WELLE is Professor of Romance Languages and Literatures, and of Film, Television and Theatre at the University of Notre Dame. He is the author of *The Poetry of Andrea Zanzotto*, the editor of 'Film and Literature', *Annali d'Italianistica* (1988); and the translator of *Peasants Wake for Fellini's Casanova and Other Poems* by Andrea Zanzotto. His research on early Italian cinema appears in journals and edited volumes including *Bianco e Nero*, *Cinema & Cinema*, *Film History* and *The Printed Media in Fin-de-siècle Italy*.

MARY P. WOOD is Emeritus Professor of European Cinema and a Fellow of Birkbeck, University of London. She currently holds a Leverhulme Emeritus Fellowship. She is the author of *Italian Cinema*, *Contemporary European Cinema* and numerous articles and book chapters on Rosi, Zeffirelli, Sorrentino, Italian film noir and popular Italian film genres.

VITO ZAGARRIO is Professor of Cinema and Television at the University of Rome III and a film-maker. He is the author of numerous books, including: *Cinema e fascism*; *La meglio gioventù – Nuovo cinema italiano*; and the editor of *Storia del cinema italiano 1977–1985*.

Federico Fellini directs Anita Ekberg on the set of *La dolce vita* (*La Dolce Vita*, 1960), one of the landmark films of postwar Italian cinema

General Introduction

Rethinking Italian Cinema

Peter Bondanella

The Italian Cinema Book provides a readable, reliable, provocative and innovative treatment of the most important historical, aesthetic and cultural aspects of the Italian cinema throughout its long and glorious history. It offers the film student and film enthusiast a broad and clear understanding of the major developments in what may be called twentieth-century Italy's greatest and most original modern art form. This collection of essays comprises five chronologically organised sections devoted to the silent era (1895–1922); the birth of the talkies and the fascist period (1922–45); post-war cinematic culture: neorealism and beyond (1945–59); the golden age of the Italian cinema and the triumph of genre and the art film (1960–80); and an age of crisis, transition and consolidation (1981 to the present). A sixth section dealing with new directions in critical approaches to Italian cinema concentrated primarily on the future of criticism, Italian cinema's future, its impact on other cinemas and cultures, and outside influences that are currently influencing its present development. Each essay contains suggestions for further reading that are narrowly focused upon the topic of the individual essay, while the more general bibliography at the end of the book will give the reader a broader but necessarily selective view of the voluminous critical and historical literature the Italian cinema has inspired.

The thirty-nine contributors represent an international team of writers and scholars from Italy, France, the United Kingdom, Australia and the United States. It includes not only established and authoritative critics in the field who have published on Italian cinema for decades and have earned reputations as key figures in the rise of Italian cinema studies within academia, but also extremely productive and creative younger scholars at work in the United Kingdom and the United States. Indeed, *The Italian Cinema Book* embodies the belief that Italian Cinema Studies have become significant in the study of contemporary Italian culture, joining the traditional concentrations on Dante or Renaissance literature. Today, justifying the inclusion of Italy's cinema into a university curriculum no longer rests upon a somewhat parochial and tentative attempt to integrate it by teaching courses comparing literature and film; by organising classes around Italian film as primarily a 'reflection' of Italian society or daily life; or as a practical means of appealing to an undergraduate population more attracted to the cinema than to literature or language. Today, studying Italian cinema has become the driving force behind a larger and even more revolutionary movement away from a predominantly linguistic, literary or philological treatment of things Italian in the universities of the English-speaking world toward what may more generally be called a Cultural Studies approach.

Writing on Italian cinema has also evolved considerably since the immediate post-war period when Italian cinema was initially championed by French critics – foremost among them being André Bazin – whose polemical essays and intelligent reviews elevated Italian neorealism and a collection of what later became known as auteurs (Rossellini, Antonioni, De Sica, Fellini, Visconti) to a position of authority in the history of the development of the cinema. Few English-speaking critics and film historians knew much about Italian film criticism, but French publications provided a body of critical work that was enthusiastic, well informed, and persuasive. Director-oriented monographs which formed the *Cinéma d'aujourd'hui* series from Éditions Seghers of Paris were models of the kind of auteur-specific writing of the day, while thematically oriented collections of essays in the *Études cinématographiques* series from Éditions Minard of Paris or other French film periodicals such as *Positif*, offered templates for exploring larger currents in Italian cinema. Privileging neorealism as Italy's most enduring contribution to the evolution of the language of cinema and celebrating the great cinematic works of Italy's post-war auteurs in the 1950s and the 1960s, also allowed Italianists to argue that, far from lowering the academic standards of their discipline by teaching and writing about Italian film, such a development actually focused on the high-culture aspects of film and served as a useful classroom tool to deal with art and life in the peninsula in the contemporary period. For some time, the only film history available in English during the very height of Italy's golden age was also French – Pierre Leprohoun's *The Italian Cinema*, originally published by Seghers in 1966 and translated into English in 1972.

My own first attempt to provide an English-language history of Italian cinema appeared in 1982 as *Italian Cinema: From Neorealism to the Present* and went through three successive revisions, but its traditional focus on neorealism and major art-house directors could not be sustained as quite different critical approaches to the subject developed and more and more attention was paid to the silent period, cinema during the fascist era, and the many popular genres or topics that had evolved as legitimate subjects of study by the end of the twentieth century (the sword-and-sandal epic or the peplum; the *giallo* thriller; the crime film; the spaghetti horror film; films about terrorism) and that could now be combined with the two popular genres that had always attracted critical attention – the spaghetti Western and the *commedia all'italiana*. It took me the second half of my career to offer a correction to this overemphasis upon neorealism and art films with *A History of Italian Cinema* that first appeared in 2009. With entirely new chapters on the silent film, cinema during the fascist period, and separate treatments of the peplum, the *giallo*, the crime film, and the Italian spaghetti horror films, now added to chapters on the Western and the comedy and combined with the former attention to the grand tradition of neorealism and auteur cinema, I attempted to rewrite and revise Italian film history to reflect contemporary critical inquiry. As one reviewer of this work in the *Times Literary Supplement* generously noted, reading the new book 'feels like watching the tectonic plates of a discipline shifting, inexorably but at times uneasily, before your eyes'.[1]

It is my hope that those shifting 'tectonic plates' will shift even further and with greater ease and transparency in *The Italian Cinema Book*. In this case, the prime movers in this shifting are the contributors to this anthology, virtually all of whose essays reflect 'rethinking' typical of writing on Italian cinema today. Outstanding treatments of Italy's glorious heritage from the silent era and the fascist period have been produced in the last several decades, primarily by the contributors to these two sections of this book. Our consideration of post-war cinematic realism still considers neorealism worthy of further study but from different points of view than were common decades ago, and newer perspectives on other films made during the brief moment neorealism captured the attention of the world's moviegoers show that Italian cinema cannot be measured solely on the works of Rossellini or De Sica between 1945 and 1955. Neorealism was, after all, more popular abroad than in Italy, and Italian cinema was moving at the very same time toward the heyday of 'Hollywood on the Tiber', the antithesis of neorealist aesthetics. With the golden age of Italian cinema during the late 1950s and the 1960s into the mid-1970s, the great auteur films of a first generation of directors (Rossellini, Fellini, Antonioni, Visconti) gave birth to another successive generation of auteurs (Pontecorvo, Monicelli, Pasolini, Bertolucci, Bellocchio, the Taviani brothers, Olmi, Leone and many others), with entirely different aesthetic ideas and ideological perspectives. The high-brow Italian cinema was rewarded with numerous festival prizes, Oscars and considerable punch at the box office, and Italy's reputation as a workshop for great cinema reached a pinnacle during this golden age, challenging even the economic and cultural hegemony of Hollywood.

However, what represented a dramatic and revolutionary change in affairs during this period, often stimulated by the presence of Hollywood productions in Rome or co-productions with France, was the unparalleled impact of Italian genre films – not just the fame of a Fellini or an Antonioni. Beginning with the peplum in the late 1950s and continuing with the spaghetti Western; the *commedia all'italiana*; political films; thrillers and horror movies; and crime films into the early 1970s, the Italian film industry – led by a group of innovative producers and production companies that understood public taste (and sometimes exploited the public's lack of it!), a group never subsequently equalled in talent or foresight – managed to generate substantial profits from what used to be denigrated as 'B' films. And these were in addition to the equally impressive box-office results from smash hits directed by auteurs. In short, low-brow and high-brow film culture joined hands to create a boom in the industry. The most significant of these successes came in the dramatic change in the Western film as a result of the international success of Sergio Leone; more than 400 Italian Westerns followed Leone's example. Causing a major shift of direction in a Hollywood genre so integral to popular *American* culture seems to this day quite simply almost unimaginable, and the influence of Italy's version of the Western myth, as well as its other 'B' genre films, continues today in the work of such figures as the postmodern American director Quentin Tarantino. By the time the golden age drew to a close, however, Italy's love affair with the cinema, at least insofar as popular audiences were concerned, had greatly diminished. This anthology pays ample attention to the genre film, unjustly ignored for many years by historians and critics, and its treatment of the traditionally popular auteurs considers them in new critical contexts that reflect preoccupations different from those typical of the classic approach to auteur cinema.

Of course, Italian films after the mid-1970s, perhaps the high watermark of Italy's auteur cinema as well as its genre-film success at international box offices, remain worthy of study. And new theoretical approaches have brought new insights. In particular, star studies have advanced beyond the kind of writing typical of fan magazines and, armed with heuristic theories derived largely from English or American film criticism, now have much to teach us about depictions of masculinity or femininity (including feminist insights not just from critics but also from female directors). Two particularly Italian phenomena – one with an international impact (the *Mondo* craze, leading ultimately to the 'shockumentary'); and one virtually impossible to export abroad (the yearly *cinepanettone* or Christmas film) – have much to tell the Italian fan of film about cultural attitudes and the composition of film audiences in the peninsula. Examining Italian film music (particularly its practice of post-synchronisation of sound) or a representative example of how Italian auteur scripts were produced, offers insight into how Hollywood and Cinecittà film cultures differ. And Italian movies about the Mafia or the Camorra, on the one hand, and terrorists, on the other – two *filoni* or thematic preoccupations of the last several decades of Italian film-making – have produced some outstanding international commercial or critical successes in an era when the industry had slipped into an intellectual and economic decline. Moreover, these treatments of events 'torn from the headlines' of the daily newspapers have reinvigorated Italian cinema's depiction of social and economic conditions in a way that has not been seen since the post-war neorealist period.

Finally, *The Italian Cinema Book* looks forward to the future and to the questions raised by rapid technological, cultural and economic change in society and industry. To succeed in the international marketplace, must Italian films become 'international', whatever that might mean? How does a film-maker today approach the new phenomenon of a 'multicultural' Italy with hundreds of thousands, even millions of immigrants from as far as China, the Philippines and Africa, all of whom represent departures from traditional Italian linguistic, religious and cultural behaviours? What does contemporary film theory contribute to our discussions of Italian films? What contemporary impact has the best of Italy's auteur cinema had on the rest of the world? And what prospects are open to the future historian of the Italian cinema?

These and many other complex and interesting issues are considered in these essays which represent the cutting edge of contemporary thinking about Italian film, a field of interest and study that has undergone fundamental changes during the past decade. Perhaps most importantly, one result of the recent 'rethinking' of Italian cinema has been the gradual but inescapable conclusion that writing on this field must not separate the low brow from the high brow; the popular from the art-house film; elite subject matter from the nitty-gritty realm of economic and sociological data; and the results of archival research from the insights of theoretically engaged discourse. I believe all of the contributors to this volume subscribe to the view expressed in the concluding essay by Gian Piero Brunetta, who calls not for *one* history of Italian cinema but *many different histories* of Italian cinema, with *multiple* points of view and *different* and *contrasting* perspectives.

It is my hope that reading *The Italian Cinema Book* will provoke thought and encourage readers and filmgoers to explore the riches of a great national cinema, a treasure trove of delights and surprises, that readers will be challenged and amused by the questions and issues its contributors raise.

NOTE

1. Robert Gordon, 'Film History Recut', *Times Literary Supplement* (1 July 2011), p. 28. For recent reconsiderations of the issues involved in writing contemporary Italian film history, see the following essays of mine: 'New Directions in Teaching Film in Italian Studies Programs', *Italica* vol. 83 no. 1 (2006), pp. 7–19; 'My Path to Italian Cinema', *The Italianist* vol. 31 no. 2 (2011), pp. 276–80; and 'Writing Italian Film History: A First-person Account', *Italian Studies* vol. 67 no. 2 (July 2012), pp. 252–66; plus the 'Preface' to *A History of Italian Cinema* (New York and London: Continuum, 2009), pp. vii–xi.

FURTHER READING

Bertellini, Giorgio (ed.), *The Cinema of Italy* (London: Wallflower Press, 2004).

Bondanella, Peter, *A History of Italian Cinema* (New York and London: Continuum, 2009).

Brunetta, Gian Piero, *Guida alla storia del cinema italiano 1905–2003* (Turin: Einaudi, 2003); English edn, *The History of Italian Cinema: A Guide to Italian Film from Its Origins to the Twenty-first Century*, trans. Jeremy Parzen (Princeton, NJ: Princeton University Press, 2009).

——, *Storia del cinema italiano 1895–1945* (Rome: Editori Riuniti, 1979).

——, *Storia del cinema italiano dal 1945 agli anni ottanta* (Rome: Editori Riuniti, 1982).

——, *Storia del cinema italiano*, 4 vols (Rome: Editori Riuniti, 1993).

    Vol. I: *Il cinema muto 1895–1929*.

    Vol. II: *Il cinema del regime 1929–1945*.

    Vol. III: *Dal neorealismo al miracolo economico 1945–1959*.

    Vol. IV: *Dal miracolo economico agli anni novanta 1960–1993*.

Landy, Marcia, *Italian Film: The National Tradition* (New York: Cambridge University Press, 2000).

Sorlin, Pierre, *Italian National Cinema 1896–1996* (London: Routledge, 1996).

Wood, Mary P., *Italian Cinema* (Oxford: Berg, 2005).

PART ONE

The Silent Era

Introduction

Peter Bondanella

It is too easily forgotten that the cinema was initially a European, not a Hollywood invention. Between 1895 and the outbreak of the Great War, Italy's silent cinema gained enormous audiences all over the world, particularly with its production of historical epics boasting what would later become the proverbial 'cast of thousands', and by diva films starring sensual and enchanting actresses (rivals of Hollywood 'vamps' such as Theda Bara). In terms of international influence, Italian silent film was far more important and consequential than were the Italian films produced between the birth of the Italian sound film in 1930 and the end of the fascist era in 1945. Despite the almost universal international distribution of the best of Italian silent films in the second decade of the twentieth century, only a handful of films are now available on video or DVD. Even the film historian must travel to various film archives or film festivals devoted to silent cinema in order to see more than a very small percentage of the total output of the Italian film industry from this initial period. It has been estimated that of the hundreds of films produced, roughly one quarter has been preserved partially or completely.

In the essays in this first section, Giorgio Bertellini outlines the international influences that helped to give birth to the native Italian cinema, particularly those from France and the US. Foreign markets often dictated the kinds of films that were profitable for the native industry and when such markets dried up, the Italian industry fell upon hard times. John P. Welle focuses upon the rise of the specific kind of Italian stardom its silent films produced, visualised through the print media of divismo and the emergence of Italian film periodicals during this period. Between 1907 and 1920, Italy produced ninety film periodicals, an astounding figure that grew to some 200 by 1931 when soundtracks to films became the norm. Some of these periodicals reached audiences of tens of thousands of readers, and these fascinating documents tell us much about early film culture. Some of the most highly regarded avant-garde artists, novelists, playwrights and drama critics were regular contributors to these numerous publications, a great many of which (like so many of Italian silent films themselves) have received little critical attention.

Angela Dalle Vacche and Jacqueline Reich focus attention on the most important commercial and artistic genres during this period: the diva film; comedies; and epic films. Their analyses demonstrate that well before the popularity of auteur films, silent genre films of the comic, historical or adventure variety made up a fundamental part of industrial production even before the introduction of sound; they also prefigure the post-World War II success of such genre films as the peplum, the Western and the *commedia all'italiana*. Although it is difficult to underestimate the impact of the Italian diva film upon international film culture in the silent period, it may well have had less of a lasting influence on world cinema than Italy's comic and historical works.

1 Silent Italian Cinema

An International Story[1]

Giorgio Bertellini

Rather than an unmistakable index of distinct national features, the emergence and development of silent cinema in general resulted from dense international exchanges of talents, film-making styles and business practices. In this regard, the case of Italian film culture is perhaps more peculiar than emblematic. Even before the beginning of the domestic production of fiction films, which occurred only in 1905 – that is, ten years after the Lumières publicly presented the *cinématographe* – foreign elements were affecting Italian film culture through the manufacturing and distribution *in* Italy of films *about* Italy. This was not a novel phenomenon. It largely upgraded centuries of comparable image-making practices through a new technology of reproduction. After 1905, foreign cultural influences and expectations continued to inform the national film scene of production and exhibition at many levels. They affected the development of key genres (i.e. historical epics, literary adaptations, comedies, actuality films and southern melodramas), popular themes (antiquity, the Renaissance, natural disasters, crime), film-making and distribution formats (i.e. serials), casting practices of performers and technicians (i.e. comedian André Deed and cinematographer/operator Segundo de Chomòn) and even avant-garde poetics and experimentations.

At the core of how foreign factors variously affected Italian cinema's international character and address was the idea of Italy as an exotic place that entertained a distinct cultural and even anthropological relationship with history. For decades, the 'voyage to Italy' was a familiar and well-practised tradition that in paintings, prints, photographs and illustrated tourist guides had relied on two preferred aesthetic modes – antiquity and the picturesque. Such resilient vectors of representation provided the impetus behind Italian silent cinema's golden age between 1908 and 1914 –

namely, its tremendous worldwide success in sheer numbers (about 6,000 titles, out of about 10,000 for the entire silent era); and aesthetic taste. In more antagonistic fashion, the same purported relationship with the past animated a host of anti-passatist positions – inferior only in number and popular appeal – centred on futurist, anti-decadent and anti-antiquarian stances. This oppositional aesthetic mode informed scattered experimental, and overtly modernist, productions, including Anton Giulio Bragaglia's futurist *Thaïs* (*Thaïs*, 1916), André Deed's feature-length comedy *L'uomo meccanico* (*The Mechanical Man*, 1921) and Corrado D'Errico's experimental *Stramilano* (*Supermilan*, 1930). It also affected the cultural halo of certain stars (i.e. Elettra Raggio) and informed the critical work of individual writers, i.e. Bragaglia's *Fotodinamismo futurista* (*Futurist Photodynamism*, 1911). Unsurprisingly, these efforts gained little notoriety, at home and abroad – an indication of the influential role of foreign expectations in the domestic and international positioning of Italian silent film culture.

BEGINNINGS

Between 1896 and 1905, the vast majority of films produced and exhibited in Italy were of foreign origin – mostly French, American and British. Film-making in Italy followed the grand visual tradition associated with the Grand Tour, which had been relying on domestic and international networks of individual artists, print-makers and photographers as well as educated consumers. Between 1896 and 1904, the very mobile and efficient Lumière film operators shot more than 100 'views' (*vues*) in the peninsula. Other foreign operators included Thomas Edison's former chief engineer, W. K. L. Dickson; British photographers Birt Acres and Henry Short; and the British film pioneers

Charles Urban and George Albert Smith. Their films revealed choices of touristic and political relevance consonant with the desire for popularity and the recognition of the new medium's educational value. Film-makers focused on inaugurations, public commemorations and military parades held in Turin and Rome, and known urban and natural landscapes. Particularly famous were the Lumière tracking and panning views of Venice, such as *Panorama de la Place Saint Marc pris d'un bateau, Venise* (*Panorama of St. Mark's Square Taken from a Boat, Venice*, 1896), obtained by placing a camera on a moving gondola.

In Naples, film-makers opted for the picturesque angle rather than the political or archaeological view, showing volcanic eruptions (Vesuvius and Mt Etna) and scenes from nature.

For Italians, foreign films' focus on famous landscapes, monuments and individuals fostered dynamics of national self-exploration and display. Before 1905, early Italian cinematographers, whether affiliated with major foreign firms, particularly Lumière, or working independently as photographers, duplicated this fashionable taste for national history and geography. Their names may not be well known, but their impact was significant because they combined their technical, scientific or journalistic interests with their influential role as local exhibitors. In their non-fiction films, Francesco Felicetti and Filoteo Alberini in Rome, Giuseppe Filippi and Italo Pacchioni in Milan, Vittorio Calcina and Roberto Omegna in Turin, Luigi Sciutto in Genoa, Rodolfo Remondini in Florence, Giovanni Troncone in Naples, Raffaello Lucarelli in Palermo and even Luca Comerio, the famous photojournalist based in Milan, but active all over Italy and the world, corroborated familiar notions of touristic and national relevance by filming renowned urban locations and actual events of momentous and solemn significance, including state funerals and ceremonies, army parades and religious celebrations. Between 1896 and 1905, Italian non-fiction productions amounted to about 160 titles, a fraction of the more than 2,500 foreign travelogues and *actualités* that had been made in Italy during the same period. The difference in number did not imply a change in subject matter, which remained cultured and cosmopolitan. Initially, in fact, the individuals involved in making, exhibiting and viewing Italian films were members of the aristocracy and urban bourgeoisie. When the film industry began to aspire to a broader social appeal, it followed a known geographical divide variously affected by foreign forces.

In the northern regions around the Po Valley, films gained a wider circulation thanks to the established circuits of Italian and foreign itinerant exhibitors known as *ambulanti* who operated independently or within travelling circus shows. Their competition with permanent movie theatres enhanced films' interclass recognition and small-town popularity. In the south, except for Naples, full-fledged movie theatres were scarce, located only in major centres. As a result, not until the mid-1910s did southern Italian film patronage expand beyond urban, middle-class limits, when film-makers successfully co-opted local stage and musical talents to exploit their domestic and international appeal.

PRODUCTION

Italy's first film factories were located in the nation's political and industrial centres – Rome, Turin and Milan – where worldly noblemen and resourceful entrepreneurs intertwined financial and cultural goals. The transnational pattern of development of these companies was fairly similar. Their founders and managers journeyed abroad, mainly to France, to buy the newest equipment and to familiarise themselves with established modes of production or with larger film markets. Then they built new, large studios, attracted foreign artistic and technical personnel, particularly from the giant Pathé Frères, and opened distribution offices abroad. They were very quickly successful in the domestic market and even more so internationally, mainly with comedies, Shakespearian adaptations and dramatisations of French melodramas or revolutionary narratives. Distinct national recognition came with historical epics – often adapted from international

Panorama de la Place Saint Marc pris d'un bateau, Venise (1896)

La caduta di Troia (1911)

bestselling novels. Although the very first fiction film, *La presa di Roma: 20 settembre 1870* [*The Capture of Rome, 20 September 1870*, 1905], addressed a key episode in Italy's state formation, the subject of the most successful Italian films of the pre-World War I period was not the heroism of the Risorgimento, but antiquity in general. As a cosmopolitan 'beaten track' and repository of national narratives of legitimacy and officialdom, ancient Rome was a more universal basis for both political and commercial designs, in a combination of patriotic impetus and antiquarian sensationalism.

Large-scale historical epics gave aesthetic and marketing self-awareness to Italian film companies. In 1908, Turin's Ambrosio Film released *Gli ultimi giorni di Pompei* (*The Last Days of Pompeii*, 1908), an ambitious one-reeler that greatly capitalised on the established intermedial attraction for ancient calamities and Edward Bulwer-Lytton's 1834 bestselling novel of the same title. Although foreign trade periodicals mistook the Italian film as a production of its distributors (Warwick Company in England, and Raleigh & Roberts in the US), praise for its realistic *mise en scène* became prototypical of the criticism reserved for, and constantly sought after by, later Italian productions. A year later, Ambrosio Film released the toga-drama *Nerone* (*Nero; or, The Burning of Rome*) partly to capitalise on the domestic popularity of Pietro Cossa's 1872 play, but mostly to ride the wave of the international success of Barnum & Bailey's 1884 eponymous pyrodrama.

As the foreign press promoted the notion that Italian film companies could 'naturally' specialise and excel in historical epics, Italian film-makers began to aspire to archaeological and antiquarian accuracy. The ground-breaking novelty of Itala Film's *La caduta di Troia* (*The Fall of Troy*, 1911), directed by the visionary Giovanni Pastrone, was not just its comparatively colossal two-reel length, but also its unprecedented rendering of an ancient three-dimensional space in place of old painted backdrops.

Painter-director Enrico Guazzoni did the same by creating a sumptuous *mise en scène* for *Bruto* (*Brutus*, 1911), adapted from Shakespeare's *The Tragedy of Julius Caesar*, which inaugurated for Cines (Rome) a profitable agreement with the Chicago distributor and Edison Trust member, George Kleine. Attuned to the international correlation of Italian art cinema with large-scale historical representations, Kleine, who also distributed films by Ambrosio and Pasquali & Co. and later even attempted an Italian production venture, launched *Bruto* as 'a marvel of magnificence, staged in splendor, wrapped in grandeur' and catered it to the affluent American middle class. At Cines, Guazzoni continued in this vein with the multi-reelers *La Gerusalemme liberata* (*Crusaders* aka *Jerusalem Delivered*, 1911), adapted from the epic poem by Torquato Tasso; *Marcantonio e Cleopatra* (*Antony and Cleopatra*, 1913), from Shakespeare; and his masterpiece *Quo vadis?* (1913), from Henryk Sienkiewicz's bestselling novel. Italy's most modern and well-equipped film studio, Milano Films, poured its resources into *La divina commedia: Inferno*, also known as *L'Inferno* (*Dante's Inferno*, 1911). The first Italian film to be deposited for copyright, *L'Inferno* made Dante intelligible to the world's masses in fifty-four scenes. Finally, Pastrone engaged the renowned writer and poet

Gabriele D'Annunzio for the erudite intertitles of the gargantuan twelve-reeler *Cabiria* (1914), whose magisterial set design impressed D. W. Griffith to the point that he tried to duplicate it for *Intolerance* (1916) with the help of the same Italian technicians.

For cultured Italian producers and spectators, the visualisation of *Romanitas* participated in the idea of a *continuity* between modern Italy and ancient Rome, evoked in the recent celebrations of the fiftieth anniversary of the formation of a unified Italian state in 1861. As such, *Romanitas* resonated with geopolitical ideas of state officialdom and national distinction. Decades after their first US run, many Italian historical epics were still screened in American colleges, school districts and educational societies as the most accurate and entertaining visualisation of humanity's Roman historical and political patrimony. The early success of these films in the first decade of the twentieth century prompted Italian producers to replicate the same narrative and visual formulae a decade later, with costly remakes of older hits, which included *Quo vadis?* (*Quo Vadis?*, 1924) and another version of *Gli ultimi giorni di Pompei* (*The Last Days of Pompeii*, 1926).

By then the genre, having failed to renew its narrative and visual appeal, found distribution mainly among America's Little Italies. Italian immigrants had learned to appreciate historical and literary epics, although typically after their exhibition in cheaper neighbourhood theatres. In the same venues, however, from the late 1910s, the most nationalistic of Italian film genres was competing with exceptionally popular Neapolitan melodramas. By featuring regional dialect performers and by establishing crucial relationships with the local stage and music scene, Naples' productions had learned to tell stories rooted in the city's culture of vernacular *pochades*, songs and stage melodramas. Bypassing fascist censorship, countless Neapolitan productions, including Dora Films' *A Santanotte* (*The Holy Night*, 1922) and *Core 'e frate* (*Brother's Heart*, 1923), found a way into the world's Little Italies. In 1920, this kind of film was one of Italian cinema's most profitable genres, to the point that it encompassed the re-release of such classics of Neapolitan melodrama as *Assunta Spina* (*Assunta Spina*, 1915), starring Francesca Bertini and directed by Francesca Bertini and Gustavo Serena.

Assunta Spina (1915)

Maciste all'Inferno (1926)

Internationally, a few other Italian genres held great popular appeal. From the beginning, several Italian companies believed comedies could enable them to enter the lucrative market of popular and populist entertainments. Although devoid of recognisable national and cultural referents to their production origin, most comedies poked fun and jokingly subverted bourgeois customs and habits, particularly regarding sartorial and ethical codes. In addition to the clownesque and acrobatic routines borrowed from the circus and other live public performances, the French film industry was the model to which early Italian comedies turned for inspiration. In 1908, Itala Film's artistic director Giovanni Pastrone lured Pathé star André Deed, famous as Boireau, and renamed him Cretinetti. With his Italian films, Deed achieved fame again in France, this time as Gribouille, as Foolshead in most English-speaking countries, and as Toribio or Don Toribio in most Spanish-speaking ones. At Itala, Deed

starred in about ninety films, some of which he directed, mainly impersonating the character of the restless boy donning bourgeois outfits (i.e. opera hat, walking stick) in an often surrealist display of anarchic energy. He returned to France in 1912 and then back to Italy in 1915–16 (where he starred in the famous *Cretinetti e gli stivali del brasiliano* [*Foolshead and the Brazilian Man's Boots*, 1916]) and 1919–22. Other comedians who became famous in Europe and in the US (although not necessarily as performers in Italian films) included Marcel Fabre (Robinet) and Ferdinand Guillaume (known as Tontolini and Polidor).

In the mid-1910s, with mounting competition from American slapstick comedians, Fabre and Deed switched to feature films doing double duty as actors and directors. Their *Le avventure straordinarissime di Saturnino Farandola* [*The Extraordinary Adventures of Saturnino Farandola*, 1914] and *L'uomo meccanico*, while beloved by the futurists, were unsuccessful. The season of silent Italian comedy was over. Still, the genre had taught Italian producers the key practice of serial production, consisting of character recognition, formulaic narratives and intertextual repetitions. Italian producers duplicated French and American practices and applied them to crime narratives, as in the cycle of films starring the character of Za la Mort (Emilio Ghione), released from 1914 to 1924, and to the so-called 'athletic-acrobatic genre', self-contained episodes centred on the figure of the *forzuto* (strongman). First seen in circus shows and in the historical epics of the early 1910s, the *forzuto* became the familiar and benign hero of popular serials. For more than a decade after *Cabiria*, Maciste (Bartolomeo Pagano) dropped his slave costume and his blackface make-up to wear the patriotic uniforms of Alpine soldier, policeman or virtuous film star. Other recognised heroes included Ausonia, Ursus, Sansonia, Galaor, Ajax, Saetta and a few strongwomen, such as Sansonette and Astrea. Unlike the historical epics, the strongmen films maintained their appeal until the mid-1920s, but found success mainly in European and non-Western markets and infrequently crossed the Atlantic. Only with the peplum epics set in classical antiquity during the 1950s and 1960s did Italian cinema embrace the nation's ancient past successfully and with conviction.

The *forzuti* were not the only transnational stars of Italian cinema. Indebted to the stage and film phenomenon of international female stardom (of Sarah Bernhardt, Eleonora Duse and Asta Nielsen), the diva films of Lyda Borelli, Pina Menichelli and Francesca Bertini all showcased a distinctly Italian style. In films like *Ma l'amore mio non muore* (*Love Everlasting*, 1913) and *La donna nuda* (*The Naked Woman*, 1914), the aristocratic diva's silent, pantomimic, yet complex form of eloquent expressiveness participated in a mode of cinematic narration and experience that privileged decadent, anti-naturalistic and symbolic representations. This style contributed to these films' identification as Italian productions even more than their known literary sources (novels by D'Annunzio, Verga, Fogazzaro, Di Giacomo or Deledda). Yet, their intense pictorial suggestions, referencing Dante Gabriel Rossetti, Ernest Herber, Ernst Ludwig Kirchner, Alphonse Mucha and even Edvard Munch, also situated the Italian diva's operatic gestures amid refined art deco settings, lending these films a European resonance. Still, while the diva films had some success in Europe, their loose storytelling pace thwarted their wide recognition in the US. Because of their lavish long-term contracts and

their attachment to old narrative formulas, in the late 1910s and early 1920s the dive contributed significantly to the Italian film industry's loss of foreign and domestic marketability.

The Italian avant-garde could have acquired comparable continental significance. Despite the proximity to European artists and critical debates, the Italian landscape of experimental cinema remained dotted with countless projects, productive theorisations, but all too few finished, and for decades invisible, works. The beginnings were promising, considering the early activity of experimental film theorists and film-makers, particularly Anton Giulio Bragaglia and the brothers Bruno Corra and Arnaldo Ginna – at least before their association with futurism. For years, in fact, the most famous Italian avant-garde movement maintained a costly prejudice against photographic media – which futurist painter Umberto Boccioni described as 'mechanical illusions'. Such technophobia was animated by conceptual and personal motives (including Henri Bergson's influential critical stance and Fernand Léger's attack against Umberto Boccioni's painterly use of photography), and these ideas resulted in the futurists' forced juxtaposition of photographic reproductions against artists' 'vital force'. After rejecting Bragaglia's visionary treatise *Fotodinamismo futurista* and Aldo Molinari's film *Mondo baldoria* [*World Revel*, 1914], only in 1916 did the founder of futurism, Filippo Tommaso Marinetti, endorse Bragaglia's oneiric *Thaïs* and agree to collaborate on the film *Vita futurista* and the writing of the futurist manifesto *La cinematografia futurista*. Despite these efforts, however, most of these works did not circulate widely and, in conjunction with the devastation wrought by the war and the subsequent decline of the national film industry, failed to influence mainstream productions, in contrast to the much more important impact French and German avant-garde films had in their respective countries and elsewhere.

One field where Italian film-making distinguished itself was that of non-fiction, particularly in the area of education and journalism. Between the Great War and the March on Rome by Mussolini's fascists in 1922, the government had shown little interest in motion pictures in general, and even less in documentary film-making, limiting its role to censorship and control of war coverage. After the mid-1920s, the fascist regime embraced non-fiction film-making as a unique propaganda tool to promote the positive effect of the regime's policies to domestic and international spectators. Central to these efforts was L'unione cinematografica educativa, or LUCE, later renamed simply Istituto Nazionale Luce. Beginning in the mid-1920s, Italian spectators had the chance, which became an obligation in 1926, with every fiction film screened, to watch government-sponsored educational and scientific documentaries and, after 1927, to view a steady diet of newsreels (*Giornali Cinematografici Luce*, also known as *cinegiornali*). All these productions were widely distributed abroad. In 1927, the LUCE established agreements with the main German studio, UFA (Universum Film AG), whose exhibition circuits covered an enormous area from Finland and Lithuania to Holland, Poland and Yugoslavia. The same year Mussolini himself signed a distribution deal with William Randolph Hearst and shortly after with the Fox studio for their newsreel services – respectively, the Metrotone and Movietone News.

The link between politics and educational film-making reveals another strand of the international fabric of Italian film culture, one that encompassed the late silent and early sound period. As a founding member of the League of Nations in 1927, Italy played a role in the establishment of the League-sponsored International Educational Cinematographic Institute (IECI). The mandate of the IECI was to encourage the production and dissemination of educational films, create a specialised international *cinémathèque*, publish a scholarly journal, initially called *International Review of Educational Cinematograph* (1929–34) and organise dedicated conferences. Italy took central stage in the IECI's activities. In the 1930s, the IECI mandate would also include the design and organisation of specialised conventions and the publication, unfortunately never realised, of an *Encyclopedia of Cinematography* of international ambition and scope. A key concern was the encouragement of research on the impact of cinema upon children and adults – in other words, on the effectiveness of propaganda among spectators of all ages. Another one, even more important for our analysis, was the international openness that it fostered aesthetically, scholarly and critically. Such inclusiveness allowed critic/psychologist Rudolph Arnheim to move to Italy after fleeing from Nazi Germany and to collaborate with the Milanese periodical *Convegno* in the early 1930s before working for the IECI and contributing essays to Italian film journals.

Finally, an overview of the international fabric of silent Italian film culture should reference the several instances in which individual Italian films made explicit references to icons of international popular culture. In addition to the aforementioned influence of neighbouring France, with its renowned comedians, crime serials and Napoleonic dramas, one should also cite the enthusiastic Italian reception of Sherlock Holmes. Homages to the famous British literary hero (and his cultural representations) included Pastrone's *Più forte che Sherlock Holmes* (*The Death Knell*, 1913), photographed by Segundo de Chomón, Ambrosio's *Fricot emulo di Sherlock Holmes* [*Fricot Emulates Sherlock Holmes*, 1913] and Cines' *Kri Kri contro Sherlock Holmes* [*Kri Kri against Sherlock Holmes*, 1915]. Even more pervasive was the Italian response to American popular culture, particularly to the American shows and showmen associated with turn-of-the-century world's fairs in Chicago and Paris and amusement parks such as the famous one in Coney Island. The presence of Buffalo Bill's shows in Italy in 1890 and 1906, widely broadcast through posters and postcards, participated in a dense phenomenon of influence and playful pretext that resulted in Italian films' frequent references to the Western frontier, America's unbridled commercialism and its polarising racial culture. In Giulio Antamoro's *Pinocchio* (1911), some Native Americans, obviously absent from Carlo Collodi's book, burst into the scene as if in a Western. In *Maciste* (1915), Bartolomeo Pagano uses blackface make-up to play an African-American dandy and a servant to deceive his antagonists. Comedy, perhaps more than any other genres, abounded with such references, as in *Cocò negro per amore* [UK: Coco Turns Nigger for Love, 1910], *Cretinetti e la negra* [Foolshead and the Black Woman, 1910], *Kri Kri bianco e negro* [UK: Bloomer, Negro, 1913], *Kri Kri e gli apaches* [UK: Bloomer and the Apaches, 1913]. It also assimilated American sports – i.e. *Jolicoeur ama il foot-ball* [*Jolicoeur Loves Football*, 1910] and *Kri Kri e il foot-ball* [*Kri Kri and Football*, 1914] – and general customs, including crime – i.e. *Robinet sposa un'americana* (*Tweedledum Marries an American Girl*, 1911), *Robinet falso cow-boy* [*Tweedledum as Fake Cowboy*, 1912], *Kri Kri e la Mano Nera* [Bloomer and the Black Hand, 1913] and *Polidor e l'americana* [*Polidor and the American Girl*, 1915].

In conclusion, silent Italian cinema emerged within a visual culture embedded with foreign contributors and expectations. Their presence affected how the national film production positioned itself within domestic and international markets at the level of genre, stardom, characterisations and style. Along this trajectory of transnational self-reflexivity, several Italian films absorbed and quoted other cultural traditions, mainly French and Anglo-American. In so doing, they paid homage to cinema itself according to a phenomenon that all too often is thought of as postmodern, but that instead included such early key examples as *Maciste, Cretinetti al cinematografo* (*Foolshead at the Cinematograph*, 1911), and *Cinessino imita Fantomas* [UK: *Cinessino as Raffles*, 1914].

NOTE

1. Throughout this study I have adopted the following procedure to present English-language translations of Italian film titles: I use the American title under which known US-distributed Italian films appeared in the US, i.e. *La caduta di Troia* (*The Fall of Troy*, 1911), unless the two titles coincide, as in the case of *Cabiria* (1914). When no American title is available, I have included titles employed in the UK.

FURTHER READING

Bernardini, Aldo, *Cinema delle origini in Italia. I film 'dal vero' di produzione estera, 1895–1907* (Gemona: Cineteca del Friuli, 2008).

Bertellini, Giorgio, 'Early Italian Cinema', *Film History* (Special Issue on 'Early Italian Cinema') vol. 12 no. 3 (2000), pp. 235–329.

——, *Italy in Early American Cinema: Race, Landscape, and the Picturesque* (Bloomington: Indiana University Press, 2010).

——, (ed.), *Italian Silent Cinema: A Reader* (New Barnet: John Libbey, 2013).

Brunetta, Gian Piero, *Il cinema muto italiano* (Rome-Bari: Laterza, 2008).

——, *The History of Italian Cinema: A Guide to Italian Film from Its Origins to the Twenty-first Century*, trans. Jeremy Parzen (Princeton, NJ: Princeton University Press, 2009).

Bruno, Giuliana, *Streetwalking on a Ruined Map. Cultural Theory and the City Films of Elvira Notari* (Princeton, NJ: Princeton University Press, 1993).

Dalle Vacche, Angela, *Diva: Defiance and Passion in Early Italian Cinema* (Austin: University of Texas Press, 2008).

Gili, Jean A., *André Deed: Boireau, Cretinetti, Gribouille, Toribio, Foolshead, Lehman …* (Genoa: Le Mani; Bologna: Cineteca di Bologna, 2005).

Laura, Ernesto G., *Le stagioni dell'Aquila. Storia dell'Istituto Luce* (Rome: Ente dello Spettacolo, 1999).

Reich, Jacqueline, 'Slave to Fashion: Masculinity, Suits, and the *Maciste* Films of Italian Silent Cinema', in Adrienne Munich (ed.), *Fashion in Film* (Bloomington: Indiana University Press, 2011), pp. 236–59.

Welle, John P., 'Early Cinema, *Dante's Inferno* of 1911, and the Origins of Italian Film Culture', in Amilcare A. Iannucci (ed.), *Dante, Cinema & Television* (Toronto: University of Toronto Press, 2004), pp. 21–50.

Wyke, Maria, *Projecting the Past: Ancient Rome, Cinema and History* (New York: Routledge, 1997).

2 The Beginnings of Film Stardom and the Print Media of Divismo

John P. Welle

Eugenio Ferdinando Palmieri, the first Italian to attempt a history of early cinema in Italy (*Vecchio cinema italiano* published in 1940) describes the difficulties he faced:

> A precise and conclusive history of our old cinema – silent theatre, they used to call it – is not possible. A more attentive judgment on those films, almost all of them gone to the slaughter house, is not permitted: it is necessary to trust in memory, in the 'impressions' of the time; and the information gathered is not sufficient. The subject matter, as they call it, is extremely vast.[1]

Palmieri goes on to mention, in an off-handed manner, the discovery of some copies of an old film journal from the teens:

> A weekly publication from Rome comes to my assistance, *Il Tirso al Cinematografo*, heir, perhaps, of *Il Tirso*, a literary and theatrical gazette of Luca Cortese. I found a few issues from 1916 at a bookstall. *The old cinema, by now, is there, on the bookstalls.*[2]

In the late 1930s, someone interested in films from previous decades, like Palmieri, rather than having an opportunity to actually view a film, was perhaps more likely to stumble upon an old theatrical or film periodical while perusing the used-book stalls that still occupy the squares of many Italian cities and small towns.

In the second decade of the third millennium, however, as is by now clear to anyone interested in film, the situation has changed. Following the famous International Federation of Film Archives (FIAF) Brighton conference of 1978, the 'new film history' has brought about a dramatic revitalisation of attention to early cinema. Collaboration among archivists, film buffs, scholars, university students, museums, international professional organisations such as FIAF, Domitor and others, as well as film festivals such as *Le giornate del cinema muto* in Pordenone and *Il cinema ritrovato* in Bologna, have contributed to presenting films usually only accessible in archives to a wider public, not only through screenings with live musical accompaniment, but also by means of video and high-quality DVDs for private viewing and individual study. Indeed, today, with the advent of digitisation and the Internet, many early films can be accessed at websites such as www.europafilmtreasures sponsored by Lobster Films of Paris; www.sempreinpenombra managed by Armando Giuffrida and M. Teresa Antolin of Rome; the American Memory Project of the Library of Congress; and the British Film Institute's YouTube channel. Moreover, 'The Bioscope: Reporting on the World of Early and Silent Cinema' is a very comprehensive website. It features digitised books on the production, reception and appreciation of early cinema; periodicals from the silent period that have been digitised, including links to over thirty Italian periodicals; as well as catalogues and databases, blogs, discussion networks and information of all kinds.

While instructors and students now have the opportunity to adopt these new resources to expand the range of teaching and research in film history, the current situation with regard to Italian Film Studies makes one less than sanguine. Early Italian cinema still remains largely unknown in the Anglophone countries perhaps because relatively few scholars seem to be engaged in this area of research. As a case in point, one of the most important phenomena of early Italian cinema, divismo (the celebrity culture that emerged around the time of World War I in a symbiotic intermedial relationship between theatre, film, literature and print media) beckons as a still largely unmapped terrain. Recent work on the diva film by Angela Dalle

Vacche, as well as more comprehensive and probing explorations of divismo by Cristina Jandelli and Monica Dall'Asta, to name a few, have begun to address various aspects of this multifaceted phenomenon. A conference on Italian female star performers from the sixteenth century to the present, 'Desiring Divas: the Diva in Modern Italian Culture', was held at Cambridge University, on 22 and 23 September 2011.

Divismo, according to the *Dizionario Garzanti della lingua italiana*, represents: 1) 'an inordinate collective infatuation with actresses and actors, primarily of the cinema' and 2) 'the behaviour with which the actors and actresses feed this same phenomenon.'[3] Certainly, if divismo does indeed represent an 'inordinate collective infatuation with actors and actresses', then, in order to understand the phenomenon more fully, it seems logical that we should turn our attention to the forms of print media that stimulated the passions and fantasies of exhibitors, of filmgoers and of readers alike. By the same token, if divismo also encompasses the off-screen conduct of actors, then where else but in print media will we find the narratives in which their behaviour is purportedly recounted? In other words, print media constitutes nothing less than the extra-filmic component of divismo and nothing more than its material manifestation in print.

Francesco Alberoni, among other scholars, has confirmed that audiovisual forms of stardom and celebrity, whether in film or television, work hand in hand with print media. Simply put, without print media there is no divismo. Alberoni writes:

> Divismo is [...] broader than the Star System. It is not limited to the world of the spectacle even if it is above all this sector of social and cultural life that develops collective gossip. But the means of mass communication that generate and feed into divismo are not so much cinema and television that 'show' the personalities in fashion, as much as it is the press rather – above all the women's press – that comments on their lives and causes them to become everyone's nextdoor neighbors.[4]

A number of issues merit emphasis here. First of all, Alberoni makes an important distinction in nomenclature. The Italian word divismo signifies more than 'star system' and can perhaps be most accurately translated into English as 'celebrity culture', 'stardom' or 'phenomenon of the stars'. This broader categorisation embraces charismatic leaders, theatrical and film stars,

Attrici e attori in pigiama (1926), one of the first Italian books of interviews with actresses and actors

politicians, athletes and celebrities of various kinds. Second, divismo relies upon what Alberoni calls 'il *pettegolezzo collettivo*' (collective gossip), a discourse that circulates most clearly in, but is not limited to, the entertainment sector of a culture.

Mindful of Alberoni's claim that print media are vital to divismo, let us begin with a synopsis of the development of film stardom in Italy before considering some aspects of the commercial literature that arises in tandem with the actors and actresses who became prominent in the years surrounding World War I.

THE EMERGENCE OF FILM ACTING IN ITALY

Internationally, the earliest examples of acting on film consist of the photographic reproductions of performers whose acts and celebrity status pre-dated the emergence of the film medium. Examples would include Eugene Sandow flexing his muscles and Annie Oakley shooting her rifle in several early Edison films. In Italy, if we concentrate on actors, rather than the royalty, aristocracy, dignitaries and Popes who appear in many early films by Edison, the Lumières and other pioneer film-makers, then the chronology of acting on film begins with Leopoldo Fregoli. The first star in the history of Italian cinema, an internationally renowned *trasformista* and quick-change artist, Fregoli purchased a *Cinématographe* from the Lumières and worked it into his stage act renaming it the 'Fregoligraph'. His brief comic films produced between 1897 and 1903 take us 'behind the scenes' of his stage trickery. Moreover, Fregoli's adoption of the film apparatus in his variety performances forms a bridge between the 'fairgrounds' stage (or the *cinema ambulante* season following the arrival of Edison and the Lumières in 1894 and 1895, respectively) and the construction of purpose-built film theatres beginning around 1905. The identity of the new film medium originates in the apparatus and the 'animated photographs' that it projected. 'The cinema' was primarily thought of as a machine, the latest technological invention, a new form of popular spectacle, as well as a scientific discovery. Fregoli's unique contribution to film history, therefore, stems from his live performance practices that ingeniously blurred the distinction between human labour and technological apparatus, between acting and mechanical reproduction. One reviewer, for example, described him as '*un cinematografo-vivente*' (a living cinema machine).[5]

The second phase in the emergence of acting on film in Italy involves comedians and comediennes such as André Deed, Marcel Fabre, Ferdinand Guillaume and Gigetta Morano. In the years between 1909 and 1914, these actors were the protagonists of a ' comic star system' that found expression in the production of more than 1,000 film comedies. In their dealings with the production companies, these comics established strong positions from which they negotiated terms of payment, length of engagement and percentages owed them according to the length of the films in which they appeared. The website of Europa Film Treasures provides access to some ten Italian comedies featuring such stars as Robinet, Tartarin, Polidor, Ernesto Vaser, Fricot and Fabre.

With regard to chronology, it is important to acknowledge that a number of interrelated phenomena occur simultaneously in a rather short time span, making it difficult to argue in terms of cause and effect. For example, the launching of a series of artistic films in France, *Film d'art* in 1908, featuring well-known actors and actresses in classical dramas, provided a model that was exported the following year to Italy with the *Film d'arte italiana* series sponsored by Pathé Frères but located in Rome. Aniello Costagliola in a 1909 article entitled, '*Attori in pellicola*' (Actors in Film) greeted the new development with enthusiasm:

I Nostri Artisti Leopoldo Fregoli issue (c. 1904), an anecdotal biography of Italy's first film star

> Let Duse, Zacconi, Novelli, Caruso and all of our best stage artists make up their minds to *pose* for the cinema. Why not? Their illustrious French colleagues and those from other sites have already given a good example, and in this way they have paid homage to the exigencies of modernity.[6]

In 1909, *Film d'arte italiana* released titles featuring Italian actors and actresses who had already gained a national reputation on the stage, beginning with Ermete Novelli and Ferruccio Garaviglia, and continuing with Cesare Dondini, Teresa Mariani, Dillo Lombardi, Vittoria Lepanto, Giannina Chiantoni, Maria Jacobini, Gastone Monaldi, and many others.[7] Once again, an excellent example of this series of artistic films can be viewed at the Europa Film Treasures website: *Salomè* (*Salomè*, 1910) directed by Ugo Falena, featuring Vittoria Lepanto, with Francesca Bertini making her film debut in a minor role as a slave girl.

These years witnessed the transition to the feature-length film along with the arrival of modern dramas from Denmark and Germany, including Asta Nielsen in *Afgrunden* (*The Abyss*, 1910) directed by Urban Gad. These films are considered some of the first in Italy to publicise prominently the names of actors and directors. In fact, publicity surrounding *The Abyss* hailed Nielsen as 'the Duse of the Cinema', linking her with Eleonora Duse, Italy's most acclaimed and internationally celebrated stage actress of the time. In a similar fashion, Urban Gad was likened to Gabriele D'Annunzio, an Italian poet, novelist and aesthete of wide fame and great cultural prestige. The cloaking of Nielsen and Gad in the mantles of two of Italy's most-renowned artistic figures triggered a negative reaction in the trade press. At the same time, the native film industry was soon able to celebrate its own popular on-screen couples: Cines brought forth Amleto Novelli and Maria Gasparini; Ambrosio featured Alberto Capozzi and Mary Cléo Tarlarini and Pasquali showcased Ubaldo Maria Del Colle and Lydia De Roberti.

Ma l'amor mio non muore, starring Lyda Borelli, directed by Mario Caserini, is generally considered the first diva film. This important genre was constructed around the female performer: the actress, and not the character she plays, is the key element. Indeed, a culture of film celebrity from the theatre, as we have seen, had been in gestation in Italy for a number of years, preparing the terrain for the golden age of divismo, primarily female, that flowered in Italian cinema between 1913 and 1921. As Claudio Camerini writes:

> the years following 1912 mark the point of arrival of a cycle that transforms the actor, once a marginal figure, into the central character of Italian cinema. The cinema of these years is truly an actor's cinema, and the stardom phenomenon should be primarily understood as the *centrality of the actor*, that is to say, as the capacity to subordinate to himself other roles that in previous phases were of equal dignity and importance: the costume designer, the make-up specialist, the light technician, the cameraman, the scene-painter and the director all now revolve around a single person, whose intentions they support and whose projects they bring to fruition.[8]

The actor was now firmly entrenched at the centre of an industry with international distribution whose production strategies attracted a diverse audience through high-quality films featuring famous artists. The role of the actor had also expanded to supersede that of the producer, of the artistic director, of the scenario writer. Schools for film actors were founded in Palermo, Turin, Rome and Florence. Beginning in 1914–15, production companies appear that bear the names of, and belong to, the actors themselves. Examples of this tendency include Bonnard-Film

(belonging to Mario Bonnard), Azzurri-Film (belonging to Paolo Azzurri), Polidor-Film (belonging to Ferdinand Guillaume), Rodolfi-Film (belonging to Eleuterio Rodolfi), Vidali-Film (belonging to Giovanni Novelli Vidali), Cléo Film (belonging to Mary Cléo Tarlarini), Vitè-Film (belonging to Serafino Vitè), Bertini-Film (belonging to Francesca Bertini), David-Karenne-Film (belonging to Diana Karenne), Aristos-Film (belonging to Giampaolo Rosmino) and Zannini-Films (belonging to Giovanni Zannini).[9]

The close relationship between theatre and early cinema in Italy, while complex, cannot be over-emphasised. In fact, the actor-driven film-production companies listed above resemble an organisational system that had been operating in the Italian theatre world throughout the nineteenth century: the tradition of the great actor. Serving as the focal point and leading performer as well as at times the 'capocomico', a mixture of chief actor, artistic director and business manager – the 'great actor', to whom the others were subservient, was responsible for forming and managing a group of actors and actresses who signed contracts to play particular roles over a specified period of time. In fact, this system, although in crisis, would remain in effect in the Italian theatre until the 1940s. Many of Pirandello's plays, for example, were brought to the stage by companies organised around the great actor: the Angelo Musco Company, the Giovanni Grasso Company, the Lamberto Picasso Company, the Virgilio Talli Company, the Emma Gramatica Company, the Ruggero Ruggeri Company and the Maria Melato Company, among others. It should be pointed out, however, that the experimental artistic creativity, the individual performance techniques and the deeply honed craftsmanship of the great actors of the nineteenth century – such as Eleonora Duse, Ermete Novelli, Ermete Zacconi and Ruggero Ruggeri – were not implanted into the acting codes of early Italian cinema. The leadership role that the great actor embodied, nevertheless, had an impact on the direction of the film industry.

In short, whereas in the initial stages of Italian film production after the turn to fiction around 1906, the recruitment of actors had posed a problem, by the mid-1910s, stage performers had moved from the margins to the centre of production strategies. Divas who were in charge of their own companies, as noted above, include Mary Cléo Tarlarini, Francesca Bertini and Diana Karenne. Before appearing on screen, Lyda Borelli was the head of her own theatrical company. Indeed, the Italian divas brought into the cinema modes of organisation that had proved successful in the opera and prose theatre of previous centuries. 'The Italian film diva inserts herself knowingly in this track, following in many cases the model of the artistic impresario already present in the prose theatre.'[10] After Leopoldo Fregoli, therefore, and following the comic stars in his wake, with the transition to the longer feature film, the diva assumed the primary star role in Italian cinema.

Having traced the development of early film stardom in Italy, let us now turn our attention to the print media of divismo beginning with the general context of Italian film periodicals of the silent period.

FILM PERIODICALS

The Italian publishing world, as early as 1907, began to produce a significant number of periodicals devoted to motion pictures. Davide Turconi has observed that the Italian cinematic press is fertile and longstanding, with the first film periodicals being published in 1907, the same year in the United States that *The Moving Picture World* began, the latter, the first and for many years the most important, film journal in the silent period.[11] Between 1907 and 1920, Italy would produce no fewer than ninety film journals; by 1931, the number had increased to some 200.

Many of these journals were short-lived, with a declared distribution of between 30,000 and 50,000 copies reaching some fifteen Italian cities. Turin, Milan, Rome and Naples, however, were the chief centres of these periodicals, Rome being the most active with some forty film journals published during this period. Most of these publications addressed those working in the film industry. Over time, they tended to become closely aligned with regional centres of film production. Between 1910 and 1915, journals appear that consider the cinema as an intellectual phenomenon and are often associated with avant-garde artistic groups.[12] A number of Italian film journals were oriented toward literary and cultural developments and boasted attractive designs, articles of more than passing critical interest and the collaboration of distinguished writers, dramatists, actors and artists. One of the most important film journals, *La vita cinematografica*, founded at Turin in 1910, is described by Davide Turconi in this way:

> It is the most long-lived journal, lasting until 1934 and it publishes articles and debates on the situation, problems, and needs of the Italian film industry and exhibitors, also in relation to other cinemas, biographical and illustrative articles on actors, directors,

and film personalities, short stories, film news from the principal cities of Italy and from abroad, a column of film criticism, anthologies of criticism from the most important daily papers, news on films in the planning stage and in process, on the movements of actors, directors, and technicians from one production company to another, illustrated publicity of new films.[13]

Other important film journals include *L'illustrazione cinematografica* founded in 1912, *Il maggese cinematografico* of 1913, *La tecnica cinematografica* of 1914, *Apollon* founded at Rome in 1916 and the Neapolitan *L'arte muta* of the same year.

A particularly beautiful periodical, which appeared in 1917 under the title, *Penombra*, became *In Penombra* in 1918 and represents one of the most promising sources for the study of divismo. In fact, *In Penombra's* subtitle, 'Rivista d'arte cinematografica', reflects the progress that the cinema had made in acquiring the aura of art by that date. Through the collaboration of well-known writers, actors and the emerging figure of the director, these journals served to add lustre to the Italian cinema's patina of high culture. *In Penombra*, for example, claimed to be 'the first film journal compiled with criteria that are exclusively artistic'. Its list of collaborators includes such leading writers, playwrights

In Penombra magazine, one of the most lavishly illustrated early film journals

Anno 2 - N.6   *Giugno 1919*

and drama critics as Giuseppe Adami, Antonio Baldini, Sem Benelli, Roberto Bracco, Anton Giulio Bragaglia, Luigi Chiarelli, Lucio D'Ambra, Silvio D'Amico, Guido Da Verona, Salvatore Di Giacomo, F. M. Martini, Marino Moretti, Luigi Pirandello, Rosso Di San Secondo, Federico Tozzi and Trilussa. The actors, actresses and *metteurs en scène* who either collaborate by contributing articles or who are featured as subjects of interviews include Francesca Bertini, Lyda Borelli, Carmine and Soava Gallone, Augusto Genina, Emma Gramatica, Leda Gys, Diana Karenne, Febo Mari, Maria Melato, Pina Menichelli, Lina Millefleurs, Giovanni Musco, Ruggero Ruggeri, Virgilio Talli and Vera Vergani.

The journal is particularly noteworthy for the high quality of its layout, photographs and illustrations. In fact, *In Penombra*, in the words of its editor, is a 'journal in which the illustrative part has an importance not inferior to the text'. With *In Penombra*, according to Turconi, 'Italian literature unites itself happily and officially with the cinema, or, better, with the film press, through the weight of the noted literary intellectuals who figure among its collaborators.'[14]

Demonstrating key elements of divismo, *In Penombra* illustrates the importance of print media in general and of periodicals directed toward a female audience in particular for the functioning of stardom. In the third issue of 1919, for example, the editor describes the journal's success as follows:

> *In Penombra* has become in these recent months the most widely read journal of elegance, of art, of the life of the theatre and of the cinema in Italy. The augmented number of its pages rich with photographs, with original drawings, with interesting articles, with curious and novel items of every kind, regarding not only the cinema and the theatre, but every form of activity of high society, with particular attention to women's fashion, to the events that are of interest to high society, to the furnishing of the modern home, has brought about as a consequence a distribution that has more than doubled.[15]

The connection with social elites constitutes an element of divismo familiar to anyone who has viewed diva films such as *Ma l'amor mio non muore*, Giovanni Pastrone's *Tigre reale* (*Royal Tiger*, 1915), Carmine Gallone's *Malombra* (*Malombra*, 1917) and many others. Demonstrating the synergy flowing between the films and the periodicals that support them, numerous pages of *In Penombra* are dedicated to women's fashion, to the chronicles of high

society, and to the domestic private spaces of the wealthy. In this way, print media make it possible to understand more fully the social and class relations that are part and parcel of various aspects of early Italian film culture. Indeed, the high-society world portrayed in the novels of Gabriele D'Annunzio and the widespread influence of D'Annunzianism on cinematic divismo find ample expression in periodicals such as *In Penombra*.

Selected issues of *In Penombra* and many other Italian film journals of the silent period have been digitised. Some 60,000 pages from these periodicals – with more to come – can now be accessed through the website of *Il Museo nazionale del cinema* at Turin and the *Tecla digitale piemontese*. In contrast to the situation Eugenio Palmieri described in 1940 when writing *Vecchio cinema italiano*, abundant resources are now available for the study of early cinema in general and for the exploration of Italian film stardom in particular.

A panoramic treatment of the literature that arises around film acting in Italy, what I am calling here the print media of divismo, would include, in addition to *In Penombra* and other periodicals, star biographies like Franco Liberati's *Leopoldo Fregoli: Una biografia aneddotica* (*Leopoldo Fregoli: An Anecdotal Biography*, 1903); humorist writings on celebrities such as Yarro's *Viaggio umoristico nei teatri* (*A Sentimental Journey in the Theatres*, 1903); film-

Come si possa diventare artisti cinematografici (1915), an important manual of film acting

acting manuals like Paolo Azzurri's *Come si possa diventare artisti cinematografici* (*How to Become Artists of the Cinema*, published in three editions of 1915, 1917 and 1926); books about divas including those by Ottorino Modugno, *Le donne mute* (*Silent Women*, 1919) and by Tito Alacci (Alacevich), *Le nostre attrici studiate sullo schermo* (*Our Actresses Studied on the Screen*, 1919); interviews with actresses and actors in Dina Galli's *I nostri attrici ed attori in pigiama* (*Our Actresses and Actors in Pajamas*, 1926); as well as particular sections of works of early film theory that pertain to divismo: G. Gariazzo, *Il teatro muto* (*The Silent Theatre*, 1919) and S. A. Luciani, *Verso una nuova arte: il cinematografo* (*Towards a New Art: the Cinema*, 1921). These different genres of print media, perhaps not surprisingly, are also closely connected to forms of commercial literature surrounding actors and actresses of the late nineteenth and early twentieth century.

In conclusion, a treasure trove of visually attractive and historically significant material awaits both the researcher and the instructor providing rich and abundant resources for the creation of further knowledge – beyond the diva film – regarding divismo, one of the most important phenomena of Italian culture and society that took root, flourished and exhausted itself before the advent of fascism.

NOTES

1. Eugenio Ferdinando Palmieri, *Vecchio cinema italiano* (Vicenza: Neri Pozza, 1994), p. 18. All translations are my own.
2. Ibid., emphasis added, p. 102.
3. *Dizionario garzanti della lingua italiana* (Milan: Garzanti, 1965), p. 564.
4. Francesco Alberoni, 'Introduzione', in Nicolò Costa, *Il divismo e il comico* (Turin: ERI, 1982), p. 9.
5. *Il paese*, 16 October 1907, as cited by Luigi Colagreco, <http://www.trasx.it/olivieropdp/ateatro2002/fregoli.htm>.
6. Aniello Costagliola, 'Attori in pellicola', *Lux* no. 11 (October 1909), now in *Tra una film e l'altra: Materiali sul cinema muto italiano 1907–1920* (Venice: Marsilio, 1980), p. 86.
7. Claudio Camerini, 'Verso il divismo', in Riccardo Redi (ed.), *Cinema italiano muto 1905–1916* (Rome: CNC Edizioni, 1991), p. 48.
8. Claudio Camerini, 'E l'attore diventò una diva', *Bianco e Nero* vol. XLV no. 2 (April–June 1986), p. 37.
9. Ibid., p. 38.
10. Cristina Jandelli, *Le dive italiane del cinema muto* (Palermo: L'Epos, 2006), p. 1.
11. Davide Turconi, 'Prefazione', in Riccardo Redi (ed.), *Cinema scritto: Il catalogo delle riviste italiane di cinema 1907–1944* (Rome: Associazione italiana per le ricerche di storia del cinema, 1992), p. viii.
12. Giorgio Fabre, 'D'Annunzio nelle prime riviste del cinema italiano', *Quaderni del Vittoriale* no. 4 (August 1977), as cited by Turconi, *La stampa cinematografica in Italia e negli Stati Uniti d'America dalle origini al 1930* (Pavia: Amministrazione provinciale di Pavia, 1977), pp. 28–9.
13. Turconi, *La stampa cinematografica*, p. 8.
14. Ibid., pp. 8–9.
15. Tomaso Monicelli, 'Il prossimo numero', *In Penombra* vol. II no. 3 (March 1919), p. 1.

FURTHER READING

Alberoni, Francesco, 'Introduzione', in Nicolò Costa, *Il divismo e il comico* (Turin: ERI, 1982), pp. 7–14.

——, ' "The Powerless Elite": Theory and Sociological Research on the Phenomenon of the Stars', in P. David Marshall (ed.), *The Celebrity Culture Reader* (New York and London: Routledge, 2006), pp. 108–23.

Alovisio, Silvio, 'Lo spoglio delle riviste del cinema muto italiano: il corpus e i primi risultati', in Giulia Carluccio and Federica Villa (eds), *Cinema muto italiano: tecnica e tecnologia. Vol. 1. Discorsi, precetti, documenti* (Rome: Carocci, 2006), pp. 49–57.

Camerini, Claudio, 'E l'attore diventò una diva', *Bianco e Nero* vol. XLV no. 2 (April–June 1986), pp. 20–41.

——, 'La formazione artistica degli attori del cinema muto italiano', *Bianco e Nero* vol. XLIII (1982), pp. 7–43.

——, 'Verso il divismo', in Riccardo Redi (ed.), *Cinema muto italiano 1905–1916* (Rome: CNC Edizioni, 1991), pp. 47–60.

Dall'Asta, Monica (ed.), *Non solo dive: Pioniere del cinema italiano* (Bologna: Cineteca di Bologna, 2008).

Dalle Vacche, Angela, *Diva: Defiance and Passion in Early Italian Cinema* (Austin: University of Texas Press, 2008).

Elsaesser, Thomas, 'The New Film History as Media Archeology', *Cinémas: revue d'études cinématographiques/ Cinémas Journal of Film Studies* vol. 14 nos 2–3 (Spring 2004), pp. 75–117.

Jandelli, Cristina, *Le dive italiane del cinema muto* (Palermo: L'Epos, 2006).

Palmieri, Eugenio, *Vecchio cinema italiano* (Vicenza: Neri Pozza, 1994).

Redi, Riccardo (ed.), *Cinema scritto: Il catalogo delle riviste italiane di cinema 1907–1944* (Rome: Associazione italiana per le ricerche di storia del cinema, 1992).

Tra una film e l'altra: Materiali sul cinema muto italiano 1907–1920 (Venice: Marsilio, 1980).

Welle, John P., 'Film on Paper: Early Italian Cinema Literature, 1907 to 1920', *Film History: An International Journal* vol. 12 (2000), pp. 288–99.

3 The Diva Film

Context, Actresses, Issues

Angela Dalle Vacche

A 'diva' is the most important woman singer, the prima donna in an opera, but, in early Italian cinema, this word also describes an arrogant or temperamental woman. Close to the English 'divine', 'diva' means goddess, implying that she is either on a par with or competes with God for the spotlight. By contrast, in Hollywood cinema, the movie star is someone special or exceptional, even superhuman, but who is not comparable to a divinity. Striving for the absolute, and somewhat at odds with the modern age of relativity and change, the Italian silent diva involves a certain kind of ineffable spirituality, ritualistic otherness and an aura of transcendence. Most frequently, the Italian diva is a suffering mother or *mater dolorosa*, while she becomes a predatory femme fatale only out of harsh necessity. Her unusual contribution to the history of international film stardom stems from the cultural peculiarities of Italian industrialisation, an age characterised by historical nostalgia and utopian yearnings towards a technological future.[1]

New definitions of gender were raised by Italy's quest for modernity, because, in the wake of several scientific developments, European culture was confronting a new understanding of the relation between being and appearance. The topic of the turn of the century was what the new man and the new woman were supposed to be like, in order to fit into the modern world of speed, consumption, urban traffic, risk, electric signs and moving images. As a result of this widespread interrogation of gendered identity, American film stars and early Italian cinema divas became trendsetters. This new awareness that being may or may not match appearance, was tied to changing definitions of masculinity and femininity.

The year 1911 was memorable because it marked the first time an Italian woman dared to wear trousers in public. This first attack on bulky petticoats and stifling corsets failed, but the message was not lost. That same year the Turin press reported that the diva Lyda Borelli was attending a futurist event in modern clothing. Inasmuch as women's emancipation was a major theme of the period, Italian women were lagging behind their sisters in England and the United States, where the right to vote and other basic rights had been granted shortly after World War I.[2] With a discontinuous acting style oscillating between fluid and rigid motions, the phenomenon of the diva became symptomatic of Italian women's tightrope-walking act between tradition and rebellion. To this day, their efforts stand out as an exceptional page of Italian cultural history, in painful contrast with the situation of women during its twenty years of the fascist regime from 1922 to 1943.

In the early Italian film industry, 'diva' meant female star in the 'long' feature film. The latter was approximately sixty minutes long, four reels, with some close-ups for the film star or diva, artificial lighting, a fairly static camera and many-layered compositions in depth. A mixture of the Catholic *mater dolorosa*, of the Northern European femme fatale in literature and in painting and of the new woman of modernity, the Italian diva would move from the roles of prostitute to socialite, or from rags to riches in the very same melodrama, so combining stereotypes of femininity from both the upper and lower classes. Thus, she was able to appeal to a mass audience, while she also set trends by wearing outfits to practise women's sports popular among the upper classes, such as horse-riding, cycling and tennis. The diva smoked, played with her rosary-like necklaces, took the train frequently, but did not drive her own car. Occasionally, she became an aviatrix, while she was associated with image-making as an artist's model or as a socialite in the arts.[3]

From 1910 to 1913, the diva phenomenon was preceded by a slew of less internationally famous actresses dominating the short film. Between twenty and thirty minutes, with one or two reels, these short features launched minor but talented and anti-conformist actresses into domestic stardom. Lia Formia, Valentina Frascaroli, Berta Nelson, Gigetta Morano, Clementina Gay, Lidia Quaranta, Suzanne Armelle and Fernanda Negri-Pouget built their reputations by appearing in contemporary dramas about espionage and crime; they also starred in comedies about changing gender roles, or adventure stories dealing with the legal system, the police and technology, the influence of the fast and regimented American way of life and the enterprise of colonialism. Often divas played roles with foreign names in order to avoid the censors' cuts or vetoes, whenever their melodramas contained social scandal or sexual abuse.

One may wonder who was more feminist: the diva or the minor star? Less involved with the aristocracy and more at home with the professional middle class, the minor star worked in cheaper productions and was more action-oriented and urban than the diva. Most significantly, the Italian minor star was born before the ascendance of the American serial queen Pearl White, but she never engaged in the extreme action-packed cliffhangers of Hollywood. The diva's rise coincided with increased costs and more lavish sets or natural locations. She spent hours in magical, private gardens or lived near famous resorts, while she wore sophisticated clothing whenever she inhabited luxurious palaces. On the other hand, the diva could end up in the slums of the city, dressed in black and with no money, after living at the Grand Hotel or going on cruises. In short, divas were in touch with the risks of modernity, while the minor stars were more pro-active. The divas operated near the gambling table or in environments of debauchery, whereas minor stars belonged to an average neighbourhood with smaller buildings and public parks. In the end, their respective levels of feminism are comparable, in that the minor star was often daring and athletic, but still subordinate to a father figure in the role of the dutiful daughter; the diva, by contrast, was a stage performer or a fashion designer, while struggling against a cruel husband or a heartless male figure.

In rollercoaster plots filled with thrills and sensationalism, the minor star and the diva appealed to male and female audiences. Yet, between 1905 and 1911, the young medium of the cinema had a dubious reputation in both an intellectual and a social sense.

Much cheaper than the theatre, the cinema was seen as either an infantile form of leisure good for nannies and children or an insalubrious environment fostering prostitution, vice and rebellion in general. For all these contradictory reasons, the cinema was more associated with bored women than with busy men. The ordinary perception was that sons and husbands had more serious business to attend to and much less leisure time to waste during the day. At the beginning of the twentieth century, Italian women were isolated with their children and discouraged from pursuing a profession. Thus, a career in the cinema looked like a unique, yet controversial choice for personal independence. With a steady demand for seamstresses, colourists, milliners, assistants, typists and actresses, the film industry was a potential new source of employment. But this career choice could ruin a good girl's reputation.

Besides functioning as a window on the world, or a substitute for costly foreign travel, the cinema became a mirror reflecting back into the public eye the most common, but also the most secret, everyday issues in women's lives. Because women's problems were the result of paternal authority, the impossibility of divorce, the double standards of judges and physicians, the lack of basic rights such as the ability to subscribe to a newspaper or own property after marriage, the diva film became a major, autonomous genre specialising in pregnancy out of wedlock, child custody, abandonment, shame, adultery, divorce, prostitution and financial ruin. Despite its escapist indulgence in glitz and glamour at the level of clothes, décor, houses and locations, the diva film was informed by a profound and undeniable social awareness. By calling attention to the legal and economic plight of women, the diva film greatly strengthened its bond with female audiences. In fact, until around 1910, the Italian word for 'film' was used in the feminine as 'la film'. Notwithstanding this feminisation of the new medium, it is important to keep in mind that divas were frequently punished at the end of their melodramas, or subjected to conservative endings.

Throughout the silent period, the Italian film industry remained city-bound and regionally based, without ever achieving a vertical integration of production, distribution and exhibition comparable to the Hollywood system. This is why bankruptcy struck this whole shaky set-up right after the end of World War I. Within this ruinous climate, the diva film genre degenerated into a repetitive and empty formula without enough play between new narrative solutions and the development of old tropes. Mostly in the hands of old-fashioned aristocrats playing film producers, the Italian film industry and the diva phenomenon soared for a few years, until more modern film-making styles from other countries pushed Italian early and silent cinema out of the market into oblivion. Furthermore, from 1919 on, the moralistic constraints of the rising fascist regime prevailed. In this new climate, in which all women were meant to be mothers, the highly independent and contradictory figure of the diva became not only an obsolete, but also an unacceptable trope. Notwithstanding the genre's brief trajectory, between 1913 and 1919, Italian diva films sold well in Latin America, Russia, Japan, the Balkans, Egypt and Spain.

Despite the diva film genre's domestic roots, the category of stardom came to Italy from Denmark. Although trained in the theatre, the Danish Asta Nielsen is the first European actress to be associated with international film stardom. Before Nielsen, the self-promoting stage icon Sarah Bernhardt rose to star-like world fame through her acting innovations and sensationalistic way of living. Bernhardt's contemporary, meanwhile, the much more modest, yet innovative Eleonora Duse, distinguished herself for the spiritual slant of her quiet, but intense introspective approach.[4] Although she built on Bernhardt's exuberance, Duse's spirituality and Nielsen's independence, the Italian film *diva dolorosa* differed from all her predecessors, because she sought an ideal of social justice for all women in clear contrast to the Hollywood vamp's self-centred search for forms of personal gratification.

The diva's cultural context is not enough to explain the difference between this short-lived, Italian approach to female stardom and the Hollywood formula. The diva is afraid of, but also eager for, new behaviours and fresh situations. By contrast, Hollywood stardom as a whole is built on the belief that, on one hand, sexy vamps are always evil and successful, while, on the other, any new way of being, in a personal or an economic sense, is, by definition, good, a positive progression. In Frank Powell's *A Fool There Was* (1915), the femme fatale Theda Bara is as responsible for leading a married man astray as alcoholism. Significantly, the American wife in Powell's plot does not lose her social standing as a result of her spouse's vice. Thus, the American vamp was a symptom of male anxieties about self-destruction and not an indictment of female sexuality as such. On the contrary, the woman is blamed for all the male shortcomings, and berated for being a desiring and thinking being. Furthermore, in the Italian diva film, prostitution is

shown to be a means of economic survival for someone who has had the misfortune of simply being born a woman.[5] By contrast, before the 1928 establishment of the Hays Code in American silent cinema, female prostitution was an issue linked to an excess of female consumerism or urbanisation within which the cinema itself dangerously participated as a form of female entertainment.

Abandoned by institutional religion and civil society, and at odds with older female relatives and younger or wealthier rivals, the diva dreams of some kind of miraculous transformation or redemption. And when the dream fails to become a reality, either because of her own contradictions or because of patriarchal oppression, the diva kills. This is the case with Lyda Borelli's Malombra, whose mere image lit by a night-lamp in the darkness is enough to induce a fatal heart attack in her oppressive uncle. Instead of clever scheming in the dark to achieve victory like an American vamp, the diva kills in self-defence, as with Pina Menichelli who is exasperated by her own sad fate at the end of Eugenio Perego's *La storia di una donna* (*A Woman's Story*, 1920). Again, instead of money or self-empowerment, it is the abuse of women in family life and their need to conform to societal norms in gender roles, which lead Lyda Borelli to kill her own loving husband at the end of Amleto Palermi's *Carnevalesca* (*Carnevalesque*, 1918). Reduced to fear and anger, in this allegorical film about a whole society in a state of decay, the diva attacks like a beast in pain, thus coming close to resembling Cesare Lombroso's dominant stereotype of femininity as a regressive way of being, the bottom of an evolutionary scale dominated by the man of genius.[6]

The three most famous divas during the period around World War I were Francesca Bertini, Lyda Borelli and Pina Menichelli. Born out of wedlock, Bertini hid her illegitimacy all her life and taught herself to handle the challenges of screen acting after a few minor appearances on stage.[7] Unlike her two contemporaries, who mostly appeared in overwrought melodramas, Bertini took professional risks by embracing a broader variety of genres. For instance, she did well in Edoardo Bencivenga's *Mariute* (*Mariute*, 1918), a patriotic comedy with a dark subplot involving rape and a section of self-parody as an egotistical diva. In touch with her Neapolitan beginnings on stage, she rose to fame through a vernacular subject such as *Assunta Spina*. Enhanced by Bertini's vibrant interpretation, this film stood out for its proto-neorealist documentary flavour and criticism of a corrupt legal system.

Besides moving beyond the operatic type of the punished woman in Bencivenga's *La piovra* (*The Octopus*, 1919), where she marries a loving man, Bertini tried to channel her financial success into her own production house, Bertini Films. Under the pseudonym of Frank Bert, she also wrote the scenario of a fiction film about industrial espionage. Possibly, Bertini's illegitimate origins might have kindled her social consciousness in regard to the plight of women and motivated her to take on controversial roles in Alfredo De Antoni's *Il processo Clemenceau* (*The Clemenceau Affair*, 1917) and in *Il nodo* (*The Knot*, 1921; director unknown), two films about greedy and adulterous husbands eager to mentally and physically destroy their innocent and wealthy wives.

In contrast to Bertini's more intuitive, ladylike and measured acting style, Borelli relied on her family background in the theatre and training on the stage. There, after learning all of Duse's typical gestures, she proceeded to amplify and complicate them for the silver screen. Thus, she developed a unique style that entered the Italian language with the verb *borelleggiare*.[8]

The most defiant of the three, but also far less in touch with the theatre than Bertini and Borelli, Pina Menichelli was a complete cinematic construct, in the sense that she was invented as a glow of light or a leaping flame of temptation by Giovanni Pastrone with *Il fuoco* (*The Fire*, 1915). All these references to light, flame and fire are appropriate to Menichelli because, thanks to her blonde halo of hair, high cheekbones, big eyes with long lashes and well-defined mouth, the Sicilian diva fared better with artificial lighting and in close-up than her colleagues. In fact, Bertini's and Borelli's delicate features did not always show to their best advantage in harsh lighting. Their countenances seem so fragile or refined that they may switch from

youthful to fatigued in the same sequence, while their slender naked arms may look either too flat or too large, as if the black-and-white chromatic balance of the shot had started bleeding into an excess of white light. Not only did Menichelli take on all the typical diva roles, but she became Salvador Dalí's favourite actress due to her mixture of playful and devilish ways which competed with the gratuitous evil embodied by Theda Bara.

In addition to this holy trinity of worldwide renown, film historians usually include Elena Sangro, Maria Jacobini, Mercedes Brignone, Italia Almirante Manzini and Leda Gys. More specifically, launched in Pastrone's historical epic *Cabiria*, Manzini was the matronly queen, Jacobini became the girl-next-door or the Italian Mary Pickford, Brignone played the persecuted innocent and Gys specialised in the playful, Neapolitan type, reaping great success with immigrant audiences in the US.[9] The foreign-born Diana Karenne, Soava Winawer Gallone, Stacia Napierkowska and Elena Makowska were also very important. This group of expatriate actresses built their careers around the Orientalist vogue and the craze for Slavic women launched by the Ballets Russes in Italy and France around 1911. A famous proverb of the period stated: 'Slavic eyes, you cannot get away.'

By often assuming multiple roles in twisted melodramas, such as the rich aristocrat and the prostitute, the single mother and the orphan heiress, divas dramatised the female dilemmas of their age in regard to marriage, social status, intellectual independence and romantic fulfilment. At the same time, they relied on a mixture of improvisation and training from dance, theatre, fashion or acting schools specifically developed for the new medium of film.[10] At times they were rejected by their conservative families, but later rescued by a young director (Nino Oxilia with Maria Jacobini); or they were mentored by a producer (Alberto Fassini, in the case of Lyda Borelli); or by a man of letters such as Salvatore Di Giacomo who, like a Pygmalion, watched over Francesca Bertini and encouraged her to learn foreign languages. To their credit, these young actresses managed to prevail over a huge crowd of female candidates whose little-known faces proliferated in the film-trade magazines of the period. The competition was absolutely out of control and it was common for film magazines to announce the launch of a new film with a new star, even if the film did not exist and the actress had not even begun to act. The situation was chaotic, at the very least.

Pina Menichelli in Giovanni Pastrone's *Il fuoco* (1915)

Lyda Borelli in Mario Caserini's *Ma l'amore mio non muore* (1913)

The polite rivalry between Bertini and Borelli has become legendary, so that this tension also marks the tales surrounding the development of the first diva film, which is usually deemed to be Mario Caserini's *Ma l'amore mio non muore*, starring Lyda Borelli.[11] But there is, of course, much more to be said around this official birth date. In the wake of Asta Nielsen's *Afgrunden*,[12] Francesca Bertini quickly realised how stuffy and rigid were her operatic roles for Film D'Art in Italy. She wanted to be modern and ground-breaking. Thus, around 1911, she began to seek new acting roles. In 1913, the self-taught Neapolitan performer was the first Italian film actress to play a role in male garb for *L'Histoire d'un Pierrot* (*Pierrot the Prodigal*) with Leda Gys and Emilio Ghione. This short film, based on a musical pantomime by Antonio Costa, dealt with male debauchery and marital reconciliation. Although Baldassarre Negroni figures in the credits as the director, he left the production of *L'Histoire d'un Pierrot* halfway through. Thus, Francesca Bertini and her lifelong friend, Emilio Ghione, ended up doing most of

the extant work under the supervision of Baron Alberto Fassini at Celio Film, a branch of Cines in Rome. Only eighteen years' old, Bertini quickly demonstrated leadership potential and could be a director, for she could both act and be in charge of an entire production team. In 1914, with Nino Oxilia's *Sangue Blu* (*Blue Blood*), Bertini transitioned into the longer feature-film version of short modern dramas about child custody. Yet that same year, she also starred in Baldassare Negroni's *L'Amazzone mascherata* (*The Masked Amazon*) – a sort of Italian response to the hugely popular thriller from Denmark, Benjamin Christensen's *Det hemmelighedsfulde* (*The Mystery of X*, 1914). This was a short film featuring Bertini as a courageous wife defending her husband from an unjust accusation of military betrayal.

The link between Bertini and Nielsen is little known, although unerringly documented by a woman film historian, Iole Ribolzi, whose precious work has been mostly unacknowledged in decades of bibliographies about the origins of the Italian diva.[13] Traditionally, male critics and historians have blamed only the diva and not the male producers or male directors for the film industry's bankruptcy at the end of World War I, as if her fatal destruction of men on screen had overflowed into real-life budgets, banking decisions and financial investments completely outside her sphere of direct action. Ribolzi explains that one key reason for the divas' high salaries was the cost of their set wardrobes. In fact, Bertini, who preferred a more classic, European look, bought from Worth in Paris, while Borelli used the exotic styles of Poiret and Fortuny much more frequently. Although, according to Ribolzi, Bertini was the first Italian diva, the official *doxa* upheld by male historians, from Francesco Soro to Vittorio Martinelli,[14] is that the diva was born with Lyda Borelli's *Ma l'amore mio non muore* in 1913. The novelty involved here was not only Borelli's launch as a film star, but also the switch from the short to the long format. Another tale of espionage and military duty, *Ma l'amore mio non muore* features a female heroine, Elsa Holbein, who is much less pro-active than Christensen's wife in *The Mystery of X* and much more subordinate than Bertini's equestrian performer in Negroni's *L'Amazzone mascherata*. In addition, whereas Bertini had no doubt that her future was in the cinema, Borelli continued to perform on stage, while she was working for Caserini.

It is likely that Borelli was chosen to carry the diva banner, not only because of her notoriety from the theatre, but also because her acting style was aligned with Duse and not with Nielsen. In this way, the diva's origins could be removed from Denmark and relocated in Italy for the sake of a more nationalistic argument. This approach was supported by the only other major woman film historian in Italy, Maria Adriana Prolo, whose name is forever associated with the development of the Turin Film Museum.

Finally, Caserini's *Ma l'amore mio non muore* was built as a multiple filmic adaptation of the famous Bernhardt's success in *La Dame aux Camélias*, by Alexandre Dumas, combined with Borelli's 1910 theatrical hit in Oscar Wilde's *Salomé*. With mirrors, chandeliers, letters, tuxedos, horse-riding, royal dynasty and social disgrace, suicide and sacrifice, Caserini's formula for a potboiler of amazing impact was a success at the box office. In short, the official Italian film diva and the genre of the diva film were born by having the stage diva Borelli perform a double-edged role. She was a semi-naked Salomé dancing for the hungry eyes of the male public, and she died like a fully clothed Marguerite Gauthier for an impossible love in order to uphold the values of family respectability and national duty. Although *Ma l'amore mio non muore* did not rely on exotic sets, it was clear from the audiences' approval that this new genre had found its public and was going to stay around for a few years. Needless to say, exoticism went hand in hand with the longer film format. With the Borelli diva film accommodating allusions from the Middle Eastern belly dancer to the Japanese geisha, additional themes and visual solutions quickly crystallised into well-known tropes split between escape and denunciation.

In contrast to the historical film's linear trajectory with a male hero, the diva film is often marked by narrative lacunae and weak adult males. Often reduced to disobedient children or vulnerable sons whom the diva tolerates, accepts and resents, these carefree or exploitative partners fail to provide an image of a modern, constructive and responsible male agency. This is why, in the diva film, in order to compensate for the proliferation of dandies and lounge lizards, of male artists and loafing aristocrats, it is the old and tough patriarchal figures who endure. It is as if the narrative needed the previous male generation to reach some kind of closure. Yet these grandfathers or old uncles represent an anti-modern and anachronistic regime, while they behave either in an over-protective or a despotic way towards their young female relatives.

In the diva film, adult males cheat, gamble, pimp, womanise, until their behaviour becomes too intolerable even for a patriarchal society. At that point, the family elders or the government send them to some colonial or exotic outpost. In Bertini's *Mariute*, the husband is away at war and the grandfather shoots the Austrian soldier who rapes the young peasant woman. Either because adult males are fighting on the front or because they spend all their time at the *tabarin*, narratives are marked by the absence of loving parents or genuinely romantic couples.

Unable to be good husbands or civil relatives, the male actors of diva film are powerful oppressors in principle and even less interesting performers de facto. The three most important male stars for this genre were: Amleto Novelli, an epileptic stalker in Bertini's *La piovra*; Mario Bonnard, a sickly and passive prince in Borelli's *Ma l'amore mio non muore*; and Alberto Capozzi, the male lead with a variety of divas without approaching Novelli's and Bonnard's more recognisable personae. In short, despite her sufferings and punishments, it is the diva as an actress who dominated the genre, and as such, she captured the transitional and contradictory atmosphere of a remarkable age of interrogation about gender roles. Future discoveries and restorations might eventually yield an even more nuanced panorama of the early and silent film industry from 1910 to the early twenties. Whether or not the diva of early Italian cinema is an isolated phenomenon, one whose aspects have migrated into subsequent international stars or actresses in the Italian film industry, after the coming of sound, is a question that remains to be answered.

NOTES

1. For a more detailed treatment of the diva, including an extensive bibliography, filmography and timeline of the era, see my book *Diva: Defiance and Passion in Early Italian Cinema* (Austin: University of Texas Press, 2008).
2. In the US, the nineteenth amendment granting women the right to vote was passed on 26 August 1920. In the UK, women householders or those with a university degree received the franchise in 1918; universal suffrage for all adults over twenty-one years of age was achieved in 1928. Italian women did not win the right to vote until 1945.
3. Dalle Vacche, *Diva*, pp. 105–28.
4. Cesare Molinari, *L'attrice divina: Eleonora Duse nel teatro italiano fra i due secoli* (Rome: Bulzoni, 1985); Carol Ockman and Kenneth E. Silver (eds), *Sarah Bernhardt: The Art of High Drama* (New Haven, CT and London: Yale University Press, 2005).
5. Mary Gibson, *Prostitution and the State in Italy 1860–1915*, 2nd edn (Columbus: Ohio State University Press, 1999); 1st edn (New Brunswick, NJ: Rutgers University Press, 1986). For examples of films, see *La memoria dell' altro* (1913), starring Lyda Borelli, or *La storia di una donna* (1920) with Pina Menichelli.
6. Cesare Lombroso and Guglielmo Ferrero, *Criminal Woman, the Prostitute, and the Normal Woman*, trans. and with new Introduction by Nicole Hahn Rafter and Mary Gibson (Durham, NC and London: Duke University Press, 2004). Originally published as *La donna delinquente, la prostituta, e la donna normale* (Turin and Rome: Roux, 1893); originally published in English as *The Female Offender* (London: T. F. Unwin, 1895).
7. Cristina Jandelli, *Le dive italiane del cinema muto* (Palermo: L'Epos, 2006), pp. 31–3.
8. Adriano Aprà, 'Lucio D'Ambra ritrovato. "Le mogli e le arance" e L'illustre cicala formica', *Bianco e Nero* vol. 63 no. 5 (September–October 2002), pp. 5–16.
9. Giorgio Bertellini, *Italy in Early American Cinema: Race, Landscape, and the Picturesque* (Bloomington: Indiana University Press, 2010).
10. On acting schools and their ambiguous reputation, see 'Scuola per Film', *Cine Gazzetta* vol. 1 no. 18 (3 May 1917), n. p.
11. Maria Adriana Prolo, *Storia del cinema muto italiano, Vol. I* (Milan: Poligono, 1951), p. 57.
12. Marguerite Engberg, *Asta Nielsen: Europe's First Film Star* (Berkeley, CA: University Art Museum and Pacific Film Archive, 1996).
13. Iole Ribolzi, *Divi e dive: Faccende e vicende del cinema 1913* (Milan: Stellissima, [1943?]). Also *Storia aneddotica del cinema italiano* (Varese: Maj & Malnati, 1945) and *Vecchio cinema italiano* (Milan: Casa Editrice Nuova Aurora, 1940).
14. See Francesco Soro, *Splendori e miserie del cinema; Cose viste e vissute da un avvocato* (Milan: Editore Consalvo, 1935). Also Vittorio Martinelli, 'Nascita del divismo', Gian Piero Brunetta (ed.), *Storia del cinema mondiale. L'Europa, vol. I* (Turin: Einaudi, 1999–2001), pp. 221–50.

FURTHER READING

Bade, Patrick, *Femme Fatale: Images of Evil and Fascinating Women* (New York: Mayflower Books, 1979).

Bergson, Henri, *Creative Evolution*, trans. Arthur Mitchell (Mineola, NY: Dover, 1998; New York: Henry Holt, 1911; originally published as *L'Évolution créatrice* [Paris: F. Alcan, 1907]).

Bossaglia, Rossana, A. Braggion and M. Guglielminetti, *Dalla donna fatale alla donna emancipata: Iconografia femminile nell'età del Deco* (Nuoro: Ilisso, 1993).

Dalle Vacche, Angela and Gian Luca Farinelli (eds), *Silent Divas of Italian Cinema: Passion and Defiance* (Milan: Edizioni Olivares, 2000).

Dijkstra, Bram, *Evil Sisters: The Threat of Female Sexuality and the Cult of Manhood* (New York: Knopf, 1996).

Doane, Mary Ann, *Femmes Fatales: Feminism, Film Theory, and Psychoanalysis* (New York: Routledge, 1991).

Dyer, Richard, *Heavenly Bodies: Film Stars and Society* (London and New York: BFI/Macmillan, 1986).

Leonardi, Susan J. and Rebecca A. Pope, *The Diva's Mouth: Body, Voice, Prima Donna Politics* (New Brunswick, NJ: Rutgers University Press, 1996).

Morin, Edgar, *The Stars* (New York: Grove Press, 1961).

Tebano, Neerio, *Lyda Borelli e Pina Menichelli. Poesie e immagini* (Rome: Il Delfino e Lo Scorpione, 1992).

4 Italian Silent Film Genres

Comics, Serials, Historical Epics and Strongmen

Jacqueline Reich

Since its inception, Italian film productions found worldwide profit and recognition by specialising in historical epics, melodramas, elaborate costume films and, to a minor extent, *actualités* (documentaries), scientific and educational films. A different but also quite profitable production format was based on the serialisation of characters and narratives, as in comedies, detective and crime films, and the strongman adventures. While Italian silent cinema's most successful genre, the historical epic and its popular offspring, the strongman film, had a lasting impact on Italian cinema in terms of style, national and international appeal, and chronological permanence, Italian comic and crime serials also deserve serious critical attention.

While many Italian cities had thriving film industries, in particular Milan, Naples and Rome, most of these early film genres were shot in Turin, the country's vibrant centre of film production. As a 1914 article in the magazine *Secolo XX* put it, Italy's former capital was the nation's *filmopolis*, a 'cinema city', where film production and exhibition pervaded all walks of life; film periodicals thrived, including the very influential *La vita cinematografica* (founded in 1910); artists flocked to participate in set and costume design; and the Italian star system was born.[1] Turin's fairs, variety theatre and public performances in piazzas featured acts whose short vignettes and feats of strength, comedy and agility fit perfectly with the exigencies and the limitations of early film production, and provided the first attractions that found their way onto the screen.

The first Italian comic film was *Il finto storpio del castello* [The Fake Cripple of the Castle, 1896] by Italo Pacchioni, shown at the Milan fair of that year through a projection system of Pacchioni's own devising, since the Lumière brothers had denied him the use of their pioneering invention.[2] Leopoldo Fregoli, a theatrical transformist and a performer known for his rapid changes of costume and character, soon followed, creating a series of short films which were the first to feature the comic's name in the title, among them *Fregoli trasformista* [Fregoli Transformist], *Fregoli donna* [Lady Fregoli] and *Fregoli al restaurant* [Fregoli at the Restaurant], all from 1898. He was also one of the first to incorporate dialogue into his film exhibitions, as he would often hide behind the screen and voice the characters as they spoke.

The comic film went through several phases of development: the pre-industrial phase from 1896–1907/8, during which their length increased from short films of 15–17 metres to entire reels. They earned the term *comica finale* (roughly translated as 'the last laugh'), because they were often shown at the end of a film programme in order to ensure the spectators left the theatre in good humour. In the years 1908 to 1911, Italy experienced the birth and establishment of the comic series (the *comica a serie*), which appeared regularly on screen (about once per month) and featured a recurrent character in a variable situation: even though the character remained constant, in each film he (or she, in a few cases) could acquire a complexity of tone and variation.[3] With relatively few intertitles, the flow from one situation to another produced the comic rhythm.

These films were mostly farcical sketches centred on one protagonist with recognisable traits and features, and one principle action or gag. Prominent among these early comics were the French Max Linder and André Deed whose films enjoyed an immense following in Italy as well. Deed had worked with Georges Méliès before moving to Pathé and creating the successful character Boireau, and then to Italy with Turin's Itala Film company as the character Cretinetti, under the supervision of the studio's creative director, Giovanni Pastrone. In 1909, the first Cretinetti films appeared to national and international acclaim, and the series lasted through 1911, when Deed returned to France (he resumed his Italian career in 1915 when the French film industry suffered an economic crisis). What made Deed's films different from other comic characters' cinematic sketches was that they told a story rather than exclusively focusing on the gag. Also interested in experimentation, select films featured surreal special effects, the use of visual tricks and the acceleration of the hectic rhythm typical of chase comedies.[4] Other popular comic series, in addition to Cretinetti's, included those starring Fricot (Enrico Vaser), Kri Kri (Ovaro), Robinet (Marcel Fabre), and Tontolini and Polidor, played by Ferdinand Guillaume. Guillaume, who became one of early Italian cinema's great comics (and subsequently performed in Fellini's *La dolce vita*), exploited the tradition of the French farce, with his extremely expressive and easily recognisable face. His characters were emblematic of the twentieth-century figure of the *inetto*, the inept man who becomes the victim of others or objects around him, and were used to ridicule the behaviour of Italy's growing bourgeois class.[5]

Precisely what made the comic films uniquely Italian, as opposed to mere copies of their French counterparts, was this immersion in the everyday life of turn-of-the-century Italy: they appealed to both popular and bourgeois spectators, and at the same time, recorded, in an almost diary-like fashion, lower middle-class and middle-class life caught between tradition and modernity. More an urban than a rural phenomenon, these films were parodies of emerging bourgeois rituals and cultures, although, unlike many early American comics working under Mack Sennett, they had a less problematic connection to modernisation in terms of the characters' relationship to and interaction with mechanical objects, such as cars and machines. Similarly, authority, particularly law enforcement, was not the target of their jokes and gags. Instead, political institutions and public assistance bore the brunt, such the Red Cross, anti-drinking societies, feminists and suffragettes.[6]

Early comedies were significant in the development of Italian film stardom. In many ways, these short films, and the rise to prominence of the comedians featured therein, revealed the economic, commercial and psychological mechanisms at the base of what would become the Italian star system: the actors and actresses who commanded the highest salaries and achieved the greatest recognition were inextricably linked to particular generic forms and modes of expression. The comic series, however, did not prove to be a viable form as the industry shifted to multi-reel production in the mid-1910s, and these films were among the first to suffer during the post-World War I downturn in the Italian film industry. Their lack of innovation and, arguably, their one-note gags, were soon eclipsed by the charismatic and inventive short and feature-length films of Charlie Chaplin (known as Charlot in Italy), Fatty Arbuckle and Buster Keaton. The relatively underdeveloped avenue of the sophisticated comedy, exemplified in the late 1910s and early 1920s by the films of Lucio D'Ambra, yielded few lasting results. Instead, the comic one-reelers survived in the tradition of the *comica finale*: they continued to be exhibited after melodramatic or tragic films, such as the diva films (see Angela Dalle Vacche's contribution in this volume), in order for the audience to experience the necessary catharsis and leave the theatre in an appropriately good mood. In this way, older films continued to be recycled during the silent period and beyond.

Following closely on the heels of the comic film was the detective or crime series, which, instead of showcasing a recognisable performer, such as Guillaume or Deed, focused instead on recurring characters. Once again the blueprint here was French cinema, and the mysterious characters Nick Carter, Sherlock Holmes, Arsène Lupin, Zigomar and, the most popular of all, Fantômas. Essential to these more dramatically oriented series was the idea of transformation: not only were actors interchangeable, but the characters themselves could morph into other creatures.[7]

Unlike comic films, detective and crime one-reelers began to mutate successfully into longer multi-reel films. Eventually, feature-length films with overarching narratives that carried from one film to the next gave birth to what came to be known as the serial, which added the concept of continuity of narrative to the continuity of character: one story would be told over several episodes, or the plot would leave the viewer hanging – the cliffhanger – until he or she was able to go to the theatre to see it the following week. Also known as episodic films (*film a episodi*, in Italian), there were varied exhibition practices, sometimes one per week (as in Pathé's American-made serial, *The Perils of Pauline* [1914] or in Kalem's *Hazards of Helen* [1914–17]) or several episodes at once, making up, in a sense, a feature-length film. For the nascent film industries in the US and Europe, they were the perfect model to invigorate the marketplace: they standardised production, recycled materials and ideas, were easily publicised and guaranteed an audience.[8]

The Italian industry's first attempt to adapt these successful formulae to feature-length productions was through films with the character Za la Mort, starring and directed by Emilio Ghione. Ghione made many films as the thief Za la Mort, including *Za la Mort* (*Za la Mort*, 1915), *Topi grigi* in eight episodes [The Grey Mice, 1918] and *Dollari e fraks* [Dollars and Tuxedos, 1919, four episodes]. In a blatant attempt to co-opt the French *Fantômas* series, Za la Mort continued his crime spree from one film to the other, constantly evading capture. Although most serial films featured Italian characters in the service of appropriate social goals and as embodiments of the status quo, at the same time these films revealed, with their popular settings and nefarious underworld, a poor and socially arrested Italy unseen in other films of the era.[9]

In contrast, a type of film that perfectly preserved the nationalist spirit pervading Italy during this period was the historical epic, the most popular and profitable product of early Italian cinema. Like the comic films and detective serials, they owed part of their success to French film-making models, including Pathé's Film d'Arte Italiana production company, founded in 1909 and based in Rome. What distinguished Italian films from these and other national epic productions was an authenticity of settings, costumes and *mise en scène* that exuded a genuine nationalist sentiment. Historical epics served to create a mythological base onto which to construct the new Italian nation, masking its cracks and fissures with respect to geographical disparity and disunity, radical class differences and past defeats in Italy's colonialist enterprises.[10]

Many historical epics were adaptations of successful literary works; others expanded upon a contemporary theatrical trend of plays set in ancient times, whose major exponent was the playwright Pietro Cossa and whose theatrical works based on actual events – including *Nerone* (1872), *Messalina* (1876), *Giuliano l'Apostata* [Julian the Apostate, 1877] and *Cleopatra* (1877) – imbued historical characters with human attributes. With their literary origins and their recourse to the historical past, as well as their spectacularity and attractiveness, these films brought together both bourgeois and popular audiences in an attempt to educate, elevate and enlighten the Italian and international filmgoing public. The historical epic's stock characters were the bold and loyal young man who falls in love with a helpless young woman, because she is a slave or a hostage; the shifty rival; the young girl snared by individuals without scruples; the faithful nurse or slave; the good giant with superhuman force who can solve any problem; and an old man unable to understand the young people's love. Common dramatic tropes and spectacles included natural explosions and a violent encounter between opposing forces (Christians vs pagans, Romans against Jews, liberty vs slavery), serving as backdrops for the story of the individual characters.[11]

The first historical epic dates to 1908 and is the first of two eventual adaptations of *The Last Days of Pompeii*: the 1908 version was directed by Arturo Ambrosio and Luigi Maggi, the 1913 version by Mario Caserini and Eleuterio Rodolfi, and produced by Ambrosio. Based on the 1834 novel by Edward Bulwer-Lytton (translated and published in Italian in 1865), the film inspired other epic productions, such as *Nerone* (*Nero, or the Burning of Rome*, 1909), *Giulio Cesare* (*Julius Caesar*, 1909) and Giovanni Pastrone's *La caduta di Troia*. The turning point in the genre's popularity and reach was Enrico Guazzoni's *Quo vadis?* (*Quo Vadis*, 1913) which, like many of the films under discussion, continued to circulate long after its release. The rhetorical references to ancient Rome, particularly the notion of the myth of an imperial nation based on a collective of strongmen – a theme that would play itself out particularly well in Giovanni Enrico Vidali's *Spartaco* (*Spartacus*, 1913), another crucial historical epic – factored in the film's success. Its use of depth of field and the crowd, a hallmark of the early Italian historical films, increased its sophistication: the scene at the Roman Forum as the slaves are fed to the lions, while not particularly complex in terms of its editing, created realistic suspense through the use of reaction shots of the on-screen spectators and actual lions on the prowl in the frame's foreground. Heavily promoted in film magazines (it received a four-page spread announcing its imminent arrival in the January 1913 issue of *La vita cinematografica*), it cemented the industry's reliance on full-length feature film and was exported all over the world to great acclaim. Similarly, the publicity for *Spartacus* in the 30 September issue of the same publication touted its forty free-roaming lions and the gladiators' battles against them, horse races and athletic competitions, as all part of the 'greatest cinematic spectacle yet'.

The Roman Forum scene from *Quo vadis?* (1913)

Quo vadis?'s Roman Forum scene is noteworthy as well for the heroic exploits of Ursus the slave, who, as he saves a woman strapped to the back of a bull then kills the bull with his bare hands, signals the birth of the strongman as the historical epic's moral compass. Played by Bruto Castellani, the character of Ursus was celebrated in the press and by the moviegoing public, including being singled out for praise by the British Royal Family. Although Castellani remained attached to the historical epic, Luciano Albertini, the actor who played Spartacus in the eponymous film, did not, and would later go on to star in his own series of strongman films as the character Sansone (Samson).

Ironically, the success of, and the film industry's reliance on, the historical epic contributed to the crisis that plagued the Italian film industry after World War I: the soaring costs, the industry's inability to innovate the formula and its stubborn reliance on the genre in a misguided attempt to improve its fortune proved fatal to the film industry. But it would not disappear before the making of Italy's most ground-breaking silent film, Pastrone's *Cabiria* and introducing the character who would spawn the most successful Italian film series of

the silent era, Maciste, brought to life on screen by Bartolomeo Pagano, a dockworker plucked from obscurity while working at the Genoa ports.

With intertitles by the renowned poet Gabriele D'Annunzio, *Cabiria* altered the landscape of early Italian cinema. It told the story of the kidnapping of a noble Roman girl Cabiria (Lidia Quaranta) during the Punic Wars in the third century BC and her liberation by the Roman Fulvio Axilla (Umberto Mozzato) and his loyal, muscular African slave Maciste. The film's enormous impact sprang from its many cinematic innovations: the historical accuracy of its elaborate sets, its high-brow literary aspirations, its pioneering tracking and dolly shots, the strategic use of artificial lighting, ornate costume design and a complexity in plot previously absent from Italian cinema. Scenes of the eruption of Mount Etna, the human sacrifice at the Temple of Moloch and Hannibal (Emilio Vardannes) crossing the Alps revealed the unique range of special effects and inventive use of colour that the film achieved thanks to well-known Catalán film director and cinematographer extraordinaire Segundo de Chomón.[12] More than a mere film show, the initial national and international exhibitions of *Cabiria* were major and unique events, highly promoted and publicised by Itala with elaborately designed posters, brochures and programmes. Musical accompaniment featured a live orchestra playing an original score by Manlio Mazza and included an eleven-minute interlude entitled 'The Symphony of Fire' by the renowned composer Ildebrando Pizzetti, Mazza's teacher.[13]

The popular press immediately hailed Maciste as an Italian hero – they quickly dubbed him 'il gigante buono' (the gentle giant). If historical films valorised what was important in ancient Rome as spectacle – the muscular body, exhibitions of strength, gymnastics and athletic displays personified by Maciste in *Cabiria* – the strongman nevertheless remained circumscribed by the limits of slavery. Once freed from those bounds and established as the protagonist of his own series, the strongman passes from slave to master, from supporting actor to lead in a genre unique to Italian screens at a time when Italy was itself in search of its own national identity.

The strongman film, commonly referred to in Italian as the *il cinema dei forzuti, il cinema degli uomini forti* or *il cinema atletico-acrobatico*, was an extremely popular genre in the late 1910s and 1920s that revolved around a familiar character, a hero with a Herculean upper body performing feats of bravery that showed off his strength and virility, or in the case of the more acrobatic-oriented films, agility. The strongman fits somewhere in between the realist and decadent/expressionist tendencies of Italian cinema's early years. On the one hand, the films required a suspension of disbelief with respect to their plot twists, the main character's feats of strength and their often ludicrous catalytic incidents. On the other hand, they were filmed

The Temple of Moloch in *Cabiria* (1914)

on location all over Italy, although mostly in the North, in both urban and rural settings, in order to appeal to the widest possible audience.[14]

While films with circus/adventure themes began to appear on screen with such titles as Giovanni Enrico Vidali's *Il principino saltimbanco* [The Acrobat Prince, 1914], Enrique Santos's *L'acrobata mascherato* [The Masked Acrobat, 1915] and Vittorio Rossi Pianelli's *Il romanzo di un atleta* [The Story of an Athlete, 1915], among others, it was not until the end of World War I that the genre began to flourish. Between 1919 and 1922, what Alberto Farassino considers the golden age of the strongman film, 118 strongman films were produced by a variety of studios, once again mostly based in Northern Italy.[15] Its major protagonists, in addition to Maciste and Sansone (or Sansonia), included Ausonia (Mario Guaita Ausonia), Aiax (Carlo Aldini), Saetta (Domenico Gambino) and even several women; Astrea (the Countess Barbieri) and Sansonetta (Albertini's wife) were two of the most popular. Some, such as Albertini, founded their own film studios and produced their own movies. Although the strongman remained popular as the Italian film industry began its rapid decline in the 1920s, the genre too suffered due to critical pressure, the shift in the public's more sophisticated taste for American, German and French films, and the financial disarray of the whole industry.

Farassino has isolated several characteristics common to the strongman films, which continued the tradition of mining the porous boundaries of other contemporary film genres that featured action sequences: detective films, spy films, adventure films and war films, with the strongman as the added, pivotal element. In general, the strongman does not kill his enemies but rather uses his strength to subdue and deliver them to the proper law-enforcement authorities. And although not a uniquely urban phenomenon (many do in fact take place in the open countryside as opposed to closed urban environments), these films were not immune to the trappings of modernity: many featured cars, trains, factories and other signs of Italy's progressive march toward further industrialisation and modernisation. With the dominance of action over narrative, these were films made with a good heart and good wit for the entire family: their intertitles, despite remnant D'Annunzian flourishes, included strategic moments of irony that provided much of the films' humour. Lacking an overt eroticism, the strongmen were desexualised heroes representing a realistic fusion between the extraordinary and the everyday.[16] Their familiarity via popular theatrical traditions, their naturalistic acting, even with incredible and incredulous feats of strength, ran counterpoint to the overwrought acting style of their female counterparts, the dive.[17]

The Maciste films remained the most influential of the strongman films and Italy's most prominent example of the silent film series based on a popular protagonist. It all began with *Cabiria*'s phenomenal international success. Following the unexpected but widespread popularity of Maciste, Itala Film decided to produce a series of adventure films with the strongman as protagonist, beginning with Vincenzo Dénizot and Romano Luigi Borgnetto's *Maciste* (*Marvelous Maciste*, 1915). In his transition from supporting character in *Cabiria* to the series' leading man, Maciste undergoes several radical alterations: he moves from ancient Rome to modern-day Italy and, most significantly, he changes from a black-bodied African slave to a white, northern Italian. The fact that Maciste's skin colour shifts from black to white has racial and national significance. Maciste's metamorphosis popularised current anthropological tenets of northern Italian and white superiority through the classic cinematic devices of heroic sacrifice, spectacular feats and moral righteousness, embodied in the muscled body. These temporal and racial shifts cement and legitimise Maciste's emergence as an acceptable, and highly marketable, national symbol.

Pagano made a total of nineteen films as Maciste: nine by Itala Film, including Pastrone's widely praised *Maciste alpino* (*The Warrior*, 1916), one of the most influential World War I fiction films of its time, and two films by Romano Luigi Borgnetto *Maciste innamorato* (Maciste in Love, 1919) and *Maciste in vacanza* (Maciste on Vacation, 1921). During the 1920s, Pagano, like many other performers, found work in Germany's thriving national cinema, where he made three 'sensation' films (the German term for action-packed adventure films) but ultimately returned to Italy in 1924 to make some of his most successful films for the distributor/producer Stefano Pittaluga and his company Fert: they include Brignone's *Maciste imperatore* (Maciste the Emperor, 1924) and *Maciste all'inferno* (*Maciste in Hell*, 1926) and Camerini's *Maciste contro lo sceicco* (Maciste against the Sheik, 1926). In Italy, Pagano became the highest-paid male star of the day, and his films were

distributed worldwide. Maciste clones began to appear in the United States and elsewhere: advertisements for Elmo Lincoln, star of the original Tarzan series, billed him as the 'Yankee Maciste'.[18]

Maciste played a crucial role in Italian cinema's narrativisation of a unified national identity before, during and after World War I for both national and international audiences. His charismatic appeal and associations with strength and bravery raised him to a heroic, national status and Maciste became the model Italian to lead the relatively young nation by entertaining example. The transposition of his heroic narratives to contemporary Italy aligned him with pressing contemporary national and political imperatives: Italy's intervention in World War I, modernisation, the birth of fascism and its colonial aspirations. Maciste effectively bridged Italy's past and present and, in a convergence of Italian politics and popular entertainment, his fame anticipated later occurrences of Italian political stardom, notably that of Benito Mussolini. He remained an iconic reference well into the 1930s, even after Pagano had stopped making films, because many of his earlier films were released with added sound, including *Cabiria* in 1931, once the technology permitted. They later inspired another serial incarnation, the 1960s peplum films (see Jon Solomon's chapter in this collection) and countless other film-makers, including Sergio Leone and, perhaps surprisingly, Federico Fellini. As Fellini himself famously said, 'So many times I say jokingly that I am always trying to remake that film, that all the films I make are the repetition of *Maciste in Hell*.'[19]

In conclusion, genre production, be it comic, historical or adventure/athletic, was the basis of much of the Italian film industry during its first three decades and before the introduction of sound, often aligned and in tune with the many political, social and cultural changes of a rapidly changing twentieth-century Italy. As this volume of diverse essays demonstrates, genres remained at the heart of Italian cinema and showcased significant artistic merits years before the national production witnessed its postwar auteuristic turn. The spaghetti Western, peplum and comedy Italian-style films had their roots in these first films as they came to reincarnate their predecessors' iconography and characters for the modern and postmodern era.

NOTES

1. Gianni Rondolino, *I giorni di Cabiria* (Turin: Lindau, 1993), originally published as *Torino come Hollywood* (Bologna: Cappelli, 1980).

2. Throughout this study, I have adopted the following procedure to present English-language translations of Italian film titles: I use the American title under which known US-distributed Italian films appeared in the US, i.e. *La caduta di Troia* (*The Fall of Troy*, 1911), unless the two titles coincide, as in the case of *Cabiria* (1914). When no American title is available, I have included a literal translation *in square brackets*: *L'ultima battaglia* [The Last Battle, 1914]. My source for the American titles is Aldo Bernardini (ed.), *Archivio del cinema italiano, Volume I: Il cinema muto, 1905–1931*, (Rome: Edizioni ANICA: 1991).

3. Aldo Bernardini, 'Appunti sul cinema comico muto italiano', *Griffithiana* vol. 7 nos 24–5 (October 1985), pp. 21–35.

4. Paolo Cherchi Usai, 'Italy: Spectacle and Melodrama', in Geoffrey Nowell-Smith (ed.), *The Oxford History of World Cinema* (Oxford: Oxford University Press, 1996), pp. 123–9, here p. 125.

5. Gian Piero Brunetta (ed.), *Storia del cinema italiano, Vol. I* (Rome: Editori Riuniti, 1993), p. 197.

6. Gian Piero Brunetta, 'Il clown cinematografico tra salotto liberty e frontiera del West', *Griffithiana* vol. 7 nos 24–5 (October 1985), pp. 11–20.

7. Monica Dall'Asta, 'La diffusione del film a episodi in Europa', in Gian Piero Brunetta (ed.), *Storia del cinema mondiale, Vol. I* (Turin: Einaudi, 1999), pp. 277–315; and Monica Dall'Asta (ed.), *Fantômas. La vita plurale di un attore* (Pozzuolo del Friuli: Il Principe Costante Edizioni, 2004).

8. Ben Singer, 'Serials', in Richard Abel (ed.), *Encyclopedia of Early Cinema* (New York: Routledge, 2005), pp. 582–3.

9. Gian Piero Brunetta, *Il cinema muto 1895–1929, Vol. I* (Rome: Editori Riuniti, 1993), p. 209; Denis Lotti, *Emilio Ghione, l'ultimo apache. Vita e film di un divo italiano* (Bologna: Cineteca di Bologna, 2008).

10. Giovanni Calendoli, *Materiali per una storia del cinema italiano* (Parma: Maccari Editore, 1967), p. 30; James Hay, *Popular Film Culture in Fascist Italy: The Passing of the Rex* (Bloomington: Indiana University Press, 1987), p. 152; and Irmbert Schenk, 'The Cinematic Support to National(istic) Mythology: The Italian Peplum 1910–1930', in Natascha Gentz and Stefan Kramer (eds), *Globalization, Cultural Identities, and Media Representations* (Albany: State University of New York Press, 2006), pp. 153–68.

11. Monica Dall'Asta, *Un cinéma musclé. Le surhomme dans le cinéma muet italien (1913–1926)* (Crisnée: Yellow Now, 1992), p. 27; Maria Wyke, *Projecting the Past: Ancient Rome, Cinema and History* (London: Routledge, 1997), p. 25.

12. Silvio Alovisio and Alberto Barbera (eds), *Cabiria & Cabiria* (Turin: Il Castoro, 2006); Paolo Bertetto and Gianni Rondolino (eds), *Cabiria e il suo tempo* (Milan: Il Castoro, 1998); Gian Piero Brunetta (ed.), *Storia del cinema italiano, Vol. I*, pp. 173–7; Calendoli, *Materiali per una storia del cinema italiano*, pp. 63–111; Angela Dalle Vacche, *The Body in the Mirror: Shapes of History in Italian Cinema* (Princeton, NJ: Princeton University Press, 1993), pp. 27–52; Marcia Landy, *Italian Film: The National Tradition* (New York: Cambridge University Press, 2000), pp. 33–40; Pierre Sorlin, *Italian National Cinema 1896–1996* (London: Routledge, 1996), pp. 35–8; and Jon Solomon, *The Ancient World in Cinema*, rev. and expanded edn (New Haven, CT: Yale University Press, 2001), pp. 47–9.

13. Martin Miller Marks, *Music and the Silent Film: Contexts and Case Studies, 1895–1924* (New York: Oxford University Press, 1997), pp. 103–8.

14. Alberto Farassino and Tatti Sanguineti (eds), *Gli uomini forti* (Milan: Mazzotta, 1983); Michele Giordano, *Giganti buoni: Da Ercole a Piedone (e oltre) il mito dell'uomo forte nel cinema italiano* (Rome: Gremese, 1998); Vittorio Martinelli and Mario Quargnolo, *Maciste & Co. I giganti buoni del muto italiano* (Gemona del Friuli: Cinepopolare Edizioni, 1981); and Mario Verdone, 'Il film atletico e acrobatico', *Centrofilm* no. 17 (1971).

15. Alberto Farassino, 'Anatomia del cinema muscolare', in Farassino and Sanguineti, *Gli uomini forti*, pp. 29–50.

16. Ibid.

17. Martinelli and Quargnolo, *Maciste & Co.*, pp. 9–10.

18. *The Sandusky Star Journal* (8 July 1919), p. 12.

19. Federico Fellini, 'Amarcord Maciste', in Farassino and Sanguineti, *Gli uomini forti*, p. 182.

FURTHER READING

Bertellini, Giorgio (ed.), *Italian Silent Cinema: A Reader* (New Barnet: John Libbey, 2012).

Cherchi Usai, Paolo, 'Italy: Spectacle and Melodrama', in Geoffrey Novell-Smith (ed.), *The Oxford History of World Cinema* (Oxford: Oxford University Press, 1996), pp. 123–9.

Dalle Vacche, Angela, *The Body in the Mirror: Shapes of History in Italian Cinema* (Princeton, NJ: Princeton University Press, 1993).

Solomon, Jon, *The Ancient World in Cinema*, rev. and expanded edn (New Haven, CT: Yale University Press, 2001).

Wyke, Maria, *Projecting the Past: Ancient Rome, Cinema and History* (London: Routledge, 1997).

PART TWO

The Birth of the Talkies and the Fascist Era

Introduction

Peter Bondanella

The first Italian feature film with sound was Gennaro Righelli's *La Canzone dell'amore* (*The Song of Love*, 1930). Ironically, this first talkie was based on a short story by Nobel Prize-winning writer Luigi Pirandello entitled 'In silenzio' or 'In Silence'. The Italian film industry produced almost 800 feature films during this second and very important stage of Italian film history. Unlike the early phenomenal success of Italian silent films in foreign markets, the productions between 1922 and 1943 (when Benito Mussolini ruled the country as a dictator) were far less successful abroad, often due to obstacles created by political, economic or ideological conflicts with other nations. Besides the fact that Italian cinema during the fascist period did not achieve wide distribution abroad, its critical reputation after the fall of the regime was naturally suspect, and the rise and subsequent international fame of Italian neorealist cinema immediately after the war encouraged Italians and non-Italians alike to see an abrupt separation between this period and the period after 1945.

Yet, such a perspective has been progressively challenged by film scholars in the past few decades. David Forgacs outlines the issues involved in determining whether there was a 'fascist' cinema or whether we need to speak of 'cinema under fascism' – the two things are quite different. Moreover, we must, on the one hand, be careful to distinguish between the overtly propagandistic products turned out in newsreels made by the Istituto Luce (in which Mussolini seemed to be single-handedly responsible for everything worthwhile across the entire peninsula) and, on the other, the hundreds of feature films obviously more concerned with entertaining than with brainwashing the population. Hollywood continued to dominate the Italian film market, as it would in the immediate postwar neorealist period.

Marcia Landy's contribution on the matinee idols of this time emphasises how the major directors – individuals such as Blasetti, Camerini, Gallone, De Sica and Rossellini who we would now probably label auteurs – expanded the generic boundaries of silent cinema, particularly in comedies and adventure films. Vito Zagarrio's chapter analyses how Blasetti, Camerini and De Sica defined a kind of comic film we now more clearly see as the foundation of Italy's most popular postwar film genre, the so-called *commedia all'italiana* or 'comedy, Italian style'. Italian comic films produced during the fascist era have much to teach us about how Italian audiences envisioned modernity, modernisation and entertainment in a newly nascent consumer society. And in this regard, comparisons to contemporaneous Hollywood comedies lead to some surprising conclusions.

Guido Bonsaver offers a panoramic treatment of Italian film censorship from the fascist period to the present, and his discussion goes beyond the chronological boundary of the fascist regime (1922–43) because much fascist censorship legislation endured after the dissolution of Mussolini's regime. Bonsaver examines how the legacy of fascism lived on until the last several decades of the twentieth century, during which major directors such as Fellini, Pasolini and Bertolucci had to deal with threats to their artistic freedom. Times change: the Italian government now sponsors a website allowing free access to documents related to the censorship of films between 1913 and 1955.

5 Fascism and Italian Cinema

David Forgacs

Italy had a fascist government for just over twenty years, from October 1922, when Benito Mussolini and his Blackshirts seized power, to July 1943, when a majority of his own cabinet ousted him in order to pull the country out of a world war in which it had suffered disastrous reversals. In October 1943, a rump fascist regime known as the Republic of Salò, again headed by Mussolini, was set up with the backing of Nazi Germany in the north of Italy, then occupied by German forces. It claimed to be the legitimate government, but it was opposed by the anti-fascist resistance and by the advance of British and American troops from the south. Fascism's final demise came in April 1945 when Mussolini was captured and shot by Communist partisans and Italy was liberated.

What relations existed between fascism and the cinema over this period? There is no clear consensus about this among film scholars and historians. Some argue that the cinema was strongly shaped by fascism, while others maintain that its effect was more limited. The former generally point to the propaganda newsreels, bans on some foreign films and revisions by censors of treatments and scripts for Italian films. They also argue that there was a distinct fascist ideological influence on many feature films, not just those with an overt political content. The latter highlight the limits of state control on private film production, the Italian film industry's commercial orientation, including its attempts to emulate Hollywood and French cinema, and the numerical prevalence of entertainment films. They also note that from 1922 to 1939, in other words for most of the period of fascist government, many more American films were being screened in Italy than Italian ones. In 1938, for example, American films accounted for 74 per cent of box-office gross in Italy. So, until 1939, the cinema in Italy could, from the audience's point of view, be said to have been more

American than Italian. Hardline fascists repeatedly complained about the seemingly irrepressible 'esterofilia' (love of foreign things) of the Italian public and of certain film critics.

These differences of opinion do not derive, as one might think, simply from the particular aspects of the relationship that one chooses to highlight. These choices often reflect different underlying ideas and judgments about how pervasive fascist ideology was, what happens to people when they watch a film and whether the regulation of the content of Italian feature films in the fascist era was really all that different from that exerted, say, by the Hays Code in the US or by the British Board of Film Censors. They also involve, at least for Italian scholars, a difficult and at times ambivalent relationship with Italy's fascist past, where the desire to know and appreciate the cinema of the period comes up against the equally legitimate desire not to allow a depoliticised or nostalgic image of fascism to circulate. This can make it hard to assert positive value judgments – for instance to declare that a certain Italian film made under fascism is good rather than just informative as a historical source or interesting as an ideological text – and to reconcile such judgments with one's political stance on fascism. Although it is now nearly seventy years since the fascist government fell, these problems have become, if anything, more acute because of the rise since the mid-1990s of a political right in Italy that has sought to minimise the crimes and injustices of fascism, emphasise the allegedly positive aspects of its prewar record and 'balance out' the violence of the fascists by that perpetrated by anti-fascists in and after the resistance of 1943–5.

The question of cinema and fascism, therefore, is a complicated one. In order to untangle it, we need to draw out a number of smaller questions and try to answer each in turn. First, in what ways did the fascist state intervene in the film industry and did these interventions amount overall to strong control? Second, how far did the films made under fascism embody fascist ideas and values? Third, who were the audiences and were their responses to films shaped by fascism? Fourth, was the cinema of the fascist period a self-contained era or did aspects of it persist after World War II?

THE STATE AND CINEMA

When the fascists took power in 1922 they did not immediately take over the Italian state. This process took several years, in which, without abolishing the existing constitution, they outlawed other political parties, destroyed the law-making powers of parliament and enabled the government increasingly to rule by decree. The fascist government enjoyed the support of industrialists, to whom it offered protection against the threat of militant organised labour, as well as of many small property owners. Unlike the leadership in the Soviet Union, the fascist government in Italy was content at first to leave most of the economy, including the film industry, in the hands of private companies, over whom it exercised a light regulatory touch. During the 1930s, however, state intervention expanded, just as in other capitalist economies, including the US, Germany, Japan and Britain, in response to the Great Depression. The Italian state rescued ailing firms and failing banks, and in 1933 it created Italy's first major state holding company, the Istituto per la Ricostruzione Industriale (IRI).

The evolution of relations between the state and the cinema broadly followed this pattern of a move from an early *laissez-faire* phase to one of growing intervention and regulation. In the early years, 1922–4, it was film producers who initially approached the state for its support, rather than the state moving to intervene in the film industry. Italian film production was in deep crisis when the fascists came to power and it would not begin to recover until the end of the 1920s. Distributors, exhibitors (cinema owners) and audiences were increasingly seeking American films, although German ones also did well enough in Italy in the early 1920s to outperform domestic films at the box office. The admiration for American films, in particular for their technical quality and acting, was evident in many Italian reviews of the 1920s. Italian producers sought assistance from the state and asked, variously, for protectionist measures to defend them from foreign competition, exhibition quotas to guarantee screenings

of their films on the home market and measures to facilitate export, including relaxation of customs duties and diplomatic aid.

The fascist government's initial lack of interest also reflected the fact that it did not yet consider the cinema to be significant either as an industry – in the early 1920s its contribution to Italy's gross domestic product was almost negligible – or as a cultural activity. Or, to be more precise, the fascists did not yet believe *entertainment* cinema to be of much importance. They understood very well from early on, by contrast, the political potential of *information* cinema as well as the need to be vigilant about controlling the flow of news images and reports into and out of Italy. This distinction is crucial. By 1924–5, the fascists were taking control of what they saw as the most influential channels of information in Italy and, just like the Bolsheviks in the Soviet Union, they realised that newsreels could reach and influence large numbers of people in a country where rates of literacy and newspaper reading were low but cinema attendances were rising. As for censorship, a law of 1923 transferred the responsibility for examining both film scripts and completed films to the prefects in each of Italy's seventy-three provinces (rising to ninety-three in 1927 as a result of boundary changes) who depended directly on the Ministry of the Interior.

In line with its recognition of the importance of newsreels, in 1925, the state took over and recapitalised a private company that had been founded a year earlier to make educational films and turned it into the Istituto Luce. 'Luce' means 'light', and the name played both on the idea of projected film and on that of mass enlightenment, but it was also officially an acronym for L'Unione Cinematografica Educativa. The Istituto Luce produced documentaries, educational films and, from June 1927, regular newsreels (*cinegiornali*). On 3 April 1926, a decree-law recognised 'the urgent and absolute necessity of carrying out a constant and intense action of civil and national education by showing in public cinemas films of national propaganda and culture' and it made the screening of LUCE films obligatory in all cinemas in Italy. Initially silent, by 1930, sound newsreels were being produced, up to five each week. Each one lasted around ten minutes and consisted of a series of short news items of one or two minutes' length.

From the early 1930s, the state began to develop more systematic kinds of support for the commercial cinema. The change is attributable in part to the assiduous activity of Stefano Pittaluga, who headed the

Although enduring difficult economic times, Cinecittà ('Cinema City'), Italy's historic film studio, still stands in Rome's suburbs where it was founded by Mussolini's regime

The Centro Sperimentale di Cinematografia still stands today near Cinecittà on the outskirts of Rome

film studio Cines, founded in 1930, and who started the practice of talking directly to government representatives to get their support for the film industry. But it was also a result of the transition of the film industry at just this time from silent to sound, which involved costly technical refurbishments both of film production and of cinemas. This drove the industry to request state support again, but it also offered new hope that sound films could enter foreign markets and restore Italy's international competitiveness. In 1931, a mechanism of rewarding producers of commercially successful films was introduced: they would receive a premium or top-up from the state in proportion to their box-office takings. In addition, a tax was levied on foreign producers of sound films dubbed into Italian and the quota of Italian films that exhibitors in Italy were required to screen was increased.

Mussolini himself now began to realise that a strong and modernised film industry could enhance Italy's cultural prestige abroad. In 1932, the world's first international film festival was held in Venice. Initially a spin-off from the art Biennale (its official name was Esposizione Internazionale d'Arte Cinematografica), from 1934, it became an annual showcase for new Italian and foreign films and began awarding prizes. After the Nazis came to power in Germany, their centralised control of cultural activity, including cinema, influenced the fascist government in Italy. In 1934, the latter set up a similar umbrella body for culture that included a film section, Direzione Generale della Cinematografia, to oversee production as well as censorship. Luigi Freddi, an able fascist journalist who had visited American and German production facilities and had a clear vision of what the Italian film industry needed, was appointed its first head. In 1935, the state set up a centralised loan fund at the Banca Nazionale del Lavoro (BNL) to bankroll film production as well as

a film school, the Centro Sperimentale di Cinematografia (CSC). The CSC's teachers of theory, including Luigi Chiarini and Umberto Barbaro, were receptive to the work of Soviet writers on film and to that of two Jewish theorists, the Hungarian Béla Balázs and the German Rudolf Arnheim. The latter had moved to Italy after the Nazi takeover and would teach for two years at the CSC, but then left for England in 1938 when the fascist government introduced anti-Semitic laws. In 1937, Cinecittà, the largest and most modern film-production facility in Europe (16,000 square metres, ten sound stages), was opened on the outskirts of Rome, initially as a private initiative, but in 1939 it was handed over to the state. It was subsequently joined to Ente Nazionale Industrie Cinematografiche (ENIC), which contained both a distribution arm and a national exhibition chain, to create a powerful, vertically integrated, state-controlled cinema sector.

Through these combined measures Italy, whose film industry had been in the doldrums throughout the 1920s, acquired by the late 1930s a reputation for its high technical quality of film production, its advanced film education and its openness to quality foreign cinema, as well as a substantial film sector under direct state control. These measures also established the centralisation of film production in Rome, after its dispersed beginnings in several Italian cities, with a centralisation that would continue. There was, however, a brief interlude in 1943–5 when film production followed the relocation of the fascist government in the Republic of Salò and resumed in Venice and Turin. Individuals who collaborated with the cinema of Salò were to face some difficulty working again after the liberation.

The creation of the Direzione Generale della Cinematografia also changed the nature of film censorship. This too became centralised in Rome and organised in a series of phases, from the compulsory vetting of treatments and scripts, at which stages revisions and cuts might be required, to the censors' preview of the completed films to possible seizure of prints after release (see Chapter 8 of this anthology, 'Censorship from the Fascist Period to the Present'). State intervention in the cinema also changed in the later 1930s, leading to a more assiduous promotion and organisation of film export, to help Italian producers and compensate in part for the massive imports of foreign films. The US market was so well protected as to be virtually impenetrable, except for the small circuit of Italian-language cinemas frequented by the emigrant communities, but there were viable export markets in other parts of Europe, particularly in those countries without a strong production sector themselves, as well as in the parts of South America and north and east Africa where there were large Italian communities. The import–export balance was not modifed significantly, however, until the Monopoly Law, passed in 1938, came into force at the beginning of 1939. This gave ENIC a monopoly over domestic distribution of imported films and it infuriated the Hollywood majors, who retaliated by withdrawing their new films from Italy. This led to a sharp decline in the circulation of American films during the war years, though they by no means disappeared, since the smaller Hollywood studios, like United Artists, did not join the boycott and prints of older American films continued to be shown in second- and third-run cinemas, where in 1942, imports still outnumbered Italian films. It also led to an increase in the number of Italian films produced and in their market share, as well as more imports of films from other European countries, including Germany, France and Hungary, to substitute for those withheld by the US majors.

FASCIST IDEAS AND VALUES

If newsreels were already explicit instruments of fascist government propaganda by 1925, most feature films made under fascism were not. The majority were genre films – comedies, costume dramas, romantic dramas, adventures – and some of these were adaptations of foreign stage plays or novels or Italian ones written before the fascists came to power. Their plots, production design and acting styles were all influenced in the 1930s by foreign models, and some of them were made by non-Italian directors who worked briefly in Italy. There are, for example, family resemblances between the plot device of *Darò un milione* (*I'll Give a Million*, 1935), directed by Mario Camerini from a story by Cesare Zavattini and Giaci Mondaini, in which a millionaire (Vittorio De Sica) trades

places with a homeless man (Luigi Almirante) who has planned to drown himself, and that of Frank Capra's *Lady for a Day* (1933), where a poor woman poses as a society matron, and that of Jean Renoir's *Boudu sauvé des eaux* (*Boudu Saved from Drowning*, 1932), where a tramp who has tried to drown himself gets made over as a bourgeois, even though each of these three films is also quite distinctive in tone and style. Some Italian films were adaptations or remakes of foreign films. Max Neufeld's *Mille lire al mese* (*A Thousand Lire a Month*, 1937) and Vittorio De Sica's *Teresa Venerdì* (*Doctor Beware* aka *Do You Like Women?*, 1941) were more or less straight remakes of Hungarian films, respectively Béla Balogh's *Havi 200 fix* (*200 Pengő Fixed per Month*, 1936) and László Vajda's *Péntek Rézi* (*Teresa Friday*, 1938). In other words other external influences shaped these films rather than the fascist regime.

Yet if these films were in several respects the typical products of a commercial cultural industry operating in an international context, this was also an industry that had to work within a system of increasing domestic political constraint, particularly from the mid-1930s, and to comply with its ground rules of censorship. The Italian films that got vetted by the censor and went into production were often the result of a certain amount of push and pull behind the scenes between writers, producers, directors, distributors and censors. However, the end result was nearly always compliance with the rules. Although some workers in the film industry disliked some aspects of the regime or harboured liberal or leftist sympathies, most producers, writers and film-makers either genuinely supported fascism or adjusted their values to fit with it.

'Entertainment' and 'ideology' were not, therefore, so much conflicting principles as elements that could be combined. The comedies directed by Camerini from the early 1930s, as well as those made between the late 1930s and the early war years, which some film historians refer to as 'white telephones' or 'Hungarian-style comedies', are good examples of this combination. Like many comedies produced in other countries at the time, they involved complicated intrigues and awkward situations that unravelled into happy endings. In ideological terms, there is little that is obviously fascist about them. They make no reference to the regime's mystique of patriotism, militarism or self-sacrifice for the nation, to its public-works projects, its wars, its campaigns to raise the birth rate or for economic self-sufficiency. Their plots do, however, largely resolve themselves according to values

Crowd scenes in *Scipione
l'Africano* (1937) with Italian extras
giving the fascist salute to link
Mussolini's imperial adventures
abroad with the ancient Roman
Empire

and a moral code that were compatible with the more
conservative end of the fascist and Catholic ideological
spectrum: that class privilege could be challenged but
not changed or that girls and young women could be
self-assertive and transgress in minor ways but in the
end their fulfilment lay in marriage, submissiveness
and a stable family. On the face of it, these values are
not all that different from those of many Hollywood
films made in the New Deal era under the Hays Code
or in central Europe in the 1930s. Hungary under the
Horthy regime, for instance, was ideologically aligned
with Mussolini's Italy, with which it had signed a
Treaty of Friendship in 1927. However, some historians
have argued cogently that several of these films did
effectively project fascist ideas. Ruth Ben-Ghiat notes,
for instance, that Camerini's *Gli uomini, che mascalzoni!*
(*What Rascals Men Are!*, 1932), starring Vittorio De Sica
and Lia Franca, flaunts the attractions of modernity
but at the same time shows its dangers, such as
consumerism. She claims that, in this way, it served
fascism's ideological project of offering Italians the
promise of modernisation while safely containing it
within the boundaries of nation, tradition and the
established class structure.

An alternative approach to some of these films is to
suggest that they contained tensions between different
ideological impulses. James Hay was one of the first
scholars to have applied to the cinema of fascist Italy
the argument from Cultural Studies that one needed to
see filmgoing as a social practice, where audiences
bring expectations and desires to films, and that the
films themselves operated within a field of

'contradictory models'. Hay acknowledged that most of
these films conformed outwardly to a conservative
ethos but he noted that their narrative structures and
characters were often riven by 'paradoxes and
ambivalences' and he suggested that contemporary
audiences responded to these in complex ways. Vito
Zagarrio and Marcia Landy, independently, have drawn
attention to the intricate symmetries of some of these
films, with their doublings of characters and their
reflexive stagings of theatre within a film or film within
a film. Both *La signora di tutti* (*Everybody's Woman*, 1934),
starring Isa Miranda and directed by Max Ophüls (the
only film he made in Italy, for Rizzoli), and Mario
Soldati's *Dora Nelson* (*Dora Nelson*, 1939) are about film
actors and studios. They draw attention to the way the
woman's image is produced as a commodity as well as
to their own fabrication as screen fictions.

There were, however, a smaller number of films that
did have an overt fascist ideological character. In 1932,
the Istituto Luce produced *Camicia nera* (*Black Shirt*),
directed by Giovacchino Forzano, as part of the
celebrations of the first decade (Decennale) of fascist
power. In 1934, Alessandro Blasetti co-wrote and
directed *Vecchia guardia* (*Old Guard*) about the early
fascist action squads. Guido Brignone's *Passaporto rosso*
(*Red Passport*, 1935) was about a young Italian born in
South America who returns to fight for the fatherland in
World War I and is killed. His daughter becomes a loyal
fascist and receives her father's posthumous medal.
Carmine Gallone's *Scipione l'Africano* (*Scipio Africanus: The
Defeat of Hannibal*, 1937), a historical epic about ancient
Rome's conquest of Carthage, alluded transparently to

fascist Italy's campaigns in East Africa and Libya (which included the site of ancient Carthage) and embodied one of fascism's central myths about itself in this period, that it was a modern extension of the imperialist mission of ancient Rome.

As the fascist government geared its actions increasingly towards foreign policy and war from the second half of the 1930s, it produced several war-themed films and films about colonial settlement, most of which received state production loans. Italy invaded Ethiopia in 1935 and proclaimed its empire in East Africa in 1936. Camerini's *Il grande appello* (*The Great Call*, 1936) and Goffredo Alessandrini's *Luciano Serra pilota* (*Luciano Serra, Pilot*, 1938) both mobilised patriotic feelings through the story of men who, after being out in the cold, respond to the 'appeal' to fight for Italy's conquest of Ethiopia. Between 1936 and 1939, nine features were set or partly set in Italy's African colonies. After Italy joined World War II in June 1940, a number of film dramas were funded by the armed forces. These included Roberto Rossellini's first three features: *La nave bianca* (*The White Ship*, 1941; co-directed with Francesco De Robertis); *Un pilota ritorna* (*A Pilot Returns*, 1942); and *L'uomo dalla croce* (*The Man with a Cross*, 1943).

AUDIENCES UNDER FASCISM

Cinema was popular in Italy before the fascists came to power and it became even more popular under the regime. Most films were seen in commercial cinemas, but there were also the smaller circuits of the parish cinemas and the Dopolavoro (the workers' leisure organisations). The Istituto Luce also had a small fleet of cinema trucks (*carri-cinema*) that could take their films to villages without a cinema. The statistics collected by the Società Italiana Autori e Editori (SIAE), which monitored ticket sales for all paid public entertainments in every province, show a steep decline in variety theatre audiences and a rise in cinema audiences between 1924 and 1933, a period approximately coinciding with the first decade of fascism. Cinema's share of the revenue of all kinds of entertainment rose in those nine years from under 40 per cent to 64 per cent. By 1945, it was 72 per cent. However, these figures also hide a process by which cinemas gradually usurped variety shows, many of which, particularly in working-class areas of cities, staged a live entertainment (*avanspettacolo*) in a mixed programme with screenings of the feature film, newsreels and advertisements.

This growth in cinema audiences was, however, geographically and socially uneven. In other words, during the fascist regime, not all Italians went to the movies and those who did were not seeing the same films in the same places. SIAE figures for 1936 show that twice as many people went to the cinema in the north as in the south. In the main towns in the northern regions of Piedmont, Liguria and Lombardy, average expenditure on film box office for that year was between 35 and 40 lire per inhabitant, whereas in the southern regions of Campania, Sicily and Sardinia it was between 16 and 19 lire and in those of Basilicata and Calabria just 9 lire. The same statistics also showed wide discrepancies in each region between expenditure in main towns and rural areas. In Lombardy, over ten times more was spent in its main towns, such as Milan, Como or Bergamo, than in its small towns and villages. Cinema, in other words, remained still largely an entertainment of urban populations, rather than of rural areas, where most of Italy's poorer population lived, and of the regions of northern and central Italy more than the south.

Although in the towns cinema was popular with all social classes and both sexes, different genres and films appealed to certain subsections of the audiences and some attracted more women than men. There was a social and economic hierarchy of cinemagoing, which corresponded to a three-tier distribution structure. Higher-paying audiences went to see films on their first run (*prima visione*) in the picture palaces of the city centres. The films then moved out to the second-run and then third-run cinemas in the suburbs, where ticket prices were lower, and in the surrounding rural areas, where they might arrive a year or more after their first run in the city centres. Freddi complained in 1936 that the urban audiences for first-run films tended to be snobbish pseudo-intellectuals who lapped up the 'latest foreign rubbish' ('l'ultima porcheriola straniera'), whereas the loyal mass audience for Italian films was to be found in the second- and third-run houses of the suburbs and provinces. His comment suggests, importantly, that the fascists did not feel themselves to be in control of cinema audiences, their choices of films or their reactions. And indeed, if we consider the social and geographical fragmentation of those audiences, the evidence we have of their behaviour – in the provinces it was reported that they were often noisy, chewed salted and roasted pumpkin seeds (*bruscolini*), and spat out the husks and sometimes stayed to watch the same film twice over – and the large number of imported films in circulation, it does seem highly improbable that the fascists could have shaped their tastes or their responses to films in a hegemonic way.

We can put the SIAE figures into perspective by comparing them with those of the first decade after World War II, the last decade before television, which saw the biggest all-time expansion of cinemas and cinema audiences in Italy: from under 3,000 cinemas in 1942 to over 10,000 in 1955, with a large increase in rural areas and in the south. In the south, the number of cinemas more than doubled between 1950 and 1955. The fascist period thus appears comparatively to be one of conspicuous growth in filmgoing, but the growth was less rapid than it would be after the war and filmgoing remained predominantly an urban and northern-central phenomenon, with relatively little penetration into rural areas and the south, apart from the larger southern towns, such as Naples and Palermo.

What is harder to reconstruct, simply because we do not have much good evidence, is what audiences thought about the individual films they saw. No systematic investigations of cinema audiences were done in Italy in the 1930s like those being carried out then in the US by the Payne Fund which, for all their limitations, have left us with unique testimonies of filmgoers from different social classes, or even like the 1939 major survey of the radio audience in Italy. The evidence we have consists mainly of miscellaneous written records and allusions, mostly by educated filmgoers, either produced at the time or in subsequent recollections, including those semi-fictionalised in novels. For those who read Italian, Gian Piero Brunetta's book *Buio in sala* is a useful source with extracts from several such accounts. In 1933, in other words early in the sound era, Antonio Baldini reported that audiences were almost splitting their sides watching the re-release of the 1913 silent classic *Ma l'amor mio non muore* starring Lyda Borelli because they already found her style of gestural acting ridiculous. Vasco Pratolini's postwar novels about young people growing up in the 1930s in a working-class area of Florence contain flashes of interesting information about the social impact and rituals of filmgoing. The main character of *Le ragazze di San Frediano* (1949), for instance, is called Bob after Robert Taylor, whom he and his friends had seen playing the romantic lead in George Cukor's *Camille* (1936). Giacomo Debenedetti, a Jewish intellectual and screenwriter who would be barred from working in the film industry after the passing of the race laws of 1938, wrote in 1927 of how

The cinema auditorium, with its darkness, gives us back the sense of an unbounded freedom and allows us to relax and let ourselves go morally. As the faces of those around us disappear in the shadows, all conventions disappear.

In English translation, there is Italo Calvino's 'A Cinema-Goer's Autobiography', a recollection of his adolescent filmgoing in San Remo in which, among other things, he describes the different sexual pull on him of French and American female stars. There are also a handful of oral testimonies by ordinary Italians of cinemagoing in the fascist period quoted in David Forgacs and Stephen Gundle's *Mass Culture and Italian Society from Fascism to the Cold War*.

THE POSTWAR LEGACY

When Mussolini was executed on 28 April 1945 the first anti-fascist-themed films were already in production. With them would come a sharp ideological rejection of most of Italy's immediate cinematic past. Rossellini's *Roma città aperta* (*Rome, Open City*, 1945) was being filmed in Rome, which had been liberated in June 1944, and the first long documentary about the Italian Resistance, *Giorni di gloria* (*Days of Glory*) was being edited by Mario Serandrei and others and directed by Serandrei. Both these films would first be screened in September 1945. Rossellini's film would launch the tendency that critics would label neorealism, a term which consciously negated and disavowed the entertainment cinema of fascism.

Despite the understandable rejection of the fascist past by film-makers and critics at that time, we can now see more clearly that there were some fundamental continuities between the cinema of the fascist period and that of the early postwar years. In the first place, the system of state funding, through the BNL, the mechanism of premiums and the production infrastructure laid in the 1930s, would act as springboards for the postwar film industry. Cinecittà restarted production in 1947 and, as well as being used over the next decade to shoot several American runaway productions, starting with the Technicolor *Quo Vadis* (Mervyn LeRoy, 1951), it was used for many Italian films, including neorealist ones such as Visconti's *Bellissima* (*Bellissima*, 1951) and De Sica's *Umberto D.* (*Umberto D.*, 1952). Second, there was a substantial continuity of personnel at all levels in the film industry, from producers to directors to actors and crews. The encouragement of creative talent and an advanced culture of film criticism in the later years of fascism, through the Centro Sperimentale, its journal *Bianco e nero*, and other quality film journals like *Cinema*, would launch many of the key creative personnel of the postwar cinema, from directors such as Michelangelo Antonioni, Giuseppe De Santis and Luigi Zampa to cinematographers, editors, production and costume designers and actors. Directors such as Blasetti, Genina, Alessandrini, but also De Sica, Rossellini, Matarazzo and many others, also 'carried over'. Third, despite the undeniable cultural importance of the films associated with neorealism, the pattern of genre production established in the 1930s quickly resumed and it provided the commercial backbone also of the first decade of postwar cinema, with its comedies and melodramas. Fourth, the centralised system of censorship was also carried over, with the fascist Direzione Generale della Cinematografia now replaced by a Sottosegretariato di Stato per lo Spettacolo, and it continued to operate in a very similar way. Critics and film personnel on the left complained of treatments and scripts being rejected, ideologically challenging films being refused production funding, and a return after 1948, when the Christian Democrats won a resounding election victory, to the production of bland, commercially successful genre films with a strongly conservative ethos.

It is more difficult to assess *ideological* continuities between the cinema of the fascist period and that of the postwar years. Here too, however, we can say that the overemphasis on neorealism has distorted the picture. Not only were several films made under fascism put back into distribution after 1945, sometimes in modified versions which adapted their political meaning, but several new films were made in the late 1940s and 1950s about World War II and about the colonial past, which suggested that a good collective memory of the war and colonialism could be retrieved and separated from fascism. One example of re-release was Blasetti's film about Garibaldi, *1860*, which in its original version (1932) had ended with a scene showing fascist Blackshirts saluting the elderly veterans of Garibaldi's campaign. The Italian Communist Party, which had adopted Garibaldi as a figurehead in the resistance, screened Blasetti's film during its election campaign in 1948, after shearing it of its fascist ending. Another example was *Bengasi* (*Benghazi*), originally released in 1942, about the Italian community in Libya during the war, which was re-released in 1955 with some newly shot scenes. As for the question of ideological continuity between the

1930s and 1950s, the way one answers this depends on how far one sees the films of the earlier period as having been pervaded by a distinctly fascist ideology, as opposed to a more loosely clerico-conservative one. If they are characterised in terms of the latter then continuities can certainly be found.

The question of whether neorealism itself had its roots in the fascist period is also a difficult one to answer. André Bazin, who contributed decisively to the elaboration of the critical category of neorealism, himself argued in 1948 that neorealist films had precursors before 1945, and he named as one of them Blasetti's *Quattro passi fra le nuvole* (*A Walk in the Clouds*, 1943), of which Cesare Zavattini was one of the writers. Since then, critics have also singled out Blasetti's *1860* for its location shooting and use of non-professional actors and Camerini's *Gli uomini, che mascalzoni!* for its sequences shot in the streets and at the Milan trade fair. It has also been pointed out that there was a turn towards a realist aesthetic in some Italian film criticism from the mid-1930s, with multiple influences, including French cinema, Soviet film theory, American literature and the British documentary movement. However, it is worth pointing out that, as Bazin and others also argued, postwar neorealism was decisively determined by the political conjuncture of anti-fascism and the emergence of a strong humanist ethos at the end of the war. It is also important to note that the emphasis on the 'royal road' of realism was itself a product of the discourse of neorealism and it served to sideline all the other 'roads' of Italian cinema, including the popular genres as well as non-realist experimentation – from the futurists' short films to Camerini's modernist *Rotaie* (*Rails*, 1930), influenced by the city symphony films, and Walter Ruttmann's *Acciaio* (*Steel*, 1933), set in the steel town of Terni, from a story idea by Luigi Pirandello – as not only less important but also as tainted by association with fascism. The view of fascist popular cinema as 'escapist', 'just entertainment' and therefore by implication less serious and less important than neorealism, led to a critical downgrading not just of fascist cinema but also of postwar entertainment cinema and effectively stigmatised its audiences for taking pleasure in these sorts of films. Yet, as feminist writing on melodrama began to argue in the 1970s, these pleasures were shared by many women and they could be equally political. And, as Marcia Landy has suggested, the notion of 'escapism' itself needs to be critically interrogated and 'enlarged to a level of complexity that redeems it from the familiar charge of vacuity, frivolity and evasion of conflict'.

FURTHER READING

Aprà, Adriano and Patrizia Pistagnesi, *I favolosi anni trenta. Cinema italiano 1929–1944* (Milan: Electa, 1979); English edn, *The Fabulous Thirties: Italian Cinema 1929–1944* (Milan: Electa, 1979).

Baratieri, Daniela, *Memories and Silences Haunted by Fascism: Italian Colonialism MCMXXX–MCMLX* (Bern: Peter Lang, 2010).

Ben-Ghiat, Ruth, *Fascist Modernities: Italy, 1922–1945* (Berkeley and Los Angeles: University of California Press, 2001).

Brunetta, Gian Piero, *Buio in sala. Cent'anni di passione dello spettatore cinematografico* (Venice: Marsilio, 1997).

Calvino, Italo, 'A Cinema-Goer's Autobiography', in *The Road to San Giovanni*, trans. Tim Parks (London: Cape, 1993). (Originally published as 'Autobiografia di uno spettatore' as the Preface to Federico Fellini, *Quattro film* [Turin: Einaudi, 1974]).

Cavallo, Pietro, Luigi Goglia and Pasquale Iaccio (eds), *Cinema a passo romano. Trent'anni di fascismo sullo schermo (1934–1963)* (Naples: Liguori, 2012).

Faccioli, Alessandra (ed.), *Schermi di regime. Cinema italiano degli anni trenta: la produzione e i generi* (Venice: Marsilio, 2010).

Fanchi, Mariagrazia, 'Sale e pubblici', in Orio Caldiron (ed.), *Storia del cinema italiano, vol. V: 1934/1939* (Venice: Marsilio and Rome: Edizioni di Bianco e Nero, 2006), pp. 176–82.

Forgacs, David and Stephen Gundle, *Mass Culture and Italian Society from Fascism to the Cold War* (Bloomington: Indiana University Press, 2007).

Freddi, Luigi, *Il cinema* (Rome: L'Arnia, 1949). Reprinted as *Il cinema: il governo dell'immagine* (Rome: Gremese, 1994).

Hay, James, *Popular Film Culture in Fascist Italy: The Passing of the Rex* (Bloomington: Indiana University Press, 1987).

Landy, Marcia, 'Theatricality and Impersonation: The Politics of Style in the Cinema of the Italian Fascist Era', in Jacqueline Reich and Piero Garofalo (eds), *Re-Viewing Fascism. Italian Cinema, 1922–1943* (Bloomington: Indiana University Press, 2002).

Laura, Ernesto G., *Le stagioni dell'aquila. Storia dell'Istituto Luce* (Rome: Istituto Luce, 2004).

Martinelli, Vittorio, *L'eterna invasione. Il cinema americano degli anni Venti e la critica italiana* (Gemona: La Cineteca del Friuli, 2002).

Mosconi, Elena and Roberto Della Torre, 'Consumo cinematografico e funzioni sociali del cinema: critica, dati di consumo e manifesti', in Mariagrazia Fanchi and Elena Mosconi (eds), *Spettatori. Forme di consenso e pubblico del cinema italiano, 1930–1960* (Rome: Fondazione Scuola Nazionale di Cinema, 2002), pp. 23–61.

Muscio, Giuliana (ed.), *Prima dei Codici 2: alle porte di Hays, retrospettiva del Cinema Americano 1929–1934* (Venice: La Biennale Editrice and Milan: Fabbri, 1990).

Pinna, Luca, 'Indagine sul pubblico cinematografico', *Bianco e Nero* vol. XIX no. 2 (February 1958), p. 3.

Redi, Riccardo (ed.), *Cinema italiano sotto il fascismo* (Venice: Marsilio, 1979).

Ricci, Steven, *Cinema and Fascism: Italian Film and Society, 1922–1943* (Berkeley: University of California Press, 2008).

Soro, Francesco, *Splendori e miserie del cinema: cose viste e vissute da un avvocato* (Milan: Consalvo, 1935).

Zagarrio, Vito, *Cinema e fascismo. Film, modelli, immaginari* (Venice: Marsilio, 2004).

——, *L'immagine del fascismo. Le re-visione del cinema e dei media nel regime* (Rome: Bulzoni, 2009).

Zinni, Maurizio, *Fascisti di celluloide. La memoria del ventennio nel cinema italiano (1945–2000)* (Venice: Marsilio, 2010).

6 Italian Matinee Idols in the Era of the Talkies

Marcia Landy

Living in a different constellation than the film actors did, but still a star, Mussolini attracted interest and admiration; he projected aura and awe. And the regime seems to count on the political trajectory in order to satisfy the consuming needs of the population. The image of Mussolini sold well, whether in postcards or as a model of style. Records and radio diffused his words, the cinema propagated his icon, posters, and calendars commemorated his deeds.[1]

Stardom is an invitation to think of the cinema as more than storytelling but as an intimate involvement with the creation of images, their designs and impact on their viewers. The spectator is solicited through the cinema as a mirror to contemplate the human body and the landscape as a world intrinsic to the historic imaginary. Not invented by the movies but significantly altered through media technology (radio, popular romances, journalism, newsreels and cinema), the fascination with the star provides critical insights into the creation of a profitable and appealing mass culture of Italian cinema in the silent and sound era.

Through personal memory of the fascist era in a darkly comic vein, Fellini's *Amarcord* (*Amarcord*, 1973) connects stardom to the culture of the fascist era through the figure of Mussolini. The film evokes Mussolini's persona, caricaturing newsreels of his visits to various Italian towns and the orgiastic response of the townspeople. Fellini's film captures how stars played both a direct and indirect, adoring and even parodic role in the film culture of the fascist era, endowing significance to an everyday world. Through media and his self-invention, Mussolini became an idol of the masses by exploiting numerous duplications of his persona in posters, newsreels and implicit associations with characters in feature films. His image belongs to the evolution of media from the silent

cinema of divismo to a more familiar world of stardom that my essay traces by tracking the technical innovations, key figures and film forms involved in the emergence of the cinematic and political star, both masculine and feminine.

THE CINEMA OF DIVISMO: THE DIVA

In the early cinema, the female diva, a precursor of the contemporary star, was a creation of light, shadow and affect. The diva's power was not primarily her physical beauty, though she was attractive. It arose from her mysterious character, her otherworldliness and her imperiousness.[2] She was the consummate interpreter of gesture and the lack of a soundtrack created a quality of remoteness, enhancing her appeal.

The narratives of divismo focus on the desires and fears of this exceptional feminine creature in her tempestuous and transgressive inner world of longing, passion, loss and eroticism. In Nino Oxilia's *Rapsodia satanica* (*Satanic Rhapsody*, 1915), Lyda Borelli, a major diva of the 1910s, appears in a dual role, as an ageing woman and as an eternally young seductress who makes a Faustian compact to reverse ageing and to attain eternal youth. Her relation to the objects of the world (e.g., the symbolic hourglass and the clock that in the intertitle is a reminder of the 'fatal laws of time') emphasises her desire to overcome mortality and to distance herself from ordinary existence.[3] The narrative entails an upper-class woman (rather than the familiar male scientist/magician) who seeks knowledge and power at the expense of the renunciation of love.

Affective intensity is a requisite of the diva's self-absorption expressed in her struggle to communicate desire. By contrast and not as sympathetically, Antonio Gramsci captured a quintessential aspect of her cinematic persona as a creature 'who is a part of prehistoric and primordial humanity. No one can explain what is Borelli's art, because it doesn't exist. Borelli does not know how to interpret any diverse creature other than herself'.[4] Her presence on screen was writ large by her 'languid poses, slow gestures, affected speech, dress of a classicizing and Orientalist taste',[5] suggesting that the theatricality and the power of the diva's performances relied heavily on the expressiveness of the body as much as on that of the face to convey emotional resonances.

The diva as a fascinating portrait of conflicting femininity went into decline in the post-World War I era in the changing cultural and political climate. With its emotionally charged dramas, divismo was no longer successful at the box office. Thanks in part to the excessive salaries demanded by the divas, the diva film ceased to be economically viable. New and everyday images of femininity derived from popular Hollywood films and from negative fascist propaganda concerning the masculinised woman, as well as the destructive femme fatale, were to diminish the reign of the diva, although the figure of the male divo, the strongman, was to retain its power.

THE DIVO AND THE SUPERMAN

The mythic Maciste, played by Bartolomeo Pagano, first appeared in Pastrone's *Cabiria*, as a freed slave, 'the benevolent unselfish giant, who would be a darling of the 1920s'.[6] With his large, muscular and athletic body and his humorous and clever reactions to injustice, Pagano became the model of a positive cultural hero associated with the nationalist values cultivated first by the writer/political activist Gabriele D'Annunzio and later appropriated by Mussolini. Maciste's myth was forged largely through action-adventure narratives identified with the body and physical feats of the strongman disseminated through popular culture. If the diva was a figure of power as passion, rebelliousness and intense sensation, the divo transformed affect into action. Maciste's character was endowed with human attributes: his love of food, his identification with the common man and his ruses as a trickster who used humour to ensnare his enemies. The framing and choreography of the spectacular *Cabiria* capture Maciste's virility in a dizzying array of moving images geared to physical exploits.

Two years after *Cabiria*, Pagano appeared again as Maciste in a film set in World War I, *Maciste alpino*. Here, Maciste is the driving force behind the war effort against the Austrians. In this anachronistic film, he plays a classical hero of a twentieth-century war film and Pagano displays his penchant for comedy within his feats of bravery. In encounters with the enemy, he is portrayed as one man against many and as a member of the Alpine regiment distinguished by his exceptional physical qualities.

Pastrone's narrative places the protagonist in a situation where he must overcome the threatening milieu of war to restore moral order. Maciste inhabits the image of the strongman as leader, patriot and common man, qualities personified by Mussolini, in adventure and historic films during the sound era. Pierre Sorlin compares a photo of Mussolini to that of Bartolomeo Pagano as Maciste that emphasises their postures, their muscular arms embracing their large torsos.[7]

Maciste, one man against many, in
Maciste alpino (1917)

TRANSFORMING THE DIVA/DIVO TO STAR

By the end of the 1920s, Italian cinema had gone into decline. Audiences in Italy and in the Americas no longer thronged to see Italian films. Hollywood had begun its long march into Italy. Among numerous economic, cultural and political factors responsible for this reversal of fortune was the fact that the industry remained disorganised. Technical facilities were in need of modernisation, as were the kinds of films produced. The successful films from the early 1910s – the historical films and melodramas – had become formulaic and did not address the changing tastes of audiences. After the establishment of the fascist dictatorship under the aegis of a powerful leader, the regime insisted upon new conceptions of femininity, masculinity, interpretations of Italian history and changed notions about work and leisure time, all of which would have some impact upon popular cinematic culture. Although the media were to occupy an important position in this altered world, the commercial cinema was economically unstable until the mid-1930s.

EVOLUTION OF THE NEW ITALIAN MATINEE IDOL

Attempts were made to improve the film industry, to meet the growing challenges of foreign competition through modest protection measures in relation to quotas, the easing of taxation and state support through the nationalisation of LUCE in 1926, an organisation designed to produce educational films, newsreels and documentaries. Crises in the industry were also gradually ameliorated through the advent of sound, the uses of dubbing, new cinematic and narrative techniques in the production of comedies, musicals, melodramas, historic films and biopics, as well as the encouragement of new technicians, writers and directors. Through his Società Anonima Stefano Pittaluga and Cines studio, distributor and producer Stefano Pittaluga played a major role in the transformations that took place from the late 1920s until his death in 1931. Alessandro Blasetti and Mario Camerini introduced new techniques of visual and sound narration to rejuvenate genres, experimenting with melodramas, comedies and historical films.

Stardom increased in prominence in Italian cinema of the 1930s and early 1940s, thanks to the competitive influence of Hollywood and the arrival of sound. The Dopolavoro, a fascist organisation created to regulate mass leisure, also contributed to the creation of stardom by encouraging new views of modern life associated with the newsreels and feature films it screened for workers and their families. While aristocrats and the rich had not totally disappeared from the narratives, the dominant characters were often workers and peasants depicting tensions between modern and traditional life, city and country, industrious, loyal and devoted peasant women in contrast to city women (as in Blasetti's *Terra madre* [*Mother Earth*, 1931]) or young women in search of employment who end up getting married to the boss (e.g. in Goffredo Alessandrini's successful *La segretaria privata* [*Private Secretary*], 1931). These comedies and melodramas were socially, if indirectly propagandistic, oriented with an eye to creating an Italian everyday and modern milieu in conjunction with images denoting leisure and mobility, such as the automobile, the department store, the aeroplane and tourism, aided by the introduction of sound.

One of the first films converted to sound through the uses of voice and music was Mario Camerini's *Rotaie*. The film portrays the vicissitudes of a young petit-bourgeois couple bereft of employment, money and hope for the future who contemplate suicide. They are led astray by promises of wealth via gambling but are ultimately converted to acceptance of a working-class and familial milieu, a recurrent motif in the films of Mario Camerini. The film's visuals and soundtrack associate the wheels of a railroad train (the source of the film's title) with a roulette wheel. The reiterative circular images and sound of the wheels, the rhythmic editing, the chiaroscuro lighting and the minimal dialogue develop a tension between the couple's entrapment in a cycle of self-destruction and their struggle to extricate themselves from an obsession with wealth that almost destroys their relationship. If the film was self-conscious in its uses of sound and silence to develop the material and psychic dimensions of the couple's relationship to their milieu, its actors and a modern, even quotidian, landscape differed from the physical appearance and actions of the models of divismo, though it was not yet a star vehicle. The creation of distinctive forms of stardom was yet to come.

MELODRAMA AND THE EMERGENCE OF A STAR

German-born Max Ophüls was invited to Italy to make the melodramatic *La signora di tutti*, a film instructive for its self-conscious exploration of the formation of the star in the context of a mass cinema. As a consequence,

The luminous Isa Miranda as 'everybody's woman' in Max Ophüls' *La signora di tutti* (1934)

blonde Isa Miranda (often advertised as an Italian Marlene Dietrich) became a star, but one who seemed more international than specifically Italian.[8] The film is filled with images of the movie industry (highlighting the role of agents, producers, publicity) and other artefacts associated with the business of film-making. Unlike the sovereign diva, the star becomes an industrial assemblage of qualities captive to the director, agent and producer, the camera, narrative, publicity, changing fashions in clothing, make-up and hairdo, and the box office. The sound image introduced 'a new dimension of the visual image'[9] that altered the spectator's views of the landscape and actors.

Isa Miranda's portrayal of her character in *La signora di tutti* is an excellent example of a star performance. The viewer's first visual contact with her is while she is under anesthesia after a suicide attempt. Flashbacks dramatise her transformation from youth to adulthood. Her rise to stardom is enacted through various technologies: the printing press, medical equipment, a record player, the soundtrack, a voiceover on film and conversations on the telephone with her producer and with the men in her life. The viewer observes her metamorphosis from commonplace life to an exceptional and successful persona through the use of make-up, glamorous and fashionable apparel, lighting and extreme close-ups of her face.

The tension between a 'real' person and public star, so essential to star lore, is further accentuated by an inability to realise personal desire through love and marriage. In this portrait, the star is just an image derived from the visual and sound images that blur the boundaries between a real and imaginary world to be elaborated in other Italian star vehicles of the 1930s, if in more upbeat fashion often through comedy, as in the films of Blasetti and Camerini.

POPULAR STARS AND COMEDY

Comedy was a popular genre in the era of the talkies and generated its own matinee idols. Mario Camerini's popular sentimental comedies and melodramas were to become profitable for the director and for the stars they helped to popularise. His films evoke the populist comedies of Frank Capra as well as those of René Clair. The style and subjects of the city films of Walter Ruttmann and Jean Vigo, with their emphasis on mobility, traffic, streets, shops and the people in this mundane milieu, are also central to Camerini's fictional world. Most vital to Camerini's comedy is the motif of impersonation; disguise and doubling play a critical role in his stars' performances and serve as a critical exploration of escapism that entails a doubling, a tension between the real world and that of cinema. In *Gli uomini, che mascalzoni!*, De Sica is a mechanic who temporarily impersonates a rich industrialist; in Camerini's *Il signor Max* (*Mister Max*, 1937), he assumes dual roles, as newspaper vendor and aristocrat; in *Darò un milione* remade in Hollywood as *I'll Give a Million* (Walter Lang, 1938), De Sica is a millionaire who exchanges roles with a beggar. Sound became critical to the director's portraits of different social classes, urban and rural landscapes, with contrasts in language, gesture and costuming. The culprit in Camerini's films is the desire for wealth, success and upward mobility expressed through the protagonists' attempts to escape their everyday existence. After masquerading in the upper-class world through assuming another identity, the chastened protagonists generally find safety in restored familial, work and community relationships.

Thanks to his role in *Gli uomini, che mascalzoni!*, Vittorio De Sica became a major matinee idol eliciting comparisons to Hollywood stars (Cary Grant in particular). His popularity (and that of the director Camerini) was reinforced by his ability to romanticise commonplace existence, to capture the slippery relationship between the ordinary and the exceptional world, the cinema and real life. This film and De Sica's roles in *Il signor Max* and *Darò un milione* captured the two sides of his star persona, as 'a sort of ordinary Joe, the typical middle-class or working-class guy',[10] and as a wealthy or upper-class figure, endowing his star image with protean characteristics.

Gli uomini features De Sica as Bruno, a chauffeur, who pursues Mariuccia (Lia Franca), a saleswoman who lives with her taxi-driver father, Tadini (Cesare Zoppetti). Through masquerade and impersonation, Bruno seeks to impress Mariuccia as a wealthy man. The film's popular appeal is evident not only in De Sica's acting and singing, but also in the film's emphasis on machines, movement and action and in its treatment of commonplace situations and attractive, sympathetic petit-bourgeois characters. Through their physical appearance, their domestic lives and the forms of leisure and work in which they engage, the characters are identified within a contemporary realistic landscape and with the working-class tension between economic survival and the desire for pleasure and mobility. Through sound as well as visual images, close-ups of Bruno, dancing with Mariuccia at a country inn in the suburbs of Milan, and crooning to her, 'Parlami d'amore Mariuccia', the song he made famous, De Sica transformed the new Italian film actor 'into a faithful mirror and accomplice of the new dreams of Italians'.[11] His persona is enhanced by his romantic and often inept struggle (in contrast to the strongman) to accommodate himself to the contradictions between social stability and the lures of modern life. The climax is significantly situated at an industrial fair in Milan (La Fiera Campionaria) at which De Sica becomes an interpreter not only of this showcase of contemporary commodities, but also a guide to the spectator's engagement with him as an object of fascination and desire. De Sica as star is central to both the film's diegetic and intra-diegetic look: his role-playing

De Sica the millionaire exchanges roles with a beggar (Luigi Almirante) in Camerini's *Gli uomini, che mascalzoni!* (1932)

highlights the role of cinema as a carrier of personality in which his image creates a belief in the vicissitudes of everyday life as appealing spectacle, a cinematic world different from otherworldly divismo.

Assia Noris, who co-starred with Vittorio De Sica in Camerini's comedies, was also a burgeoning star in the resurgence of Italian cinema effected by the advent of sound. Born in Russia, of an aristocratic family, her first appearance was in 1932 in *Giallo* (*Mystery*, Camerini, 1933) and she continued to star in films through the 1930s and early 1940s. Although she made films with other directors, her greatest successes were in Camerini comedies. Her physical appearance was not exotic but rather ordinary, enhanced by her understated make-up, costuming and acting, though she would also less successfully play upper-class and aristocratic women (e.g. Goffredo Alessandrini's *Una donna tra i due mondi* [*Between Two Worlds*, 1936] and Mario Soldati's *Dora Nelson*. Noris's persona is enhanced by an illusion of freshness and sincerity, the assumed opposite of a glamorous movie star. Compared to and billed as a Carole Lombard type, she could also do screwball comedy (evident in her witty dialogue in Camerini's *Batticuore* [*Heartbeat*, 1939]). In *Dora Nelson*, she plays two roles, Dora and Pierina, through the convention of a film within a film, with Dora as its aristocratic diva. Dora, like Noris in real life, is an ex-Russian aristocrat, a wilful princess who cannot acclimatise to bourgeois existence. Dora as diva is temperamental, imperious and hostile to a bourgeois life that entails conjugal responsibilities, while Pierina is loyal, submissive and domesticated (in contrast to Noris's numerous marriages).

More successfully in *Batticuore*, Noris plays a dual role as a graduate of a school for thieves and as an upper-class spy. Her victim, a count, apprehends her in a movie theatre while an Astaire/Rogers vehicle is on, underscoring the film's motif of playing roles. Dressed in a gown reminiscent of Ginger Rogers's character and bought by the count, Arlette (Noris) is coerced into attending a ball where she becomes involved in a scheme to blackmail the ambassador of Stivonia. In her metamorphosis from thief to aristocrat, she is identified with the artifice of cinema and its fascination with glittering, often international, upper-class society. The film's reiterative focus on other media and on spectatorship (as in the movie-theatre sequence), the use of television during the ball scene, and the deceptive uses of photography, all serve as reflections on cinematic spectacle as an unstable

currency. The film offers a gloss on moviegoing and the star as an imaginary but affectively engaging incarnation to render cinematic artifice familiar and accessible to the viewer, if only then to insist through the figure of Noris on the difference between material acquisition and domestic values.

HISTORY, ACTION AND THE SPECTACLE OF THE VIRILE STAR

Alongside the comedies, there were action and adventure films tied to the historic aspirations of the regime in the films of Augusto Genina, Carmine Gallone and Goffredo Alessandrini and their masculine stars. While De Sica's persona was only indirectly attached to the values of the regime, Amedeo Nazzari and Fosco Giachetti played roles that incarnated the values of fascist leadership, virility, commitment to patriotism and sacrifice. Their star images were often tied to films that dramatised the founding moments of fascism such as Alessandro Blasetti's *Vecchia guardia* and Giovacchino Forzano's *Camicia nera*; and allegories involving militarism and war (e.g. Alessandrini's *Cavalleria* [*Cavalry*, 1936] and Gallone's *Scipione l'Africano*). The stardom of both actors might be said to evoke images of Mussolini disseminated in the patriotic newsreels and documentaries of LUCE, the government institute charged with newsreel propaganda for the regime, though altering aspects of il Duce's flamboyant behaviour to suit the melodramatic solemnity of the feature films, endowing them with monumentality and sacredness.

Amedeo Nazzari was a star formed on the basis of an Italian cinema that took cues from Hollywood but transformed them for the Italian cultural and political milieu. Often said to look like Errol Flynn, Nazzari began acting in the theatre, turning to cinema in 1935.

He made a number of films under fascism and his career continued until his death in 1979, with a legacy of over 120 films. His career burgeoned after the release of *Cavalleria*. Playing the dashing but ill-fated Captain Solaro, he loves an aristocratic woman whom he cannot marry for reasons of his inferior class and economic status. He is converted to a quasi-religious figure prefiguring fascist ideals. Set in an earlier historic moment during the era of the politician Giovanni Giolitti, the film dramatises the change from a traditional to a modern society. The heroism and national glory identified with the cavalry are transferred to aviation where the earlier aspirations are now embodied in the modern role of the aeroplane

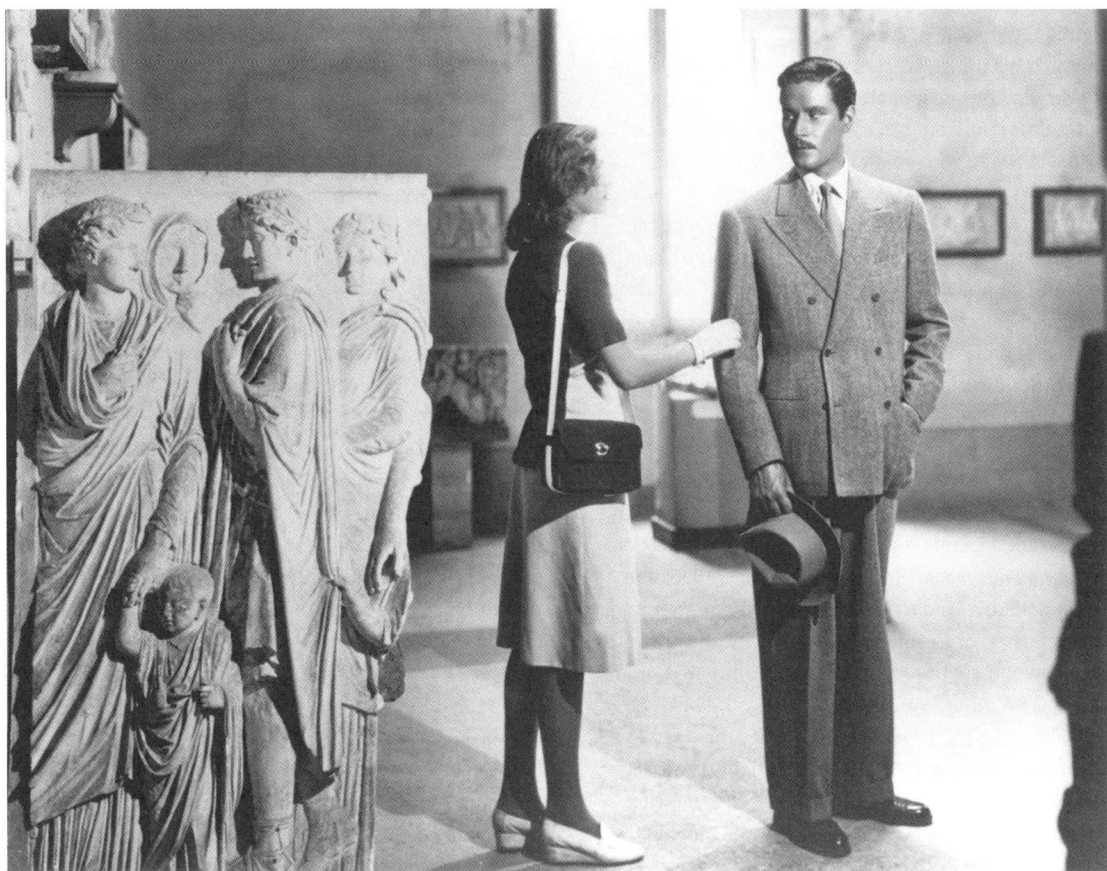

Amedeo Nazzari, one of fascist Italy's most popular matinee idols, often compared to Errol Flynn, in Renato Castellani's *La donna della montagna* (1944)

pilot as in *Luciano Serra pilota* (also starring Nazzari), fusing the technology of modern warfare and cinema through the popular figure of the aviator (e.g. Italo Balbo and Mussolini). His physical body becomes identified with the machine, lending itself to the moral imperatives of heroism and sacrifice, expressing human transcendence over imperfection through the technology of war and through media.

Similarly, Fosco Giachetti was identified with films that dramatised fascist characters and situations: in *Vecchia guardia* as a militant and committed fascist of the first hour; in Augusto Genina's *Squadrone bianco* (*The White Squadron*, 1936) as the mythic Captain Santelia fighting the colonial war in Africa on behalf of the Italian nation and in Genina's celebration of Spanish fascist military victories, *L'assedio dell'Alcazar* (*The Siege of the Alcazar*, 1940). Giachetti appeared in melodramas and war films, fashioning the strongman into a man of iron in public with deep but disciplined emotion. His physical appearance, craggy face, posture and deportment

remained constant in his films. His facial expressions were key to the stylised character of his performance, underlining his control even in extremely emotional moments. His choreographed body movements were most evident in the war films where he embodied the virility exalted in the propaganda of the time and identified with Mussolini. He was the Italian cinema's riposte to the perceived image among Italians of the 'effeminate' Rudolf Valentino and Ramon Novarro, actually embodying a form of stoic and restrained masculinity evocative of the idealised iconography of Mussolini displayed in documentaries and newsreels.[12]

The history of Italian fascist culture and politics reveals an equivocal relation between politics and cinema. If the figure of Mussolini celebrated through newsreels and documentaries played a prominent role in the creation of a cult of virility through rituals and spectacles associated with his persona and style of rule, the commercial feature films and their stars served as 'codifiers of gender roles, value systems, and certain ideas about national identity'.[13] But the faces of stardom also provide insights into the way in which the regime totalitarianism as expressed through cinema was not seamless or unified. Since the power of cinema relies on an intimate appeal to the diverse emotional and social world of the spectator, the figure of the star is the carrier of desires and conflicts that cannot easily be resolved. The stars and their films were not rigidly programmed despite totalising, though often inconsistent, pressures from the regime and censorship. Their personae and the landscapes they inhabit reveal conflicts resulting from the changing cultural currency, along with the imperative to conjoin profit, pleasure and persuasion.

NOTES

1. Simonetta Falesca-Zamponi, *Fascist Spectacle: The Aesthetics of Power in Mussolini's Italy* (Berkeley: University of California Press, 1997), p. 145.
2. Gian Piero Brunetta, *Storia del cinema italiano: Il cinema muto 1895–1929*, Vol. 1 (Rome: Editori Riuniti, 2001), pp. 81–6.
3. Angela Dalle Vacche, *Diva: Defiance and Passion in Early Italian Cinema* (Austin: University of Texas Press, 2008), p. 20.
4. Antonio Gramsci, *Letteratura e vita nazionale* (Turin: Einaudi, 1972), p. 273.
5. Victoria De Grazia, *How Fascism Ruled Women: Italy 1922–1945* (Berkeley: University of California Press, 1992), p. 211.
6. Pierre Sorlin, *Italian National Cinema, 1896–1996* (London: Routledge, 1996), p. 35.
7. Ibid., pp. 48–9.
8. See Giuliana Muscio, 'I Am Not Greta Garbo. I Am Not Marlene Dietrich. I Am Isa Miranda', in Tytti Soila (ed.), *Stellar Encounters: Stardom in Popular European Cinema* (New Barnet: John Libbey, 2009), pp. 90–9.
9. Gilles Deleuze, *Cinema 1: The Movement Image*, trans. Hugh Tomlinson and Barbara Habberjam (Minneapolis: University of Minnesota Press, 1986), p. 226.
10. Stephen Gundle, 'Film Stars and Society in Fascist Italy', in Jacqueline Reich and Piero Garofalo (eds), *Re-viewing Fascism: Italian Cinema 1922–1943* (Bloomington: Indiana University Press, 2002), p. 324.
11. Gian Piero Brunetta, *The History of Italian Cinema: A Guide to Italian Film from Its Origins to the Twenty-first Century*, trans. Jeremy Parzen (Princeton, NJ: Princeton University Press, 2009), p. 90.
12. Gundle, 'Film Stars and Society in Fascist Italy', p. 334.
13. Ibid., p. 316.

FURTHER READING

Brunetta, Gian Piero, *The History of Italian Cinema: A Guide to Italian Film from Its Origins to the Twenty-first Century*, trans. Jeremy Parzen (Princeton, NJ: Princeton University Press, 2009).

——, *Storia del cinema Italiano: Il cinema muto 1895–1929*, Vol. 1 (Rome: Editori Riuniti, 2001).

Dalle Vacche, Angela, *Diva: Defiance and Passion in Early Italian Cinema* (Austin: University of Texas Press, 2008).

Deleuze, Gilles, *Cinema 1: The Movement Image*, trans. Hugh Tomlinson and Barbara Habberjam (Minneapolis: University of Minnesota Press, 1986).

Falesca-Zamponi, Simonetta, *Fascist Spectacle: The Aesthetics of Power in Mussolini's Italy* (Berkeley: University of California Press, 1997).

De Grazia, Victoria, *How Fascism Ruled Women: Italy 1922–1945* (Berkeley: University of California Press, 1992).

Gundle, Stephen, 'Film Stars and Society in Fascist Italy', in Jacqueline Reich and Piero Garofalo (eds), *Re-viewing Fascism: Italian Cinema 1922–1943* (Bloomington: Indiana University Press, 2002), pp. 315–41.

Landy, Marcia, *Stardom, Italian Style* (Bloomington: Indiana University Press, 2008).

Mancini, Elaine, *Struggles of the Italian Film Industry during Fascism, 1930–1935* (Ann Arbor, MI: UMI Research Press, 1985).

Muscio, Giuliana, 'I Am Not Greta Garbo. I Am Not Marlene Dietrich. I Am Isa Miranda', in Tytti Soila (ed.), *Stellar Encounters: Stardom in Popular European Cinema* (New Barnet: John Libbey, 2009), pp. 90–9.

Passerini, Luisa, *Mussolini Imaginario: Storia di una biographia 1925–1939* (Rome: Laterza, 1991).

Reich, Jacqueline and Piero Garofalo (eds), *Re-viewing Fascism: Italian Cinema, 1922–1943* (Bloomington: Indiana University Press, 2002).

Ricci, Steven, *Cinema & Fascism: Italian Film and Society, 1922–1943* (Berkeley: University of California Press, 2008).

7 The First Comedy, Italian Style

Blasetti, Camerini and De Sica

Vito Zagarrio

Italian and Hollywood comedies of the 1930s may be compared along the thematic axes of 'modernity' and the 'double' through focusing upon three key figures of the industry: Alessandro Blasetti, the leading man of fascist cinema and at the same time an inspired, sophisticated film-maker; Mario Camerini, specialist in genre films and light-hearted comedies highlighting the theme of of modernity in Italian society; and Camerini's pupil Vittorio De Sica, a successful young actor first and later an expert director of genre films before his postwar neorealist period. Several theoretical questions arise in dealing with this subject matter. First, must we speak of a 'fascist' cinema or of cinema 'during' the fascist era or a cinema 'despite' fascism? Second, what does 'modernity' mean in terms of 1930s film and how does it differ from 'modernisation' in the period? Were the comedies of the 1930s part of the fascist 'factory of consensus' or were they, because of their escapist quality, 'a-fascist' or even 'anti-fascist'? Is there continuity or a break between the fascist era and the postwar neorealist period? And finally, is there continuity between comedies of the 1930s and the so-called *commedia all'italiana*, Italian film's most important mega genre in the postwar period?

The issue of continuity has always concerned Italian historians. The centralised industrial policies of the fascist regime were instrumental in the creation of professions, personalities and the technological and linguistic tools that nourished a whole generation of film-makers who became popular with the advent of neorealism. The belief that cinema was the 'strongest weapon', substantial public investments in the industry and the frequent exchanges with foreign film industries – Hollywood, the Soviet Union and Germany, in particular – led to the creation of government boards and organisations, the building of Cinecittà studios; the foundation of the Centro Sperimentale di

Cinematografia (Rome's national cinema school); and the launch of the Venice Film Festival. All this was fertile ground for the theoretical and stylistic elaborations of the neorealist film-makers to be.

MODERNITY AND THE HOLLYWOOD MODEL

Comedy provides an important training ground for crews, actors and directors, and the Italian comic film of the 1930s can be defined quite well as the 'first comedy, Italian style'.[1] 'Modernisation' is a consequence of social and technological processes; 'modernism' is a formula derived from the history of art; and 'modernity' pertains to filmic language, in reference to style and gaze. More traditional historians identify modernity with modernisation. In *Fascist Modernities*, Ruth Ben-Ghiat uses the plural to underline the existence of different types of 'modernities' during the fascist regime. Modernity is thus seen as a process of transformation of mores and taste in both the public and private spheres. Nicola Tranfaglia offers a different interpretation, describing modernity as a large-scale social change involving the main economic, political, administrative, familial and religious structures of a given society, heading gradually towards a model of modern society.[2]

The first hint of modernity in Italian comedy is introduced by the very first shot of Mario Camerini's *Gli uomini, che mascalzoni!*. Here, Camerini renders the dynamics of a changing Italy, with a fresh style and sense of immediacy depicting the new industrial soul of Milan, inhabited by cars and ever-present signs of a capitalist society built on the obsessive quest for consumer goods. The series of long sequences set at the huge warehouses of the Fiera (the expo), partly reproduced on sound stages, but frequently photographed at real exterior locations, exemplifies the economic boom. Camerini insists on displaying popular brand names like Fiat, Alemagna, Cinzano and Philips

Lia Franca is the prototype of the modern young woman in Camerini's *Gli uomini, che mascalzoni!* (1932). The film popularised the period's most famous song, 'Parlami d'amore Mariù'

in relief against the industrialised urban landscape. Sometimes publicity is used with an ironic undertone, as in the scene when the car driven by Bruno (De Sica) crashes into a billboard publicising another expo (the Fiera del Levante). Other testimonials of modernity are fashion (the hairstyle of the female protagonist, the women's magazine read by Mariuccia [Lia Franca] on the tramway, the swimsuits seen at the expo) and above all else, speed. Bicycles, cars, taxis, carousels and bumper cars all represent the dynamism of speed, as in the scene when an odometer explodes and the camera closes in upon whirling wheels.

Another symptom of modernity is self-reflexivity. The use of metalanguage allows the expression of modernity and, at the same time, shows cinema as apparatus. Max Neufeld's *Mille lire al mese* is rife with mass media, including the popular eponymous song being broadcast on the radio. Several more instances of cinema within films can be noted, such as the sound stage that bookends Mario Soldati's *Dora Nelson*, or the dark, unethical side of the cinema world in Camillo Mastrocinque's *Inventiamo l'amore* (*Let's Invent Love*, 1938), where the comedic conventions encapsulate a dramatic backstory that remains unresolved: two lovers escape their provincial lives and move to Rome to make their fortune. Tempted by the lures of the cinema, the man wants to become a screenwriter, the woman an actress. This compassionless portrait of Italian society accurately reproduces the microcosm of cinema (its sets, its production apparatus, the fans) against the backdrop of a Roman milieu inhabited by the *nouveau riche* and profiteers, while the

claustrophobic atmosphere of this vanity fair sheds a negative light on Italian society as a whole.

There are important affinities between the Italian and American comedies of the 1930s. Andrew Bergman, for instance, ties the appeal of the screwball comedy to its warm and reassuring qualities despite its typically unusual twists, the lack of a clear divide between urban and rural settings as well as its irresistible combination of unlikely elements, such as the simultaneous presence of all social classes.[3] Despite some obvious differences, Italian comedies also question the very society and culture that produce them. Bergman highlights two opposed views on the debate around the screwball: on the one hand, some scholars view these comedies as self-portraits of a mid-1930s America trying to show everything in a positive light (Lewis Jacobs, in particular, describes the screwball genre as a sort of paint used to conceal the alienation caused by the Great Depression); on the other hand, the screwball comedy (according to Arthur Knight) exposes the bleakest side of the reality of the time: unemployment, hunger and fear. Bergman's thesis confirms a view of this particular kind of comedy as both a response to the Great Depression, and as a form that aims to cement the links between social classes and urges the audience to work toward a common goal. Despite obvious historical differences between the US and Italy (in the US, the Great Depression is followed by the democratic New Deal, not an authoritarian fascist regime), some important affinities exist: an attitude towards social appeasement (what Bergman defines as 'reconciliation' I would call an 'aesthetics of corporatism'); an interest in 'modernity' reflecting a period of history dominated by Americanism and Fordism; and the development of the 'American myth', especially insofar as mass behaviour and imagery are concerned, since Italian comedy during the fascist period derives its cultural and industrial models from Hollywood (in part due to the influence of Vittorio Mussolini, the dictator's son and film buff director of the important journal *Cinema*).

James Hay's seminal study of fascist popular culture argues, using Fellini's classic film *Amarcord* as a template, that one key cultural myth during the 1930s in Italy was that of America, a myth popularised by Italian cinema.[4] Hay calls these images 'cose dell'altro mondo' ('things from another world'), punning on the title of a 1939 film by Nunzio Malasomma, where citations and homages to Hollywood abound. In Amleto Palermi's *Non c'è bisogno di denaro* (*There's No Need for Money*, 1933), an emigrant (played by Nino Besozzi) who has just come back from America is nominated president of a small bank on the brink of failure. Bragging about the riches the man has accumulated in America, the bank attracts its savers back until the bluff is revealed. Eventually, the banker is forgiven thanks to the honesty and good heart of the protagonist. The narrative device is identical to the one Frank Capra develops in *American Madness* (released one year before Palermi's film). The plot of Raffaello Matarazzo's *Giorno di nozze* (*Wedding Day*, 1942) recalls the classical structure of Capra's *Lady for a Day* (1933): a poor couple disguise themselves as well-off people in order to arrange their daughter's marriage with a wealthy family's son, leading not only to a comedy of errors but also the representation of the kind of corporate dream of classlessness typical of the later years of the fascist regime. The embrace between the two fathers-in-law recalls the reconciliation between Anthony P. Kirby (Edward Arnold) and Martin Vanderhof (Lionel Barrymore) in Capra's *You Can't Take It with You* (1938) and constitutes a metaphoric embrace between rich and poor, master and peasant, tycoon and worker, much theorised and idealised by fascist corporatism. As with the puritan ethics of the New Deal, money is not always a good in itself. In any case, money cannot follow you everywhere, as the case of the industrial tycoon satirised in Matarazzo's film demonstrates. Even a formalist film-maker like Ferdinando Maria Poggioli in an adaptation of a classic Shakespeare comedy shows a modern Rome made of identical tower blocks, all white and ominous, over which clouds of war loom in *La bisbetica domata* (*The Taming of the Shrew*, 1942). Petruccio (played by Amedeo Nazzari) is an emigrant returned from America who feels nostalgic about the older Rome he used to know, with all its small shops along its narrow lanes, and he does not approve of this modern Italy that is not like America: 'Here comes the American', says Catina's father, 'He comes from America, from another world … he's not like all those other idiots that hang around here.' Another emigrant returning to Italy is Joe (Armando Falconi) in Raffaello Matarazzo's *Joe il rosso* (*Joe the Red*, 1936), which contains a parody of the American gangster film with car chases, shootouts and escapes, and a comic portrait of an Italo-American with a pronounced Little Italy accent. Thus, Italian film comedy of the 1930s owes an important debt to American screwball comedy: it simplifies the Hollywood themes and, at the same time, emphasises strategies of social appeasement and control of consensus that serve as useful tools for the fascist regime.

BLASETTI AND THE SCREWBALL COMEDY

Another central director of the 1930s, Alessandro Blasetti, was indebted to both Soviet and Hollywood cinema, and he is best known for great historical films and for prefigurations of postwar neorealism. But a film like *La contessa di Parma* (*The Duchess of Parma*, 1938) contains a treatment of American mythology in a screwball comedy that can stand comparison with the best American titles of this genre. Blasetti relies on a team of excellent collaborators – scriptwriter Aldo De Benedetti, cinematographer Otello Martelli, with Mario Soldati as assistant director – to make a film that presents its audience with a formalist world of fiction from the beginning of its opening credits: neon signs on top of drawn buildings are sketched out in a style that mingles futurism and rationalism. The film was shot at the FERT studio, near the headquarters of Fiat, the emblematic automobile factory in Turin, one of the main cities of the industrial region in northern Italy and so a symbol of progress. Blasetti represents this kind of modernity, partly realised and partly just dreamed of, through imaginary models and codes or through mythopoeic projections into the worlds of fashion and football (i.e. the spheres of action of the two protagonists), seen as the symbolic spaces of a society that is rapidly going through radical changes. But the film also features racehorses, typical of Hollywood comedies, as well as grand hotels, cars and telephones, all status symbols of mass society, poised between slump and progress, between depression and change. The narrative relies on the classical device of role switching, a tradition that stretches back from Plautus to the *commedia dell'arte*, Mozart and Da Ponte's *Don Juan*. Marcella (Elisa Cegani) is the average girl-next-door, far from the femme fatale stereotypes found in contemporary media representations of top models. When she happens to wear a fashion designer's dress (named 'Contessa di Parma') at the racetrack, she is mistaken for a true aristocratic lady by Gino Vanni (Antonio Centa), a successful soccer player, who chases after her to return the 2,000 lire she won at the races. The entire plot revolves around this symbolic amount of money: Gino uses it to pay a creditor, who then gives it to Gino's tedious aunt. Eventually, Gino regains the money and both he and Marcella pretend not to care about it. Money is thus charged with a fetishist value in a film about the fetishism of commodities. This traditional comedy of errors shows a clearly paternalistic attitude in resolving the whole story by means of a metaphoric marriage between two different social classes; at the same time, however, it reflects a strong critical view of society. Stanley Cavell points out how marriage was the ever-present symbolic happy ending of most comedies made in Hollywood.[5] In the case of Blasetti's film, we have an ironic variation that suggests more symbolic readings. When Gino finally catches up with Marcella at a fashion catwalk in the Sestriere ski resort, she is wearing a designer's bridal dress. Gino – who had previously pretended to be engaged to another girl –misunderstands the whole situation until the happy ending. At first unaware that a movable platform is taking them among the audience, the two protagonists keep on flirting: as in a fairytale, the bridal dress comes in handy as they walk out among the applauding people lined on either side, just like two newlyweds would do. The boundary between fiction and reality is no longer discernible; reality itself has become spectacle and artifice.

Maurizio Grande wittily observes that Blasetti's film is the finest example of how a film can portray the entrepreneurial attitude of a new social milieu whose specialty is the fabrication and, above all, the marketing of dreams.[6] According to Grande, Blasetti's film is 'stylistically sordid' in the way it masks bitter smiles and treacherous embraces behind a comedy of errors and disguise. Under the surface of apparently innocent plots lies a deep inner drama. Each time the two protagonists try to free themselves from their social masks, the doomed 2,000 lire restore the boundaries that separate two worlds. La contessa di Parma can be associated with other comedies of the 1930s (for instance, Darò un milione and Il signor Max treated below) whose characters do not go through any visible transformation but disguise themselves and fake a new identity. Visual and narrative devices such as role switching, disguise and the double are instrumental in telling stories that subvert easily recognisable fascist stereotypes. They also suggest a diffused social schizophrenia that, in the long term, may end up undermining the ideology of consensus that they only apparently reinforce. In other words, the double is a subtle thematic underpinning hiding learned references and political commentary. 'I'm tired of looking like what I'm not', Marcella sadly admits before accepting the job at Sestriere. Just as she seems to give up her romantic dreams, Marcella's line ironically hints at her doubleness and, perhaps, it can be read as a sign of impatience at what Torquato Accetto called centuries ago the 'honest dissimulation' forced upon intellectuals during the fascist dictatorship.[7]

Sometimes unconscious, often deliberate, this double nature is a peculiar aspect of cinema during the fascist regime. Blasetti's films contain several such instances. The much-celebrated Quattro passi tra le nuvole's narrative situations take inspirations from classical American genres: in particular, its plot is quite derivative of Capra's It Happened One Night (1934). Clear examples are the sequence on the coach and the subsequent crash. The scene when the soon-to-be newlyweds Paolo (Gino Cervi) and Maria (Adriana Benetti) are left alone in the bedroom, with a blanket draped over a rope, clearly recalls the famous 'Jericho's wall' scene at the motel with Gable and Colbert. At the same time, Blasetti's comedy shows the symptoms of a deep malaise, since the opening and end sequences of the film, do not merely function as narrative bookends, but frustrate any fairytale resolution and pave the way for the imminent arrival of neorealism.

CAMERINI AND THE DOUBLE: METACINEMATIC ASPECTS OF 1930s FILM COMEDY

The themes of the double and schizophrenia are constant elements of Mario Camerini's films, to the extent that they become a stylistic, authorial trait of his cinema, in particular the films featuring Vittorio De Sica as an actor. In Darò un milione, De Sica plays a bored millionaire who one day decides to exchange clothes with a suicidal tramp so that, for a short time, he can live as a homeless person.

Narrative complications are assured by an intricate twist when a local newspaper manipulates the tramp as part of a publicity stunt and announces that the millionaire, disguised as a tramp, will donate one million lire to anybody who commits one act of true altruism. Again, this device ignites a comedy-of-error mechanism: all the middle-class inhabitants of the French town chosen as the setting of the story suddenly become 'good', welcoming and pampering tramps in the most unusual ways, with the hope of getting the coveted reward. Meanwhile, the owner of a circus organises a show for tramps only, with the secret goal of identifying the 'real' millionaire. Assia Noris plays an unaffected girl who works in the circus.

Eventually, the millionaire decides to marry her, as she is the only one who sincerely loves him for who he is and not for his money. The happy ending is only temporarily liberating: the millionaire gives a lot of money to the town tramps so that they can enjoy at least one night (but one night only, like the 'lady for a

In Camerini's *Darò un milione* (1935), Vittorio De Sica and Luigi Almirante switch places

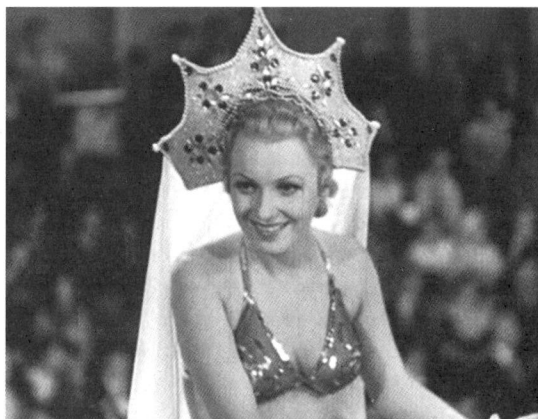

Assia Noris, one of the most famous stars of the period's comic films, in *Darò un milione*. Noris was married to Camerini from 1940–3.

day' …) having fun. As this subplot about tramps recalls the storyline of the future neorealist classic by De Sica, *Miracolo a Milano* (*Miracle in Milan*, 1951), we can see that Cesare Zavattini contributed to the script. His homeless tramps also recall the American movies of the Great Depression era even though *Darò un milione* was made before the most typical of Capra's films on poverty and media manipulation: *Meet John Doe* (1941). But Camerini does invent the narrative incident that Capra's film will exploit: the tale of a penniless tramp who wants to commit suicide and who is manipulated by an ambitious journalist and a cynical media tycoon to set up a press and political campaign around a false piece of news. Another similar situation occurs when the tramp is taken to the radio station: in *Meet John Doe*, Gary Cooper, who plays the Everyman John Doe, is tempted to flee before his speech is broadcast; in *Darò un milione*, the tramp actually runs away. Much later, in 1948, Capra directs *It's a Wonderful Life*, and once again, one scene seems to be lifted right out of Camerini's film, when the protagonist dives into the water to save the suicidal tramp.

Role switching is a main device of the film's subplots: Assia Noris takes on the role and look of the circus owner's wife, a plump starlet unable to perform her act any longer after she is injured by a horse. The female protagonist is also acclaimed in her role as a beauty queen. Still building upon the true–false dichotomy, Camerini adds a highly symbolic subplot around a sapphire owned by the millionaire. The jewel is authentic, but everybody thinks the opposite. Eventually, it ends up adorning the girl's finger, just like a nuptial ring, but also as the emblem of a commoditised society. Camerini's films are filled with

clues of this metonymic mechanism: sexual or consumerist fetishes representing the fascist ideology. In *Grandi magazzini* (*Department Stores*, 1938), the mild clerk played once again by Assia Noris hides in the women's department of a shopping mall and pretends to be a dummy in order to dodge the night guard. The sequence is rather surreal and is vaudevillian in inspiration (Totò, the great Italian comedian, will probably cite this gag in *I pompieri di Viggiù* [*The Firemen of Viggiù*, 1949], a scene which is also quoted in Giuseppe Tornatore's *Nuovo Cinema Paradiso* [*Cinema Paradiso*, 1988]). Another unlikely scene is focused on the idea of the fetish: her colleagues provide her with an incredibly realistic dummy with the exact same features as Bruno (De Sica), just as she complains about his ambiguity.

Because it was not allowed to put poor people and aspiring suicides on display in fascist Italy, *Darò un milione* is set in an unlikely location on the French Riviera where the millionaire's yacht is berthed. *Batticuore* is also set in France, in a stereotyped and rather theatrical Paris, populated by thieves and ambiguous ambassadors of imaginary foreign countries. This time Assia Noris plays an astute but good-hearted thief, whose misfortune led her down the wrong track in life. Not only she will redeem herself, but she will also manage to redeem the boss of a famous school of thieves. Driving the main storyline is the protagonist's involvement in a crime-caper plot centred around a double-role mix-up. First, she is caught stealing a brooch and forced to pretend to be the niece of a foreign diplomat. Later on, all sorts of misunderstandings originate from a risqué photograph found inside a pocket watch. Finally, she turns into a fair lady, completing her transformation into a rather ambiguous Cinderella. This conclusion is the triumph of the fairytale and, at the same time, of metalinguistic devices. A first instance occurs when, caught in the act of stealing the brooch, the beautiful thief takes refuge in a cinema. In the darkness, the viewers can watch the detective story projected on the screen: a lady is interrogated by a policeman, trying to justify herself. When the ambassador finally catches her, she replies with the same lines uttered by the character of the film within the film. This metafilmic device amplifies and reveals the apparatus in order to emphasise the dual nature of the character. In a second instance, a pioneer television show suggests once again the device of the double. At the embassy, an agreement between the two imaginary countries is being celebrated and broadcast live via a bizarre TV set, dressed with curtains that make it resemble a theatrical stage. The metalinguistic devices alone suffice to make this film an interesting experiment; however, Camerini and his writers manage to emphasise the metacinematic theme by making fun of the new, still futuristic, mass medium. The live broadcast is technically very flawed, the quality of sound is awful, and the two austere diplomats 'double up' as two thin ballerinas, by means of an interesting split-screen effect that shows their upper bodies above dancing, soft-footed legs. The most blatant example of Camerini's self-reflexivity can be found in *Grandi magazzini*. In one scene, Lauretta (Assia Noris) is offered a lift by her boss as she walks down the street. On the opposite side of the street, there is a poster for another Camerini film, *Batticuore*, released in the same year, and with Noris as Arlette, its female lead: Lauretta looks at herself in the poster. Ironically, the boss asks the girl: 'Can I take you to the movies?' A last example of Camerini's use of the metacinematic double can be found in his best-known film, *Il signor Max*, whose eponymous protagonist, played by De Sica, is a lower-class newsagent who finds himself in the shoes of an aristocratic man attending high-society clubs. Misunderstandings ensue when he meets Lauretta, the typical girl-next-door (played again by Assia Noris), who works as a babysitter for a wealthy woman infatuated with Max.

CAMERINI'S DOUBLE: VITTORIO DE SICA

The double is a fundamental metacinematic theme in Vittorio De Sica's early films as well. De Sica's first movies behind the camera are clearly inspired by Camerini, with the addition of Cesare Zavattini's artistic contribution. These include the films made before *I bambini ci guardano* (*The Children Are Watching Us*, 1943), which already marks a turn towards neorealism. In the 1930s, De Sica was one of the most successful actors in the Italian star system, one of the few to audition for Hollywood. His first films as director lay the technical and aesthetic foundations of his imminent maturation as a neorealist auteur. However, from a historical and methodological perspective, a correct reading of these films should not be influenced by our knowledge of his future neorealist productions. Instead, we must search for traces of continuity and rupture, and identify his models and influences from other cinemas and film-makers. The Camerini/Hollywood comedy model is a primary source of inspiration, of course, although a hybrid one that welcomes elements from other genres: Westerns, war movies, period dramas and melodramas, are all conflated into a certain degree of un-realism in De Sica's early films. They reveal a tendency to use sound stages (which we still find years later, in the neorealist *Sciuscià* [*Shoeshine*, 1946]) and the frequent occurrence of closed, claustrophobic spaces.

A good example is *Rose scarlatte* (*Red Roses*, 1940). Entirely shot at Cinecittà studios, this film has a rather theatrical appeal based on the classical pattern of the comedy of errors. Spaces are bidimensional and the action is restricted to the interior of a luxurious mansion. The *mise en scène* is clearly inspired by Hollywood continuity style and customs: soft filters on the close-ups of the female protagonist, smooth camera movements, rear projection doubling up for the few exterior locations. In short, studio shooting dictates stylistic choices. The plot relies on a misunderstanding, as is typical of American and Camerini's comedies: a bunch of roses that De Sica sent to another woman is intercepted by his wife, who believes they come from a mysterious and unidentified admirer. A potential betrayal is resolved with a reassuring ending, thanks to a minor character who deceitfully confesses to being the secret lover. Still, this is the story of an unhappy wife, ready to enter a romantic affair in order to punish her husband for his lack of appreciation. Despite the happy ending, we can find *clues* of the malaise and the adultery that drives the plotline of *I bambini ci guardano*.

Maddalena zero in condotta (*Maddalena, Zero for Conduct*, 1940) is a light-hearted comedy entirely focused on modernity. This time the misunderstanding is triggered by a love letter written (for a test in foreign languages) by a student named Maddalena (Carla Del Poggio) to an imaginary man called Alfredo Hartman,

which she sends to the address of the publisher of her
school handbook. Due to a lack of communication, the
letter is actually sent to Vienna, where not one, but
three Alfredo Hartmans live: grandfather, father and
son (all played by De Sica). Intrigued by the letter, the
young Hartman goes to Rome hoping to meet the
person who wrote it. Complications ensue and further
misunderstandings are assured. This offbeat pattern
would make for a perfect screwball comedy, although
all the characters belong to the same upper middle-
class milieu. The only exception is found in one of the
few sad moments of the film, when Elsa the teacher
(Vera Bergman) reproaches her pupils: 'You have no
idea what it means to lose your job, your daily bread
…'. The action alternates between a stereotyped Vienna
and Rome (both cities belonged at that time to the
historical German–Italian Axis, although Vienna is also
a romantic city). Alfredo, the son, flies in comfort to
Italy and reaches Maddalena's wealthy household.
There is no mention of the war taking place, no hint
of personal or collective anguish and fear. However,
Maddalena is an extraordinarily modern protagonist:
she triggers the various couples' affairs and is the
driving force behind the whole romance plot. It is no
accident that she has a bad conduct mark at school,
as the title of the film states.

Teresa Venerdì further explores a world inhabited
by females living in a girls' orphanage. The male
protagonist, Dr Pietro Vignali (De Sica), is a paediatrician
dragged into an unpleasant situation of misunderstandings. Young, broke, ridden with debts, harassed by
creditors who search his house for money, he is forced
by his father to take on the post of physician at the
orphanage, replacing an old doctor who used to
prescribe castor oil for everything. Here occurs the
charming encounter with Teresa Venerdì (Adriana
Benedetti), who takes her nickname (in English, Friday)
after the day she was found. The ironic citation of
Robinson Crusoe's servant underscores how isolated
Dr Vignali feels in such an environment, and Teresa
becomes the only person he can rely on for support.
Their love is hampered by all sorts of obstacles: above
all, he is forced to get engaged to a rich, vain girl he
does not love. The happy ending is eventually assured,
but not before a final sequence of further
misunderstandings: when Teresa sneaks out of the
orphanage and breaks into the paediatrician's house,
she is confronted by his lover who mistakes her for his
new fiancée. Playing the role of the luscious lover is
Anna Magnani (Pina of Roma città aperta) who is the

femme fatale of a vaudeville show whose function is to
reveal how everybody plays a part, wears a mask or acts
in disguise, as did the protagonists of Rose scarlatte and
Maddalena. In Teresa Venerdì though, the metalinguistic
device is openly declared by the theatre within the
film, and by other examples of texts within the text:
Magnani's rehearsals on the stage are influenced by the
ups and downs of her private life; the rich fiancée
recites couplets; Teresa rehearses Shakespeare's Juliet
monologue unbeknownst to the headmaster. When one
of her school friends tells on her, her monologue is
mistaken for a striking declaration of love. As in many
of De Sica's previous works, the modernising of Italy
is represented by high-tech vacuum cleaners and
constantly ringing telephones.

After Maddalena and Teresa, Un garibaldino al
convento (A Garibaldian in the Convent, 1942) takes us
back in time to the Italian Risorgimento, but also fits
a hybridised comedy model. An old lady tells a few
young girls about an event that occurred to her when
she was their age. This precipitates a long flashback to
the imaginary town of Latium and brackets the whole
narration within a fairytale, lending it a 'once upon a
time' atmosphere. Two young girls, Gertrude (Clara
Auteri Pepe) and Mariella (Maria Mercader), daughters
of two families who live opposite each other, spend all
their time bickering. They end up in the same college
run by nuns and, despite their initial competitive
spirit, they gradually bond and become friends. The
tranquil life at the convent is suddenly disrupted by
the arrival of a follower of Garibaldi fleeing the troops
of the Bourbons. Gertrude is soon infatuated with the

Comedy marries history with Leonardo Cortese and Maria
Mercader in Un garibaldino al convento (1942); Mercader later
marries De Sica

young man, unaware that he is an earl and already engaged to Mariella. When the soldiers break into the convent looking for him, the young man hides in the stable with the help of the comic handyman who sees this as a good chance to show his patriotism besides trying to teach his blackbirds to sing the Italian national anthem. The film shifts towards the generic conventions of the Western until the eventual providential attack by Garibaldi's Redshirts, much like the Union army in so many Hollywood films, summoned by Gertrude, who manages to enlist the help of Captain Nino Bixio (Garibaldi's second-in-command), a cameo by De Sica himself. A few visible flaws in this work exist: its acting is too stereotyped and theatrical; Maria Mercader's Spanish accent makes her character less believable; and the setting, confined within the sound stages of the studio, is unexciting. The originality of the film is found in its unusual mix of genres: De Sica makes a romantic comedy centred around a coming-of-age plot, but includes elements of the war film, period drama, melodrama and surreal comedic twists.

Shortly after the war, De Sica began producing his brilliant neorealist classics, but his work in the metacinematic vein championed by his mentor Camerini underscores the continuity between prewar and postwar Italian cinema. Prewar comedy seemed to ignore the imminent tragedy caused by the outbreak of World War II and the collapse of the fascist regime, but the 'first comedy, Italian style' of the 1930s would soon give way to the more dramatic stories of *I bambini ci guardano*, *La porta del cielo* (*The Gate of Heaven*, 1945) and the neorealist masterpieces of the late 1940s and early 1950s.

NOTES

1. See also Adriano Aprà and Patrizi Pistagnesi (eds), *I favolosi anni Trenta, Cinema italiano 1929–1944* (Milan: Electa, 1979); or its English version: *The Fabulous Thirties: Italian Cinema 1929–1944* (Milan: Electa, 1979). For an analysis of postwar Italian film comedy, usually labelled by the critics and film historians as *commedia all'italiana* or 'comedy, Italian style', see the essay in this collection by Rémi Fournier Lanzoni.
2. Nicola Tranfaglia, *Fascismi e modernizzazione in Europa* (Turin: Bollati Boringhieri, 2001).
3. See Andrew Bergman, *We're in the Money. Depression America and Its Films* (New York: Harper Colophon Books, 1971).
4. See James Hay, *Popular Film Culture in Fascist Italy: The Passing of the Rex* (Bloomington: Indiana University Press, 1987).
5. Stanley Cavell, *Pursuits of Happiness. The Hollywood Comedy of Remarriage* (Cambridge, MA: Harvard University Press, 1981).
6. Maurizio Grande, *Il cinema di Saturno* (Rome: Bulzoni, 1992), p. 22.
7. Torquato Accetto (1590/98 to 1640) was a Neapolitan who wrote an important treatise on conformity and the hypocrisy required by life in baroque society: *Della dissimulazione onesta* (*On Honest Dissimulation*). See Rosario Villari, *L'uomo barocco* (Rome/Bari: Laterza, 2006). The formula of 'honest simulation' has since been applied to the consent Italian intellectuals offered to fascism; see Andrea Martini (ed.), *La bella forma. Poggioli, i calligrafici e dintorni* (Venice: Marsilio, 1992).

FURTHER READING

Argentieri, Mino and Umberto Rossi, *Risate di regime. La commedia italiana 1930–1944* (Venice: Marsilio, 1991).
Ben-Ghiat, Ruth, *Fascist Modernities. Italy, 1922–1945* (Berkeley: University of California Press, 2001).
Grande, Maurizio, *Il cinema di Saturno* (Rome: Bulzoni, 1992).
Hay, James, *Popular Film Culture in Fascist Italy: The Passing of the Rex* (Bloomington: Indiana University Press, 1987).
Landy, Marcia, *Fascism in Film: The Italian Commercial Cinema, 1931–1943* (Princeton, NJ: Princeton University Press, 1986).
Miccichè, Lino (ed.), *Il neorealismo cinematografico italiano* (Venice: Marsilio, 1999).
Reich, Jacqueline and Piero Garofalo (eds), *Re-viewing Fascism: Italian Cinema, 1922–1943* (Bloomington: Indiana University Press, 2002).
Zagarrio, Vito, *Cinema e fascismo. Film, modelli, immaginari* (Venice: Marsilio, 2004).
——, *L'immagine del fascismo. La re-visione del cinema e dei media nel regime* (Rome: Bulzoni 2009).

8 Censorship from the Fascist Period to the Present

Guido Bonsaver

CENSORSHIP LEGISLATION DURING FASCISM

When Benito Mussolini took over Italy's prime ministership, the legislation on film censorship was well established and so was left untouched for a few years. The pre-fascist decree-laws of 31 May 1914 and 9 October 1919 laid down the general rules of what could not be screened in public cinemas: anything offensive to morality and public decency; glorification of crime, violence and superstition; adultery for sexual gratification; and insulting institutions of the state. Moreover, the decree-law of 1919 introduced pre-production censorship of film scripts by an officer of the Directorate of Public Security and, as of April 1920, a whole commission composed of one magistrate, a mother, a representative of a humanitarian association, a critic and a journalist. In practice, however, this directive was not strictly imposed, hence it was rarely followed by production companies which, instead, submitted the script together with the final cut of the film.

From a legal viewpoint, the fascists concentrated on two main issues. First they aimed at adding a political dimension to the censorship commission. This was initially done through the decree-law of 9 April 1928 which introduced appointed members of the National Fascist Party and of the Ministry of National Education. Much more important, however, was the move in September 1934 of the entire administration of censorship from the Ministry of the Interior to the newly created Directorate General for Cinematography (Direzione Generale per la Cinematografia, or DGpC) which was part of the then Undersecretariat for Press and Propaganda (in future years to be renamed first Ministry of Press and Propaganda, in 1935, and then Ministry for Popular Culture, in 1937). Under the firm hand of its head, Luigi Freddi, the DGpC became a

central player in the development of the Italian film industry. It was under the aegis of the DGpC that pre-production censorship of scripts was made compulsory. By January 1935, the censorship commission had also been entirely politicised, with all its five appointed members serving in either a ministry or in the party. In the mind of Luigi Freddi, however, censorship could be pre-empted if the state were more active in all sectors of the industry. Patronage became an effective tool in ensuring ideological orthodoxy. Following increased government funding, scripts were discussed and modified with the involvement of DGpC officials long before they reached the table of the censorship commissions. Formal political censorship was rarely necessary. No production company could afford the risk of displeasing their potential patrons and protectors. The financial benefits of co-operating with government departments also engendered a high degree of self-censorship and opportunistic choice of subject matter.

The second issue derived from the fascists' nationalistic agenda. Despite his admiration for the American studio system, Luigi Freddi was determined to defend Italian national cinema through protectionist policies. The first step was the law of 16 June 1927, which imposed a minimum of 10 per cent share of distribution for Italian films. By October 1933, the percentage was raised to 25 (in towns with over 50,000 inhabitants) and, by July 1937, each cinema in Italy had to devote at least one third of its schedule to Italian films. Foreign films were never boycotted entirely, not even during the war years, but a decisive form of control was the imposition in September 1938 of a single importing agency, ENIC, whose selection of films was clearly directed against American, British and French imports. As a consequence, four Hollywood major companies (20th Century-Fox, Metro-Goldwyn-

Mussolini opening Cinecittà with Luigi Freddi to his right

Mayer, Paramount and Warner Bros.) decided to write off the Italian market altogether. This provoked a massive drop in the number of imported US films, descending from 162 in 1938 to 64 the following year, with only 36 in 1940.

Entirely distinct from fascist film censorship, during the mid-1930s, the Catholic Church created its own institution whose aim was to provide guidance with regard to film screening. Following Pope Pius XI's Encyclical 'Vigilanti cura' of 29 June 1936, the Catholic Centre for Cinematography (Centro Cattolico Cinematografico or CCC) was created. Its periodical publications listed all films released in Italy with clear indications as to their permitted audience, moving in alphabetical degrees from A (for all) to E (unsuitable for anybody). One example of an E-rated film is Alessandro Blasetti's La cena delle beffe (The Jesters' Supper, 1941), mainly due to the overt sensuality and scanty clothing of lead actress Clara Calamai. The indications of the CCC bore no legal status, however; their importance derived from the fact that, in parallel with this initiative, the Vatican created a vast network of local parish cinemas which naturally strictly followed those indications.

EROS, THANATOS AND NATIONALISTIC POLICIES IN FASCIST CENSORSHIP

As already suggested, ideological orthodoxy was guaranteed and to a great extent emerged spontaneously during the 1920s and 1930s. Topics which were not in line with fascist cultural policies were either discouraged – such was the case of films in dialect – or, in the case of foreign films, denied national distribution. The latter was the case with war films which were either considered too critical of warfare – such as Lewis Milestone's All Quiet on the Western Front (1930) and Jean Renoir's La Grande illusion (The Grand Illusion, 1937, which paradoxically won a prize 'for its artistic merit' at the Venice Film Festival), or those accused of depicting the Italian army in too critical a light, such as Frank Borzage's adaptation of Hemingway's World War I novel, A Farewell to Arms (1932).[1] An unintentionally ironical case of censorship in order to defend the dignity of the Italian nation is the case of Archie Mayo's The Adventures of Marco Polo (1938). Because of its allegedly disrespectful representation of the famous Italian traveller as impersonated by Gary Cooper, the Samuel Goldwyn Company was asked to adjust the dubbing of the dialogue so that the nationality of the protagonist could be altered improbably to Scottish, hence the Italian title *Uno scozzese alla corte del Gran Khan*. More seriously, early gangster films centred on Italian-American criminals, such as Mervyn LeRoy's *Little Caesar* (1931) and Howard Hawks's *Scarface* (1932), were denied distribution in Italian cinemas during the fascist rule. The same fate befell Jean Renoir's *Toni* (*Toni*, 1935) depicting the troubled life of an Italian migrant in southern France.

The censors still primarily focused on perceived excessive sensuality. This was the case with Mitchell Leisen's *Murder of the Vanities* (1934), for which Paramount was ordered to reduce the length of shots dedicated to the naked legs of ballerinas. A similar fate was destined for a German production, Max Neufeld's *Opernredoute* (*Opera Ball*, 1931) in which cuts extended to an intertitle describing the house of the male protagonist as a love nest. Scenes perceived to be traumatically violent were also censored, hence images of torture were cut from David Butler's *A Connecticut Yankee* (1931) and Edward G. Robinson's *The Little Giant* (1933). Finally, it is interesting to note that the horror genre, inspired by German expressionist films and developed in Hollywood in the early 1930s, was often considered unpalatable by Italian censors for both its fearful and darkly sensual traits. Classics, such as Tod Browning's *Dracula* (1931) and Charles Brabin's *The Mask of Fu Manchu* (1932) did not reach Italian cinemas, neither did the much-celebrated *Nosferatu* (*Nosferatu, A Symphony of Horror*, 1922) by F. W. Murnau. Others were tamed with various cuts or given an age 16 certificate (introduced in 1926), as in the case of Rouben Mamoulian's *Dr. Jekyll and Mr Hyde* (1932).[2]

During the last years of fascism, with Italy's intervention in World War II and its following disastrous military campaigns, censorship control became more stringent, particularly on foreign films. At the same time, the growing disillusionment with fascism began to find expression in cinema too. Two Italian films, in particular, deserve attention since they provide complementary examples of the wide-reaching nature of fascist censorship: Alessandro Blasetti's *Nessuno torna indietro* (*Responsibility Comes Back*, 1943) and Luchino Visconti's *Ossessione* (*Obsession*, 1943). The fortunes of *Nessuno torna indietro* were closely related to those of the homonymous novel by Alba De Céspedes. Published by Mondadori in 1938, the novel had acquired instant success for its disillusioned depiction of a group of female university students living in contemporary Rome. Initially, the book was not censored but De Céspedes' non-fascist views, coupled with attacks on

moral grounds on her collection of short stories, *Fuga* (1940), caused the proscription of the novel at the very time in which its film adaptation was about to enter production. In a prolonged negotiation with censorship officials, De Céspedes, and later Blasetti, introduced a number of cuts and modifications to the script in order to ensure it conformed to a more orthodox view of womanhood. Some characters were dropped; more uplifting endings were provided for others. Mussolini himself was involved, and it was his decision that the film should be distributed with another title, *Pensione Grimaldi*, in order to detach it from the literary work. Due to the political crisis in 1943, the film was not distributed and it was only in November 1944 that, amid the chaos of the last months of the war, it received the *nulla osta* (paperwork for the ministerial permission) by the fascist authorities in northern Italy with the reinstated title, *Nessuno torna indietro*.[3]

The case of *Ossessione* was simpler at the outset, since the group of young film-makers involved in the production were close to Mussolini's son, Vittorio, a film enthusiast and scriptwriter himself, then editor of the journal *Cinema*. Despite relocation of the story from California (as in James Cain's novel of 1934) to the desolate plains of the Po valley, and the presence of a new character, a quasi-anarchist and crypto-homosexual called lo Spagnolo ('The Spaniard'), the script was approved and production began. When Visconti entered the editing studio, one of the five scriptwriters, Mario Alicata, was arrested on 29 December 1942 for being a member of the underground Italian Communist Party. As his correspondence shows, Alicata continued to contribute to the production from his prison cell, and the film did not suffer any form of direct censorship. However, as stated by another scriptwriter, Giuseppe De Santis, a scene was added in order to throw a more negative light on lo Spagnolo (he reports his friend to the police) in order to counterbalance his ideological heterodoxy. The paperwork for the ministerial *nulla osta* was submitted on the eve of the fall of the regime, in May 1943, but it was only during the short-lived period of the fascist Repubblica Sociale Italiana, once Mussolini was reinstated in power in September 1943, that *Ossessione* received the go-ahead. The only cuts imposed were the removal of the name of Luchino Visconti from the credits (by then he had also joined the Communist resistance) and a detail in which some Italian flags with the by-then-repudiated royal crest in the middle, could be seen in the background. Once distributed in the spring of 1944, the film encountered the disapproval of local authorities in a few cities in northern Italy, such as Bologna, where it was withdrawn.

THE EARLY POSTWAR YEARS

After the fall of the regime, as early as October 1945, the legislation on pre-production censorship of scripts was annulled. However, in 1947, the Constituent Assembly opted for the maintenance of pre-distribution censorship. This was confirmed in Article 21 of the Constitution, which, after granting freedom of speech and information, stated the need to monitor and prevent any insult to public morality ('buoncostume'). Each film was vetted by one of the eight commissions which then provided a *nulla osta* certificate and defined the age specification (for all or over 16). In many respects, it was a system which was similar to that of other democratic countries. As first decreed by the law of 16 May 1947, the censorship commissions were depoliticised, and they returned to a panel composed by members of society at large. Censorship was also renamed with the euphemism 'cinematographic revision'. All appointments, however, were the responsibility of the institution which had replaced the DGpC: the Department for Cultural Events (Dipartimento per lo Spettacolo), under the Prime Minister's Office (Presidenza del Consiglio). With regard to this institution, a worrying degree of continuity with the fascist years was evident since Luigi Freddi's DGpC survived practically intact in both organisation and personnel (with the exception of its directors).[4] At the time, the Department for Cultural Affairs was headed by a young Christian Democrat Undersecretary, Giulio Andreotti, who was to become one of the most influential politicians in Italy for over forty years. Moreover, if pre-production censorship had been abolished, the prospect of government funding for national productions introduced a similar process of government vetting of scripts. Productions could not be stopped, but at the same time a certain element of self-censorship and conformism was inevitably encouraged. Indeed, Giulio Andreotti made his intentions to promote 'good cinema' very explicit in a speech in parliament on 28 September 1948 when he spoke of the need to 'incoraggiare una produzione sana, moralissima e nello stesso tempo attraente' ('to encourage a healthy, highly moral and at the same time attractive production').[5] Andreotti's open criticism of neorealist films, owing their focus on Italy's social tensions and economic problems, was best interpreted

by the censorship commission which judged De Sica's *Umberto D.* too crude for an audience of minors (the film was given a certificate 16) and imposed the cut of a scene in which a patient in a hospital could be seen reciting the rosary with a visibly jaded expression.

Perceived disrespect towards state institutions also triggered a number of renowned incidences of censorship. The most extreme resulted in the arrest of scriptwriter Renzo Renzi and film critic and journal editor of *Cinema nuovo*, Guido Aristarco, for the publication of the treatment of a film entitled *L'armata s'agapò* (*The S'agapò/I Love You Army*), in September 1953. Centred on the Italian wartime occupation of Greece, the film treatment was considered so insulting by a retired general that, once alerted, the military magistrates decided to intervene. The two spent forty-five days in a military prison, followed by a trial (both had served in the army as reserve officers and hence could be judged by a military court) at the end of which, and in the midst of a unrelenting press campaign in their support, they were acquitted. Another case, limited to imposed cuts, was that of Mario Monicelli's *Totò e Carolina* (*Toto and Caroline*, 1955). Its humorous satire of the Italian police was curbed with a total of 573 metres of film lost, 20 per cent of the entire length. More frequently, the censorship commissions requested the removal of entire scenes or selected shots considered offensive to public morality. In those years, many popular films by leading directors fell foul either of the censors or, once distributed, of local magistrates: from Federico Fellini's *I vitelloni* (*I Vitelloni*, 1953), to Visconti's *Rocco e i suoi fratelli* (*Rocco and His Brothers*, 1960) and Michelangelo Antonioni's *Il grido* (*The Cry*, 1957) and *L'avventura* (*L'Avventura*, 1960).[6]

At the same time, the influence of the CCC increased post war, helped by its political allies in government and more so by the exponential growth of the Vatican's network of parish cinemas. This grew from about 450 units in 1938 to 2,500 by 1948, thus providing the Church with a powerful tool with which it could influence the film industry.

CENSORSHIP BY TRIAL

By the mid-1960s, censorship commissions seem to reflect the more permissive atmosphere in wider society (and, in politics, with the first coalition governments with Christian Democrats sharing power with Social Democrats and Socialists), often limiting their intervention to the imposition of an age certificate. This relaxation is also a result of the new legislation on theatre and film censorship introduced with the decree-law of 21 April 1962. In a move towards self-governance, censorship commissions were opened up to representatives of the film industry (three out of seven; the others being a magistrate and three teachers/lecturers respectively in Law, Pedagogy and Psychology). Age certification was divided into two bands: fourteen and eighteen.

However, if censorship commissions became more lenient, a considerable number of films were still the subject of court cases triggered by local magistrates, with the latter either acting on their own initiative or reacting to an accusation of disrespect for public morality by an individual or an association. Pier Paolo Pasolini's films recurrently met with criticism resulting in court proceedings. This had begun in a lower key with his debut film *Accattone* (*Accattone* aka *The Scroungers* aka *The Procurer*, 1961), which was subject to four small modifications in the dialogue (in order to soften the harsh reality of mothers taking to prostitution) and an exceptional certificate 18 (only later introduced across the board by the 1962 legislation). More important was the case of Pasolini's episode of the multidirected film *Ro.Go.Pa.G* (*Ro.Go.Pa.G*,

1963). 'La ricotta' was accused, directly by a Roman judge, of blasphemy against the Catholic Church (which in those years was still the official religion of the Italian state). Found guilty by the court, it was only after the Court of Appeal reversed the verdict that the film was re-released, more than a year later. Equally controversial was *Il Decameron* (*The Decameron*, 1971), which featured the first male nude in Italian cinema.

Despite its Certificate 18, the film was attacked and temporarily sequestered in some cities. Piously, a delegation from the southern city of Lucera even asked the magistrature to prevent any moral disorder by banning the film within its city walls. A similar misfortune befell Pasolini's *I racconti di Canterbury* (*The Canterbury Tales*, 1972) which was distributed the following year. In this case, too, court proceedings, delayed by two levels of appeal, postponed the free circulation of the film for more than a year. This time, colour was added by the fact that a Franciscan monk joined the proceedings, alleging that his religious order had been defamed. One should also mention the posthumous case of *Salò o le 120 giornate di Sodoma* (*Salò or the 120 Days of Sodom*, 1975). Approved with a certificate 18 during the weeks following Pasolini's death, the film was immediately sequestered, then released in Milan on 10 January 1976, then sequestered again until February of the following year.[7]

A most tortuous case is that of Bernardo Bertolucci's *Ultimo tango a Parigi* (*Last Tango in Paris*, 1972). On 21 December 1972, only six days after its premiere, a Roman magistrate ordered its withdrawal for its obscene content. Director, scriptwriters, producers and actors were asked to testify at the trial which took place in Bologna and ended in February 1973 with full acquittal and the redistribution of the film. However, the Roman magistrature appealed and was successful, first with the Court of Appeal forbidding the film was in November 1974, and then with the Court of Cassation confirming the guilty verdict and requesting the destruction of every copy of the film, in January 1976. In reality not all the copies of the film were destroyed, but *Ultimo tango a Parigi* did remain banned throughout Italy until 1987.[8] The censorship excesses of the magistrature became the subject of a strike of all workers in the film industry, on 26 April 1974, triggered by the impounding of Liliana Cavani's *Il portiere di notte* (*The Night Porter*, 1974).

With the 1980s, there is a sharp drop in the activity of the magistrature. This was not due to a change in the legislation but the result of a combination of factors. First, a generation of particularly intolerant magistrates neared the end of their career. The most renowned among them was Donato Massimo Bartolomei, Procuratore Generale at L'Aquila, who in previous years had distinguished himself as the initiator of dozens of sequestrations. One of his last acts, only a few weeks before retirement, was the impounding of Renzo Arbore's comedy *Il Pap'occhio* (*In the Pope's Eye*, 1980) for allegedly offending the Catholic Church. Second, the massive expansion of television audiences with the liberalisation of the private market in the late 1970s moved the focus of censorship to the small screen. The mushrooming of private television channels transmitting pornographic material which could be viewed by spectators of any age and at any time of day radically dwarfed the perceived dangers of the cinema as a place of mass public entertainment. Third, film historians highlight a generational change

among film-makers. Radical directors such as Pasolini or the young Bellocchio, Fellini and Antonioni, were replaced by a generation which seemed less interested in pushing the boundaries of the permitted, despite an evident political and social commitment, such as in the films of the Taviani Brothers, Nanni Moretti or, in later years, Gabriele Salvatores and Giuseppe Tornatore.

A case of self-censorship on the part of distributors concerns a foreign film, *Lion of the Desert* (1981) by Syrian director Moustapha Akkad. It is a biopic of Libyan rebel leader Omar al-Mukhtar, captured and executed by the Italian colonial army in 1931. Financed by the Libyan government, the film presented a first-class cast, with Anthony Quinn as the rebel leader, Oliver Reed as General Rodolfo Graziani and Rod Steiger impersonating Mussolini. Unsurprisingly, the plot depicted the fascist Italian colonisers as cruel and calculating. The film provoked a parliamentary discussion in January 1982 in which a member of the government, then led by Giovanni Spadolini, the first non-Christian Democrat Prime Minister in postwar years, expressed his disappointment at the representation of the Italian army. The producers never asked for the *nulla osta* of the censorship commissions, hence the film was never distributed. On 10 March 1987, it was sequestered by the police when a pacifist association (Coordinamento per la Pace) attempted to

screen it. Amid political polemics, *Lion of the Desert* was eventually allowed to be seen at the film festival Riminicinema the following year. The same form of self-censorship was practised by the Italian state and independent television channels. *Lion of the Desert* was finally broadcast by Sky Cinema in 2009 on the eve of the official visit of Muammar Gaddafi, hosted by then Prime Minister Silvio Berlusconi.[9]

At the turn of the millennium, official film censorship in Italy is limited to the decisions of the censorship commissions with regard to age certificates. Intervention by the magistrature is still legal but has not taken place for years. The last case was the banning of the controversial dark comedy *Totò che visse due volte* (*Totò Who Lived Twice*, 1998) by cult Sicilian directors Daniele Ciprì and Franco Maresco. The film was unusually refused the *nulla osta* by the censorship commission, which deemed it offensive to 'the dignity of the Sicilian people, Italians and humanity in general' and for its blasphemous scenes. Given that the film had already been selected at the Berlin Film Festival and, following complaints by film critics and politicians, a few months later the regional court responsible for appeals related to administrative acts (Tribunale Amministrativo Regionale) sentenced in favour of its free circulation with a certificate 18. In the wake of this *querelle*, then Deputy Prime Minister and Minister for Culture and Environment Walter Veltroni tabled a modification to the 1962 legislation on censorship. The modification deprived censorship commissions of the power to ban the circulation of a film.

As for the promotion of Italian films, it should be mentioned that protectionist policies are still in place. This happens in the form of tax breaks and 'quality prizes' reserved for cinemas which devote a certain percentage of their schedule to European art films and Italian ones identified as of 'National Cultural Interest' ('interesse culturale nazionale').[10]

Finally, there is no doubt that the years of direct involvement in politics of media tycoon Silvio Berlusconi (Prime Minister in 1994–5; 2001–6 and 2008–11) greatly intensified the public debate on the reciprocal influence of politics and the media. With regards to cinema, however, it can be stated that government censorship institutions and the magistrature showed a reassuring degree of independence and maturity. No controversial censorship cases directly concerned the film industry. With regard to television, on the other hand, one should quote an example of self-censorship regarding Nanni Moretti's dark satire of Berlusconi, *Il caimano* (*The Caiman*, 2006). Despite the fact that Italian state broadcaster RAI had acquired the expensive television rights for the film, *Il caimano* was not scheduled for years. It was only broadcast on 19 June 2011, by RAI 3, after the director and prominent journalists had publicly complained about the delay in its projection on national television.

NOTES

1. On the film production and reception of *A Farewell to Arms*, see Stephen Gundle's essay: 'Hollywood, Italy and the First World War: Italian Reactions to Film Versions of Ernest Hemingway's *A Farewell to Arms*', in Guido Bonsaver and Robert Gordon (eds), *Culture, Censorship and the State in Twentieth-Century Italy* (Oxford: Legenda, 2005), pp. 98–108.

2. Thanks to a vast research project called 'Italia Taglia', sponsored by Italy's Ministero per i Beni e le Attività Culturali and run by the Cineteca in Bologna, studies on film censorship have recently benefited from the digitisation of the ministerial archives related to film censorship. The results of this project can be found in Tatti Sanguineti (ed.), *Italia Taglia* (Ancona: Transeuropa, 1999) and more importantly in the project's website which allows free access to hundreds of digitised reports by the censorship commissions, ranging, at the time of writing, from 1913 to 1955. The web address, last used here on 29 February 2012, is: <http://www.italiataglia.it/home>.

3. This latest development in the fortunes of the film was probably a consequence of the fact that the then Secretary of the Fascist party was hardliner Alessandro Pavolini, whose lover, the actress Doris Duranti, played a lead part in *Nessuno torna indietro*.

4. This is directly satirised in the film *Gran varietà* (*Great Vaudeville*, 1954) by Domenico Paolella. In one of its episodes, the then popular comedian Renato Rascel plays both parts of a variety artist who is persecuted by a censorship official, first during the fascist years, and then by the same person in different clothing in the postwar ones.

5. Quoted in Domenico Liggeri, *Mani di forbice: La censura cinematografica in Italia* (Alessandria: Falsopiano, 1997), p. 107. It should also be mentioned that some protectionist policies were maintained in the postwar years. As late as 1952, Italian cinemas were under the obligation of screening a percentage of national films: a minimum of twenty days of programming every three months (about 20 per cent) had to be devoted to Italian films.

6. Federico Fellini satirised the image of the obsessive censor in his episode of *Boccaccio '70* (1961), entitled 'The Temptations of Doctor Antonio' ('Le tentazioni del dottor Antonio'). On *Umberto D.*, see Enzo Sallustro (ed.), *Storie del cinema italiano. Censure* (Milan: Silvana Editoriale, 2007), pp. 18–19. On *L'armata s'agapò* and *L'avventura* see Tatti Sanguineti (ed.), *Italia Taglia*, pp. 28–39 and 99–100. On *Totò e Carolina*, see Tatti Sanguineti (ed.), *Totò e Carolina* (Bologna: Transeuropa, 1999).

7. On Pasolini, see Francesca Romana Massaro (daughter of Gianni Massaro, the lawyer who represented many Italian directors in court), *Il cinema come nessuno ve l'ha mai raccontato: Storie di grandi film, di grandi personaggi, di grandi censure* (Florence: Emmebi, 2011), pp. 35–46, 67–78; see also Sallustro, *Storie del cinema italiano*, pp. 74–7, 232–45. A better documented study is offered by Laura Betti (ed.), *Pasolini: cronaca giudiziaria, persecuzione, morte* (Milan: Garzanti, 1977); see also Sallustro, *Storie del cinema italiano*, pp. 74–7, 232–45.

8. On the censorship of Bertolucci's film, see Liggeri, *Mani di forbice*, pp. 147–50.

9. Given the disagreements and competition at the time between Silvio Berlusconi and media tycoon Rupert Murdoch, it is easy to imagine that the scheduling of the film by a Sky channel was planned in order to exploit the situation and at the same time embarrass the Italian Prime Minister.

10. I am grateful to cinema managers Roberto Roversi and Gabriele Caveduri for their update on current legislation on the scheduling of Italian and European art films (*film essai*).

FURTHER READING

Bonsaver, Guido and Robert Gordon (eds), *Culture, Censorship and the State in Twentieth-Century Italy* (Oxford: Legenda, 2005).

Forgacs, David and Stephen Gundle, *Mass Culture and Italian Society: From Fascism to the Cold War* (Bloomington: Indiana University Press, 2007).

Freddi, Luigi, *Il cinema* (2 vols) (Rome: L'Arnia, 1949). Reprinted as *Il cinema: il governo dell'immagine* (Rome: Gremese, 1994).

Gili, Jean A., *Stato fascista e cinematografia: repressione e produzione* (Rome: Bulzoni, 1981).

Landy, Marcia, *Fascism in Film: The Italian Commercial Cinema 1931–1943* (Princeton, NJ: Princeton University Press, 1986).

Nowell Smith, Geoffrey, 'Italian Cinema under Fascism', in David Forgacs (ed.), *Rethinking Italian Fascism* (London: Lawrence & Wishart, 1986).

Reich, Jacqueline and Piero Garofalo (eds), *Re-viewing Fascism: Italian Cinema, 1922–1943* (Bloomington: Indiana University Press, 2002).

Ricci, Steven, *Cinema & Fascism: Italian Film and Society, 1922–1943* (Berkeley: University of California Press, 2008).

Sanguineti, Tatti (ed.), *Italia Taglia* (Ancona: Transeuropa, 1999).

Zagarrio, Vito, *Cinema e fascismo: Film, modelli, immaginari* (Venice: Marsilio, 2004).

PART THREE

Postwar Cinematic Culture – Realism and Beyond

Introduction

Peter Bondanella

In recent years, part of 'rethinking Italian cinema' involves moving away from an exclusive emphasis upon postwar Italian neorealism or traditional art-house auteurs to a consideration of other compelling topics. Such an adjustment in critical attention does not, however, imply that the moment in international film history identified with Italian neorealism is anything less than one of Italy's artistic treasures worthy of continued study, only that we should acknowledge and explore the work of the many important Italian directors after 1945 in appropriate and innovative ways.

Stephen Gundle's assessment of neorealism's relationship to the Italian left in politics reveals that, contrary to popular belief, directors associated with the Communist Party (Visconti, Lizzani, De Santis) often encountered criticism and opposition from that source as well as from ideological adversaries on the right. In addition, more moderate or conservative figures associated with the cinema industry during the fascist period, such as Vittorio De Sica or Rossellini, could be criticised not only by the left for their rapprochement to Hollywood genres or locating financing to make their films, but also by the political right. In De Sica's case, *Umberto D.* provoked a famous scolding from the then young Christian Democrat politician Giulio Andreotti for washing dirty laundry in public!

Traditional treatments of Italian neorealism overemphasised how 'realistic' these films were; how 'true to life' their external locations were as opposed to the supposedly 'artificial' work on sound stages with artificial lighting; how neorealists managed to avoid conventional film genres and traditional dramatic plotting and employed non-professional actors; and how the neorealists embraced an ideology of progressive thought, if not leftist ideology. Moreover, almost everyone in Italy had an interest in finding a dramatic break between cinema under fascism and cinema after 1945. Yet, today we see things from a broader perspective. An examination of Rossellini's *Roma città aperta*, the masterpiece universally accepted as the film that ushered in international interest in postwar Italian neorealism, underscores how earlier emphasis upon realism in these films may have obscured their artistic complexity. *Roma città aperta* actually combines non-professionals with consummate professionals. The film's impact rests upon performances by Anna Magnani and Aldo Fabrizi, cast against type by Rossellini, since they were at the time identified with the variety theatre or comic films rather than tragic dramatic roles. Certain of the film's most dramatic scenes take place within traditionally constructed film sets, particularly the horrifying torture scenes of Giorgio Manfredi (Marcello Pagliero) and the partisan priest Don Pietro (Aldo Fabrizi) in Gestapo headquarters, where the dramatic lighting recalls expressionist cinema rather than reflecting the natural. Far from being a completely realistic film, the dominant generic content of the narrative is pure melodrama, with Italians representing Good and Germans representing Evil. And to top off this Manichean division, Rossellini depicts Nazis as not only evil but perverse – they are stereotyped as decadent homosexuals in the process. Rossellini's sugar- coating of Italian complicity with Nazi Germany in pushing Europe into a world war and the film's implicit goal of portraying Italians as victims rather than as accomplices certainly points to some suspicious loss of national memory (not to mention Rossellini's desire to have his audience forget for whose armed forces he was shooting films just before the end of the war). In short, if the film is a masterpiece (and it is), realist aesthetic principles are not sufficient to explain why this is so. And, like many of the best neorealist masterpieces, *Roma città aperta* was initially not enormously popular within Italy. In most cases (and there are a few important exceptions), neorealist films were greeted abroad with more praise and larger audiences than they were at home; they represented a very small percentage of Italian film production between 1945 and 1955, as Hollywood imports dominated the national market.

Nevertheless, that much remains to be said about Italian neorealism is clear from the original ideas contained in three separate essays. Mark Shiel explores the implications of the urbanism of neorealism, connecting its focus upon city life to contemporary developments in architecture and urban development but changing the modernist emphasis upon the city typical of films shot during Mussolini's reign. In a consideration of Italian neorealist cinema that includes the contemporaneous neorealist literary production, Torunn Haaland suggests that there existed what might well be defined as a neorealist period style common to both film and fiction, one that allowed directors to explore empty spaces for new thoughts. More often than not, neorealist fiction was not 'realistic' and its frequent use of subjective, non-reliable narrators might have suggested more caution to critics of the day, who celebrated neorealism as a cinema of the 'real'. Finally, Giovanna De Luca explores neorealism's famous practice of employing children in important roles and how this new view of the child as agent (and not merely as subject) expands the power of cinema's vision. She also traces how this neorealist predilection for children as protagonists becomes a long-standing tradition down to the present day.

Three other essays deal with what some critics or film-makers have called the 'road beyond neorealism' or other trends of the period. Danielle Hipkins analyses depictions of female friendship in films made in the early 1950s from a feminist perspective and considers how these same bonds of friendship may be pictured in contemporary Italian films. Pauline Small examines the popular phenomenon of the *maggiorata fisica*, or what Americans called the 'sweater girl' of the period – the essence of film stardom for women in the late 1940s and 1950s. Paradoxically, this obsession with actresses as pin-ups and material for pulp fan magazines was given an enormous push by Silvana Mangano's performance in Giuseppe De Santis's neo-Marxist neorealist classic *Riso amaro*, even though nothing could be further from traditional notions of neorealist 'realism' than the triumph of buxom female actresses at the box office, especially when they played proletarian figures up to their knees in water, harvesting rice. Robert Gordon's thought-provoking analysis of two key 1950s films set in the Eternal City uncovers further deviations from the orthodox view of film realism in the period. One is the superb Hollywood import (Wyler's *Roman Holiday*) released during the first part of the decade (1953); and the other is a blockbuster auteur masterpiece by Fellini (*La dolce vita*) that marks the end of one era of Italian film history and the dawn of another, leading to a period often defined as Italian cinema's golden age.

9 Neorealism and Left-wing Culture

Stephen Gundle

On the face of it, the trajectories of neorealist cinema and the Italian left were inextricably entwined. Both emerged on the scene as fascism, resurrected and propped up by Nazi Germany, entered its vicious final phase and eventually succumbed to defeat. In the postwar years, both appeared to offer the prospect of a new departure in national life predicated on human solidarity and reform. Both stressed the importance of neglected, suffering or weak subjects in their idea of Italy and sought to give voice to their problems and concerns. Both, moreover, underwent serious setbacks as the Cold War provoked division and conflict in domestic politics and the Christian Democrats asserted their dominance over government. When neorealism was attacked by the Church and members of government, the forces of the left stepped in to defend and encourage it, thus cementing a link that supporters and opponents alike had considered natural. Although some of the most prominent neorealist directors, notably Roberto Rossellini and Vittorio De Sica, had no previous personal affiliation with the left, the themes of resistance and sacrifice that marked the first wave of films and the focus on social issues that emerged a little later, broadly keyed in with a left-wing outlook.

In fact, the relationship between neorealism and the left was fraught and often problematic. The largest leftist force, the Italian Communist Party (PCI), was certainly favourable to cinematic realism. As David Forgacs has observed, 'realism' featured in the cultural arguments being put forward in Communist publications as soon as they emerged out of clandestinity. It was

associated with engagement as against detachment, with the involvement of intellectuals in the working-class movement as opposed to ivory-tower intellectualism, with philosophical materialism as against idealism, with the concrete versus the abstract, with clarity of expression and the need for divulgation as against stylistic preciosity and difficulty.[1]

But the liberal humanism of the first neorealist films clashed with the left's increasing emphasis on ideological rigour. While the moral impulse behind postwar cinema was welcomed, the particular international mode of address adopted by the most acclaimed neorealist films, and especially the engagement they sought of the US in their treatment of the country's problems and future prospects, did not dovetail readily with the hostility to US policies and culture that marked the left's position in the early Cold War period.

In this chapter, these issues will be explored in relation to, first, the political response to Rossellini and De Sica; second, the efforts made, especially through Visconti, to anchor realism to national traditions; and third, the controversy over *Riso amaro*, a highly 'impure' example of realism directed by the Communist Giuseppe De Santis.

ROSSELLINI AND DE SICA

After the war, the PCI actively courted artists and intellectuals who, following Gramsci, were seen as an important 'connecting tissue' of the nation.[2] The party drew thinkers, teachers, writers and artists who, it believed, could play an important role in shaping the new Italy that would emerge from the conflict. In the period between the liberation of Rome in 1944 and the PCI's removal from government in 1947, the party's approach to cinema was not specific. It was merely one of several cultural spheres which the party addressed as it aimed to draw to it as many creative talents as it could, creating or supporting contexts and platforms where issues could be aired in a way that fitted the priorities of the left. However, cinema was unusual

Roberto Rossellini and Ingrid Bergman; while their personal relationship angered conservatives, it was their professional one that angered the left

because, unlike literature or art, it was by definition collective and popular. Moreover, the field had given rise to a flurry of oppositional activity in the late fascist period. It was well known that the state film school, the Centro sperimentale di cinematografia, had been a hotbed of non-conformist ideas and that theoretical debates published in the journal *Cinema* in 1941–3 about the future of Italian cinema had pointed in the direction of realism. Visconti's *Ossessione*, which had only had a limited release before the deluge of July 1943, had been a testing ground for left-wing talent. The writing team on the film included two men, Mario Alicata and Pietro Ingrao, who would become prominent party officials and others who would either join the party or actively support it, including Giuseppe De Santis, Gianni Puccini and Antonio Pietrangeli.

Given that realism had been, since the late 1930s, 'a sort of sign of recognition between actual or potential political oppositionists',[3] works like *Ossessione* and De Sica's *I bambini ci guardano* were regarded as important breaks with the past and bridges towards a possible future of greater freedom and truth. Although Rossellini, with his recent past in fascist propaganda cinema, was a surprising author of the first dramatic film of the occupation and the resistance, the search for elementary humanity, the crude treatment of tragic and painful recent events that marked *Roma città aperta*

resonated widely. By offering a harsh and ostensibly truthful account of the suffering of the Italian people during the war and under dictatorship, the film also corresponded with the PCI's broad approach at this time. The epic nature of the film, with its positing of a common morality and purpose uniting the priest Don Pietro and the Communist Manfredi, perfectly suited the party's commitment to national unity, while *Paisà* (*Paisan*, 1946), which was centred on the experiences of the Allies in Italy, featured the heroism and sacrifice of the resistance in the context of the traumatic experience of war and liberation. The films offered a vision of the Italians not as allies of the Nazis or perpetrators of atrocities but as resisters and victims. For a party like the PCI, which was keen to wipe the slate clean and win over former rank-and-file fascists, this was exactly the view it was keen to encourage.

Rossellini was happy to engage with a party that in the early postwar years renounced dogma for dialogue. He was friendly with the Communist writer Sergio Amidei, who worked on *Roma città aperta*, and the politician Giorgio Amendola, as well as the cultural organiser Antonello Trombadori and others. This friendship, Carlo Lizzani has written in his memoirs, 'was consolidated in the first two postwar years thanks also to the warmth of all those who, together with their newspaper *L'Unità*, supported the first efforts of neorealist cinema, and in particular *Roma città aperta* and *Paisà*'.[4] These recollections highlight two key ways in which the PCI developed its activity in cinema: first, by creating an immediate circle of influence around directors and, second, by providing support for neorealism in civil society. Initially, this occurred reasonably spontaneously but, as a climate of political conflict replaced the cooperative atmosphere of the anti-fascist alliance, both these practices became more rigid and programmatic. Communist cultural organisers exchanged respectful observations for a more dogmatic view and the party came to act as the most vocal and forceful public defender of Italian cinema.

Germania anno zero (*Germany Year Zero*, 1948), the third film in Rossellini's war trilogy,[5] saw Lizzani join his inner circle, ostensibly to provide political input so that the film would deliver a picture of Germany similar to the one of Italy in *Roma città aperta*. Amid the ruins of Nazism, the heroic role of an anti-Nazi minority would be underlined. This, Lizzani has written, was what Trombadori expected, along with the French production company and 'all of us in the group that had taken shape around the magazine *Cinema*, that

Carlo Lizzani worked with Rossellini before directing two films produced by a left-wing cooperative

from the start of the 1940s had supported the nascent neorealist movement'.[6] Seeking to play down suggestions of political control, he went on,

> Around Rossellini, in brief, was concentrated in those years ... a shared purpose which united everyone, from the production staff to the screenwriters and the director. My candidature as assistant director and co-writer, supported by Trombadori, was not therefore an expression of an astute political surveillance or of a cold and calculating attempt at conversion.[7]

Whatever the intention, it did not work, for the returned political exile who figured so strongly in the screenplay is barely noticeable in the finished film.

For Lizzani, it was the failure of the Christian Democrats to accord the film industry protection against foreign imports or to provide it with financial support, as well as the use of various forms of censorship, that supplied the Communists, and the left parties more widely, with a campaign opportunity that they were quick to exploit. As Gian Piero Brunetta has written, from initially being a secondary arena, cinema rapidly became the cultural terrain on which the PCI made its presence felt most forcefully.[8] For some ten years, starting from the run-up to the first parliamentary elections in 1948, it conducted concerted action in defence of Italian national cinema. As a result, it won the allegiance of many of the most important film-makers in the country.

One of the most significant events cementing the PCI's role came on 22 February 1949 when the Communist-dominated CGIL union (the Confederazione generale italiana del lavoro) held a public rally to highlight the plight of cinema in Rome's Piazza del Popolo. Among the celebrity speakers on that occasion was De Sica. Although he had been both a star and a director under fascism, and was regarded as a man of the centre, his commitment to neorealism made him a crucial ally of the left. He encountered trouble with his first postwar film, *Sciuscià*, whose focus on juvenile waywardness and criminality fuelled the anger of conservatives, who demanded that cinema tackle 'more noble themes and motives', to quote one influential member of parliament.[9] When the film was denied an export licence, the PCI sprang to its defence. The party also drummed up support for *Ladri di biciclette* (*Bicycle Thieves*, 1948) after its initial lack of success at the box office.

Perhaps more than any other director, De Sica antagonised conservatives and moderates. Their dislike of his approach to cinema was compounded by the support he won from the left, a fact that revealed the political nature of his films. *Miracolo a Milano* was openly attacked by right-wingers, who saw its pitching of poor against rich as infused with 'Soviet ideology'. They were in no doubt at all that the poor shanty-town dwellers who fly off on broomsticks in the final scene of the film were heading east and were destined for Russia.[10] When *Umberto D.* was released in 1952 the cinema minister Giulio Andreotti was so incensed that he wrote an open letter to the director, telling him that he 'will have rendered a very bad service to [the] country' if people were to take it as a portrait of Italy in the mid-twentieth century.[11] He called instead for a

Giulio Andreotti, as the government minister responsible for cinema from 1948 to 1954, was accused of bringing an end to neorealism

'minimum commitment to a healthy and constructive optimism which might truly help humanity to advance and to hope'.

While the left, despite some grumbling about his repeated focus on social isolation and penchant for depressing endings, backed De Sica, the director never tailored his films to its priorities. Indeed, precisely when worsening international relations fed a burgeoning Communist hostility to American 'imperialism' and mass culture, he entertained the option of securing backing from an American studio, engaging in negotiations with David O. Selznick during the preparation of *Ladri di biciclette*. Although it was entirely in keeping with neorealism's outward address – and particular interest in dialogue with the US (a phenomenon illuminatingly explored most recently by Karl Schoonover)[12] – it could not have won approval from the left.

When Rossellini undertook a much-publicised trip to the US to seek finance, the PCI's interest in him waned. On his return to Rome in March 1949, the Communist illustrated weekly *Vie Nuove* published a picture of him alighting from the plane accompanied by the following caption:

> With a Hollywood smile on his lips and a pack of Chesterfields sticking out of his pocket, Roberto Rossellini has returned from America with a contract for 'The Girl from Stromboli,' who will be Ingrid Bergman, protagonist and co-producer of the film. After *Germania anno zero* and above all the questionable effort of *Amore* – and at a time when some are attempting to undermine our cinematic realism in the field of criticism – it is to be hoped that the injection of Americanism will not make the cinematic style of Rossellini … Hollywoodian as well.[13]

When the magazine sent a correspondent to the island of Stromboli to interview Rossellini on his set, it was unable to extract from him the expected condemnation of American culture: 'Can you imagine, in Hollywood there are no pedestrians. The roads are populated with shiny cars all full of flowers', was his comment, a response that led the journalist to observe bitterly: 'This courageous Italian director … seems to me to be already distant from his barely born neorealism.'[14]

VISCONTI AND LEFT-WING CINEMA

Visconti's connections with the Communists were both personal and thematic. The director enjoyed close relations with a number of senior party officials,

including Mario Alicata and especially Trombadori, who advised him and worked with him in devising projects. His interest in the Italian south fitted perfectly with the emphasis the PCI accorded the southern question after the publication of the first volume of Gramsci's prison notebooks in 1948 and the poor result the left achieved in the southern regions in the 1948 election. In the immediate postwar years, Visconti was mainly active in theatre. He had however been cultivating the idea of filming an adaptation of Verga's novel *I Malavoglia* (*The House by the Medlar Tree*, 1881) since 1941, the year he bought the film rights. The film would finally be made following a suggestion from the PCI that the director might wish to consider making a propaganda film in Sicily. The resulting drama was no simple transposition of a well-known novel. Produced by Visconti himself, the PCI, and the Universalia company, and made with an entirely non-professional cast, *La terra trema* (*The Earth Trembles*, 1948) recounts the odyssey of 'Ntoni Valastro (Antonio Arcidiacono), a fisherman of the Sicilian village of Aci Trezza who leads his fellow workers in a doomed revolt against the wholesalers who run the anchovy trade. By revising Verga's pessimism and sarcasm to focus on the historical, economic and cultural aspects of the southern question and connect 'Ntoni's revolt to a nascent class consciousness, the director conducted an operation that was entirely in line with the approach that the party was proposing for national development.[15] In an article published in 1960, possibly written by Trombadori, he made this connection explicit, stating that his work was inspired by the ideals in Gramsci's writings.[16]

For many years, Visconti was the central figure in left-wing film culture. Unlike Rossellini, who had temporarily been the darling of the left, and De Sica, a liberal whose films evinced a sympathy for the poor and weak that broadly dovetailed with the left's outlook, Visconti was regarded by the party leadership as the most valid and 'useful' of film-makers. Like most of the Communist cultural elite, his background was traditional and literary and his films were treated as intellectual artefacts. For most of his postwar career, they were read in a highly political light, as reflections on the historical strengths and weaknesses, and future prospects, of the working-class movement in the peninsula.

For this reason, Visconti was often the subject of criticism on the part of a small and heterogeneous, but significant, group of Marxist critics – some inside, some outside the PCI – who disputed the attempt to weave

Marxism into the Italian tradition. Neither the pro-Soviet wing of the party nor more ideologically rigorous Marxist critics like the Lukacsian Guido Aristarco were satisfied with this approach. The model, in their view, was to be found not in literary antecedents but in certain currents of national cinema (realist works of the silent period) or Soviet cinema. The Russian film-maker Pudovkin, at a conference held in Perugia in 1949, had announced in line with prevailing policy that 'the common tendency of Soviet films is to show on the screen the figure of the positive man, to show him as a living example, who incites imitation'.[17] Evidently this approach had not been embraced in Italy. While André Bazin argued that, with *La terra trema*, Visconti achieved 'a paradoxical synthesis of realism and aestheticism',[18] Umberto Barbaro, a key figure at the Centro sperimentale in the fascist period and an admirer of socialist realism, denounced the film's lack of 'clear ideas'.[19] Barbaro had not liked *Ossessione* and would continue his polemic for years, arguing that Visconti stood outside realism on account of the decadent origins of the form and themes of his film work.[20] Writing in the mid-1950s, the critic Pio Baldelli repeated the accusation that Visconti was more concerned with stylistic virtuosity than Marxism.[21] His work was cold and detached while at the same time insufficiently analytical. 'The anti-capitalist polemic [of *La terra trema*] is conducted in an approximate manner which is matched, on the formal plane, by the excessive order of the composition', Baldelli argued.

These polemics and debates show the vitality of the critical discourse born around neorealism. Visconti continued to be the main focus of argument, with *Bellissima* attracting criticism for its depiction of the Roman working class, and the Risorgimento-set *Senso* (*Senso* aka *The Wanton Countess*, 1954) dividing critics over its melodramatic depiction of Italian history. While party officials endorsed his work without reservation, non-official Marxism continued to highlight his heterodox and bourgeois inspirations and the ambiguity of his message that would continue into the 1960s, long after the demise of neorealism as a cultural current.

Visconti's early films did not always go down well with the rank and file. Antonio Pietrangeli and others put some effort into building up a network of film circles to educate the public, and in left-dominated areas of the country, despite government opposition, there were numerous opportunities to see films that did poorly in commercial distribution. But even activists sometimes preferred less demanding fare. A twenty-three-year-old student interviewed in *Rassegna del film* confessed that he found *La terra trema* 'too intellectual and difficult', while a Communist worker said that he found 'complicated' films like Visconti's empty and sterile and preferred American adventure films that 'may be improbable but are harmless'.[22]

DE SANTIS AND POPULAR CINEMA

While Rossellini, De Sica and Visconti had all been active before the war, new energies and talents also contributed to the renewal of cinema. Rossellini interpreted the resistance, but other films sought to record or commemorate the struggle for liberation. These included the documentary compilation *Giorni di gloria*, which included footage shot by Visconti of the trial and execution of important Nazi collaborators. In the north, Aldo Vergano shot *Il sole sorge ancora* (*The Sun Rises Again*, 1946). Produced by Geo Agliani, the president of the partisan's association ANPI (Associazione nazionale partigiana d'Italia), the film featured several themes first seen in *Roma città aperta*, including the execution of a priest and a Communist, played respectively by Lizzani and Gillo Pontecorvo, but unlike Rossellini's film it ended with the triumph of the liberation.[23] The relative success of this film at home and abroad induced Agliani to produce a further film, this time entrusting the direction to Giuseppe De Santis. Set in the Romagna region and made with extensive support from Communist organisations and

Giuseppe De Santis, director of *Riso amaro* (1949), was accused by some fellow Communists of pandering to American fads

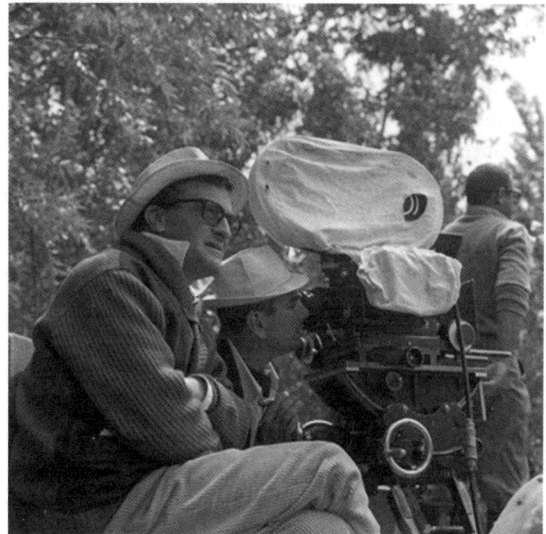

the league of cooperatives, *Caccia tragica* (*Tragic Hunt*, 1947) explored another chapter of Resistance history.

As had occurred with Rossellini and De Sica, the success of the film brought its director commercial opportunities. De Santis was given the chance to make a film with the Lux company, operative since before the war, which was in the forefront of efforts to tie the rebirth of Italian cinema to forms of co-production. *Riso amaro* would enjoy considerable domestic and international success while provoking bitter disputes on the left. As a Communist, De Santis opted to set his film among the rice fields of the northwest, highlighting the working conditions of the female rice weeders. Moreover, in a manner that dovetailed with the Soviet preference for imitable types, he structured the plot around four characters, two of whom emerge as incontrovertibly positive. However, the film incorporated elements of melodrama and of the gangster film and it featured American popular music and dance as well as American-inspired products of mass culture. The film's negative heroine, a beautiful Americanised young rice weeder named Silvana,[24] is lured into wrong-doing by a charming outlaw. Played by Silvana Mangano, she became its poster girl, her proudly curvaceous figure and skimpy outfit adorning its advertising like a pin-up.

Trade unionists wrote to *L'Unità* to denounce the depiction of the rice weeders while Trombadori attacked De Santis for suggesting that the working class was anything other than united in its resistance to American mass culture.[25] In fact, the left knew that workers liked American culture, to the extent that *Vie Nuove* put starlets on some of its covers and ran an annual beauty contest for several years; furthermore, it published numerous advertisements, a practice also criticised by Trombadori.[26] In truth, the only way for the Communists to have avoided commercial deviations and ideological heterodoxy would have been to produce films themselves. In fact, the Cooperativa spettatori produttivi cinematografici, an organisation born in the left-dominated regions of Emilia-Romagna and Tuscany, did produce two films, both directed by Lizzani. The first, *Achtung! Banditi!* (*Attention! Bandits!*, 1951), was another Resistance drama; the second was an adaptation of Vasco Pratolini's highly popular novel of working-class life in Florence, *Cronache di poveri amanti* (*Chronicles of Poor Lovers*, 1953). Despite their low budgets, the two films did well, to the extent that the latter was even considered for the Golden Palm at Cannes, a prospect that so horrified the government

that officials even lobbied jury members against it.[27] Like other films, it was denied an export licence. This measure, it has been noted, deprived the cooperative of the profits it needed to continue producing.[28] Recently, Lizzani has revealed that he appealed personally to Togliatti for financial support, receiving in response a refusal to commit the party to any role in film production. He said:

> I certainly don't have the experience that you have in this field, but I think that, with the prestige that by now neorealist cinema has won, it would be better for you to navigate the open seas. Is there really a need for production that in the end would be branded 'PCI'?[29]

In answer to this question, some would have responded positively. But it is doubtful that an opposition party, even one as large and as well-organised as the PCI, could ever have intervened with sufficient force in the areas of production, distribution and exhibition to prevent neorealism's project for a socially concerned cinema from failing. But then neorealism was never a unified phenomenon either politically or aesthetically, and its use of images of suffering and sacrifice 'as a means of opening up Italian national history and politics to international viewers while simultaneously imagining what it would mean to grant an international audience authority within the political arena of Italy' had more in common with the direction Italy took from the late 1940s than either the Communists or the Christian Democrats realised or cared to admit.[30]

NOTES

1. David Forgacs, 'The Making and Unmaking of Neorealism in Postwar Italy', in Nicholas Hewitt (ed.), *The Culture of Reconstruction: European Literature, Thought and Film, 1945–50* (London: Macmillan, 1989), pp. 52–3.
2. See Stephen Gundle, 'The Legacy of the Prison Notebooks: Gramsci, the PCI and Italian Culture in the Cold War Era', in Christopher Duggan and Christopher Wagstaff (eds), *Italy in the Cold War: Politics, Culture and Society, 1948–58* (Oxford: Berg, 1995), pp. 131–47; and Stephen Gundle, *Between Hollywood and Moscow: The Italian Communists and the Challenge of Mass Culture, 1943–91* (Durham, NC: Duke University Press, 2000), especially Chapter 1.
3. Nello Ajello, *Intellettuali e PCI 1944–1958* (Rome/Bari: Laterza, 1979), p. 202.

4. Carlo Lizzani, *Il mio lungo viaggio nel secolo breve* (Turin: Einaudi, 2007), p. 72.

5. Ibid., pp. 71–84.

6. Ibid., p. 71.

7. Ibid., p. 72.

8. Gian Piero Brunetta, *Storia del cinema italiano dal 1945 agli anni Ottanta* (Rome: Editori Riuniti, 1982), especially the chapter entitled 'La battaglia delle idee: il fronte della sinistra'.

9. Mino Argentieri, *La censura nel cinema italiano* (Rome: Editori Riuniti, 1974), p. 70.

10. Ibid., pp. 82–3.

11. Giulio Andreotti, 'Lettera aperta a Vittorio De Sica', *Libertas*, 24 February 1952.

12. *Brutal Vision: The Neorealist Body in Postwar Italian Cinema* (Minneapolis: University of Minnesota Press, 2012).

13. *Vie Nuove*, 13 March 1949, p. 19.

14. M. Schettini, 'L'inventore del vulcano', *Vie Nuove*, 15 May 1949, p. 19.

15. Alessandro Bencivenni, *Visconti* (Milan: Il Castoro, 1995), pp. 22–3.

16. See Gundle, *Between Hollywood and Moscow*, p. 100.

17. See Ugo Finetti, 'Cenni sulla critica marxista e il neorealismo', in Lino Micciché (ed.), *Il neorealismo cinematografico italiano* (Venice: Marsilio, 1975), p. 268.

18. See Bencivenni, *Visconti*, p. 26.

19. Finetti, 'Cenni sulla critica marxista', p. 269

20. Ibid., p. 270.

21. Ibid.

22. Stephen Gundle, 'Il PCI e la campagna contro Hollywood 1948–58', in D. W. Ellwood and G. P. Brunetta (eds), *Hollywood in Europa: industria, politica, pubblico del cinema 1945–1960* (Florence: La Casa Usher/Ponte alle Grazie, 1991), p. 125.

23. Triumphant representations of the resistance were preferred over suffering bodies in the left's subculture. For a discussion of this issue in relation to art and sculpture, see my 'The "Civic Religion" of the Resistance in Postwar Italy', *Modern Italy* vol. 5 no. 2 (2000), pp. 113–32.

24. For a discussion of the polemics in this film, see Christopher Wagstaff, 'The Place of Neorealism in Italian Cinema from 1945 to 1954', in Hewitt, *The Culture of Reconstruction*, pp. 68–70.

25. Gundle, 'Il PCI e la campagna contro Hollywood', pp. 121–2.

26. Gundle, *Between Hollywood and Moscow*, pp. 68–70.

27. Lizzani, *Il mio lungo viaggio*, p. 108.

28. Massimo Mida, 'Perche sono morte le cooperative', *Cinema Nuovo*, 1 April 1957, reproduced in Guido Aristarco (ed.), *Sciolti dal giuramento: il dibattito critico-ideologico sul cinema negli anni Cinquanta* (Bari: Dedalo, 1981). See also Eligio Imarisio (ed.), *Come uccidere un'idea: in memoria della Cooperative Spettatori Produttori Cinematografici, 1950–1961* (Genoa: Le Mani, 2012).

29. Lizzani, *Il mio lungo viaggio*, p. 109.

30. Schoonover, *Brutal Vision*, p. 147.

FURTHER READING

Forgacs, David and Stephen Gundle, *Mass Culture and Italian Society from Fascism to the Cold War* (Bloomington: Indiana University Press, 2007).

Gundle, Stephen, *Between Hollywood and Moscow: The Italian Communists and the Challenge of Mass Culture, 1943–91* (Durham, NC: Duke University Press, 2000).

Schoonover, Karl, *Brutal Vision: The Neorealist Body in Postwar Italian Cinema* (Minneapolis: University of Minnesota Press, 2012).

10 Cityscapes and Cinematic Space

Mark Shiel

Although much postwar Italian cinema drew attention to the hardship and lyrical beauty of rural landscape and society, the cityscape was arguably its most distinctive representational feature. The neorealist aesthetic predominated among film-makers, but it had to compete with several relatively conservative forces: the Catholic Church, the Christian Democratic Party, the US government, the Hollywood film industry, Italy's own genre-based commercial film industry and the restrictive cultural politics of the Soviet Union. In that context, the image of the city took on an ideological charge, a formal and thematic complexity, and an unconventional beauty which remains exceptional in the history of motion pictures. The neorealist film was notable for shooting on location in real places and for documenting the intertwined conditions of war, poverty and decay in contemporary society and the built environment. It foregrounded the layers of human history in urban space, fragmented the iconography of classical and modern architecture and planning, and increasingly reflected on the universal, philosophical meaning of urban crisis as well.

While they all made films with rural settings, the most important directors were firmly metropolitan. *Sciuscià*, *Ladri di biciclette*, *Miracolo a Milano*, *Umberto D.* and *L'oro di Napoli* (*The Gold of Naples*, 1954) give the impression that their director Vittorio De Sica almost never set foot in the countryside. Roberto Rossellini's *Paisà* was split between rural and urban scenes but the latter dominated his war trilogy, which also included *Roma città aperta* and *Germania anno zero*, encompassing Naples, Rome, Florence and Berlin. In later films, Rossellini remained in the city – as in *Europa '51* (*The Greatest Love* aka *No Greater Love*, 1951) and *Viaggio in Italia* (*Journey to Italy* aka *Strangers* aka *The Lonely Woman*, 1953) – or used rural settings to comment on urban modernity obliquely – as in *Stromboli* (*Stromboli, terra di*

dio aka *Stromboli*, 1950) or *La macchina ammazzacattivi* (*The Machine to Kill Bad People*, 1952). Visconti made two rural films, *Ossessione* and *La terra trema*, in which the modernising effects of the city were encroaching, and followed them by three resolutely urban films, *Bellissima*, *Senso* and *Le notti bianche* (*White Nights*, 1957). Fellini's *Luci del varietà* (*Variety Lights*, 1950, co-directed with Alberto Lattuada) and *La strada* (1954) had rural settings but *Lo sceicco bianco* (*The White Sheik*, 1952), *I vitelloni* (1953), *Il bidone* (*The Swindler*, 1955), and *Le notti di Cabiria* (*The Nights of Cabiria*, 1957) were urban, and much of *La strada* was meaningfully set on the *outskirts* of Rome without entering the city as such. Antonioni's first films were a rural and an urban documentary respectively – *Gente del Po* (*People of the Po Valley*, 1943) and *Nettezza urbana* (*N.U.*, 1948), but his feature films – from *Cronaca di un amore* (*Story of a Love Affair*, 1950) through *La signora senza camelie* (*The Lady without Camelias*, 1953), *I vinti* (*The Vanquished*, 1953) and *Le amiche* (*Le amiche*, 1955) – nearly always unfolded around the city, and on the odd occasions they went into the

Michelangelo Antonioni's *Nettezza urbana* (1948)

Pietro Germi's *La città si difende* (*Four Ways Out*, 1951)

Vittorio De Sica's *Ladri di biciclette* (1948)

countryside, it, too, was a place of anguished modernisation, as in *Il grido* (*Il grido* aka *The Outcry*, 1957).

In that film, the despair and suicide of Aldo (Steve Cochran), a factory worker in the Po valley whose lover leaves him for another man, is closely linked to the impending destruction of the local community of Goriano by the construction of an airport. Hence, the film highlighted what Fabio Sforzi calls the 'diffusion' of the urban into the rural which characterised postwar Italian life and which included not only rural-to-urban migration and the suburban growth of cities, but also the expansion of communications, media and transport.[1] This diffusion was evident earlier too: in *Ossessione*, Giovanna Bragana's trattoria, in a quiet wayside on a busy trunk road between cities, becomes a scene of adultery and plotting for murder; in *La terra trema*, Sicilian youth are lured from their remote village by military service and the chance of work in major ports; in Giuseppe De Santis's *Riso amaro*, the natural silence of rice fields is disturbed by trainloads of workers who arrive from Turin accompanied by boogie woogie on the radio.

The urbanism of postwar Italian cinema was noted by two of its most important chroniclers. Discussing *Roma città aperta* and *Paisà*, Bazin was drawn to the 'prodigiously photogenic' character of the Italian city, and the continuity between its cinematic image and Italy's long urban and architectural history: 'From antiquity, Italian city planning has remained theatrical and decorative. City life is a spectacle, a *commedia dell'arte* that the Italians stage for their own pleasure.'[2] Citing the prevalence in *mise en scène* of terraces, balconies, courtyards, facades and sunshine, Bazin preferred the 'open city' to the 'closed-in countryside',

mistrusting the latter as a feature of what he called 'neorealist superspectacle' – that is, a debased, commercialised form of neorealism in Pietro Germi's *In nome della legge* (*In the Name of the Law*, 1949) and other films.[3] Against that, *Ladri di biciclette* was wholeheartedly authentic: its 'lower-class' tenements and its multiplicity of ordinary streets, bridges and tunnels, were the setting for a 'story of a walk through Rome' which was so lacking in conventional cinematic action that it 'would not deserve two lines in a stray-dog column' in a newspaper.[4] Added to this, the film derived authenticity from the fact that the lead roles – Antonio (Lamberto Maggiorani) and Bruno (Enzo Staiola) – were played by non-professional actors who actually lived lives like those portrayed. And yet Bazin's view of neorealism was flexible enough to encompass Antonioni's abstract film noir *Cronaca di un amore*, in whose Milan streets the lead characters are 'caught in the maze of the plot like laboratory rats', a 'poetico-realist' version of that city in De Sica's *Miracolo a Milano*, Rossellini's 'mental landscape' of Naples in *Viaggio in Italia*, and Fellini's Rome in *Le notti di Cabiria*, whose realism was 'social in content' but 'not social in intent'.[5] Similarly, Siegfried Kracauer argued that *Umberto D.* exemplified 'cinematic films' which took advantage of the unique technical ability of the medium to articulate the 'the flow of life'.[6] This was most evident in settings where the materiality of built space was matched by density of social interaction: 'The street is in the extended sense of the word not only the arena of fleeting impressions and chance encounters but a place where the flow of life is bound to assert itself.'[7] These characteristics were heightened by the turmoil of war: as Kracauer put it, 'When history is made in the streets, the streets tend to move onto the screen.'[8] But Kracauer, like Bazin, admired the tendency of neorealist films to reject celebration of the modern city and the obvious iconic value of Italy's many landmark buildings – what Kracauer called 'pictorial diversions'.[9]

In neorealist cinema, the city does not emblematise urban modernity in the way that it did, for example, in films about Weimar Berlin, such as Walter Ruttmann's *Berlin: Die Sinfonie der Grosstadt* (*Berlin, Symphony of a Great City*, 1927), or about 1940s New York, such as Stanley Donen's *On the Town* (1948). In contrast, the neorealist city existed *between* modernity and the premodern, its accumulated layers of ancient, medieval and Renaissance history always reminding us of the past rather than thrusting us into the future. Indeed, Donald Pitkin has convincingly argued that the Italian city must be conceptualised differently to its European and North American counterparts.[10] Ancient Rome was a highly urbanised society for centuries before others emerged, developing advanced technologies of engineering, architecture and urban planning to manage large, high-density populations and also prioritising the symbolic use of the city for imperial spectacle and control. In the medieval and Renaissance eras, Italian cities were again at the cutting edge. Its city-republics were often authoritarian (for example, the Borgias and Barberinis in Rome, the Estes in Ferrara), but they were key centres of capitalist expansion through mercantile trade, and of humanistic learning and art. Then, in the eighteenth century, the Italian city stagnated, falling behind by the height of the Industrial Revolution because of Italy's increasingly peripheral position in southern Europe and its internal division that lasted until the 1860s. Even after unification, Italy remained outside the main zone of European industrialisation. The UK, the Netherlands, Belgium, Germany and France all had more people living in cities than in the countryside by the early twentieth century, but Italy did not until the 'economic miracle' of the 1960s.

The built environment that neorealist cinema presents is often less concentrated and metropolitan than that of other cinemas. In addition to Rome, we frequently see Milan, Naples and a well-dispersed range of smaller cities and towns which reflect what Giuseppe De Matteis has called the distinctly 'polycentric' character of Italy's urban system.[11] In Visconti's *Ossessione*, although the primary setting is the Po valley, significant action takes place in Ancona, where Gino (Mario Girotti) and the Spaniard (Elia

Marcuzzo) dream of bohemian escape, and Ferrara, where Gino and Giovanna (Clara Calamai) fall out over their murder of Bragana (Juan De Landa). In Rossellini's *La macchina ammazzacattivi*, Salerno has a traditional tightly knit community, but also a busy street life, with the narrative revolving around the modern figure of a photographer and the opening sequence making it clear that the town will soon be redeveloped as a tourist destination. In *I vitelloni*, Fellini presents his native Rimini as a succession of more or less empty streetscapes, which nullify the restless energy of the young protagonists and drive the most interesting of them, Moraldo (Franco Interlenghi), to escape by train for a new life in Rome.

Indeed, the notion of urban modernity as productivity, abundance and opportunity, was out of the question in neorealism given the physical destruction of Italian cities by war, which led to a lack of buildings and infrastructure, the collapse of the economy, and in turn a lack of food and other commodities, and the moral and existential implications of Italian fascism, Nazi occupation and the Cold War which the neorealist city helped to exteriorise. As Stephen Barber has explained, newsreels in 1945 presented mass audiences with detailed accounts of 'the destroyed cities of Europe' which remain 'one of *the* punctuation points in the depiction by film of urban space'.[12] Two of the six episodes of *Paisà* concentrate on the bombed-out terrain of Naples and Florence, buildings once precisely defined now blurred into fields of rubble, most citizens hiding indoors, the streets ruled by occupying armies and pedestrian navigation difficult or impossible, even for locals. *Germania anno zero* uses long, brooding tracking shots and a striking score by Renzo Rossellini to express the moral disorientation of a twelve-year-old boy in a Berlin so flattened by bombs that it is barely recognisable as a city at all. The still-imposing ruins of Hitler's headquarters, the Reichschancellery, serve as an architectural index of his predicament, surrounded by the defeated Third Reich, the lingering Nazism of his elders, the threat of homelessness, and constant hunger.

However, *Paisà* and *Germania anno zero* are two of the relatively few neorealist films which spend time among bombed-out ruins – and the latter is unusual for giving a well-known architectural landmark such a central role. Other films treat iconic buildings differently, but always at arm's length. In *Ossessione*, when Gino meets a young prostitute in a park in Ferrara, in the background of the shot is Castello Estense, prominent but ignored, the provincial prefecture and former seat of the

Roberto Rossellini's *Germania anno zero* (1948)

powerful Este dynasty, one of Italy's most renowned medieval and Renaissance palaces. In the final shot of *Roma città aperta*, after the Germans' execution of the resistant priest Don Pietro, the dome of St Peter's on the horizon appears tentatively symbolic of Rossellini's hope for a better Italy after the war, but it sits uncertainly in a frame divided equally between worn asphalt, rooftops and sky. In *Europa '51*, which tells the story of a high-society wife driven insane by the suicide of her young son (his death partly caused by the trauma of wartime air raids), the Piazza del Campidoglio of Michelangelo Buonarotti appears shrouded in darkness in a short but significant scene as the woman confides her grief to a friend. In *Umberto D.*, the classical portico of the Pantheon appears as a formless but menacing wall of shadow whose bulk looms over the impoverished elderly gentleman Umberto (Carlo Battista) as he begs for small change in desperation and shame. The deployment of these urban icons is off-

centre and circumspect. It contrasts clearly with the myth of the Italian city as a place of classical beauty or exotic decadence which had been well established for centuries in Renaissance painting, the European Grand Tour, and the nineteenth-century novels of Henry James. It also implicitly criticises the bombastic ways in which Italian architecture had been deployed by the fascist regime for which the city and its buildings were a means to project fixed ideological meaning.

Although Italian fascism relied greatly on rural support at first, it soon placed the city at the centre of its agenda. In part inspired by a faith in the heroism of the machine which it inherited from futurism, the regime stressed the need for the city to be an efficient unit of production, an orderly habitable space and a powerful symbolic terrain. Its widespread projects of urban expansion and construction showed a preference for planning which emphasised monuments and major axes, *sventramenti* to clear old slums for modern

buildings and thoroughfares and design which
expressed fascist 'pride, power and discipline', first in a
distinctively Italian brand of modernist architecture
known as *razionalismo* and later in an increasingly
kitsch reiteration of Greco-Roman styles.[13] Such
principles were enacted in Marcello Piacentini's grand
plans for the redesign of Rome (1925 and 1931), the
foundation of the Istituto Nazionale di Urbanistica
(1930), the reorganisation of government offices around
Rome's central Piazza Venezia, relocations of inner-city
communities to new mass housing in the urban
periphery and the creation of new roads such as the Via
della Conciliazione, which linked St Peter's Basilica
with Rome's historical centre. The streamlined
functionalism in concrete, steel and glass of
razionalismo was promoted by the influential journal
Casabella and major architectural expositions in 1928
and 1931, and found expression in landmark buildings
such as the regional fascist headquarters in Como,
Giuseppe Terragni's Casa del Fascio (1932–6). The
increasing return to ancient precedents was most
evident in the regime's largest project, the Esposizione
Universale Roma (EUR), a coordinated arrangement of
specialised 'cities' on the capital's western edge (the
Città dello sport, Città universitaria, Città militare and
Cinecittà). This was planned to be the largest world's
fair in history, an expression of the city's 'Twenty-Seven
Centuries of Civilisation' and of Italian imperial
ambitions in the Mediterranean Sea and Africa.
Continuity between fascism and classical tradition
was also deliberately suggested by the regime's
prioritisation of archaeological excavations and
restorations at the Forum of Trajan and other sites.

Cinematic representations of the city in the fascist
era showed urbanisation as evidence of the providential
rule of Mussolini. The regime invested heavily in the
production, distribution and exhibition of historical
epics such as Gallone's *Scipione l'africano*, which
presented a lavish reconstruction of ancient Rome
during the Second Punic War, its *mise en scène* consisting
of extensive sets of monumental architecture in the
Roman Forum, recreated at Cinecittà, and heaving
crowds paying homage to conquering heroes.[14]
Mussolini was directly associated with real public-works
projects through newsreels and press accounts of his
visits to construction sites – for example, during the
reclaiming of the Pontine marshes for housing
development featured in Alessandro Blasetti's *Sole* (*Sun*,
1929). And *I grandi magazzini* and other films by Mario
Camerini used romantic comedy and cosmopolitan

Milan settings to emphasise economic productivity, the
value of work, friendly social interaction and the
benevolent order of family and the state.

By contrast, neorealist cinema sought to undo the
fascists' ideological investment in architecture and
planning by sidelining them in *mise en scène*. In *Roma
città aperta*, Rossellini undercuts the fascist symbolism
of the EUR by displacing one of its most prominent
buildings, the Palazzo della Civiltà del Lavoro (1938–43),
to the distant horizon while resistance fighters
heroically ambush a German convoy in the foreground.
In *Ladri di biciclette*, the Ponte Duca d'Aosta, inaugurated
in 1942 to commemorate the hero of World War I Duke
Emanuele Filiberto di Savoia-Aosta, is the site where
Antonio Ricci, the father whose bicycle has been stolen,
is momentarily horrified by the thought that his little
boy Bruno has fallen into the Tiber and drowned. De
Sica's *Miracolo a Milano* makes architectural distinctions
between the makeshift homes of the tramps, who live
on the city's outskirts and the ornate neoclassical
offices of the greedy property developer Mobbi
(Guglielmo Barnabò) which bear an uncanny
resemblance to Il Duce's famous Gymnasium at the
Foro Mussolini. Visconti's *Bellissima*, which centres on a
mother who seeks to make her daughter a child movie
star, delivers a critique of commercial cinema by
counterpointing the synthetic ambience of the
Cinecittà studios with the authentic inner-city,
working-class community of Prenestina.

As Agnoldomenico Pica has put it, in architecture
too 'it was easy to speak in apocalyptic terms of "Year
Zero"' in 1945.[15] Like film-makers, many architects were
motivated by a sense of collective guilt, renewed
creative liberty and a desire to break with the fascist
past. The physical destruction of Italian cities and
towns presented them with unprecedented challenges.
In journals such as *Domus* and *Urbanistica*, solutions to
the country's infrastructural problems were earnestly
debated, architectural triennials were held regularly in
Milan, and schools of architecture expanded under new
leaders such as Ernesto Rogers in that city and Pier
Luigi Nervi in Rome. While conflict raged between
neorealist cinema and profit-oriented film-making as
popular entertainment, it also existed between leftist
and free-market models of urban development. The
former prioritised social housing, environmental
manageability and ethical architecture, while the latter
prioritised industrial and commercial recovery. For
architectural historians such as Pica, Vittorio Gregotti
and Aldo Rossi, the leftist tendency was in the

ascendancy in the late 1940s and early 50s and, like the best cinema of the day, it too was 'neorealist' in its social orientation, philosophical reflection and sense of moral responsibility.[16]

Manfredo Tafuri has explained that 'neorealist' architecture was allied to the anti-fascist politics of the resistance and neorealist architects such as Ludovico Quaroni and Mario Ridolfi were convinced of the urgent need for 'an encounter with active politics' in their work.[17] This could be best achieved by tackling Italy's most pressing and symbolic problem – its acute shortage of housing. Taking into account the large numbers of people made homeless by the war, inner-city communities displaced by fascist planning to outlying *borgate* and the thousands who chose to migrate from rural poverty, Peter Rowe has estimated that in Rome, for example, almost 7 per cent of the population was homeless by 1951, and a further 22 per cent lived in unsanitary conditions.[18] This crisis was central to neorealist cinema: in the haunting image in *Paisà* of destitute families living in caves outside Naples in filthy conditions akin to the real-life caves of Matera, which caused an international scandal; in the depiction in *Ladri di biciclette* of the overcrowding of workers and their families in the tenements of the Roman suburb of Valmelaina; in Luigi Zampa's *L'Onorevole Angelina* (*Angelina*, 1947), which recounts the efforts of poor working women to organise politically to ensure their families have access to rice, running water, public transport and decent housing; and in Fellini's *Le notti di Cabiria*, which revolves around the physical and metaphorical isolation of the prostitute Cabiria who lives in a makeshift cottage in the *borgata* of San Francesco in Acilia outside Rome.

Luigi Zampa's *L'Onorevole Angelina* (1947)

The neorealist architecture of Quaroni and Ridolfi, and of the publicly funded housing authority INA-Casa (1949–56), sought to relieve the endemic conditions of homelessness, poverty and marginalisation by building numerous clusters of low-rise housing in vernacular styles on low-cost marginal lands on the cities' edges. This approach meant to recapture the social cohesion of village life at a time when displacement generated great demand for a sense of social and psychic stability. In cinema, the challenges to social cohesion were typically emblematised by patterns of arduous movement and contrasts in *mise en scène*. For example, the protagonists of both *Ladri di biciclette* and *Le notti di Cabiria* have to struggle to make a living despite the challenge of commuting long distances between the periphery and core of Rome, sometimes by streetcar but often on foot. They testify to the gap which persisted between the physical expansion of Italian cities and the development of adequate public transport to serve them. This problem was compounded by the fact that, although the *quartieri* of Italian cities tended to be more socioeconomically mixed than those of cities elsewhere, after World War II, many Italian cities experienced new degrees of social segregation, because their historical centres were increasingly dominated by luxury housing for the bourgeoisie.[19]

However, the cinematic cityscape evolved in two broad and overlapping phases – the first, from the end of the war to the beginning of the 1950s and the second from then to the following decade, when Italian cinema was transformed once more by the emergence of 'art cinema'. The immediate postwar phase was dominated by neorealist films which nearly always attempted to present the predicaments and challenges faced by their protagonists as typical of society as a whole. *Roma città aperta* insists upon the grassroots solidarity of the people of Rome in resistance to German occupation. Giuseppe (Rinaldo Smordoni) and Pasquale (Franco Interlenghi) in *Sciuscià* are closely bonded not only to each other as friends but to the community of boys they hang out with on the streets of Rome and in the reformatory to which they are sent for handling stolen blankets. *Ladri di biciclette* situates Antonio as just one out-of-work Roman among many whose lives unfold in tenements, labour exchanges, pawn shops, police stations and soup kitchens, especially in the open-ended final shot in which Antonio and his son disappear into the city's hurrying crowds. *L'Onorevole Angelina* foregrounds one woman of that name from the *borgata*, and Anna Magnani as a charismatic star in the lead role, but the film uses frequent crowd scenes to locate her repeatedly within a large disenfranchised collective of men, women and children on whose behalf Angelina attempts a political career. This tendency is reinforced by the newsreel footage in the film of the physical damage and evacuation of residents caused by the severe flooding of the Tiber in February 1947. The protagonists of these films share the experience of hardship and displacement which was the common lot of so many Italians in the first years after the war.

During the 1950s, however, a shift of emphasis occurs from solidarity to disconnection in the relationship between the protagonist and his or her urban milieu as the Italian city shows increasing signs of a return to the normal routines and material comforts of peacetime. As austerity breeds community, increased affluence breaks it down. *Bellissima* exposes the self-centred vanity which popular film encourages among its fans. *I vitelloni* offsets the lazy hedonism of its young characters against the hard-working but conformist monotony of their parents. In Pietro Germi's *La città si difende* (Four Ways Out, 1951), the film's narrative of a payroll heist divides into four subplots, one for each of the thieves, who are increasingly isolated as the narrative progresses and only some of whom are motivated by desperate poverty. In *L'Amore in città* (Love in the City, 1953), a collective film of Roman life in six episodes, the three which stress widespread suffering – Lizzani's film about prostitutes ('L'Amore che si paga'), Antonioni's about suicides ('Tentato suicidio'), and Zavattini's about impoverished single mothers ('Storia di Caterina') – are counterbalanced by three comedic accounts by Fellini ('Agenzia matrimonial'), Dino Risi ('Paradiso per 4 ore'), and Alberto Lattuada ('Gli Italiani si voltano') of a marriage broker's, a nightclub and men getting aroused watching curvaceous women in the street. The first two episodes of *L'Oro di Napoli* present images of that city as a place of 'love of life, patience, and eternal hope', full of schoolchildren, shoppers, street musicians, gallerias and cafés. But this touristic vision is demolished in the next two episodes which focus on the sense of entrapment tormenting a compulsive gambler and a prostitute forced into an arranged marriage with a man who is still in love with his late wife. These protagonists are members of an urban society, but their experiences are less closely related to the mass, their crises more private and their cinematic depiction more reflective. No film better encapsulates this evolution than Antonioni's *Cronaca di un amore*, which concentrates on representing the excessive artificiality, absence of humanity and suffocating luxury of bourgeois society and its distinctive architectural environments (*palazzine*, fashion boutiques and executive offices). The alienating buildings and spaces of cosmopolitan Milan which fascinate Antonioni witness the disheartening eclipse of neorealist architecture and planning in the 1950s by a resurgent rationalism now backed by big business rather than by fascism.

Tafuri has lamented that decade's slow decline in neorealist architecture due to the growth in private sources of investment and the increasingly individualistic vision of society which accompanied the recovery of free-market capitalism in Italy. That recovery ushered in architecture and urban sprawl of the kind which Antonioni loved to critique. In cinema, it led to the proliferation of escapist, entertainment-oriented movies of the kind epitomised by Luigi Comencini's *Pane, amore e fantasia* (Bread, Love and Dreams, 1953), one of the best-known examples of so-called *neorealismo rosa*, increasingly numerous and also invested in location shooting in the city, responding to Christian Democratic calls for a 'healthy and constructive optimism' by subordinating urban realism to conventional comedy and romance.[20] Similarly, Renato Castellani's *Sotto il sole di Roma* (Under the Sun of Rome, 1948), Luciano Emmer's *Domenica d'agosto* (Sunday in August, 1950) and Dino Risi's *Belle ma povere* (Poor Girl, Pretty Girl, 1957) acknowledged urban hardship but emphasised a sense of a happy and growing Italy despite it. Such films displayed neither the political commitment nor the artistic innovation of neorealism and what realism they had was reassuring rather than questioning or revealing. Alongside them, a return to the celebration of the iconic value of Italian cities was evident in Hollywood films set in Rome, as in William Wyler's *Roman Holiday* and Jean Negulesco's *Three Coins in the Fountain* (1954).

In subsequent years, while *neorealismo rosa* was displaced by *commedia all'italiana*, some of the most established and internationally renowned directors continued to innovate against generic expectations. In *La dolce vita* (La Dolce Vita, 1960) and later films, Fellini's Rome became increasingly anti-rational and enchanted while Antonioni explored urban modernity, tradition and the primitive in *L'avventura* and subsequent work. Films by emerging directors –

for example, Pier Pasolini's *Accatone*, Francesco Rosi's *Le mani sulla città* (*Hands over the City*, 1963) and Bernardo Bertolucci's *Prima della rivoluzione* (*Before the Revolution*, 1964) – extended but also frequently overturned the neorealism which had prevailed, becoming more and more self-reflexive in filming the urban condition. In the 1960s, the tension between conflicting cinematic visions of the city was not only not resolved – if anything, it increased.

NOTES

1. Fabio Sforzi, in Giuseppe De Matteis, Piero Bonavero and Fabio Sforzi, *The Italian Urban System: Towards European Integration* (Brookfield, VT: Ashgate, 1999), p. 51.

2. André Bazin, *What Is Cinema, Vol. 1*, trans. Hugh Gray (Los Angeles and Berkeley: University of California Press, 1971), pp. 28–9.

3. Ibid., p. 48.

4. Ibid., pp. 49–50.

5. Ibid., pp. 66, 80, 87 and 98.

6. Siegfried Kracauer, *Theory of Film: The Redemption of Physical Reality* (Princeton, NJ: Princeton University Press, 1997), p. 71.

7. Ibid., p. 72.

8. Ibid., p. 98.

9. Ibid., p. 118.

10. Donald S. Pitkin, 'Italian Urbanscape: Intersection of Private and Public', in Robert Rotenberg and Gary McDonogh (eds), *The Cultural Meaning of Urban Space* (Westport, CT: Bergin and Garvey, 1993), p. 96.

11. De Matteis, in De Matteis *et al.*, *The Italian Urban System*, p. 144.

12. Stephen Barber, *Fragments of the European City* (London: Reaktion Books, 1995), p. 56.

13. Robert C. Fried, *Planning the Eternal City* (New Haven, CT and London: Yale University Press, 1973), p. 31. See also Richard A. Etlin, *Modernism in Italian Architecture, 1890–1940* (Cambridge, MA: MIT Press, 1991), p. 93.

14. See Marcia Landy, *Italian Film* (Cambridge: Cambridge University Press, 2000), pp. 55–60, and Maria Wyke, *Projecting the Past: Ancient Rome, Cinema and History* (London and New York: Routledge, 1997), pp. 20–2.

15. Agnoldomenico Pica, *Recent Italian Architecture* (Milan: Edizioni del Milone, 1959), p. xix.

16. Vittorio Gregotti, *New Directions in Italian Architecture*, trans. Giuseppina Salvadori (London: Studio Vista, 1968); Aldo Rossi, *Three Cities: Perugia, Milano, Mantova* (Milan: Electa, 1984).

17. Manfredo Tafuri, *History of Italian Architecture, 1944–1985*, trans. Jessica Levine (Cambridge, MA: MIT Press, 1989), p. 3.

18. Peter G. Rowe, *Civic Realism* (Cambridge, MA: MIT Press, 1997), p. 107.

19. Tafuri, *History of Italian Architecture*, p. 43.

20. These were the words of the Christian Democrat, Undersecretary of Public Entertainment, Giulio Andreotti, later Prime Minister of Italy; quoted in Lorenzo Quaglietti, *Il cinema italiano del dopoguerra* (Rome: Mostra Internazionale del Nuovo Cinema, 1974), p. 37.

FURTHER READING

Bruno, Giuliana, *Atlas of Emotion: Journeys in Art, Architecture, and Film* (London and New York: Verso, 2002).

Forgacs, David, *Rome Open City* (London: BFI, 2000).

Reichlin, Bruno, 'Figures of Neorealism in Italian Architecture', trans. Antony Shugaar, Branden W. Joseph, *Grey Room* no. 5 (Autumn 2001), pp. 78–101 and *Grey Room* no. 6 (Winter 2002), pp. 110–33.

Restivo, Angelo, *The Cinema of Economic Miracles: Visuality and Modernization in the Italian Art Film* (Durham, NC and London: Duke University Press, 2002).

Rhodes, John David, *Stupendous. Miserable City: Pasolini's Rome* (Minneapolis: University of Minnesota Press, 2007).

Shiel, Mark, *Italian Neorealism: Rebuilding the Cinematic City* (London: Wallflower Press, 2006).

Steimatsky, Noa, *Italian Locations: Reinhabiting the Past in Postwar Cinema* (Minneapolis: University of Minnesota Press, 2008).

Wrigley, Richard (ed.), *Cinematic Rome* (Leicester: Troubador, 2008).

11 Dislocated Spaces for New Thought

Paths of Nomadic Wandering in Neorealist Film and Literature

Torunn Haaland

> There is a kind of nomadism, a perpetual
> displacement in the intensities [...] that
> interpenetrate each other at the same time that they
> are lived, experienced by a single body.[1]

Among the films we today would consider neorealist
and whose denied life testifies to a governmental
'crusade' aligned with Cold War sensitivities for 'a
moralisation of the Italian cinema', Cesare Zavattini's
unrealised *Italia mia* (*My Italy*) constitutes a particularly
sad loss.[2] Conceived as a cinematic journey of
encounters void of narrative premises, if it had actually
been shot, the film would probably have been more
erratic than the quest for liberation reconstructed in
Rossellini's *Paisà* and more confrontational than Pietro
Germi's *Il cammino della speranza* (*The Path of Hope*, 1950),
wherein Germi follows some Sicilian immigrants' illegal
flight to France.[3] Most importantly, *Italia mia* might have
magnified the neorealist gaze which, in opposition to
the 'invisibility of fascism',[4] would have unravelled both
shared and separating social experiences in order to
construct new images of the country and its
population.[5] The emergence in postwar neorealist
culture of this 'manifold discovery of the different
Italies' reflected, according to some of its most
influential contributors, the popular origins of the
Resistance[6] and the anonymous narrative voice it
inspired.[7] More recent critics have emphasised other
factors, including the 'sense of defeat and of paradoxical
euphoria' brought about by the Armistice in 1943;[8] as
well as the 'collective amnesia' that obfuscated recent
national history by locating the redefinition of
nationhood in the postwar present.[9] There are, however,
moments when the journey towards the diverse truths
of the country deviates from normative ideals of
material and moral rebuilding for experiences of
opposition and abandonment; fantasy and

contemplation; encounters and isolation. By
approaching these singular passages as nomadic – as
anti-sedentary strategies of defiance and de-codification
– we can better see that the revolutionary quality of
neorealism was not ultimately its anti-illusionist ethos
or its sociogeographical discoveries, but the juncture
these qualities found in a narrative in which style
becomes political and national history inspires new
thinking about artistic creation and human essence.

Notions of singular paths to universal experiences
are precisely what inform Deleuze's understanding of
neorealism as having introduced characters who,
'caught in certain pure optical and sound situations,
find themselves condemned to wander about or go off
on a trip. These are pure seers who no longer exist
except in the interval of movement.'[10]

Reflecting the ordeals and uncertainties of recent
disasters, such stasis in front of external situations
provokes the type of 'time-images' Visconti
experimented with in *Ossessione*, where the 'protagonists
invest the setting and the objects with their gaze' while
failing to seize the freedom for which they kill.[11]

The self-destructive affair between the wavering
vagrant Gino and the conveniently but unhappily
married Giovanna replicates James Cain's novel
A Postman Always Rings Twice (1934), whose irresolute,
vagabond and elliptical narrative had already shaped
the passage Cesare Pavese relates in *Paesi tuoi* (1941)
following the whimsical Berto from jail in Turin to
archaic rites of destructive vitality in the country. Cain's
melodrama yields, however, to the 'anthropomorphic'
poetics we in particular recognise in the tired postures
and resigned expressions of Visconti's murderous lovers
whose dwelling within the provincial squalor of the Po
River's languid plains denies fascist rhetoric of action
and determination. Visconti's notion of 'frames' filled
by 'living people; people alive among things'[12] echoed

Giovanna's accidental death in *Ossessione* (1943)

not only Mario Alicata and Giuseppe De Santis's call for a cinematic return to the humanity of Verga's Sicilian stories,[13] but also the 'nomadic' cinema the painter Domenico Purificato had proposed as a 'migration' towards 'scenarios only nature can prepare'.[14] A point of reference for these visions of a new culture was the strategy of estrangement Vittorini developed in his novel *Conversazione in Sicilia* (1937), where Silvestro's unmotivated homecoming to Italy's most unimperial and historically diverse sphere unfolds as a formation of consciousness.[15] Written with anti-nationalistic references to Faulkner's lyricism and Hemingway's dialogues, the narrative oscillates between poeticised sociogeographic specificities and iterative conversations with interlocutors typified either as fascist, indifferent or anti-fascist. The latter's insistence on 'the pain of the offended world' and the need for 'other duties' induces Silvestro to see something 'more human' in the sick and impoverished people to whom his mother introduces him, whereas the appearance at the churchyard of his brother who died in one of Mussolini's imperial wars dismantles the rhetoric of glory and heroism typical of the regime. Moving through abstractions and fragmentations, the initially apathetic wanderer indicates a road to opposition that escaped fascist censors until 1942 when the novel was withdrawn from publication.

While disclosing the social and moral crises fascist portrayals of nationhood systematically excluded, the drifting these deviant characters experience in Italy's unrepresented provinces also localise the shady locales, deserted spheres and disjointed settings that Deleuze sees proliferate in the neorealist landscape. Rooted as they are in perception that unleashes thought rather than action, such 'any-space-whatevers' relocate the images from 'space and movement' to 'topology and time':[16] from the concreteness, in the case of *Roma città aperta*, of Saint Peter's dome to spheres marked by everyday life and heroic deaths rather than papal pomp and imperial glory. Rossellini's choral portrayal of solidarity and resistance during the German occupation reaches a standstill with Pina's (Anna Magnani) last scream in her war-torn working-class neighbourhood while the claustrophobic spaces of betrayal, persecution and torture fade behind the vast fields of anti-fascist martyrdom at Forte Bravetta where Don Pietro says his last prayer. Invested by the revitalising force of sacrificial blood, these anonymous spaces evoke an earlier scene where the urgency of a clandestine mission forces the Resistance priest to postpone Pina's confession. Once they reach the road where he will encounter his partisan contact, she nonetheless addresses both her premarital pregnancy and wartime scarcity, opening a dialogue Don Pietro quickly refocuses from individual culpabilities to collective sins. Relocating the Holy Communion from the Church's spheres and mediation towards uncontrolled hills associated with the people's war and the political reform it was thought to bring about, their walk actualises the nomadic alternative to the 'sedentary, bourgeois, and reputable' studio-shot films that Purificato championed,[17] as well as Deleuze's analogous conception of nomadism as a strategy to defy 'laws, contracts and institutions' – codes upon which every bureaucratic organisation thrives. His concrete example derives not incidentally from imperial times when excessive coordination and developments would stir such resentment among the despot's subjects as to drive entire communities towards the type of undesignated and unconstrained space Rossellini's wanderers perceive of as the foundation for a truly 'open city'.[18]

The freedom immanent in the personal and national tragedies of *Roma città aperta* is as absent from Carlo Levi's contemporary *Cristo si è fermato a Eboli* (1945) as is the hope that nomadic opposition can actually end centuries of suppression. Retreating from the context of Nazi-fascism in which the defiant anti-fascist painter and doctor was clandestinely writing in favour of the southern province of Basilicata to which he had been interned between 1935 and 1936, Levi's account *of* and *about* resistance discloses an isolated and resourceless village, where exploited peasants are subjected to incompetent local servants of the fascist regime. Deprived of all means of progress and abandoned, in their own view, by Christ and state alike, these peasants live their own dehumanisation with a circular notion of time and with space as a restrictive dimension of agency. When the mayor announces a mandatory celebration of Mussolini's campaign in Africa, farm workers arise two hours before fascist law-enforcers close the roads, leaving for labour in faraway fields to ensure a day's meagre income. This rejection not only of a cause they acutely see as a waste of money better spent at home, but also of a state and a regime they only know through the tax collector, culminates when Levi's medical assistance to the poor of the area is prohibited to protect the incompetent local doctors. As Levi barely prevents the peasants' violent reactions and discourages democratic initiatives that are doomed to failure, they determine to channel ancient and powerful resentments by performing a self-composed satirical sketch outside the homes of the authorities. Whereas the peasants' previous protest illustrated the separation of an 'extrinsic nomadic unit' from the 'intrinsic despotic unit', this artistic occupation of what for them are exclusive spaces points to the correlations Deleuze identifies between the imperial machine whose excessive codification aims at internalising the nomads' ways, and the nomadic 'war machine' which breaks

down traditional codes and barriers. Deleuze's interest in this fundamentally dynamic and creative strategy of opposition resides in its ability to operate, intellectually, at the limits of linguistic and textual laws to assist in the 'decodification' of increasingly deregulated modern societies. If the nomadic is a question of 'style', and as such, a 'politics',[19] we should be able to localise the nomadic in Levi's fusion of anthropological analysis, lyrical description and sociohistorical critique, and, before that, in Vittorini's surreally accentuated conversation pieces. Both testify to the search of 'a modern taste, style, and world' that, from the 1930s had unleashed a literary 'discovery' of America and a subsequent wave of translations and critical debates. This was a dissident and enormously successful evasion the fascists 'pretended not to see' rather than admitting that what young writers sought, as Cesare Pavese observed after the war, was 'a human warmth that official Italy did not offer us. And even less, that we were searching for ourselves'.[20]

For those who in 1945 came out of 'war, civil war [...] full of stories to tell', the formal and thematic defiance of Vittorini and Pavese offered tools with which to seize the 'explosive load of freedom' brought about by the Liberation; an unprecedented atmosphere that, as Italo Calvino later recalled, inspired not 'to inform' but 'to *express*' lived and unrepresented experiences.[21] In his *Il sentiero dei nidi di ragno* (1947), this anti-naturalistic intent evolves along the picaresque trajectory of Pin, an orphan intruder who steals a pistol from his prostitute sister's German client, escapes from a fascist jail with the mythical communist Red Wolf, and joins a detachment of opportunist partisans that is soon dissolved. Except for the misogynist Cousin, they all confirm Pin's distrust of adults, convincing him to run away from the camp for spaces that preserve his hope of finding a friend. While the child's unrestrained enunciations and distorted perceptions provoke vernacular voices and grotesque caricatures, his imagination allows Calvino to move beyond the Ligurian hills where he had fought with far more heroic companions towards the 'magic place where spiders construct nests'. When Cousin appears like a wizard on these enchanted paths, leading Pin by the hand from the spiders' intricate tunnels through the illumination of fireflies, the story's historical frame is breached by visions of a 'faraway land' of freedom none of them found in the people's struggle for justice.[22] Their idyllic walk away resonates in the broomstick flight with which Totò (Francesco Golisano) and the other squatters go in search of free land in *Miracolo a Milano*, escaping a country where the solidarity of the Resistance lies buried beneath private property signs. This connection of surrealist continuity also relates the disconcerting subtexts of Calvino's fable to the poetic-denunciatory discourses De Sica and Zavattini had previously presented in *Sciuscià*.[23] Like the many street urchins in Allied-occupied Rome, Giuseppe and the orphaned Pasquale make a living shining soldiers' shoes. Their good spirit relies on unconditional togetherness and carefree moments of horse-riding as well as shared dreams that seemingly materialise when the reward for obliviously assisting Giuseppe's criminal brother in a robbery enables them to purchase a horse. This living toy unravels sunlit spaces of an unworried pleasure too fugitive to last beyond the boys' dehumanising encounter with the reformatory and the judiciary – forces of injustice that, along with Giuseppe's family, spread enmity between them and punish the least guilty. After a violent fight in a haunting wood from which Pasquale is left crying over Giuseppe's accidental death, the white-haired horse continues their search for freedom, vanishing into fantastic surroundings in a rejection of a world where levels of material and moral destruction are mirrored in lost childhoods.

To what extent alarming deprivation, exploitation and neglect had turned children away from the road to liberation upon which Pina's son Marcello (Vito Annichiarico) embarks was a question Rossellini himself addressed, not only in *Paisà* which traces Pasquàle's

(Alfonsino Pasca) paths of survival in a ruined Naples after Allied bombing killed his parents, but, more troubling still, with Edmund's wanderings across postwar Berlin in *Germania anno zero*. Facing the end of the only value system he ever knew as well as the impossible imperative of supporting a household where his sister endures endless ration lines and their ex-soldier brother hides from Allied occupiers, Edmund (Edmund Moeschke) poisons their ailing father, thus acting on the ideologies of a former Nazi teacher who, out of fear rather than remorse, reproaches him for his act. When Edmund returns to their temporary housing and realises that there is no longer a home for him, he immerses himself in the city's ruins and follows its desolate roads back to witness his father's funeral procession from the heights of a destroyed building. Marking a defeated country's year zero, Edmund's fatal fall and lifeless body call for an entire new system of morality. Between the child abandoned to an abyssal solitude and the *seer* irreversibly marked by recent disasters, there runs a line of continuity that Pavese outlined, *ante* Deleuze, in *La luna e i falò* (1950), wherein the flashback structure of Anguilla's narration establishes acute parallels between past and present rootlessness. Returning after the war to the Piedmont hills where he grew up as a miserable foundling and farmworker before military service brought him to ideological formation in Genoa and fascist persecution sent him onward to America, Anguilla reflects on the destiny that realised his desire to escape and rise above poverty without resolving his need to

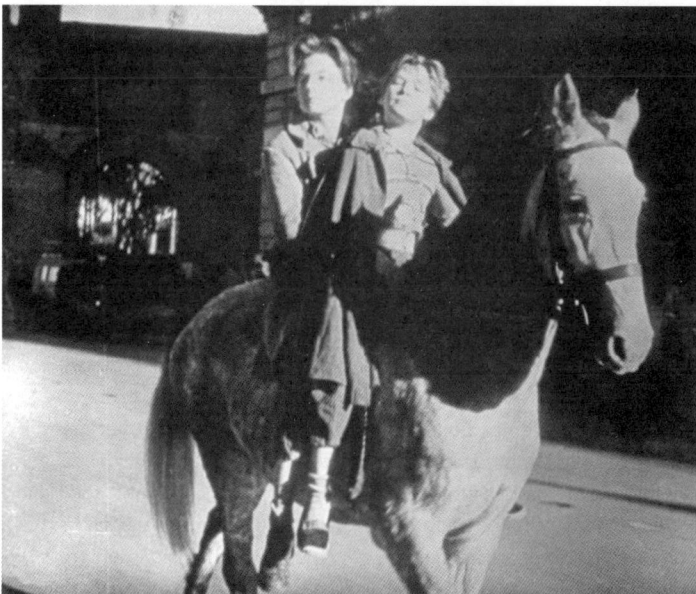

Giuseppe and Pasquale on a ride in via Veneto in De Sica and Zavattini's *Sciuscià* (1946)

belong. How much twenty years on the move between casual relations, business enterprises and political internment in the Californian provinces have alienated him from a community where only people's misery is unchanged Anguilla discovers in relation to the abused boy Cinto who mirrors his childhood persona as well as to Nuto, a Communist carpenter who in the past convinced him to read and seize the world without himself ever leaving the village. Notwithstanding the many disillusions of the Reconstruction, Nuto still insists on the need for social reform, while at the same time relating agricultural life to the cycles of the moon and the celebratory bonfires. What distances the businessman from the carpenter is not only newly won wealth or archaic myths and political ideals Anguilla can no longer believe in, but also the Resistance: a civil war and a failed revolution he can only relive as narratives that testify to his own non-participation.

There are some significant parallels between Edmund, who launches himself into a necropolis to annihilate his own roots, and Anguilla, who observes himself living in the past and seeking perpetual escape from geographical and emotional settlement. While disregarding any possibility of redemption and reconstruction, their trajectories unfold as a 'process of intensity'; a continuous flux of physical and mental wandering that breaches the narrative frame to connect with something outside itself. Like the revolutionary works of Nietzsche, Kafka and Godard who confound linguistic and visual codes 'to transmit something uncodifiable', the introspective narratives Rossellini and Pavese construct do not seek to codify the postwar condition but rather to engage in thoughts that await their 'meaning from a new external force', from the encounter with other intensities of inner life and with the audience.[24] The ability of such displacements to make thought itself nomadic is theorised in *A Thousand Plateaus* wherein Deleuze and Guattari discuss the production of counter-thought as a matter of 'rhizomatic' thinking. In contrast to roots and trees which evolve from a beginning to 'a centred or segmented higher unity', the rhizome channels out infinitely and non-hierarchically from a 'plateau' in the middle; as is the case with nomads, the rhizome evades sedentary points in favour of multiplicities and assemblages in infinite expansion into new terrains.[25] To what extent the opening towards something exterior to themselves offered postwar writers the means to denounce totalitarian power and reject the populist imageries and nationalist rhetorics of fascism becomes clearer in the light of trajectories that deviate from the historical struggle to connect with an exteriority of universal experiences. Pavese's novel *La casa in collina* (1949) develops symptomatically as a long retreat, following Corrado who observes both Allied bombing and the beginnings of German occupation from the hills outside Turin where his proletarian friends prepare for armed struggle. Among them is Cate, a past love whose child, Dino, he suspects is his own. In seeing his friends arrested and deported while he, by chance, escapes persecution as Dino joins the partisans, the intellectual inclined to shrug his shoulders at the war and to exclude the possibility of historical change seeks refuge in his childhood home while questioning whether his accidental survival is actually his salvation.

More than refusing to renounce class privileges for social liberation – an historical exigency Giaime Pintor addressed in his last letter before dying on a partisan mission[26] – Corrado greets the war as a protective 'nest' that excuses his desire for isolation and nurtures the illusion that he can live detached from history.[27] What eventually awakens him is his realisation that the massacred fascists he witnesses resemble him and that his own survival rests on their deaths. Vittorini had discovered something similar during the Resistance in Milan, and his fictionalisation of these experiences in the novel *Uomini e no* (1945) crucially juxtaposes surreally horrific images of Nazi-fascist terror with lyrical portraits of their victims, to conclude that offences against humanity are no less 'within man' than suffering. Reflecting on the enemy's nature is an abstract Narrator whose comments on and interference in the events are italicised; the non-italicised sections gravitate around a character known by his *nom de guerre* as Enne 2 who directs 'peaceful' and 'simple' workers in anti-fascist attacks while involved in an anguished affair with the married Berta.[28] Whereas the Narrator engages with Enne 2's desires, transporting him and Berta back to his childhood in Sicily so as to invert the chronology and impossibility of their love, in the omniscient narrative, Enne 2 is sought by the enemy following an unsuccessful attempt to eliminate Black Dog, the mastermind of fascist violence. Tired of waiting and resisting, the partisan leader reflects on his own incapacity to aid fallen companions and refuses to go underground, deceiving himself that Berta will return while subconsciously anticipating Black Dog's arrival. The moment when their bullets cross is, however, withdrawn from the book's pages in favour of new narrative dimensions: whereas the italicised section closes in around the Narrator's decision to liberate Enne 2's seven-year-old persona before the mutually fatal encounter with Black Dog, the factual storyline follows a worker who, after Enne 2 declines his escape plans, honours the Resistance leader's sacrifice by launching himself into patriotic action.

Enne 2's inclination to let himself be carried away is as far removed from the opportunism of Pin's companions as it is from the tragedies of *Paisà*. In this ascent of the peninsula, partisans encounter fascist opponents in the battle for Florence, whereas in the flooded Po River they fight with inadequate means and against the order General Alexander communicated in November 1944 for all partisans to return to their homes. Some Allied soldiers have joined the guerrilla war and, in assuming the partisans' desperate refusal to wait for external liberation, the Allies also share their defeat by well-equipped Nazi troops.

Witnessing his Italian comrades being tied up and thrown into the river, the American Dale jumps up in a gesture of protest only to be penalised the way Pina is in *Roma città aperta*. In contrast to these manifestations of commitment, Enne 2's self-destructive immobility and Corrado's defensive retreat from the present both betray a scepticism towards the political struggle their working-class counterparts embrace instinctively or consciously, but even more importantly, their detachment reflects an existential exhaustion that, along with recent national history, forges 'a new type of tale [récit]'.[29] Symptomatically, *La casa in collina* identifies neither an end nor a precise beginning as Corrado writes while the war is still raging and while recollections better serve the auto-analytical objective. Proceeding from physical and mental paths into unresolved junctures between inner and external conflicts, his confession articulates a dialectics between sought isolation and the exigency of confronting the present that breaches the work's disconcertingly closed sphere of thought. In what ways a text may reside in 'intermezzos' of suspended meaning[30] and breach both solipsist perspectives and historical frames is even more evident in *Uomini e no*, where the binary structure confuses beginnings and endings as well as codes of unity and mimetic representation in order to eclipse the tragic moment of nihilistic abandonment. Between the child persona abstracted from spatiotemporal anchorages and the worker who on his first mission shoots a fascist officer while sparing an enlisted German out of empathy, there emerges a 'rhizomatic realm of possibility' that, as is the case with Corrado's enlightening recognition of himself in the defeated

enemy, rests on the need to address the darkness uncovered by recent historical disasters and formulate adequate stylistic means to reconsider the subject's understanding of self and relations to others.[31]

That civil war and final solutions had brought forth demons and entirely jeopardised past perceptions of human essence is a premise for some works that, to narrate neglected and muted micro-histories, traverse the emptiness of a shattered country or the concentric circles of an earthly underworld. It is not to formulate historical accusations that Primo Levi outlines the year of violence endured after he was captured as a Jewish partisan and deported to Auschwitz, but to engage us in the question embedded in his work's title *Se questo è un uomo* (1947). Wandering in the present tense among SS guards, Kapos and prisoners unified in a single internal desolation, the combined protagonist/narrator/author immediately affirms that what he describes is Hell itself, and although he belongs to the collective of damned souls, he is, like Dante, destined to return with a message to the world containing both graphical descriptions, sociological analysis and moral lessons. If the three-year-old Emilia, who is executed upon arrival, epitomises a machinery impeccably designed to bury everyone's humanity, and Alex, the Kapo who mechanically wipes his oily hand on Levi's shoulder, becomes the standard against which he judges all offenders against humanity, Alberto's fraternal companionship and Lorenzo, a civil worker who brings Levi food from the outside, remind him that he is still human. The awareness of a presumed lost dignity is a key to survival, but also a punishment Levi endures more frequently during the moments of 'ceasefire' in the laboratory where he works the last months before Russian troops arrive.[32] Amid this relative luxury, to write and destroy what he cannot tell anyone becomes a therapy he reassumes after a long journey of repatriation when the nightmare tormenting him in the concentration camp – that his experiences, were he ever to return, would only meet incomprehension or indifference – materialises as another traumatising reality. Against the collective desire to forget and move on, the almost biological need to tell others assumes such urgency that the chronology develops, erratically, as fragments of life wherein the absence of a divine providence is as certain as the remediating force of solidarity. Moments of human warmth and systematic dehumanisation are, in fact, equally at work in Levi's determination to bring his story to the world outside the barbed wire; an act of testimony that while it deconstructs assumptions of the rational and moral nature of the human race also formulates a humanistic interpretation of the Hebraic mandate to transmit an uncodifiable memory of discrimination and persecution.

It is an altogether different form of documentation we follow in *Paisà*. Anchoring fictional storylines to archival footage, it conveys the agony of loss rather than of a persistent nightmare and is even more disjointed as each of the six episodes introduces new characters with different experiences of the almost two-year-long struggle against Nazi-fascist repression. Characteristic of both journeys is, however, their picaresque quality and the unifying theme of strangers brought together by extreme historical circumstances. In Sicily, Carmela (Carmela Sazio) has hardly met Joe (Robert Van Loon) from Jersey when they are both killed by Germans and his colleagues judge erroneously that she betrayed him; in Naples, the Afro-American Military Policeman Joe sees both the effects of the Allied campaign and his own marginalised life mirrored in Pasquale (Alfonso Pasca), who steals to survive and lives with thousands of war victims in the caves, whereas in Rome, Francesca's (Maria Michi) incidental re-encounter with Frank (Gar Moore) who entered the city as a liberator five months earlier, confronts her with the moral degradation she has undergone during the winter crisis of 1944–5. As there is neither a resolution nor any point of transition between the episodes, the disconcerting passages of lost love and deprived innocence fail to sustain the optimistic tone and popular unity narrated in *Roma città aperta*. Instead, they affirm the country's sociocultural and ideological disjunctions: whereas the Allied-invaded south never saw an anti-fascist Resistance, Florence is riven by battlegrounds and forbidden passageways. Harriet (Harriet Medin), an American nurse, nonetheless crosses the river in search of a Resistance hero only to learn from a mortally wounded partisan that he has just been killed. In Emilia-Romagna, some friars have lived protected from the war and are happy to accommodate three American chaplains until it appears that one is Jewish and the other Lutheran. Their refusal to engage in a human dialogue is denounced by the final episode in which Allied soldiers and civilians are captured or killed for supporting the partisans and a desperate child left abandoned after the massacre testifies to the nature of all intolerance.

It is such 'facts' that, as Bazin observed, compose the unity of cinematic narration in *Paisà*, and they exist ambiguously and independently from causal relationships. Only when the viewer relates these facts

A surviving child cries into a dawn void of promises in Rossellini's *Paisà* (1946)

to each other does the film's meaning emerge.[33] Beyond the last shot of *Paisà*, national liberation awaits at last, but contemporary viewers will probably relate the issues highlighted in the film, such as victims of war and problems of marginalisation, deprived childhoods, political violence, racial and religious intolerance to their modern-day incarnations.

Were we to trace these paths towards a point of conjuncture, to a point of 'contact and transmission', that, in its intensity embodies both irresolution and abandonment; immobility and directionless wandering,[34] we would arrive at the entirely inconsequential passage along Roman streets featured in *Ladri di biciclette*. Although Antonio is accompanied by his son Bruno and encounters a variety of institutions and social ambiences, the desperate search for a stolen bike radiates a solitude and meaninglessness that cannot exclusively be reduced to the postwar crisis most obviously on De Sica and Zavattini's agenda. Antonio's story is axiomatically simple. To accept a position as a billposter after two years of job-hunting, the disillusioned worker needs the bicycle he just pawned. Once his wife has resolved this dilemma, he cycles the stretch from the peripheral wastelands where he lives in poor conditions to the city centre and assumes his duties with an optimism that soon disintegrates when the bike is stolen and the malefactor escapes right before his very eyes. A taxi driver, some street cleaners, a fortune teller and two police officers are all engaged in the futile search, but Antonio fails himself to seize chance encounters with the thief and the old beggar who bought the bike. When Bruno notices this error, Antonio slaps him and spends his last money on a lunch to re-establish their alliance, only to jeopardise everything following a mortifying defeat in the thief's own neighbourhood. When he finally seeks to change the course of events, the gesture hardly belongs to him but the humiliation he suffers certainly does. The honest worker who steals a bike is 'out of himself' and, incapable of escaping from the crowd of men who observed his violation, he 'lets himself get caught [...] like someone who has given up'.[35]

Besides the incapacity to act and the counterproductive gestures with which he seeks either to ignore or to confront his own predicament, Antonio's trajectory is also characterised by narratively purposeless moments such as the rain sequence, when father and son come in alienating contact with some Austrian priests, and the dead time of wandering along narrow alleys, deep riverbanks and disconnected topologies that disorient our perceptions of the characters' environment while aligning us with their displacement within it. In such uncoordinated spheres invested with the inertness of a seer who may leave the frame or vanish in the depth of temporalised images, we discern the search for a new style capable of accommodating both an anti-totalitarian unity and a modern subjectivity. What we are left with when Bruno takes his father's hand and the two merge into the waves of the urban crowd, so indifferent to their tragedy, and with the film's languid texture, so embracive of their tacit isolation, are lands of unresolved ambiguity; a web of connections and continuities that while they leave scarce hope for a solution to the worker's drama, project new dimensions of dissident possibility. More specifically, in affirming not only the political pessimism but also the disconcerting tone of loss and solitude that, as we have seen, increasingly accompanies the neorealist nomad, Antonio's trajectory outlines foundations for a cinema that, rather than signifying pre-established meanings, seeks to survey and map out 'realms that are yet to come'. If the rhizome, as Deleuze and Guattari write, connects 'semiotic chains, organisations of power and circumstances relative to the arts, sciences and social struggles,'[36] then we can also conclude that among the most significant achievements of neorealism was that of bringing Purificato's call for a mobile cinema towards fields of narration in which cineastes and viewers engage in forms of contemporary thought unknown to pre-existing systems of meaning.

NOTES

1. Gilles Deleuze, 'Nomad Thought', in Daniel W. Conway et al. (eds), *Nietzsche: Critical Assessments* (London: Routledge, 1998), p. 82.

2. See Gian Piero Brunetta, *Storia del cinema Italiano. Dal neorealismo al miracolo economico, Vol. 3, 1945–1959* (Rome: Editori Riuniti, 2001), p. 75. For a detailed account of government opposition to social criticism in Italian films during the fascist and neorealist periods, see Guido Bonsaver's chapter in this anthology.

3. The direction of *Italia mia* was assigned first to De Sica, who instead directed *Stazione termini* (*Indiscretion of an American Wife*, 1953) for David Selznick and, successively, to Rossellini, who embarked on the completely different road movie that is *Viaggio in Italia*. The loss of this project remained a 'thorn in Zavattini's heart'(Mino Argentieri in Cesare Zavattini, *Cinema: Diario cinematografico, Neorealismo ecc* [Milano: Bompiani, 2002], p. 740).

4. See Giulia Fanara, *Pensare il neorealismo* (Rome: Lithos, 2000), p. 78.

5. See Giovanni Falaschi, 'Alla scopera dell'Italia e degli italiani: Zavattini e altri autori (1944–1963)', *Cuadernos de Filología Italiana* no. 14 (2007), p. 176; and Mirco Melanco, 'Il motivo del viaggio nel cinema italiano (1945–65)', in Gian Piero Brunetta (ed.), *Identità italiana e identità europea nel cinema italiano dal 1945 al miracolo economico* (Turin: Fondazione Giovanni Agnelli, 1996), p. 218.

6. See Zavattini, *Cinema*, pp. 770–5; and Giuseppe De Santis in 'Confessioni di un regista', in Sergio Toffetti (ed.), *Rosso fuoco. Il cinema di Giuseppe De Santis* (Turin: Lindau, 1996), pp. 227–45.

7. See Italo Calvino, *Il sentiero dei nidi di ragno* (Milan: Mondadori, 1993), p. vi.

8. Emiliano Morreale, 'Nel paese dei neorealisti. Scrittori e cinema nel secondo dopoguerra', in Luca Venzi (ed.), *Incontri al neorealismo. Luoghi e visioni di un cinema pensato al presente* (Rome: Fondazione Ente dello Spettacolo, 2008), p. 62.

9. Brunetta, *Identità italiana*, p. 19.

10. Gilles Deleuze, *Cinema 2. The Time-Image*, trans. Hugh Tomlinson and Robert Galeta (Minneapolis: University of Minnesota Press, 1989), p. 41.

11. Ibid., pp. 1–4.

12. Luchino Visconti, 'Il cinema antropomorfico', *Cinema* nos 173–4 (1943), pp. 108–9 (author's translation).

13. See Mario Alicata and Giuseppe De Santis, 'Verità e poesia. Verga e il cinema italiano', *Cinema* no. 12 (1941), pp. 216–17.

14. Domenico Purificato, 'L'obiettivo nomade', *Cinema* no. 7 (September 1939), pp. 195–6 (author's translation). Purificato was the editor of *Cinema* in the crucial years (1940–3) when the journal's redaction became the de facto centre of the Roman underground movement.

15. *Conversazione in Sicilia* first appeared in instalments in the literary magazine *Letteratura* between 1938 and 1939. Visconti, who visited Sicily in 1941 and there envisioned the adaptation of Verga's *I Malavoglia* (1881) that later became *La terra trema* (1948), recalled the 'alarm' Vittorini's novel had stirred up: see 'Da Verga a Gramsci', in Giuliana Callegari and Nuccio Lodato (eds), *Leggere Visconti. Scritti, interviste, testimonianze e documenti di e su Luchino Visconti* (Pavia: Arte grafiche La Cittadella, 1976), pp. 48–50. De Santis remembered how his generation's 'desire and need for revitalisation' was encouraged not only by Vittorini, but also by Visconti's *Ossessione* and Renato Guttuso's *Crocifissione* (*Crucifixion*, 1941): see 'Il Guttuoso di Riso amaro', in Toffetti, *Rosso fuoco*, pp. 195–8.

16. Deleuze, *Cinema 2*, pp. 5, 125.

17. Purificato, 'L'obiettivo nomade'.

18. See Deleuze, 'Nomad Thought', pp. 77–8, 84.

19. Ibid., p. 79.

20. Cesare Pavese, *La letteratura americana e altri saggi* (Turin: Einaudi, 1968), pp. 194–7 (author's translation).

21. Calvino, *Il sentiero dei nidi di ragno*, pp. vi–vii (author's translation).

22. Lucia Re, *Calvino and the Age of Neorealism: Fables of Estrangement* (Stanford, CA: Stanford University Press, 1990), p. 307.

23. Bruno Falcetto points to the surrealist connection between *Il sentiero dei nidi di ragno* and *Miracolo a Milano* in *Storia della narrativa neorealista* (Milan: Mursia, 1992), pp. 42–3.

24. Deleuze, 'Nomad Thought', pp. 79–82.

25. Gilles Deleuze and Felix Guattari, *A Thousand Plateaus. Capitalism and Schizophrenia*, ed. and trans. Brian Massumi (Minneapolis: University of Minnesota Press, 1987), pp. 22–3; 377.

26. Pintor's 'Lettera al fratello Luigi' (28 November 1943) was published in the Communist Party's organ *Rinascita* in 1946 and is reprinted in Claudio Milanini (ed.), *Neorealismo. Problemi e polemiche* (Milan: Il Saggiatore, 1980), pp. 35–9.

27. Cesare Pavese, *La luna e i falò* (Turin: Einaudi, 1968), pp. 95 and 24.

28. Elio Vittorini, *Uomini e no* (Milan: Mondadori, 1965), pp. 174–81 and 51.

29. Gilles Deleuze, *Cinema 1. The Movement-Image*, trans. Hugh Tomlinson and Barbara Habberjam (Minneapolis: University of Minnesota Press, 1986), p. 211.

30. Deleuze and Guattari, *A Thousand Plateaus*, p. 377.

31. Ibid., p. 190.

32. Primo Levi, *Se questo è un uomo* (Turin: Einaudi, 1958), p. 126.

33. André Bazin, *Qu'est-ce que le cinéma?* (Paris: Les Éditions du Cerf, 2002), pp. 281–2.

34. Deleuze, 'Nomad Thought', p. 82.

35. Guglielmo Moneti, *Lezioni di neorealismo* (Siena: Nuova Immagine, 1999), p. 42.

36. Deleuze and Guattari, *A Thousand Plateaus*, p. 82.

FURTHER READING

Bonsaver, Guido, *Elio Vittorini: The Writer and the Written* (Leeds: Northern Universities Press, 2000).

Calvino, Italo, *The Path to the Spiders' Nests*, trans. Tim Parks (London: Penguin, 2009).

Fanara, Giulia, *Pensare il neorealismo* (Rome: Lithos, 2000).

Gordon, Robert (ed.), *The Cambridge Companion to Primo Levi* (Cambridge: Cambridge University Press, 2007).

Haaland, Torunn, *Italian Neorealist Cinema* (Edinburgh: Edinburgh University Press, 2012).

Levi, Carlo, *Christ Stopped at Eboli: The Story of a Year*, trans. Frances Frenaye (New York: Farrar, Straus, 1947).

Levi, Primo, *If This Is a Man and The Truce*, trans. Stuart Woolf (London: Everyman's Library, 2000).

Oberbey, David (ed. and trans.), *Springtime in Italy: A Reader in Neo-Realism* (Hamden, CT: Archon Books, 1979).

Pallotta, Augustus (ed.), *Italian Novelists since World War II, 1945–1965* (Detroit, MI: Gale Research, 1997).

Pavese, Cesare, *American Literature: Essays and Opinions*, ed. and trans. Edwin Fussell (Berkeley: University of California Press, 1970).

——, *The Harvesters*, trans. A. E. Murch (London: Owen, 1961).

——, *The Moon and the Bonfires*, trans. R. W. Flint (New York: New York Review Books, 2002.

——, *The Selected Works of Cesare Pavese*. trans. R. W. Flint (New York: New York Review Books, 2001).

Re, Lucia, *Calvino and the Age of Neorealism: Fables of Estrangement* (Stanford, CA: Stanford University Press, 1990).

——, 'Neorealist Narrative: Experience and Experiment', in Peter Bondanella and Andrea Ciccarelli (eds), *The Cambridge Companion to the Italian Novel* (Cambridge: Cambridge University Press, 2003), pp. 104–24.

Vittorini, Elio, *Conversations in Sicily*, trans. Alane Salierno Mason; Preface by Ernest Hemingway (New York: New Directions, 2000).

——, *Men and Not Men*, trans. Sarah Henry (Evanston, IL: Northwestern University Press and Marboro Press, 1987).

12 Seeing Anew

Children in Italian Cinema, 1944 to the Present

Giovanna De Luca

The position of the child in Italian society has inspired film directors since the beginning of cinema. He is at once an eternal child, never relinquishing his dependence on family, and the *enfant roi* who dominates his parents. In a patriarchal society that grants ultimate importance to motherhood and defines itself according to family values, films with children in them have reflected the history and culture of Italian society. Contemporary discourse about childhood is based on multiple perspectives – mythological, psychoanalytical, anthropological and historical – that make it difficult to define the child as a subject. As Karen Lury put it, the study of the child becomes possible 'once the child and childhood is understood to never have fully been encompassed by these stories and discourses'.[1] Once we have recognised that the role of the child in film is that of agent rather than subject, his demystifying gaze offers us a new perspective of the world. For many Italian movie-makers, the child's perspective provides a panoramic view of life, an important device in film-making, as a single frame can contain much essential information.

The child in cinema has two essential functions: he is a character involved in the drama on screen and, at the same time, a proxy for the viewer. This enables moviegoers to experience his reality, and their own, viewed through his eyes. His perspective provides a double view of the world, close and distant. The child is completely involved in the present moment while the adult spectator watches the proxy, thus observing himself as a child.[2] The child in Italian cinema has functioned as a thermometer of society, morphing into different signifiers that range from the innocent victim of a degraded society to a nostalgic figure longing for a lost past or better future.[3] In early cinema, children played relatively minor roles, in folkloric portraits of street urchins (like Gennariello [Eduardo Notari] in

Elvira Notari's films) or images of innocent, sacrificial children as in Pastrone's *Cabiria*. Fascism, instead, used children to advance a political agenda; they mostly appeared in documentaries from the government-run Istituto Luce and other propaganda sources. Children, divided by gender and age, marched and saluted in parades or performed physical activities, helping to promote fascism's goals. Youth were portrayed as the future representatives of a rejuvenated Italy taught the ideals of this new society, who would in turn become exemplars of the system and impose discipline on society. Only after World War II did the child in cinema achieve an independent status. The physical and moral destruction of the war reverberated within cinema, and movie-makers attempted to rebuild a national purpose through their art form. Neorealism, the postwar film movement born in Italy, reflected this new national feeling and assigned children the task of restoring a cohesive national consciousness. Children represented the future; they became a symbol of confidence in the aftermath of the war. The child as witness is a very common trope in neorealist cinema. But children are not used simply as passive spectators, but rather as active participants who have been transformed by traumatic experiences.

Italian directors who made more than one film about childhood defined a realistic aesthetic that mostly eschews sentiment or nostalgia, instead incorporating humanistic and thought-provoking values. The director Vittorio De Sica is among the neorealist directors that best expressed this new style. De Sica's *I bambini ci guardano*, *Sciuscià* and *Ladri di biciclette* each reveal the director's instinctive relationships with child actors.[4] *I bambini ci guardano* is the first of De Sica's movies with a child protagonist. It marks the first collaboration between De Sica and screenwriter Cesare Zavattini, who also worked with De

Sica on *Sciuscià* and *Ladri di biciclette*. Though shot during the fascist period (1942) and still subject to censorship, this proto-neorealist movie borrows from the classic love triangle and attacks the conformity of the Italian petit-bourgeoisie. The movie reveals the latent conflicts in traditional Italian families despite fascist proclamations about the moral solidity of the Italian household. Little Pricò (Luciano De Ambrosis) is the silent witness of the collapse of his family. He quietly watches his mother's encounters with her lover and the consequent pain of his father. At the beginning, he doesn't understand what he sees so he keeps everything to himself. But when he is sent to a boarding school after his mother again abandons him to join her lover, he stares at her in judgment. When she comes to his school to inform him of his father's suicide, Pricò cries. Unable to trust her, he walks away from her, exhibiting great strength in his solitude. Pricò's gaze becomes the spectator's gaze on an inept and dysfunctional society.

With *Sciuscià* and *Ladri di biciclette*, De Sica moves into neorealism. The title *Sciuscià* is a Neapolitan alteration of the English word 'shoeshine'. Plying this trade on the streets after the war, the children hoped to attract customers. The plot of the movie was inspired by two real *sciuscià* De Sica met in Rome, Scimmietta and Capellone, who, after a day of work, spent all their money at a racetrack in Villa Borghese. In the film, the characters Pasquale and Giuseppe were in Rome immediately after World War II, working hard so they could buy a horse. Like all the young orphans and outcasts who surrounded them, they got involved in the black market and other illegal activities organised

A child loses his innocence as he observes his mother's adultery in De Sica's *I bambini ci guardano* (1944)

by family members. Caught selling stolen American blankets to a fortune teller, the boys were sent by authorities to a reform school. There the coldness and indifference of the authorities and family members broke them. In a tragic ending, Giuseppe's death is accidentally caused by Pasquale. Filmed among the ruins of Rome, the movie established what would be considered the main features of De Sica's style. A master of *mise en scène*, as per André Bazin's definition, De Sica used settings from real life and moved actors through actual landscapes, where outcast, postwar youth hung out and real people lived. We see them interacting in a self-sufficient way in the poverty-stricken streets and in the sterile institutional buildings. The film, however, is different from a typical neorealist film, with the white horse as a symbol of innocence, the mannered minor characters, the dense narrative structure and a melodramatic ending. Nevertheless, it lays the path for *Ladri di biciclette*, a masterpiece of cinema about childhood.

Formally, *Ladri di biciclette* distinguishes itself through its narrative style. Unlike traditional cinema, there are no cause-and-effect relationships between events. Casual digressions and *tempi morti* (dead time) are employed to provide a nuanced view of reality. At one point, Bruno stops to urinate against a wall. This process enhances the spectator's perception of chronological time and his identification with the characters. Enzo Staiola, who played little Bruno Ricci in *Ladri di biciclette*, was defined by Bazin as the real 'stroke of genius' that made a simple story – the theft of, and search for, a bike – such a success.[5] Bruno – like Pricò, Giuseppe and Pasquale – is part of that group of children who are victims of adult irresponsibility. However, unlike the other children, Bruno does not succumb to events and circumstances that bring him down but, rather, fights back, embodying hope for a better future. The role reversal of the father–son relationship means that it is Bruno who takes care of his family, both financially and emotionally. Bruno's behaviour is that of a 'little man' who is dealing with a father defeated by the war and its subsequent poverty. In the first dialogue between father and son, the reversed roles are already established. It is early in the morning, the first day of work for Antonio. Bruno is cleaning the bike his father retrieved from the pawn store. When he sees a dent on it, he says: 'They (the people at the pawn office) did it. Who knows how they take care of things over there? Had I been you, I would have told them what they did!'

Bruno cleans the bicycle upon which Antonio's livelihood depends in De Sica's *Ladri di biciclette* (1948)

The implication is that his father had been submissive and did not fight for his rights. Antonio is often portrayed as inept in his search for the stolen bike. However, the final scene achieves an emotional balance between the two. When a desperate Antonio steals a bike, the son understands his father's condition – and desperate act – as an adult would, and the emotional parity between father and son is regained. Bruno sees his father captured and roughed up by the crowd, and he immediately runs towards him crying, until a passing tram pulls between them. There follows a powerful midshot of Bruno alone, walking and crying among the stadium crowd. When he reaches the group of passersby holding his father, the bike owner decides to let Antonio go. As father and son walk next to each other, Bruno, crying, watches him but the father does not return his gaze. Antonio is in a state of shock. Finally, he reciprocates his son's look and starts crying. Bruno gives him his hand and together they dissolve into the crowd. By extending his hand to his father the child is initiated into the adult world, recognising that his father's mistake is transcendent, belonging to all humanity.

Like De Sica, Roberto Rossellini also portrayed children of the war. In his war trilogy: *Roma città aperta*, *Paisà* and *Germania anno zero*, children are vital members of the varied populations during and immediately after the war period. Rossellini began the trilogy with historically defined characters but moved toward characters with metaphysical dimensions, culminating in the figure of Edmund in *Germania anno zero*. Rossellini uses child characters to personalise historical situations. Thus the spectator is not surprised if Romoletto, the young crippled boy of *Roma città*

aperta, participates with his friends in the Italian Resistance, attacking Germans with bombs. Like his friend Marcello, whose mother was killed by Germans, the war forced him to take sides, despite his tender age. Often accused of presenting a pessimistic vision of reality, Rossellini's children are, instead, symbols of a promise for a better tomorrow. The first film of the trilogy concludes with a panning camera following the children after their mentor, the partisan priest, has been executed by the Germans: St Peter's Basilica is visible in the distance, a kind of symbolic destination where compassion might gain a footing in a new and spiritually enriched society.

If in *Roma città aperta*, Rossellini describes a national reality through a local perspective, in *Paisà*, he illustrates how the stories of gradual understanding between Italians and Allied troops assumed a wider meaning. The film is divided into six episodes and follows the Allied invasion (July 1943 through the winter of 1944), from Sicily to the Veneto, showcasing the reception given to the Americans. In the Neapolitan episode of the film, the *scugnizzo* Pasquale (another street urchin) robs Joe (Dots Johnson), a drunken African-American military policeman. Like Pasquale and Giuseppe in *Sciuscià*, Pasquale lives in the ruined streets of Naples. He belongs to the same category of cinematic street kids who, although poor and uneducated, are resourceful and often outsmart their adult counterparts. Pasquale befriends the American soldier Joe and waits for him to become drunk again before stealing his boots. Rossellini skilfully uncovers the common experiences of these two opposing characters. Joe is an African American who drinks to forget that his home in America is an 'old shack with tin cans at the door' and that when he returns, there will be no hero's welcome awaiting him, as he had fantasised. Alcohol and his military position in Italy allow him to live between illusion and reality in contrast to the young Pasquale, an orphan of the war who is guided only by the reality of his abject poverty. In the finale, Joe finds the boy in the street and insists on getting his boots back. Joe then drives Pasquale to his 'home', a cave that he shares with many other victims of the war. In this moment of epiphany, the military man realises that the 'law' he represents is inadequate in the face of the human tragedy he witnesses, and he leaves his boots with the boy. As in the other episodes of the movie, the encounters between different cultures establish a brief human empathy before each individual is left to his loneliness.

Roberto Rossellini's *Germania anno zero* (1948): Edmund's lonely walk through the ruins of Berlin

Germania anno zero, the last film of Rossellini's war trilogy, is his least spontaneous. It came out in 1948, after a long gestation, in conjunction with the unexpected death of Rossellini's son Romano, to whom the film is dedicated. With *Germania anno zero*, the director reflects on the other side of the war, with a poignant vision of a completely destroyed postwar Berlin. For Rossellini, the young protagonist Edmund is the victim of 'distorted utopic education'. Because he was indoctrinated by a former teacher and by his brother (metonyms of Nazi doctrine), Edmund kills his own ailing father, convinced by the teacher that destroying the weak for the sake of the larger community is the means to survive the postwar misery. Edmund will not be able to understand his actions, and he will subsequently kill himself. In the exposition of this tragic story, Rossellini's eye is utterly unbiased; neither pity nor judgment are communicated. The stylised camerawork – alternating light and shade, with sudden cuts at the beginning and end of shots – tends to create a neutral and non-judgmental view of

Edmund's life. What emerges is Edmund's solitary walk through a spiritual wasteland lacking humanity.

Among those ruins, Rossellini seems to suggest it is now impossible to find meaning in life. Edmund's suicide is sudden and unexpected. He walks alone among the debris of a church, following the path of a filtering sunbeam, when he suddenly launches himself into the void. For Rossellini, Edmund's death is as absurd as the world he lives in.

In the multifaceted panorama of the *cinéma des auteurs*, which characterised the post-neorealist cinema, it is hard to find common denominators in childhood cinema. The social and cultural revolution of the 1960s highlighted the psychological traits and insecurities of young people. But one common theme that emerges in this post-neorealist cinema is the loss of the father figure, or the guidance a child depends on. The Italian-French director Luigi Comencini has often tackled this topic. The director himself confessed that his interest in the father figure was determined by the fact that as a child he did not communicate with his

Comencini underlines the loneliness of his children in *Voltati Eugenio* (1980)

father, who died when Comencini was eighteen. He fathered twelve movies for cinema and television about childhood: *I bambini in città* (*Children in the City*, 1946), *Heidi* (*Heidi*, 1952), *Finestra sul luna park* (*Window on the Amusement Park*, 1956), *Incompreso* (*Unacknowledged*, 1967), *Infanzia, vocazione e prime esperienze di Giacomo Casanova* (*Childhood, Vocation and First Experiences of Giacomo Casanova*, 1969), *I bambini e noi* (*Children and Us*, 1970), *Le avventure di Pinocchio* (*The Adventures of Pinocchio*, 1972), *Voltati Eugenio* (*Eugenio*, 1980), *Cuore* (*Heart*, 1984), *La storia* (*History*, 1986), *Un ragazzo di Calabria* (*A Boy from Calabria*, 1987) and *Marcellino* (*Miracle of Marcellino*, 1991). Comencini's style has its roots in his past as a documentary film-maker and in the so-called *neorealismo rosa*, a less critical strain of neorealism, containing elements of comedy and melodrama designed for a mass audience. In his films, children face adult incomprehension, inadequate mothers and loneliness.[6] Comencini's interest in portraying childhood derives from his belief that childhood is 'the greatest moment of freedom of the individual'. In his films, Comencini dwells on the deep duality of his children. On one hand, they rely on their parents; on the other hand, they are independent from the adults. Thanks to their naivety, the children are liberated from the pre-established structures to which parents and educators want to subject them. Children are often alone in Comencini's movies. In *Finestra sul luna park*, a father has to leave his child when he moves away to work; in *Voltati Eugenio*, a family of inadequate 1968 activists (and egotistical grandparents) are all unprepared and unwilling to raise a child. Thus the

young Eugenio (Francesco Bonelli), for his own sake, escapes from the world of the adults, liberated but alone.

In the tearjerker *Incompreso*, the uptight noble father becomes aware of how his emotional detachment has hindered his children's grieving after their mother's death, but only once the oldest child dies. The young Giacomo Casanova (Claudio De Kunert), in *Infanzia, vocazione e prime esperienze di Giacomo Casanova*, is raised by a mediocre father when he becomes motherless at eight. But his motherless status (and the fact that he was sent to a boarding school at the age of nine) will not prevent him from becoming a success in Venice's highly competitive society. In *La storia*, Useppe's (Andrea Spada) frail existence is linked to the tragic episode of his mother's rape by a German soldier. In *Un ragazzo di Calabria*, Mimì's father is too busy fighting hunger and misery to be aware of his son's emotional and intellectual needs. Nonetheless, Comencini's children are reactive and manage to overcome parental abandonment and miscommunication by pursuing freedom and independence. In Comencini's *bildungsroman*-style movies, the element of the fable is very strong. In *Casanova*, Venice and its citizens inhabit the space between a realistic portrayal of the landscape and the fictional representation of carnival. In *Pinocchio*, Comencini's famous television rendition of Collodi's book, the director personalises and enhances Collodi's depiction of the voyage between fable and reality. Thus the set design flawlessly reproduces the physiological activities of a whale's stomach, and uses costumes to humanise animals (Il Gatto and La Volpe). Fantastic characters, like the Fata Turchina (Gina Lollobrigida) are trivialised. The fable is used to express sarcasm and wit, as illustrated by the dialogue between Eugenio and Baffo, the unsympathetic family friend who kicks Eugenio out of his car when the boy makes fun of him. Baffo is reminiscent of fictional characters such as the jester or those created by Jonathan Swift. Baffo the jokester is the one to tell the truth, encouraging the boy to leave his family, a choice that ultimately will benefit him.

The director Francesca Archibugi can be included among the representatives of the so-called 'New Italian Cinema', movies of the last twenty years, made after the creative and budgetary crisis of the 1980s. 'New Italian Cinema' is a cinema in progress, exploring through themes and style the flux of Italian history. Archibugi's style borrows from neorealism and Italian comedy, and the influence of the politicised 1970s cinema is also apparent in her films. Her interest in children stems from her belief that there is continuity between childhood and adulthood. Grown-ups should be able to reconnect to their younger selves, or be aware that they maintain the imprint of childhood. Children in Archibugi's films are 'young individuals'. So far, she has directed five long features with children as protagonists: *Mignon è partita* (*Mignon Left*, 1988), *Verso sera* (*Towards Evening*, 1990), *Il grande cocomero* (*The Big Pumpkin*, 1993), *Con gli occhi chiusi* (*Closed Eyes*, 1994) and *L'albero delle pere* (*Shooting the Moon*, 1998).

Though she is one of the few female film directors to have shown a strong interest in children, Archibugi's observation of childhood is not gender-based. Rather, she prefers a more neutral and lyrical cinema with a strong literary component. She directs what she defines as 'novels written with light'.[7] Her films narrate private stories of contemporary Italian families in flux, migrating from traditional to modern life. The extended family portrayed in *Mignon è partita* includes the pre-adolescent Giorgio (Leonardo Ruta) who, in voiceover, reads from his diary. He recounts the pains of his unrequited love for his visiting cousin Mignon (Céline Beauvallet), a relationship that was abruptly interrupted when she suddenly returned to Paris.

Verso sera takes place during the political turmoil of the 1970s. The movie portrays generational and gender conflicts between the old Communist Professor Bruschi (Marcello Mastroianni) and his activist daughter-in-law Stella (Sandrine Bonnaire). The conflict is mitigated by Papere (Lara Pranzoni), daughter of Stella, granddaughter of Bruschi. The unexpected departure of Stella and

Papere from Professor Bruschi's home causes him to painfully confront, and try to understand, the violent radicalism of a younger generation. The story is revealed in Bruschi's voiceover, in which he reads a long letter he wrote to Papere promising to help her to understand the social and historical moments that shaped her past, a letter she is meant to read once she turns eighteen.

Family crisis and its psychological consequences on the life of young Pippi (Alessia Fugardi) is the topic of *Il grande cocomero*. It is an adaptation by the psychiatrist and political activist Marco Lombardo Radice from the book *Una concretissima utopia* (*A Very Concrete Utopia*, 1991). The film shows the reciprocal healing process of Pippi, affected by psychosomatic epilepsy, and her psychiatrist Arturo (Sergio Castellitto), a man separated from his wife and struggling with solitude. The title of the movie refers to Charles Shultz's *Peanuts* episode 'The Great Pumpkin' in which Charlie Brown and Linus wait in vain, and with undying hope, every year for the Great Pumpkin to arrive. Schultz's Great Pumpkin is a symbol of Arturo's never-ending hope, finally rewarded by Pippi's healing. When he understands that Pippi's problem is a cry for help in dealing with an uncomfortable situation, he stops administering drugs and starts psychological treatment. The cinematography is purposefully very plain to avoid any distraction from the story. The self-proclaimed 'naturalistic' director dwells on the aseptic but crowded interiors of the psychiatric ward and the equally crowded exteriors of the street. Encouraged by Arturo's new approach, all the young patients try to live a regular life as a way to fight social injustice.

A contemporary of Francesca Archibugi, Gianni Amelio has often been described as a 'neo-neorealist' movie-maker, as he brings us back to the observation of reality in progress with a great focus on the ethical aspects of human relationships. Amelio's first movies about childhood were for television: *La fine del gioco* (*Endgame*, 1970), *Il piccolo Archimede* (*The Young Archimedes*, 1979), *I velieri* (*The Sailing Ships*, 1983). These were followed by the feature films *Il ladro di bambini* (*Stolen Children*, 1992) and *Le chiavi di casa* (*The Keys to the House*, 2004). The investigative movie *Porte aperte* (*Open Doors*, 1991) also features children, but in a less central way. Like Archibugi, Amelio envisions children as 'disguised' adults. The recurring themes of polarity between degenerative and educative knowledge, chaos and order and the disappearance of a guiding figure disclose that the children's solitude is rarely relieved by a human touch.

The initial setting for *Il ladro di bambini* is Milan. The Sicilian siblings, eleven-year-old Rosetta (Valentina Scalici) and nine-year-old Luciano (Giuseppe Ieracitano), live with their destitute mother. She regularly prostitutes Rosetta until she is discovered and arrested. Her children are taken away by the police and assigned to the *carabiniere* Antonio (Enrico Lo Verso), who will escort them south in search of a foster institution. The trip is not easy due to the hostility the children feel towards their guardian and the unfriendly institutions they visit. Nevertheless, during the road trip their relationship grows, and Antonio, a symbol of humanity and grace, tries to give the children a normal, loving experience by temporarily keeping them from an uncertain future. Filmed immediately after the political bribery scandals of 1992, the movie expresses a national sentiment for ethical redemption. Amelio's focus on the two young non-professional actors – and the judgmental gaze they cast upon a corrupted and ice-cold society – cleverly recapitulates the main function of neorealism's children: factual observation of reality. But whereas children in neorealism reflect a universal condition, Rosetta and Luciano expose the dysfunction of Italian society. The threesome's unscheduled stop in Calabria, at Antonio's childhood home, reveals the political and moral corruption of those years. They stay in illegally constructed buildings. Antonio wants to provide the needy kids with the warmth of a real family. In a telling scene, the camera follows Antonio as he moves among the unfinished pillars (made possible by his brother-in-law, a corrupt politician) to reach his grandmother. She is struggling to cultivate her little orchard, being suffocated by a new

highway. Amelio makes a point of contrasting the decorum of Antonio and his grandmother with the vulgarity of younger family members. Antonio's desire to show the children a good home is crushed, yet in the context of this ethical dissolution, Amelio shows the significance of an authentic family, however briefly forged by Antonio.

Amelio's latest movie on childhood, *Le chiavi di casa*, considers the delicate topic of disability and how it affects a family. A young father, Gianni (Kim Russi Stuart), feeling inadequate to the task of caring for his disabled child Paolo (Andrea Rossi), and enraged by the fact that the child's birth caused the death of his wife, leaves the boy in the care of relatives. Years later, after creating a new family, he feels obliged to reconnect with his son. The film is freely inspired by Giuseppe Pontiggia's novel, *Nati due volte* (2000). As in Pontiggia's book, the idea of rebirth is explored by Amelio when he raises the prospect of a second chance for Gianni and Paolo. As in his other movies, human interactions happen in transient places, neutral settings (Berlin in this case) or institutions (hospitals, convents, prisons). The camera dwells on the physical deformity – and gaiety – of Paolo, and on the emotional life of Gianni, with a certain detachment, demonstrating how the needy son will reassure the discouraged father, who feels inadequate.

In his films, Amelio approaches the portrayal of children with a respect for their individuality, keeping the camera at a safe distance and avoiding any interference in their forward progress. His endings are borrowed from Antonioni's cinema, where the protagonists are shot from the back, and we are unable

Antonio tries to cheer Luciano up during their trip toward a foster home in southern Italy in Gianni Amelio's *Il ladro dei bambini* (1992)

to glimpse expressions. Both *Il ladro di bambini* and *Le chiavi di casa* end with a long shot from behind the protagonists. In *Il ladro di bambini*, Luciano and Rosetta sit at dawn on a pavement in Gela, waiting to be taken to a foster institution by Antonio, who is asleep. Rosetta for the first time gets closer to her brother and reassures him, with her hand on his shoulder, that they will let him play soccer at the institution. In *Le chiavi di casa*, we see the father facing away from the camera, sitting on a rock, as he contemplates how difficult it will be to take care of his son. Paolo reaches him, and in a gesture of human solidarity embraces him to give him courage. Amelio keeps us at a distance from the lives of these children, reminding us that we can only observe them and not judge them or interfere. We can infer by their actions that their future belongs only to them; they will determine its course, and that is enough.

NOTES

1. Karen Lury, 'The Child in Cinema and Television', *Screen* vol. 46 no. 3 (Autumn 2005), p. 307.
2. Giovanna De Luca, *Il punto di vista dell'infanzia nel cinema italiano e francese: rivisioni* (Naples: Liguori Editore, 2009), p. 2.
3. Marcia Landy, *Italian Film* (Cambridge: Cambridge University Press, 2000), p. 234.
4. The actor Franco Interlenghi remembers that when De Sica directed him in *Sciuscià*, he worked on the same scene with him for fifteen hours (Stephen Harvey, *Vittorio De Sica* [Rome: Cinecittà International, 1991], p. 28).
5. André Bazin, *What Is Cinema?*, vol. II , trans. Hugh Gray (Berkeley: University of California Press, 1974), p. 50.
6. Robert Benayoun, 'Luigi Comencini', *Positif* no. 156 (February 1971), p. 56.
7. Plinio Perilli, *Mignon è partita* (Pescara: Edizioni Tracce, 1991), p. 32.

FURTHER READING

Alonge, Giaime, *Vittorio De Sica, Ladri di biciclette* (Turin: Lindau, 1997).

Bondanella, Peter, *The Films of Roberto Rossellini* (New York: Cambridge University Press, 1993).

Cattini, Alberto, *Le storie e lo sguardo: il cinema di Gianni Amelio* (Venice: Marsilio, 2000).

Curle, Howard and Stephen Snyder, *Vittorio De Sica: Contemporary Perspectives* (Toronto: University of Toronto Press, 2000).

De Luca, Giovanna, *Il punto di vista dell'infanzia nel cinema italiano e francese: rivisioni* (Naples: Liguori Editore, 2009).

De Luca, Giovanna, 'Il piccolo Archimede e Le chiavi di casa di Gianni Amelio: Autorialità e testo letterario', *Forum Italicum* vol. 42 no.1 (2008), pp. 184–99.

Gili, Jean, *Luigi Comencini* (Paris: Edilig, 1981).

Grazzini, Giovanni, *Dolci pestiferi perversi, i bambini del cinema* (Parma: Pratiche Editrice, 1995).

Hardcastle, Anne, Roberta Morosini and Kendall Tarte (eds), *Coming of Age on Film: Stories of Transformation in World Cinema* (Cambridge: Cambridge Scholars, 2009).

Laviosa, Flavia, 'Francesca Archibugi's Cinema: Minimalism or Micro-history? Italian Cinema: 1980s–2000s', *Studies in European Cinema* no. 4 (2007), pp. 99–109.

Lebeu, Vicky, *Childhood and Cinema* (London: Reaktion Books, 2008).

Lury, Karen, *The Child in Film: Tears, Fears and Fairytales* (New Brunswick, NJ: Rutgers University Press, 2010).

Marcus, Millicent, *After Fellini: National Cinema in the Postmodern Age* (Baltimore, MD: Johns Hopkins University Press, 2002).

Proto, Carola (ed.), *Francesca Archibugi* (Rome: Dino Audino Editore, 1996).

13 Italian Cinema from the Perspective of Female Friendship[1]

Danielle Hipkins

Luciano Emmer's *Le ragazze di Piazza di Spagna* (*Girls of the Spanish Steps* aka *Three Girls from Rome*, 1952) opens as the voice (and implicit gaze) of an avuncular middle-aged male[2] frames the film's narrative of the loves and fortunes of three Roman girls. Further scenes throughout the film underline his fondness for and fascination with the group of seamstresses (one an aspiring model played by Lucia Bosè) who spend their lunch-hours chatting on the Spanish Steps, just outside his window.

Over fifty years later, his voiceover commentary and his ambivalent gaze (paternal, lustful, wistful, probably all three?) is echoed in Federico Moccia's recent popular hit *Scusa ma ti chiamo amore* (*Sorry, If I Love You*, 2008), which features a similar scene towards the beginning of the film in which the central female friendship group, le ONDE (an acronym based on their names, Olly, Niki, Diletta and Erica) do not sit so demurely on the steps of a Roman suburb, but play with the idea of fashion modelling more actively, treating the steps as a catwalk, drinking beer and openly discussing sex.

The intradiegetic male narrator (Giorgio Bassani) chats with the three friends in Luciano Emmer's *Le ragazze di Piazza di Spagna* (1952)

Le ONDE friendship group on another set of Roman steps in Moccia's *Scusa ma ti chiamo amore* (2008)

Their performance of 'girlpower' is firmly situated under the male gaze by another intradiegetic paternalistic male voice, that of the private detective, Tony Costa (Luca Ward), who sits spider-like at the centre of the story's web, a clear stand-in for the author/director Moccia himself. The resonances between these two films encapsulate many of my questions about the role of female friendship in Italian cinema. In a cinema made predominantly by men, but for and about men and women, who is the female friendship on screen for? This theme persists on the margins of the history of Italian cinema, and reconsidering Italian cinema from the perspective of female friendship might open up new ways of thinking about the place of femininity in its history. Feminist film criticism, still relatively underdeveloped in Italian film studies, has tended to focus on the representation of striking individual female characters, most often incarnated by female stars, who are nonetheless inevitably a product of a process of selection and individualisation, in which it is difficult to escape from discourses about the objectification of women. However, if we start to think about the ways in which cinema also places women in relation to one another, new discourses can emerge that unsettle that male gaze, which just as in the films mentioned above, suddenly has to justify itself with a voiceover. When women connect with one another on screen, according to Lucie Arbuthnot and Gail Seneca, 'the possibilities for the female viewer's identification with characters are greatly enhanced. The female characters' connection with each other facilitates the female viewer's connection and identification with them.'[3] It is important for us to re-read a cinema that stands accused of sexism and male domination, often with good reason, and to think about the moments and genres in which female friendship is foregrounded and how, asking when it works against and when for that positive identification.

SERAGLIOS AND PRISON CELLS

One of the most important questions to pursue initially, however, concerns what kinds of female friendship exist on screen. One can distinguish between the group female friendship, such as that outlined in the films above, and the dyadic female friendship. Critical debate still rages about which one of these might be more or less progressive,[4] but without rooting these representations in specific historical and textual contexts that question itself is hardly helpful. Melanie Bell argues that 'British cinema has been rather more hospitable to the female group film' because of a 'tradition of ensemble-playing in British cinema', which she attributes to 'Britain's lack of a star system (relative to Hollywood) and the close relationship between theatre and cinema'.[5] Bell's argument can be extended to the Italian tradition, whose lesser dependency on the star system has lent itself to the ensemble film in which different femininities are simultaneously foregrounded, allowing for different possibilities of identification for female viewers, but it is worth remembering that such representation is still heavily circumscribed by the demands of the patriarchal gaze.

Jacqueline Reich emphasises that, under fascism, there was an attempt to 'appeal directly to the female reader/spectator, the primary consumer of the cinematic and extracinematic discourse during the fascist period',[6] during which time the 'schoolgirl comedy' emerged as a key genre, which she has examined for its subversive foregrounding of proactive femininity in characters such as the tomboy Nicola/Nicoletta (Chiaretta Gelli) in Raffaello Matarazzo's *Il birichino di papà* (*Papa's Little Devil*, 1943).[7] A film from the previous year, Carlo Ludovico Bragaglia's *Violette nei capelli* (*Violets in Their Hair*, 1942), concentrated even more intensely on the potential of female friendship to subvert the status quo: at one point the heroine, Carina (Lilia Silvi), ends up caring for

the child of one of her two close friends, Oliva (Irasema Dilián), a successful ballerina and single mother, so that the latter can pursue her career. Even if the film ends with a dissolution of the friendship between seamstress Carina and the two wealthier sisters who adopted her as one of their own, Carina renouncing her own professional ambitions as an actress in order to marry, for the most part, the film sustains a striking focus on the development of the playful and passionate bonds between the girls. This tendency to permit young girls more leeway in terms of female bonding, because they are not yet women, is one we can return to in the context of the contemporary re-emergence of the female girl-group friendship film.

Another product of this emphasis on female spectatorship under fascism was Alessandro Blasetti's adaptation of proto-feminist Alba de Céspedes's bestselling novel about eight girls in a Roman boarding house of the 1930s, many of them university students, exploring, as its title indicates, the way in which decisions women make in their early twenties fix their destinies irrevocably: *Nessuno torna indietro* (*Responsibility Comes Back*, 1943). The film produces some striking results, involving conversations between the girls which address ambitions beyond the romantic, and plotlines that connote understanding and love between women, such as when wealthy Emanuela (Doris Duranti) does not report Xenia's (Mariella Lotti) theft of her emerald ring, because she understands the desperation of Xenia's impoverished background. Nonetheless, Reich has also drawn attention to the way in which 'many of the more blatantly and even ambiguously subversive elements were eliminated from the film version'.[8] Such shifts included the total elimination of one of the girls, Augusta, a character defined by the director as 'resistant to a translation onto the screen'.[9] On closer examination, Augusta's opening description in the novel makes quite clear why: 'she was the oldest of the girls [...] she looked over thirty – she was tall, but fat, with a mop of curly black hair. She was Sardinian, a remarkable character.'[10] This exclusion tells us much about one purpose of the ensemble film in Italy: to showcase young female beauties, and to create a series of *visually acceptable* stereotypes of femininity, in which only the young and beautiful are considered such. The film starred Doris Duranti, Maria Mercader, Elisa Cegani and Mariella Lotti, among others, and much of the critical material emphasises the notion of the 'seraglio of leading ladies'.[11] This tendency to juxtapose women's stories, as examples of different (stereo)types betrays a curiosity about femininity that grew in the postwar period, reaching its apex in the 1950s, when such ensemble films recurred without necessarily allowing much space for bonds to actually emerge. Giuseppe De Santis's *Roma ore 11* (*Rome 11:00*, 1952), for example, was driven by a Zavattinian curiosity about women's lives and their social status, using a female friendship and its impossibility as a cipher for social injustice in its dramatisation of the real-life collapse of a staircase in Rome in 1951. One of the girls, Luciana (Carla Del Poggio) befriends a girl while in the queue for a job as a typist. When Luciana impatiently pushes ahead, she causes the unrest that eventually leads to the death of the girl she has befriended. The failure of friendship between women is repeatedly used in Italian cinema to address something besides itself, from Antonioni's *Le amiche*, which addresses his recurrent theme of the aridity of all human relations, to Michele Placido's more recent *Le amiche del cuore* (*Close Friends*, 1991), which purports to represent a group female friendship, but features so few scenes between the girls that it acts instead as a vehicle for Placido's bravura performance as an abusive father. All three of these films underline the powerlessness of the female network in the face of patriarchy but, in doing so, run the risk of reinforcing that power structure.

Nonetheless, almost all storylines about groups of women, even in their sometimes desultory attempts to hold the plot together through the pretext of friendship, do throw up more positive instances of the female gaze. In the 1950s, a preoccupation with women involved in the fashion industry, while providing the opportunity to showcase both young beautiful stars, and Italy's booming industry, could appeal to audiences attracted to that glamour and also generate a more positive female gaze upon women.[12] If in Antonioni's *Le amiche*, this is inevitably an opportunity for rivalry, in *Le ragazze di Piazza di Spagna*, a lesser investment in the psychological motivations of the gaze upon Marisa Benvenuti, Lucia Bosè's character, means that her friend can take a moment of genuine delight in Marisa's ticket to success and in her glamour, surely an instance of the positive female connection described by Arbuthnot and Seneca.

This possibility is also evident a decade earlier as Carina and Mirella (Carla Del Poggio) gaze upon Oliva's dancing in *Violette nei capelli*. In the titular scene, after the girls have sworn eternal friendship, they put flowers in their hair, and in a clearing in the woods Carina and Mirella sing, while Oliva dances. Ultimately,

Lucia (Liliana Bonfatti) praises her friend Marisa (Lucia Bosè) for her performance in a fashion show in Emmer's *Le ragazze di Piazza di Spagna* (1952)

the scene is captured on camera by Carina's future husband as he walks through the woods, but the scene of female performance, for female pleasure, framed belatedly by the male gaze, might stand in as synecdoche for many depictions of female friendship groups in Italian cinema.

In particular, such instances tend to coalesce around the figure of the female prostitute, whose depiction dominated the screen in the 1950s during the prolonged debate about the state-approved brothel, leading up to its closure in 1958. Already beyond the pale, and the containing influence of heterosexual coupling, friendship narratives rotating around prostitution and criminality, including less conventional female stars, like Anna Magnani, and Simone Signoret in Antonio Pietrangeli's *Adua e le compagne* (*Adua and Company* aka *Adua and Her Friends*) 1960), enable the exploration of 'fascination, critical proximity, identity in production', dynamics of friendship that Emma Wilson also sees dissected in late 1990s film.[13] In Renato Castellani's *Nella città l'inferno* (*Caged* aka ... *and the Wild Wild Women*, 1959), for example, Anna Magnani plays Egle, a prisoner whose impassioned interaction with her fellow cellmates elicits fascination, and imitation on the part of her friend Lina (Giulietta Masina), but ultimately self-criticism, and through that a renewed sense of solidarity towards other women on Egle's part.

The powerful articulation of female friendship through the criminal margins, which dominates 1950s film-making, speaks of course to its lack of social legitimation, but also to its perceived potential threat. Either way, its visibility and incarnation through such powerful stars as Magnani is significant. The film was based on a novel by a female author,[14] and highlights how important it is to interrogate further the contribution that female-authored literature makes towards the development of a picture of female friendship on screen, even if those novelists and scriptwriters tend to remain out of the spotlight.

POSTWAR SHIFT: FRUSTRATED FRIENDSHIPS?

If cinema under fascism recognised the power of the female friendship to attract female audiences, in the postwar period of reconstruction, an increasing emphasis on a sexualised female beauty, through the emergence of the *maggiorata fisica*, brought the notion of female rivalry to the fore, self-reflexively foregrounding women in competition across a myriad of films.[15] The dyadic bond between women is a trope that lends itself to antagonistic polarisation, particularly given the almost inevitable tendency to contain female friendships within the discourses of heterosexual coupledom, and also towards a need to allocate women in the melodramatic categories of good and bad. The postwar emphasis on beauty contests and auditions, and the rise of the Italian female star, unavoidably reinforced this, and it is no surprise that in a period in which women had been granted the vote, it seemed more necessary to deconstruct the female bond than to promote it, but screening such a scenario in the films of this period inevitably opened up alternative perspectives. We only need to look to that key film of the late 1940s to see this story of a frustrated female friendship in action. De Santis's *Riso amaro*, which purports to be about solidarity among female workers, in fact foregrounds a plot about female rivalry. Catherine O'Rawe points out that, in the light of intense debate about Silvana (Silvana Mangano) and the legitimacy of her body in a neorealist text, the character of Francesca (Doris Dowling) has not garnered much attention, but her strength and the space given her to reform (from abortion and attempted robbery) is impressive.[16] If we ask the ubiquitous question about female friendship on screen (sometimes known as the 'Bechdel test'); whether the women talk about anything other than men, the answer for *Riso amaro* is a resounding 'yes'. On one level, the interaction between Francesca and Silvana does revolve around the appeal of Walter (Vittorio Gassman), the gangster, but on another, they talk about lifestyle choices and politics – the dispute over the

clandestine rice workers, for example. So, there are two representations of women in tension with one another – on one level, women are subservient to men and on another, they attempt to negotiate female solidarity. These two levels are not as separate as we might think and there are moments in the film in which Francesca and Silvana come close to sympathy, understanding and friendship, as even towards the very end, Francesca tries to persuade Silvana to forget the fairytale. Here I would turn towards theories about the representation of women that focus on the female spectator, and how she might be situated in relation to Silvana and Francesca. The couple Francesca/Silvana does in fact occupy more screen time than any of the heterosexual combinations of Francesca/Walter. We might ask whether their differences, 'forms of otherness between women characters which are not merely reducible to sexual difference', allow for the complication of female spectatorship pleasures, extending beyond the desire or identification dichotomy, as Jackie Stacey has suggested?[17] Furthermore, it could be argued that male homosocial triangles, in which men exchange women, structure cinema of this period, but in this film, the opposite configuration emerges: it is the women who exchange men, making space for female desire and a female homosocial economy.

We can of course go for a 'straight' reading of Francesca and Silvana's swapping of places as yet another postwar attempt to divide good girls and bad girls with reference to sexual propriety. The work of Lucy Fischer on the splitting of women in melodrama is useful here, since it enables us to understand how the pairing of women in opposites can be used to express and contain anxiety about female sexuality.[18] However, it could be argued that a southern Mediterranean emphasis on kinship bonds inflects this model differently, particularly in the period of melodrama's great popularity in the late 1940s and early 1950s. In several melodramas of this period, the sisterly bond (ultimately frustrated in Marcello Pagliero's *Desiderio* [*Desire*, 1946] and *Riso amaro*) is allowed to triumph as women repeatedly help one another. Anna Magnani's murder of her sister's pimp in William Dieterle's *Vulcano* (*Volcano*, 1949) is one such example, but such vigorous defence is not merely the prerogative of the unconventional star. In Luigi Comencini's noirish *Persiane chiuse* (*Behind Closed Shutters*, 1951) Sandra (Eleonora Rossi Drago) risks her life and her domestic idyll with architect fiancé (Massimo Girotti) in order to rescue her sister, Lucia (Liliana Gerace), who has disappeared into the netherworld of prostitution. Sandra is successful, and the film ends with the sisters re-entering the family home, in defiance of their father's veto. The impact that such a film might have had on female viewers is referenced playfully in the later *Le ragazze di Piazza di Spagna*, when Lucia secretly follows her beautiful friend Marisa home from a party to make sure the same fate does not befall her (Marisa's gentleman friend turns out to be driving her home because she is drunk).

This parodic reference reminds us that if 1950s melodrama lent itself to the emergence of such bonds, they are also present in comedy from that time. The figure of Franca Valeri in particular, who was often involved in the scripting of her films, enables female solidarity to emerge out of the most unlikely coupling: that of the 'bella' and the 'bruttina' (always played by Valeri). In Dino Risi's *Il segno di Venere* (*The Sign of Venus*, 1953), for example, the interaction between the cousins, Agnese (Sophia Loren) and Cesira (Valeri) brings out a sympathy between women not usually associated with Loren's comic star performance. Although Agnese cannot seem to help stealing away the attention of any man Cesira sets her eyes on, the affection between the cousins is not diminished. As Pauline Small points out, despite the polarisation of the pair, the film suggests that neither of their options, low-paid work or marriage, is particularly glittering.[19] This potential strand of Italian comedy was arguably lost in the new genre of the late 1950s, the *commedia all'italiana*, which, with the exception of the work of Antonio Pietrangeli, emerged powerfully as 'a genre of masculine, homosocial identities and concerns'.[20]

FEMMINE CONTRO FEMMINE?: FEMINISM, POSTFEMINISM AND THE FEMALE FRIENDSHIP FILM

The increasingly masculinist bent of Italian cinema from the 1960s may to some degree be related to the relaxation of censorship with regard to sexually explicit material and nudity. Depictions of women became much more obviously sexualised, and therefore less open to multiple readings. Friendships between women in this context have a tendency to collapse into gratifying scenes of lesbian performance, of which Tinto Brass's cinema presents the most notorious mainstream example. However, if Karen Hollinger identifies in the wake of second-wave feminism the rise of a 'female friendship film' in Hollywood, is it possible to map a similar tendency in Italian cinema?

Certainly, some recourse to the female ensemble film occurs in the cinema of the 1980s, from Mario Monicelli's *Speriamo che sia femmina* (*Let's Hope It's a Girl*, 1986) to Giuseppe Bertolucci's *Segreti, Segreti* (*Secrets Secrets*, 1985), both of which bear obvious traces of the impact of feminism, in showing how women tentatively develop alternative communities to that of the traditional nuclear family. However, it is in this period that the lack of integration of women into the Italian film industry becomes much more evident, particularly in comparison with other nations (France, for example). When films that draw upon the feminist tradition and female writing are made, they tend to disappear due to poor funding and promotion. Anna Negri's *In principio erano le mutande* (*In the Beginning There Was Underwear*, 1999) is one good example. A thoughtful exploration of the boundaries between female friendship and the erotic relationship, the film attempts to reflect upon the lack of space for female friendship within heterosexual bonds and within Italian cinema itself. Towards the end of the film one flatmate goes off travelling after the friends have slept together and rejected the idea of a lesbian relationship. In answering Emma Wilson's question of contemporary film: 'If ignoring the erotic, can female friendship films still pose a challenge to heterosexism and patriarchal configurations of desire?',[21] the film appears to say no. The film directly references its own (canonical) cinema heritage, showing two endings, one in which one of the women is reconciled to life alone, and a second in which she watches the final scene of a family reunion in a Matarazzo family melodrama, while she awaits her 'Prince Charming', a fireman who appears *deus-ex-machina* style at her window. Based on a novel by Rossana Campo, the film seems interested in the idea of female friendship, but defeated by a notion of Italian cinema that appears to reinscribe women within the heart of the family.

The work of Rossana Campo represents a field of popular female-authored literature aimed at women that is growing in Italy, and is increasingly associated with a second flowering of interest in female friendship in the contemporary period that draws upon the tradition of so-called 'chick lit' to give rise to the 'chick flick' or the 'girlfriend flick'. Inevitably associated with the hit HBO TV series *Sex and the City* (1998–2004), representations of the female friendship group in a 'postfeminist' context are controversial. For many critics, while appearing to create a women-only space, this new trope only reinscribes the limits of 'neoliberal' femininity.[22] However, looking at Italian cinema can shed new light on this debate. The simple question might be: would Italian cinema even allow women to make it to the wine bar for a chat about anything? Such instances are rare. The difficulty in narrating adult female friendships is glaringly evident in Fausto Brizzi's recent pair of hit films *Maschi contro femmine* (*Men vs Women*, 2010) and *Femmine contro maschi* (*Women vs Men*, 2011). While the men and women are supposedly aligned in opposing friendship groups, homosocial male bonds emerge much more powerfully in both, as Catherine O'Rawe suggests.[23] More screen time is dedicated to the male friendship groups as they play Risk or form a band together, and create comedy through banter. In contrast, the women are occasionally seen drinking tea and moaning, and perhaps a more telling insight into female interaction is when the older woman, Nicoletta (Carla Signoris), is offered a seat on the bus by well-meaning youngster, Francesca (Sarah Felberbaum), provoking the former to label her youthful benefactor a 'puttanella' on account of her dress. The dependence of Italian comedy on antagonism between women would make *Femmine contro femmine* a better label for the film enterprise. This problem is in part related to the failure to develop space for connections between women within Italy's most popular genre, comedy, in which women are most frequently the butt of the joke.

Other recent generic developments offer more hope. The teen movie, which has seen a boom in the past decade, enables a different set of discourses. Luis Prieto's *Meno male che ci sei* (*Thank Goodness for You*, 2009), for example, imagines a connection between generations of women that can overcome sexual rivalry. Even though the teenage heroine sleeps with the boyfriend of her adoptive mother (Claudia Gerini), the two are reconciled and female rivalry itself is shown to be a fantasy construct rather than an inevitable reality. The teen movie has also seen the re-emergence of the female ensemble film. On the one hand, one might regard the teen movie as a pretext to enable a titillating reconstruction of the taboo around female virginity, as in Federico Moccia's *Amore 14* (*Love at 14*, 2009), or even the possible re-narration of a Lolita-style intergenerational narrative, harking back to the likes of Alberto Lattuada's *I dolci inganni* (*Sweet Deceptions*, 1960), as in *Scusa ma ti chiamo amore*. On the other, the screentime dedicated to female friendship as a space for fun, aiming to draw in teen audiences, contrasts greatly with a set of films depicting group

teenage girl friendships as a source of potential threat. Films ranging from Paolo Virzì's *Caterina va in città* (*Caterina in the Big City*, 2003) to Matteo Rovere's *Un gioco da ragazze* (*Girls' Games*, 2008) reflect and reinforce a moral panic about what happens when girls get together. In this respect these films speak to a particular Italian inflection of the debates within Anglophone culture about the limits of 'postfeminist' representations of young women.[24]

CONCLUSION

The debates that rage in postfeminist criticism about what the newly emergent 'girlfriend flick' might mean are cast in a new light by the tenuous hold that female friendship has in Italian cinema. If the vogue for the female friendship group represents a popular contemporary translation of the 1970s feminist group, albeit with the inevitable dilution of political intent that may entail, what does it mean if we do not see that group on screen? Or rather, what does it mean for Italian audiences, if that group is only seen on screen in Hollywood or other 'foreign' films? What this brief outline of female friendship's history in Italian cinema suggests is that, while it may be framed by discourses of female beauty, heterosexuality and inevitable maternity, as long as female friendship is screened there exists the possibility for it to be open to multiple interpretations. For the present, we might conclude that the best chances for the nuanced representation of female friendship lie in female-authored literature. The choice to adapt Silvia Avallone's bestselling novel of 2010, by Stefano Mordini in *Acciaio* (*Steel*, 2012), might well sound a warning bell about how female-authored literature is selected and adapted, however. Avallone's purple prose descriptions of female sexual development and lesbian-tinged passion are going to be difficult to present visually without falling into heavy-handed voyeurism. Another strand of intermediality that deserves further investigation is the potential for dialogue between cinema and television. The recent film adaptations of *Sex and the City* (2008) and *Sex and the City 2* (2010) made manifest the limitations that the cinematic narrative imposes on female friendship, which television might leave open. Was this why a director like Anna Negri moved from film to television? How have TV series such as *Il bello delle donne* (2001, Canale 5, three seasons) or *Amiche mie* (2008, about four single women living in Milan) depicted female friendship and how might they resonate with film experience? How might viewers read stars, like Margherita Buy, who cross between film and television? This preliminary approach to the theme suggests that female friendship provides a welcome opportunity to refresh a series of received ideas about women's role within Italian cinema.

NOTES

1. I would like to thank colleagues Fiona Handyside, Kate Mitchell and Catherine O'Rawe for their ideas and advice for this essay.
2. This figure (a professor) was played by the novelist Giorgio Bassani, although his voice was dubbed.
3. Lucie Arbuthnot and Gail Seneca, 'Pre-text and Text in Gentlemen Prefer Blondes', in Patricia Erens (ed.), *Issues in Feminist Film Criticism* (Bloomington: Indiana University Press, 1990), pp. 113–25 (p. 115).
4. Karen Hollinger, *In the Company of Women: Contemporary Female Friendship Films* (Minneapolis: University of Minnesota Press, 1998), p. 25.
5. Melanie Bell, '"A Prize Collection of Familiar Feminine Types": The Female Group Film in British Popular Cinema', in M. Bell and M. Williams (eds), *British Women's Cinema* (New York: Routledge, 2009), pp. 94–110.
6. Jacqueline Reich, 'Fear of Filming: Alba di Céspedes and the 1943 Film Adaptation of *Nessuno torna indietro*', in Carole Gallucci and Ellen Nerenberg (eds) *Writing beyond Fascism: Cultural Resistance in the Life and Works of Alba de Céspedes* (Cranbury, NJ: Associated University Presses, 2000), pp. 132–52 (p. 132).
7. Jacqueline Reich, 'Reading, Writing, and Rebellion: Collectivity, Specularity, and Sexuality in the Italian Schoolgirl Comedy, 1934–1943', in Robin Pickering Iazzi (ed.), *Mothers of Invention: Women, Italian Fascism and Culture* (Minneapolis: University of Minneapolis Press, 1995), pp. 220–51.
8. Ibid.
9. 'Refrattario ad una traduzione cinematografica', from Alessandro Blasetti's report on the film to the Ministry of Popular Culture (provided in the booklet accompanying the RHV dvd).
10. 'Era la più anziana delle ragazze [...] dimostrava oltre trent'anni: era alta, ma grassa, i capelli, che aveva neri e ricciuti, erano tagliati a zazzera. Era sarda, un tipo singolare', Alba de Céspedes, *Nessuno torna indietro* (Milan: Mondadori, 1963, originally published 1938), pp. 8–9. Jacqueline Reich also highlights the role that Augusta's ambiguous sexuality played in her excision.
11. 'Serraglio di prime donne'; see interview with Maria Mercader, taken from Tullio Kezich (ed.), *Cinecittà Anni '30, 1930–1943* (Rome: Bulzoni, 1979).
12. In the context of fashion photography, Diane Fuss described this as the 'homospectatorial look' in 'Fashion and the Homospectatorial Look', *Critical Inquiry* vol. 18 no. 4 (Summer 1992).
13. Emma Wilson, 'Identification and Female Friendship in Contemporary French Film', in Alex Hughes and James Williams (eds), *Gender and French Cinema* (Oxford: Berg, 2001), pp. 255–67 (p. 256).
14. Isa Mari, *Roma via delle mantellate* (Rome: Edizioni Corso, 1958). Suso Cecchi D'Amico wrote the screenplay.
15. For a discussion of the *maggiorata fisica*, see Pauline Small's chapter in this volume.
16. Catherine O'Rawe, 'Gender, Genre and Stardom: Fatality in Neorealist Cinema', in Catherine O'Rawe and Helen Hanson (eds), *Femmes Fatales: Images, Histories, Contexts* (London: Palgrave, 2010), pp. 127–44.
17. Jackie Stacey, 'Desperately Seeking Difference', in E. Ann Kaplan (ed.), *Feminism and Film* (Oxford: Oxford University Press, 2000), pp. 450–65 (p. 456).
18. Lucy Fischer, 'Two-faced Women: The Double in Women's Melodrama of the 1940s', *Cinema Journal* vol. XXIII (1983), pp. 24–43.
19. Pauline Small, *Sophia Loren: Moulding the Star* (Bristol: Intellect, 2009), p. 101.
20. Maggie Günsberg, *Italian Cinema: Gender and Genre* (New York: Palgrave Macmillan, 2005), p. 66.
21. Wilson, 'Identification and Female Friendship', p. 257.
22. See Alison Winch, '"We Can Have It All": The Girlfriend Flick', *Feminist Media Studies* vol. 12 no. 1 (2012), pp. 69–82.
23. See Catherine O'Rawe's chapter in this volume.
24. See, in particular, Angela McRobbie, *The Aftermath of Feminism* (London: Sage, 2009).

FURTHER READING

Cardone, Lucia and Sara Fillipelli (eds), *Cinema e scritture femminili. Letterate italiane fra la pagina e lo schermo* (Pavona: Iacobelli Edizioni, 2011).
Deleyto, Celestino, 'Between Friends: Love and Friendship in Contemporary Hollywood Romantic Comedy', *Screen* vol. 44 no. 2 (Summer 2003), pp. 167–82.
Hollinger, Karen, 'From Female Friends to Literary Ladies: The Contemporary Woman's Film', in Steve Neale (ed.), *Genre and Contemporary Hollywood* (London: BFI, 2002), pp. 77–90.

14 The *Maggiorata* or Sweater Girl of the 1950s

Mangano, Lollobrigida, Loren

Pauline Small

The cinema of early postwar Italy was characterised by two main trends. Just as it was marked by an urgency to articulate the social problems of the country through the medium of neorealism, so was there a strong impulse to entertain, and convey the aspirations of the new social order through the medium of popular cinema. The *maggiorata* or 'sweater girl' gave significant momentum to this second, vital strand of postwar production and, given the wide circulation of these star images in both the national and international press, she could fairly be termed the face of 1950s Italian film-making. The label *maggiorata* in fact covers a range of stars whose presence was crucial to a successful run of genre films, mainly comedy and melodrama, in 1950s film-making. The full expression *maggiorata fisica* means 'physically well-endowed', and was coined in Alessandro Blasetti's *Altri Tempi* (*In Olden Times*, 1952), with specific reference to the character Frine, played by Gina Lollobrigida. The term was quickly applied retrospectively to several personalities either already established or just emerging on screen, with career paths that are in truth widely contrasting and divergent in nature. This chapter will identify and give greater understanding to the complexity of meanings referenced in this single, apparently uncomplicated label.

CAREER BEGINNINGS
Although the careers of the *maggiorata* stars are generally aligned with the decade of the 1950s, their origins are identifiable in earlier writings. Before the end of the war, we find evidence of the urge for cultural renewal in the short-lived publication *Star*, which was published weekly from 1944 to 1946. In the opening edition, dated 12 August 1944, the magazine's editor, scriptwriter Ercole Patti, asserted that, 'non è concepibile un'Italia rinnovata senza una sua cinematografia (it is inconceivable that Italy can renew itself without also

renewing its cinema)'. The following year, in the issue of 11 August 1945, the magazine duly inaugurated a competition to find a new lead actress for the film *L'angelo e il diavolo* (*The Angel and the Devil*), to be produced by Ambrosiana Film and directed by Mario Camerini. The list of competition judges – Cesare Zavattini, Vittorio De Sica, Giuseppe Marotta and Antonio Pietrangeli, with Camerini, Patti and producer Angelo Giavilli – is itself remarkable. Despite the constraints exerted by fascism on artistic expression, the regime had clearly not entirely restricted the creativity of certain film-makers. In a country barely liberated from war and occupation, we can see that these leading figures were already actively seeking to reinvigorate their craft.

A find-the-star competition suggests, somewhat erroneously, a dearth of established talent, but the war had severely disrupted production and, by 1945, it is apparent that some 1930s stars would be unable to revive their careers. Career progress can be said to divide largely according to gender, and possibly also age lines: the fortunes of Amedeo Nazzari (born 1907) and De Sica (born 1901) were strongly reasserted in the postwar period, while Clara Calamai (born 1909) was assigned 'older woman' roles, however striking her performance in Luchino Visconti's *Ossessione* proved to be. In 1945, rising star Alida Valli was on the point of leaving Italy for a Hollywood contract, a career route that proved to be of questionable value both for her and other European stars. Only the very exceptional Anna Magnani flourished during and beyond the fascist regime. More generally, the fact that women had been allotted a subordinate position under fascism gives logic to the implicit proposal that new faces in cinema might be instrumental in altering the profile of national female identity. The 'requirements' for the film role proposed by *Star* afford considerable insight into the anticipated nature of a new star: 'La protagonista dovrà naturalmente essere bella, di una

Sophia Loren as Paramount pin-up (1957)

bellezza semplice e viva, non artefatta non "costruita".'
(The female lead we are looking for must of course be
beautiful, but her beauty should be simple and fresh, not
at all artificial or 'manufactured').

All star profiles are manufactured, but the stardom
of the *maggiorata* was marked from the outset by
insistent associations with 'simplicity' and 'naturalness'.
The construction of the *maggiorata* image functioned
in two main ways: through assertions in press and
publicity of her humble, off-screen origins; and through
the foregrounding of an equivalent lack of sophistication
in the on-screen roles that she played. The three key
figures of the group – Silvana Mangano, Gina
Lollobrigida and Sophia Loren – share remarkably
similar, unassuming backgrounds: Loren in the poverty
of Pozzuoli near Naples; Lollobrigida in Subiaco, a small
town in the Rome hinterland; and Mangano from the
working-class area of San Giovanni in central Rome.
Their entries into the film business were also alike. If
the *Star* talent competition gives insight into the
beginnings of the *maggiorata* phenomenon, the key route
for aspiring stars was in fact via local beauty pageants
and the national Miss Italia event that had its origins in
fascist times, but was quickly revived in the postwar
period. The much-cited competition of 1947 won by
Lucia Bosè also included Gina Lollobrigida, Gianna Maria
Canale, Silvana Mangano and Eleonora Rossi Drago. The
degree of familiarity (or lack of familiarity) with which

the reader will now register these names shows that a
beauty-contest prize did not in any way guarantee
screen success and, even if success were then to result,
it arrived in varying degrees for those who participated.
The image of the *maggiorata* is found in pin-up poses,
as this photograph of Sophia Loren (a Hollywood studio
publicity shot from 1957) shows. It is an image that
attempts to locate her in the mould of the classic
Hollywood sweater girls Rosalind Russell, Lana Turner
and Rita Hayworth but, as subsequent illustrations will
show, Italy nurtured stars who specifically did not
display the 'manufactured' looks associated with the
Hollywood industry.

The era of the *maggiorata* has a clear-cut and
relatively short-lived chronology, and only a few of the
celebrity names cited remained prominent beyond the
1950s. In 1949, the Giuseppe De Santis film *Riso amaro*
finally brought to fruition the search for a new face for
Italian female stardom. The success of *Riso amaro*, and
of Mangano in its lead role, set the agenda for the era of
the shapely star. The naturalness of her look, embodied
in the photograph below, is evident in her (apparently)
unadorned hair and make-up, and in the costume of a
mondina (rice picker) labouring in the fields.

This pattern of looks and associations with the rural
and the provincial was not fully reinforced, however,
until Gina Lollobrigida's role as the *bersagliera* (the

Silvana Mangano as a *mondina* in *Riso amaro* (1949)

Gina Lollobrigida, *bersagliera* in *Pane amore e fantasia* (1953)

girlfriend of the *bersagliere* soldier), in Luigi Comencini's *Pane amore e fantasia* (*Bread, Love and Dreams*, 1953). The above photograph of Lollobrigida in this role shows similarly humble dress and naturalness of appearance though here, in contrast to the melodrama of the De Santis film, the tone is decidedly comedic.

Lollobrigida's star trajectory took longer to reach its apex than that of her counterpart. She and Mangano had shared the screen as extras in Mario Costa's *L'Elisir d'amour* (*Elixir of Love*, 1947) but it was Mangano whose profile assumed the first and greater prominence. Lollobrigida instead spent several years in a series of lesser parts (including an abortive attempt at a Hollywood career) before assuming this defining role as the *bersagliera*. In the same way, Sophia Loren's supposed 'breakthrough' role as the *pizzaiola* (the pizza seller) in Vittorio De Sica's *L'oro di Napoli* confirmed her as a key *maggiorata* figure, but prior to this she had been for several years prominently featured in illustrated romance magazines termed *fotoromanzi*, and in opera films such as Clemente Fracassi's *Aida* (*Aida*, 1953).

The role these actors most consistently played was the female lead in romantic comedy. Though a rural or provincial setting was common, there was an equally pronounced emphasis on urban locations. The city of Rome, so strongly favoured in neorealist productions, is also used in several fine comedies, from Luciano

Emmer's *Le ragazze di Piazza di Spagna* early in the decade, to the series that began with Dino Risi's *Poveri ma …* (*Poor but …*, 1956–8), featuring the last of the major *maggiorata* roles played by Marisa Allasio. These comedy productions, using both rural and urban locales, repeatedly focus on the perspective of the female figure, gauging the possibilities, romantic and social, available to her in postwar society. In the films, the ethos of subordinate femininity pertaining to fascist ideology is manifestly replaced by a centralised image that is strongly assertive in nature. The *maggiorata* figure, through the power of her image, threatens to destabilise the reassertion of gender norms that marks the traditional conclusion – the capitulation of the female figure – enacted in standard comedy narratives. Popular cinema productions such as these were the mainstay of film-making in early 1950s Italy and, irrespective of their light-hearted tone, they were marked by assured scripting that charted emerging social trends and the complexities of gender relations. However, the era when the *maggiorata* figure held sway shows little coherence in terms of career or production patterns, and this is in keeping with the broad lines of all European film industries. Above all, it needs to be emphasised that, unlike practices in the era of Classical Hollywood cinema, there was in Italian film-making no such thing as a 'star system' in operation to support leading screen figures. To understand better the context in which the *maggiorata* operated, it is important to consider the wider industrial context that shaped their fortunes.

INDUSTRIAL BEGINNINGS

The citations from *Star* provide good evidence of the climate of opinion in the film industry in the immediate postwar period, but enthusiasm for renewal was tempered by the struggle to ensure regular sources of funding. The inevitable instability of this time made the position of the industry particularly precarious, and the call to give impetus to the country's film-making activities was made manifest by artists in a major demonstration on 20 February 1949 in Rome's Piazza del Popolo. Leading participants Vittorio De Sica, Gino Cervi and Anna Magnani issued what the press termed a 'grido d'allarme' (emergency call) to the government regarding the struggles of the industry that continued to display low production figures.[1] What transpired soon after shows how these difficulties were right at the forefront of political and commercial awareness. 1949 became not only the year of release of *Riso amaro* but also of two major industrial initiatives significant to the era of the *maggiorata*.

In February of that year a co-production agreement between Italy and France became fully operative, and companies quickly seized the opportunity to access a broader European market. Almost simultaneously, the newly elected Christian Democrat government of 1948 had appointed Giulio Andreotti as Minister of Culture and his strategy to stabilise the industry was established by means of the 'Andreotti Law' that entered the statute book in December 1949.

Collaboration between Italy and France benefited the progress both of individual careers and of the Italian film industry in general. Effectively, it enabled production companies to tap into two separate sets of government support. Aldo Bernardini's meticulous year-by-year summary of production histories shows a system labelling producers as either major (*maggioritario*) or minor (*minoritario*) contributors; this was based on the financial and, to a much lesser degree, artistic input to individual productions.[2] The 'French connection' was a particularly important component of Lollobrigida's career. Within a month of the co-production agreement becoming operative, Lux, one of the major producers of the period, proudly proclaimed Duilio Coletti's *Miss Italia* (Miss Italia, 1950) as their first film funded by the deal: Lollobrigida took the lead role, and France was the subsidiary contributor.[3] Thereafter French producers were the majority players in two Lollobrigida films from 1952, Rene Clair's *Les belles de nuit* (Beauties of the Night) and Christian-Jaque's *Fanfan la Tulipe* (Fan-Fan the Tulip aka Fearless Little Soldier). The latter production, a swashbuckling historical romp with feisty women in tight-fitting bodices and lusty, uniformed soldiers, is rightly seen as a forerunner to key elements of the *Bread and Love* franchise. Co-production policy in Italy evolved largely on a trial-and-error basis with due attention to market responses. This was the case with popular comedy, and the fortunes of the *Don Camillo* series were important to the trend. The first film, produced in 1952, was based on the writings of Giovanni Guareschi, and cast French comedian Fernandel in the lead role, with French director Julien Duvivier. It was filmed on location in Italy with Italian lead Gino Cervi and partial funding by producer Angelo Rizzoli. In the first two films, Italy was the minor contributor, but thereafter, Carmine Gallone took over the director's role, with Rizzoli (and Italy) assuming the majority holding. The series enjoyed enormous box-office success in both participating countries,

demonstrating the lucrative commercial potential of comedy in co-production initiatives. Loren's 1950s films with Mastroianni, as well as the third of the *Bread and Love* series, all carried the Franco-Italian co-production label. There were many such co-productions during the period, including, later in the decade, major art-house productions, such as Fellini's *La dolce vita*.

While their films generated significant revenue, the *maggiorata* stars also benefited from other key activities of the European film circuit. The newly inaugurated Cannes Film Festival supported the artistry of Italian film-makers by allocating many individual prizes to the films of Rossellini, De Sica and Fellini, but importantly it also invited a national, multiple-film submission. In the early 1950s, the Italian national industry entered a vibrant combination of art-house and, very notably, popular comedy productions, winning the 'Best National Selection' prize in consecutive years with entries that in 1951 included De Sica's *Miracolo a Milano* and Eduardo De Filippo's *Napoli Millionaria* (Side Street Story) and in 1952 De Sica's *Umberto D.* and Mario Monicelli's *Guardie e ladri* (Cops and Robbers). The momentum of Italian success was maintained in 1953 when the festival screened two Lollobrigida films, emigré Hollywood director Robert Siodmak's *Le grand jeu* (Flesh and the Woman), a co-production with France as the majority contributor; and *La provinciale* (The Wayward Wife), an all-Italian production directed by Mario Soldati. By the following year, Lollobrigida was generating her own headlines: the festival news-sheet of 2 April 1954 announced 'Gina Lollobrigida arrive ce matin à Cannes (Gina Lollobrigida arrives this morning in Cannes)', indicating that she would be available to sign autographs on the Croisette that very day. This resulted in a frenzy of public and press activity, considered for many years one of the high points in festival memories.

Lollobrigida and Loren continued to attend Cannes assiduously throughout the 1950s, always elegantly attired and manifestly courting press attention. Hollywood premieres had long carried such allure, but the fact that the aura of glamour was now displayed so prominently in Europe enhanced the profile of European cinema, its festivals and these particular Italian stars. The *maggiorata* thus also evolved off screen into a kind of ambassador for Italian film on the international stage. In August 1950, Unitalia, a government-funded organisation administered by the producers association ANICA, was established with the aim of developing the international dimension of Italian film-making. It funded delegations for a range of film festivals, including Cannes and Berlin, as well as a series of highly successful Italian film weeks. Unitalia's own promotional journal shows that nine of these events took place in 1951, its first full year of operation; throughout the 1950s, we see the *maggiorata* stars prominently on display at these events that served as an alternative promotional gambit in the circulation of their image, beyond the single medium of the cinema screen.[4]

HOLLYWOOD AND THE *MAGGIORATA*

In the early 1950s, the American film industry, seriously dented at home by cultural shifts away from mass cinema-going and by changes to the structure of the established studio system, urgently courted European audiences. As a result, in addition to the practices of European co-productions the decade was marked also by collaboration between Hollywood and Italy. However, the impact of this on the fortunes of the *maggiorata* is less clear-cut. The Andreotti Law of 1949 required a fixed fee from US companies to pay for dubbing on the films they exported to Italy: revenues were held in a *fondo speciale* and released (*sborsati*) to ambitious blockbuster successes from *Quo Vadis* (1951) to *Ben-Hur* (1959). These productions drew on the skills of those involved in the local industry and boosted it economically, especially at Cinecittà, which was used for interior shooting and post-production work not only in these high-profile international projects but also in national popular and art-house productions. Nowell-Smith argues that films with a contemporary focus such as William Wyler's *Roman Holiday* were instrumental in constructing an image of Europe, and more particularly Italy, as 'a site of fantasy, particularly sexual' for international audiences.[5] The Italian industry certainly drew benefit from the mix of national and international casts that triggered its crowning in *Time* as 'Hollywood on the Tiber' on 16 August 1954, with a cover shot of Lollobrigida. However, despite the strong sexual charge of the *maggiorata* figure, Italy is proposed as a site of sexual fantasy in narratives where the fantasy is in fact predicated on a *non*-Italian female figure experiencing the liberating qualities of the country's allure. *Roman Holiday* and David Lean's British-funded *Summer Madness* (1957) present Audrey Hepburn and Katharine Hepburn as seduced by, respectively, the beauties of Rome and Venice, and the charms of Gregory Peck and Rossano Brazzi. While Lollobrigida's image is used to illustrate *Time*'s edition of 'Hollywood on the Tiber', there is considerable irony when one reflects on the failure of this star's own American

career. Equally, Loren's associations with Hollywood demonstrate a very mixed picture in terms of the benefits accrued to Italy and to her individual career. She starred in a number of high-profile runaway productions while still based in Europe, but Stanley Kramer's *The Pride and the Passion* (1957) and Henry Hathaway's *Legend of the Lost* (1957) were filmed outside Italy, with a predominantly non-Italian cast and crew. At the same time the films featuring her earlier, skilful comic performances were accorded little distribution in the US market that, with its own range of comedy stars, displayed instead a marked preference for importing and awarding European art-house productions.

Like Alida Valli and others before her, Loren transferred to Hollywood on a major Paramount contract in 1957: the move was financially lucrative, but of limited commercial success. It was timed, not coincidentally, to tie in with the hunt on the part of a number of studios to find 'the newest queen of sweaterdom' – a comment on the career of Jayne Mansfield, seen in turn as following the path marked out by 'love goddess' Rita Hayworth and, later, Marilyn Monroe.[6] However, the cultural climate that sanctioned studio practices designed to manufacture a passive female figure for Hollywood stardom was by now being vigorously challenged. By the late 1950s, the career narratives of Hayworth, Monroe and Kim Novak present instead a complex discourse where the stars themselves work to assert agency and a much more pronounced control over the shaping of their own personae. The rigid structures of the Hollywood studio system, although now clearly in decline, throw into sharp relief the fundamentally different nature of Italian stardom. The various production arrangements traced in this chapter present a contrasting picture of producers operating a multiplicity of funding arrangements for both art-house and popular films in varying combinations of Italian-national, co-production and runaway production status. The trajectory of the Italian star is, logically, characterised by an equal degree of flexibility if not fragility in his/her career prospects, thereby discounting entirely the notion that she or he was supported by a structured star system. In this respect the history of Italian cinema undervalues the *maggiorata*'s achievement by consistently focusing primarily on the skills of auteurs and producers. Loren and Lollobrigida merit much greater recognition for the personal and professional skills they exercised to forge successful careers in a film-making context described by Barbara Corsi as 'a random mix of high-minded projects and improvised adventures'.[7]

BEYOND THE *MAGGIORATA*

If the era of the *maggiorata* began with Silvana Mangano in *Riso amaro*, it can be said to conclude in 1957 with Mario Monicelli's *I solti ignoti* (*Big Deal on Madonna Street*), which featured an all-male ensemble cast. Thereafter, a male-orientated discourse, with appropriate casting, becomes a constant in Italian comedy productions. The skills of the scriptwriters then focused on masculine-dominated narratives, whether in the ensemble performance of the Monicelli film, a central pairing such as Vittorio Gassman and Alberto Sordi in Monicelli's *La grande guerra* (*The Great War*, 1959), or the many productions of the only solo comedy stars, Totò and Alberto Sordi. The female stars moved away from comedy performances, and notably, when Loren returned from Hollywood she achieved Oscar and Cannes success in a melodrama, De Sica's *La ciociara* (*Two Women*, 1960). Lollobrigida secured high-budget funding for the ambitious productions *La donna più bella del mondo* (*The Most Beautiful Woman in the World*, 1955) and the later *Venere imperiale* (*Imperial Venus*, 1962) but despite these major box-office successes, in the 1960s, her career went into sharp decline. More generally, comedy film-making in the economic boom focuses increasingly on the instabilities of male identity within this period of rapid cultural change. The meanings of the *maggiorata*, of a fresh image in a revived social agenda, were not sustained and the assertiveness of her on-screen femininity was not matched by an equivalent advancement in women's social position. Paul Ginsborg identifies a quite different agenda for women in 1960s Italy, noting a pronounced emphasis in the press on their being increasingly associated with an 'idealized confinement to the home [that] removed them even more than previously from the political and public life of the nation'.[8]

Nevertheless the image of the *maggiorata* continued to exert an influence, one might say, in informing the personae of its lead players, but with less pronounced emphasis. In the 1960s, as Lollobrigida's career faded, Loren adapted to large-scale Euro-funded productions, and continued to balance successfully the contrasting elements of her humble origins/cinema roles with elegant images of her fashion house and publicity promotions. These tensions and contradictions, undeniably present in the persona of the *maggiorata* figure, are most strongly pronounced in the details of Silvana Mangano's career, where we find a wealth of reliable anecdotal evidence of her personal struggles and disinclination to sustain her original star image.

Furthermore, films such as Camerini's *Il brigante Musolino* (*The Brigand Musolino*, 1950) and *Ulisse* (*Ulysses*, 1954) are regularly cited as featuring her in a starring role, guided by her producer-husband Dino de Laurentiis although close attention to the filmic text shows that these films give centrality to the role and, most interestingly, to the body of the male star, respectively Amedeo Nazzari and Kirk Douglas. Mangano, increasingly reluctant in the *maggiorata* role, explicitly enacts this duality in Alberto Lattuada's *Anna* (*Anna*, 1951), where her role as a nun is occasionally punctuated by sequences showing her former existence as a nightclub singer. The beauty of her body is completely concealed, with only her sculpted facial features prominent below a severe religious head covering; but in a dance sequence performed in close-fitting, sequined attire, she moves briefly and sensually to a Latino rhythm, summoning memories of the transgressive associations of her boogie-woogie dance in *Riso amaro*. The image becomes a memory that is largely discarded, and her subsequent screen appearances are sporadic until she accepts a series of

Silvana Mangano as Tadzio's mother in Visconti's *Morte a Venezia* (1971), transformed from the *maggiorata* role that made her famous

major roles with directors Pasolini and Visconti, some twenty years after her screen debut. The entirely separate associations of her image in these great works are encapsulated in this last photograph, a still from Visconti's *Morte a Venezia* (*Death in Venice*, 1971): the figure is distant in time (the force of the period costume), but the idea of 'distance' is also conveyed in the refined, consciously mannered stance she adopts.

The esoteric quality of her persona is further enhanced by the origins of the productions themselves, from classical tragedy in Pasolini's *Edipo re* (*Oedipus Rex*, 1967) and *Medea* (*Medea*, 1969) to the Thomas Mann novella on which Visconti's film is based. Contrasts between this image and her early image as *mondina* are self-evident. Within the persona of all three stars, the *maggiorata* remains as a memory appraised perhaps as no longer relevant to the contemporary social context and, in the case of Mangano, an image certainly long since resisted and without relevance to the individual performer. This last photograph is evidence of a career direction, chosen freely by Mangano, within which she may be said to enact the antithesis of the major *maggiorata* roles. As the country and the industry moved away from the aspirations of the early postwar period to the economic boom, the *maggiorata*, for a complexity of reasons – industrial, professional and personal – did not find a place in the films and the social agenda that followed the 1950s.

NOTES

1. See the (unidentified) press headlines on display in Fabio Cavalli, 'Attori sulle barricate: gli anni di lotta per la dignità del lavoro'. Available at www.enricomarisalerno.it/eventi_e_mostre_italia60.htm; accessed on 12 June 2011.
2. See the two volumes by Aldo Bernardini: *Il cinema sonoro (1930–1970)* and *Il cinema sonoro (1970–1990)* (Rome: Anica, 1993) for these statistics.
3. See Lux correspondence, dated 18 March 1949, in the *Miss Italia* production file, Archivio Centrale dello Stato.
4. *Unitalia* vol. 2 no. 4 (December 1951), p. 12.
5. Geoffrey Nowell-Smith, *Hollywood and Europe: Economics, Culture, National Identity 1945–1995* (London: BFI, 1998), p. 138.
6. Matthew Solomon, 'Reflexivity and Metaperformance: Marilyn Monroe, Jayne Mansfield and Kim Novak', in R. Barton Palmer (ed.), *Movie Stars of the 1950s* (New Brunswick, NJ: Rutgers University Press, 2010), pp. 107–19 (p. 110).
7. Barbara Corsi, *Con qualche dollaro in meno: storia economica del cinema italiano* (Rome: Editori Riuniti, 2001), p. 10.
8. Paul Ginsborg, *A History of Contemporary Italy: Society and Politics 1943–1988* (London: Penguin, 1990), p. 244.

FURTHER READING

Crisp, Colin, *The Classic French Cinema, 1930–1960* (Bloomington: Indiana University Press, 1993).

De Laurentiis, Veronica and Anne M. Strick, *Rivoglio la via vita* (Rome: Edizioni e/o, 2006).

Gili, Jean A. and Aldo Tassone (eds), *Parigi-Roma: 50 anni di coproduzioni italo-francesi* (Milan: Edizione Il Castoro, 1999).

Kaufman, Hank and Gene Lerner, *Hollywood sul Tevere* (Milan: Sperling and Kupfer, 1982).

McLean, Adrienne, *Being Rita Hayworth: Labor, Identity and Hollywood Stardom* (New Brunswick, NJ: Rutgers University Press, 2004).

Masi, Stefano and Enrico Lancia, *Goddesses: Over 80 of the Greatest Women in Italian Cinema* (Rome: Gremese, 1997).

Rocca, Federico, *Silvana Mangano* (Palermo: L'Epos, 2006).

Small, Pauline, *Sophia Loren: Moulding the Star* (Bristol and Chicago, IL: Intellect, 2009).

15 Hollywood and Italy

Industries and Fantasies

Robert S. C. Gordon

*A famous woman flies into Rome sometime in the
1950s and is feted by noisy crowds. She makes public
appearances, holds press conferences, hosts parties, and is
pursued by the local and international press. She manages
to escape her entourage and immerse herself in the city of
Rome, on a secret journey of pleasure. But she is not quite
alone: with her is a handsome, renegade member of the
press pack, trailed by a photographer companion. It is not
clear if he is trailing her for pure pleasure or for a possible
scoop. She visits famous sights, dresses up, has something
like a romantic encounter with the journalist; but soon she
returns to her 'real' life of fame and glamour.*

Arrival ceremonies for Hepburn in *Roman Holiday* (1953) and
Anita Ekberg in *La dolce vita* (1960)

This plot summary describes more or less
adequately two of the key films of the 1950s in
which Hollywood and Italy came into complex and
pleasurably symbiotic contact. The first film was
American and mainstream, a hugely successful genre
movie and star vehicle (but one which offered a heavily
Europeanised version of Hollywood genre and the
industry behind it), William Wyler's *Roman Holiday*,
starring Audrey Hepburn and Gregory Peck. The second
film, released six years after Wyler's, was Italian and
'art-house', a high point of what came to be known as
'auteurist' cinema (but one which, like much of this
'high' European cinema, was heavily obsessed with the
glamour of Hollywood), Fellini's *La dolce vita*, especially
its first and most famously iconic segment, featuring
Anita Ekberg and Marcello Mastroianni.

The links between these two remarkable films can
be used as a lens through which to view the dynamic
interactions, hybridisations and cross-fertilisations
between Hollywood and Italian culture in the 1950s and
as a case study in how film – film industries and film
fantasies – of the period engaged with and acted as
a filter for the wider intercultural web of relations
between Hollywood and Rome, and through Rome,
Italy and Europe as well.

INDUSTRIES

The 1950s was a period of especially intense interaction
and collaboration between Europe and Hollywood. After
the end of World War II, the tightly controlled and
vertically integrated Hollywood studio system entered
a phase of tension and crisis which was eventually to
lead to its break-up and reconfiguration in the late
1960s. In particular, a 1948 anti-trust ruling meant that
the studios had to relinquish their monopoly of the
chain of production and distribution. There were also
problems of rising costs, of union pressures, of

intrusions into Hollywood business by Senator McCarthy and the House Un-American Activities Committee (HUAC) and of the threat posed by the new but rapidly growing medium of television. The economic consequences of this were cushioned to a degree by a growing dependence on non-US audiences to bring films into profit, but foreign markets were not without their own problems; in particular, many foreign countries controlled and restrained the export of profits back to the US. One of the more creative solutions to this whole web of problems was to outsource entire blocks of production abroad to create something like self-standing overseas outposts of the studios, where labour and production talent were cheap and less constrained, where profits could be reinvested in more local production and where, in general, the studios could operate with more freedom and flexibility. Paris was one key location for this new, internationalised Hollywood industry, as was London, for obvious reasons of language; but Rome, too, presented distinct advantages and became one of the iconic sites where Hollywood reinvented itself, tapping into a seam of glamour and a new dimension of cosmopolitan celebrity alongside the striking visuals in the 'Eternal City' of empire, church and art. For economic and production reasons also, Rome had much to offer, the Cinecittà studios on the edge of the city, founded by Mussolini in 1937 to modernise the Italian industry as a challenge to dominant US imports, offered a convenient concentration in one place of cheap sets, stages and skilled labour after it returned to high-level production in 1948. Like much of Europe, Italy was still recovering from war, civil war and occupation, still dependent on Marshall Plan funding and more than keen to encourage the investments of this major US industry. Rome soon became associated with productions on a massive scale – scale was one of Hollywood's concerted responses to the small screen of television – in particular, costume dramas and historical epics set in Biblical and/or imperial Rome. So, between 1950, with the appearance of *Quo Vadis* (1951), and 1959, with the extraordinary achievements of *Ben-Hur*, Hollywood rediscovered in Rome its vocation for the grandest of epic film-making and, conversely, Rome rediscovered its own vocation, which had flourished in the days of silent cinema and the early sound period, for the films of empire. It would be another epic of ancient history, Joseph Mankiewicz's *Cleopatra* (1963), which would destroy this happy synthesis of traditions and practical economics, as costs overran, Burton and

Taylor argued, the film bloated and the studio, Twentieth Century-Fox, nearly collapsed around it.

This was the so-called era of 'Hollywood on the Tiber'. It was not only characterised by collaborative, outsourced production, but by an entire subculture that grew up around it. Stars moved to Rome, renting villas on the via Appia; restaurants, bars and clubs sprouted to cater for them and their production crews and entourages. A local print and photo media developed and a culture of gossip, scandal and glamour – previously associated with far-off and exotic America – came to Italy. Stars got married in Rome (Linda Christian and Tyrone Power in 1948); stars had affairs and fell out in Rome (Roberto Rossellini left the iconically Italian Anna Magnani for the coolly northern European Hollywood icon Ingrid Bergman in 1949); and the news press and their readers lapped it all up. At a certain point in the history of this offshoot of the Hollywood system, something of a cheap, convenient and commercially canny second string to the studio-based epics that were driving the success of Roman Hollywood emerged. It made sense to use the stars stationed in Rome and the beauty of the contemporary city on location shoots to produce some romance movies, which would promote the Rome experienced by the modern, particularly American, tourist. Films such as *Three Coins in the Fountain* or José Quintero's *The Roman Spring of Mrs Stone* (1961) told stories of love across the cultural divide between Americans and Italians, against the background of the Trevi Fountain or the Spanish Steps. Other graftings were also underway in these films: *Three Coins in the Fountain* came packaged with a hit song by Italo-American and youth-culture icon Frank Sinatra; for *The Roman Spring of Mrs Stone*, a torrid story by Tennessee Williams made the Mediterranean summer echo the southern American summers of the playwright's signature dramas and screenplays.

The film which launched this other wave of films set in contemporary, 'tourist' Rome was the hugely successful, star-making, romantic genre piece and screwball comedy, *Roman Holiday*. Unlike the later examples, the 'love across the divide' in *Roman Holiday* is not between Italians and Americans; but instead in the fairytale divide between princess and commoner. The Roman elements of *Roman Holiday* seem, at first, entirely confined to background and local colour, and the stars are both products of the Hollywood star system. Crucially, however, this first foray into the streets of present-day Rome plays games, in a highly self-conscious manner, with the very world of media celebrity that 'Hollywood on the Tiber' had brought in its wake. It captures both the streets of Rome and the playground of the famous (and their attendant media) the city had become. In opening up this world for cinema's own representation and playful interrogation, it paved the way for a great deal of later metacinema about celebrity; and, more specifically, for the terrain Fellini would make so characteristically his own with *La dolce vita* (but also with *8½* [*Otto e mezzo*, 1963], *Ginger e Fred* [*Ginger and Fred*, 1986], and *Intervista* [*Interview*, 1987]).

La dolce vita, in turn, recodified Rome for Italian film (and for Italian culture, the Italian imaginary, even the Italian language), in the light of the new Americanised glamour and decadence. Here, Rome was the playground of Hollywood, which brought new prosperity, but also a new strangeness and a moral vacuum in its wake. Coinciding as it did with the most dramatic of economic and sociocultural transformations in modern Italian history, the so-called 'boom' or 'economic miracle' of the late 1950s and the arrival of mass consumerism, Fellini's film – along with two other iconic products of 1959–60: Michelangelo Antonioni's *L'avventura* and Luchino Visconti's *Rocco e i suoi fratelli* – seemed to offer a portrait and a critique of everything that modernity meant for Italy. At least one of the multiple sources of the imagery and narrative world of *La dolce vita* was *Roman Holiday*. For all its exquisite lightness of touch, Wyler's film, and Fellini's riff on it, engaged with a web of contemporary cinematographic and representational issues rooted in the same global origins as those driving Italy's postwar boom.

Beyond the intriguing parallels in plot noted earlier, the industrial or film-historical links between the two films are threefold, working through screenplay, stars and production. First, *La dolce vita* knowingly acknowledges its debt to *Roman Holiday* in an easily missed moment of throwaway dialogue: early in the film Mastroianni's character is mockingly nicknamed by a prostitute, in her heavy Roman accent, '*agregoripec*' (i.e. Gregory Peck). The appropriation of the Hollywood name into the street slang of a Roman prostitute (an archetype of Roman film-making of the time, associated especially with the work of Pier Paolo Pasolini, who scripted some street dialogue for *La dolce vita*) speaks volumes of the hybridisation between the two industries. Second, there is the backstory of Anita Ekberg: in 1958–9, she had been in Rome to make a peplum movie, Guido Brignone's *Nel segno di Roma* (*Sign of the Gladiator/Sheba and the Gladiator*, 1959), and had

very much lived the 'Hollywood on the Tiber' star treatment, including being photographed in the Trevi Fountain in a scene famously restaged in *La dolce vita*. Further, she had starred in a film knowingly echoing Wyler's in its title, Gerd Oswald's *Paris Holiday* (1958), with Bob Hope and others. Ekberg, in other words, was like a B-string, sexualised and fetishised version of the Hollywood star figure embodied by Bergman and Hepburn. Third, there is a hidden but direct link at the level of screenwriting and production, which might directly explain the plot parallels. The treatment of *Roman Holiday* is credited to Ben Hecht and the screenplay to Ian McLellan Hunter and John Dighton. In fact, these were covers for the blacklisted writer Dalton Trumbo, a member of the Hollywood Ten who had gone to jail for refusing to testify to the HUAC, several of whom subsequently found work more easily outside America, but not necessarily outside the American industry. As was common practice, however, local 'script doctors' were also employed: for *Roman Holiday*, two of the most significant screenwriters in the history of Italian cinema – Suso Cecchi d'Amico and Ennio Flaiano – were signed up to add some local flavour to Trumbo's script. Flaiano was already one of Fellini's closest collaborators and, along with Fellini himself, Tullio Pinelli and Bruno Rondi, would be responsible for the screenplay of *La dolce vita*. The point here, however, is not so much to establish lines of plot or production links between *Roman Holiday* and *La dolce vita* – although they certainly exist – but rather to see the two films as symptomatic of the porous interface between Hollywood and Italy in the 1950s, in production terms and also, and by way of this, in patterns of fantasy.

FANTASIES

A series of dynamic fantasies circulate around and between *Roman Holiday* and *La dolce vita*. We can touch on three of the most compelling: fantasies of star bodies, fantasies of celebrity and its teeming subcultures, and fantasies of tourism and its intercultural pleasures and practices.

1   *Star bodies.* Both our films revolve – and were heavily marketed – around the cultural iconography and erotic play of stars, especially their female stars. Hepburn and Ekberg share as stars a hybridity of identity and cultural marking, between Europeanness and a real or imagined glamorous Americanness, which powerfully evokes the transnational hybridity we are exploring. Hepburn's

rise to fame followed a classic Hollywood 'star system' path, from unknown to stage success to film star, carefully moulded by both director and studio. *Roman Holiday* was her first major role on screen, following her great stage success on Broadway in Colette's *Gigi* in 1951. Wyler in particular was self-consciously looking to create a new, modern-looking star image with Hepburn in *Roman Holiday*. He explained as much to his script doctors, Flaiano and Cecchi d'Amico, saying he wanted the script stripped so bare that all eyes would be on Hepburn all the time. In reality, Hepburn's background and look, the source of her 'Hollywood' glamour were European: born in Belgium, she had grown up in Holland (including under Nazi occupation), London and Paris before coming to Broadway. Her face, too, her body and sexuality, were also crucial: Wyler moulded her characteristic star look somewhere between the infantile and the androgynous, or the 'gamine', as she was often labelled (Fellini would perform a comparable operation with his wife and muse, Giulietta Masina, in films such as *La strada*).

Ekberg was like a polar opposite to the new model for the female star body represented by Hepburn. In *La dolce vita*, and in its defining image of her wading in the Trevi Fountain at dawn, she is all fetishised, hyperbolic sexuality, almost a caricature of an infantile or adolescent male fantasy of adult sexuality. The bodily star image of Ekberg – only a minor star in the pantheon herself – further connoted two dominant images of female stardom of the 1950s, one Italian, one American. First, there was the postwar tradition of Italian stars known as the *maggiorate fisiche* (like Silvana Mangano, Gina Lollobrigida and Sophia Loren, Ekberg came to acting through beauty contests and was sold largely on her physical attributes); second, there was a line of comparison with an emerging Hollywood star phenomenon of the 1950s, which she and Fellini consciously exploited in *La dolce vita*, that of Marilyn Monroe.

Insofar as Ekberg's character in *La dolce vita* represents the descent upon Rome of Hollywood stardom and American glamour, of modernity and its embodied sexuality, this is conveyed through her use of the English language, her apparent sexual freedom, her distinctly un-Italian blondness and her look *à la* Marilyn Monroe. In the panorama of A-list female stars of the 1950s, the archetypal anti-Hepburn was Monroe; or rather Wyler's moulding of Hepburn was as an anti-Monroe, since the latter had recently become the major box-office draw of the day. In fact, Hepburn's and Monroe's careers had close parallels: 1953 brought them both their first starring roles, Monroe in a cluster of hit films (Henry Hathaway's *Niagara*, Howard Hawks's *Gentlemen Prefer Blondes* and Jean Negulesco's *How to Marry a Millionaire*), Hepburn in *Roman Holiday*. Further, over the course of the 1950s, the two not only competed as icons of modern female stardom; they also competed on the terrain of Hollywood in Europe. Where Hepburn and Ekberg present contrasting icons of feminine stardom as occupying a fantasy of the site of Rome, Hollywood's Rome, so Monroe and Hepburn competed over the site and city of Hollywood's Paris in two Parisian vehicles of the mid-1950s, *Gentlemen Prefer Blondes* and Stanley Donen's *Funny Face* (1957). And the Parisian connection points to a further emblematic figure of the play between Hollywood, Italian and European stardom and sexuality, Brigitte Bardot; another blonde, eroticised, 'natural' (and, therefore, anti-Hollywood) body to emerge in this period, with Roger Vadim's *Et Dieu … créa la femme* (*… And God Created Woman*, 1956). Fellini's games with the body and iconicity of his female star, then, are in elaborate dialogue with practices of stardom and the image of the female body of the 1950s, *Roman Holiday* included, as filtered and twisted through layers of Hollywood, Italian and European star genealogies.

2 *Celebrity*. Stars in cinema have always been created by the symbiotic and cannibalistic culture of celebrity that surrounds them. Both *Roman Holiday* and *La dolce vita* address directly, diegetically, the world of 1950s celebrity. In a period of weakening studio control and management of stars, thousands of miles from Hollywood, a new gossip media was born in Rome, modelled on American magazine culture, but if anything more aggressive (not least in the photographer packs, who found their name in Fellini's character Paparazzo). In both films, the narrative is centrally driven by the interplay of male star/journalist and female star/celebrity. In *Roman Holiday*, the celebrity is a beautiful princess; in *La dolce vita*, a glamorous film star. In other words, between the two films, two historical forms of charisma or mythology of the persona – royalty and stardom – are set against each other and the modern subcultures of fame.

As the mock newsreel at the start of *Roman Holiday* tells us, Hepburn's Princess Ann is on a grand European 'royal tour', taking in London, Paris and Amsterdam, before moving to Rome. In a public speech, she declares her desire to 'modernise' her royal household; but it is her girlish escape from the stultifying rituals of the royal tour that, in a sense, takes the ultimate 'modernising', democratising lunge. In a complete character and physical 'makeover', she becomes for a brief time an everyday, ordinary girl, falling for the decent, everyday guy, thereby transgressing the terms of royalty's core mystique (just as the real British Princess Margaret had done in her 'scandalous' affair with a commoner, which broke in the same year as *Roman Holiday*). Of course, this interplay of the ordinary and the aura of the extraordinary is the same that propels modern, cinematic stardom. Stars are both special and just like us. Like the two bodies of the medieval monarch – at once divinely appointed and humanly frail – the two bodies of the film star exist in the modern imaginary firmament, as both magical and banal, perfect on film, and all too human in the gossip and scandal media. In fact, the two worlds of ancient European royalty and Hollywood beauty, glamour and stardom had literally collided in 1956 – halfway between the releases of our two films – when Prince Rainier of Monaco married Grace Kelly, reversing the modern (and impossible) fantasy of *Roman Holiday*: Kelly went from modern screen star to ancient royal household, where Princess Ann enacted her fantasy of escape from her household to her hack in a garret.

The movement from old royalty to new royalty to Hollywood royalty is also staged in the movement from *Roman Holiday* to *La dolce vita*, from Hepburn to Ekberg, from Ann to 'Anita', and in all the parallels between their two journeys to Rome that we have noted. Fellini's most telling contribution to this cluster of discourse on modern celebrity is to be found first of all in his teeming portrait of the media pack that surrounds Sylvia, Marcello's washed-out, languid character included; but also, as the film progresses (and lengthily digresses) from its opening segment, in the extraordinary, desiccated media circus that sets up camp outside Rome on hearing news of miraculous visions of the Virgin; or, indeed, outside the apartment of Marcello's intellectual acquaintance Steiner (Alain Cuny) who has murdered his family and killed himself. In other

words, Fellini's overarching narrative is stitched together through an acute commentary on the fake religious iconography and the complicity with violence of the modern media and its prime object of attention, the 'star'. At the same time, he is also stitching together elements of a specifically Italian identity in its mid-twentieth-century form – through the structuring roles of the Church and popular religion, and of the 'intellectual' in film and Italian culture – with the Americanised culture that permeates the local one in so many ways, direct and indirect, including through new cultures of celebrity.

3   *Tourism*. A third thread that binds together *Roman Holiday* and *La dolce vita*, and so Hollywood and Italy, lies in the pleasure Ann and Anita take in touring the sights of Rome – the Spanish Steps, the Coliseum, St Peter's, the Trevi Fountain and so on. In other words, as well as stars and royalty, they are also merely tourists in a tourist city.

The Trevi Fountain as tourist site and backdrop in *Roman Holiday* (1953) and *La dolce vita* (1960)

Rome, of course, holds a very particular place in the history of tourism and in the history of visual culture associated with travel and tourism. Classical and Renaissance Rome was an essential stop on the Grand Tour of Italy in the eighteenth and nineteenth centuries by northern Europeans and later by wealthy Americans (chronicled by Henry James, Edith Wharton and others). In the twentieth century, the Grand Tour gave way to forms of middle-class and mass tourism, with all the infrastructure, paraphernalia and rites of record that went with it. In all these phases, tourists visited the city, imbibed its aura as outsiders and recorded it for visual reproduction back home. Hollywood on the Tiber, too, came searching for imperial Rome (*Quo Vadis?* etc.), but also took home images of the frivolous and decayed present-day Italy. Both *Roman Holiday* and *La dolce vita* are acutely conscious of this aspect of Rome's cultural and visual history, showing a new star-aristocracy 'touring' Rome, but also hinting at the newly accessible everyday tourist experience and image of the city.

Traditional tourism brought novel 'ways of seeing' Italy, from the the *vedutismo* of Canaletto to the fantastic neoclassical ruins of Poussin to Piranesi's prisons. And it brought also new technologies of seeing – photography, panoramas, dioramas, picture postcards and the like – which paralleled the invention of film. Tourism, and the visual modes it invented or appropriated for itself as 'paratexts', run strongly through *Roman Holiday* and obliquely *La dolce vita* also. Both films move with ease – just like the modern tourist – between the sites of tourist transit, such as airports and hotel lobbies, and the ancient and ruined city the tourist has come to see. *La dolce vita*'s stunning opening sequence is closely related to this movement: the modern and the ancient or Renaissance city are brought together as a helicopter lifts a sculpture of Christ over the roofs of glamorous apartments with women tanning and flirting and ancient Roman ruins or temples or viaducts towards St Peter's, all as a prelude to Anita's touchdown at the airport and her regal procession into town along the ancient Appian Way.

Further, the city is edited in these films just as it is for the tourist. In *Roman Holiday*, for example, from the opening credits, the film cuts between photogenic historic sites and iconographic stock images of Rome (as the mock documentary at the start edits its way around Europe's royal and tourist capitals). Even the key modern icon of the film – the Vespa scooter – acts as a technological marker of this 'editing', since it is the means with which Hepburn and Peck speed through the city, pleasurably taking it all in. And, in what became a famous but entirely characteristic symbiotic inversion of roles, where Hollywood and the tourist industry fed off each other, *Roman Holiday* also launched its very own historic Roman sight as a tourist destination: the 'Bocca della verità' at the Church of Santa Maria in Cosmedin, where Peck (according to Hollywood lore, improvising the scene) instructs Hepburn of the local legend that the mouth of a fountainhead will bite off your hand if you lie. *Three Coins in the Fountain* repeated a similar trick of convergence – dusting off an old local legend for a Hollywood audience figured as 'future' tourists to Italy – with its title song (a hit for Frank Sinatra) referring to throwing a coin in the Trevi Fountain as an augury to return to Rome. *La dolce vita*, ever arch and knowing, reconfigured (eroticised, made glamorous) the touristic meaning and attraction of the same fountain site and its postcard representations, in Ekberg's grand gesture and Mastroianni's melancholic perspective on it.

Finally, photography is also germane. Journalistic photography is central to both films, as we have seen. In *Roman Holiday*'s romantic ending, there is a hint of an interplay between the public function of photography and the private pleasures of tourist photos: Peck's scoop is held in a reel of photos of Princess Ann's private escapade in Rome. His first plan is to sell the story, but, the romance of the decent man (that the princess has turned him into – he started out as a hack) leads him to relinquish the photos. In the closing scene, Peck encounters the princess for one last time, in the public and highly formal setting of a royal reception. Peck palms the negatives of the photos to the princess, thereby restoring her privacy and her trust in him, and sealing their romance *manqué* as a magical hidden memory. In this gesture, he also transforms the photos from the stuff of a media scoop to private snaps from a holiday romance. Ann is allowed to preserve in this small way, at least, her brief time as an ordinary tourist in Rome and thus as an ordinary person with her private emotions and memories, through the iconic power of a studiedly banal kind of tourist photography.

In the dense, refractory, intertextual interplay between two iconic films, a great deal of insight can be gleaned into the on-screen and off-screen symbiosis in the 1950s between Hollywood and Italy (or, more narrowly, Rome; or, more broadly, Europe). The complexity of the interplay underscores the plural exchanges and cross-fertilisations that characterised the relation of the two industries, places, cultures and film languages, as hard economics channelled them into contact in this particular moment in the history of the global film industry and of US–European geopolitical relations. In the process, issues of a fundamental nature within film language but also within the shifting grounds of cultural discourse – gender roles, the nature of celebrity, modern ways of seeing and moving, through space, leisure and pleasure practices – were tapped into, narrated and represented, and reconfigured in forms of narrative and audiovisual fantasy. *Roman Holiday* meeting *La dolce vita* is never simply a question of American meeting Italian, in a relation of binary difference or derivation. *Roman Holiday* is already imbricated with the discourse of cultural encounter and exchange – with both Hollywood and Italian/European traditions of representations of the city, of female identity and stardom, or Europeanness itself and the tourist encounter with it – while also being a highly polished and successful Hollywood comedy product and star vehicle. *La dolce vita*, in amongst its myriad influences and intertextual nods, looks to the example of *Roman Holiday*, back towards a European's notion of Hollywood, and outwards towards an Italian's self-conscious fantasy of a newly decadent Rome and the play of sexuality within it. The two films, then, represent snapshots from a proliferating web of connection and hybridisation between 1950s Hollywood and Italy.

FURTHER READING

Angelucci, Gianfranco (ed.), *'La dolce vita': un film di Federico Fellini* (Rome: Editalia, 1989).

Bondanella, Peter, *The Eternal City: Roman Images in the Modern World* (Chapel Hill: University of North Carolina Press, 1987).

Bruscolini, Elisabetta, *Rome in Cinema between Fiction and Reality* (Rome: Fondazione Scuola Nazionale di Cinema, 2001).

Di Biagi, Flaminio, *Il cinema a Roma: Guida alla storia e ai luoghi del cinema nella capitale* (Rome: Palombi Editore, 2003).

Gomery, Douglas, 'Transformation of the Hollywood System', in Geoffrey Nowell-Smith (ed.), *World Cinema* (Oxford: Oxford University Press, 1996), pp. 443–51.

Gundle, Stephen, *Death and the Dolce Vita. The Dark Side of Rome in the 1950s* (London: Canongate Books, 2011).

Kaufman, Hank and Gene Lerner, *Hollywood sul Tevere* (Milan: Sperling and Kupfer, 1982).

Krämer, Peter, ' "Faith in Relations between People": Audrey Hepburn, *Roman Holiday* and European Integration', in Diana Holmes and Alison Smith (eds), *100 Years of European Cinema. Entertainment or Ideology?* (Manchester: Manchester University Press, 2000), pp. 195–206.

Nemiz, Andrea, *Vita, dolce vita* (Rome: Network Edizioni, 1983).

Pinkus, Karen, *The Montesi Scandal: The Death of Wilma Montesi and the Birth of the Paparazzi in Fellini's Rome* (Chicago, IL: University of Chicago Press, 2003).

PART FOUR

The Golden Age of Italian Cinema

Introduction

Peter Bondanella

For some ideologically motivated film-makers and critics, neorealism seemed to offer Italian cinema an alternative to Hollywood movie-making. But by the mid-1950s, a cinema of realism became less appealing to Italian audiences than more traditional film genres, such as melodrama or comedy. And Hollywood eventually came to Rome, where Cinecittà and the Eternal City experienced the phenomenon known today as Hollywood on the Tiber. This important conjunction of two national cinemas in a single location led to all sorts of important developments. As Réka Buckley's study of Italian costume design shows, when native or local fashion designers geared up to furnish exquisite costumes for all sorts of films shot in Rome, both domestic and foreign, many famous American actresses helped to promote Italian couture on the screen and in the movie fan magazines. Jon Solomon's survey of pepla or sword-and-sandal films emphasises the profitability and influence of this adventure genre set in the ancient world; it was but the first of a series of genre films to have an impact all over the world, followed immediately by the vogue of the spaghetti Western, whose huge audiences are analysed by Flavia Brizio-Skov. The *giallo* thriller, as well as the spaghetti nightmare horror genre – treated in Mikel J. Koven's essay – also became popular and profitable. Today, such genre films enjoy cult status with film buffs and collectors, with numerous websites, blogs and DVDs rivalling those devoted to more traditional auteur figures; they have received postmodernist homages from Quentin Tarantino, who has emerged in Hollywood as the champion of the Italian genre film.

It is in fact the conjunction of extraordinary art-house movies with creative genre films that makes the period between the mid-1950s and the mid-1970s golden. Federico Fellini, Michelangelo Antonioni, Roberto Rossellini, Luchino Visconti, Pietro Germi, Alberto Lattuada, Lina Wertmüller, Luigi Comencini, Dino Risi, Mario Monicelli, Ettore Scola, Pier Paolo Pasolini, Paolo and Vittorio Taviani, Gillo Pontecorvo, Bernardo Bertolucci, Marco Bellocchio: such a list compiled from two successive generations of directors reflects but does not exhaust the variety and richness of auteurs during the period, individuals consistently recognised with awards at the world's most prestigious film festivals or by the American Academy of Motion Pictures with Oscars in various categories. Yet, to do justice to the diversity of this golden age, we need to juxtapose these renowned names with a list made up predominantly of less familiar faces: Mario Bava, Pietro Francisci, Riccardo Freda, Sergio Leone, Luciano Salce, Mariano Laurenti, Dario Argento, Antonio Margheriti, Giorgio Ferroni, Mario Caiano, Sergio Corbucci, Gianfranco Parolini, Duccio Tessari, Enzo C. Castellari, Enzo Barboni, Lucio Fulci and Aldo Lado. Our second list contains those directors originally considered 'B' or genre film directors, although some of these figures – particularly Bava, Leone and Argento – would be eventually 'promoted' by film buffs and critics to the status of popular film genre auteurs. The golden age also profited from the energetic activities of ambitious and imaginative Italian film producers, men who risked their fortunes and reputations to back the making of so many good and profitable films (as well as many spectacular flops): Carlo Ponti, Dino De Laurentiis, Franco Cristaldi, Riccardo Gualino, Alberto Grimaldi,

Alfredo Bini, Mario Cecchi Gori and Angelo Rizzoli. Jean A. Gili examines the international co-production, primarily with the French but also with Hollywood during this period, one important economic strategy embraced by Italian producers and production companies.

Both art films and genre films made substantial profits, as Christopher Wagstaff's detailed analysis of Italian film production around 1960 underlines quite clearly. Very few films in Italy have had more impact at the box office than Fellini's *La dolce vita*, Antonioni's *Blow-up*, Pasolini's *Il Decameron* or Bertolucci's *Ultimo tango a Parigi* – all films identified with the art-house circuit as opposed to the popular genre film. Still, genre films such as Francisci's *Le fatiche di Ercole* (*Hercules*, 1958), Leone's *Per qualche dollaro in piú* (*For a Few Dollars More*, 1965), Barboni's *… continuavano a chiarmolo Trinità* (*Trinity is STILL My Name*, 1971), Germi's *Divorzio all'italiana* (*Divorce Italian Style*, 1961) and Argento's *L'uccello dalle piume di cristallo* (*The Bird with the Crystal Plumage*, 1970), to name only a few, were box-office smash hits as well. After all, this period represented not only the golden age of the Italian cinema and its directors, its producers, its technicians and its actors but also the high-water mark of the European and American film audience, the period in which cinema was finally taken seriously as an art form, largely because French critics and their European and American followers stressed the key role of the director (defined precisely as a film's auteur or 'author') in the creation of film as an art in its own right, and not just mere entertainment. During this era, the quality of traditional film comedy – the Italian *commedia all'italiana*, analysed here by Rémi Fournier Lanzoni – also reached its aesthetic and ideological apex, casting a cynical and jaundiced eye upon Italian social customs and economic conditions. A surprisingly popular ideological film genre – the Italian political film (discussed by Gaetana Marrone) – attracted a number of outstanding artists who had large followings in Italy and Europe, and the best of such films (for example, Elio Petri's *Indagine su un cittadino al di sopra di ogni sospetto* [*Investigation of a Citizen above Suspicion*, 1970]) managed to combine a clear left-wing message with dramatic and broad appeal to a wide and popular audience not necessarily sympathetic initially to the film's political position or interested in tedious intellectual polemics.

The rich range of Italian cinema during this period, its economic success at a variety of artistic levels and its extremely high critical profile among both audiences and film historians make this period a moment in time that could not have lasted for ever. Every golden age must eventually fade away. But for several decades, Cinecittà managed to challenge the economic and cultural hegemony of Hollywood. The final chapter in this section of the collection by Pierre Sorlin discusses how Italian audiences eventually came to care less about their own national cinema than imports from Hollywood, and how other popular pastimes began to erode interest in the cinema among what were, by European or even American standards, relatively large audiences in the postwar period.

16 Material Dreams

Costume and Couture Italian Style: From Hollywood on the Tiber to the Italian Screen

Réka Buckley

Ava Gardner, Ingrid Bergman, Audrey Hepburn, Gina Lollobrigida, Sophia Loren, Silvana Mangano and countless other stars besides – both Hollywood and home-grown – stare out of the pages of weekly and monthly illustrated magazines like *La Settimana Incom Illustrata, L'Illustrazione Italiana, La Domenica del Corriere, Eva, Epoca, Oggi* and *Annabella*. They are captured in photos being fitted for clothes in Italy's leading ateliers, or shown fully costumed on the set of their latest film. It is the golden age of Italian cinema; when Silvana Mangano titillated many a young male spectator as she stood thigh-deep in water clad in a tight-fitting top and hotpants in *Riso amaro*, and Lucia Bosè aroused attention dressed in her sumptuous white tulle dress, fur stole and diamonds as she ran through the rain-drenched streets of Milan in the final sequence of *Cronaca di un amore*. Gina Lollobrigida, dressed in the carefully constructed rags of the Bersagliera, tempts and taunts the Maresciallo Carotenuto (Vittorio De Sica) in *Pane, amore e fantasia* and its sequel, *Pane, amore e gelosia* (Frisky, 1954) while Sophia Loren, as Antonietta, in *La fortuna di essere donna* (*What a Woman!*, 1955), is sent to Mirella Fontanisi (the director of a fashion atelier) where she learns how to dress in a more sophisticated style. It is the era when fashion models like Elsa Martinelli emerged as leading stars of the Italian screen and when couture and costume became an essential component of star discourse. It is also the infamous era of Hollywood on the Tiber, a time when countless Hollywood productions relocated to Italy in search of authenticity and cheaper labour (among other things). It is the heyday of the epic Hollywood sword-and-sandal movie, like *Quo Vadis* (1951) and *Ben-Hur*, filmed mostly in Cinecittà and around Rome, with vast casts of extras all requiring historically specific costumes. And with Hollywood on the Tiber also came an influx of American stars all in search of a wardrobe (for both on and off screen).

This chapter will offer an overview of some key figures working in Italy, who were involved in the provision of costumes for the screen. In many cases, the supply of costumes in Italian cinema was a collaboration, and it is necessary to see how some leading costume designers, dressmakers, tailors and couturiers pulled together to create both historical and contemporary costumes for films made in Italy. In particular, the work of costume designer Piero Tosi, arguably one of the greatest costume designers of all time (both in Italy and internationally), will be considered. In addition, the role of dressmakers and tailors like SAFAS (Studio artistica fornitura abbligliamento e spettacolo), Sartoria Umberto Tirelli and Annamode will be explored. Finally, it is important to establish how fashion couturiers also contributed to screen costumes and star wardrobes. The couturiers Emilio Schuberth and the Fontana sisters will be discussed in detail, but some attention will also be paid to two other designers, Ferdinanda Gattinoni and Ferdinando Sarmi.[1] The aim is to analyse their contribution to film costume, focusing specifically on Italy's golden age of glamour, the late 1940s to the late 1960s, a time when Italian fashion and style became synonymous, the world over, with elegance, quality and craftsmanship. The handmade garments showed careful attention to detail and were often celebrated for their elaborate and laborious surface decorations and the use of extravagant draping, innovative materials and designs. It was also during this period that some of Italy's most renowned costume designers for the cinema, such as Piero Tosi and Piero Gherardi,[2] established themselves and that their work garnered international recognition. Furthermore, the 1950s and 1960s were important in terms of the shift that took place in discourses on (female) stardom, with a far greater emphasis being placed on star image and fashion in the burgeoning Italian popular press. In the opening sentence of Sarah Street's *Costume and Cinema: Dress Codes in Popular Film*, the author notes that the study of film costume has only recently been considered a legitimate field. Although she was referring here largely to the study of Hollywood cinema and costumes, more than a decade has passed since this comment and still relatively little has been published on film fashion and costume by scholars of Italian cinema. Thus, there is much scope for investigation into the fascinating realms of film costume 'Made in Italy' and the exquisite creation of Italian material dreams. While this chapter focuses primarily upon the sourcing of costumes for films shot in Italy, distinctions will be drawn with Hollywood as this is the area of film costume studies that has, to date, received the greatest amount of scholarship. Comparisons with Hollywood also highlight differences in the provision of costumes for Hollywood spectaculars produced at Cinecittà during the period.

COSTUME DESIGNERS, DRESSMAKERS AND COUTURIERS: DRESSING THE SCREEN IN ITALY

Due to the fact that Italy did not have a studio system as such, there were no resulting vast wardrobe departments like those in Hollywood. MGM and Paramount were especially known for their lavish costumes, and the studios boasted sizeable research departments and libraries dedicated to the history of costume. The studios employed a large and highly skilled workforce consisting of designers, seamstresses, pattern cutters, fitters, embroiderers and drapers, dedicated solely to making on-screen costumes. MGM and Paramount were also known for spending a large percentage of their production budgets on costumes. In *Forever Amber* (1947), for example, the film's star, Linda Darnell, wore a staggering forty-two outfits in the film comprising of eighteen evening gowns, twenty daytime dresses, three negligees and one wedding dress, with each requiring on average ten people to work on it.[3] In Italy, the provision of costume was more reliant on personal connections between designers, directors, fashion ateliers, boutiques, dressmakers and tailors, and leading stars, rather than on an organised structure such as the one in operation in Hollywood. In many instances, designers would visit boutiques and fashion ateliers to borrow garments and accessories for films. Lucia Bosè's furs in *Cronaca di un amore* were lent to *haute couture* designer Ferdinando Sarmi (who was in

charge of the wardrobe) by the Rivelli Company, while her jewellery was loaned to him by the Corsi Company. In Italy, where funding was still quite limited during the reconstruction period, stars opened up their personal wardrobes to the costume designers, allowing them to choose their on-screen outfits from their own clothes. The importance of personal connections in the provision of star wardrobes (both on and off screen) was also clearly evident in the popular cinema of the period. The couturier Sarli (who made his debut in film costume design under the guidance of Sarmi, creating some of Bosè's costumes in *Cronaca di un amore*) has suggested that the relationship stars enjoyed with particular dressmakers was important and that when a film was in production in the 1950s, often the actresses would contact the dressmaker directly, as was the case with Ava Gardner and the Fontana sisters. The actress would explain the scenes from the film to the dressmaker and together, they would choose what she would wear on the set.[4] In addition, though costume design in Italy is celebrated for its attention to detail and – as we will see here – historical accuracy, its creation was also often spontaneous and improvised, an example of which was the white evening dress used in the final sequence of *Cronaca di un amore* which was fashioned from the undergarment of a wedding dress that Sarmi found in an old trunk.[5]

The costume designer has the important task of mediating between the director, art director, cinematographer, actor, fashion, hair and make-up stylists, wardrobe mistress and scriptwriter, among others. Usually brought in at the pre-production stage of a project, they carry out extensive research in order to ensure authenticity and accuracy (especially for historical films), and also consider contemporary tastes. A costume designer needs to structure their designs carefully around the actor's body and the costumes should enable the actor to get into character. Lighting and scenery, as well as the angle of the shots, must also be considered and might entail the creation of several versions of the same costume according to the angle from which it must be photographed. Hair and make-up might also be part of their remit, in order to ensure a cohesive overall styling of the actors. Indeed, the costume designer Piero Tosi is known for undertaking the task of both hair and make-up design in such works as *Fellini Satyricon* (*Fellini Satyricon*, 1969), although in this particular film he remains uncredited. In Francesco Costabile's recent documentary, *Piero Tosi: L'abito e il volto: L'incontro con Piero Tosi* (2009), Tosi voiced his concern about stars using their own make-up artists or hairdressers on a film, stating that this often results in a concentration on maintaining the star image rather than on upholding continuity with the character image and aesthetic accuracy.

Tosi has pointed out how, up until the interwar years in Italy, costume was very much influenced by contemporary trends and the aesthetics of the moment. He suggests that the costume designer Gino Carlo Sensani was, in large part, responsible both for revolutionising the way that actors were dressed on screen and radically altering the craft of the costume designer. Sensani sought to break away from contemporary aesthetics and to adhere to a notion of authenticity when creating costumes (both contemporary and historical). Close attention was paid to the types of fabrics used, the cut of the cloth and the colours with a view to recreating 'real' costumes.[6] Tosi, who was greatly influenced by the work of Sensani, is celebrated for his astounding attention to detail; for the creation of some of the most exquisite period costumes ever devised for the screen, as well as for his ability to conceive and create contemporary apparel. For example, Tosi was famed for the innovative method that he utilised to procure some of the costumes for Anna Magnani in the first film he worked on, *Bellissima*:

I had to walk the street looking for people who most resembled the characters and get their clothes off them. And without washing them or changing them, I had to put them on the actors. [...] In those days the cinema held a great appeal for people, a lot more than today. [...] I only had to say I needed their clothes for a film by Visconti with Anna Magnani and they would suddenly be astonished and they would not believe their dirty clothes would be used by Anna Magnani.[7]

Tosi is also known for employing, where he could, authentic materials or clothes in order to recreate as truthfully as possible the period and the aesthetics of historical costumes. He has commented on the problems related to this, saying that every era has its own physique, which changes on average every ten years.[8] Tosi noted how Claudia Cardinale's small waist meant that she was able to wear an original corset in Visconti's film *Il gattopardo* (*The Leopard*, 1963);[9] the actress, however, in an interview that appeared in Francesco Costabile's documentary on Tosi, revealed that the corset used in the ball scene was so tight (Tosi and Tirelli managed to reduce her waist from 68 to 53–54 centimetres) that it lacerated her waist, causing it to bleed.

In a recent question-and-answer session with Piero Tosi that I attended at the Casa del Cinema, Rome

Piero Tosi's ball gown – worn over the authentic corset – for Claudia Cardinale in *Il gattopardo* (1963)

(13 September 2011) following the screening of *Piero Tosi: l'abito e il volto*, the costumier explained that the most difficult part was obtaining the correct fabrics. This was particularly true during the 1960s, he claimed, when fashion designers like Courrèges (famous for his space-age collections) instigated the trend for using more rigid, manmade materials such as polyester, acrylic, nylon and PVC, which were unsuitable for costumes from earlier eras. Tosi explained how he obtained some of the costumes, materials and accessories for his on-screen creations by scouring flea markets or by improvising – using, for example, the satin crepe from the linings of old fur coats in order to create the softer, draped look of earlier decades. Tosi (like Visconti, the director most closely associated with him), believed in the importance of costumes looking 'lived in' and 'real'. In order to achieve this, Tosi would rub the pockets of coats to give the effect of their having been worn; he would leave fabrics out in the sun for weeks on end so that the sun would bleach them, giving them a used appearance, and he would submerge material in tea to lend it a naturally aged look.

Where original clothes and materials were not available, Tosi undertook extensive research into the clothes and accessories of the era to ensure historical accuracy. Visconti gave Tosi the task of designing the military costumes as well as the apparel of the secondary characters, the peasants and bourgeoisie in his melodrama *Senso*. Marcel Escoffier was responsible for designing the costumes for the female protagonist, Alida Valli. Tosi visited many museums in order to understand the appropriate colours and types of materials required to recreate most effectively the clothes of the era.[10] For the military costumes in *Il gattopardo*, for example, Tosi visited the Museo del Risorgimento in Palermo. Here, he discovered to his surprise that no two trousers, cravats or shirts of the *Garibaldini* were exactly the same. He also noted that the red shirts were of different hues and were cut and sewn in a variety of ways which, Tosi opined, was due to the fact that they were probably handmade by the soldiers' mothers, wives, sisters or sweethearts. To recreate a similar effect in the film, Tosi enlisted the aide of the Sartoria Tirelli. Ten Tirelli tailors were responsible for handmaking 300 shirts (among other items) in order to ensure that, like the originals, the cut and sewing of the garments would not be identical.[11]

In a close analysis of Tosi's contribution to film between 1951 and 1969, it was observed that he participated in the provision of costumes for thirty-eight films and designed the set for nine films. He also created the hair and make-up for a number of films. Tosi has stipulated that the role of the costume designer is collaborative and involved contact with dressmakers and couturiers. Generally speaking, a middle- to-large-scale production required involvement from four to five fashion houses.[12] As a result, dressmakers, tailors, haute couturiers and boutiques were drawn in to create both period and contemporary clothes for films. The Rome-based theatrical dressmakers, SAFAS, run by the Maggioni sisters (the Baroness Emma Cappabava and Giuditta [Gita] Roux),

Some of the 300 shirts created by the Sartoria Tirelli for *Il gattopardo*

were key suppliers of period stage costumes. Visconti was personally acquainted with the Maggioni sisters since childhood through his mother, and he enlisted their expertise. SAFAS was one of Piero Tosi's most prolific collaborators (alongside the Sartoria Tirelli and Annamode), working on ten of the thirty-eight films he was involved with between 1951 and 1969. According to the tailor Umberto Tirelli, Tosi would take his set drawings and costume sketches to SAFAS for them to carry out the creation of his ideas. The SAFAS dressmakers also provided costumes for a great number of sword-and-sandal Hollywood movies produced in Italy from the late 1940s through to the 1960s, including *Quo Vadis* (1951) and *Spartacus* (1960).

The SAFAS dressmakers alone, however, could not supply all the necessary costumes for films being produced in Italy following the international success of Italian cinema in the wake of neorealism and the influx of Hollywood productions to Italy in the late 1940s to the 1960s. Umberto Tirelli, also employed by SAFAS in the early part of his career and a close collaborator with Tosi while at SAFAS, went on to set up his own concern in Rome in 1964: the Sartoria Tirelli. Inspired by Tosi, as well as the meticulous attention to detail learnt at SAFAS, the artistic vision of Visconti and the teachings of Sensani, Tirelli developed a keen eye for authenticity and for original costumes. Tirelli's interest in authentic costumes led him to start collecting clothes and theatrical costumes; he also received donations from the personal wardrobes of numerous stars, such as Gina Lollobrigida and Ingrid Bergman. Tirelli's collection amounts to some 20,000 pieces, some of which date back to the seventeenth century. The vast stock of original clothes provides an invaluable source of costume for both screen and stage. Most of Silvana Mangano's costumes in Visconti's *Morte a Venezia* come from Tirelli's collection, and some clothes reportedly even originally belonged to members of the House of Savoy.[13] The Sartoria Tirelli has since become one of the most notable providers of costume for film and theatre in the world.

The Sartoria Annamode, like the Sartoria Tirelli, is a leading provider of costumes for both Italian and international film productions. Established by Anna Allegri in 1946 as a fashion atelier, Annamode has gone on to become one of the most significant theatre and cinema dressmakers in Europe. In the postwar years, young aspiring apprentices of Italian cinema – and fellow Tuscans, like Franco Zeffirelli, Piero Tosi and Mauro Bolognini – requested Anna's assistance in lending them ready-to-wear clothes for the films on

which they were working. The link between the Sartoria Annamode and the costume designer Tosi dates back to his first film, *Bellissima*, when he commissioned several outfits from Annamode. SAFAS also frequently called upon the Sartoria Annamode to provide the more contemporary costumes. Luciano Emmer's *Le ragazze di Piazza di Spagna*, for example, commissioned the Sartoria Annamode to supply the contemporary daywear of the film's leading ladies, while the Fontana sisters created the *haute couture* designs in the movie.

The demand for period costumes, however, was considerable in the 1950s. As only a limited number of historical costumes were available for hire from repertoire companies, productions were forced to invest in commissioning and buying costumes. Costume designers had a limited range of dressmakers and tailors to whom they could turn to for assistance. Seeing that there was scope for development in this area, the costume designer Maria De Matteis advised her friend Teresa Allegri, Anna's younger sister, to branch out and to specialise in cinema costume (not only contemporary ready-to-wear fashions, but period costumes as well). Annamode contributed costumes for such contemporary films as *Caccia tragica* (*The Tragic Hunt*, 1947 – the company's first venture into film costume), *La donna del fiume* (*The River Girl*, 1955), *Il bell'Antonio* (*Bell'Antonio*, 1960), *La ragazza di Bube* (*Bebo's Girl*, 1963), and period films such as *Casta diva* (*Casta Diva*, 1954), *La grande guerra*, and *The Bible: In the Beginning* (1966), to name but a few. Teresa also decided that, instead of selling the costumes to the production companies, she would loan the clothes to them (although some film companies did insist on purchasing costumes at the request of the stars, once filming had been completed). Such was the case with Sophia Loren, who wished to keep her on-screen wardrobe from *Peccato che sia una canaglia* (*Too Bad She's Bad*, 1954). Annamode has thus built up one of the most extensive collections – as well as become one of the most notable providers – of film costumes internationally today, with an archive of over 100,000 costumes stored in their 2,000 square-metre-costume deposit in Formello, outside Rome.[14]

Italian couturiers also made important contributions to film costume. Of particular significance here are Emilio Schuberth and the Fontana sisters (Zoe, Micol and Giovanna), whose relationship with the stars not only sealed the success of their fashion houses but also brought mass, international

Gina Lollobrigida being fitted for a gown by Schuberth in *Epoca* (9 December 1956)

attention to Italian fashion in the 1950s and 1960s. The flamboyant couturier Schuberth (sometimes spelt Schubert), whose extravagant, handmade designs paid great attention to precision and detail, was particularly admired by the soubrettes and young female stars of Italy's popular cinema, such as Gina Lollobrigida and Sophia Loren. Off screen, these two stars wore Schuberth designs and advertised his clothes in women's magazines and daily newspapers.[15]

Schuberth also provided many of their on-screen costumes. For example, in De Sica and Lastricati's *Anna di Brooklyn* (*Fast and Sexy*, 1958). Lollobrigida's wardrobe was designed by Schuberth, while the film's costume designer was Valerio Colosanti.[16]

Micol Fontana stressed the intrinsic link between Italian fashion and cinema when she suggested that 'Fashion was launched through the cinema and the cinema could not do without our fashion atelier – it was a spontaneous, organic union.'[17] The success of the Fontana sisters is bound up with their collaboration with cinema and more specifically with their links to film stars. Luciano Emmer, for example, chose their atelier as the setting of his film *Le ragazze di Piazza di Spagna* starring Lucia Bosè, and the Fontana sisters provided some of the *haute couture* collections for the film, while the ordinary daywear clothes were created by the dressmakers Annamode. Antonioni also looked

to the Fontana sisters for the wardrobe of Eleonora Rossi Drago in *Le amiche*, the story of a young woman who sets up a fashion atelier in Turin.

While couturiers designed the more extravagant evening wear or star costumes for film, boutiques such as Emilio Pucci would often be called upon by costume designers to produce contemporary daywear costumes. Emilio Pucci's bold colours, beachwear, infamous Capri pants and casual designs became *de rigueur* among the international set that flocked to Italy's exclusive holiday resorts during the height of the *dolce vita* era. The role of boutiques in providing ready-to-wear fashions for the Italian screen became particularly noteworthy in the late 1950s. It was at this time that the fresh, youthful, bright and innovative boutique fashions were becoming a staple of the growing number of light-hearted comedies located in holiday destinations. Films like Gianni Franciolini's *Racconti d'estate* (*Love on the Riviera*, 1958), Vittorio Sala's *Costa azzura* (*Wild Cats on the Beach*, 1959) and Camillo Mastrocinque's *Vacanze d'inverno* (*Winter Holidays*, 1959) emphasised the importance of leisure, sport and comfort, all encompassed in the boutique fashions seen on screen.

HOLLYWOOD ON THE TIBER: FROM SCREEN COSTUMES TO STAR WARDROBES

With the relocation of many Hollywood productions to Italy in the late 1940s through the 1960s and the large-scale production of sword-and-sandal epics, there was a mounting demand for period costumes for the stars and the hordes of extras. Gianfranco Calderoni reveals in an article in the weekly magazine *L'Illustrazione Italiana* (13 August 1950) that 30,000 costumes had been designed for the Hollywood production of *Quo Vadis*, 10,000 of which had been created by Italian tailors and fashion houses.

Calderoni also states that the production team used textile companies from Como to create a special lightweight silk for the costumes, suitable for Technicolor film. He stipulates that great care needed to be taken during filming as the very thin and delicate material was prone to igniting under the hot studio lights.[18] The journalist Art reveals in *La Domenica del Corriere* (29 September 1957) that DeMille's epic *The Ten Commandments* (1956) employed a total of 125 dressmakers to create the 25,000 costumes required in the film, including one worn by Debra Paget made from gold extracted from the filaments of a shell. Mario Zanelli, writing in the illustrated magazine *Gente* (5 March 1958), discusses how the costume designer for

Hollywood on the Tiber: 10,000 of the 30,000 costumes needed for the cast of *Quo Vadis* (1951) were created by Italian dressmakers, tailors and fashion houses

Ben-Hur, Elizabeth Haffenden, together with a small army of collaborators, had just completed the sketches for the 50,000 costumes required for leading actors and the vast cast of extras.

Not only did Hollywood studios (and their costume departments) provide the on-screen apparel for the stars, but the head costume designers (in a bid to maintain a seamless star image) often created their off-screen wardrobes as well. With the influx of Hollywood stars to Rome in the postwar period, stars looked to the various fashion houses for both their on- and off-screen wardrobes. Fashion historian Elda Danese writes that 'the presence of American cinema stars was an extraordinary occasion for the promotion of the designs of Italian ateliers',[19] for there was considerable interest in them from mass media and the general public and their fame brought attention to the clothes that they wore and the designers who made them, thus simultaneously publicising Italian fashion. Sofia Gnoli has commented on how, in between takes, the stars would take leave to visit the ateliers of the capital –

many of which were positioned in the vicinity of the Spanish Steps. These ateliers actually became the hub of star life at that time, the place for socialising, intrigue and love affairs. The stars often allowed themselves to be photographed in the fashion ateliers and accompanying articles were published about them in magazines and newspapers.[20] In a sense, as the dressmaker Bruno Piattelli suggested, these stars became ambassadors for Italian fashion in the US.[21]

With Hollywood on the Tiber, the Sorelle Fontana atelier became a key point of reference for the stars of the moment, from Linda Christian (Power) to Audrey Hepburn and Liz Taylor. Perhaps, however, it was their collaboration with Ava Gardner which provided the most valuable publicity, as Gardner became the most significant ambassador of the Fontana sisters' style abroad. Gardner approached them to make her personal wardrobe while filming the *The Barefoot Contessa* (1954) in Italy, but then famously demanded that it be written into her contracts that the Fontana sisters designed and made all her screen costumes as well.

Ava Gardner in *The Barefoot Contessa* (1954) wearing a
Sorelle Fontana creation

The Fontana sisters also made Gardner's costumes
for *The Sun Also Rises* (1957), *On the Beach* (1959) and
The Bible: In the Beginning. Gardner was frequently
photographed in the Fontana atelier by the Italian
popular press, examples of which include articles that
appeared in *Annabella* (7 February 1954) and *Gente*
(16 October 1957).

The relocation of Hollywood productions to Cinecittà
proved fruitful for the couturier Ferdinanda Gattinoni.
After having worked in various ateliers in London, Paris,
Milan and Rome, Gattinoni established her own atelier
in Rome in 1945, building up a successful concern which
employed some 120 staff. Gattinoni's links with the
world of cinema dated back to the very origins of her
atelier as her first client was the star of Visconti's
Ossessione, Clara Calamai. Gattinoni was subsequently
approached by many a star to create not only their
personal wardrobes, but also their on-screen costumes.
Particularly notable is Gattinoni's relationship with
Hollywood star Ingrid Bergman. She designed Bergman's
costumes for *Stromboli*, *Europa '51* and *Viaggio in Italia*.
Gattinoni was also contacted by costume designers to
create the wardrobes of specific characters in large-scale
productions, such as King Vidor's *War and Peace* (1956).

For this historical epic, the costume designer Maria De
Matteis asked a number of dressmakers, tailors and
couturiers to supply the wardrobes of specific leading
actors. The Sartoria Annamode created the costumes for
Annamaria Ferrero, while Ferdinanda Gattinoni made
over twenty costumes for Audrey Hepburn for her role
as Natasha. Not only did Gattinoni make the clothes
for Hepburn's character, but she also provided the
accessories to go with each outfit: hats, gloves, bags and
even underwear. This film was particularly significant
in Gattinoni's career as a contributor to film costume
because she won an Oscar nomination for Hepburn's
costumes. The film costumes also provided the
inspiration for her Autumn–Winter 1955–6 collection,
which was appropriately called the *Natascia* collection.
Gattinoni's designs were also popular with home-grown
stars; in particular, Gattinoni was renowned for being
Anna Magnani's preferred couturier. Not only did the
Italian diva dress in Gattinoni off screen, but she also
chose Gattinoni to provide her on-screen costumes in
Siamo donne (*Of Life and Love*, 1953) where the actress
appeared as herself, thus firmly linking Gattinoni
fashions to Magnani's star image.

In the absence of a well-established studio system
like that of Hollywood, with its in-house costume
departments and vast workforce, in Italy the provision
of costumes was heavily reliant on personal
connections and the cooperation of a variety of
artisans: costume designers, *haute couture* ateliers,
dressmakers, tailors and boutiques. Collaboration was
an essential part of the process in postwar Italy, both in
terms of Italy's national productions and its role in
creating costumes for Hollywood films shot in Italy. It
was also during the *dolce vita* era of film-making in Italy
that the provision of cinema costumes – though still
heavily artisanal in nature – became more of a large-
scale concern. From Hollywood on the Tiber to the
Italian screen, from the costuming of vast crowds of
extras, to the provision of star wardrobes, from period
costumes to contemporary clothes, certain key figures –
costume designer Piero Tosi, dressmakers and tailors
SAFAS, Sartoria Tirelli and Annamode, couturiers Emilio
Schuberth, the Fontana Sisters, Ferdinanda Gattinoni
and Ferdinando Sarmi — contributed to the costuming
of the screen in Italy from the late 1940s to the 1960s,
creating in the process many an exquisite material
dream, Italian style.

NOTES

1. Sarmi is discussed in greater detail in Réka Buckley, 'Dressing the Part: "Made in Italy" Goes to the Movies with Lucia Bosè in *Chronicle of a Love Affair* (1950)', in Louis Bayman and Sergio Rigoletti (eds), *Popular Italian Cinema* (London: Palgrave Macmillan, 2012), pp. 166–7.

2. Limitations of space prohibit a detailed discussion of Gherardi, who won Academy Awards for Best Costume (in black and white) for Fellini's *La dolce vita* and 8½.

3. Edward Maeder, 'The Celluloid Image: Historical Dress in Film', in Edward Maeder (ed.), *Hollywood and History: Costume Design in Film* (Los Angeles, CA: Thames & Hudson, 1987), pp. 9–42 (pp. 11–12).

4. Fausto Sarli is cited in Stefania Giacomini, *Alla scoperta del set: con venti personaggi che il cinema lo fanno* (Rome: RAI, 2004), p. 20.

5. Buckley, 'Dressing the Part', p. 168.

6. Caterina d'Amico de Carvalho and Guido Vergani, *Piero Tosi: Costumi e scenografie* (Milan: Leonardo Arte, 1997), p. 11.

7. Drake Stutesman, 'Hide in Plain Sight: An Interview with Piero Tosi,' *Framework* vol. 47 no. 1 (2006), pp. 107–21 (p. 114).

8. D'Amico de Carvalho and Vergani, *Piero Tosi*, p. 92.

9. Ibid., p. 47.

10. Ibid., p. 14.

11. Ibid., p. 46.

12. Stefano Masi, 'Le due anime', *Fashionset: Annamode: 60 anni di moda femminile sul set* (Annamode 68), pp. 10–16 (p. 12).

13. Sofia Gnoli, 'Il collezionismo di moda di Umberto Tirelli', in Paola Colaiacamo (ed.), *Fatto in Italia: La cultura del made in Italy (1960–2000)* (Rome: Maltemi Editori, 2006).

14. Masi, 'Le due anime', p. 16. Note that Annamode is now known as Annamode '68.

15. See Michele Quiriglio, 'Schubert veste le dive', *Cinema* (16 June 1956), pp. 286–8. See also *Epoca* (9 December 1956), p. 79.

16. Buckley, 'Dressing the Part', p. 165.

17. Fontana's interview is recorded in *La storia siamo noi: Il filo d'oro – 50 anni di moda italiana*, available at http://www.lastoriasiamonoi.rai.it/puntata.aspx?id=242; accessed 9 September 2009. See also Eugenia Paulicelli, 'Framing the Self, Staging Identity: Clothing and Italian Style in the Films of Michelangelo Antonioni (1950–64)', in Eugenia Paulicelli and Hazel Clark (eds), *The Fabric of Culture: Fashion, Identity and Globalisation* (London: Routledge, 2008), pp. 53–72.

18. Gianfranco Calderoni, 'Il Quo Vadis costerà 6 miliardi', *L'Illustrazione Italiana* vol. 77 no. 32 (13 August 1950), pp. 18–19 and 36 (p. 36).

19. Eda Danese, in Leopoldina Fortunati and Eda Danese, *Manuale di sociologia e cultura della moda, Vol. III. Il Made in Italy* (Rome: Meltemi Editori, 2005), p. 79.

20. See Irene Brin, 'Le attrice di Hollywood si vestono a Roma: le sarte del capitale hanno conquistato il cuore di Myrna, di Irene, di Deborah e di Linda', *L'Illustrazione Italiana* vol. 77 no. 26 (2 July 1950), pp. 23–4. Brin highlights the relationship between Linda Power (née Christian) and the Fontana sisters, and this article includes a full-page photograph of the star being fitted for an outfit in the Fontana atelier in Rome.

21. Bruno Piattelli cited in Giacomini, *Alla scoperta del set*, p. 30.

FURTHER READING

Buckley, Réka, 'Elsa Martinelli: Italy's Audrey Hepburn', *Historical Journal of Film, Radio and Television* vol. 26 no. 3 (2008), pp. 327–40.

——, 'Glamour and the Female Film Stars of the 1950s', *Historical Journal of Film, Radio and Television* vol. 28 no. 3 (2006), pp. 267–89.

Gnoli, Sofia, *Moda e cinema: La magica del abito sul grande schermo* (Citadel Castello: Edimond, 2002).

Kaufman, Hank and Gene Lerner, *Hollywood sul Tevere* (Milan: Sperling & Kupfer Editori, 1982).

Masi, Stefano, *Costumisti e scenografi del cinema italiano*, 2 vols (L'Aquila: La Laterna Magica, 1989–90).

Merlo, Elisabetta, *Moda italiana: Storia di un'industria dall'Ottocento ad oggi* (Venice: Marsilio, 2003).

Paulicelli, Eugenia, *Fashion under Fascism: Beyond the Black Shirt (Dress, Body, Culture)* (London: Berg, 2004).

17 Italian Film Music

M. Thomas Van Order

Although Italian film music presents an abundance of musical genius, including such renowned composers as Mario Nascimbene, Alessandro Cicognini, Giovanni Fusco, Nino Rota, Ennio Morricone and Nicola Piovani, the value of Italian soundtracks surpasses the beauty of the music itself, and any examination of film music must take into account the cinematic functions of sound – the various styles of selecting, mixing and editing music. Cinematic sound conventions – the rules of matching music, dialogue and ambient sound to the visual track – have often been different in Italy than in Hollywood, and this is especially true of the period of film-making that begins in the early 1930s, when the first Italian sound films are recorded, and extends into the 1960s, when Italian films begin to adapt to international conventions based upon direct takes (the simultaneous recording of dialogue and ambient sound with the image). One of the principal reasons for a divergence from Hollywood sound conventions in early Italian *cinema sonoro* is the practice of post-synchronisation in Italy – a technique in which all sound, including dialogue, ambient sound, as well as both diegetic and non-diegetic music, is recorded separately from the visual track and later synched to the moving images in post-production.[1]

Unlike Italian sound conventions based upon post-synchronisation, which begins with the early sound films in the 1930s and remains the dominant convention for the better part of four decades, Hollywood studios quickly coalesce around conventions based upon direct takes, and in the first few years of Hollywood 'talkies' both diegetic and non-diegetic music are recorded on the set simultaneously with dialogue and ambient sound on a single audio track parallel to the film stock. Although this system produces a fairly close synchronisation of sound with action, and therefore is remarkably more realistic than

earlier audiovisual technology – and certainly more realistic than post-synchronisation – the constraints on musical intervention are significant, since both diegetic and non-diegetic music have to be played on the set during filming. Because of the complexity of producing all diegetic and non-diegetic sound on the set, non-diegetic comment music is used sparingly in these early American sound films, in large part because cuts between camera angles require either new musical cues or synchronised cameras shooting simultaneously. The cameras themselves, which produce a considerable amount of noise, have to be wrapped in insulating materials and/or housed in soundproof boxes – limiting camera mobility. These almost motionless cameras cause the early Hollywood talkies to be more visually static than silent movies, and the acceptance of these significant recording limitations demonstrates just how essential audiovisual 'realism' was for early Hollywood sound conventions.

Hollywood overcomes some of these limitations with the advent of multitrack audio, which, beginning in the mid-1930s, allows for sound effects and comment music to be added to the soundtrack in post-production, but the primary focus of sound in Hollywood from the earliest sound films has always been to support the 'realism' of the dialogue track. Hollywood music, and in particular non-diegetic comment music, has almost always functioned as an inconspicuous and even subconscious support of 'realism' as defined by dialogue and ambient sound, and for this reason American sound editors and technicians have generally gone to great efforts to hide comment music behind layers of artifice so that it will be emotionally perceived but not consciously heard.

By separating the recording of sound from the recording of images early on, Italian sound film sets off in a somewhat different aesthetic direction from Hollywood. Because the entire audio track is assembled separately from the film itself, early Italian cinema tends to view the components of sound (dialogue, ambient sounds and music) as all equally artificial (as opposed to Hollywood where the 'realism' of dialogue is supported by the artifice of comment music), and this approach has repercussions not only for the synching of dialogue and ambient sound, but for the functions of musical comment as well.

ITALIAN SOUND FILMS 1933–45

Early Italian sound film does not have the Hollywood fixation with audiovisual verisimilitude, but what the films lose in terms of realism they more than make up for in terms of efficiency and economy, because recording the visual and audio separately is both faster and cheaper. The resulting Italian sound is characterised by a fairly loose synch of dialogue, a limited bag of tricks for ambient sounds, an inability to closely adapt sound to spatial dynamics (how music, voices and ambient sounds change in different settings), and a willingness to allow some confusion between diegetic and non-diegetic musical sources – including an often indistinguishable recording quality of diegetic and non-diegetic sound.

Hewing an aesthetic line closer to the piano accompaniment of the silent film era than the more detailed and rich sound design of contemporary Hollywood cinema, Italian soundtracks from the fascist period have little musical colouring – subtle changes in instrumentation, melody, volume, rhythm and tempo that guide the actions on screen or foreshadow subsequent narrative developments. As Richard Dyer notes,

> often played quietly and without readily grasped melodies, music is used to provide an overall emotional feeling to a sequence: tension, drama, sentiment, tragedy. Sometimes louder music and stronger melodies heighten the emotions of a scene; rather more rarely, music underscores in the Hollywood manner, closely following the movement and minute emotional shifts within a scene.[2]

Unlike the rigid subservience to visual narration that characterises Hollywood soundtracks from the same era, early Italian film music provides a background mood for sequences rather than for scenes within a

sequence, and the score generally does not follow the subtle nuances of narrative development – with the exception of particularly intense moments (first kiss, death, etc.), in which cases, the comment music is often overly obvious and manifestly manipulative. Viewers today are more likely to consciously perceive music in these early Italian films because, unlike the subtle Hollywood film music of the same period, the background music seems at times unrelated to the action on screen (and indeed is sometimes used to fill a perceived acoustic void rather than add emotional depth), and the music that underscores emotions is often so emphatic that it distracts the viewer from the visual narration. For example, when a man unexpectedly arrives at his lover's family home in Vittorio De Sica's *I bambini ci guardano*, Renzo Rossellini's score is so sinister and menacing that viewers are denied a reading of the encounter as anything other than an evil threat (to give an idea of the level of threat the music evokes, the same cue in *Roma città aperta* expresses the danger represented by Nazi troops surrounding a tenement house shortly before arresting the partisan Francesco). In another Rossellini score, for his brother Roberto's *Un pilota ritorna*, the soundtrack erupts with sudden melodramatic insistence in the middle of a sequence in which an Italian bomber pilot is killed by anti-aircraft fire over Greece, while two similar sequences of bombing raids have no comment music at all, even though in one of them a plane is shot down and the protagonist is subsequently captured by enemy troops. Rossellini's soundtrack highlights the sorrow of the heroic death of an Italian combatant in one sequence, but in a way that is awkward and intrusive. The lack of comment music in the other two nearly identical sequences diminishes dramatic tension and fails to differentiate, on an emotional level, a routine mission from a bomber being shot down over enemy territory. Since all three of these sequences have roaring airplane engines, the director and sound technicians probably did not feel that music was required to fill an unnatural silence, but the three bombing runs have such different outcomes (successful mission, pilot killed, plane shot down) that some musical comment would help the viewer follow the logic of the story. Music in *Un pilota ritorna*, however, as in much of fascist-era cinema, tends to either mitigate the awkwardness of silence or telegraph moments of emotional intensity with overbearing transparency.

MUSIC IN ITALIAN NEOREALISM

Neorealism revolutionises many aspects of film-making, including on-location shooting with available light, increasingly mobile cameras and the use of non-professional actors, but one thing that neorealist directors do not change is their musical soundtracks, which in the first years after World War II are indistinguishable from film music from the fascist period. This is not only true of the conventions for editing and mixing sound and music, but also of the conventional meanings implicit in different musical genres. In both fascist-era films and in neorealist films, the non-diegetic soundtrack is almost always orchestral concert music – a musical form that is perceived as expressing the necessary seriousness and the requisite cultural authority to guide viewers' emotional responses to action on screen. As Richard Dyer reminds us, there is a certain irony in the fact that neorealist directors chose to score their films with an elitist musical form with which the masses, that were both the subject and the ostensible public for these films, did not identify.[3] Even more striking are the almost identical uses and meanings of most diegetic music in both fascist-era and neorealist films. Italian folk music, in both instances, generally represents authenticity and the natural order of things, while foreign music, in particular American jazz, often indicates moral shortcoming if not perversion, and is often presented in contrast with idealised local songs. In Rossellini's *Roma città aperta*, for example, the exuberant American jazz that the nightclub dancer Marina chooses to play on the radio shortly after her childhood friend, Pina, tragically dies at the hands of Nazi troops, separates Marina, both emotionally and morally, from the sorrow shared by both the audience and Pina's fiancé Francesco, and defines her character in terms of evasion from reality (a definition further supported by the escapist lyrics of popular songs heard earlier in the film in the background of her *varietà* dressing room). The musical antipode of this avalanche of jazz notes is the simple three-note call that the partisan children whistle to recognise each other, music that the film portrays as eminently local and natural, expressing solidarity, sacrifice and a willingness to engage with the historical present.[4]

The negative functions of jazz in fascist cinema are not surprising, since the regime frowned upon foreign music in general and saw jazz as 'primitive' because it was composed and performed primarily by African-Americans, but in *Roma città aperta*, the use of jazz to

Marina (Maria Michi) turns on the radio to a station that plays lively American jazz in Rossellini's *Roma città aperta* (1945)

portray Marina as frivolous and materialistic is problematic since her primary sin is aiding the Nazis in their fight against Italian partisans, while the grieving Francesco and Manfredi are ostensibly allied in their fight against Nazi-fascism together with the advancing American troops. In this case, however, jazz does not represent the uneasy alliance between Italian partisans and the Allies so much as the spirit of capitalism and the value of competition as a means to social advancement, and therefore it is not surprising that neorealist directors continue to use American popular music as an indicator of materialism and greed opposed to the more wholesome Italian folk tradition. This musical opposition becomes more and more untenable in the late 1940s, however, as it becomes clear that Italian audiences like and appreciate jazz, and many commercial films from this period, both American and Italian, use jazz as a positive indicator of both sensuality and economic progress.

The tension between the alluring representations of American popular music in commercial films and their negative associations in neorealism reaches a climax of sorts in Giuseppe De Santis's *Riso amaro*, where a dance that Silvana Mangano performs to a raucous boogie-woogie is filmed with such appreciation for its sensual charge that the music undermines narrative logic. Although the boogie-woogie has clear associations with criminality and materialism throughout the film, and is presented in contrast to the indigenous authenticity of the *mondine*'s call and response songs and folk music associated with the idealised masculinity of the Communist soldier Marco, there is no sense of justice

at the end of the film when Mangano's character dies,
nor is there a sense that the Marxist cultural and
ideological assumptions inherent in the indigenous
music have necessarily carried the day. On the contrary,
the boogie-woogie's seductive energy erodes the appeal
of class solidarity that the staid folk music supports,
casting a moral ambivalence over the film that is out of
character with the intentions of much of neorealist
cinema.

FELLINI AND NINO ROTA IN THE 1950s

> Italian film music only truly escaped from the
> melodramatic shackles of a stagnantly operatic idiom
> – one that had continued to feature diminished
> sevenths and string tremolos – when the eccentric
> talents of director Federico Fellini and composer Nino
> Rota collided headlong in the 1950s.[5]

There is no doubt that Nino Rota's scores for Fellini's
early films represent a high point in Italian film music,
but it is also true that Fellini's style of editing and
mixing music are at least as important as the quality
of Rota's compositions, seeing that Rota had already
composed music for nearly fifty films when he met
Fellini, and that some of Rota's earlier scores are
stylistically similar to his music for Fellini. Fellini's new
style of editing sound is determined not so much by

breaking existing rules, but rather by exaggerating the
quirks and conventions of previous Italian sound films.
Where Italian films in the 1930s and 1940s synch
dialogue loosely, and the 'freedom allotted … for the
synching of voices is already enormous', Fellini 'breaks
all records with his voices that hang on the bodies of
actors only in the loosest and freest sense, in space as
well as in time'.[6] While earlier Italian films generally
limit ambient sound to noises that are logically related
to action on screen, Fellini further limits the quantity
and relative volume of ambient sounds, with the result
that his actors often glide across the screen in a
dreamlike silence, without background noises or even
footsteps. And while Italian film music in the 1930s and
1940s occasionally confuses musical sources, Fellini
consistently blurs distinctions between diegetic and
non-diegetic sound, thereby drawing added attention to
the artifice of the musical comment. As Nino Rota
himself notes, Fellini 'gives more weight to music than
I myself would. In scenes with a musical comment, he
often irritates the sound technicians by eliminating all
natural sounds, all realism.'[7] The resulting Fellini
soundscape is aesthetically and epistemologically
opposed to the Hollywood ideal because the Italian
director's purposeful mismatching of the dialogue
synch and simplification of ambient sound undermine
the audiovisual realism that forms the basis of
Hollywood sound. Examples of this include: actors who

The Fool (Richard Basehart) plays a song on his miniature violin in Fellini's *La strada* (1954)

count off numbers on the set rather than recite lines, use of different actors for voice and screen, and the substitution of one diegetic tune for another in post-production.[8] Fellini further draws attention to the soundtracks of his films by substantially reducing the qualitative differences between diegetic and non-diegetic music – in both cases, Fellini prefers a more popular sound that undermines the traditional divide between diegetic orchestral concert music and non-diegetic popular/folk music. Fellini also mixes music at a much higher volume relative to the dialogue track than conventions would have allowed previously, with the result that the confusion between diegetic and non-diegetic musical sources is even more apparent. While comment music in Hollywood is almost always subordinate to image, and the editing of film music is often judged positively insofar as it is imperceptible, Fellini gives so much emphasis to music in his films that the musical soundtrack, as Sergio Miceli notes, takes on many of the qualities of a character.[9]

ITALIAN FILM MUSIC IN THE 1960s: INNOVATION AND EXPERIMENTATION
Italian film music in the 1960s represents a unique moment of experimentation in the uses of sound that stands in stark contrast to the more conservative soundtracks of the 1930s, 1940s and 1950s. With the exception of Fellini's idiosyncratic soundtracks, the

editing and mixing of Italian film music from the beginning of the sound-film era in the 1930s through neorealism and into the 1950s are relatively conventional, with diegetic music supporting the verisimilitude of the setting and/or expressing regional identity, and non-diegetic music guiding the viewers' emotional reaction to the narration. For a variety of reasons, including the social and economic transformation of the *miracolo economico*, the end of the studio system in Hollywood and a concurrent experimentation with film music in American film, and the example of Fellini's earlier experimentation, many Italian films in the 1960s break with established conventions of sound editing, offering new paradigms of music/image pairing.

An important factor in the sound innovation in the 1960s in Italian cinema is the prominent role of Italian directors in selecting and editing music. Since dubbing dialogue and synching ambient sound usually requires the director's presence, Italian directors in the 1960s often have more control over post-production in general, and over their soundtracks in particular, than their American counterparts (who, in the compartmentalised and specialised Hollywood studio system, control dialogue and ambient sound during direct takes on the set, but often have little control over the editing of sound effects and non-diegetic music during post-production). With in-house composers, musicians, technicians, recording engineers and sound editors, each Hollywood studio produces a distinct sound that is often unrelated to individual directors. Italian directors, in contrast, have far more artistic freedom in defining the soundscapes of their films, and, beginning in the late 1950s, develop idiosyncratic approaches to sound editing that are often unique and immediately recognisable as a style.

Many of the most famous Italian directors active at the time develop or refine a distinctive cinematic sound in the years leading up to the student protests of 1968. Luchino Visconti, who 'conceived of the structure of the music destined for his films as a Romantic symphony articulated in the traditional structure of four contrasting movements', begins to more clearly articulate a melodramatic aesthetic in which visual narration is often determined by musical logic, for example, in many sequences following Rota's soundtrack in *Rocco e i suoi fratelli*.[10] Ennio Morricone's brilliant scores for Sergio Leone's spaghetti Westerns include *Per un pugno di dollari*, *Per qualche dollaro in più*, *Il buono, il brutto, il cattivo* (*The Good, the Bad and the Ugly*, 1966), and *C'era una volta il West* (*Once upon a Time in the West*, 1968), and are characterised by unusual instrumentation, complex relations with the careful pacing and dramatic tension on screen, and melodies with narrative as well as emotive functions. Fellini, whose soundtracks in the 1950s were already often marked by significant ironic distance, begins 8½ with a series of classical zingers that immediately draw attention to the artificial construction of the story unfolding on screen, reflecting the director's belief that there is no unequivocal truth beneath narrative form, but only more layers of narration. Giovanni Fusco's score for Antonioni's *L'eclisse*, with its threatening minor chord progressions and unwillingness to reach harmonic resolution, shares the same soundtrack with popstar Mina's rendition of an exuberantly simplistic *Twist*, and the chasm between these two musical forms reflects the incommunicability between the way capitalist society expresses its appeal through a popular mass culture predicated upon the continual expansion of consumption and production (*Twist*) and the potentially catastrophic consequences of such a society (Fusco's comment music). The experimentation with the soundtrack in these years is not limited to auteur directors. In Dino Risi's *Il sorpasso* (*The Easy Life*, 1962), for example, Riziero Ortolani's complex and brooding jazz score opens the film, while a long series of diegetic popular hits played on an in-dash record

player in the protagonist's car form almost the only music in the film (a novelty at the time).

Pier Paolo Pasolini's *Accattone* represents something of an exception to the rule, in that it returns to neorealist-era sound conventions. In *Accattone*, J. S. Bach's final chorus from *St Matthew Passion*, arranged by Carlo Rustichelli, functions as both an ironic counterpoint to the violent outbursts of the protagonist, and as a support of the mythological iconography depicted throughout the film. The soundtrack emphasises the distinction between the reality of the Roman sub-proletariat, musically represented on screen by numerous popular songs in Roman dialect sung by the characters, and the filmic representation of this reality, non-diegetically supported by the epitome of musical high culture (Bach). The first time Bach is heard on the soundtrack, after the opening credits, the viewer is immediately struck by the artificial nature of the musical montage: the music begins at full volume with no fade-in, and is mixed at a constant volume, with virtually no colouring or matching of musical phrases with the action. The sudden contrast between the elevated musical comment and the base violence on screen abruptly sharpens aesthetic distance and seems clumsy and inappropriate. But through formal repetition (the Bach extract repeats without fades or artificial manipulation of the volume) the chorus slowly accumulates lyrical depth by associating the visual narration to mythological patterns of tragedy in a way that a conventional soundtrack could never accomplish.

CONCLUSION

By the beginning of the 1980s, Italian cinema has almost completely switched over to direct takes (with some notable exceptions, including Fellini) and, with the demise of post-synchronisation, Italian soundtracks quickly become almost indistinguishable from their Hollywood cousins. Although some Italian films in recent years have been recognised for their musical excellence, including Academy Awards for best original score – for example, Nicola Piovani's score for *La vita è bella* (*Life Is Beautiful*, 1997) and Luis Bacalov's score for *Il postino* (*Il Postino: The Postman*, 1995), there is little that distinguishes the editing and mixing of most recent Italian soundtracks from increasingly globalised sound conventions.[11] Although there are many reasons for the recurring sense of crisis in Italian cinema since the 1970s, including limited state funding and enormous budgets for even modest films, it is interesting to note that the more that Italian cinema becomes technologically similar to Hollywood the less Italian the films sound. Perhaps, in some small way, the heyday of Italian film-making was determined by the use of the relatively inferior sound technology of post-synchronisation.

NOTES

1. Diegetic music emanates from within the story and is logically perceived by the characters on screen (i.e. a radio, a nightclub band, etc.). In contrast, non-diegetic music – or comment music – does not have a logical source from within the story (e.g. an orchestral piece playing while a cowboy rides a horse across a deserted landscape).
2. Richard Dyer, 'Music, People, and Reality: The Case of Italian Neo-realism', in Miguel Mera and David Burnand (eds), *European Film Music* (Aldershot: Ashgate Publishing, 2006), p. 30.
3. Ibid., p. 28.
4. Recognition is also the function of Alberto Rabagliati's 'Mattinata fiorentina', a popular tune that Don Pietro whistles as a means to identify himself at a secret partisan rendezvous.
5. Mervyn Cooke, *A History of Film Music* (Cambridge: Cambridge University Press, 2008), p. 366.
6. Michel Chion, *The Voice in Cinema*, trans. Claudia Gorbman (New York: Columbia University Press, 1999), p. 85.
7. Borin, Fabrizio, *La filmografia di Nino Rota* (Florence: Olschki, 1999), p. x.
8. Rota's famous 'Fool's Theme' from *La strada* was composed after shooting, and Gelsomina's trumpet and the Fool's violin are clearly out of synch with the music on the soundtrack. Similarly, Rota's 'Passerella di addio' at the end of 8½ is not the music that was used on the set, and the synch with the musicians on screen is imperfect at best (the sound technicians were so furious with Fellini's last-minute change that they stormed out of the studio).
9. Sergio Miceli, *Musica e cinema nella cultura del Novecento* (Milan: Sansoni, 2000), p. 409.
10. Franco Sciannameo, *Nino Rota's The Godfather Trilogy* (Toronto: Scarecrow Press, 2010), p. 15.
11. There are obviously many exceptions, including, for example, some recent films by Marco Bellocchio (*Buongiorno, notte* [*Good Morning, Night*, 2003] and *Vincere* [*Vincere*, 2009]) where the soundtracks break the audio equivalent of the fourth wall and demand to be actively interpreted.

FURTHER READING

Brown, Royal S., *Overtones and Undertones: Reading Film Music* (Berkeley: University of California Press, 1994).

Chion, Michel, *Audio-Vision*, trans. Claudia Gorbman (New York: Columbia University Press, 1994).

Dyer, Richard, 'Music, People, and Reality: The Case of Italian Neo-realism', in Miguel Mera and David Burnand (eds), *European Film Music* (Aldershot: Ashgate Publishing, 2006).

——, *Nino Rota: Music, Film, and Feeling* (London: BFI/ Palgrave Macmillan, 2010).

Gorbman, Claudia, 'Music as Salvation: Notes on Fellini and Rota', *Film Quarterly* vol. 28 no. 2 (Winter 1974–5), pp. 17–25. Rpt Peter Bondanella (ed.), *Federico Fellini: Essays in Criticism* (New York: Oxford University Press, 1978), pp. 80–94.

——, *Unheard Melodies* (Bloomington: Indiana University Press, 1987).

Miceli, Sergio, *Musica per film* (San Giuliano Milanese: Universal Music MGB, 2009).

Van Order, M. Thomas, *Listening to Fellini: Music and Meaning in Black and White* (Madison, NJ: Fairleigh Dickinson University Press, 2009).

18 Production around 1960

Christopher Wagstaff

May I take the liberty of puncturing certain assumptions often held about cinema? They are assumptions which have never, of course, been held by any of the readers of this volume. Nevertheless, they trickle into people's thinking, and it is well to guard against them.

First, the cinema is assumed to be a 'popular' cultural pursuit embraced above all by 'the masses'. Audience surveys have consistently shown that half of the population of a European nation never goes to the cinema. Among those higher in the social scale, around a third never go; among those lower in the social scale, more than two-thirds never go. Relatively speaking, therefore, the market for films is dependent on richer and more culturally sophisticated consumers. Moreover, the historical decline in cinema audiences is accounted for not by more people joining the ranks of the non-cinemagoers, but rather by the same group of cinemagoers attending less frequently. The extraordinary 'popularity' of Italian Westerns in the period from 1965 to 1968, and their astonishing performance at the Italian box office neither changed the social profile of the cinemagoers, nor did it have any effect on the progressive decline in the frequency with which they were willing to watch films.

In most books about Italian cinema, the films would appear to have been made by directors; but in reality, of course, they are made by commercial companies. Those companies, in their turn, operate within a context determined by international, national, legal and market structures. The most obvious material determinant is the tripartite structure of the cinema industry, resting on the huge base of *exhibition* (where money is extracted, in the period covered by this essay, from purchasers of cinema tickets). An often undervalued intermediate stage is the *distribution* sector, which is where most of the control of the industry is located, because this is where money goes in one direction for

the making of films, and in the other direction is collected from their distribution by a rigid and often monopolistic control of the exhibition sector. Ascending the pyramid brings us to the tiny pinnacle of the *production* sector which gets all the attention and publicity. The characteristics of the films themselves (let us say, for example, artistic or meretricious) are determined more at the level of the broader-based sectors of the industry than at the summit. The relations between the 'art films' on the one hand and the less culturally ambitious (though often commercially more ambitious) films on the other, which characterise the history of postwar Italian cinema, emerge from an initial assessment of their commercial and industrial context. What I should like to do in this very brief chapter is describe what I think a healthy state of the Italian cinema looked like – and I say *describe* what it looked like, rather than *explain why* it was that way, because I do not think I have the answer to the latter question – and draw attention to some of the producers who helped to make it that way.

A tiny case history. On the evening of 22 December 1961, Tullio Kezich and Ermanno Olmi rowed out to the Isolino in Lake Maggiore to finalise an agreement with the general secretary of the Edison Volta company, Bruno Janni, to set up a film production company duly named 22 Dicembre Società Editoriale Cinematografica Italiana (Milano). Working for Edison as a documentary film-maker, Olmi had shot a feature film, *Il tempo si è fermato* (*Time Stood Still*, 1959) for 18 million lire. A year later he was filming his own script of *Il posto* (*The Job*, 1961) using the streets, friends' houses and Edison's offices as locations and without professional actors. It was financed by a group of friends each chipping in what they could afford, calling themselves 'The 24 Horses'. Edison had been turning a blind eye to Olmi's moonlighting, and had been accepting a notional rent

Ermanno Olmi being his own cameraman

for the equipment. Edison's sternly right-wing managing director had no time for the cinema, but his general secretary, Janni, was a much more cultivated man. Meanwhile, Goffredo Lombardo, the young heir of the large production company Titanus, had seen and liked *Il tempo si è fermato*, and bought outright *Il posto* for distribution. He also agreed to distribute Vittorio De Seta's self-produced first feature film, *Banditi a Orgosolo* (*Bandits of Orgosolo*, 1961), intending the two as his slate for the Venice Film Festival, and announcing a programme of renewal of authorial Italian cinema. Meanwhile, Olmi moved from Edison to 22 Dicembre, which was constituted by 51 per cent Edison and the rest by six members, each contributing 2 million lire. Olmi was the animating figure, but Tullio Kezich took on the artistic directorship. Janni pushed for a diversified programme of features, documentaries and television projects. Lombardo followed developments with interest. Galatea's president, Lionello Santi asked 22 Dicembre to produce one of its films, Eriprando Visconti's *Una storia milanese* (*A Milanese Story*, 1962) and

with Santi's Galatea once again they produced Lina Wertmüller's *I basilischi* (*The Lizards*, 1963). While Olmi was shooting *I fidanzati* (*The Fiancés*, 1963) in Sicily they took on a nearly completed cinéma vérité film by Alberto Caldana, *I ragazzi che si amano* (*Children Who Love*, 1963) and agreed to another project with Galatea, Damiano Damiani's *La rimpatriata* (*The Reunion*, 1963), above all to get into partnership on Gianfranco De Bosio's very interesting *Il terrorista* (*The Terrorist*, 1963). The company produced Rossellini's *Età di ferro* (*The Iron Age*, 1965) for television. Meanwhile Titanus more or less went bust as a production company over Robert Aldrich's *Sodoma e Gomorra* (*Sodom and Gomorrah*, 1962), and Lombardo approached Edison to take over Titanus as a distribution company – which it did, whereupon Titanus bought 22 Dicembre, paying off, in the process, the debts incurred by distributors' and exhibitors' fear of the explosive politics of *Il terrorista*.[1]

Large production companies obviously lie behind costly prestige films. Smaller production companies usually lie behind films that are often incorrectly referred to as B-movies. In the 1960s, Italian cinemas did not show double bills, and so there were no B-movies as such. True, Italian formula films were cut down in length and used as B-movies in the UK and the US, but that is a different matter. The genres both of the peplum and of the Western in the 1960s grew out of an original operation carried out by artists: in the case of the peplum, the innovation was carried out by Ennio De Concini (scriptwriter) and Pietro Francisci (director) with *Le fatiche di Ercole*, and in the case of the Western, the innovation was carried out by Sergio Leone with *Per un pugno di dollari*. After that, the waves that followed were producer-driven; not in every case, of course, but Florestano Vancini's reflections on his own Western make it clear that the impulse was not an artistic one, while Carlo Lizzani, talking about the two Westerns he directed, nicely illustrates the distinction between doing a professional job and taking ownership of a film.

> Florestano Vancini: I too made a Western, *I lunghi giorni della vendetta* [*Days of Vengeance*, 1967] but I didn't make it in the real sense; I made it in a sort of technical sense. I'm not responsible for it as its author, but rather in the sense of a professional service that was asked of me and which I supplied. I didn't sign it with my own name but with the pseudonym Stance Vance, not because I wanted to hide my identity – even if there are a lot of people working in the Italian cinema industry, we all know what everybody's doing in any given moment. I didn't sign it because using another name was a way of saying: 'I don't feel responsible for it, I am not its author, it is a confection to which I have devoted my best professional talents.'[2]

> Carlo Lizzani: In 1966 I made *Un fiume di dollari* [*The Hills Run Red*, 1967] among other things with an American pseudonym Lee Beaver, because this was at the height of the Western wave and I wanted to repay [the producer] De Laurentiis for his help in giving me work during the period of McCarthyism in our cinema industry. I had made *Il gobbo* [*The Hunchback of Rome*, 1960] and *Il processo di Verona* [*The Verona Trial*, 1963] with him and so, to pay him back, when he asked me to make a Western, using an American name, I did it. And I did it for the same reasons that many directors make television advertisements. I also, however, made *Requiescant* [*Kill and Pray*, 1967] –which had rather higher pretensions, and in fact I put my own name on it – in order to get together some funds for a company we had set up with some friends.[3]

Antonio Margheriti recounts:

> In twelve weeks in 1965 I conceived, prepared and shot four science-fiction films all in the same period. Shooting them was incredible! We had to resort to clapperboards of different colours so as to know which film the scenes belonged to. I had a reduced budget and had to make savings. [...] I'm not the least bit happy with these films, except perhaps for two of them. *I criminali della galassia* [*Gamma I Quadriology Vol. 1* aka *Wild, Wild Planet*, 1965] won a prize in Prague, for technique. It was the story of an invasion of the Earth by mutants. *I diafanoidi vengono da Marte* [*Gamma I Quadrilogy Vol. 2* aka *The War of the Planets*, 1966] showed extraterrestrials who, in the form of phantom lights, were also trying to invade the Earth. *I diavoli dello spazio* [*Gamma I Quadrilogy Vol. 4* aka *The Snow Devils*, 1967] explained the extraterrestrial origin of the Yeti, and *Missione pianeta errante* was a sort of remake of *Il pianeta degli uomini spenti* [*Battle of the Worlds*, 1961]. [author's note: *Missione pianeta errante*, produced by Mercury Film International in 1966 and known by the title of *Pianeta errante* in Italy, was made for the US market – *Gamma I Quadrilogy Vol. 3*, 1971 – and only subsequently imported into Italy].[4]

Sergio Corbucci alludes to points that have been made in more technical detail by many figures in the industry:

> At my level and that of Sergio Leone we could have made twice as many Westerns as we did because they were so much in demand. As for me, I hardly had the time to finish one before I had to start on the next. [...] Our films were so much presold on foreign markets that their budgets were amply covered right from the start. Where coproductions were concerned, many of the clauses in the contracts were slightly fictional, a bit fiddled, and the conditions laid down for them were never accurately followed. People would always work out agreements among themselves.[5]

In Table 18.1, obvious examples of this kind of film are the Westerns, and the musicals directed by Ettore Fizzarotti with Gianni Morandi: quickly and cheaply made to exploit the captive market of the fans of the singer's latest hit, they circulated throughout the 'depths' of the market (provincial and third-run cinemas), and fans often went to see them more than once. In the 1980s, the producer Cecchi Gori would

Pier Paolo Pasolini on the set of *Accattone* (1961)

specialise in a parallel operation with comedians whose enormous following derived from television.

If we turn to 'authors' seriously identifying with their own films, Italy can be said to have had its own 'new wave' around the turn of the decade, with the debuts of Marco Bellocchio, Bernardo Bertolucci, Mauro Bolognini, Tinto Brass, Gianfranco De Bosio, Vittorio De Seta, Marco Ferreri, Alfredo Giannetti, Ugo Gregoretti, Nanni Loy, Giuliano Montaldo, Ermanno Olmi, Pier Paolo Pasolini, Elio Petri, Gillo Pontecorvo, Francesco Rosi, Florestano Vancini, Lina Wertmüller – to name just those who come immediately to mind. Already among established film-makers there was a movement towards what one could call a new didacticism, with Rossellini's *Età di ferro*, the quite daring revision of World War I in Monicelli's *La grande guerra* and Comencini having this to say about his equally daring revision of the Resistance in *Tutti a casa* (*Everybody Go Home*, 1960):

> I said that we needed to make a 'didactic' film, and I didn't mean this in a limiting sense: it had to be a film that would explain this period of history in a simple manner, so that it could be easily understood even by young people who knew nothing about it, and had never had this period explained to them in school.[6]

Of the new authors, Ermanno Olmi would be an obvious example of this stance:

> This company [22 Dicembre] would produce both documentaries and feature films. This didn't mean industrial documentaries, which in reality are just a sort of advertising medium for companies, but rather investigating the issue of work through documentaries, while with feature films 22 Dicembre would create a kind of cinema that was not a commercial cinema in the normal sense, but one which would approach without commercial presuppositions the problems of our time, and here too in particular those surrounding work, in as much as work constitutes one of the main pivots of society and of the personal life of every one of us.[7]

An argument can be mounted that all this owed a great deal to a group of producers, from the larger companies right down to the smallest. When relations over *La dolce vita* broke down with De Laurentiis, Giuseppe Amato dragged Angelo Rizzoli kicking and screaming to produce the film. Fellini set up a production company, Federiz, together with Clemente Fracassi and Rizzoli to foster new talent, but it never produced a single film that was not directed by Fellini himself. When Pasolini, Fellini's good friend, brought his project for *Accattone* to him, Fellini rejected it, and Alfredo Bini of Arco Film stepped in. Mauro Bolognini took Pasolini's script to Bini: 'I have to say that Bini immediately realised the worth of the script he had in his hands, and didn't hesitate for a moment about producing it.'[8]

> Alfredo Bini: Pasolini was really desperate, he was ready to kill himself. I went to see him, read the script and saw the material he had shot which was truly horrible, but you could see that it was just for the lack of experience and help. So I got hold of Tonino Delli Colli [Director of Photography], who hadn't been working for quite a while, I surrounded him with reliable people, and gradually we got it going again. Certainly, it was a technically idiosyncratic film, but that was part of its attraction. [...] No distributor was willing to take up a film rejected by Cineriz. [...]
> In the end I asked a delightful person, Sciscione, who was working at the time for Cino Del Duca's company. [...] We went to Deauville, because that's where Cino Del Duca had his horses and was racing them. I remember that it was raining and Sciscione and I were huddling under an umbrella and he with his binoculars was following his horses while I was telling him about this film that cost very little, but had a great story, the story of a pimp who is redeemed by love and becomes a thief, an entertaining story. And almost without listening to me, still following his horse which was in a race, Cino del Duca agreed to take it on at 50 per cent. So with that 50 per cent which was real money, we managed to make the film, and I rustled up the other 50 per cent.[9]

Del Duca was repeating the help he had given Bini with Bolognini's *Il bell'Antonio*. When Antonioni's *L'avventura* stalled because of poor budgeting, Cino Del Duca completely took over production.[10]

The actor Gino Cervi's son, Tonino Cervi, either alone in his Compagnia Cinematografica Cervi or together with Alessandro Jacovini in Ajace, launched Florestano Vancini and Bernardo Bertolucci.

> Florestano Vancini: Still today, twenty years later, I have to say that *La lunga notte del '43* [*It Happened in '43*, 1960] was the easiest film to set up of my career. In November 1959 I took what I had worked up into an eighty-page treatment from a short story by Bassani to Alessandro Jacovoni and Tonino Cervi, who were then two very young producers, and on 18 February 1960 we began shooting. It was a classic case of a subject wrapped up and disposed of. Everything happened with a speed and simplicity that in subsequent years have never been repeated.[11]

> Bernardo Bertolucci: After having been assistant director on *Accattone*, I found myself scripting, together with Sergio Citti, for Tonino Cervi, a treatment of Pier Paolo's [Pasolini] that he no longer wanted to direct [*La commare secca*, *The Grim Reaper*, 1962]. It was Cervi, who was then young and full of initiative, who said why didn't I direct it. Very irresponsibly I replied yes. It cost very little, 50–60 million [lire], and launched me as a director at the age of 21.[12]

Bertolucci's next film was the product of a similarly supportive producer:

> Bernardo Bertolucci: If I was able to make *Prima della rivoluzione*, it is thanks to Gianni Amico, who helped me to write the script and who put me in touch with someone in Milan, Bernocchi, who really liked the idea of the film and enabled us to shoot it by setting up a production company for the purpose, Iride Cinematografica.[13]

Bellocchio's *I pugni in tasca* [*Fists in the Pocket*, 1965] was made in the family, because neither producers nor distributors saw any value whatever in such scabrous material:

> Marco Bellocchio: For months I searched together with [Enzo] Doria [the film's producer] for people who could participate in financing the project. We couldn't find a single person. So my brother Piergiorgio asked for a small loan from the bank which he guaranteed. The loan was around 20 million and with this 20 million the film got made.[14]

While Lionello Santi of Galatea played an important role in producing Francesco Rosi's first films, Franco Cristaldi's Vides was responsible in this period for the first significant films of Petri, Giannetti and Pontecorvo, as well as of Rosi.

> Francesco Rosi: Cristaldi has the great merit of having been a producer who was always open to innovative initiatives. In that period he emerged as the young producer who launched, or at least supported, young directors. He started out that way and I have to say that he has kept up a policy of almost always supporting projects that didn't conform to the norm. I owe him in *La sfida* [*The Challenge*, 1958], *I magliari* [*The Magliari*, 1959], *Salvatore Giuliano* [*Salvatore Giuliano*, 1962], all my early films.[15]

> Nanni Loy: As a first film, I had proposed to Cristaldi's Vides, who in turn proposed it to Titanus, *Un giorno da leoni* [*A Day for Lionhearts*, 1961], a story about the Resistance in Lazio that I had been working on for a number of years. But Titanus told Vides that it was willing to distribute *Un giorno da leoni* only if Vides first made *Audace colpo dei soliti ignoti* [*Fiasco in Milan*, 1959], the sequel to *I soliti ignoti* [*Big Deal on Madonna Street*, 1958], which Monicelli either didn't want to or didn't have the time to direct. Negotiations took place with Vides, and Cristaldi undertook with me to make both films. Once *Audace colpo* was finished, Vides kept his word, but not Titanus, which refused to distribute *Un giorno da leoni*, which got distributed by Lux. However I consider it my first real film because the other one, which made a lot of money, was just a technical job without me being really involved in the initiative.[16]

Tullio Kezich summarised some of what he saw as the principles operating in film production at the time:

> Two things lie at the heart of the cinematographic initiatives around 1961: a general realisation of the renewed importance of Italian cinema at the international level, and the influence of France. The *nouvelle vague* had provided the orders of the day: the *politique des auteurs*, the *caméra stylo*, low-cost film-making. The secrets behind Parisian-style cinema are: having something to say, being able to express oneself freely, and not letting oneself be conditioned by the capitalist system.[17]

What had happened was that the production conditions of neorealism had heavily influenced the young French cineastes of the *nouvelle vague*, whose inspiration had then come back home to Italy in the younger generation of 1960.

NOTES

1. Tullio Kezich, 'La "22 dicembre"; ovvero un capitolo di storia minore della Titanus', in Vito Zagarrio (ed.), *Dietro lo schermo. Ragionamenti sui modi di produzione cinematografici in Italia* (Venice: Marsilio, 1988), pp. 73–9.
2. Franca Faldini and Goffredo Fofi (eds), *L'avventurosa storia del cinema italiano raccontata dai suoi protagonisti 1960–69* (Milan: Feltrinelli, 1981), p. 306. All English translations in this essay from this book are by the author.
3. Ibid., p. 306.
4. Ibid., p. 211.
5. Ibid., p. 298.
6. Ibid., p. 90.
7. Ibid., p. 79.
8 Ibid., p. 42.
9. In Ezio Di Monte et al., *La città del cinema (produzione e lavoro nel cinema italiano 1930/1970)* (Rome: Casa Editrice Roberto Napoleone, 1979), p. 102.
10. See Federico Vitella, *Michelangelo Antonioni, 'L'avventura'* (Turin: Lindau, 2010), pp. 115–16.
11. *L'avventurosa storia del cinema italiano*, p. 70.
12. Ibid., pp. 71–2.
13. Ibid., p. 249.
14. In Di Monte et al., *La città del cinema*, pp. 90–1.
15. *L'avventurosa storia del cinema italiano*, p. 69.
16. Ibid., p. 70.
17. Tullio Kezich, 'La "22 dicembre"', p. 74.

TABLE 18.1: Production costs, gross box-office receipts, and notional estimated returns to producers in historical and constant currency

Year	Title	Director	Type	Nationality	Production company	Cost in historical lire	Cost in 1983 USD	Notional estimate of returns to producer in 1983 USD	Gross receipts in 1983 USD	Gross receipts in historical lire
1945	Roma città aperta	Roberto Rossellini	neo-realist	Italy	Excelsa Film	12,000,000	$111,111	$706,019 (not in fact received)	$1,157,407	125,000,000
1947	Vivere in pace	Luigi Zampa	neo-realist	Italy	Lux Film/ Pao Film	14,000,000	$104,634	$574,439	$941,704	126,000,000
1957	La sfida	Francesco Rosi	art	Italy Spain	Lux, Vides, Suevia, Madrid	110,000,000	$626,335	$1,722,762 + Spanish receipts and subsidies	$2,824,199	496,000,000
1957	L'ultima violenza	Raffaello Matarazzo	melo	Italy	Lux, Par	72,000,000	$409,964	$1,649,822	$2,704,626	475,000,000
1957	L'uomo di paglia	Pietro Germi	art melo	Italy	Lux, Cinecittà, Vides	240,000,000	$1,366,548	$1,035,046	$1,645,552	289,000,000
1958	Ercole e la regina di Lidia	Pietro Francisci	peplum	Italy France	Lux, Galatea, Lux CCF	323,000,000	$1,788,235	$3,005,675 + French receipts and subsidies	$4,927,336	890,000,000
1958	I giovani mariti	Mauro Bolognini	comedy	Italy France	Lux, Nepi, Zodiaque, Silver Films	135,000,000	$747,405	$1,040,166 + French receipts and subsidies	$1,705,190	308,000,000
1958	I soliti ignoti	Mario Monicelli	comedy	Italy	Lux, Vides, Cinecittà	250,000,000	$1,384,083	$3,046,201	$4,993,772	902,000,000
1959	Cartagine in fiamme	Carmine Gallone	peplum	Italy France	Lux, Gallone, Lux CCF	922,000,000	$5,069,416	$1,821,196 + French receipts and subsidies	$2,985,567	543,000,000
1959	Il generale Della Rovere	Roberto Rossellini	art	Italy France	Zebra Film, S.N.E. Gaumont, Paris	*220,000,000	$1,300,000	$2,391,368 + French receipts and subsidies	$3,920,275	713,000,000
1959	Il tempo si è fermato	Ermanno Olmi	art	Italy	Edisonvolta	18,000,000	$98,969	$30,186	$49,485	9,000,000
1959	Vento del sud	Enzo Provenzale	melo	Italy	Lux, Vides	180,000,000	$989,691	$261,608	$428,866	78,000,000
1960	L'avventura	Michel-	art	Italy	Cino Del Duca,	195,000,000	$1,054,054	$1,124,378	$1,843,243	341,000,000

Year	Title	Director	Type	Production company	Nationality	Cost in historical lire	Cost in 1983 USD	Notional estimate of returns to producer	Gross receipts in 1983 USD	Gross receipts in historical lire
		angelo Antonioni		Cinémato-graphique Lyre, Paris [originally Imera, Faro, Ariel]	France					
1960	I delfini	Francesco Maselli	art	Lux, Vides	Italy	209,000,000	$1,129,730	$1,615,676	$2,648,649	490,000,000
1960	Rocco e i suoi fratelli	Luchino Visconti	art	Titanus, Films Marceau, Paris	Italy France	480,000,000	$2,594,595	$5,572,432 + French receipts and subsidies	$9,135,135	1,690,000,000
1960	La dolce vita	Federico Fellini	art	Riama Film, Gray Films, Paris S.N. Pathé Cinéma, Paris	Italy France	600,000,000	$3,243,243	$7,320,000 US: 20m dolls to now + French receipts and subsidies	$12,000,000 (in Italy)	2,220,000,000 (in Italy)
1961	Banditi a Orgosolo		art	De Seta, V.	Italy	*50,000,000	$267,559	$456,990	$749,164	140,000,000
1961	Barabba	Richard Fleischer	peplum colossal	Dino De Laurentiis Cinematografica	"Italy" in Italy, Germany, UK; "USA" in France, Norway	5,000,000,000	$26.7m	$5,314,140 (in Italy)	$8,711,706 (in Italy)	1,628,000,000 (in Italy)
1961	Il brigante	Renato Castellani	art	Cineriz di Angelo Rizzoli	Italy	98,000,000	$524,415	$1,090,24	$1,787,291	334,000,000
1961	Divorzio all'italiana	Pietro Germi	com	Lux, Vides, Galatea	Italy	325,000,000	$1,739,130	$4,122,702	$6,758,528	1,263,000,000
1961	Un giorno da leoni	Nanni Loy	resistance	Lux, Vides, Galatea	Italy	262,000,000	$1,402,007	$1,015,171	$1,664,214	311,000,000
1961	Orazi e curiazi	Ferdinando Baldi, Terence Young	peplum	Tiberia, Lux	Italy	650,000,000	$3,478,261	$1,165,324	$1,910,368	357,000,000

Year	Title	Director	Type	Production company	Nationality	Cost in historical lire	Cost in 1983 USD	Notional estimate of returns to producer	Gross receipts in 1983 USD	Gross receipts in historical lire
1961	Il posto	Ermanno Olmi	art	The 24 Horses, Milano	Italy	20,000,000	$107,023	$479,839 Titanus bought it from the producers for 25m lire=$133,779	$786,622	147,000,000
1961	Salvatore Giuliano	Francesco Rosi	art	Lux, Vides, Galatea	Italy	403,000,000	$2,156,522	$2,382,876	$3,906,355	730,000,000
1962	Colpo segreto di D'Artagnan	Siro Marcellini	cloak & dagger	Liber Film, Films Agiman, Paris	Italy France	130,000,000	$688,742	$778,861 + French receipts and subsidies	$1,276,821	241,000,000
1962	La commare secca	Bernardo Bertolucci	art	Cineriz di Angelo Rizzoli, Compagnia Cinematografica Cervi	Italy	55,000,000	$291,391	$135,735	$222,517	42,000,000
1962	I compagni	Mario Monicelli	art, comedy	Lux, Vides, Mediterranée Cinéma	Italy France	582,000,000	$3,083,444	$1,173,139 + French receipts and subsidies	$1,923,179	363,000,000
1962	La leggenda di Enea	Giorgio Rivalta	peplum	Mercury Film, Sirius Film, Paris	Italy France	208,000,000	$1,101,987	$1,551,258 + French receipts and subsidies	$2,543,046	480,000,000
1962	Maciste il gladiatore più forte del mondo	Michele Lupo	peplum	Leone Film	Italy	222,000,000	$1,176,159	$1,438,146	$2,357,616	445,000,000
1962	La monaca di Monza	Carmine Gallone	hist melo	Globe Films Int'l, Produzione Gallone, Paris-Elysée Films	Italy France	550,000,000	$2,913,907	$2,165,298 + French receipts and subsidies	$3,549,669	670,000,000
1962	Omicron	Ugo Gregoretti	art science fiction	Lux, Ultra, Vides, Lux CCF	Italy France	255,000,000	$1,350,993	$219,762 + French receipts and subsidies	$360,265	68,000,000
1962	Senilità	Mauro Bolognini	literary	Zebra Film, Aera Film, Paris	Italy France	160,000,000	$847,682	$1,140,821 + French receipts and subsidies	$1,870,199	353,000,000

Year	Title	Director	Type	Production company	Nationality	Cost in historical lire	Cost in 1983 USD	Notional estimate of returns to producer	Gross receipts in 1983 USD	Gross receipts in historical lire
1962	Le sette folgori di Assur	Silvio Amadio	peplum	Apo Film	Italy	373,000,000	$1,976,159	$691,603	$1,133,775	214,000,000
1962	Sodoma e Gomorra	Robert Aldrich	peplum colossal	Titanus, S.G.C., Pathé Cinéma, Twentieth Century-Fox (US)	Italy France	3,125,000,000	$16m	$3,716,556 (in Italy) + French receipts and subsidies	$6,092,715	1,150,000,000 (in Italy)
1962	Una storia milanese	Eriprando Visconti	art	Galatea, 22 Dicembre, Lyre, Paris	Italy France	180,000,000	$953,642	$584,954 + French receipts and subsidies	$958,940	181,000,000
1962	Le tentazioni del dottor Antonio (ep. in Boccaccio 70)	Federico Fellini	art	Cineriz, Concordia Compagnia Cinematografica, Francinex, Gray Films	Italy France	450,000,000 (just that episode alone)	$2,384,106	$3,878,146 + French receipts and subsidies	$8,476,821	1,200,000,000
1962	Una vita violenta	Paolo Heusch, Brunello Rondi	literary	Zebra Film, Aera Film, Paris	Italy France	160,000,000	$847,682	$504,159 + French receipts and subsidies	$826,490	156,000,000
1962	La voglia matta	Luciano Salce	comedy	D.D.L./Umbria Film, Perugia/Lux Film	Italy	373,000,000	$1,976,159	$1,813,033	$2,972,185	561,000,000
1963	I basilischi	Lina Wertmüller	art	Galatea, 22 Dicembre	Italy	*120,000,000	$627,451	$263,529	$418,301	80,000,000
1963	I fidanzati	Ermanno Olmi	art	22 Dicembre, Titanus Sicilia, Palermo	Italy	*50,000,000	$261,438	$124,392	$203,922	39,000,000
1963	Il fornaretto di Venezia	Duccio Tessari	cloak & dagger	Lux, Ultra, Gaumont	Italy France	410,000,000	$2,143,791	$590,065 + French receipts and subsidies	$967,320	185,000,000
1963	Il gattopardo	Luchino	art	Titanus, S.G.C.,	Italy	2,900,000,000	$15m	$7,090,353	$11.6m	2,223,000,000

Year	Title	Director	Type	Production company	Nationality	Cost in historical lire	Cost in 1983 USD	Notional estimate of returns to producer	Gross receipts in 1983 USD	Gross receipts in historical lire
		Visconti		Pathé Cinéma	France					
1963	Gli indifferenti	Francesco Maselli	art	Lux, Ultra, Vides, Lux CCF	Italy France	751,000,000	$3,926,797	$1,215,216 + French receipts and subsidies	$1,992,157	381,000,000
1963	La rimpatriata	Damiano Damiani	art	Galatea, 22 Dicembre, Lyre, Paris	Italy France	*80,000,000	$418,301	$334,902 + French receipts and subsidies	$549,020	105,000,000
1963	Sedotta e abbandonata	Pietro Germi	comedy	Lux, Ultra, Vides, Lux CCF	Italy France	550,000,000	$2,875,817	$3,154,458 + French receipts and subsidies	$5,171,242	989,000,000
1963	Il terrorista	Gianfranco De Bosio	art	Galatea, 22 Dicembre, Lyre, Paris	Italy France	*50,000,000	$261,438	$133,961 + French receipts and subsidies	$219,608	42,000,000
1963	Il vendicatore mascherato	Pino Mercanti	cloak & dagger	Lux, Ultra	Italy	205,000,000	$1,071,895	$577,307	$946,405	181,000,000
1964	Per un pugno di dollari	Sergio Leone	Western	Jolly Film, Roma, Constantin Film, München, Ocean Films, Madrid	Italy Spain Germany	120,000,000	$619,355	$10,021,316 (in US 3.5m dollars) + Spanish and German receipts and subsidies, as well as worldwide receipts	$16.4m	3,183,000,000
1965	Agente 3S3: passaporto per l'inferno	Sergio Sollima	007	Cineproduzioni Associate, Films Copernic, Paris, P.C. Balcazar, Barcelona	Italy France Spain	80,000,000	$406,349	$653,765 + French and Spanish receipts and subsidies	$1,071,746	211,000,000
1965	In ginocchio da te	Ettore Fizzarotti	musical	Ultra Film – Sicilia Cinematografica, Palermo	Italy	80,000,000	$406,349	$1,812,571	$2,971,429	585,000,000
1965	Una pistola per Ringo	Duccio Tessari	Western	P.C. Balcazar, Barcelona,	Spain Italy	115,000,000	$584,127 (70% Spain)	$6,196,825 + Spanish receipts	$10.2m	2,000,000,000

Year	Title	Director	Type	Production company	Nationality	Cost in historical lire	Cost in 1983 USD 30% Italy)	Notional estimate of returns to producer and subsidies	Gross receipts in 1983 USD	Gross receipts in historical lire
1965	I pugni in tasca	Marco Bellocchio	art	Doria Cinematografica	Italy	30,000,000	$152,381	$458,565	$751,746	148,000,000
1965	Se non avessi più te	Ettore Fizzarotti	musical	Mondial Te.Fi. – Televisione Film	Italy	80,000,000	$406,349	$4,957,460	$8,126,984	1,600,000,000
1966	La Bibbia	John Huston	peplum colossal	Dino De Laurentiis Cinematografica	Italy	10.78 billion	$53m	$9,606,370 (in Italy)	$15.7m	3,189,000,000 (in Italy)
1966	Django	Sergio Corbucci	Western	B.R.C. – Produzione Film, Tecisa, Madrid	Italy Spain	*120,000,000	$592,593	$3,072,593 + Spanish receipts and subsidies	$5,037,037	1,020,000,000
1966	Mi vedrai tornare	Ettore Fizzarotti	musical	Mondial Te.Fi. – Televisione Film	Italy	80,000,000	$395,062	$1,298,321	$2,128,395	431,000,000
1966	Per pochi dollari ancora	Giorgio Ferroni	Western	Fida Cinematografica di Amati Edmondo/ Productions Jacques Roitfeld, Paris, Epoca Films, Madrid	Italy France Spain	195,000,000	$962,963	$3,916,049	$6,419,753	1,300,000,000
1966	Ramon il messicano	Maurizio Pradeaux	Western	Magic Films	Italy	120,000,000	$592,593	$753,086	$1,234,568	250,000,000
1966	Sette pistole per i MacGregor	Franco Giraldi	Western	Estela Films, Madrid, Jolly Film, Roma, Produzione D.S.	Spain Italy	195,000,000	$962,963 (70% Spain 30% Italy)	$2,921,975 + Spanish receipts and subsidies	$4,790,123	970,000,000

EXPLANATION OF TABLE 18.1
Year
The period I have chosen starts with what is generally considered the beginning of the boom in quantity and quality of Italian film production at the end of the 1950s, and stops partly for reasons of space, but also because the inflation of low-quality genre cinema in the second half of the 1960s, accompanied by a reassertion of US distributors' control of the Italian market, is seen as where the eventual decline of the Italian cinema took root.[1] I include two low-cost neorealist films from just after World War II in order to show how, once their costs and receipts are made measurable against those of later films, they compare with similar films made twenty years later.

Type
This designation is merely intended as an indicative label, and perhaps not all the films labelled 'art' deserve the honour bestowed on them; but part of the aim of the exercise is to see how culturally 'serious' films fared in a very large and frenetic market.

Nationality
A film's 'nationality' determined its eligibility for special conditions in exhibition (the reimbursement of entertainments tax to cinemas that projected it) and subsidies to producers from the state (also in the form of the reimbursement of taxes paid on cinema tickets). A co-production (see Jean A. Gili's chapter) benefited from privileges in both contributing nations.

Cost in historical lire
How much money it cost at the time to make the film. We do not know production costs; they have not been published. I have gathered together from many sources what people have said about the production cost of a given film, and where a figure has an asterisk (*) by it, I have made a guess based on deduction.

The next three columns are the product of calculations that I have made to help the reader make comparisons, first, between one film and another and second, between costs and the receipts that actually find their way back to the producers. For example, while *Roma città aperta* and *Il tempo si è fermato* cost roughly the same (about $100,000), Rossellini's film brought returns to the producer of seven times its cost, and Olmi's only a third of its costs.

Cost in 1983 USD
The sum in lire (in the previous column) for a given year has been converted into dollars at the exchange rate applying in that year, and this sum in dollars has been adjusted in line with the consumer price index to the dollar in 1983.

I have converted the cost and gross receipts into 1983 dollars so that all the films in this table can be compared to one another easily. I have also made a calculation of what portion of the receipts made their way back to the producer. This data is listed in the following three columns so that the reader can easily compare cost, revenue and profitability between the various films.

The *last three columns* are explained in *reverse order: from right to left.*

Gross receipts in historical lire (column on the far right)
These are the generally accepted published figures in Italy for box-office receipts. Admittedly, we are not always sure what is being included and what is not, and the fact that we are unsure is probably a scandal, but this is the world we live in.

Gross receipts in 1983 USD (next to last column)
The result of the same operation on receipts that has been carried out on costs.

Notional estimate of returns to producer in 1983 USD
This column is printed in bold so as to be easily readable together with its neighbour, the cost in 1983 dollars. It is the result of a further calculation. If we compared the raw box-office receipts with the production costs of a film, we would learn little about whether the film covered its costs, and how much profit or loss the makers of the film incurred. From those gross box-office receipts, the state takes 28 per cent in taxes, the exhibitor takes 43 per cent, the distributor 9 per cent, leaving the producer with about 20 per cent at most. To the producers of a film qualifying for 'Italian' nationality, the state gives a subsidy (it is given different pseudonyms, the most frequent is 'ristorni' signifying a reimbursement of taxes and duties paid) amounting to 16 per cent of gross box-office receipts. Furthermore, Italian films had foreign earnings in addition to domestic box-office receipts. Indeed, in very rounded figures published by

the Italian film producers' association ANICA, in 1960, the total Italian investment in Italian production was 27 billion lire, while returns from the domestic market were claimed to be 8 billion lire, the 'ristorni' from the state 7 billion lire, and revenue from foreign markets 20 billion lire. ANICA's figures are the product of deductions and calculations. In a 1957 market report on Italy, the MPEA (Motion Picture Export Association of America) recorded investment in Italian film production as totalling 21 billion lire [adjusted $120 million] – exclusive of interest payments, estimated at 10 per cent – and the producers' returns from domestic box office, export and government subsidy totalling 21.8 billion lire [adjusted $124 million].[2] I have used a very conservative estimate of an amount corresponding to 25 per cent of gross domestic receipts as a purely notional gesture towards the fact that producers got money from selling their films abroad. Clearly, while some films sold phenomenally well abroad, others did far less trade, and so my calculation is no more than an indication of a source of revenue about which we have little detailed information. In short, this column adds together the producer's 20 per cent, the ristorni's 16 per cent and export's 25 per cent of the dollar-adjusted gross receipts.

Official figures are not reflecting the full facts, because the market was not running at as much of a loss as all the figures I am recording would suggest. Let us listen to Suso Cecchi D'Amico:

> Producers have always made a song and dance about Luchino's [Visconti] films costing too much, particularly [Goffredo] Lombardo [of the production company Titanus], whose real disaster was *Sodoma e Gomorra* and certainly not *Il gattopardo*, on which he lost very little and perhaps nothing at all, while *Sodoma e Gomorra* was a real disaster. But for him it looked much better to say that his disaster was due to Visconti and *Il gattopardo*.[3]

In the table, the film *Agente 3S3: passaporto per l'inferno* (*Agent 3S3: Passport to Hell*, 1965) is recorded as having box-office receipts of 211 million lire (adjusted to $1,071,746, and giving producer's returns of $653,765), whereas its director, Sergio Sollima, says that gross receipts were 800 million lire, which would give adjusted returns to the producers of $2,560,000.[4] Demofilo Fidani says about one of his Westerns, *Inginocchiati straniero … i cadaveri non fanno ombra!* (*Dead Men Don't Make Shadows*, 1970), that it was made together with another film in five weeks:

> That way I could say that I had spent 90 million lire (adjusted $371,134), when instead it cost me at most 25 million lire (adjusted $103,093). Even the stupidest of my films earned 350 million lire (adjusted $1,443,299, giving producer's returns of $880,412). I have always made money.[5]

There is a lot we don't know, in other words.

NOTES

1. The most authoritative accounts of this decline are two monographs: Barbara Corsi, *Con qualche dollaro in meno. Storia economica del cinema italiano* (Rome: Editori Riuniti, 2002); and Francesco Contaldo and Franco Fanelli, *L'affare cinema. Multinazionali produttori e politici nella crisi del cinema italiano* (Milan: Feltrinelli, 1979).
2. MPEA memo, *Survey of Motion Picture Market – Italy*, dated 1957, from the Warner Bros. Archive at the School of Cinematic Arts, University of Southern California, kindly shown to me by my colleague at the University of Reading, Peter Miskell.
3. *L'avventurosa storia del cinema italiano*, pp. 261–2.
4. Ibid., p. 212.
5. *Nocturno*, n.s., 11, 1999, quoted in Alberto Pezzotta, *Il western italiano* (Milan: Il Castoro, 2012), p. 51.

19 The Muscleman Peplum

From *Le fatiche di Ercole* (1958) to *Hercules and the Princess of Troy* (1965)

Jon Solomon

In Europe, peplum, the Latin word for an ancient Greek-style garment (plural, pepla), usually applies to all the 'Ancients' – films set in classical antiquity – from the silent era to the present. In the US the phrase 'sword-and-sandal' more often applies specifically to the several hundred Ancients produced, with few exceptions, in Italy from 1958 to 1965. Eventually spreading beyond the confines of antiquity, this corpus covers a wide range of historical and metahistorical subjects in a spectrum of geographical settings, but at its nucleus was always the heroic male bodybuilder protagonist performing feats of strength while righting wrongs, originally and predominantly within the mythological and historical parameters of the Greco-Roman world.

Although none of the films is an exemplary cinematic achievement, the corpus as a whole offers a uniquely comprehensive vision of bygone eras and distant worlds, recreating an unparalleled sweep of history from the bronze age to the nineteenth century and the world from Rome to China. As Italian and international consortia produced and distributed a steady stream of films throughout Europe and America for these eight years, they entertained audiences with brawny action, titillating sex and morally sanctioned heroism triumphant over unrelentingly evil villains. The bodybuilders worked beside a host of international stars and a corps of Italian players, who ably enlivened the secondary roles, not to mention dozens or sometimes hundreds of costumed Italian extras. Like their predecessors, who for centuries had adapted ancient tales to operatic librettos, pepla writers freely conflated myths and reinvented history, inserting beautiful princesses, femmes fatales and dance numbers as well as monsters, torture contrivances and apocalyptic destruction scenes. The films were almost all shot in appropriate Mediterranean exteriors and upon budget-conscious but inventive sets exhibited in brilliant Eastmancolor and eye-catching widescreen formats like Dyaliscope and Supertotalscope. Because the casts were usually international, the films were dubbed before distribution. The translations and dubbing were often quite competent, even if the result often created a lack of immediacy and occasionally unintended amusement. Nonetheless, it was the visual action, not poetry, which audiences came to see. In addition, a host of composers helped to compensate by creating original scores filled with spirited introductions, vibrant brass and timpani orchestrations for the many action scenes, string passages for the intermittent romantic scenes and exotic rhythms for dance sequences.

The continued production of the peplum corpus allowed a number of directors from the silent era to resurrect their careers, while a new generation, most notably Sergio Leone, began building theirs. Overcoming many significant obstacles – lean budgets and tight production schedules, complicated action scenes and effects sequences, unfamiliar settings, multilingual dialogue and dubbing – film-makers generated an adoring (if often lovingly ridiculing) audience continually rejuvenated for decades by broadcast, VHS, DVD and online screenings. Although the genre abruptly yielded to the Italian Western genre in late 1965, one could easily argue that the renascence of the Ancient genre evidenced in Ridley Scott's *Gladiator* (2000) and Zack Snyder's *300* (2006) with its muscular Spartans, resulted from the worldwide popularity of Sam Raimi's syndicated 1990s television series, *Hercules: The Legendary Journeys*, which in turn owed its very conception to the most prominent of all the pepla, Pietro Francisci's *Le fatiche di Ercole*.

PREDECESSORS

The postwar international success of Universalia's *Fabiola* (Fabiola, 1949) and *Gli ultimi giorni di Pompei* (1950),

Carmine Gallone's *Messalina* (*The Affairs of Messalina*, 1950) with Maria Felix, and the Cinecittà location shooting of MGM's *Quo Vadis* inspired a short-lived but trendsetting series of films about familiar ancient characters featuring rising actors: Francisci's *La regina di Saba* (*The Queen of Sheba*, 1952) with Leonora Ruffo; Riccardo Freda's *Spartaco* (*Sins of Rome*, 1953) with Massimo Girotti; Camerini's *Ulisse* with Kirk Douglas; Freda's *Teodora, imperatrice di Bisanzio* (*Theodora, Slave Empress*, 1954) with Gianna Maria Canale; Francisci's *Attila* (*Attila*, 1954) with Anthony Quinn and Sophia Loren; Carlo Ludovico Bragaglia's *Cortigiana di Babilonia* (*Queen of Babylon*, 1954) with Rhonda Fleming; and Guido Brignone's *Le schiave di Cartagine* (*Slaves of Carthage* aka *The Sword and the Cross*, 1956) with Gianna Maria Canale. There were also several comedies: Mario Soldati's *O.K. Nerone* (*O.K. Nero*, 1951) with Gino Cervi; Mario Mattoli's *Due notte con Cleopatra* (*Two Nights with Cleopatra*, 1953) with Sophia Loren and Alberto Sordi; and Steno's *Mio figlio Nerone* (*Nero's Mistress*, 1956) with Alberto Sordi, Gloria Swanson and Brigitte Bardot. This cluster came to an abrupt halt in 1956. There was only one entry in 1957, Fernando Cerchio's *La Venere di Cheronea* (*Goddess of Love*, 1957), but then 1958 brought the very influential *Le fatiche di Ercole*, a loosely conflated mythological contamination of Apollonius's *Argonautica* with several Herculean labours. The three other 1958 releases, all from long-established directors, were more traditional: Vittorio Cottafavi's *La rivolta dei gladiatori* (*The Warrior and the Slave Girl*, 1958), a fictional story about gladiators; Bragaglia's biblical *La spada e la croce* (*The Sword and the Cross*, 1958); and Mario Bonnard's romantic *Afrodite, dea dell'amore* (*Aphrodite, Goddess of Love*, 1958).

INITIAL SUCCESS

Dino de Laurentiis and Carlo Ponti co-produced *Ulisse* and *Attila*, employing veterans Mario Camerini and Francisci to direct. Francisci then teamed with Mario Bava for *Le fatiche di Ercole*, featuring the former Mr Universe, Steve Reeves. But it was Joseph E. Levine, who was primarily responsible for turning this film into an international sensation. His Embassy Pictures had successfully designed the international distribution of the Japanese *Gojira* (*Godzilla*, 1956) and *Attila* in 1958. Levine purchased *Le fatiche di Ercole* in Rome for $125,000 and began an unprecedented $1 million publicity campaign in March 1959. Then, in mid-July, he saturated American cities, exhibiting the film in hundreds of theatres simultaneously, capturing the attention of suburban and rural drive-in and matinee promoters, and

Steve Reeves performs his first feat of strength by uprooting a tree and halting Sylva Koscina's runaway chariot in the opening segment of *Le fatiche di Ercole* (1958)

coinciding serendipitously with the pre-release publicity for MGM's *Ben-Hur*. By 1965, according to an interview in the *New York Times* (26 October 1965, p. 48), *Le fatiche di Ercole* alone had earned $20 million worldwide.

In addition to the massive publicity and innovative theatre-saturation campaigns, the international release of *Le fatiche di Ercole* in 1959 fuelled the ongoing renascence of Greek mythology. It was in this year that Marcel Camus's *Orfeu Negro* (*Black Orpheus*) was released and won the Academy Award for Best Foreign Language Film. The *Larousse Encyclopedia of Mythology* was published in 1959, as was Rose's *A Handbook of Greek Mythology*, with Guthrie's *Mythology and Religion of the Ancient Greeks* soon to follow. In the spring, NASA announced that they would now call their spacemen 'astronauts' à la Apollonius's Argonauts, the work that had also been incorporated into the plot of *Le fatiche di Ercole*. The same week the film was released, Searle applied for FDA approval of their birth-control pill, claiming in advertisements that Enovid was 'symbolized in an illustration from ancient Greek mythology: Andromeda freed from her chains'. At the same time, a muscular body was rapidly becoming a desirable aesthetic, as sport and exercise had now become mainstream. The World Amateur Bodybuilding Championships were established in 1959, and in the US, ABC began broadcasting *The Jack Lalanne Show* coast to coast.

Europeans had long ago become enamoured of Hollywood and enjoyed a reciprocal exchange of current fads, so the raging success of *Le fatiche di Ercole* in the US revived its popularity in Europe. The film was an innovation that catered in particular to the younger demographic, eager to spend their cash to have fun. Even if the reinvented narratives and nuanced, stereotyped characters of a film like *Le fatiche di Ercole* had long been a part of European literary history and its dramatic repertoire, now audiences could see widescreen, full-colour, close-up images of Hercules' well-developed musculature swinging chains at the hapless minions of an evil tyrant. This made for thrilling and entertaining action, particularly because the films simultaneously featured voluptuous women along with heretofore taboo homoerotic attractions.

EXPANDING THE GENRE

The success of *Le fatiche di Ercole* spawned more than Francisci's sequel, *Ercole e la regina di Lidia* (*Hercules Unchained*, 1959), loosely adapted from Aeschylus' *Seven against Thebes* and Sophocles' *Oedipus at Colonus*. As Asclepius says in the former film, 'They've all become fanatics since Hercules arrived. They seem to worship nothing but strength.' Within eighteen months, some thirty more Ancients would appear, many of them using the *Le fatiche di Ercole* formula. Opportunistic individual producers as well as long-established companies competed and collaborated in attracting a steady stream of marquee English, American and French actors to join the variety of statuesque bodybuilders, who would physically enliven the roles of Hercules, Samson, Maciste, Ursus, Goliath, Colossus, Atlas and, ultimately, the 'sons of Hercules'.

Galatea Film, under the guidance of Lionello Santi, followed *Ercole e la regina di Lidia* by expanding into the historical genre. It collaborated with Lux to produce *La battaglia di Maratona* (*Giant of Marathon*, 1959), with Steve Reeves as Phillipides leading the Athenians to victory over the Persians, highlighted by innovative naval-battle and underwater sequences directed by Jacques Tourneur (and Mario Bava). (Notice the insistence on the irrelevant word 'Giant' in the American release title.).

Francisci's *L'assedio di Siracusa* (*Siege of Syracuse*, 1959) was co-produced with Glomer Film. Here Francisci pointedly varied the formula by emphasising the intelligence of Archimedes (Rossano Brazzi) while recreating the *Cabiria* episode in which Archimedes ignites the enemy fleet by using solar mirrors. When Steve Reeves moved on to play in Carlo Campogalliani's *Il terrore dei barbari* (*Goliath and the Barbarians*, 1959), Galatea, along with Glomer, found a different bodybuilder, Ed Fury, for Vittorio Sala's *La regina delle Amazzoni* (*Colossus and the Amazon Queen*, 1959), also featuring Rod Taylor. Realising that the name of the strongman protagonist was critical, Alta Vista distributed these films in the US with titles that included such recognisable and vivid names as Goliath and Colossus. Meanwhile, Galatea collaborated with Twentieth-Century-Fox and the venerable Titanus to

Chelso Alonso performs the *de rigueur* dance number and Steve Reeves outmuscles two horses in *Il terrore dei barbari* (1959)

issue Raoul Walsh's *Esther and the King* (1960), starring Joan Collins and Richard Egan, with a full complement of Italian players. Mario Bava was put in charge of preparing the Italian version. Glomer Film itself also produced Brignone's *Nel segno di Roma*, with Anita Ekberg playing Zenobia, the historical, third-century Queen of Palmyra.

Other Italian studios took a different path. Liber Film, for instance, which had produced *La spada e la croce*, issued Bragaglia's *Annibale* (*Hannibal*, 1959) starring Victor Mature in an effort to recreate history and another episode from *Cabiria*. But rather than continue with historical mini-epics or take the strongman route, the company focused on swashbucklers, such as Luigi Capuano's *La tigre dei sette mari* (*Tiger of the Seven Seas*, 1962); or comedies like two films by Cerchio – *Totò e Cleopatra* (*Toto and Cleopatra*, 1963) and *Totò contro Maciste* (*Toto vs Maciste*, 1964).

Independent producer Achille Piazzi was among the first to challenge Galatea and Glomer with different Hercules scripts and a different bodybuilder to play the role. First was Cottafavi's *La vendetta di Ercole* (*Goliath and the Dragon*, 1960), released in mid-August. Here, Brooklyn-born Mark Forest plays Emilius, 'who, because of his tremendous strength and prowess, was given the name of Goliath'. He struggles against a villainous version of Eurystheus (Broderick Crawford) of Oechalia, Eurystheus being originally the name of the ancient Tirynthian king for whom Hercules performed his canonical twelve labours. Just one week later, Grandi Schermi Italiani released Bragaglia's *Gli amori di Ercole* (*The Loves of Hercules*, 1960) starring the Hungarian-born former Mr Universe, Mickey Hargitay and his wife Jayne Mansfield. Piazzi followed almost immediately with *Ercole alla conquista de Atlantide* (*Hercules and the Captive Women*, 1961), also directed by Cottafavi and now with the British Reg Park as Hercules. This warranted an atmospheric sequel, *Ercole al centro della terra* (*Hercules in the Haunted World*, 1961) directed by Mario Bava, which also included Christopher Lee, Hammer's horror star.

As roles for Hercules proliferated, Italian film-makers resurrected the original strongman hero of Italian cinema. Maciste was well remembered from *Cabiria* and Itala Film's series of eighteen films of the 1910s/20s. Bartolomeo Pagano had owned the role, but now there would be a variety of actors and production companies. First was Carlo Campogalliani's *Maciste nella valle dei re* (*Sons of Samson*, 1960) starring Mark Forest, set in ancient Egypt. The producers Donati and Carpentieri, along with Gallus Films, did not think the name Maciste would be marketable in the US or France, where they released it two years later as *Son of Samson* and *Le Géant de la vallée des rois*. Following the same strategy, Gallus exported Freda's *Maciste alla corte del Gran Khan* (1961) as *Samson and the Seven Miracles of the World*, and Dino de Laurentiis exported Sergio Corbucci's *Maciste contro il vampiro* (1961) in 1964 as *Goliath and the Vampires*.

Another revival from the silent era was Ursus, the strongman bullwrestler from *Quo vadis?*. Campogalliani had directed several of Itala's original Maciste films and now, after *Il terrore dei barbari* and *Son of Samson*, he directed *Ursus* (1961), starring Ed Fury. Fury would play the role again in Carlo Ludovico Bragaglia's *Ursus nella valle dei leoni* (*Ursus in the Valley of the Lions*, 1961), but because there was no specificity to this or the other strongman roles, Ursus would in short order be played by Samson Burke in Capuano's *La vendetta di Ursus* (*Revenge of Ursus*, 1961); by Joe Robinson in Remigio Del Grosso's *Ursus e la ragazza tartaruga* (*Tartar Invasion*, 1961); and by Dan Vadis in Domenico Paolella's *Ursus, il gladiatore ribelle* (*The Rebel Gladiators*, 1962).

Many of these films would be developed by consortia. Piazzi, for instance, produced *Ercole alla conquista di Atlantide* and *Ercole al centro della terra* in an international collaborative effort with SpA Cinematografica and Comptoir Français de Productions Cinématographiques (CFPC). Some of the consortia productions developed non-Herculean programmes. Alexandra Produzioni Cinematografiche, for instance, teamed variously with Atenea, CFPC and others to follow their *La rivolta dei gladiatori* with such films as *Le legioni di Cleopatra* (*Legions of the Nile*, 1959) and *I giganti della Tessaglia* (*The Giants of Thessaglia* aka *The Giants of Thessaly* [*The Argonauts*], 1960). Aiming at a superior product, they hired Cottafavi and Freda respectively to direct and adapt historical material (the story of Cleopatra and Antony) and mythological epic (Apollonius' *Argonautica*). Nonetheless, English-language advertisements for the March 1960 New York premiere of *La rivolta dei gladiatori*, though starring Ettore Manni, feature a muscular hero swinging an iron mace on a long chain à la Hercules. Similarly, Cinematografica Associati (CI.AS) along with the Spanish company Procusa (Productores Cinematográficos Unidos S.A.) produced two films with interesting variations. Employing Steve Reeves and Ennio De Concini, the lead writer for *Le fatiche di Ercole*, they first issued Mario Bonnard's *Gli ultimi giorni di Pompei* (1959), freely adapting Bulwer-Lytton's 1834 novel, which had been filmed several times in the silent era when director Mario Bonnard had begun his career. Sergio Leone also worked on the script, having recently completed his work on the second unit of *Ben-Hur*, and he then co-wrote and directed *Il colosso di Rodi* (*The Colossus of Rhodes*, 1961), where his signature technique was already taking shape. Heading in a different direction, was Faro Film, which had produced Cerchio's *La Venere di Cheronea* with Belinda Lee and then collaborated with CFPC and Explorer in succession to produce two films about Biblical villains: *Erode il grande* (*Herod the Great*, 1959) and *Giuditta e Oloferne* (*Head of a Tyrant*, 1959) directed by two other veterans, Victor Tourjansky (as Arnaldo Genoino) and Fernando Cerchio.

SUBGENRES IN THE FIRST HALF OF THE 1960s

Between 1960 and 1965, Italy produced three or four dozen sword-and-sandal films per year. The plots usually involved Greco-Roman myth and history, but some were derived from Biblical tales or were set in more exotic Eastern courts, and an ever-increasing number of producers found success in historically unrelated swashbucklers. Like their contemporary Hollywood counterparts, some of the Biblical films again featured well-known actors, e.g. Orson Welles in *David e Golia* (*David and Goliath*, 1960), and Jean Marais, Jeanne Crain and Basil Rathbone in Glomer's *Ponzio Pilato* (*Pontius Pilate*, 1962). But these were hardly mechanical Biblical re-enactments or imitations of Hollywood prototypes. Even more Americanised than *Esther and the King*, *Sodoma e Gomorra* (*Sodom and Gomorrah*, was directed by an American (Robert Aldrich)

Sergio Leone lowers the bell to torture Georges Marchal in
Il colosso di Rodi (1961)

and distributed by Joseph E. Levine and Twentieth
Century-Fox. But it plays like a quintessential peplum,
produced by a European consortium, filled with Italian
actors and extras, and culminating in an apocalyptic,
dam-breaking climax. Gianfranco Parolini's *Il vecchio
testamento* (*The Old Testament*, 1962) went so far as to
create a muscleman role for Brad Harris in a quasi-
Biblical war between Jews and Syrians. By far the most
popular Old Testament figure was that of a legitimate
strongman, Samson, who would make nearly a dozen
additional appearances, whether as the lead character,
e.g. Brad Harris in Parolini's *Sansone* (*Samson*, 1962), or
not, e.g. the aforementioned *Maciste alla corte del Gran
Khan*. Fittingly, the last film of our corpus, released on
8 October 1965, was Marcello Baldi's *I grandi condottieri*
(*Samson and Gideon*, 1965).

Maciste alla corte del Gran Khan provides an excellent
example of Orientalisation. Just as popular Italian
operas had often employed Egyptian (*Aida*) and Oriental
(*Madama Butterfly*) settings, pepla could be set in such
exotic locations within the Roman Empire as Egypt
(Cerchio's *Il sepolcro dei re* [*Cleopatra's Daughter*, 1960]; or
his *Nefertiti, regina del Nilo* [*Nefertiti*, 1961]), the Greek
islands (Francisci's *Saffo, Venere di Lesbo* [*The Warrior
Empress*, 1960]) and Carthage (Sergio Grieco's *Salambò*
[*The Loves of Salammbo*, 1960]). Further East, Babylon was
particularly evocative of cinematic sin, as in Silvio
Armado's *La sette folgori di Assur* (*War Gods of Babylon*,
1962); Siro Marcellini's *L'eroe di Babilonia* (*Hero of Babylon*,
1963); Michele Lupo's *Maciste, l'eroe più grande del mondo*
(*Goliath and the Sins of Babylon*, 1963); Paolella's *Ercole
contro i tiranni di Babilonia* (*Hercules and the Tyrants of
Babylon*, 1964); and, by association, the Assyrian *Io
Semiramide* (*I Am Semiramis*, 1963), directed by Primo
Zeglio. Such exotic locations inspired even greater
villainy in the tyrants and sensuality in the femmes
fatales for the musclemen to overcome. Particularly
challenging in this regard were the (originally) foreign
Amazons in *La regina delle Amazzoni* and Antonio
Leonviola's *Le gladiatrici* (*Thor and the Amazon Women*,

1963), which developed the Amazon sequences found
in *Le fatiche di Ercole*.

Further afield geographically, André De Toth's
I Mongoli (*The Mongols*, 1961) represented barbarians *par
excellence*, particularly with Jack Palance playing Ogatai.
Such barbarian stereotypes, whether at the fringes of
the Roman Empire or elsewhere, offered a number of
attractive features and motifs for film-makers –
inexpensive but effective fur-like costumes and unruly
hair and beards, implements of torture, wild women
with bare thighs and warrior spirits, 'barbaric' cruelty
and rustic simplicity. Several examples appeared early.
Steve Reeves as 'Goliath' in *Il terrore dei barbari* was
followed by Tourjansky's *I cosacchi* (*The Cossacks*, 1960);
Guido Malatesta's *La furia dei barbari* (*Fury of the
Pagans*,1960); Sergio Grieco's *La regina dei Tartari* (*The
Huns*, 1960); and the previously cited *Ursus e la ragazza
tartara*. The Mongols were visited again in Paolella's
Maciste contro i Mongoli (*Hercules against the Mongols*,
1963). Increasing the crew of sons that pepla film-
makers often invented for famous film heroes, Roberto
Montero's *Tharus, figlio di Attila* (*Colossus and the Huns*,
1962) featured a son of Attila.

Those films were set primarily in Central Asia. Pepla
were set also in Africa (e.g. Piero Regnoli's *Maciste nelle
miniere di re Salomone* [*Samson in King Solomon's Mines*,
1964]); and even the Americas (e.g. Osvaldo Civirani's
Ercole contro i figli del sole [*Hercules against the Sons of the
Sun*, 1964]; and Piero Pierotti's *Sansone e il tesoro degli
Incas* [*Hercules and the Treasure of the Incas*, 1964]), a
transitional film between the peplum and the Italian
Western. Additional hairy and scary antagonists would
appear as cannibals in Guido Malatesta's *Maciste contro i
cacciatori di teste* (*Colossus against the Headhunters*, 1963)
and the vampire in *Maciste contro il vampiro*. Several
films were placed in metageographical Atlantis,
whether in the cinematically traditional desert setting
in Alfonso Brescia's *Il conquistatore di Atlantide* (*Conqueror
of Atlantis*, 1965), or during the most distant time period
in the entire corpus, the Atlantidean futuristic past
(20,000 BC) in Umberto Scarpelli's *Il gigante di Metropolis*
(*The Giant of Metropolis*, 1961). But even space aliens
appear in Giacomo Gentilomo's *Maciste e la regina di
Samar* (*Hercules against the Moon Men*, 1964).

Non-Greco-Roman locations proliferated particularly
in the swashbuckling subgenre, which was
chronologically and geographically but not narratively
or formulaically distinct from the Greco-Roman style.
Many of these films also cast the same feature and
supporting players that populate the more 'traditional'

types of Greco-Roman films. Steve Reeves helped to validate this branch of the corpus with relatively early (but post-Herculean) leading roles in Freda's *Agi Murad il diavolo bianco* (*The White Warrior*, 1959) set in nineteenth-century Tsarist Russia; De Toth's *Morgan, il pirate* (*Morgan, the Pirate*, 1960); and Arthur Lubin's *Il ladro di Bagdad* (*The Thief of Bagdad*, 1961) which revisits the earlier Hollywood venture. Subsequent works range from Mario Costa's *La venere dei pirati* (*The Queen of the Pirates*, 1961) and Capuano's *Il leone di San Marco* (*The Lion of St Mark*, 1963) to Vertunnio De Angelis's *L'uomo mascherato contro i pirati* (*The Masked Man against the Pirates*, 1964); Civirani's *Kindar l'invulnerabile* (*Kindar the Invulnerable*, 1965), and Capuano's *L'avventuriero della Tortuga* (*The Adventurer of Tortuga*, 1965), all of them still featuring the triumphant solitary action hero.

MYTHOLOGICAL FILMS

After the success of *Le fatiche di Ercole* and its many descendants, subsequent film-makers mined the major Greco-Roman mythical cycles for additional filmable material. The pre-story of Homer's *Iliad* was dramatised in Marino Girolami's *L'ira di Achille* (*Fury of Achilles*, 1962). Homer's *Odyssey* had already been featured in the 1954 *Ulisse* and, in both Francisci Hercules films, Ulysses [Gabriele Antonini] played an integral role by representing, as our ancient sources indicate, a younger generation. Ulysses was revived for the sole Ancient produced by Compagnia Cinematografica Mondiale and the French Fidès – Mario Caiano's *Ulisse contro Ercole* (*Ulysses against Hercules* aka *Ulysses against the Son of Hercules*, 1962) – and this character returned as subsidiary to Hercules (Kirk Morris) and Samson (Iloosh Khoshabe) in Francisci's *Ercole sfida Sansone* (*Hercules, Samson and Ulysses*, 1963), another feature with two musclemen. Steve Reeves portrayed the Trojan warrior Aeneas in Giorgio Ferroni's *La guerra di Troia* (*The Trojan Horse*, 1961), an inventive adaptation of the final weeks of the Trojan War, including two duels between Aeneas and Ajax. In keeping with Virgil's Roman perspective, three of the Greeks are portrayed as villainous characters (Ulysses, Achilles, Sinon), as is the Trojan Paris. Rounding out the Trojan cycle, the account popularised by Stesichorus and Euripides, claiming that Helen spent the war in Egypt, was adapted for Ferroni's *Leone di Tebe* (*The Lion of Thebes*, 1964). Again echoing historic Italian interests, Greek tragedy for the most part had relatively little allure for Italian dramatists and screenwriters.

Individual mythological heroes warranted only single films. Two-time Olympic Decathlon champion

Bob Mathias played Theseus in Silvio Amadio's *Teseo contro il minotauro* (*Minotaur, the Wild Beast of Crete*, 1960); Perseus (Richard Harrison) slew Medusa (Angel Jordán) in Alberto De Martino's *Perseo l'invincibile* (*Perseus against the Monsters* aka *Perseus the Invincible*, 1964); and Jason (Roland Carey) sought the Golden Fleece in Freda's *I giganti della Tessaglia*. Atlas now joins the other mythological heroes, making his first appearance in Roger Corman's American-Greek production of *Atlas il trionfatore di Atene* (*Atlas*, 1961), using the reconstructed Stoa of Attalus in Athens as a backdrop. Then Atlas becomes the subject of translated name substitutions in two films: Antonio Leonviola's *Maciste nella terra dei ciclopi* (*Atlas against the Cyclops*, 1961); and Tanio Boccia's *Maciste alla corte dello zar* (*Atlas against the Czar*, 1964).

Of course this is not the mythological Atlas who supports the heavens upon his shoulders. In general the sword-and-sandal film-makers portray the Greco-Roman gods in fully anthropomorphosed representations. Even if we discount Hercules' role as a demigod, when the Olympian gods make an appearance, their entrances and exits are rarely lavished with special effects à la the contemporary *Jason and the Argonauts* (1963), directed by Don Chaffey. And the roles they play fall entirely within the range of genres and purposes accorded them in centuries of Italian opera – romance, free adaptations of Greek tragedy, messengers of exposition, voices of warning and arguments relating to their allegorical functions. Emimmo Salvi's *Vulcano, figlio di Giove* (*Vulcan, Son of Jupiter*, 1962) visits Pluto (Gordon Mitchell), Mars and Jupiter in the realm of the Olympian gods as Vulcan (Iloosh Khoshabe aka Rod Flash) who seeks the love of Venus. Dionysus makes a visit to his native Thebes in Ferroni's *Le baccanti* (*Bondage Gladiator Sexy*, 1961), an adaptation of Euripides' *Bacchae*. Mercury as messenger god establishes the plot of Caiano's *Ulisse contro Ercole* (*Ulysses against the Son of Hercules*, 1962). Mars and Venus argue in a Roman temple about the relative merits of war and love in Bonnard's *Il ratto delle sabine* (*Romulus and the Sabines*, 1961), and the same two divinities are featured in Marcello Baldi's *Marte, dio della guerra* (*Mars, God of War*, 1962). Gods associated with the inferno loom in *Ercole al centro della terra* and the imaginative *Arrivano i titani* (*Sons of Thunder* aka *My Son, the Hero*, 1962), directed by Duccio Tessari. The latter also includes an appearance by Prometheus, the creator of mankind, as does Freda's *Maciste all'inferno* (*The Witch's Curse*, 1962), along with other Titans, who would destroy it. Several films, most notably *Le fatiche di Ercole* and *Ercole al centro della terra*, include prophetesses or sibyls who speak the words of the celestial gods, but only to have Hercules reject his own divine powers. The peplum genre was predominantly about men and their heroic exploits: traditional Homeric heroes may invoke the gods to support them in battle, but these films instead celebrate human power and achievement. Hercules insists on maintaining a human existence.

After a few years the successful formula of *Le fatiche di Ercole* inspired Cintematografica Associati to innovate further by placing two mythological strongmen in a single film, usually in combat against each other, at least in their initial encounter. Parolini's *Sansone* starred Brad Harris along with Sergio Ciani (Alan Steel) as Macigno/Hercules. *Sansone* was released in December 1961, as was Corbucci's *Romolo e Remo* (*Duel of the Titans*, 1961), which typically featured two rivals – Romulus (Steve Reeves) and Remus (Gordon Scott). In the action climax of *Maciste contro il vampiro*, released the previous August, the villain Kobrak (Guido Celano) metamorphoses himself into Maciste/Goliath, so Gordon Scott engages in combat with a lookalike.

HISTORICAL FILMS

Roman history was by nature integral to the Italian film industry and our corpus reflects this tradition. However, the films cover a wide chronological range of Roman history but focus on relatively few major figures, be they strongmen, heroes or villains: Aeneas, Romulus, Spartacus, Caesar, Nero and Commodus. Most of the earliest Roman historical films are quasi-mythological, rich in legendary material passed on to us by Livy, Virgil and others, and well suited for loose filmic adaptation. Set during Rome's archaic Etruscan period, Ferroni's *Il colosso di Roma* (*Hero of Rome*, 1964) recounts the overthrow of Tarquin, and Bragaglia's *Le vergini di Roma* (*Amazons of Rome*, 1961) offers prominent roles for Porcenna and Horatius Cocles. The famous Horatii and Curiatii triplets who battled for Rome and the Albans are featured in Ferdinando Baldi's *Orazi e Curiazi* (*Duel of the Champions*, 1961), with Alan Ladd playing the victorious Horatius. The early fourth-century BC attack of the Gauls was the subject of Gentilomo's *Brenno il nemico di Roma* (*Brennus, Enemy of Rome*, 1963). Steve Reeves played Romulus in *Romolo e Remo*, while Roger Moore played him in *Il ratto delle sabine*. Reeves played Aeneas again in Giorgio Venturini's *La leggenda di Enea* (*The Avenger* aka *The Last Glory of Troy*, 1962), adopted from Virgil's *Aeneid*.

The apocalyptic conclusion of Carmine Gallone's *Cartagine in fiamme* (1960)

Appropriate to the filmic genre, the legendary period is much better represented than the expansion of the Roman Republic, as was Gallone's fascist *Scipione l'africano*. Only Francisci's *L'assedio di Siracusa* and Bragaglia's *Annibale* are set during the Second Punic War; subsequently Lux Film hired Carmine Gallone to revisit his 1937 film in one of his last directorial assignments, *Cartagine in fiamme* (*Carthage in Flames*, 1960), which is set during the Third Punic War.

In contrast, our detailed information about Spartacus and Julius Caesar, two of the most colourful historical personages who lived during the last century of the Republic, inspired a number of films. Because Kirk Douglas's *Spartacus* ended with the survival of a son, screenwriter Adriano Bolzano, who had worked with director Sergio Corbucci on *Romulo e Remo*, developed a new role for Steve Reeves. In Corbucci's *Il figlio di Spartacus* (*The Slave*, 1962), Reeves played Randus, the son of Spartacus, caught in an Egyptian confrontation between the triumvirs Crassus and Caesar. In 1964–5, just the name Spartacus would evoke the spirit of the rebellious gladiator. Spartacus is the alleged leader of the rebellion in Michele Lupo's *La vendetta di Spartacus* (*The Revenge of Spartacus*, 1964) and the name of one of the ten in Nick Nostro's *Gli invincibili dieci gladiatori* (*Spartacus and the Ten Gladiators*, 1964). The name only is used for the German release of *Il colosso di Roma* (*Spartacus: Der Held mit der eisernen Faust*). In his last of nearly a dozen sword-and-sandal films, Domenico Paolella would direct Peter Lupus (Rock Stevens) as Spartacus in his native Thrace, in *Il gladiatore che sfidò l'impero* (*Challenge of the Gladiator*, 1965).

None of the five films involving Julius Caesar attempted either to serve as a lengthy biopic or an adaptation of Shakespeare's tragedy, demonstrating the continuing inventiveness of the genre and the ability of the writers to create full-length films out of single encounters. Sergio Grieco's *Giulio Cesare contro i pirati* (*Caesar against the Pirates*, 1962) focuses on Caesar

The Capitoline Hill is reconstructed in a set for Cottafavi's *Messalina Venere imperatrice* (1960)

(Gustavo Rojo) in Bithynia; Grieco's *La schiava di Roma* (*Slave of Rome*, 1961) features Guy Madison as Marco Valerio, one of Caesar's lieutenants in Gaul; Tanio Boccia's *Giulio Cesare, il conquistadore delle Gallie* (*Caesar the Conqueror*, 1962) is limited to the struggle between Caesar (Cameron Mitchell) and Vercingetorix (Rik Battaglia); the plot of Antonio Margheriti's *I giganti di Roma* (*Giants of Rome*, 1964) revolves around Caesar (Alessandro Sperli) and Britain's Druids; and Piero Pierotti's *Una regina per Cesare* (*A Queen for Caesar*, 1962) focuses on his involvement with Cleopatra in Egypt.

The villainous emperors of the Roman Empire had already caught the attention of Hollywood, which in turn inspired refurbishings of earlier silent Italian and high-profile American releases. The Neronian court intrigue of *Quo Vadis?* inspired Guido Malatesta's *L'incendio di Roma* (*Fire over Rome*, 1965), while the reign of Commodus in Anthony Mann's *The Fall of the Roman Empire* (1964) was revisited four and seven months later in Caiano's *I due gladiatori* (*Two Gladiators*, 1964) and Grieco's *Una spada per l'impero* (*Sword of the Empire*, 1964). Similarly, Cottafavi revisited Gallone's evil Messalina (with Maria Felix) in *Messalina Venere imperatrice* (*Messalina, Imperial Venus*, 1960), now with Belinda Lee, reprised once again in Umberto Lenzi's *L'ultimo gladiator* (*Messalina against the Son of Hercules*, 1964). Not surprisingly, only the first Christian emperor warranted a positive biopic, Lionello De Felice's *Constantino il Grande* (*Constantine and the Cross*, 1962), in which he was played by Cornel Wilde.

In the final productions of the genre, some producers realised that most of the mythological and historical highlights had already been captured on film, so they were content to contrive plots which had only a vague historicity, for example, Luigi Vanzi's *Sette a Tebe* (*Seven from Thebes*, 1964); Malatesta's *Revolt of the Barbarians* (1964); Roberto Mauri's *I tre centurioni* (*Three Swords for Rome*, 1964); and Michele Lupo's *Sette contro tutti* (*Seven Rebel Gladiators*, 1965). An interesting example is the trilogy of Parolini's *I dieci gladiatori* (*The Ten*

Gladiators, 1963), Nick Nostro's *Il trionfo dei dieci gladiatori* (*Triumph of the Ten Gladiators*, 1964), and Nostro's *Gli invincibili dieci gladiatori* – all starring Dan Vadis as 'Rocca'. The first of these CI.AS co-productions takes place during the reign of Nero, but the second and third instalments move into metahistory. In doing so, this trilogy continued the concept of including multiple strongmen within one film, as would Giorgio Capitani's *Ercole, Sansone, Maciste e Ursus gli invincibili* (*Samson and the Mighty Challenge*, 1964). Some of these late films had essentially no historicity whatsoever, such as Giuseppe Vari's *Roma contro Roma* (*Rome against Rome*, 1964), which postulates a Roman war against zombies. The film was one of Galatea's final productions, as the genre would dissipate by the end of the next year and Galatea would go out of business. Starring Ettore Manni, who also starred in *La rivolta dei gladiatori* that Cottafavi directed in 1958. And this brings this part of our survey full circle, as will our denouement.

ADDITIONAL AMERICAN DISTRIBUTION
Under the guidance of Joseph E. Levine, *Le fatiche di Ercole* had already made the sword-and-sandal genre a staple in the US at drive-in theatres and Saturday theatrical matinees. Galatea even handled the distribution of the National Broadcasting Company's derivative peplum, *Revak, lo schiavo di Cartagine* (*Revak* aka *Rivak the Barbarian* aka *The Barbarians*, 1960), with Jack Palance and an entirely American cast but an Italian crew. Three years later Levine's Embassy Pictures began to import the 'Sons of Hercules' series from Italy, repackaging fourteen Maciste, Ursus, Goliath and other films with exciting but lengthy names including the

Muscular Dan Vadis leads a large group of muscular gladiators in *Il trionfo dei dieci gladiatori* (1964)

phrase 'Son of Hercules'. *Hero of Babylon*, for instance, became *The Beast of Babylon against the Son of Hercules*, and *Perseo l'invincibile* was now known as *Medusa against the Son of Hercules*. Embassy grouped all these films together with a Western-style musical theme song sung by a male chorus accompanied by a solo guitar. At the peak of production, in 1964, professional bodybuilder Dave 'the Gladiator' Draper hosted these and other sword-and-sandal films every Saturday night on KHJ-TV in Los Angeles, and many local television stations followed suit in the US and Europe. There were even a few attempts to reproduce the genre for American television. Following the cool reception afforded *Revak*, Trans-Lux offered an animated television series, *The Mighty Hercules* (1963), and then none other than Levine served as the executive producer for *Hercules and the Princess of Troy* (1965), an ABC TV pilot starring Gordon Scott. It was broadcast in September 1965, too late in the genre to be successful. One month later, Levine reminisced to the *New York Times*: 'Hercules' was lousy, wasn't it? Still, I'm not ashamed of it. In this business, to survive, you naturally cater to different levels of taste.'

FURTHER READING

Aziza, Claude, *Le Péplum: l'antiquité au cinema* (Condé-sur-Noireau: Corlet, 1998).

Bondanella, Peter, *A History of Italian Cinema* (New York: Continuum International, 2009).

Cammarota, Domenico, *Il cinema peplum* (Rome: Fanucci, 1987).

D'Amelio, Maria Elena, 'Hercules, Politics, and Movies', in Michael G. Cornelius (ed.), *Of Muscles and Men: Essays on the Sword and Sandal Film* (Jefferson NC: McFarland & Company, Inc., 2011), pp. 15–27.

Graitson, Jean-Marie (ed.), *Péplum: L'antiquité dans le roman, la BD et le cinema. Les Cahiers des para-littératures* no. 5 (Liege: Éditions du CÉFAL, 1988).

Günsberg, Maggie, 'Heroic Bodies: The Culture of Masculinity in Peplums', in Maggie Günsberg (ed.), *Italian Cinema: Gender and Genre* (London: Palgrave Macmillan, 2005), pp. 97–132.

Hughes, Howard, *Cinema Italiano: The Complete Guide from Classics to Cult* (London: I. B. Tauris, 2011).

Legny, Michèle, 'Popular Taste: The Peplum', in Richard Dyer and Ginette Vincendeau (eds), *Popular European Cinema* (London: Routledge, 1992), pp. 163–80.

Lucanio, Patrick, *With Fire and Sword: Italian Spectacles on American Screens, 1958–1968* (Metuchen, NJ: Scarecrow Press, 1994).

Solomon, Jon, *The Ancient World of the Cinema*, 2nd rev. edn (New Haven, CT: Yale University Press, 2001).

Wyke, Maria, 'Herculean Muscle!: The Classicizing Rhetoric of Bodybuilding', *Arion* no. 4 (1997), pp. 51–79.

Gino Moliterno

Mondo [...] the ugly bastard child of the documentary
and the peepshow[1]

Critically reviled, when not largely ignored, in canonical
histories of postwar Italian cinema, the *mondo* film has
been rehabilitated in more recent times. In the new
millennium, and particularly following the issue of the
eight-disc *Mondo Cane Collection* by Blue Underground in
2003, a number of major studies have appeared, all
attempting to revalorise both the aesthetic credentials
and the cultural import of the *filone* that soon came to
be known internationally as the 'shockumentary'. Mark
Goodall has closely analysed the shock aesthetics of
the genre to reveal, at least in its best incarnations, an
audacious experimentation and auteurist expressivity
characteristic of nothing less than avant-garde art.[2]
Sébastien Gayraud and Maxime Lachaud have sought
to place it within an even wider cultural context,
leading them to conclude that the *mondo* film, 'a much
more intelligent genre than hitherto accepted, [...] was
a genuine engagement with cinematic expression,
even as it propagated the channel-hopping and reality
television that would follow'.[3] Martin Roberts, in an
analysis of a late variant of the genre, *Baraka* (*Baraka*,
1992), also underscored how the genre's appearance
in the early 1960s constituted the first sign of the
emergence of a global imaginary in Euro-American
commercial cinema.[4] A more contemporary appraisal
of the *mondo* film, then, evaluates it as a timely and
paradigmatically postmodern genre, whose voracious
gaze and visual shock tactics anticipate the most
characteristic features of the global mediatised
televisual culture of our twenty-first century.

JACOPETTI AND COMPANY
The roots of the *mondo* film, however, reach back to the
very beginnings of cinema, to that spectacle of the real

offered up in the 'optical reports' of the Lumière
actualités and to that 'cinema of attractions' which
catered to the same voyeuristic taste for sights of the
freakish and the bizarre previously satisfied by the P. T.
Barnum circus and the fairground sideshow. The
genre's planetary imaginary and its obsessive interest
in big game animals and the rituals and habits of
'primitive' cultures can also be traced back to the long
tradition of the exotic nature documentaries and the
jungle exploitation films of explorer-cinematographers
like Martin and Osa Johnson. It is generally agreed,
however, that the *mondo* shockumentary really begins
with *Mondo cane* (*Mondo Cane*, 1962).

Directed jointly by Gualtiero Jacopetti, Franco
Prosperi and Paolo Cavara, thereafter regarded as the
'godfathers' of the genre,[5] and released into a crowded
marketplace in 1962, *Mondo cane* achieved the
extraordinary success of becoming, as the publicity for
once could accurately claim, one of the most talked-
about films of the period. Nominated for the Golden
Palm at Cannes, in Italy it shared the David award for
Best Production of the year. Two years later, with the
film still being screened throughout the world and
'More', derived from Riz Ortolani's memorable score,
having become one of the most widely recorded songs
in recent history, it also garnered an Academy
nomination for Best Music. Most importantly, perhaps,
it became the fifth highest-grossing film of the season
in Italy, going on to do as well if not better on the
international market.[6]

While the film achieved great box office
everywhere, critical reaction remained mixed.
In Italy, oddly enough, it received a relatively positive
review from the Vatican-based Centro Cattolico
Cinematografico which lauded its 'impressive' realism,
its colour photography and its rhythmic editing even
as it noted a 'questionable inclination towards the

macabre'.[7] Others highlighted its sadistic voyeurism and its misanthropic inspiration.[8] Abroad, English critics also underscored the misanthropy in the film's insistent presentation of the world as a theatre of cruelty, with the *Monthly Film Bulletin* deploring it as a 'catalogue of horrors [...] a hymn to death and mutilation embellished with a giggle and tickle'.[9] In the US, however, Bosley Crowther was moved to invoke Hamlet's 'more things in heaven and earth' speech to characterise what he called an 'extraordinarily candid factual film' which presented a profusion of weird and bizarre things in the world in 'a sort of cinematic compilation of believe-it-or-not vignettes'.[10] The more conservative Pauline Kael, on the other hand, characterised it as a brutal series of shocks and falsifications designed merely to titillate.[11] And the term that emerged most often, in both criticism and publicity alike, was indeed 'shock', the central element of what Goodall has called 'the Jacopetti effect' and the indispensable component of all *mondo* films to come.[12]

Filmed in eye-catching Technicolor and introduced by a written declaration that everything shown would be absolutely real and unstaged – another element that

Publicity for *Mondo cane* (1962) stresses the Jacopetti effect

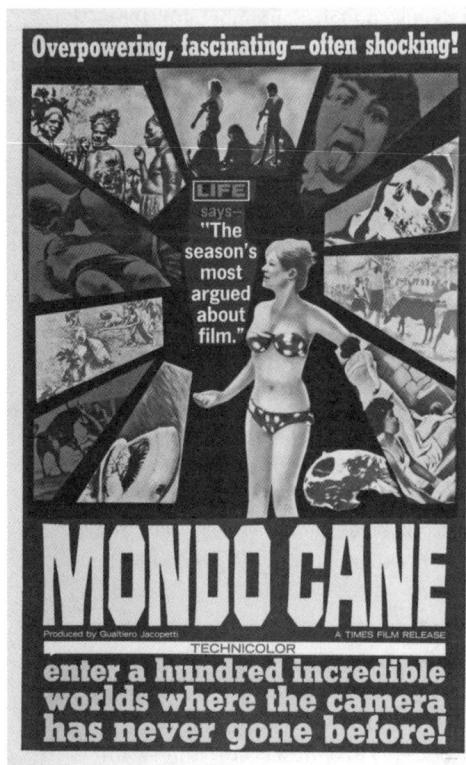

would become standard in the genre – the film presented some thirty sequences which took the viewer on what *Life* called 'a journey to jar your innards'.[13] In a series of ironic juxtapositions which on the surface often seemed arbitrary but which in reality were tightly governed by a logic of contiguity, the film mixed together in startling promiscuity scenes of banality and brutality, 'civilised' customs and 'savage' rituals, sexual titillation and religious fanaticism. A hectic cinematography which panned and zoomed relentlessly was further energised by Jacopetti's expressive editing which privileged the 'shock cut' and the abrupt transition, often disconcertingly pairing rebarbative images of suffering and death, human or animal, with the sweet strains of jazz or lounge music. All of this was controlled and held in place by a distinctive voiceover commentary, penned by Jacopetti but spoken by veteran actor-dubber, Stefano Sibaldi, in a tone which oscillated between empathetic and cynical, in places rising almost to poetry, in others sinking to condescension.

In spite of the film's claim to absolute authenticity, some of the scenes were clearly staged, a fact noted and decried by many commentators. Yet this itself constituted what would remain a characteristic of the genre. As knowledgeable enthusiast, Dr Mondo (Charles Kilgore), would later explain,

> A true mondo movie [...] has to be somewhat inauthentic, because that's what makes it a mondo movie rather than a straight documentary. [...] not that straight documentaries are always authentic, but the mondo movie is a little more boldfaced in its use of inaccurate or staged sequences.[14]

Blurring all boundaries, then, mixing the authentic and the staged, the mundane and the taboo, *Mondo cane* precipitated the *mondo* formula as an intense but fundamentally sceptical engagement with the world in the form of carnival.

The film's overwhelming international success at the box office made a sequel inevitable and, in any case, producer Rizzoli's generous budget had allowed the troupe to shoot much more footage than could ever have been incorporated into one film. With what must have been minimal effort and a repetition of the formula, *Mondo cane 2* was assembled and released the following year.

Mondo cane 2 proved popular enough but, predictably, less successful than its predecessor.

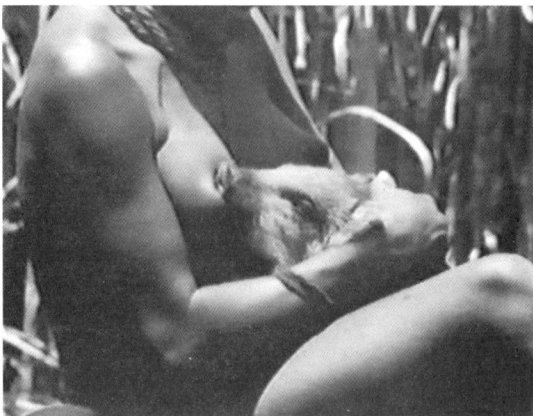

In Jacopetti's *Mondo cane* (1962) starlets on boats waving to sailors are juxtaposed with a native woman suckling a piglet

Ironically, by the time it was released, it found itself competing with a flood of films all sporting the *mondo* label, some, like Roberto Bianchi Montero's *Mondo infame* (*Abominable World*, 1963) and Francesco De Feo's *Mondo nudo* (*Naked World*, 1963) which followed *Mondo cane*'s own stratagem of parading, as Amy Staples would put it, a world of 'primitive rites and civilised wrongs',[15] and others, like Mino Loy's *Mondo sexy di notte* (*Mondo Sexuality*, 1962) and Carlo Veo's *Mondo matto al neon* (*Mad World in Neon Lights*, 1963) which were more directly in the line of the titillating 'sexy nocturne' initiated by Alessandro Blasetti's *Europa di notte* (*Europe by Night*, 1959), a film to which Jacopetti himself had significantly contributed by scouting locations and writing the distinctive commentary.[16]

Puzzlingly, however, in subsequent interviews, Jacopetti would continue to disown *Mondo cane 2* emphatically, denigrating it as nothing but a pale imitation and blaming its existence on the financial greed of producer, Angelo Rizzoli. And yet this can only

have been disingenuous. The two films are clearly cut from the same cloth, both photographed and produced by largely the same team and, perhaps most significantly, both authorially governed by the distinctive voiceover commentary written by Jacopetti himself, imposing on both a similar structure and tone. Rather than imitation, then, *Mondo cane 2* would seem to be simply a second take on the world in a carnival mode, cleverly seizing the opportunity of its later release to provide something of a rejoinder to scandalised critics of its predecessor.

The original *Mondo cane* had been particularly criticised in England for its scenes of animal cruelty, especially in its opening sequence. With extraordinary cheek, *Mondo cane 2* begins with the camera quietly stealing into a similar dog pound to that in the opening of the earlier film but with the dogs now wearing blood-stained bandages around their necks and their barking muted to almost a whisper. The voiceover begins by extolling the many virtues of the English, among which it includes a love of dogs. In deference to this, the commentator declares, the film's makers explicitly undertake not to show any more scenes of cruelty to canines which appeared in the earlier film and caused so much consternation among British audiences – except for this one, which appears precisely dated 'London, September 4th, 1963'. The vocal chords of these dogs, we are told, have been cut so that their barking will not disturb the surgeons who perform vivisection on them (and we cut to a scene in what purports to be a London clinic where white-smocked doctors do appear to be operating on conscious dogs). Mischievously punning on the word 'cut', the voiceover explains that, very obligingly, the film-makers have placed this scene at the beginning of the film enabling the British censors to cut it, if they wish, without affecting the rest. Even more truculently, the next sequence, apparently set in Italy, reprises the dog being dragged along on a leash in the opening sequence of *Mondo cane* but in a more 'civilised' key, with a number of unwilling poodles, their coats dyed and their hair coiffed, being pulled along a catwalk by elegant models as part of what, we are told, are this season's obligatory fashion accessories.

The film then proceeds in a way that continues to echo its earlier incarnation, provocatively cutting together scenes that intermix the mundane and the sensational, the sacred and the lurid, the 'primitive' and the 'civilised', in a mosaic structure again superficially arbitrary but at base determined by a principle of contiguity. So, the look of the dogs and the mention of dog hair prompts the camera to highlight the exaggerated coiffure of the women watching the fashion show which, as a visual bridge, leads into a sequence showing poor peasant women in a southern Italian village having their hair cut off to be sold for the manufacture of wigs. Cut to a large workshop in America where female workers are both making and trying on wigs, which leads us to transvestites in wigs performing burlesque in a French nightclub, the cross-dressing conjuring up the next sequence in which burly police officers in an undisclosed American city dress up as women in a sting to entrap sexual offenders. At this point 'police' becomes the linking motif as we cut to a scene where Mexican policemen are dangerously honing their marksmanship in what appears, to all intents, to be a fairground sharpshooting act. Here, however, 'Mexico' motivates a segue to a sequence which shows Mexican children on All Souls' Day eating the innards of corpses made of marzipan and ice-cream from what appear to be human skulls. At this point, the 'bizarre food' motif is engaged as we are taken to a Mexican village where peasants add handfuls of crawling insects to their tortillas and eat them with relish – a situation that seems to echo in reverse the sequence in the earlier film in which sophisticated American diners in an expensive New York restaurant urbanely consume fried ants and cooked insects à la carte. And so the film proceeds as a kaleidoscopic narrative refracting through a series of audacious, indeed at times outrageous, connections.

As in the earlier film, scenes that were, or at least seemed to be, unquestionably authentic were liberally mixed with ones that were patently staged. The issue of authenticity, however, came particularly to the fore in the sequence which implicitly purported to show graphically the actual death of Quang Duc, the Buddhist monk who set himself on fire in Saigon in 1963 in protest against the persecution of Buddhists by the ruling Christian government. The idea that the sequence *was* true in all its horrifying reality certainly contributed to the film's overall shock value and to supporting its boast of breaching any and all taboos in order to show the natural and human world in all its terrifying aspects. And the real event, of course, *had* actually taken place and been widely reported, although less graphically shown, in the media only a few months before the film's release. All the same,

nagging doubts about its veracity persisted, giving the film its *mondo* edge. It was only in 1993 that Kerekes and Slater, after close analysis of the sequence on videotape, were able to persuasively conclude that 'mondo's first cultural kill, on closer examination, is nothing but an elaborate reconstruction; a convincingly staged technicolour suicide [...] marketed as genuine and sold to the public as a real-death spectacle'.[17] A decade later, interviewed separately for *The Godfathers of Mondo* documentary (2003), both Prosperi and Jacopetti admitted that the sequence had indeed been faked.

If *Mondo cane 2* might thus be considered less a derivative sequel and more of a double-take on its predecessor, *La donna nel mondo* (*Women of the World*), released in the same year, would appear to complete a triptych. In spite of, as the title implies, narrowing its voracious look specifically to the world of women, *La donna* is also clearly cut from the same cloth as the other two: produced by the same troupe, similarly photographed and structured, and again authorially controlled by the very distinctive commentary written by Jacopetti himself. Indeed, two unsourced but credible press reports recently posted in the entry for *La donna nel mondo* on Wikipedia suggest that, in spite of the chronology of the films supplied by Prosperi and Jacopetti in *The Godfathers of Mondo* interviews, *Mondo cane* and *La donna* (and presumably much of what ended up as *Mondo cane 2*) may originally have been part of the one extended project of documenting the whole world in all its most sensational aspects, all probably filmed at around the same time.[18] Significantly the film is dedicated to the American actress, Belinda Lee, who had been Jacopetti's constant partner at the time they had been photographing *Mondo cane* and who had died in the car accident in California in 1961 which Jacopetti himself had only just narrowly survived.

Mondo aficionados have generally considered *La donna* less shocking and thus less successful as a *mondo* movie. Nevertheless, and despite strong competition from the many other sexy *mondos* at the time it was released, the film did extremely well at the box office, becoming the eighth highest-grossing film in Italy in the 1962–3 season. And if undoubtedly tamer than the other two *Mondo cane* films in some respects, and disconcerting in many places more for its moralising tone than for its libertinism, *La donna* in some ways seems to push the *mondo* formula further, particularly when, in a number of sequences, the camera's obsessive desire to 'reveal all' turns back upon itself to show the camera and the film-makers themselves photographing the event, thus creating the effect of a *mise en abŷme*.

Exploitation cinema's traditional obsession with the 'dark continent' and 'primitive peoples', after having already been so much indulged in all the 'savage' sequences of these three films, came to occupy the very centre of Jacopetti and Prosperi's next film, *Africa addio* (*Goodbye Africa*, 1966), a fully fledged shockumentary that took death and destruction to new heights of spectacle. By Jacopetti's own account, as they were putting the finishing touches to the *Mondo cane* films, a letter from a friend in Africa alerted him to the fact that, in the process of decolonialisation, the continent was undergoing massive changes, which cried out for documentation. Accepting the challenge, Jacopetti and Prosperi together with now regular cinematographer, Antonio Climati, and production manager, Stanis Nievo, immediately moved to Africa where, for the next three years, they crisscrossed the continent filming, in graphic gory Technicolor detail, everything from the gruesome destruction of wildlife at the hands of poachers to the continuing and violent crisis in the Congo. In a grisly media coup, they managed to capture from the air the only visual documentation of the wholesale massacre of the Arab population of Zanzibar by African ASP insurgents as it occurred, as well as photographing many of the enormous mass graves into which the thousands of bodies were being shovelled. In the final edit of the film, all this carnage was slyly juxtaposed with sequences of relative happiness and well-being in South Africa, thus supporting the voiceover commentary's contention that all the chaos and destruction derived predominantly from a too hastily instituted process of decolonialisation at a time when Africans were not ready for independence.

As a declared valediction to 'the old Africa of the explorers, the adventurers and big game hunters', the film was undoubtedly indulging in what Renato Rosaldo has termed 'imperialist nostalgia'[19] and its colonialist and racist sympathies provoked widespread denunciation. Indeed, the film became enmeshed in controversy long before its completion. In late 1964, Carlo Gregoretti, a journalist from the left-leaning Italian weekly, *L'Espresso*, had visited the troupe, which had been for some time embedded with a column of mercenaries allied to the Congolese Army of Moise Tshombe, attempting to take back the strategic city of Boende from Simba separatists. Returning to Italy, Gregoretti published several articles recounting how the gung-ho mercenaries carried out their deadly missions and atrocities often at the behest, and for the benefit, of the troupe's camera.[20] On the basis of these reports, the Italian Senate called for prosecution and, returning to Italy, Jacopetti was forced to defend himself from charges of complicity to murder. He was eventually exonerated of direct responsibility for any of the deaths graphically shown in the film but, ironically, only by proving that, in true *mondo* style, a considerable number of the most gruesome 'genuine' sequences had in fact been staged.[21]

Finally released amid continuing controversy in 1966, the film nevertheless shared the David di Donatello award for Best Production of the year although the Minister for Culture refused to actually present the prize. As with Jacopetti and Prosperi's previous films, *Africa addio* also proved extremely popular at the Italian box office, achieving fifth place in the 1966 season. Outside Italy, the film was generally reviled. In West Germany, vocal opposition to the film became an effective rallying cry for the emerging anti-authoritarian Left movement.[22] In the US, where it was released for a short season in 1967, it was publicly denounced by American UN Ambassador, Arthur J. Goldberg, while a young Roger Ebert branded it 'a brutal, dishonest, racist film [which] slanders a continent and at the same time diminishes the human spirit'.[23] Soon withdrawn from circulation in the US, the film was re-released in 1971 by exploitation specialist, Jerry Gross, in an unauthorised shorter version titled *Africa Blood and Guts*, tellingly taglined 'Every scene looks you straight in the eye – and spits.' Jacopetti always condemned Gross's version as a travesty.

As Prosperi explained in *The Godfathers of Mondo* interviews, it was in response to the charge of racism levelled at *Africa addio* that he and Jacopetti decided to make an epic documentary on slavery in the US under the ironic title of *Addio zio Tom* (*Goodbye Uncle Tom*, 1971). Originally to be shot in Brazil to economise on costs, the huge production with a cast of thousands ended up being filmed for the most part in Haiti, strongly facilitated by the active support of President 'Papa Doc' Duvalier. In keeping with the myth of non-involvement in the reality which they were documenting, in *Africa addio*, the film-makers themselves only appeared in a sequence in which the cameraman continued to film as a soldier smashed the windscreen of the troupe's car and pulled a bloodied Jacopetti from the vehicle to line him up against a wall with other prisoners.[24] In *Addio zio Tom*, the notion of non-involvement is abandoned from the start, with the film-makers openly declaring their presence as two contemporary cine-journalists (somehow) journeying back in time to a reconstructed American south, fat and flourishing under all the benefits bestowed by the slave system. At first, their presence is acknowledged as being behind the camera, as they are directly addressed by a number of historically based characters including Harriet Beecher Stowe, author of *Uncle Tom's Cabin* (1852), but as the film proceeds they come to be ever more part of their patently staged 'historical documentary' whose constructedness is further underscored by the frequent interpolation of found footage of 1960s America. The film-makers literally advertise their own presence when, in a bustling slave market shown, as so often in the film, as a grotesque carnival, the camera zooms out from the side of a wagon on which we see 'Jacopetti & Prosperi/Traveling Photographers' in huge lettering. This active participation is taken to its limit in a later sequence where Jacopetti, Prosperi and assistant director, Giampaolo Lomi, actually (and convincingly) play the part of professional slave hunters mercilessly shooting down hundreds of escaped slaves and then standing next to the pile of bodies like African game hunters posing for their commemorative photo. For all its gory realism, however, the massacre turns out to have been more an assault on the viewer than on the hapless slaves for as soon as the camera has clicked to record the scene, Jacopetti, breaking out from actor to director, dismisses everyone and all the 'dead bodies' happily resurrect themselves and gleefully run off to prepare for the next set-up.

As what Goodall styles 'nearly the most supreme mondo film' and 'one of the most staggering contributions to the history of film art',[25] *Addio zio Tom*

Film-makers as slave-hunters, next to their kill in Jacopetti's *Addio zio Tom* (1971)

presents a profoundly horrifying vision of slavery as the very grotesque carnival and theatre of cruelty it really must have been, although no one had previously had the barefacedness to employ all the resources of cinema to restage it in such stunning pornographic detail. Inevitably, however, such a vision offended critical sensibilities, especially in the US where Roger Ebert called it a 'vomit-bag of racism and perversion-mongering' and 'the most disgusting, contemptuous insult to decency ever to masquerade as a documentary'.[26] Pauline Kael went even further in seeing it a rabid incitement to race war. Outraged at what she called 'the voyeuristic hypocrisy of the movie' she nevertheless conceded that 'No-one has ever before attempted a full-scale treatment of slave-ship misery; how degrading to us all that by default it has fallen into the hands of the most devious and irresponsible film-makers who have ever lived'.[27] The film had a short season with an X-rating and soon disappeared. It only reappeared in a special BFI screening in London in 2008 when it was presented in context by Goodall and others. It still proved capable of provoking shock and outrage in a mixed-race audience, although in post-screening discussions many spectators admitted that their reaction probably stemmed more from the facts of slavery so spectacularly shown than from the apposite grotesquerie of their presentation.[28] Perhaps the ethical dimension of the Jacopetti effect had finally surfaced.

CONTINUING THE *FILONE* IN ITALY

These films by Jacopetti and Prosperi rightly appear as the classics of a genre which, however, could also quickly become weak and repetitive. Indeed, even as Prosperi and Jacopetti were making *Africa addio*, their former co-director, Cavara, released *I malamondo* (*Malamondo*, 1964), a touted 'wild exposé' of emerging youth culture gathered from around the world which, seen today, looks decidedly twee. Cavara's best solo effort before he moved on to the *giallo* was undoubtedly *L'occhio selvaggio* (*Savage Eye*, 1967), a fictional feature about a ruthless cine-journalist which accurately depicts, but at the same time clearly critiques, both the methods and ethos of *mondo* film-making. This, however, in no way discouraged newcomers to the genre like Alfredo and Angelo Castiglioni, who would soon become its foremost practitioners. Beginning in 1969, the Castiglioni brothers enthusiastically took up the lesson of *Africa addio* to produce no less than five Africa-centred para-

Filming the horror in Deodato's *Cannibal Holocaust* (1979), a work deeply indebted to the *mondo* tradition

documentaries with shock values disconcertingly well above what Prosperi and Jacopetti had been able to achieve. Ranks were also soon swelled by Jacopetti's regular cinematographer, Antonio Climati, and editor, Mario Morra, who in 1975 embarked on what came to be known as their 'savage trilogy': *Ultime grida dalla savana* (*Zumbalah* aka *Savage Man Savage Beast*, 1975); *Savana violenta* (*This Violent World*, 1976); and *Dolce e selvaggio* (*Sweet and Savage*, 1983). Boasting, among its other spectacles of carnage, a scene showing a hapless German tourist being eaten alive by lions (generally thought, in true *mondo* fashion, to have been faked), *Ultime grida* confirmed the *mondo* film's continuing purchase on the morbid curiosity of Italian audiences by becoming that season's tenth highest-grossing film.[29] A decade later, however, the release of an obvious clone like Stelvio Massi's *Mondo cane oggi – l'orrore continua* (*Savage World Today*, 1985) would stir much less interest.

A major spin-off of the *mondo* film in Italy proved to be the emergence during the 1970s of the cannibal film.[30] Beginning tentatively in 1972 with Umberto Lenzi's *Il paese del sesso selvaggio* (*Deep River Savages*, 1972), the genre found its definitive form in Ruggero Deodato's *Ultimo mondo cannibale* (*Last Cannibal World*, 1977) and its most extreme expression in *Cannibal Holocaust*, a film that quite patently, as Mikita Brottman points out, 'appropriated the Italian mondo tradition and, while pretending to denounce it [...] was, in its way, even more gruesome, exploitative, and scandalous'.[31] The shocking realism of the animal and human deaths in the film led not only to its being banned in most countries around the world but also to Deodato being forced, like Jacopetti before him, to defend himself legally from the charge of murder.

Inaccessible until recently except in second-rate pirated video copies, *Cannibal Holocaust* nevertheless clearly influenced one of the most talked-about films of the end of the millennium, *The Blair Witch Project* (1999).

THE *MONDO* OUTSIDE ITALY

The extraordinary international success of *Mondo cane* inevitably sparked off a host of imitations worldwide. With a certain prurience, the sexy *mondo* formula was propagated in England in films such as Arnold Miller's *London in the Raw* (1964) and *Primitive London* (1965). In France, too, budding director, Claude Lelouch, made *La femme spectacle* (*Night Women*, 1964), a film he later disowned. In the US, which had its own long tradition of exploitation cinema, the *mondo* label at first came to be adopted largely for sexploitation in films like Lee Frost and Bob Cresse's *Mondo Freudo* (1996) and *Mondo Bizarro* (1966), and Russ Meyer's *Mondo Topless* (1966). Eventually the more ethnographic dimension of the *mondo* formula came to the fore in films like Robert Carl Cohen's *Mondo Hollywood* (1967) and later Romano Vanderbes's *This Is America/Jabberwalk* (1977) and *This Is America: Part 2* (1980). However, it was that willingness to defy the ultimate taboo of looking death in the face, which had characterised the two original *Mondo cane* films that came to govern the most disturbing development of the *mondo* film in the US, the *Faces of Death* series beginning in 1978 and continuing through more than a dozen reiterations through to the end of the 1990s. It was death, too, that governed what is generally regarded as the other last two 'genuine' incarnations of *mondo*: *Shocking Asia* (1977) and *Shocking Asia II: The Last Taboos* (1985) by German director Rolf Olsen (as Emerson Fox).

We began by noting that recent critics see the Italian *mondo* film as in many ways anticipating our own postmodern mediatised televisual environment. Tellingly, however, in *The Godfathers of Mondo* interviews both Prosperi and Jacopetti ventured to suggest that *Mondo cane* itself could simply not be made today. The reason, it would seem, is obvious enough: in our contemporary, image-saturated, Google-Earthed, YouTubed, but fiercely politically correct, media landscape, the world is now not only one all-encompassing reality film set but one technologically geared to image itself automatically as its own global spectacle.

NOTES

1. Dr Mondo (Charles Kilgore) in Amy J. Staples, 'An Interview with Dr Mondo, *American Anthropologist* vol. 97 no. 1 (March 1995), p. 111.

2. Mark Goodall, *Sweet & Savage: The World through the Shockumentary Film Lens* (London: Headpress, 2006).

3. Sébastien Gayraud and Maxime Lachaud, *Reflets dans un œil mort: mondo movies et les films de cannibals* (Paris: Bazaar & Co, 2010), pp. 352–3 (author's translation).

4. Martin Roberts, '*Baraka*: World Cinema and the Global Culture Industry', *Cinema Journal* vol. 37 no. 3 (Spring 1998), p. 67.

5. See David Gregory, *The Godfathers of Mondo* (Blue Underground DVD, 2003), part of the 8-DVD *Mondo Cane Collection*. The DVD contains extensive interviews with Jacopetti and Prosperi although none with Cavara, who died in 1982.

6. Italian box-office figures taken from Carlo Celli and Marga Cottino Jones, *A New Guide to Italian Cinema* (London: Palgrave Macmillan, 2007), Appendix 2, pp. 171–87.

7. *Segnalazioni cinematografiche* vol. 52 (1962) (author's translation).

8. See, for example, G. P. Brera's review as cited in Roberto Poppi and Mario Pecorari, *Dizionario del cinema italiano: I film, Vol. 3, Dal 1960 al 1969* (Rome: Gremese, 1992), p. 343.

9. *Monthly Film Bulletin* vol. 30 nos 348–59 (1963), pp. 3–4.

10. *New York Times*, 4 April 1963.

11. See Pauline Kael, *I Lost It at the Movies* (Boston, MA and Toronto: Little Brown, 1965), p. 10.

12. Goodall, *Sweet & Savage*, p. 49.

13. *Life*, 15 March 1963.

14. Staples, 'An Interview with Dr Mondo', p. 117.

15. Amy Staples, 'Mondo Meditations', *American Anthropologist* vol. 96 no. 3 (September 1994), p. 662.

16. Jacopetti never mentioned it, but one wonders whether the dog motif in the title and the ubiquitous presence of canines in the two *Mondo cane* films (and beyond) may not be an ironic take on the two dogs friskily preceding Domenico Modugno's horse-drawn carriage in the closing sequence of *Europa di notte*.

17. David Kerekes and David Slater, *Killing for Culture: An Illustrated History of Death Film from Mondo to Snuff* (London: Creation Books, 1993), p. 170.

18. Available at http://en.wikipedia.org/wiki/La_donna_nel_mondo; accessed 20 November 2011.

19. Renato Rosaldo, 'Imperialist Nostalgia', *Representations* no. 26 (Spring 1989), pp. 107 ff.

20. Carlo Gregoretti, 'Una guerra privata in cinemascope', *L'Espresso*, 20 December 1964, pp. 6–7 and 'Gualtiero Jacopetti alla presa di Boende', *L'Espresso*, 27 December 1964, p. 5.

21. Years later Jacopetti admitted that a horrific scene like that of a mountain of amputated hands had 'of course' been faked. He *had* seen that sort of thing, he said, but real amputated hands immediately shrivel up and do not look like hands, and so the scene obviously had to be reconstructed. See the interview with Daniele Aramu in *Nocturno*. Available at http://www.nocturno.it/intervista/intervista-a-gualtiero-jacopetti; accessed 16 December 2011.

22. See 'The *Africa Addio* Controversy in West Germany', in Katrina M. Hagen, 'Internationalism in Cold War Germany', unpublished dissertation (Ann Arbor, MI: University Microfilms International, 2008), pp. 183 ff.

23. Available at http://rogerebert.suntimes.com/apps/pbcs.dll/article?AID=%2F19670425%2FREVIEWS%2F70425 0301%2F1023&AID1=%2F19670425%2FREVIEWS%2F70425 0301%2F1023&AID2=; accessed 12 December 2011.

24. Clearly always in some danger, the troupe at this point was apparently really on the point of being killed. Lined up with other prisoners about to be shot, they were apparently only saved at the last minute by an official running to the firing squad and shouting that he had discovered they were 'not whites but Italians'! Jacopetti often repeated this story in interviews, including in *The Godfathers of Mondo*.

25. Goodall, *Sweet & Savage*, p. 85.

26. Ebert in *Chicago Sun-Times*, 14 November 1972. Available at http://rogerebert.suntimes.com/apps/pbcs.dll/article?AID=/19721114/REVIEWS/211140301/1023; accessed 15 December 2001.

27. Now in Pauline Kael, *Reeling* (Boston, MA and Toronto: Little, Brown, 1976), pp. 66–7.

28. Some of the presentation and subsequent audience reaction can now be seen on YouTube. Available at http://www.youtube.com/watch?v=72mvQmWYLjs; accessed 30 January 2012.

29. Celli and Cottino Jones, *A New Guide to Italian Cinema*, p. 179.

30. The filiation of the Cannibal film from *mondo* is detailed in Chapter 4 of Gayraud and Lachaud, *Reflets dans un oeil mort*, pp. 127–48. See also 'Cannibali!', in Antonio Bruschini and Antonio Tentori, *Mondi incredibili: il cinema fantastico-avventuroso italiano* (Bologna: Granata Press, 1994), pp. 14–60.

31. Mikita Brottman, *Offensive Films* (Westport, CT: Vanderbilt University Press/Greenwood Publishing Group, 2005), p. 114.

FURTHER READING

Bentin, Doug, 'Mondo Barnum', in Gary D. Rhodes and John Parris Springer (eds), *Docufictions: Essays on the Intersection of Documentary and Fictional Filmmaking* (Jefferson, NC and London: McFarland, 2006), pp. 144–53.

Brottman, Mikita, 'Mondo Horror: Carnivalising the Taboo', in Stephen Prince (ed.), *The Horror Film* (New Brunswick, NJ and London: Rutgers University Press, 2004), pp. 167–88.

Bruschini, Antonio and Antonio Tentor, *Nudi e crudeli: i mondo movies italiani* (Bologna: PuntoZero, 2000).

Bussi, Marcello, *Mondo Cane Addio: Un delirio su Gualtiero Jacopetti* (lulu.com: 2011).

Castiel, Elie, 'The Mondo Film: Bizarre Rituals and Steamy Nights', *Offscreen* vol. 9 no. 4 (30 April 2005). Available at http://www.offscreen.com/index.php/phile/essays/mondo_film; accessed 14 October 2011.

Farassino, Alberto, 'Dal documentario esotico ai "mondo movies"', in *Fuori dal set: viaggi, esplorazioni, emigrazioni, nomadismi* (Rome: Bulzoni, 2000), pp. 172–88.

Goodall, Mark, 'Shockumentary Evidence: The Perverse Politics of the Mondo Film', in Stephanie Dennison and Song Hwee Lim (eds), *Remapping World Cinema: Identity, Culture, and Politics in Film* (London: Wallflower Press, 2006), pp. 118–26.

Jacopetti, Gualtiero, Interview, in Stuart Sweeney (ed.), *Amok Journal: Sensurround Edition* (Los Angeles, CA: Amok, 1995), pp. 132–68.

Persiani, Luca, 'Introduzione ai mondo movies', *Offscreen*. Available at http://www.offscreen.it/saggi/mondomovies.htm; accessed 20 November 2011.

Rice, Boyd, 'Mondo Films', in V. Vale and Andrea Juno (eds), *Incredibly Strange Films* (San Francisco, CA: RE/Search Publications, 1985).

Shipka, Danny, *Perverse Titillation: The Exploitation Cinema of Italy, Spain and France, 1960–1980* (Jefferson, NC: McFarland: London, 2011).

Tombs, Peter, *Mondo Macabro: Weird and Wonderful Cinema around the World* (London: Titan Books, 1997).

21 Spaghetti Westerns and Their Audience

Flavia Brizio-Skov

When Sergio Leone's *Per un pugno di dollari* was released on the Italian cinema circuit in August 1964, nobody would have predicted that this low-budget film – the result of an Italian-Spanish-German co-production costing only 120 million lire – would have triggered one of the most prolific and money-making cinematic trends (what Italian film critics call a *filone*) of the 1960s. Between 1964 and 1968, the film made more than 4.5 million dollars in Italy and 3.5 million dollars in the US, where it was not released until 1967 due to a legal dispute over copyrights with Japanese director Akira Kurosawa.[1] Leone's second film, *Per qualche dollaro in più*, also an Italian-Spanish-German co-production, earned 5 million dollars in Italy between 1965 and 1968 and equally as much in the US. The third Leone Western *Il buono, il brutto, il cattivo*, an entirely Italian production, earned more than 4 million dollars in Italy and 6 million dollars in the US between 1966 and 1968.[2] The enormous success of these three films unleashed the spaghetti Western phenomenon: Italy produced 462 of them in a decade, with an average of more than seventy per year between 1967 and 1968 and more than forty-five per year between 1971 and 1972, all with respectable box-office earnings. Between 1976 and 1977, production fell sharply to three spaghetti Westerns per year and even decreased to two per year in 1978.

Economic factors are usually cited for both the spectacular rise and the eventual decline of the spaghetti Western. In the 1960s, cinema was still one of the most popular forms of entertainment with annual sales of 700 million tickets and a national production of around 300 films per year. Toward the end of the 1960s, Italy produced even more films than Hollywood, a situation that had not occurred except during a few years before the outbreak of World War I, when Italy was a major global exporter of silent films, particularly historical epics. During the decade when such Westerns were phenomenally popular, competition from television was not yet a major factor, and generous financing for film production in Italy was available from US and European sources. By the end of the 1970s, however, this favourable economic climate no longer existed and overall Italian cinematic production decreased to around 100 films per year, and yearly ticket sales dropped to around 100 million, with 80 per cent of earnings going to Hollywood films, not Italian ones.[3]

We can form some hypotheses about the sociology of Italian film audiences during this period, although it is now impossible to conduct empirical research on this matter. Vittorio Spinazzola maintains that 10,517 various kinds of movie theatres existed in Italy in 1964: 20 per cent charged less than 100 lire (the equivalent at the time of $.16); 57.8 per cent charged between 100 and 200 lire; 14.3 per cent charged between 200 and 300 lire; 6.9 per cent charged between 300 and 1,000 lire; and only 0.2 per cent sold tickets for more than 1,000 lire.[4] Thus, given that most Italian theatres were of the low-cost variety, and that the profits earned by the spaghetti Westerns were enormous, we are most certainly confronted with an authentic popular success. On the other hand, the assertion that the monetary success of the Italian Western was, above all, a phenomenon linked to the second-run and third-run theatres and only to a certain type of popular or uneducated audience, is negated by the list of the box-office earnings at first-run theatres during these years, which often saw spaghetti Westerns ranking in the top ten for ticket sales. From this data, it is clear that the old claim, according to which the spaghetti Western obtained success primarily via secondary theatres or, in other words, in rural, peripheral or southern areas with an audience comprised mostly of working or uneducated classes, obviously cannot be considered valid. The distinction between cinema *engagé* for the intellectual/urban classes and commercial cinema for the inferior/rural/southern classes, or, as some say, between the 'high and low culture', is an untenable model for popular genre films of the 1960s. The Italian Western shattered the barrier between popular cinema and elite cinema; the genre was appreciated by all, by the bourgeois of the cities as well as by the proletarians of the outskirts, by women as well as by men. We are facing a mass phenomenon,[5] one that raises several important questions: what kind of pleasure did an audience derive from watching these films; what did a diversified and heterogeneous mass of people find so fascinating in this genre; why did people, for over a decade, flood theatres to watch films that were not always very well made; and what type of relationship did these films have with the reality of the time, if they had any at all?

The study of film reception is considered by many problematic due to the difficulty of conducting empirical research on the audience in terms of gender, age or class. However, in the case of the spaghetti Western, given the abundance of sociological-historical-economic studies on the 1960s and the copious data on the cinematographic industry of the period, we believe that it is possible to formulate a posteriori some theoretical hypotheses on film reception, especially considering the fact that, beginning with Christopher Frayling's seminal study in 1981, *Spaghetti Westerns: Cowboys and Europeans from Karl May to Sergio Leone*, there exists an abundance of solid critical texts, both Italian and foreign, which analyse the Italian Western and much (if not all) of the filmic production of the decade in question. As we all know, the filmic text addresses the spectator and, by doing so, solicits a certain response. At the moment of reception, however, other factors come into play because the 'message' is filtered by the subject through his/her age, class, gender, ideology, ethnic group and culture. There is a notable lag between the ideal viewer that the filmic text implies or, at the theoretical level, presupposes (the one who would fully identify with the message), and the real spectator who, seated in the theatre, receives the message. The ideal spectator as a passive subject, or as an object onto which the project of dominant ideology, designed to homogenise and dominate the masses, is poured, seems no longer sustainable. On the other hand, the subject that rebels and totally refuses the hegemonic message also seems to be a chimera. Film critics, therefore, need to reconstruct the type of filmic messages that the spaghetti Western directed toward the various kinds of

viewers of the time, arguing retrospectively on processes of both *identification with* and *refusal of* the figure of the protagonist, without which the filmic fruition would be impossible.

Unlike the classic American Western in which the hero is often a pure, fearless knight errant, the hero of the Italian Western is usually driven by personal motives that oscillate between vendetta and the acquisition of money. The Italian Western protagonist is fundamentally an anti-hero: a bounty hunter, a stranger with no name, or an outlaw who, in the course of events, acting to achieve a certain goal, commits some good deeds, not for the good of society, but only because he hates the arrogant and the pushy. The anti-heroes of the spaghetti Western operate in a way that recalls the Far West, but only as a cinematographic myth, as an echo of faraway things. The US cinematographic myth was affected by Turner's Frontier Thesis, by Henry Nash Smith's idea of 'virgin land', and by the archetypes produced by an impressive production of novels, which, in their turn, found inspiration in the epic conquest of the West, completed in the remote 1890s. Such ideals, though far removed from their chronological origins, were still present in the US imagination when the classic Western film was born. The spaghetti Western, instead, deals with the 'myth of the myth'. By the time of the creation of the Western Italian style in the 1960s, Italy had little to do with the historical events that occurred in the nineteenth-century Far West. The Italian Western, as a consequence, shows no preoccupation with historical verisimilitude. In the spaghetti Western there are no cities to build, nor communities to save: the future, like the past, is out of the frame, only the present exists.

These anti-heroes, like the heroes of the classic Western, come from an unknown place and are going towards a place just as unknown; they have no home, no family, no ties to others but, unlike their Hollywood counterparts, they are seeking gold or revenge, not justice. In this world, the sheriffs are corrupt, the power is in the hands of violent clans, and the citizens are divided into victims and executioners. In short, the law of the jungle prevails. In order to survive in such a world, one needs quickness of hand and mind, determination, a huge dose of cruelty and expertise with firearms. For spectators to absorb the hegemonic message of these films, they must identify fully with the filmic anti-hero in his celebration of ruthless individualism.

After the economic boom of 1958–63, Italy became an industrialised country. The idea of a single person who achieves success through skill and cold determination represents a celebration of the new industrial professional. He must stand out in a capitalist society and depend upon his own resources in order to survive in a world in which technological knowledge and intelligence must be used to overpower in order not to be overpowered, in which money equals power. The new law of the survival of the fittest is the new law of the capital market. Those who profited from the economic boom – merchants who have amassed wealth, the lower classes that have become working class and have improved their lot – view Italy's change from an almost rural country to an industrial power as a positive development. In the eyes of such spectators, who in various ways have been positively affected by the economic well-being of the period, the Western hero appears as a reconfirmation of the values of professionalism, wealth, individualism and tenacity in which they firmly believe. But, paradoxically, those who have profited from this economic boom and those who have not, both fall under the spell of the spaghetti Western protagonist, both identify with the *pistolero*: the successful feel further reconfirmed by this model, while the unsuccessful may still vicariously live the exhilarating experience of being a winner during the film's ninety minutes. On the other hand, spectators, ideologically opposed to the arrival of this new, industrialised Italian society, who rejected monetary gain as the ultimate end of every action and saw in the rise of the consumer society the source of many social evils, refused identification with the anti-hero as a symbol of capitalism. Nevertheless, even such spectators succumb to the charm of the spaghetti Western's protagonist. After all, the anti-hero arrives, destabilises society, kills the bad guys and, having achieved his goal, goes away, assuming it will be someone else's job to eventually re-establish law and order. The anti-hero, in his outsider position as a man who lives at the margins of society, is able to destroy a system that does not work, and by doing this, enacts a form of rebellion. The *pistolero*'s actions show he detests society because it is unjust; his attitude implies that in a world such as this, suffering and injustice are everywhere, and for this reason, violence becomes the only possible response. For those who in the mid-1960s began to rebel against the world of their fathers and denounce the hypocrisy of the dominant Italian political system and the corruption of the Christian Democrats who ran it, the extreme violence of the anti-hero could not but appear as an additional confirmation of their revolutionary

convictions. Unlike the hero of the peplum epic – a popular genre set in the ancient world that directly preceded the 'explosion' of the spaghetti Western – the gunfighter in the spaghetti Western embraces an anarchic view of society that was extremely popular among young people. The *pistolero* embodied a rebellious attitude absent in the various Hercules, Macistes and Ursuses of the sword-and-sandal epic films.

Critics often claim that the Italian Western is an excessively masculine universe, in which women practically do not exist, or if they do appear, are reduced to sexual objects that are used and then forgotten. Consequently, it seems logical that such films have principally attracted a male audience. However, if, as some critics argue, identification with the protagonist is fundamental, it is also possible for such identification to cross gender boundaries in the audience. Such enormous ticket sales would have been virtually impossible if the female spectators of the time who would, in a few years, enter Italian squares for the first feminist battles over divorce, equality and abortion, were not also captivated by the appeal of this popular genre. While there is no doubt that in the spaghetti Western, women are frequently treated quite violently, however, such anti-female violence is usually perpetrated by the antagonists of the anti-hero. Furthermore, the female audience of the time could not help but note that the anti-hero of the Italian Western, in his position of outsider, as a man who has no ties and wants no ties, in his refusal of family and, therefore, of domestic life, makes a decisive break with the rules of patriarchy and rebels against the ideals sponsored by the Catholic Italian culture of the time. The *pistolero* may be a bit misogynistic, but at the same time, he is anti-patriarchal; he does not need to force his authority on wife and children or hand down his name to posterity because he loves freedom.

Many female viewers of the time were raised in a postwar society that still judged women according to the dictates of the fascist era, which maintained that the woman's place was at the fireside, a set of beliefs designed to marginalise females in the home so as to impede their emancipation. If such emancipation were to have taken place in the sexual arena, it would rapidly have extended to other areas of life, such as politics and labour. The outcome would be sexual and economic independence, and this freedom would end up unhinging patriarchy's rigid rules. Therefore, oppressed female spectators had to admire the *pistolero*. As chauvinist as the protagonist was, by identifying with him, these female spectators could vicariously enjoy in brief filmic moments the benefits that such a position of power entailed: absolute independence, courage, tenacity and sexual freedom – conditions denied to them in everyday life, but temporarily available via the filmic text.

Finally, most viewers in the 1960s were part of the workforce that had made the 'economic miracle' possible but this miracle, with its consequent migration and urbanisation, had been achieved at a terrible price: a more stressful pace of life in the workplace that often created tension and frustration. From the psychological point of view, it should certainly have been liberating for those who were part of the new working world – the majority of the audience of the time – to identify with the *pistolero* and dream of killing the bosses of real life with a quick pistol shot. Thus, the identification with the protagonist of the spaghetti Western offered all viewers, female and male, the possibility of shifting through fantasy to a much more exciting world than the real one, a world far away from the drabness and routine of daily life.

In a cinematographic market such as the Italian one where, from 1916 until 1950, the film diet tendered to the audience was, besides the parentheses of the war years, almost completely Hollywoodian in tone if not in national origin, the fact that the spaghetti Western dressed itself in Anglophone clothing was a determining factor. Even relatively little known US actors often appeared in the main roles – Clint Eastwood, Lee Van Cleef and Charles Bronson being the classic examples. Italian native directors, cinematographers, photographers, musicians and all the crew members generally appeared with English

pseudonyms in the credits. This produced two effects: it enticed Italians to see the films with the appeal of the exotic, returning the viewer to the classic US Western world created by men like Ford, Hawks, Mann and John Wayne. At the same time, it supported the export of these films to Italy's major foreign market, the US. Naturally, Leone's films are the exception to the rule, as Leone employed both lesser-known US actors such as Eastwood or Van Cleef (both of whom became stars with the success of his movies) and well-known actors, such as Henry Fonda, James Coburn or Rod Steiger, all of whom were attracted to work with him precisely because of the enormous impact on US and foreign markets his films enjoyed.

In the years between 1961 and 1965, more Italian films were shown in Italy than Hollywood productions, which was very unusual. Following the success of the peplum epic and the spaghetti Western, other popular film genres garnered the lion's share of Italian screens. With alternating luck, the peplum films, the 'spaghettis', the *commedia all'italiana*, the *giallo* thrillers, the horror films, the homemade spy movies à la James Bond, and exotic-sexy pseudo-documentaries such as *Mondo cane*, continued to return huge profits for the Italian industry. These successful genres must have responded, in some measure, to the enormous social, political and ideological changes occurring in Italy during this decade. The 1960s mark the end of 'Italietta', and it is in this decade that we see, in the words of one perceptive critic, 'the passage from a reality tied to outdated forms of development to one that attempts to grasp the idea … of *modernity*'.[6] Italy moves from a heavy political, ideological and cultural

Joe (Clint Eastwood) grins with a *toscano* in his mouth before dispatching four opponents in Sergio Leone's *Per un pugno di dollari* (1964)

Manco (Clint Eastwood) and Colonel Mortimer (Lee Van Cleef) help a young boy harvest apples with their guns in Leone's *Per qualche dollaro in più* (1966)

heredity, that of fascism, into a chaotic period later defined as the 'crisis of ideologies'. Italian cinema found itself immersed in an era of transition in which everything that concerned both the public and private spheres was called into question. The cinema of these years, therefore, records, comments on and exposes these changes with the tools at hand. The success of the spaghetti Western could be attributed to the plurality of the messages that it transmitted to its audience. Its filmic text was open to multiple interpretations: from the hegemonic (a celebration of the capitalist individual) to the revolutionary (the use of violence to attack an unjust society); from the quasi-feminist (a refusal of patriarchy) to the escapist (fleeing from daily life into a fantastic and exciting world). In its best expression, the Italian Western was a hybrid product encompassing multiple messages; the fact that it could be interpreted in numerous ways made it a genre of great flexibility and success.

On the other hand, although the spaghetti Western is heir to the classic American Western, at the level of content and style, it is the product of a new era. Examine, for instance, the case of Sergio Leone, whose success initiated the 'spaghetti phenomenon', sometimes giving rise, in his own words, to 'perverted offspring' in his imitators.[7] Leone creates the figure of the *pistolero*, an anti-hero dressed in an unusual way, riding a mule, wearing a poncho, moving about in an inhospitable setting whose adventures usually take place in small towns that often resemble ghost towns. Leone replaced the well-groomed and immaculate hero of the classic Western with an anti-hero who seems never to shave or take regular baths. Leone reveals his dishevelled, badly

kept *pistolero* on the screen in a series of extreme close-ups, concentrating on the details of his figure: his eyes emerging from beneath the rim of his cowboy hat, his hand clasping his pistol, his belt buckle, his spurs, his *toscano* cigar, the type of weapons he uses and so forth. The focus of the camera on such seemingly insignificant minor details emphasises that this is an outsider, a man who lives outside the law. His attire and his actions are also underlined by the soundtrack, which, thanks to the skill of such great composers as Ennio Morricone, Bruno Nicolai and others, ceases to be a generic accompaniment to the film, as in the classical Western, and becomes an essential commentary. From the opening credits, even before the film begins, the music creates a sense of amazement in the viewer with its unusual arrangements of electric guitars, trumpet solos, organs, singers and classical music mingling with sounds, noises, animal cries, squeaks and the clinking of spurs, Winchester rifle shots, cannon fire, whistles, chimes and harmonicas. Every musical note moves in unison with the protagonist and underlines his every act and movement. Such music and minute details evolved into a new Western iconography, allowing Leone to reduce dialogue to a minimum, often only a few lapidary phrases.

Thanks to his unusual choice of camera shots (primarily extreme close-ups), his music soundtrack and his brilliant and original use of flashbacks (a technique usually associated with the thriller/horror genre, but which Leone successfully employed to give psychological depth to his characters), Leone's gunfighters need few words to make themselves understood. In 1964, the audiences who saw Leone's first Western were confronted by an anti-hero who not only no longer followed the rules of behaviour of the classic Hollywood Western, but did not even dress or act appropriately. The familiar prairies, herds, Indians and good sheriffs disappear; an off-centre world remains, where the church no longer serves as the centre of the community, but may even house or support the villains, where families are criminal clans and violence and death are part of daily life. The setting of these films underscores the displacement of this society: decaying towns are shot in bright desert areas or in a treeless countryside burned by the sun; characters move in a world in which just surviving would be difficult enough even without the presence of injustice and violence. In such an iconic and imaginary filmic universe, history only enters through the back door, and when we encounter the American Civil War, the Mexican Revolution or the arrival of the railroad system in this terrain, history dissolves into a continuous series of massacres.

The iconoclastic impact of the filmic style together with the versatility of the filmic message make the spaghetti Western a typical product of the confusion and ideological turmoil of the 1960s. After Auschwitz, after colonial wars (Algeria, Vietnam), after the assassinations of the Kennedy brothers, Martin Luther King and Che Guevara, after the various revolutions against imperialism and colonialism fought in the Third World, after the Cold War's grimmest years, after the tough years of reconstruction in postwar Italy, the ideals displayed by the classic American Western of the 1940s and 1950s were no longer valid. The presence of violence and injustice in the world could no longer be ignored. The *pistolero*'s shocking violence, compared to the legal violence in the real world, seems a trifle; his dishonesty, if stealing from the dishonest represents dishonesty, amounts to a venial, not a mortal, sin. The iconography, the music, the virtuosity of the shots, the pluralism of the filmic message, in short, all the novelties brought to the Western genre by the Italians

The bandit Tuco (Eli Wallach) has to earn his share of the stolen loot in Sergio Leone's *Il buono, il brutto, il cattivo* (1966)

were noted by the audiences who thronged the cinemas to see these films, but this novelty was rarely understood by the film critics.

Various factors contributed to this critical disinterest. First of all, due to the Cold War, after 1947, Italy stood polarised between the Communist Party and the Christian Democrats. The intelligentsia divided itself between Marxists and Catholic conservatives: the Marxists championed neorealism and its implicit social criticism, while the Christians aspired to the continuation of older, conservative values, some of which could be traced to fascist origins. All of Italian culture, from literature to cinema, was assessed under these fixed parameters. Leftist critics failed to realise that the Italian society of the 1960s was not heading toward a more just world, as neorealist ideals would have preferred, but toward a capitalist economic miracle and a more monetarily thriving society that wanted to forget as quickly as possible the heroic years of the Resistance and the difficult ones of the postwar period and, as a consequence, of Italian neorealism. Critics on both the right and the left were only interested in the cultural products that fitted into the aesthetic canons of their political and ideological beliefs. Unfortunately, all Italian popular cinema of the 1960s suffered from the critics' myopia. The genre cinema of the time was accused by the Marxists of being a 'cinema of evasion': its emphasis on the mythological, on the Far West, or on Gothic horror castles, resulted in the maintenance of ignorance in the proletariat and distance from the intentions of social change implicit in neorealism. This popular cinema was branded by the Marxists as a 'hegemonic-conservative cinema'. On the other hand, the critics of the right, horrified by the violence and immorality of the Italian Western and by the social satire of the *commedia all'italiana*, and shocked by the iconoclastic attack on old patriarchal moral values, rejected this popular cinema without analysing it, simply defining it as 'consumable cinema for the masses'.

In the past several decades, both Italian and foreign critics and film historians have moved beyond these outmoded views, and there are several excellent critical studies of both popular Italian cinema in general and the spaghetti Western in particular. Moreover, it has become clear to all film historians that the Italian version of the classic American genre had a profound impact on Hollywood cinema, from Sam Peckinpah's *The Wild Bunch* (1969) via Clint Eastwood's Westerns down to Quentin Tarantino, whose *Django Unchained*

Django (Franco Nero) dispatches an army of villains with a Gatling gun and great pleasure in Sergio Corbucci's *Django* (1966)

(2012) is an homage to the Italian Western.[8] Thus, in retrospect, it seems clear that at an ideological and aesthetic level, the spaghetti Western represented a far more realistic and prophetic film genre than its early critics imagined, a genre that has, in its finest moments, found an important niche in the history not only of the Italian cinema but of world cinema as well.

NOTES

1. Leone used elements of Kurosawa's *Yojimbo* (1961) and when the legal problems arose, he claimed that he had actually been inspired by Carlo Goldoni's play *The Servant of Two Masters*. The dispute was settled by giving Kurosawa distribution rights to the film in Japan, Taiwan and South Korea, along with 15 per cent of international profits. See Christopher Frayling, *Sergio Leone* (London: Faber and Faber, 2000), pp. 148–50 for more details.
2. For information on film earnings, see ibid., pp. 130, 168, 186 and 203; and Christopher Frayling, *Spaghetti Westerns* (London: I. B. Tauris, 2006).
3. For these figures on Italian film production, ticket sales, and the economic structure of the industry at this time, see Christopher Wagstaff, 'Cinema', in David Forgacs and Robert Lumley (eds), *Italian Cultural Studies* (New York: Oxford University Press, 1996).
4. *Cinema e pubblico – Lo spettacolo filmico in Italia 1945–65* (Milan: Bompiani, 1974), pp. 337–47.
5. Spinazzola distinguishes popular cinema from cinema of the masses by asserting: 'The films made for the exclusive consumption of the lower classes can be labeled popular cinema; mass cinema, on the other hand, is programmed with the desire of merging together the bourgeois and proletarian audience, and is, therefore, against anti-class division' (ibid., p. 339, author's translation).
6. Marcello Garofalo, *Tutto il cinema di Sergio Leone* (Milan: Baldini and Castoldi, 1999), p. 113 (author's translation).
7. Ibid., p. 115 (author's translation). Among Leone's

'offspring', two other major directors of spaghetti Westerns should be noted – Sergio Corbucci and Sergio Sollima. Other successful figures include Damiamo Damiani, Carlo Lizzani, Giulio Questi, Domenico Paolella, Duccio Tessari, Bruno Corbucci, Tonino Valerii and Enzo Barboni. They created Django, Sartana, the Big Silence, Trinity and other *pistoleri* too numerous to list here.
8. Sergio Corbucci's *Django* (*Django*, 1966) starring Franco Nero, a *pistolero* who uses a Gatling-type machine gun, began the Django franchise in Italian cinema, initiating an astonishing number of sequels, the most important of which is Giulio Questi's *Se sei vivo spara* (*Django Kill*, 1967).

FURTHER READING

Beatrice, Luca, *Al cuore, Ramon, al cuore: la leggenda del Western all'italiana* (Florence: Tarab, 1996).

Brizio-Skov, Flavia, *Popular Italian Cinema: Culture and Politics in a Postwar Society* (London: I. B. Tauris, 2011).

Cox, Alex, *10,000 Ways to Die: A Director's Take on the Spaghetti Western* (Harpenden: Kamera Books, 2009).

Fisher, Austin, *Radical Frontiers in the Spaghetti Western* (London: I. B. Tauris, 2011).

Frayling, Christopher, *Once Upon a Time in Italy: The Westerns of Sergio Leone* (New York: Abrams, 2005).

——, *Sergio Leone: Something to Do with Death* (London: Faber and Faber, 2000).

——, *Spaghetti Westerns: Cowboys and Europeans from Karl May to Sergio Leone* (London: Routledge & Kegan Paul, 1981; rev. edn, London: I. B. Tauris, 2006).

Giusti, Marco, *Dizionario del Western all'Italiana* (Milan: Mondadori, 2007).

Grant, Kevin, *Any Gun Can Play: The Essential Guide to Euro-Westerns* (Godalming: FAB Press, 2011).

Hughes, Howard, *Once Upon a Time in the Italian West: The Filmgoers' Guide to Spaghetti Westerns* (London: I. B. Tauris, 2004).

——, *Spaghetti Westerns* (Harpenden: Olcastle Books, 2010)

Nash Smith, Henry, *Virgin Land: The American West as Symbol and Myth* (New York: Vintage, 1950).

Roth, Lane, *Film Semiotics, Metz, and Leone's Trilogy* (New York: Garland, 1983).

Staig, Laurence and Tony Williams, *Italian Western: The Opera of Violence* (London: Lorrimer, 1975).

Turner, Frederick, J., *The Frontier in American History* (New York: Henry Holt, 1921).

Wagstaff, Christopher, 'A Forkful of Westerns: Industry, Audiences and the Italian Western', in Richard Dyer and Ginette Vincendeau (eds), *Popular European Cinema* (London and New York: Routledge, 1992), pp. 245–61.

22 Chronicles of a Hastened Modernisation

The Cynical Eye of the *Commedia all'italiana*

Rémi Fournier Lanzoni

Commedia all'italiana (1958–79) offered a macroscopic view of Italian society through satirical comedy. It revealed the many defects of a nation prey to hastened modernisation and the commensurate demands for radical sociocultural change. The purpose of these new comedies was not only to 'de-sacralise' traditional Italian institutions (politics, bureaucracy, religion, the family nucleus) but also to highlight corruption, social disenchantment, repressed needs and unfulfilled desires. This essay focuses on the second half of *commedia all'italiana*, that of the post-boom era (1968–79).[1] This period was marked by that domestic terrorism that inspired its historical designation as the *anni di piombo*, or 'years of lead'. While the *commedia all'italiana* underwent a shift around 1968, the genre was led by the same directors who had already experienced success beginning in the late 1950s. Authors such as Dino Risi, Mario Monicelli and Pietro Germi ensured popular and critical success by bringing innovation to comedy, the most conservative of all film genres. They achieved this by offering a sharp psychological examination of reality, which forced a re-evaluation of a society with newly acquired social rights.[2] Unlike films from the early 1960s, comedies of the post-boom era scrutinised human behaviour with a more extreme cynical lens to emphasise the grotesque. Directors/authors accomplished this by making the thematic of death a predominant feature. The cynicism employed earlier, such as the promotion of individualistic humour in films like Dino Risi's *I mostri* (*The Monsters*, 1963), gradually gave way to a comedy based on collective perspectives by the turn of the 1970s. The advent of this second half of the *commedia* ultimately showed an uncompromising solution to indict the excesses of Italian society as a whole, and film-makers' utilised death as an element of the grotesque to produce a candid tragicomic satire of society and an exploration of a nation's difficult reality.

THE AESTHETICS OF CYNICISM IN THE YEARS OF THE ECONOMIC MIRACLE

The major innovation of Mario Monicelli's *I soliti ignoti*, the forerunner of the *commedia all'italiana*, was the co-option of death as a comical device, and many subsequent comedies began to follow suit. The *commedia all'italiana* was recognisable for often unexpectedly halting the narrative progression with the death of a protagonist, thus avoiding discomforting or unwanted compromise. Mario Monicelli's *La grande guerra* showed Oreste (Alberto Sordi) and Giovanni (Vittorio Gassman) executed by an Austrian firing squad, and Dino Risi's *Il sorpasso* ended with the abrupt accidental death of Roberto (Jean-Louis Trintignant) caused by Bruno's (Vittorio Gassman) reckless driving. The curious combination of death with sharp cynicism stood at the forefront of comedy directors' inspiration. However, they rarely intended a moralistic implication. As Dino Risi once said: 'Spectators must form their own opinion … . Morality is only a behaviour. One cannot identify it *a priori* out of necessity: neither categorical nor hypothetical.'[3] In other words, for the new comedy film-makers, morality and its cinematographic rhetoric were never to be part of the humour. This explains why the new satires of the early 1960s, with (tragically) open-ended questions, represented a substantial change compared to the postwar comedies of *neorealismo rosa*. At the turn of the 1970s, the same film-makers took their representation of society's evils to a new level. This time, they added a grotesque dimension to pre-existing cynicism, imposing a new cognitive format on popular viewership. Thanks to a hyperbolic vision of society, these satires presented spectators with a different perspective on reality, transcending the banality of quotidian life.

CHRONICLES OF A HASTENED MODERNISATION

A NEW RHETORIC: DEATH AND ABSURDITY

In an attempt to understand the semantics of death in Italian comedies, one must ask the following question: does removing the solemn nature of death ultimately demystify it? In the 1970s, film-makers recognised the need to rejuvenate the comedy genre. However, not all topics were deemed appropriate for humorous treatment, as domestic terrorism and its deadly toll shocked the nation. Tragic events such as the terrorism of the Brigate Rosse, bomb attacks at Piazza Fontana or the train station of Bologna, the assassination of Aldo Moro, the threat of a right-wing *coup d'état* were not suitable as subjects or sources for comedy. Mario Monicelli was one of the first to recognise the inherent possibilities of such subject matter; he realised that a grotesque mode within comedy, a more audacious type of cynicism, had popular appeal. In achieving this, these new comedies left their mark, moving beyond the sphere of the economic boom's popular comedies. Stripped of any conventional logic, grotesque humour no longer exclusively relied on dark comedy but rather on psychological provocation and caricature. It used human mannerisms and mental perversions as tools of predilection. Fausto Tozzi's *Trastevere* (*Trastevere*, 1971), Dino Risi's *Sessomatto* (*Sessomatto*, 1972) Marco Ferreri's *La grande abbuffata* (*The Big Feast*, 1973) and Mario Monicelli's *Un borghese piccolo piccolo* (*An Average Little Man*, 1977) no longer presented contemporary issues through a satirical lens but built up their comedy style by using the vitriolic force of the grotesque.

The implementation of death as a thematic device in comedy was more than just a phenomenological trend. In a society prey to violence, death was no longer an external constituent limited to minor functions (i.e. *I soliti ignoti*, *Il sorpasso*, *La grande guerra*) but rather a fully fledged element that reached maturity on screen.[4] It became a topic, a subject matter, and no longer simply a visual concept, as Aldo Viganò argues:

> The dramatic development of *Profumo di donna* [*Scent of a Woman*, 1974, Dino Risi] is the opposite of that in *Il sorpasso*: in a spasmodic attempt to seize life by its outer manifestations, Bruno Cortona suddenly faces the absurd act of death; while captain Fausto [Vittorio Gassman], once at the end of what he had programmed to be his last journey, finds out that his survival instinct is stronger than his own will. In both cases, life and death transcend the projects of the individual: everyday tragedy takes on the shape of the failure of intentions.[5]

Symptomatic evidence of the transformation that took place during the 1970s could be seen in the mutation of the script, which became more concentrated on the common sphere of Italian society. With the success of the new grotesque comedies, in particular the ones featuring mortality, the focus of a film was rarely only one individual (as was common in the 1960s). Rather, authors designated groups of individuals or society itself as the ultimate architect of this destructive labyrinth of social monstrosities and/or perceived social constraints.

In 1975, Monicelli's *Amici miei* (*My Friends*) revolved around death. The narrative featured an atypical analysis of the Tuscan way of life: an epicurean vision of an ensemble of five close friends, bonded by an enduring solidarity and humour that defied the tedium of monotonous existence. The nucleus of the clan was composed of Perozzi, a journalist (French actor Philippe Noiret), decadent nobleman Mascetti (Ugo Tognazzi), municipal architect Melandri (Gastone Moschin) and bar owner Necchi (Duilio del Prete). Finally, the last member to join the crew was Sassaroli (Adolfo Celi), a well-off surgeon and unquestionably the most cynical member of the group. The comedic dynamic of the film employed the ancient art of the 'beffa', a callous and sarcastic practical humour going back to the antique origins of medieval farce dear to Boccaccio's *Decameron* and the French fabliaux. As expected, the characterisation of all prominent protagonists took a new twist as no one in this human comedy escaped a contemptuous lens. One of the comedic devices was the juvenile art of the 'supercazzola' Tuscan style, often employed by Ugo Tognazzi. It was a discourse where nonsensical phrases were interjected as a scheme to perplex interlocutors; half-invented neologisms and half-recognisable Italian words composed the entire speech, bringing any interpersonal interaction to a

Perozzi's funeral in the final scene of Mario Monicelli's *Amici miei* (1975)

state of chaos. In a memorable scene, Perozzi, on his deathbed, receives the last sacraments but nevertheless still enjoys confusing the priest through his unintelligible dialogue.

Monicelli's characters had to face the contradictions of a conventional life versus juvenile desires. Perozzi's death can be understood as a short allegory of life and death, a common theme in Monicelli's films as it elevated mortality to a highly symbolic level. Perozzi's death, as comedic as it could be, was the only truthful event. He died in the end with the sour joy of one who, at least in death, had succeeded in distinguishing himself. The desire to create laughter, irony and cynicism in order to exorcise death and defeat its solemnity was at the centre of the film's rationale. Perozzi's end was glorious as his life and torment were transformed into a victory; he refused to compromise his awareness of the absurdity of his own situation. In a society subjugated to violence, terrorism and corruption, most of which remained without explanation, comedy dragged its protagonists towards a truth: death. All of

the members of the Florentine fraternity were deeply concerned with the significance of death, its inevitability and its finality. Not only did they express the oppressive, Kafkaesque nature of existence through their language and actions, but the indoor *mise en scène* produced a sense of claustrophobia, evoking in the characters and audience the feeling of being trapped in a universe where death was the only escape.

Unlike many comedy authors who wrote under predictable precepts, Monicelli was one of the few to maintain a strictly interrogative attitude towards Italian society. He implied to the spectator that the profound reason why he wrote comedies was to reveal his own perplexity. His effort was, therefore, to upset the submissiveness of Italian spectators and to have them experience through his narratives the 'strangeness' of modern society and the enigmatic nature of their existence.

The strategy of the assimilation of absurdity and death can be best illustrated by Monicelli's contribution – 'Pronto soccorso' ('First Aid') – to the episode film

Alberto Sordi in Mario Monicelli's 'Pronto soccorso,' one of the stories in the episode film *I nuovi mostri* (1977)

I nuovi mostri (*The New Monsters*, 1977).[6] In this segment, the rhetoric of Monicelli's cynicism was effectively combined with the art of associating antithetical characters.[7] While driving his luxurious white Rolls Royce late at night in the streets of Rome, nobleman Giovan Maria Catalan Belmonte (Alberto Sordi) comes across a wounded man lying on the steps of a monument. After some hesitancy, he drives him to a nearby hospital while unsympathetically narrating to the agonising man his latest safari vacation in Africa in exhaustive detail. At the gate of the emergency room, he must interrupt the guards (who are playing cards!) to ask permission to enter. The hospital is full, and he is advised to take the dying man to the Misericordia Hospital. He drives there and upon arriving, the Mother Superior tells him that they do not accept patients after midnight and to try a military hospital instead. Finally, at the gates of the third hospital, the guards tell him that civilian patients are not allowed. After repeated failure to secure help, the nobleman leaves the man, now lifeless, where he had found him earlier, on the steps of the same monument. Typically, Monicelli showed little concern for morality. Rather, the grotesque aspect of complex personalities was emphasised in order to trigger the spectator's response. Once again, a pervading dimension of distrust in human nature replaced the naive optimism of the 1960s. As amoral as his narratives may be, Monicelli somehow managed to capture a raw and compelling vision of modern social decadence. This permissive/transgressive cinematographic approach reminded spectators of the extremely narrow line between order and chaos, tragedy and laughter – all closely interrelated.

The representation of death ultimately functioned as a metaphor to represent the collapse of Italian society during the *anni di piombo*. Monicelli's *Un borghese piccolo piccolo* exemplified a new type of comedy, one viewed through the dark lens of tragicomedy. The director defined it himself as 'a step toward the absurd whose grotesque element coincided with despair and solitude'.[8] The movie recounts the story of Giovanni Vivaldi (Alberto Sordi), a veteran accountant, who has spent his entire existence working as a civil servant in Rome. His only child, Mario (Vincenzo Crocitte), whose future holds the same fate, is accidentally killed by bankrobbers the very same day he is about to take an entrance examination to the government agency for tax collection. Devastated, Giovanni decides to kidnap the alleged killer and takes him to his modest countryside cabin, where he attaches him to a chair with a metallic

string around his throat. The next day, the young man suffocates and dies. Giovanni returns to his conventional lifestyle, hiding his Dr Jekyll and Mr Hyde personality and the enacted rage of a violent killer. What made this story compelling was not the violence itself, but the film's suggestion that innocent passion, as an inherently human characteristic, could potentially lead to violence and death. The film was alarmingly evocative of Italian society and indirectly alluded to contemporary violent incidents taking place all over the country.

Un borghese piccolo piccolo has been frequently catalogued as the conclusive chapter of a decade of satirical comedies as well as the final testament of *commedia all'italiana*. It displayed a visible compulsive quest for a particular boundary, a point of no return after which laughter was no longer the appropriate response among spectators (laughter becoming a rather uncomfortable experience triggered by an overdose of cynicism). In response to allegations of cruelty, Monicelli defended his choice of cynical humour in the following way: 'The lack of compassion is a sign of intelligence: it is the one that sharpens the mind. This is how, between laughter and tragedy, I chose, and continue to choose, laughter.'[9] At the end of two prolific decades of *commedia all'italiana*, the substance of film comedies had reached complete maturity, as authors continued to push the limits with taboo subjects. As a theatrical genre, the grotesque took away the mask worn by its protagonists to expose the hidden inner anxieties of Italian society.

FUNERALS AND COMEDY

Beyond the 'act' of death, a critical step was eventually taken by a few authors to demystify its most iconic emblem: funerals. One of the many social targets of the *commedia all'italiana*, funerals were viewed as the ultimate manifestation of duplicity. So did the *commedia all'italiana* treat death and funerals with sincerity?

This question could be best answered by Ettore Scola's 'Elogio funebre' ('Funeral Eulogy', the final episode of *I nuovi mostri*), where the members of a former *avanspettacolo* gather for the funeral of one of their own most brilliant stand-up comedians, Formichella. At the cemetery, in front of the open grave, one of the prominent members of the group (Alberto Sordi) begins with what seems to be a classic eulogy. This soon gives way to a revival of the acts that were the flagship of the theatrical company, with the unfettered participation of all actors, including music, dancing and laughter. In homage to the *avanspettacolo*

Alberto Sordi remembering his fellow actor in Ettore Scola's
'Elogio funebre,' part of the episode film *I nuovi mostri* (1977)

legacy, an art by then relegated to the past, Ettore Scola
treats death through a comic lens. The episode directly
disparaged any ritual and any romanticised image of
death. During the funeral of Formichella, death was
actually derided in a sarcastic, although never
contemptuous mode. As the funeral ceremony unfurls,
the different jokes convincingly convert the present
weeping assembly; they no longer hold in the actors'
tears, and the funeral procession slowly becomes a
carnivalesque crowd. At one point, Sordi remembers
one of Formichella's famous quotes: 'Io sogno sempre i
baci tuoi! I baci mendaci tuoi! I baci mordaci tuoi!
Mortacci tuoi!'[10] The regenerating laughter of the
collective hysteria here was meant to temporarily defy
death and the essence of conventional mourning.
Similar to medieval popular culture, this 'liberating'
laughter effectively functioned as a tool to de-sacralise
death and its daunting subjugation. According to film
scholar Jean A. Gili, 'the eulogy for the deceased comic
actor turns again into a show in which hedonism and
the pleasure of living prevail once more'.[11] Though it
would seem coherent to position humour and death as
antithetical entities, hypocritical weeping and sincere
laughter were both cathartic in this story: they simply
mirrored the disaffected, anarchic mood of the time,
propelled to a new order without rules, a hyperbolical
vision of Italian society. This is probably one reason
why Scola, like many comedy authors, brought the
representation of death into the public eye, to negate
its pre-eminence. The funeral procession ending at
the cemetery was then the appropriate metaphor for
society's nightmares gathered in a single limited space
(a sort of modern-day unity of space and time in the
style of ancient Greek tragedies).

In his own Tuscan style, Monicelli condensed the
discussion of funerals by shortening the funeral
dimension before it 'reached' the cemetery. In the final
scene of *Amici miei*, the director removed all spiritual

dimensions of death by concluding both narration and
funeral in the street. To overcome their own sorrow,
the 'fraternity' members walk behind the hearse and
eventually play a last-minute hoax by telling an
aspiring new member that they had to 'liquidate'
Perozzi because he is a traitor. For Monicelli, the choice
to associate humour with the funeral was personal:

> Funerals are the most exhilarating thing there is. I go
> to my friends' funerals because when I see my other
> friends, I start to joke about their upcoming mortality.
> That type of humor is rather amusing, not macabre.[12]

The act of exorcising death through humour, whether in
real life or on the screen, was the ultimate derision. It
was the obvious device to prolong the state of childhood
happiness by dodging the responsibilities and
vicissitudes of a dreary adult life, even the grim image
of death. Here, the general audience was dealing with a
rather uncommon conclusion, the precariousness of
humanity, far from the happy ending and uplifting
quality of the Italian comedies of the 1950s.

Comencini's *L'ingorgo: una storia impossibile* (*Traffic
Jam*, 1979) captured a sophisticated sense of humour
and an emotional dark streak, outside the realm of
conventional comedy. Written by Ruggero Maccari
and Bernardino Zapponi, *L'ingorgo* proffered a broad
reflection on the aftermath of post-consumerism and
capitalistic society in general. Iconographic themes of
death and funerals recurred in his comedies,
encouraging the audience to reflect upon cinematic
conventions. The story had no single plot, but rather a
myriad of subplots, all interacting with one another
during a thirty-six-hour traffic jam somewhere
between Rome and Naples. The protagonists,
representing different classes and regions of Italy,
compared the quintessential substance of the story. To
illustrate the deep malaise of Italian consumer society,
the narrative frame was organised into a series of
confrontations. One of Comencini's strategies involved
incongruity, as unexpected and illogical situations were
juxtaposed. The film raised questions about the nature
of identity, and how at times, the individual could
stand completely free when his/her real self was
hidden behind a mask or beneath a costume,
exemplified by the 'anarchist' priest's speech. In the
middle of the traffic jam, and during the agonising
wait, a wounded patient (Ciccio Ingrassia) dies in an
ambulance. Shortly after, a priest is called into the
vehicle in order to administer the last sacraments.

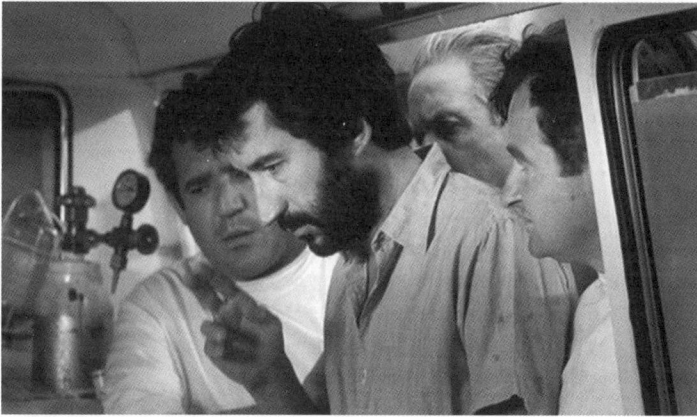

José Sacristán in the role of the anarchist priest in Luigi Comencini's *L'ingorgo: una storia impossibile* (1979)

Instead of what would be expected, the priest begins a rather singular liturgy:

> Lord, we thank you for calling and sheltering this man, removing him from the disasters of this world. Save us, O Lord, from plastic products. Save us from radioactive waste. Save us from the politics of power. Save us from multinationals. Save us from the reason of state. Save us from parades, uniforms, and military marches. Save us from the contempt for the weak. Save us from the myth of efficiency and productivity. Save us from false morality. Save us from lies and propaganda. Respect nature, love life. Copulate carnally in the respect of the next. Fornication is not a sin if done with love, amen.[13]

Traditionally, death and funerals were represented through a strategy of abstraction where protagonists were defined by their emblematic presence and function. Now comedy made its characters struggle to fit into the landscape, involving society at large and bringing confusion instead of the usual codes and order. Here Comencini hoped to engage an audience with an appreciation of incongruity as well as an awareness of cultural codification. The marked over-characterisation of the protagonist (the priest) took the characters to the edge of sanity, questioning the nature of human identity. As an uncompromisingly satirical moment, the scene of the last sacrament was an explicit indictment of capitalist values and their hypocritical expression of insincere grief over human mortality. Italian society became more chaotic, just as anarchical as the violent world that surrounded it. In addition to the satire of religious sacrament and death, the priest's revolutionary tone was a satire in itself, intense enough to border on brutality. Its message was

clear: contemporaneous monsters are among us and also provoked within each one of us in a group dynamic.

Was the presence of the grotesque a coherent metaphor for the collapse of Italian social order or a premonitory sign heralding the end of the *commedia all'italiana*? In the final stage of a glorious career, the *commedia all'italiana* was able to look into the gloomiest areas of the human psyche while never disregarding the intended target. It incriminated a society without structure that had been lost in the tormented aftermath of the economic miracle of the 1960s. The film-makers' representation of a society devoid of civility represented an opportunity to re-evaluate hastily imposed social values. While denouncing the daily violence of the 1970s, comedy authors portrayed society without thinking ahead to the practical survival of their own genre. Authors remained intensely focused on the subject matter intrinsic to the period – the illusion of well-being initiated during the economic boom; the alienation emanating from the atomisation of Italian society; the lack of communication between Italians; and the apathy of Italians and their passive acquiescence to social evils – to the detriment of the *commedia all'italiana*, which came to an end by the end of the decade. Through a cinema of disclosure and disconnection, the rhetoric of these films was a social barometer. It transported its spectators to an apocalyptic world, one that mirrored an entire nation exhausted by a decade of social ills. Authors had the difficult task of representing reality without altering, symbolising or sublimating it. By creating collective chronicles, they orchestrated their own repertoire, the phenomenological representation of society with its ultimate signifier. Death became the exit strategy.

NOTES

1. Although this late period of the *commedia all'italiana* remains just as famous as the early one, most scholarly discussions tend to dwell on the early 1960s rather than the 70s.
2. Finally, in 1968, women's adultery was no longer penalised by the 1930 law. The Penal Code's Article 559 punished women with up to two years of prison for having committed adultery. Later, in 1970, divorce was legalised (Legge 898) and in 1978, abortion became legal (Legge 194).
3. Valerio Caprara, *Mordi e fuggi: La commedia secondo Dino Risi* (Venice: Marsilio, 1993), p. 8. Unless otherwise noted, all texts are translated by the author.
4. 'Death, which at the time of *Il sorpasso* was still an intrusion, a premonition, was now in vogue.' Enrico Giacovelli, *Non ci resta che ridere: una storia del cinema comico italiano* (Turin: Lindau, 1999), p. 111.
5. Aldo Viganò, *Dino Risi* (Milan: Moizzi Editore, 1977), p. 77.
6. Written by Agenore Incrocci, Ruggero Maccari, Giuseppe Moccia and Bernardino Zapponi, also co-directed by Dino Risi, Mario Monicelli and Ettore Scola, the film was nominated for Best Foreign Film Award at the 1978 Academy Awards.
7. The benefit of the episode format was the inherent ability to push the limits of the grotesque beyond socially acceptable terms in order to accentuate the caricatures' depth: misogynous attitudes, egotism, immoral behaviour, adultery and deception.
8. Sebastiano Mondadori, *La commedia umana: conversazioni con Mario Monicelli* (Milan: Il Saggiatore, 2005), p. 44.
9. Mario Monicelli, *Autoritratto* (Florence: Edizioni Polistampa, 2002), p. 21.
10. 'I always dream of your kisses! Your fake kisses! Your biting kisses! Your damned ones!'
11. Jean A. Gili, *Arrivano i mostri. I volti della commedia italiana* (Bologna: Cappelli, 1980), p. 188.
12. Monicelli, *Autoritratto*, p. 29. The reader should remember that Monicelli ended his own life by jumping out of a hospital window in 2010 at the age of ninety-five.
13. Taken from Luigi Comencini's *L'ingorgo: una storia impossibile* and translated from the screenplay.

FURTHER READING

Aprà, Adriano (ed.), *Comedy Italian Style 1950–1980 (Catalogo degli incontri internazionali d'arte)* (Turin: Edizioni Rai, 1986).

Caprara, Valerio (ed.), *Mordi e fuggi: La commedia secondo Dino Risi* (Venice: Marsilio, 1993).

D'Amico, Masolino, *La commedia all'italiana: Il cinema comico in Italia dal 1945 al 1975* (Milan: Mondadori, 1985).

De Franceschi, Leonardo, *Lo sguardo eclettico: Il cinema di Mario Monicelli* (Venice: Marsilio, 2001).

De Gaetano, R., *Il corpo e la maschera: Il grottesco nel cinema italiano* (Rome: Bulzoni, 1999).

Giacovelli, Enrico, *La commedia all'italiana* (Rome: Gremese, 1990).

——, *Non ci resta che ridere: una storia del cinema comico italiano* (Turin: Lindau, 1999).

Gili, Jean A., *Italian Filmmakers. Self Portraits: A Selection of Interviews* (Rome: Gremese, 1998).

Lanzoni, Rémi Fournier, *Comedy Italian Style: The Golden Age of Italian Film Comedies* (New York: Continuum, 2009).

Micciché, Lino, *'Una vita difficile' di Dino Risi: Risate amare nel lungo dopoguerra* (Venice: Marsilio, 2000).

Pintus, Pietro, *Commedia all'italiana. Parlano i protagonisti* (Rome: Gangemi, 1986).

Risi, Dino, *I miei mostri* (Milan: Mondadori, 2004).

23 The Political Film

Gaetana Marrone

DEFINING POLITICAL CINEMA

Nothing unites the films made in Italy in the 1960s and the 1970s as much as the question of *what* constitutes a 'political film'. A sample of representative works of that era – *Salvatore Giuliano*, *La battaglia di Algeri* (*The Battle of Algiers*, 1966), *Il conformista* (*The Conformist*, 1970), *Il portiere di notte* and *Padre Padrone* (*My Father My Master*, 1977) – shows the difficulty of defining the concept of political cinema. These films, regardless of their artistic merits and degrees of engagement, serve as important reminders of the complexity of the issues involved in bringing together art and politics.

While one may identify the political dimensions of virtually all films, even those that present themselves as pure entertainment, the term 'political cinema' generally denotes films that raise particular social issues by challenging prevailing viewpoints. A 'political film' signals something quintessential about the director's manner of interpreting and representing key aspects of social experience, such as the national character or the cultural mode of production. In Italy, the radical film-making of the 1960s and 1970s was born during a period of economic and social transformation that accompanied the industrialisation of a country that was prevalently rural. Responding to these new economic and social developments was a group of young directors who had inherited the ethics, political commitment and social awareness of neorealism. They endorsed a practice of film-making that, however subversive, defined the author as a figure with morally or ideologically pronounced opinions. Nevertheless, as Peter Bondanella suggests, the 'political film' is better understood as a *filone*, or a 'thread' that runs through the work of many directors and through different genres of different periods up to the present day.[1] What follows is a critical overview of the most important examples of this *filone* during a period which is commonly considered to constitute the climatic moment of political cinema.

THE CINEMA OF SOCIAL INQUIRY

The year 1960 was a remarkable one. The Italian film industry overtook Hollywood films in popularity in the domestic market and reaped greater rewards than ever before: for the first time since 1946, box-office receipts grew as the number of filmgoers increased.[2] There was also an increase in exported films. The Italian cinema reached the peak of its success with the release of Federico Fellini's *La dolce vita*, Luchino Visconti's *Rocco e i suoi fratelli*, Michelangelo Antonioni's *L'avventura* and Vittorio De Sica's *La ciociara*. Acknowledging the international recognition of these films in January 1962, *Variety* referred to 1961 as 'the great year of the Italian Cinema'.[3] While De Sica and Visconti can be traced back to canonical neorealism, Antonioni and Fellini endow their characters with an existential vulnerability that prefigures the developments to come.

The neorealists' social critique was intensified by new directors identified with leftist ideologies. More than anyone else Ermanno Olmi continued to work in the spirit of Christian humanism found in the works of De Sica or Rossellini. His films *Il posto* and *I fidanzati* examine the effects of industrialisation on agrarian Italy's rapid economic transformation. With dispassionate lyrical objectivity, Olmi draws attention to his characters' sense of loss and anguish at being uprooted, their feeling of alienation in an environment where all the rules have changed. In 1978, Olmi expanded his realistic vision into the metaphoric realm with *L'albero degli zoccoli* (*The Tree of the Wooden Clogs*), a film in which personal and collective memory help create an emotionally charged homage to the vanishing world of nineteenth-century peasant civilisation.

With the exception of the neorealist period, the 1960s would prove to be years of the greatest experimentation and expressive freedom in Italian cinema. Every technical aspect of film-making underwent profound changes: from storytelling to editing, sound effects and photography, to costume design and make-up.[4] Nowhere are these changes more striking than in the 'political' *filone*, which breaks new ground in photographic technology, music and sound, modes of narration, editing techniques, settings and décor. The remarkable debuts of directors like Pier Paolo Pasolini, the Taviani brothers (Paolo and Vittorio), Bernardo Bertolucci, Marco Bellocchio and Liliana Cavani, among others, demonstrate how films may express a desire for radical economic and political change, or more simply give voice to *un impegno civile* (a civic engagement). The new art directors made their first films largely unhindered by production restraints.

No one took better advantage of these new freedoms than Francesco Rosi, whose *Salvatore Giuliano* is perhaps the more aesthetically innovative film of the 1960s. Generally considered his masterpiece, *Salvatore Giuliano* established Rosi as the brilliant craftsman of a new genre the so-called 'docudrama', a form of critical social commitment. As Rosi's lens probes the Sicilian landscape, it suggests visual and moral connections between the details of local life and larger national political practices. A character like the legendary bandit Giuliano (Pietro Cammarata) is at once an outlaw, a man of the south, and an emblem of power relations. From the beginning of his career, Rosi disdained simplistic solutions to such complex problems as the Mafia, political corruption and the *questione meridionale* (southern question) that is central

A dramatic scene from Francesco Rosi's *Le mani sulla città* (*Hands over the city*, 1963)

to Antonio Gramsci's writings. His films have often investigated issues of great public concern: civic corruption in the figure of a ruthless Neapolitan property developer and his political allies in *Le mani sulla città*; the cruelty of trench warfare in the Great War in *Uomini contro* (*Many Wars Ago/Men Opposed*, 1970); the unexplained death in a plane crash of oil tycoon Enrico Mattei in *Il caso Mattei* (*The Mattei Affair*, 1972); the portrait of a Mafia boss in *Lucky Luciano* (*Lucky Luciano*, 1973); or political conspiracy in *Cadaveri eccellenti* (*Illustrious Corpses*, 1975). Later films feature more reflective characters who journey to the past in order to interpret the present, as in *Cristo si è fermato a Eboli* (*Christ Stopped at Eboli*, 1979). For Rosi, the cinema acts as a historic witness in bringing to light what he calls 'another possible truth', a truth that is then set against the official historical point of view. Rosi does not attempt to retrieve or reconstruct the missing part of the truth. He rejects closure and fixity in favour of an open form that points to the future and all its challenges. As many critics have noted, his is a cinema of civic witness. Rosi adopts a viewpoint intended to provoke an informed response from his audience. This is the key structuring concept subtending the director's definition of political cinema: to engage the viewer actively in a dialectical exchange of ideas.

Unlike Rosi's early work, Gillo Pontecorvo's first films were not received enthusiastically by critics. *Kapò* (*Kapo*, 1960), an Italian/French co-production, was dismissed for its heavy-handed sentimental treatment of a concentration-camp Jewish prisoner who collaborates with the Nazis. Critical recognition came six years later with *La battaglia di Algeri*, rightly hailed as an act of civic courage for its re-creation of the end of the French colonisation of Algeria in 1954–7. The Algerian revolution was for many years a taboo subject in France and, to a certain extent, in Western Europe. Scripted by one of Rosi's writers (Franco Solinas), and produced by a former military commander for the National Liberation Front (Yacef Saadi), this film is indebted to *Salvatore Giuliano* for its rigorous documentation, extensive use of non-professional actors and non-linear chronological narration. The film highlights violent action scenes depicting terrorist attacks as well as military torture. Pontecorvo's Marxist and anti-colonialist reading of history (the irreversibility of the revolutionary process) resonated with an audience receptive to radical ideals. He is among the first directors to portray subversive characters seeking romantic revolutionary adventure,

Pontecorvo's *La battaglia di Algeri* (1966) uses a feigned documentary style to reconstruct the Algerian revolution

as in *Queimada!* (*Burn!* aka *The Mercenary*, 1969) and to depict the destruction brought to the Portuguese Antilles by the British conquerors. His last film *Ogro* (*The Tunnel* aka *Operation Ogro*, 1979) treats ETA's assassination of Spanish Prime Minister Carrero Blanco on 20 December 1973. Interestingly, Pontecorvo has recently enjoyed well-deserved reconsideration, but much forgotten terrain remains to be explored.

Like many directors of their generations, Paolo and Vittorio Taviani were attracted by historical, political and civil subjects. They debuted in 1962 with *Un uomo da bruciare* (*This Man Must Die* aka *A Man for Burning*), about the Sicilian union organiser Salvatore Carnevale who returns to the island to lead the peasants' revolt against the local Mafia. The film was co-directed by Valentino Orsini with whom the Tavianis had formed an artistic partnership in the early 1950s. The Tavianis' films are rich in neorealist influences, especially in the repertory of characters, topographical choices and spectacular allegorical *mise en scène*. Their *I sovversivi* (*The Subversives*, 1967) is one of the defining films of the socially committed cinema of the 1960s. It follows four Communist Party members, each facing personal crises, in the days preceding the funeral of Palmiro Togliatti in 1964, attended by an estimated 1 million people. The Tavianis (who were among the film-makers assigned by the PCI to film the funeral) well understood that Togliatti's death signalled the end of an epoch as well as of a political line. They intercut documentary

footage to dramatise Togliatti's death as a traumatic passage for more than one generation of Communists. In this climate of lost certainties, the Tavianis champion a dream of change and fervid hopes, while addressing the crucial issues for the militants and film-makers who lived through this ambivalent time: the confused entreaties of the young projected in an undefined primitive era in *Sotto il segno dello scorpione* (*Under the Sign of Scorpio*, 1969); the loneliness of the unarmed prophet in *San Michele aveva un gallo* (*St Michael Had a Rooster*, 1971), adapted from Tolstoy's story 'The Divine and the Human'; the seductions of the return to traditional order in *Allonsanfan* (*Allonsanfan*, 1974); the insurmountable barrier that isolates the remote areas of the country from the forces of modernisation in *Padre Padrone*. Based on Gavino Ledda's autobiographical novel, this film won the Golden Palm at Cannes from a jury chaired by Roberto Rossellini. In the aftermath of May 1968, the Taviani brothers came to distrust the political revolutionary ideals of the extra-parliamentary Left.

The most heterodox film-maker of the generation of the 1960s is Pier Paolo Pasolini, whose life and tragic death reflect his irrepressible desire to provoke scandal, often at the risk of his own safety. For Pasolini, cinema is an extension of the literary and political discourse of poetry, fiction, painting and critical writings. Painting, in particular, was for him a magical means of accessing filmic space. Although Pasolini lacked technical expertise, his collaboration on Fellini's *Le notti di Cabiria* and his artistic education allowed him to translate words into the cinematic equivalent of the paintings of Masaccio, Piero della Francesca and Caravaggio. Pasolini uses the camera as a paintbrush and even goes so far as to play a Giotto-like character in *Il decameron*. From the beginning of his career, he sets out to explore the mimetic nature of the filmic image: *Accattone* (which means 'beggar') and *Mamma Roma* (*Mamma Roma*, 1962) depict the alienated world of the Roman periphery, of the *ragazzi di vita*, the subproletarian youth with whom Pasolini identified for years. In these films, Pasolini experiments with the narratively rewarding effect of casting non-professional actors. At the same time, he displays a tendency to commingle styles and forms. In *Il Vangelo secondo Matteo* (*The Gospel According to St Matthew*, 1964), he plays with a wide range of aural and visual materials, while his depiction of the body becomes bolder and more candid, often in defiance of heterosexual norms. Pasolini's young men belong to a culture where, in the rundown suburbs of the big cities, poverty, sexual promiscuity, crime and prostitution define daily life. Their insolent faces scream their difference, their displacement, their inability or unwillingness to fit into national history and bourgeois society.[5] Such an unsettling depiction of marginality defines the subversive performance of the Neapolitan comedian Totò in *Uccellacci e uccellini* (*Hawks and Sparrows*, 1966). As P. Adams Sitney puts it, this film is a palinode to the film-maker's hope of revitalising the sociology and iconography of cinematic neorealism.[6] It is also a palinode to his didactic Communism. In the finale, scenes of Togliatti's funeral stand for the leader's historic fight against fascism, the shared postwar revolutionary spirit, but also for the ideological transformation that had been taking place during the 1960s.

An unorthodox Marxist, a public defender of homosexuality, Pasolini continues to explore the tension between individual and collective life in new registers. From *Edipo re*, *Medea* to *I racconti di Canterbury* and *Il fiore delle mille e una notte* (*Arabian Nights*, 1974), he uses the literary space to wander through history and mythology. The classics function as a natural milieu in which to reveal himself. They project his obsessive search for a lost Eden, and are a site from which to gaze on the present and the future, as in *Teorema* (*Theorem*, 1968), a parable of contemporary capitalist society; *Porcile* (*Pigpen* aka *Pigsty*, 1969), a poetic tale about human beings striving for conformity; and *Salò o le 120 giornate di Sodoma*, a clinical examination of the nature of fascism set in the capital of Mussolini's Socialist Republic in 1944. This frighteningly prophetic work, which explores human perversions, left critics and viewers perplexed and embarrassed. Pasolini's voice was silenced on 2 November 1975 near the beach at Ostia: a *ragazzo di vita*, Pino Pelosi, confessed to the murder.

1968 AND AFTER

By the mid-1960s, belief in the Italian state and institutions was disintegrating at all levels. These were years when the nation's sense of direction began to crumble and organised political parties no longer seemed to be in touch with citizens' lives. The would-be sons of May 1968 began to question the power exercised by their fathers. Two films, in particular, that presage times of protest and Oedipal rebellion are Bertolucci's *Prima della rivoluzione* and Bellocchio's *I pugni in tasca*. Marx and Freud, politics and sexuality underlie the film-makers' detachment from their bourgeois family roots. Alternating between poetic nostalgia and angry disillusion, their films help us

Class distinctions become more clearly drawn at a performance of Verdi's opera *Macbeth* in Bertolucci's *Prima della rivoluzione* (1964)

understand what would unravel during the academic year 1967–8, when the anti-authoritarian student movement challenged the Italian establishment at every level. Someone close to political militancy, however, did not spare the young activists his contempt. Pasolini published a controversial poem 'Il PCI ai giovani' ('From the PCI to the Youth') in *L'espresso* on 16 June 1968, in which he calls the student revolutionaries desperate, petit-bourgeois cowards, spoilt rich brats and sympathises with the policemen, the true sons of the proletarian class. For Pasolini, the confrontation between students and police showed the extent to which bourgeois ideology controlled every aspect of Italian life.

At nineteen, Bertolucci was assistant director on *Accattone*, and Pasolini supplied the story for his first film, *La commare secca* (*The Grim Reaper*, 1962). From the very beginning, Bertolucci seemed in search of a father figure. The Godard-influenced *Partner* (*Partner*, 1968) tells the story of the ideological alienation and political failures faced by the 1968 generation. In 1970, *La strategia del ragno* (*The Spider's Stratagem*) and *Il conformista* signal a decisive turning point in his work partly due to his close collaboration with cinematographer Vittorio Storaro. In these films, Bertolucci investigates the fascist past through a plot that mirrors the Oedipal myth. In particular, *Il conformista*, a psycho-political drama adapted from Alberto Moravia's 1951 novel, presents a vivid picture of the moral apathy and tumultuous violence indigenous to the fascist regime. The protagonist, Marcello Clerici (Jean-Louis Trintignant), exemplifies the decadent way of life of the upper middle class during the 1930s. Marcello's body becomes the site for the negotiation of

Giulia (Stefania Sandrelli) and Anna (Dominique Sanda) perform a provocative tango in Bertolucci's *Il conformista* (1970)

the personal with the political. This film confirms the director's exceptional talent. Arresting and expressive camera movements, the clever placement of light and shadow and, most importantly, the film's colour scheme, which signifies the inner conflicts of the main character, become the defining features of Bertolucci's cinema from that point on. As in *Ultimo tango a Parigi* and the monumental *Novecento* (1900, 1976), in which the historical legacies of landowners and peasantry find an underlying homoerotic correlative in the lifelong bond that unites Berlinghieri, the padrone's son (Robert De Niro), and Olmo, the bastard child of a farmer (Gérard Depardieu). *Novecento* tackles the political tensions between nation and class at a time when the Italian Left had become the strongest in Western Europe.

Among the film-makers who captured a time of widespread transformation in ideological and cinematic models, Bellocchio stands out for his ability to interpret contemporary history. His *I pugni in tasca* was hailed as the most momentous debut of his generation, a symbolic manifesto of 1960s youth. The film, with its depiction of a ravaged Italian society, reveals his special gift for scriptwriting and direction. *I pugni in tasca* focuses on a provincial middle-class family that exemplifies the decay of established moral codes. The home becomes the place for pathological sexuality. With *La Cina è vicina* (*China Is Near*, 1967), Bellocchio continues his attacks on the institution of the family even as he questions the actions of the

revolutionary student movements. In this highly politicised film, the cultural revolution against established hierarchies and values is viewed in the context of Maoist China and events in the Third World (Che Guevara). Bellocchio dramatises the angry youth's rupture with traditional party politics and the beginning of a new period in Italian history in which comforting ideological beliefs were being undermined. The film was too abstract to be widely appealing except to the most rigorously minded intellectuals. During the 1970s, Bellocchio pursued his anti-institutional themes in films aimed at a more commercial market. With *Nel nome del padre* (*In the Name of the Father*, 1971), *Sbatti il mostro in prima pagina* (*Slap the Monster on the Front Page*, 1972) and *Marcia trionfale* (*Victory March*, 1976), he appears more interested in recording the psychological reality and burdens of his characters' daily lives.

The secular spirit of 1968 affected film directors who shared similar experiences. Unlike Bertolucci and Bellocchio, who started by producing low-budget feature films, Liliana Cavani began working as a freelance director for the RAI, the state television network. Her first major assignment was a series of historical documentaries. Her work impressed Angelo Guglielmi, head of special programming at RAI-2, who proposed the idea of a film on Francis of Assisi. Cavani divests the figure of Francesco (Lou Castel) of all legendary attributes, and portrays him as a normal individual who has performed a revolutionary social role. An archetypal story of class, family and generational conflict, *Francesco di Assisi* (*Francis of Assisi*, 1966) provides striking evidence of Cavani's stylistic techniques and also serves as an ideal transition from her documentary films to *Galileo* (*Galileo Galilei*, 1968), *I cannibali* (*The Cannibals*, 1969), *L'ospite* (*The Guest*, 1971) and *Milarepa* (*Milarepa*, 1973). The protagonists of these early films are idealists who transgress the boundaries of conventional society in a quest for self-realisation. *Galileo* depicts the tragedy of a revolutionary intellect who finds himself at the centre of the most scandalous scientific case of the Counter-Reformation. It exposes the emptiness and decay of the papacy's repressive mechanisms. *I cannibali*, freely adapted from Sophocles' *Antigone*, perceives the collapse of traditional assumptions about the stability of political authority at a time when the protests of 1968 were just beginning. The film opens with a horrendous scene of decomposing corpses amassed upon the wet streets of downtown Milan. The bodies of the rebels who conspired against a totalitarian regime are left on

Lucia performs a seductive dance for her Nazi captors in Cavani's *Il portiere di notte* (1974)

display to serve as a deterrent to future conspirators. Only the daring Antigone (Britt Ekland) defies the order. *L'ospite* exposes the harm done to individual autonomy in incarcerating structures before mental institutions became a politicised issue. With *Il portiere di notte*, Cavani enters a new phase. The passion that led her earlier protagonists to confront the social, political and religious hierarchies of their times, now translates into a psychological drama centred in a scandalous love affair. The characters' despotic obsession with a love of darkness and a taste for lawless sexual rites becomes a metaphor for violation and power. The story concerns the accidental encounter between a former war criminal, Max (Dirk Bogarde), and a concentration-camp prisoner, Lucia (Charlotte Rampling), in a Viennese hotel in 1957, where Lucia, now married to an American conductor, is staying while on tour. Through a series of stylised flashbacks, we learn that Max, who also acted as a

sadistic doctor, had once saved his 'little girl' from death. A strange bond developed between them that is self-destructive and tragic. The couple re-enacts the master–slave relationship. After moving into Max's apartment, into a new kind of concentration camp, while being haunted by a group of ex-Nazis, Lucia carries the fateful affair to mutual annihilation. This tendency to entertain new experiences and to explore fantasy and the limits of cultural conventions is fully displayed in *Al di là del bene e del male* (*Beyond Good and Evil*, 1977), which recounts the affairs of Lou Salomé (Dominique Sanda) with Nietzsche (Erland Josephson) and Paul Rée (Robert Powell). Cavani's non-conformist cinema is not, however, a response to the guilt-ridden crisis of the Italian Marxist intellectuals of the 1960s. From the beginning of her career, Cavani speaks of the death of ideology and rejects all dogmatism. Unlike most of the film-makers of her generation, Cavani never accepted a party membership. If her cinema remains political, it is in the Aristotelian sense: as participation in the social and civil life of the polis.

While Cavani's formal education was literary and classical, Lina Wertmüller was connected with the performing arts: she attended the acting Academy of Pietro Sharoff and later joined the puppet theatre of Maria Signorelli. From her first film, *I basilischi*, a cautionary comedy set in a small southern Italian town, Wertmüller mounted a sharp critique of chauvinist males trapped in their own subjectivity. But it is in her films with Giancarlo Giannini that she established an international reputation as a political director depicting the breakdown of traditional societal codes. In *Mimì metallurgico ferito nell'onore* (*The Seduction of Mimì*, 1972), *Film d'amore e d'anarchia* (*Love and Anarchy*, 1973), *Travolti da un insolito destino nell'azzurro mare d'agosto* (*Swept Away*, 1974), and *Pasqualino Settebellezze* (*Seven Beauties*, 1975), social interaction is reduced to a struggle for survival. Careful not to glorify the years of the 'economic miracle', Wertmüller examines the transformation that had been taking place in the country through an ideological lens that defies Togliatti's belief in the unitary nature of class identity. Instead she highlights the composite nature of contemporary Italian society. A member of the Communist Party, Wertmüller became a socialist after the Soviet invasion of Hungary in 1956, and later assumed more independent anarchical positions.

Her films reflect these ideological concerns through stories that mix with sex, love, politics and gender roles. For her choice of controversial themes, Wertmüller enraged many feminists for what they perceived as a degrading portrayal of women. But Wertmüller's males are also depicted with baroque exaggerations, their bodies express a practice of domination. *Film d'amore e d'anarchia*, in which a politically naive individual sets out to assassinate Mussolini during the 1930s, is an example. Wertmüller opens the film with a photo montage of Il Duce in dictatorial poses. The fast cutting is supported by a soundtrack that does not match the mood of the images. Her cinematic approach relies on extreme wide-angle lenses (to distort the male/female body), extreme close-ups (to reveal facial texture), on mimicry based on eye movements with rhythmic cuts set to music. In perhaps her most controversial film, *Travolti da un insolito destino nell'azzurro mare d'agosto*, the Mediterranean Sea is the backdrop for a love story between a stunning female capitalist and a southern Communist deckhand who works on her husband's yacht. When the two find themselves marooned on an island, their roles are reversed and political antagonisms metamorphose into desire. Wertmüller's gallery of female characters does not validate a pernicious view of women, as some feminist critics have argued. Her female characters are more politically aware than their male counterparts, who are often ignorant and unable to understand their environment. Ultimately her films are about moments of choice. As the Anarchist says in *Pasqualino Settebellezze*, citing Thomas Mann: 'I believe in man but in a different man, not in this beast, who has brought the world total destruction.' This is Wertmüller's sombre credo, an artist who loves to provoke.

NATIONAL IDENTITY AND POLITICAL LEGITIMACY

The social unrest in May 1968 was followed by a decade of re-evaluation. The everyday life of Italians was grafting new forms and practices onto their cultural values, consumption habits, even sexual mores. By the early 1970s, it became clear that the postwar popular image of the poor southern male and the northern industrial landscape were no longer in a dialectical class conflict. Films like Wertmüller's *Mimì metallurgico ferito nell'onore* examine the world of the factory workers, who now seemed increasingly distanced from the political struggles of the 'Hot Autumn' of 1969. At the same time, Elio Petri's *La classe operaia va in paradiso* (*The Working Class Goes to Heaven*, 1971) elaborates a Brechtian parable on the workers' social and political situation from a negative polemical point of view. From his first films, which include *L'assassino* (*The Assassin*, 1961), *I giorni contati* (*His Days Are Numbered*, 1962) and *Il maestro di Vigevano* (*The Teacher from Vigevano*, 1963), Petri blends political ideology with entertainment. In 1970, his *Indagine su un cittadino al di sopra di ogni sospetto* (*Investigation of a Citizen above Suspicion*), a box-office hit and winner of an Oscar for Best Foreign Film, became a testing ground for the Italian political cinema. The film tells the story of a police officer who murders his mistress; assigned to suppress the radicals with the assistance of his superiors, he remains 'above suspicion'. Petri's attack on government corruption continues in *Todo Modo* (*Todo Modo*, 1975), adapted from Leonardo Sciascia's novel. Released during the national elections, this film attacks the Christian Democratic Party and anticipates the crisis precipitated by Aldo Moro's execution by the Red Brigades in 1978.

During the restless times preceding the years of terror (*anni di piombo*, 1973–80), political film-makers represented a series of ideological and personal crises not fully or adequately addressed by other cultural forms of expression. Since then, the loss of confidence in political alternatives and the change in systems of economic financing for independent film-making have brought a politically conscious radical cinema to a halt. Individual film-makers continue to produce work that asks difficult questions, but this work of social inquiry no longer amounts to the kind of international movement that political cinema could once be said to constitute. The political film-makers of the 1960s and 1970s represent the last great commitment to socially engaged cinema. Their creative, experimental films are important and vital sources for understanding Italian history from the death of Togliatti to the assassination of premier Aldo Moro.

NOTES

1. Peter Bondanella, *A History of Italian Cinema* (New York and London: Continuum, 2009), p. 242.
2. See Gian Piero Brunetta, *The History of Italian Cinema: A Guide to Italian Film from Its Origins to the Twenty-first Century* (Princeton, NJ: Princeton University Press, 2009), pp. 167–70.
3. Cited in Mira Liehm, *Passion and Defiance: Film in Italy from 1942 to the Present* (Berkeley, Los Angeles and London: University of California Press, 1984), p. 347, note 1.
4. Brunetta, *The History of Italian Cinema*, p. 171.
5. See Angela Dalle Vacche, *The Body in the Mirror: Shapes of History in Italian Cinema* (Princeton, NJ: Princeton University Press, 1992), p. 231.
6. *Vital Crises in Italian Cinema: Iconography, Stylistics, Politics* (Austin: University of Texas Press, 1995), p. 14.

FURTHER READING

Attolini, Vito, *Sotto il segno del film (cinema italiano 1968–76)* (Bari: Mario Adda Editore, 1983).

Bondanella, Peter, *A History of Italian Cinema* (New York and London: Continuum, 2009).

Brunetta, Gian Piero, *The History of Italian Cinema: A Guide to Italian Film from Its Origins to the Twenty-first Century* (Princeton, NJ: Princeton University Press, 2009).

Dalle Vacche, Angela, *The Body in the Mirror: Shapes of History in Italian Cinema* (Princeton, NJ: Princeton University Press, 1992).

Fofi, Goffredo, *Il cinema italiano: servi e padroni* (Milan: Feltrinelli, 1971).

Liehm, Mira, *Passion and Defiance: Film in Italy from 1942 to the Present* (Berkeley, Los Angeles and London: University of California Press, 1984).

Micciché, Lino, *Cinema italiano: gli anni '60 e oltre* (Venice: Marsilio, 1995).

Michalczyk, John J., *The Italian Political Filmmakers* (Rutherford, NJ: Fairleigh Dickinson University Press, 1986).

Pintus, Pietro, *Storia e cinema: trent'anni di cinema italiano (1945–1975)* (Rome: Bulzoni, 1980).

Quaglietti, Lorenzo, *Storia economico-politica del cinema italiano 1945–1980* (Rome: Editori Riuniti, 1980).

Sitney, P. Adams, *Vital Crises in Italian Cinema: Iconography, Stylistics, Politics* (Austin: University of Texas Press, 1995).

24 The *Giallo* and the Spaghetti Nightmare Film

Mikel J. Koven

The term spaghetti nightmare comes originally from the title of Palmerini and Mistretta's 1996 book of interviews with various personnel in the Italian fantasy and horror film industry. The coinage is obviously in reference to the spaghetti Western, although Peter Bondanella uses the phrase to refer to Italian horror cinema *per se*.[1] Despite this, the phrase does little to recognise the diverse range of subgenres and trends which make up the spaghetti nightmare strand. Most sources agree that Italy was relatively late in exploring the horror genre, since its history really only goes as far back as Riccardo Freda's *I vampiri* (*I Vampiri* aka *Lust of the Vampire*, 1956). And yet, despite its short history, Italian horror films have generated a substantial amount of controversy. For example, during the media panic over 'video nasties' in the UK in the early 1980s, of the seventy-two film titles put on the so-called 'video nasty' list by the Director of Public Prosecutions likely to be liable for prosecution if found in a video store's stock, almost 40 per cent were Italian, more than those from any other country. A dubious honour perhaps, but such publicity drew increased attention to

An example of Bava's Gothic interiors in *I vampiri* (1956)

Italian horror cinema in the period of the genre's decline, and elevated these films to collectors' items among horror cineastes.

Although Riccardo Freda is credited with the film's direction, most histories of the genre recognise Mario Bava, the film's cinematographer, as the true director of *I vampiri*. The work is a bizarre Edgar Wallace-like murder mystery set in contemporary Paris, where the bodies of several young women have been discovered, ex-sanguinated; this is believed to be the work of a vampire. Historically, the film is significant, since many of the themes and motifs of later developments in the genre can be identified here in a developmental stage. For example, while its setting is contemporary, the film evokes a strong sense of the Gothic, mainly through the interiors shot by Bava.

The film also introduces the ubiquitous black-gloved killer to Italian horror movies, a motif almost synonymous with the *giallo*. Also central to the *giallo* is the role of the amateur detective, and almost ten years before *gialli* make a proper appearance, *I vampiri* features a young reporter, Pierre Lantin (Dario Michaelis) playing amateur detective as he tries to solve the mystery of these vampire murders. Thus, *I vampiri* represents not only the first recognised Italian horror film, but in many respects it is also a prototype for the *giallo*.

Bava and Freda teamed up again for another early Italian horror, a Hollywood-style monster movie, *Caltiki – il mostro immortale* (*Caltiki: The Immortal Monster*, 1959). What makes *Caltiki* noteworthy, an otherwise fairly uninteresting story about an ancient Mayan goddess awakened by clumsy archaeologists, manifesting as a consuming blob of evil, is the film's similarity to the US hit, Irwin Yearworth's *The Blob* (1958). Produced the year following *The Blob*, *Caltiki* should be read as an early example of how home-grown Italian films copy

American successes on much smaller budgets. More
than straight 'rip-offs', such Italian copies may be said
to embody a vernacular rethinking of contemporary
American popular culture.

THE ITALIAN GOTHIC

While US horror movies in the 1950s tended to focus on
horrific invasions from outer space, the British were
reinventing the Gothic horror tradition with Hammer
Film Production's release of two works by Terence
Fisher: *The Curse of Frankenstein* (1957); and *Dracula*
(1958). US studios responded to this box-office
challenge by starting their own (albeit smaller) Gothic
revival with a series of Roger Corman-directed films
loosely based on the stories of Edgar Allan Poe.
Meanwhile in Italy, Mario Bava trumped them both
with his accredited directorial debut, *La maschera del
demonio* (*Black Sunday*, 1960), effectively launching the
Italian Gothic horror film.[2]

The Italian Gothic horror film is characterised by a
preoccupation with a decaying aristocracy, usually
cursed, and its displacement by an emerging
professional class (doctors, solicitors, journalists, etc).
The films' *mise en scène* reflect this preoccupation with
its dark, cavernous and, most importantly, empty
interiors of crumbling and draughty castles and long-
neglected cemeteries. If aristocratic rule is predicated
on lineage and family history, the Gothic focus on
ruined sepulchres and crumbling mausoleums is a
direct commentary on the decline of the aristocracy.
In the best of these films, like *La maschera* and Sergio
Corbucci and Antonio Margheriti's *Danza macabra* (*Castle
of Blood*, 1964), the story is progressed, not through the
stilted dialogue and clumsy expositions, but, instead,
through mood and atmosphere – a true Gothic
sensibility. The narrative is ultimately secondary to the

Barbara Steele in Mario Bava's *La maschera del demonio* (1960)

films' visuals. But the main difference between the
Italian Gothic horror films and those of either Hammer
or Corman lies in the surprising amount of blood, even
in films shot monochromatically, typical of the Italian
products. For example, in *La maschera* alone, the violent
nailing of the titular mask onto the witch Asa's (Barbara
Steele) face includes spurts of blood from around the
edges. In the same film, we also see on-screen
brandings, glutinous eyeballs forming in the sockets of
Asa's corpse, eyes being poked out and even necrophilia.
The Gothic sensibility of Italian horror permeated the
films produced in the 1960s, but its influence was also
felt throughout the 1970s and beyond. Despite the
influence of the *giallo* and other horror subgenres, the
Gothic sensibility is still prevalent in Mario Bava's *Gli
orrori del castello di Norimberga* (*Baron Blood*, 1972) and *Lisa
e il diavolo* (*Lisa and the Devil*, 1974), Sergio Martino's *Tutti
i colori del buio* (*All the Colours of the Dark*, 1972) and even
in Dario Argento's *Suspiria* (*Suspiria*, 1977) and *Inferno*
(*Inferno*, 1980).

THE *GIALLO*

No other subgenre of horror cinema is more associated
with the Italians than the *giallo*. In fact, and erroneously,
giallo is often used within popular discourse as a
synonym for Italian horror as a whole. But the term
has a very specific usage and meaning. Literally, *giallo*
means 'yellow' in Italian and is the metonymic term
used to describe any murder mystery. Historically, this
derives from the fact that Italian publisher Mondadori
popularised the mystery novel through a series of
Italian translations of English-language mysteries
published in distinctive yellow covers in the mid-1920s.
The term has become synonymous in Italian with
mysteries and thrillers. In film terms, the *giallo* has
come to refer specifically to the Italian style of psycho-
killer movies, which dominated much of Italian
vernacular film-making in the 1970s, and, in many
respects, were the precursors to the 'slasher' films from
Canada and the US in the late 1970s and early 1980s.
The first Italian horror film, *I vampiri*, could be
considered a *giallo*, insofar as it features an amateur
detective figure investigating a series of bizarre
murders, the narrative plotline of many later films. But
rarely, if at all, is *I vampiri* included in discussion of the
giallo. Film historians generally consider the first 'semi-
official' *giallo* to be Mario Bava's *La ragazza che sapeva
troppo* (*The Girl Who Knew Too Much*, 1962), wherein a
young girl/amateur detective finds herself embroiled in
a mystery while on vacation in Rome. Bava followed this

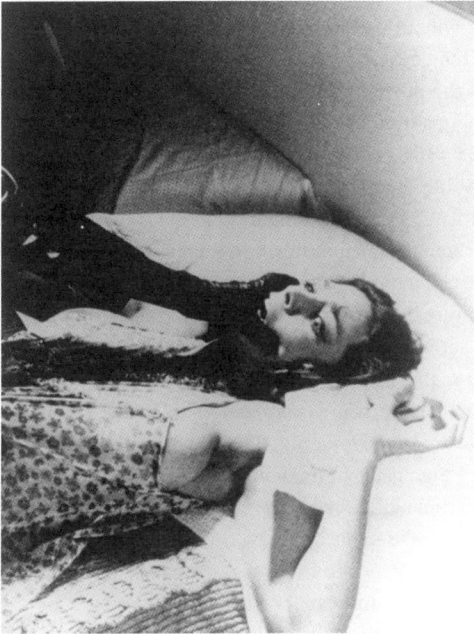

The *giallo*'s archetypal killer from *L'uccelllo dalle piume di cristallo* (1970)

up with 1964's *Sei donne per l'assassino* (*Blood and Black Lace*), about a series of gruesome murders in an Italian fashion house. In *Sei donne*, Bava further establishes the style of the genre with both the increased gruesomeness of the murders and the killer's disguise: black gloves and wide-brimmed black hat. While Bava (and Freda) had already introduced the black gloves motif in *I vampiri*, only after *Sei donne* does this type of disguise become the norm in the *giallo*.

Gialli were sporadically produced throughout the 1960s as a possible replacement for Italian Gothic, interest in which had waned due, in part, to how horror cinema changed in the wake of Alfred Hitchcock's *Psycho* (1960). Umberto Lenzi, for example, made three psychological thrillers with American actress Carroll Baker: *Orgasmo* (*Paranoia*, 1969), *Così dolce ... così perversa* (*So Sweet ... So Perverse*, 1969) and *Paranoia* (*A Quiet Place to Kill*, 1970). Lucio Fulci, although more famous for the gore-soaked zombie movies, directed the proto-*giallo* *Una sull'altra* (*One on Top of the Other*, 1969). Giulio Questi's self-consciously abstract and arty mix of Mario Bava and Michelangelo Antonioni, a murder mystery set on a poultry farm – *La morte ha fatto l'uovo* (*Death Laid an Egg*, 1968) – tried to elevate the genre to the level of art cinema (as Antonioni had done a few years earlier with *Blow-up*), but the film never achieved this objective.[3]

While the *giallo* struggled to find its feet as a film genre, one film emerged in 1970 which successfully combined the amateur detective plotline from *La ragazza*, with the gruesome murders of *Sei donne*: Dario Argento's *L'uccello dalle piume di cristallo* (*The Bird with the Crystal Plumage*). Its success not only announced the true arrival of *giallo* in cinemas around the world, but also heralded the advent of its young director as a significant player in horror cinema. *L'uccello* also established one of the central themes of *giallo* cinema: the 'eyewitness account' (in Italian, *un testimone oculare*). In the *giallo*, the amateur detective is often involved in the mystery due to his or her attempt to reconstruct what he or she witnessed during the first murder, often leading him or her to remember a vital yet overlooked clue instrumental in identifying the killer. In a much later Argento *giallo*, *Opera* (*Opera*, 1987), the *testimone oculare* of a murder of ravens identifies the killer in the audience during a production of Verdi's *Macbeth*. The *giallo* made Argento's career, and it is a genre the director repeatedly returned to well into the present day with such films as *Non ho sonno* (*Sleepless*, 2001); *Il cartaio* (*The Card Player*, 2004); *Ti piace Hitchcock?* (*Do You Like Hitchcock?*, 2005); and *Giallo* (*Giallo*, 2009). Unfortunately, despite the intimate association between Argento and the *giallo* genre, Argento's *Giallo* presents a killer with jaundice (hence a 'yellow' appearance) and avoids a postmodernist consideration of the generic properties of the genre that made him famous, the kind of self-reflexive treatment so successful in Wes Craven's *Scream* (1996).

While Argento's films are most often associated with the *giallo*, several other directors also made

Susy Bannion (Jessica Harper) destroys the evil witch in *Suspiria* (1977)

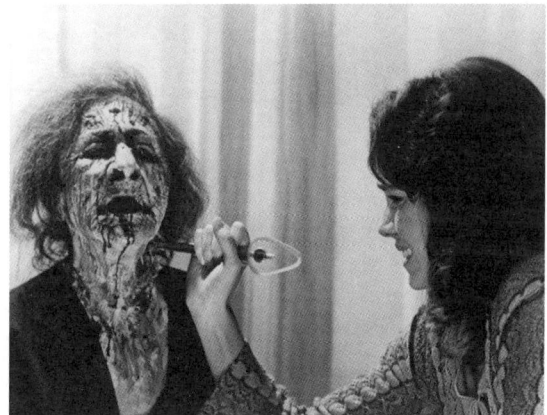

significant *gialli* throughout the 1970s. Lucio Fulci, for example, made *Non si sevizia un paperino* (*Don't Torture a Duckling*, 1972) and the hippy-trippy *La lucertola con la pelle di donna* (*A Lizard in a Woman's Skin*, 1971), although the latter film had more in keeping with the psychological thrillers of the 1960s. *Non si sevizia un paperino* typifies 1970s *gialli*, with its reporter hero investigating the murders of several young boys and a developmentally challenged girl who may have witnessed at least one of the murders. All *gialli* tend to feature gruesome murders, amateur detectives who may or may not have witnessed one of the killings and killers with a fondness for black leather gloves, they also tend to explore sexual trauma in the early life of their killer protagonists. For example, Nina Tobias (Mimsy Farmer) was raised as a boy by her abusive father in Argento's *4 mosche di velluto grigio* (*Four Flies on Grey Velvet*, 1971) and the killer in Sergio Martino's *I corpi presentano tracce di violenza carnale* (*Torso*, 1973) was traumatised by the death of his brother in an accident trying to rescue a girl's doll so she would lift her skirt for him. These films depict a world permeated by pop-culture psychology. Everyone knows a little Freud, enough at least to lend themselves to pat psychoanalytical explanations of the killer's often sexual deviancy. Identifying sexual deviancy as the source for the *giallo* killers' motives also enables the films to blend as much nudity with violence as local

censors will allow. The full Italian title of Martino's work –'the body shows signs of sexual violence' – reflects the precise combination of sex with violence that imbues these films.

If the *giallo* gave way to the North American 'slasher' film by the late 1970s/early 1980s, the favour was returned by Italian horror directors translating 'slasher' movie sensibilities into Italian. Lamberto Bava's *La casa con la scala nel buio* (*A Blade in the Dark*, 1983) is mostly a straightforward *giallo* tale, although largely set in one location – an out-of-the-way villa – thereby making it an intriguing hybrid of *giallo* and 'slasher', like Martino's *I corpi* before it. Michele Soavi's *Deliria* (*StageFright: Aquarius*, 1987) seems more 'slasher' than *giallo* in its depiction of an almost indestructible killer, recently escaped from an asylum, who stalks rehearsals of a new theatrical production. While *La casa* keeps to the *giallo*'s motifs of psychosexual trauma, black-gloved killer and a diverse array of murders, *Deliria* more or less removes those *giallo*-specific aspects of the genre. While the *giallo* was in marked decline in the 1980s, Argento still made a handful (which some identify as his best work), including *Tenebre* (*Tenebre*, 1982) and *Opera*. Newcomer Eros Puglielli's *Occhi di cristallo* (*Eyes of Crystal*, 2004) suggested a new master of the *giallo* had arrived on the scene, but to date, that promise has not been fulfilled.

Jane (Suzy Kendall) discovers her friends are all dead in the proto-slasher film *I corpi presentano tracce di violenza carnale* (1973)

HORROR CYCLES AND SUBGENRES

Italian horror cinema, particularly since the 1970s, has been largely characterised by short-lived but intensive periods of film production in certain specific subgenres or cycles. Usually, these cycles are sparked by a massive (usually Hollywood) box-office success on which Italian producers try to cash in. In this regard, screenwriter and director Luigi Cozzi remarks:

> In Italy ... when you bring a script to a producer, the first question he asks is not 'What is your film like' but 'What *film* is your film like?' That's the way it is, we can only make *Zombie 2*, never *Zombie 1*.[4]

As Donato Totaro has noted, Italian vernacular cinema reflects 'a parasitic relationship with American cinema'.[5] Often this is due, as screenwriter Dardano Sacchetti believes, to the production context: a film's concept and a vague plot would frequently be sold to international distributors not only before the film had been made, but even before the screenplay had been written. When the money had been raised, often the writer had to produce a script in less than a week.[6] Consider the strange case of Luigi Cozzi's own film *Contamination* (*Alien Contamination* aka *Toxic Spawn*, 1980). Imagine travelling through the film markets at the 1979 Cannes Film Festival and seeing only the teaser poster for the upcoming Twentieth Century-Fox blockbuster, Ridley Scott's *Alien* (1979). The poster seems to promise a scary movie about an invasion of space eggs. Whether this idea was conceived by Cozzi himself, or by producer Claudio Mancini, *Contamination* gives the vernacular film audience exactly that – a movie about scary eggs from outer space, with a little bit of plot borrowed from *Invasion of the Body Snatchers*, probably the Philip Kaufman version of 1978.

In the wake of the success of Roman Polanski's *Rosemary's Baby* (1968), a number of Italian 'versions' were produced, mostly variations on the ideas of modern witchcraft and conspiracy theories. While some, like Martino's *Tutti i colori del buio* are highly regarded, others, like Giorgio Ferroni's *La notte dei diavoli* (*Night of the Devils*, 1972), are less interesting. Aldo Lado's directorial debut, *La corta notte delle bambole di vetro* (*The Short Night of the Glass Dolls*, 1971), while partially a *giallo*, also owes its pedigree to the conspiracy horror film produced in the wake of Polanski's. As one cycle starts to decline in popularity, another Hollywood blockbuster comes along to spark a second wave. Ovidio G. Assonitis's *Chi sei?* (*Beyond the Door*, 1974) and Alberto De Martino's *L'anticristo* (*The Anti-Christ*, 1974) were both produced in the year following the massive success of William Friedkin's *The Exorcist* (1973).

One of the more controversial cycles of Italian horror film in the 1970s was the 'cannibal' strand. This began with Umberto Lenzi's *Il paese del sesso selvaggio* (*Sacrifice!* aka *The Man from the Deep River*, 1972) and ran across approximately ten feature films until 1980–1. Six of these were placed on the Director of Public Prosecutions list of 'video nasties' in the UK. 'Banned' titles included: Sergio Martino's *La montagna del dio cannibale* (*Mountain of the Cannibal God*, 1978); Ruggero Deodato's *Cannibal Holocaust* (*Cannibal Holocaust*, 1980); and Umberto Lenzi's *Cannibal Ferox* (*Make Them Die Slowly*, 1981). Typically, the cannibal films featured a scientific anthropological investigation into the dark rainforests of either the Amazon or Papua New Guinea, where the team of 'great white scientists' encounter a primitive tribe of cannibals.[7] Much of the controversy these films generated was due more to quasi-ethnographic depictions of actual animal killings and mutilations than any images of human dismemberment and consumption. Significantly, the release of Lenzi's *Il paese del sesso selvaggio* does not appear to have any immediate Hollywood precursor; although its story of a British tourist, John Bradley (Ivan Rassimov), who goes too far while trying to find the 'authentic' Thailand and strays from the tourist path, has one foot in the *giallo* (which often feature tourists who stray from the safe confines of the resort) and the other in the pseudo-ethnographic *mondo* documentaries, which depict the most sensationalist elements of their subject. Most of the latter were made in the 1960s in the wake of the highly successful, although no less ambivalent *Mondo Cane*, directed by Gualtiero Jacopetti, Franco Prosperi and Paolo Cavara; or following Jacopetti and Prosperi's 1966 documentary about the end of colonial Africa, *Africa addio*, released on the exploitation circuit as *Africa Blood and Guts*. It is likely that the cannibal cycle of films was, at least initially, influenced by these exploitation documentaries.[8] Significantly, Franco Prosperi worked with Spanish exploitation director Jess Franco on *Mondo cannibale* (*Cannibals*, 1980), a fiction film but one based on more 'anthropological' data than the previous films in the cycle.

By the late 1970s, the zombie successfully replaced the cannibal as the monster of choice in spaghetti nightmare films, largely due to the international success of George A. Romero's *Dawn of the Dead* (1978, released in Italy as *Zombi*). Marino Girolami's *Zombi*

Fulci's *Zombi 2* (1979) helps to create a new direction in Italian horror films

Holocaust (*Zombie Holocaust*, 1980) demonstrates this development rather transparently: much of the film's action centres on the hunt for a lost tribe of cannibals in Papua New Guinea (much like any other cannibal film made between 1977 and 1980), but, in a *deus ex machina*-like device, the film's heroes are saved from these savages by slave-like zombies, controlled by the Prospero-like Dr Obrero (Donald O'Brien).[9]

Lucio Fulci's *Zombi 2* (*Zombie Flesh Eaters*, 1979)[10] is perhaps the most controversial of the Italian zombie films, primarily for the shocking sequence when a woman's eye is impaled on a wooden splinter. But Fulci's *Zombi 2* was the first in a trilogy which cemented his reputation as an auteur of extreme Italian horror cinema, the next parts being *Paura nella città dei morti viventi* (*City of the Living Dead*, 1980); and ... *E tu vivrai nel terrore! L'aldilà* (*The Beyond*, 1981). These films denied the audience any concrete explanation for the walking dead beyond a vague apocalyptic metaphysics pertaining to the end of days. Along with *Quella villa accanto al cimitero* (*The House by the Cemetery*, 1981) and *The Black Cat* (1982), these few years marked a high point in Fulci's career.

While Fulci's zombies lacked concrete explanation for their resurrection, alongside the then contemporary vogue for the walking dead, other zombie films dominated the spaghetti nightmare for a few years. Umberto Lenzi's *Incubo sulla città contaminata* (*Nightmare City*, 1980), Bruno Mattei's *Virus* (*Zombie Creeping Flesh*, 1980) and even Fulci's own *Zombi 3* (*Zombie Flesh Eaters 2*, 1988) saw zombies created chemically by radiation and other pollutants, rather than because of any metaphysics. Italian zombies were also reanimated owing to the properties of the ground in which they

were originally interred. Andrea Bianchi's *Le notti del terrore* (*Burial Ground*, 1981) saw Etruscan zombies resurrected when summoned by a party of obnoxious bourgeois on a weekend getaway. Special terrain, which can bring the dead back to life, also appears in the infinitely more interesting *Zeder* (*Revenge of the Dead*, 1983) by Pupi Avati, which tries to offer a more scientific explanation for the reversal of the death process, with zombies a byproduct of this research. Michele Soavi's horror-comedy *Dellamorte Dellamore* (*Cemetery Man*, 1994), based on the novel by *Dylan Dog* creator Tiziano Sclavi, saw Francesco Dellamorte (Rupert Everett) as a cemetery's guardian who must put down, for a second time, the interred who inevitably pop back up a few hours after first being buried. By the late 1980s, the zombie craze was pretty much over and the film-makers had moved on to explore new territory.

Beyond horror movies, the spaghetti nightmare also touched upon post-apocalyptic science-fiction films. This odd cycle of films reflects an even odder array of influences and includes three films by Enzo Castellari: *1990: I guerrieri del Bronx* (*1990: Bronx Warriors,* 1982), its sequel (*Bronx Warriors 2*, 1983) and *I nuovi barbari* (*The New Barbarians*, 1983); Lucio Fulci's *I guerrieri dell'anno 2072* (*The New Gladiators*, 1984); Joe D'Amato's *Anno 2020 – I gladiatori del future* (*Texas Gladiators*, 1984); Giuliano Carnimeo's *Gli sterminatori dell'anno 3000* (*Exterminators in the Year 3000*, 1983); and Sergio Martino's *2019 – Dopo la caduta di New York* (*2019: After the Fall of New York*, 1983). In these films, we are presented with various American cities devastated by nuclear war and pollution, and neo-feudal fantasy lands controlled by gang lords and totalitarian governments. Many feature muscle-bound heroes (perhaps echoing the peplum) leading ragtag assortments of humanity through post-apocalyptic wastelands à la Snake Plisken (Kurt Russell) in John Carpenter's *Escape from New York* (1982); Mad Max (Mel Gibson) in George Miller's *Mad Max* (1979) and *The Road Warrior* (1981); or the eponymous gang in Walter Hill's *The Warriors* (1979). Lucio Fulci's *Conquest* (1983), attempts to make an Italian contribution to the fantasy peplum films produced in the wake of John Milius's *Conan the Barbarian* (1982). While none of these films is particularly controversial or really belongs in a discussion of the horror film, the directors involved – Castellari, Fulci, D'Amato, Carnimeo and Martino – had previously worked in a variety of horror genres, including the *giallo*, Italian Gothic, witchcraft, zombie and cannibal films and some, like Fulci and Martino, worked consistently across all those subgenres.

The spaghetti nightmare films also had a simultaneous influence on other aspects of Italian vernacular cinema, or, to put it another way, Italian horror-film cineastes were also exploring other types of exploitation films produced around the same time. For example, Giulio Questi's spaghetti Western *Se sei vivo spara* (*Django Kill! ... If You Live, Shoot!*, 1967) features a man physically torn apart by townsfolk looking for treasure when it is announced that he was shot repeatedly with gold bullets. Despite *Se sei vivo spara* not being a horror film (however defined), such extreme violence evokes similar pleasures to horror movies. But the most horrific non-horror genre produced in Italy in this period is likely to be the Nazi sexploitation film; softcore pornography and hardcore torture and gore films set either during the Third Reich or (worse) within concentration camps. Several of these Nazi sexploitation films were included as 'video nasties' on the Director of Public Prosecutions list: Luigi Batzella's *La bestia in calore* (*The Beast in Heat*, 1977); Cesare Canevari's *L'ultima orgia del III Reich* (*The Gestapo's Last Orgy*, 1977); and Sergio Garrone's *Lager SSadis Kastrat Kommandantur* (*SS Experiment Camp*, 1976). This cycle emerged partially from high-art precursors like Pier Paolo Pasolini's *Salò o le 120 giornate di Sodoma* and Liliana Cavani's *Il portiere di notte*.[11] But it also stemmed from the 'Black Emmanuelle' series. This sub-cycle began in 1975 with Bitto Albertini's *Emanuella nera* (*Black Emanuelle*), starring Indonesian-born actress Laura Gemser as an intrepid reporter who travels the world on assignment, investigating white-slave rings and, among other things, the last surviving cannibals, as in Joe D'Amato's *Emanuelle e gli ultimi cannibali* (*Emanuelle and the Last Cannibals*, 1977). While Gemser only played Emanuelle in a handful of films, any film starring Gemser has been marketed as part of the series, including the pornography–zombie crossover by Joe D'Amato, *Le notti erotiche dei morti viventi* (*Sexy Nights of the Living Dead*, 1980). When Emanuelle investigates the sadistic goings-on in a women's prison in Bruno Mattei's *Emanuelle fuga dall'inferno* (*Emanuelle in Prison* aka *Women's Prison Massacre*, 1983), not only is the connection made to the earlier Nazi sexploitation films, but also to the women-in-prison films popular in the early 1980s.

ITALIAN HORROR CINEMA TODAY

This period of intense horror-film diversity (roughly between the early 1960s and early 1980s) was brought to a close by several developments, not the least of which was home video, where low-budget American films received equal distribution to Italian knockoffs without the added costs of English-language dubbing. But in addition, by the early 1980s, spaghetti nightmare films had gone just about as far as they could. Consider Joe D'Amato's 1979 film *Buio Omega* (*Beyond the Darkness*), which may be the nadir of the spaghetti nightmares. While the premise about a spoilt orphan who steals and then stuffs his dead fiancée, and then proceeds to practise his taxidermy skills on a variety of young ladies he finds to try and take her place is gruesome enough, Ottavio Fabbri's script emphasises the narrative potential of visual storytelling, rather than dialogic exposition, the reliance upon which mars Argento's *Suspiria* – a visually remarkable film until the script tries to *explain* what is going on and it becomes stupid. In *Buio Omega*, a remarkably disgusting film, we see Anna's body defiled sexually before being eviscerated, as well as a portly hitchhiker chopped up for disposal in a bathtub. But that same year, 1979, also saw the 'splinter-in-the-eye' gag in *Zombi 2*; 1980 saw a foetus ripped out of a pregnant woman's body and then eaten in *Anthropophagus* (*Anthropophagous: The Beast* aka *Anthropophagous: The Grim Reaper*), as well as a woman impaled on a stake from her groin until it protrudes through her mouth in *Cannibal Holocaust*. By 1981, Umberto Lenzi tried to go even further by having Mike Logan (Giovanni Lombardo Radice) emasculated and then forcefed his own genitals in *Cannibal Ferox*. Where else could the spaghetti nightmare go from there?

Overall, Italian horror cinema production tapered off after the mid-1980s. Dario Argento seemingly tried to pass the baton first to Lamberto Bava, with *Demoni* (*Demons*, 1985), but the younger Bava was unable to compete with his father's legacy and to pass this to his protégé, Michele Soavi, who made films like *La chiesa* (*The Church*, 1989) and *La setta* (*The Sect*, 1991), but after his international success with *Dellamorte Dellamore*, Soavi put his career on hold for family reasons and has only recently begun to make films again. No film-maker since Soavi has really picked up the mantle despite continued efforts by Lenzi, Deodato, Martino, Argento and Lamberto Bava to make horror films, but the results are often a shadow of what they were in their heyday. Bruno Mattei made several straight-to-video films before he died in 2007, revisiting older subgenres like zombie and cannibal movies.

Today's young horror film-makers are clearly influenced by the spaghetti nightmares of an earlier era. Steffano Bessoni's *Imago mortis* (*Imago Mortis*, 2009) and Mariano Baino's magnificent *Temnye vody* (*Dark Waters* aka *Dead Waters*, 1993) are films distinctly rooted in the earlier Gothic tradition, while Eros Puglielli's *Occhi di cristallo* harkens back to the *giallo*. Federico Zampaglione's deeply disturbing *Shadow* (2009) takes its influence from both New French Extreme cinema, as well as American torture porn, but rather than ripping off or copying these styles, Zampaglione creates a much more personal, artistic and very enjoyable genre picture. Perhaps there is still hope for a new generation of spaghetti nightmares.

NOTES

1. See Chapter 10 of Peter Bondanella, *A History of Italian Cinema* (London and New York: Continuum, 2009).
2. *La maschera* also introduced one of Italian Gothic's biggest stars, the English-born Barbara Steele, as the witch Asa and her descendant, the ingénue Princess Katia. For a discussion of this actress, such an important figure in Italian genre cinema, see Carl Jenks, 'The Other Face of Death: Barbara Steele and *La maschera del demonio*', in Richard Dyer and Ginette Vincendeau (eds), *Popular European Cinema* (New York and London: Routledge, 1992), pp. 149–62.
3. Questi is best known as the director of the violent spaghetti Western *Se sei vivo spara*, one of the several Italian Django Westerns to influence Quentin Tarantino's *Django Unchained*.
4. Quoted in Kim Newman, 'Thirty Years in Another Town: The History of Italian Exploitation', *Monthly Film Bulletin* no. 53 (1986), p. 92.
5. Donato Totaro, 'The Italian Zombie Film: From Derivation to Reinvention', in Steven Jay Schneider (ed.), *Fear without Frontiers: Horror Cinema across the Globe* (Godalming: FAB Press, 2003), p. 161.

6. Quoted in Stephen Thrower, *Beyond Terror: The Films of Lucio Fulci* (Godalming: FAB Press, 1999), p. 15.
7. Two of the cannibal films on the list differ in their narratives: Joe D'Amato's *Anthropophagus* is about a tourist boat which washes ashore on a Mediterranean island populated by local cannibals, while Antonio Margheriti's *Apocalypse Domani* (*Cannibal Apocalypse*, 1980) imagines Vietnam veterans who return to the US with a taste for human flesh.
8. The literal translation of *Il paese del sesso selvaggio* suggests this connection too: 'Wild Sex Country' sounds very much like a typical *mondo* documentary. For more on the *Mondo Cane* phenomenon, see Gino Moliterno's chapter in this anthology.
9. Reflecting a further desire for crossover marketing, *Zombi Holocaust* was advertised as a then-popular 'slasher' film and retitled 'Dr Butcher, MD (Medical Deviant)'.
10. The Italian title demonstrates both what Cozzi is quoted previously as saying, but also that Fulci was capitalising on Romero's film by claiming this as a sequel.
11. See Mikel J. Koven, '"The Film You Are About to See Is Based on Documented Fact": Italian Nazi Sexploitation Cinema', in Ernest Mathijs and Xavier Mendik (eds), *Alternative Europe: Eurotrash and Exploitation Cinema from 1945* (London: Wallflower Press, 2004), pp. 19–31.

FURTHER READING

Bondanella, Peter, *A History of Italian Cinema* (London and New York: Continuum, 2009).

Gallant, Chris (ed.), *Art of Darkness: The Cinema of Dario Argento* (Godalming: FAB Press, 2000).

Goodall, Mark, *Sweet and Savage: The World through the Shockumentary Film Lens* (London: Headpress, 2006).

Gracey, James, *Dario Argento* (Harpenden: Kamera Books, 2010).

Howarth, Troy, *The Haunted World of Mario Bava* (Godalming: FAB Press, 2002).

Kerekes, David and David Slater, *Killing for Culture: An Illustrated History of Death Film from Mondo to Snuff* (London: Creation Books, 1993).

Koven, Mikel. J, *La Dolce Morte: Vernacular Cinema and the Italian Giallo Film* (Lanham, MD: Scarecrow Press, 2006).

McDonagh, Maitland, *Broken Mirrors/Broken Minds: The Dark Dreams of Dario Argento* (New York: Citadel Press, 1994).

Palmerini, Luca and Gaetano Mistretta, *Spaghetti Nightmares: Italian Fantasy-Horrors as Seen through the Eyes of Their Protagonists* (Key West, FL: Fantasma Books, 1996).

Slater, Jay, *Eaten Alive!: Italian Cannibal and Zombie Movies* (London: Plexus Publishing Ltd, 2002).

Thrower, Stephen, *Beyond Terror: The Films of Lucio Fulci* (Godalming: FAB Press, 1999).

25 European Co-productions and Artistic Collaborations

The Italian Response to the Hollywood Studio System

Jean A. Gili[1]

Early on, Italy became involved in a financial system of co-productions and artistic collaborations by means of recruiting artists from other countries. Even in the silent era, producers were seeking financing abroad they could not obtain from Italian banks, along with the stars most likely to ensure the distribution of their works, with *Quo vadis?* (1924) a prime example. In 1923, when Arturo Ambrosio, on behalf of the Union Cinématographique Italienne, embarked upon the ambitious project of an adaptation of Sienkiewicz's novel, he called on Gabriellino D'Annunzio, the son of the famous writer, for the direction; for added insurance, he paired him with the German director Georg Jacoby. Furthermore, he achieved international distribution by lining up an international cast: Elena Sangro, Rina De Liguoro and Bruto Castellani from Italy; Lilian Hall-Davis from England; André Habay from France; Alfons Fryland from Austria; and from Germany, Elga Brink and above all, the popular Emil Jannings in the role of Nero. *Gli ultimi giorni di Pompei* (1926) is an even better example. Filming began at the end of 1924 under the direction of Amleto Palermi, with two Italian stars – Lido Manetti and Diomira Jacobini – in the roles of Glauco and Nidia. After a few months, money dried up and shooting stopped. Palermi, who had good connections outside Italy, left for Vienna to find new financing. The director presented the material he had filmed to his contacts and gained their support for a circus scene using 5,000 extras. The Austrian financiers, however, imposed one condition: two Hungarian actors – Viktor Varkonyi and Maria Korda – would replace Lido Manetti and Jacobini. Palermi accepted the condition and richly compensated the actors. They reshot several scenes and developed the character of Arbace, thereafter played by Bernhard Goetzke, a celebrated German actor also imposed by the Austrians to promote circulation in Germanic

countries. During the filming, Palermi had to revisit Vienna several times to obtain the money to continue. In order to avoid interrupting the shooting, the production hired a second director, Carmine Gallone, who completed the film. In total, the completed film cost the considerable sum of 5 million lire.

ITALO-FRENCH COLLABORATIONS DURING THE FASCIST PERIOD

During the 1930s, concerns about Italian cinema's visibility abroad, and a dearth of trained professionals, led producers to call on numerous French film-makers with whom relationships had been important since the origins of the cinema. The most notable of these is the director Jean Renoir, who went to Rome in 1939 to prepare the shooting of *Tosca* (*The Story of Tosca*, 1941). The creation of dual-language versions of films, in which the actor who speaks the foreign language in each of the two versions is dubbed into the target language, required the movement of film-makers and actors to and from Italy. In this way, a skill especially important in Italy got its start – dubbing actors who thus appeared to be 'Italian' characters.

From 1930 on, Jean Cassagne was in Rome for *La dernière berceuse* (*The Last Lullaby*, 1931), the French version of Gennaro Righelli's *La canzone dell'amore* – the first Italian sound film. In 1934, Jacques Houssin directed Francesca Bertini in *Odette* (*Odette* aka *Déchéance*, 1935), the Italian version of which was completed by Giorgio Zambon. For their part, French actors Edwige Feuillère and Marie Bell stayed in Rome in 1935. The former took a role in Carlo Ludovico Bragaglia's *Amore* (*Love*, 1936), in which she shared the screen with Italians Gianfranco Giachetti and Gino Cervi while Georges Lacombe directed the French version, *La Route heureuse*. Marie Bell also worked opposite Fosco Giachetti and Annibale Ninchi in

Giovacchino Forzano's *Fiordalisi d'oro* (*Golden Lilies*, 1936), while Forzano himself completed the French version, *Sous la terreur* (*Under the Terror*), with help on the dialogue from Alexandre Arnoux.

In the second half of the 1930s, despite a political climate scarcely favourable to a rapprochement between the two countries, more and more film-makers, actors and other creative collaborators went to work in the transalpine studios. The fascist regime sought to attract them with a policy of openness to lend credence to the idea that Italy remained open to cultural exchanges. Besides the French embassy in Italy, the prestigious French School of Rome, or the Villa Medici, directed by the musician Jacques Ibert, saw this presence as a means of shining an indirect light on the Italian political situation. An ambitious production, based on a Luigi Pirandello novel *Il fu Mattia Pascal* (*The Late Mattia Pascal*, 1904), was entrusted to French director Pierre Chenal, who went to Rome with a constellation of celebrated French actors – Pierre Blanchar, Robert Le Vigan, Pierre Alcover, Margo Lion – and he teamed up with Armand Salacrou and Roger Vitrac to write the script. For good measure, he signed up Jacques Ibert to write the music. Chenal directed both French and Italian versions: Pierre Blanchar and Isa Miranda act in both, and the only notable difference is that Enrico Glori replaced Robert Le Vigan in the Italian version.

In 1936, two other French film-makers in Italy, Jean Epstein and Abel Gance, made *Cuor di vagabond* (*Coeur de gueux*; *The Heart of a Vagabond*), which brought together a celebrated Italian stage actor (Ermette Zacconi) and a famous French actress (Madeleine Renaud). In 1938, they completed *Il ladro di donne* (*Le voleur de femmes*; *The Woman Thief*), which included two French actors, Jules Berry and Annie Ducaux. Berry returned to Italy in 1938 to film *La signora di Montecarlo* (*L'Inconnue de Monte Carlo*; *The Woman of Monte Carlo*) by André Berthomieu (Mario Soldati did the Italian version); the film brought Dita Parlo together with Albert Préjean (replaced by Fosco Giachetti for the Italian version) and Jules Berry. Berthomieu also worked with Mario Camerini in 1943 for *T'amerò sempre* (*I'll Always Love You*). In 1936, Jean Dréville directed the French version of *Un colpo di vento* (*Coup de vent*; *A Gust of Wind*) assisted by Charles-Félix Tavano, who was also responsible for an Italian version. In the same year, Jean-Paul Paulin took the place of Carl Dreyer who had been hired earlier: Dreyer had drafted a screenplay and he began filming between June and July 1934. His name figures as the co-scriptwriter along with those of Paulin

and Ernesto Quadrone. Paulin shot what became *Jungla nera* (*L'Esclave blanc*, *The Black Jungle*, 1936) with Georges Rigaud in the title role.

In 1937, Carmine Gallone filmed a biopic – *Giuseppe Verdi* (*Le Roman d'un genie*; *The Life of Giuseppe Verdi*, 1938), for which he brought in Gaby Morlay and Pierre Brasseur to play opposite Fosco Giachetti, who had the title role. A strange Franco-Italian co-production – Nero-Film/Film Internazionali's *La principessa Tarakanova* (*Tarakanowa* in France, 1938) – was completed in this same year, directed by Fedor Ozep with Annie Vernay, Pierre Richard-Willm, Suzy Prim and Roger Karl in the lead roles. The film was shot at Cinecittà with the collaboration of Mario Soldati for the Italian version.

Despite the crisis brought on by the war in Ethiopia and the vote for sanctions against Italy by the League of Nations, Franco-Italian filming slowed only for a short period but then resumed even more successfully in 1938. The first to head back to Rome was Marcel L'Herbier who completed *Terra di Fuoco* (*Terre de feu*; *Land of Fire*, 1939) during the summer of 1938 with Jaque-Catelain as his assistant. The film brought together the celebrated Italian tenor Tito Schipa and Mireille Balin, and a script written by Jean George Auriol and Jean Sarment. At the approach of the war, despite a growing climate of tension between the two countries, the sojourns of French artists in Italy did not diminish. Dual versions of films were even more successful as some Italian companies established French subsidiaries that operated in Paris. Thus, 1939 saw the making of two films in Rome that were completed by the French: Jean de Limur filmed *Papa Lebonnard* (*Le Père Lebonnard*) with Ruggero Ruggeri, Jean Murat, Madeleine Sologne and Pierre Brasseur, with music by Jacques Ibert, while Jeff Musso shot *Ultima giovinezza* (*Dernière jeunesse*; *Last Desire*) with a group of prestigious French actors, including Raimu, Pierre Brasseur and Jacqueline Delubac.

The beginning of the war in September 1939 did not prevent these exchanges as Italy initially declared its non-belligerency. Collaboration, not entirely removed from ulterior political motives, continued within the artistic sphere. French actors went to Rome to work in Italian films: Corinne Luchaire and George Rigaud took roles in Mario Mattoli's *Abbandono* (*Abandonment*, 1940); Renée Saint Cyr plays opposite Vittorio De Sica in *Rose scarlatte*, the first film De Sica directed; Mireille Balin, a regular at the Roman studios, took part in the Italian-Spanish production of *L'assedio dell'Alcazar*, a film glorifying Francoism directed by the the veteran

Augusto Genina, marking the arrival of Spain as a new co-production partner. For their part, French film-makers continued to work in Rome. In 1939, Jean Choix finished *Rosa di sangue* (*Angelica* in French; *Blood Red Rose*) with Viviane Romance, Georges Flamant, Guillaume de Sax, from a script on which Jean Georges Auriol had collaborated, with music by Jacques Ibert. Auriol, who returned to Italy after the war to work on Alessandro Blasetti's *Fabiola* had already participated in writing the script for L'Herbier's *Terra di fuoco*. More unexpectedly, he was also involved in two fully Italian films: Palermi's *Napoli che non muore* (*Naples That Never Dies*, 1939); and Camillo Mastrocinque's *Validità giorni dieci* (*Good for Ten Days*, 1940). Jean Choux directed an Italo-Spanish co-production, filmed in two versions: *La nascità di Salome* (*Il nacimiento de Salomé*; *The Birth of Solomon*, 1940), with Conchita Montenegro, Armando Falconi, Fernando Freyre and Nerio Bernardi.

During the winter of 1939–40, Marcel L'Herbier went once again to Rome to work for Italy's most Francophile company (Scalera) on *Ecco la felicità* (*La Comédie du bonheur*; *Here Is Happiness*, 1940), an ambitious film with adaptation and dialogue by Jean Cocteau and featuring such famous actors as Michel Simon, Micheline Presle, André Alerme, Jacqueline Delubac and Ramon Novarro. During this same period, the production of *Tosca*, the high watermark of French presence in Italy, began, produced by Scalera and directed by Renoir, who remained in Rome during the winter of 1939–40 to prepare the shooting. At Renoir's side were his assistants, Carl Koch and Luchino Visconti, and actor, Michel Simon. Unfortunately, Italy's entrance into the war against France on 10 June 1940 forced Renoir to leave: shooting was completed by Carl Koch, assisted by Visconti. Another twelve years would pass before Renoir would return to Rome in 1952 to shoot *The Golden Coach* (*La carrozza d'oro*; *Le carrosse d'or*; 1952) at Cinecittà, but in English now rather than in French.

CO-PRODUCTIONS AFTER WORLD WAR II

After 1945, Italy thrust itself even more vigorously into co-productions, still mainly with the French, while also attempting to attract other international film-making to its studios. Such co-productions were launched with the obvious intention of pooling all available resources to rebuild the cinema industries in nations damaged by the war, but also to counteract troubling images of mutual misunderstanding caused by the conflict. This venture would mobilise hundreds of directors, scriptwriters, actors, creative collaborators, producers and distributors,

and in less than fifty years, it would proudce a total of around 2,000 films. One aim of this cooperative venture was to resist competition from the US, whose films swept across European screens after 1945.

The first agreements concerning co-productions were signed in October 1946. They provided that the films agreed upon could benefit in each of the two countries from the advantages in each of the two countries – quotas and premiums – given to films that were 100 per cent national productions. They allowed for the development of ambitious projects and the raising of sufficient capital to cover higher costs. In 1949, under these arrangements, the firm Universalia headed by Salvo D'Angelo produced Blasetti's *Fabiola*, an evocation of the origins of Christianity that united the artistic teams of the two countries and featured Michèle Morgan, Henri Vidal, Michel Simon (an habitué of the Italian studios since the *Tosca* of Renoir and Koch in 1940), Massimo Girotti and Gino Cervi. The following year D'Angelo followed the same path by producing another version of *Gli ultimi giorni di Pompei* (*Les derniers jours de Pompei*; *Sins of Pompei*, 1950), directed by L'Herbier with an allocation of roles that was almost exclusively French: Micheline Presle, Georges Marchal, Marcel Herrand and Adriana Benetti. In *Le Film francais* (19 March 1948), D'Angelo evokes a shared Latin culture and civilisation that 'should not be only vain words' and emphasises the complementarity of the two countries, while insisting on the economic advantages of co-productions:

> The union of our efforts must be fertile, effective, our two markets must become as one. If our experiment succeeds, producers in France and Italy will find themselves faced with a market of 10,000 cinemas that will allow a much greater and more regular profitability for their films.

It must be stressed that in this period, co-productions organised by Italian producers were much more numerous than those organised by the French. But in all other respects, Italians and French were united in their efforts to counter the omnipresence of US cinema (in 1948, 450 US films were shown in Italy as opposed to only about fifty Italian films).

New agreements for co-productions were signed in February 1949, with the details made explicit in October. They gave priority to films of quality – judged according to the interest of the subject and the prestige of the artistic teams, directors and actors –to contend with the imbalance between the number of films made in Italy and France. Indeed, it appeared that Italians gained greater advantage from the system of co-productions than the French and Rome, in particular, attracted numerous films. But, in fact, the legislation was intended to establish the principle of twin films: every film completed in Rome should correspond to one completed in France.

In September 1953, new measures further complicated the financial arrangements, proving that things were probably not working well, even if the period from 1949 to 1953 had co-produced some eighty films. It was decided that the nationality of the producer would determine whether the film would be designated Italo-French or Franco-Italian where there was a balance in the level of investments from both countries. In addition, the idea of expanding co-productions with other European countries was considered. One difficulty arose from the balance sheet: of the 120 films made in Italy as Italo-French co-productions from 1949 to 1957, only seventy-eight were actually released in France. Paradoxically, co-production did not, therefore, guarantee distribution in both countries.

Adjustments made in October 1961 give evidence of the need to continually review the working agreement. Rules governing minority investments in co-productions were much better defined (the minority participation could not fall below 30 per cent). In March 1966, the foundations for a new agreement signed in August of the same year, were laid out at the meeting of the Franco-Italian Commission. This increased the number of guarantees required of the co-producers to gain the financial benefits provided for by the law. The

accord also reconsidered the issue of equality in the number of films initiated by the Italians as opposed to those by the French. Moreover, it reversed the numerical trend in favour of the French.

After 1974, difficulties increased. The Italian Court of Accounts denounced the practice of false co-productions in which the technical or artistic participation of Italians was non-existent. Overall, the number of co-productions diminished, from thirteen films in 1975 to only six in 1976. Concurrently, cinema attendance also declined substantially. Above all, the French perception of Italian cinema as being of an excessively national character had a detrimental effect on its popularity. Even a film such as Scola's *C'eravamo tanto amati* (*We All Loved Each Other So Much*, 1974) remained without a French buyer, because it was judged to be too Italian to interest the French. Only the great classics (Visconti, Rossellini, Antonioni, Fellini) and a few directors from the younger generation found favour in the eyes of the distributors. This perception, widely endorsed by the media, endures to this day. In 1976, numerous Italian films remained undistributed despite the existence of French versions. If Italian films (including co-productions in which Italians were the major investors) represented 12 per cent of the total attendance in French cinemas in 1970, this percentage continued to diminish, falling to 5 per cent in 1975 with a sharp decrease in the following years.

Thus, since the 1980s, the system of co-productions has been in crisis, leading to an identical commercial downturn for the two national cinemas, although commissions regularly encouraged their revival, and

Gérard Philippe and Gina Lollobrigida in Christian-Jaque's *Fanfan la Tulipe* (1952)

presented co-productions as the only possible way out of economic difficulties. Taking stock of fifty years of co-productions, Catherine Burucoa wrote in the volume *Paris-Rome*:

> Above and beyond financial constraints and red tape, it appears that over the years the major problem has been, paradoxically, the cultural propensities of the two countries, each one of which had difficulty, given its bad faith, in appreciating the values, sentiments, and the ways of thinking of its neighbor. Denials, betrayals, and crises have marked the long history of a union that has often been fertile, sometimes full of conflict, and always passionate.[2]

In spite of such difficulties, Franco-Italian co-productions have given Italian cinema exceptional influence and an international presence capable, in the best of times, of competing with Hollywood. Their many successes pay tribute to the actions of Italy's dynamic film producers, individuals such as Riccardo Gualino, Angelo Rizzoli, Carlo Ponti, Dino De Laurentiis, Goffredo Lombardo, Mario Cecchi Gori, Franco Cristaldi, Alfredo Bini and Alberto Grimaldi.

The visible part of the iceberg of Franco-Italian co-production indelibly imprinted in our memory is composed of fictional couples: Gérard Philippe and Gina Lollobrigida in Christian-Jaque's *Fanfan la Tulipe*; Jean Gabin and Isa Miranda in René Clément's *Au delà des grilles* (*Le mura di Malapaga*; *The Walls of Malapaga*, 1949); Aldo Fabrizi and Gaby Morlay in Alessandro Blasetti's *Prima comunione* (*Sa majesté Monsieur Dupont*; *Father's Dilemma*, 1950) Massimo Girotti and Micheline Presle in Jean Grémillon's *L'Amour d'une femme* (*L'amore di una donna*; *The Love of a Woman*, 1953); Yves Montand and Silvana Mangano in Giuseppe De Santis's *Uomini e lupi* (*Hommes et loups*; *Men and Wolves*, 1957); François Périer and Giulietta Masina in Federico Fellini's *Le notti di Cabiria*; François Périer and Sandra Milo in Antonio Pietrangeli's *La visita* (*Annonces matrimoniales*; *The Visitor*, 1963); Jacques Perrin and Claudia Cardinale in Valerio Zurlini's *La ragazza con la valigia* (*La fille à la valise*; *Girl with a Suitcase*, 1961); Marcello Mastroianni and Micheline Presle in Elio Petri's *L'assassino* (*L'assassin*; *The Assassin* aka *The Ladykiller of Rome*, 1961); Jean-Paul Belmondo and Sophia Loren in Vittorio De Sica's *La ciociara* (*Paysanne aux pieds nu*; *Two Women*, 1960); Marcello Mastroianni and Catherine Deneuve in Marco Ferreri's *La cagna* (*Melampo*; *Liza*, 1972); Alain Delon and Monica Vitti in *L'eclisse* by Michelangelo Antonioni; Alain Delon and Claudia Cardinale in Visconti's *Il gattopardo*. The pre-eminence of masculine figures in the two national cinemas also led to the formation of numerous couples of Franco–Italian actors: Fernandel and Gino Cervi in the *Don Camillo* series but also Fernandel with Totò in Christian-Jaque's *La Loi c'est la loi* (*La legge é legge*; *The Law Is the Law*, 1958); Vittorio Gassman and Jean-Louis Trintignant in Risi's *Il sorpasso*; Alain Delon and Renato Salvatori in Visconti's *Rocco e i suoi fratelli*; Franco Citti and Laurent Terzieff in Sergio Citti's *Ostia*; Alberto Sordi and Bernard Blier in Ettore Scola's *Riusciranno i nostri eroi a ritrovare l'amico misteriosamente scomparso in Africa?* (*Nos héros retrouveront-ils leurs amis mystérieusement disparus en Afrique?*; *Will Our Heros Be*

Monica Vitti and Alain Delon in Antonioni's *L'eclisse* (1962)

In Luchino Visconti's *Rocco e i suoi fratelli* (1960), French star Alain Delon plays a young Italian boxer in Milan

Able to Find Their Friend Who Has Mysteriously Disappeared in Africa?, 1968). At the apex of these close male bondings, Mario Monicelli's *Amici miei* (*Mes chers amis*) brought Philippe Noiret, Bernard Blier, Ugo Tognazzi, Gastone Moschin and Adolfo Celi together in a perfect Franco-Italian comedic masterpiece. Furthermore, many French actors actually spent much of their careers in Italy, most notably Charles Vanel, Alain Cuny, Jean-Louis Trintignant, Jacques Perrin, François Périer, Alain Delon, Bernard Blier, Philippe Noiret, Michel Piccoli, Jean-Claude Brialy, Jean-Paul Belmondo, Laurent Terzieff, Lino Ventura, Serge Reggiani, Marina Vlady, Annie Gérardot, Anouk Aimée, Magali Noël, Catherine Deneuve and Fanny Ardant. The opposite is not true: with the exception of Marcello Mastroianni, Italian actors have rarely performed in many French films shot in France. Thus, with its strong cultural identity, Italian cinema often Italianised French actors who worked on Italian soil, and they also transformed directors as diverse as Christian-Jaque, Julien Duvivier, and René Clément into Italian film-makers at certain moments in their careers.

This represented a fundamental difference, since French actors played Italian characters in Italy: dubbing allowed them to surmount any difficulty language-wise or related to accents (even Yves Montand, Serge Reggiani and Lino Ventura were dubbed). In contrast, Italian actors in France interpreted roles of Italian characters or French characters of Italian origin: thus in Claude Sautet's *Mado* (*Mado*, 1976), Ottavia Piccolo plays the role of an Italian who has come to live in France; Lea Massari in Louis Malle's *Le Souffle au coeur* (*Murmur of the Heart*, 1971) is a beautiful young woman of Italian origin married to a rich French bourgeois. Alberto Sordi plays an Italian in Jean-Pierre Mocky's *Le Témoin* (*The Witness*, 1978), just as Gian Maria Volonté does in Jean-Pierre Melville's *Le Cercle rouge* (*Le Cercle Rouge*, 1970).

HOLLYWOOD ON THE TIBER

By the early 1950s, American producers had discovered the advantages of filming in Italy. As a result, some big-budget films were made in Rome: Mervyn LeRoy's *Quo Vadis* (1951) with Deborah Kerr, Robert Taylor and Peter

Ustinov; King Vidor's *War and Peace* (1956) with Audrey Hepburn, Henry Fonda and Mel Ferrer; William Wyler's *Ben-Hur* with Charlton Heston, Stephen Boyd and Jack Hawkins; Robert Aldrich's *Sodom and Gomorrah* with Stewart Granger, Stanley Baker and Anouk Aimée; Joseph L. Mankiewicz's *Cleopatra* with Elizabeth Taylor, Richard Burton and Rex Harrison; John Huston's *The Bible* with a constellation of actors, notably George C. Scott, Peter O'Toole and Ava Gardner. Another memorable event in the Roman studios in the course of the 1960s was the appearance of Shelley Winters, who was married to Vittorio Gassman for a time and who, in 1977, appeared in both Mauro Bolognini's *Gran bollito* (*Black Journal*, 1977) and Mario Monicelli's *Un borghese piccolo piccolo*. This practice of filming American films in Rome with American actors is far less frequent today, but one recent example was Martin Scorsese's production of *Gangs of New York* made at Cinecittà in 2001 with sets by Dante Ferretti and starring Leonardo Di Caprio, Daniel Day-Lewis and Cameron Diaz. Working in Rome had, at one time, many advantages over Hollywood: the quality of the facilities was high; labour costs were low, especially for extras. By Italian law at the time, Americans could only transfer 5 per cent of the revenue from films screened in Italy back to Hollywood – the rest had to be spent locally for shooting in Italy, paying actors and advertising new films screened in the peninsula. Thus, in order to gain some advantage from the vast amounts of capital piled up through screening their products in Italian movie theatres, US studios were obliged to do at least some work inside Italy to make sure of their profits. Such financial advantages explain why making American films in Italy once became quite popular, and Hollywood stars also became accustomed to coming to Rome. Quite rapidly, they also agreed to act in local Italian productions, even if, like Ava Gardner, they worked in Rome only under the direction of American film-makers.

However, Italian film-makers also employed American actors, aware that they could bring much greater international renown. Hence, immediately after the war, in the neorealist period, Italian directors used relatively unknown Americans to portray US soldiers: in *Paisà*, Rossellini directed Dots M. Johnson in the Neapolitan episode and Gar Moore in the Roman episode. In the same year, Luigi Zampa called on Leo Dale in *Un Americano in vacanza* (*A Yank in Rome*, 1946) and in the following year, Zampa brought Gar Moore back for *Vivere in pace* (*To Live in Peace*) and hired John Kitzmiller for the role of the black soldier. Kitzmiller

eventually enjoyed a brief career in Italy, always playing former black military personnel in Giorgio Ferroni's *Tombolo paradiso nero* (*Tombolo*, 1947); Alberto Lattuada's *Senza pietà* (*Without Pity*, 1948); Fellini and Lattuada's *Luci del varietà*. The presence of American actors was justified by the nationality of the characters they played. Things changed radically when American actors began to play Italian roles. It should be noted that the Italian film-makers' practice of recording only ambient sound during their shooting and of dubbing dialogue afterwards with post-synchronisation basically removed all the difficulties of directing US actors, who could be dubbed in the same fashion as both French and Italian actors were for the final version of a film. In 1953, Visconti inaugurated the practice of using an American actor for a non-American character with Farley Granger in *Senso*, but in this case, the character was still not Italian but Austrian. The true revolution began in 1954 with *La strada*, the film in which Fellini employs two Americans – Anthony Quinn and Richard Basehart – to play the roles of Zampanò and The Fool. Having come to Europe to gain new experiences after the triumph of Elia Kazan's *Viva Zapata!* (1952), Quinn appeared in Giuseppe Amato's *Donne proibite* (*Angels of Darkness*) in 1953 with Giulietta Masina; with Silvana Mangano in Mario Mattoli's *Il più comico spettacolo del mondo* (*Funniest Show on Earth*, 1953); and, more importantly, in Carmine Gallone's *Cavalleria rusticana* (*Fatal Desire*, 1955), playing the role of Alfio in this filmed version of the famous Mascagni opera with Quinn's singing voice dubbed by international opera star Tito Gobbi. *La strada* transformed Quinn into an international star.

At the same time, Quinn had a smaller role in Mario Camerini's *Ulisse* alongside Kirk Douglas, whose role in this was his only foray into Italian films, and then Quinn took the title role in Pietro Francisci's *Attila flagella di Dio* (*Attila*, 1954). He confirmed his physical presence on the screen in the title role in Richard Fleischer's *Barabba* (*Barabbas*, 1961), co-starring Vittorio Gassman, a film shot in Italy with a US director. In 1976, Quinn returned to Italy to work in Mauro Bolognini's *L'eredità Ferramonti* (*The Inheritance*) alongside Dominique Sanda. As for Richard Basehart, Fellini directed him again in *Il bidone* (*Il Bidone*, 1955), where he played opposite US actor Broderick Crawford – the unforgettable Augusto, the father who tries to swindle his accomplices to help his daughter. In the course of the 1950s and 60s, many American actors came to Italy to appear in sometimes surprising roles, such as Gloria Swanson's swansong in Steno's *Mio figlio Nerone* with

Alberto Sordi as Nero, Vittorio De Sica as Seneca and
Brigitte Bardot as Poppea; Steve Cochran with Alida Valli
in Michelangelo Antonioni's *Il grido*; Paul Douglas with
Giulietta Masina in Eduardo De Filippo's *Fortunella*
(*Fortunella*, 1958); Ben Gazzara in Mario Monicelli's *Risate
di gioia* (*The Passionate Thief*, 1960); Martin Balsam in Luigi
Comencini's *Tutti a casa*; Anthony Franciosa and Betsy
Blair (already seen in *Il grido*), in Mauro Bolognini's
Senilità (*Careless*, 1962); and George Chakiris in
Comencini's *La ragazza di Bube* (*Bebo's Girl*, 1963).

The statuesque Tina Louise, in Pietro Francisci's
L'assedio di Siracusa, followed by his *Saffo, venere di Lesbo*
paved the way for bringing in American actors to play
heroes of antiquity (Rory Calhoun), cowboys (Eli
Wallach, Lee Van Cleef) or cops (Henry Silva, Tony
Musante, Martin Balsam). The height of this Roman
melting pot – Vittorio De Sica's *Il giudizio universal* (*The
Last Judgment*, 1961) – brought together Jack Palance,
Ernest Borgnine, Jimmy Durante and Akim Tamiroff to
join Alberto Sordi, Vittorio Gassman, Nino Manfredi,
Silvana Mangano, Fernandel, Anouk Aimée, Lino
Ventura and Melina Mercouri. And of course, we cannot
forget Clint Eastwood, who won his stripes with Sergio
Leone in the spaghetti Western before becoming a
Hollywood star and a great director in his own right.
It is also necessary to reserve a special place for Burt
Lancaster who, after risking his reputation for Robert
Aldrich in *Vera Cruz* (1954) became a Sicilian aristocrat
thanks to Visconti in *Il gattopardo*. His performance as
the Prince Don Fabrizio Salina touches upon the
ineffable. Later in 1976, Lancaster dominated the cast
of Bernardo Bertolucci's *Novecento*, which reunites in a
kind of ideal international synthesis American actors
(Sterling Hayden, Robert De Niro and Donald
Sutherland); French actors (Gérard Depardieu and
Dominique Sanda); and native Italians (Stefania
Sandrelli, Alida Valli, Laura Betti and Romolo Valli).

Thus, when considering the international influence
of Italian cinema, it is somewhat surprising to note
that a number of the mythical figures of the Italian
cinematic imagination are based upon the faces of
foreign actors: Don Camillo (Fernandel), Zampanò
(Anthony Quinn), Rocco (Alain Delon) and Prince Don
Fabrizio Salina (Burt Lancaster) are among the icons
of a cinematography of inexhaustible richness. If
Hollywood studios produced a series of films capable
of attracting audiences from all over the world, Italian
producers succeeded, by attracting both capital and
stars to Rome, in creating works that stand up well
in comparison.

NOTES

1. Translated by Julia Conaway Bondanella.
2. Cited in Jean A. Gili and Aldo Tassone (eds), *Paris–Rome.
   Cinquante ans de cinéma franco-italien* (Paris: La
   Martinière, 1995), p. 65.

FURTHER READING

Brunetta, Gian Piero, *Storia del cinema italiano*, 4 vols (Rome:
    Editori Riuniti, 1993).
Faldini, Franca and Goffredo Fofi (eds), *L'avventurosa storia
    del cinema italiano raccontata dai suoi protagonisti*, 3 vols
    (Milan: Feltrinelli/Mondadori, 1979–84).
Giacci, Vittorio (ed.), *Neorealismo, Nouvelle Vague,
    Coproduzioni. Cento anni di collaborazione cinematografica
    italo-francese/Néo-réalisme, Nouvelle Vague, Coproductions.
    Cent ans de collaboration cinématographique franco-italienne*
    (Rome: Gallucci Editore, 2008).
Gili, Jean A., *La Comédie italienne* (Paris: Henri Veyrier, 1983).
Gili, Jean A., *Le Cinéma italien* (Paris: La Martinière, 2011).
Gili, Jean A. and Aldo Tassone (eds), *Paris–Rome, cinquante ans
    de cinéma franco-italien* (Paris: Editions de la Martinière,
    1995); (Italian edn) *Parigi–Roma: 50 anni di coproduzioni
    italo-francesi* (Assisi: Edizioni Il Castoro, 1995).
Lancia, Enciro and Fabio Melelli, *Attori stranieri del nostro
    cinema* (Rome: Gremese, 2006).
Toffetti, Sergio (ed.), *Un'altra Italia. Pour une histoire du cinéma
    italien* (Paris: Cinémathèque française/Mazzotta, 1998).

26 How the Italians Happened to Cherish and Then to Disdain Their Cinema

Pierre Sorlin

Going to the pictures is at the same time a personal initiative ('I'd like to see this film ...') and a group action ('... because they say it's very funny' or '... because it's a chance to meet my friends'). We shall never know how individuals make their decisions, but we can observe collective behaviours that, being linked to local customs and traditions, are relatively consistent in a given country. The Italians were not the greatest cine-buffs in Europe (in the best year, 1955, 800 million tickets were sold, about half of the top figure in the UK), but they were the most persevering. Attendance declined everywhere at the end of the 1950s but remained rather high till the last 1960s in the peninsula. There was an Italian way of enjoying movies, which brings out aspects of Italian cultural habits and sheds light on the social evolution that characterised the second part of the twentieth century.

BIRTH OF AN AUDIENCE

Who were the film spectators? It is not easy to identify them. A circle of people interested in films formed at the beginning of the twentieth century, but who belonged to this group? Some think that, initially, these were affluent people whose fancy did not last. The cinema soon became a popular form of entertainment despised by highbrows. According to the weekly, La cinematografia italiana ed estera (July 1908), the cinema 'is an amusement that pleases the poor who don't go to school and live in an opaque atmosphere where everything is less delicate and more dumb'. Yet others held an opposite view, Riccioto Canudo, a well-known essayist, affirmed in 1910 that spectators 'from the more uneducated to the more intellectual belong to all social classes'. Who was right?

When the agents of Lumière or Edison presented the new wonder in the most important cities, lots of well-to-do photography amateurs rushed out and bought cameras. All they wanted to do was *take* 'moving' pictures; they were not interested in images made by others. Public exhibitions began in fun fairs where films were projected either among other attractions or in stalls offering, in an hour, several amusing or instructive shorts. Admission was expensive, between twenty and fifty centimes, when an unskilled worker or a shop assistant earned two lire a day. Those who attended the shows belonged to the ill-defined 'lower middle class': they were smallholders, people in the professions, clerks and civil servants. The little we know about them suggests that they were attracted by the documentary side of films, by the impression of 'being at sea', visiting foreign cities or entering the Vatican.

The shows in fairs did not last long, but they aroused curiosity and prompted entrepreneurs to open stable premises. At the end of the first decade of the twentieth century, there were already forty-four theatres in Milan and thirty-eight in Rome. A few were huge (700 seats in the Milan Palace) and comfortable, constructed in central districts, such as the Corso and the Esedra in Rome, or the Duomo in Milan, and they exhibited feature-length films for middle-class spectators. Smaller ones, poor, cold in winter, were established in peripheral districts. Quite soon the same word, 'cinema', included both these two very distinct types of theatres, with different programmes, excellent prints of gripping stories, or random collections of old, shop-worn short films.

A STABLE PUBLIC

From the second decade of the century till the 1960s, Italian cinema attendance grew regularly, with temporary declines during the economic crisis of the Great Depression and at the end of World War II. How can we account for this long-lasting curiosity? There is no clear-cut answer. All we can do is highlight a few suggestive correlations. The massive introduction of Hollywood pictures, from 1917 onwards, played an important role. This does not mean that all spectators saw the same films, since the programme was dependent on the standard of the cinema. Sojourning in Viareggio, in August 1933, film critic Mario Pannunzio wrote: 'The films that arrive here are those we saw last winter [in Rome] and that nobody is willing to see again.' If such was the case in a medium-size sea resort, we can imagine what it was like in the distant province of Basilicata. However, thanks to US movies, it was the very idea of what constituted a film that changed. Italian film production, blossoming before World War I, nearly vanished after the conflict ended. Therefore, until the revival of the late 1930s, 90 per cent of Italian screenings came from Hollywood. Many testimonies demonstrate how significant the American mirage was in the peninsula. Intellectuals hostile to fascism admired the land of liberty, and some of those in touch with emigrants considered America to be the Promised Land, all the more so because they could not leave Italy. US comics, books and films were in vogue. In October 1931, the monthly *Cinema illustrazione* published a list of the sixteen best directors in the world: none was Italian, ten were American, three were foreigners working in Hollywood. The US was the absolute reference for film critics. It was not exceptional to read, in a paper, statements such as 'We have found an Italian Lubitsch or Capra'; or 'This Italian film is comparable to an American one, that just shows you what it is!'

Admission to the first-run theatres was costly but it was cheap in peripheral playhouses. Exhibitors, knowing that people had little money, decided to maintain low prices, with tickets costing less than a kilogramme of bread or pasta. To compensate for lower revenues, they invested little in the condition of their premises. A 1937 investigation revealed that two thirds of the picture houses were in a very bad, even unsafe, state of repair.

Fascism played its part in the popularisation of cinema. A state-owned company, LUCE, had the monopoly of newsreels, and its shorts about current affairs, or its documentaries, advertising the government's policies, were projected in all cinemas and special screenings were given in small villages. In order to prevent country people from moving to towns, where they would be unemployed and potentially menacing, Mussolini developed what he called a 'colonisation' – that is to say, the building of settlements in empty zones where people acquired

houses and pieces of land, but were forbidden from leaving. Every colony had its church, its priest and often its cinema and when there was no movie theatre the parish hall was used for Sunday projections. Previously, cinema had been a prevalently urban entertainment, but under fascism, it extended over the entire countryside. The programmes – half propaganda, half old films, some still silent despite the advent of the talkies – were miserable but the audiences, deprived of other distractions, seemed to enjoy them.

The noticeable expansion of the audience after the mid-1930s was due to the outlying and rural public, while the percentage of urban theatres diminished – not because there were fewer clients in city centres, but because there were many more elsewhere. The number of people attending motion pictures should have declined, or at least stagnated during World War II and in the dramatic postwar reconstruction years marked by malnutrition, inflation and economic stagnation. But just the reverse occurred, except for the parenthesis of the German occupation and the Liberation. Nobody has ever attempted to explain this anomaly, except for 'psychological' motivations, such as 'the thirst for amusement'. My own explanation is no more than a hypothesis, but it relies on obvious correlations. The sudden rise of seemingly aberrant forms of consumption in a depressed period is a recognised phenomenon that sociologists call 'shortage consumption'. If useful goods, especially clothes, are not available, people spend the money on something else however frivolous.

This is precisely what occurred in the middle of the twentieth century. During the 1940s and early 1950s, there was almost nothing to buy, and people were obliged to save. The black market devoured the savings of the city dwellers but benefited those living in the countryside or those, in small cities, who had a kitchen garden. The savings rate, between 1946 and 1955, exceeded 10 per cent of the gross domestic income and the Italians used it, partially, to acquire magazines, comic strips, cigarettes – and most importantly, cinema tickets. New theatres opened and, significantly, there were more created in the south and in the islands than in the north or the centre. In Eboli (a town in the remote Lucania region of Italy and immortalised by Carlo Levi's neorealist novel *Cristo si è fermato a Eboli*) soon after the end of the conflict, two cinemas were inaugurated and the same thing happened in many other similar provincial towns. I realise how disappointing my hypothesis may seem to those who love Italian cinema, but it seems that the war and postwar craze for cinema did not correspond to a surge of enthusiasm for 'cinematic art', but rather to the discrepancy between cash flow and that of consumer commodities.

THE GOLDEN AGE OF CINEMAGOING

The decade that followed World War II was the heyday of Hollywood. The GIs who disembarked in Sicily had opened the way for American film distributors. Since 1938, no American film had entered Italy, and people anxious to make up for lost time ran to see whatever Hollywood movie was on display. Since the home market and other foreign markets had already amortised Hollywood's production costs of such 'old' films, these pictures could be bought for very little. Two other factors came into play. The first was political. Careful to please Washington, the Christian-Democratic government opened the Italian home market to Hollywood, with Italian films only guaranteed one out of six days screening – a rule not respected before 1950. Another ally of Hollywood's hegemony was curiously enough the Catholic Church. Those who know contemporary Italy have difficulty in imagining the moralising atmosphere imposed by the Church and also, to a certain extent, by the Communist Party. Any hint of sex was anathema to them both. The Church had elaborated a sophisticated system of classification that told whether a film was healthy for everybody, reserved to adults or forbidden. The judgment was stuck to the door of any parish church so that, in middle-sized or smaller towns, exhibitors could not ignore it and, eager to lure in families, booked only 'good' films. Now, given the fact that the Hays Code suited perfectly the ecclesiastical hierarchy, their verdict was especially lenient with Hollywood films. In 1950, one quarter of American movies were considered suitable 'for families', while only one tenth of Italian films passed this acid test. Publishers adapted quickly to the trend, producing a series of specialised weeklies – *Hollywood*, *Cine Illustrato*, *Noi divi* – and the most popular magazines also publicised 'a new generation of stars', freer and sexually more attractive than those of the 1930s.

In 1948, Victor Fleming's *Gone with the Wind* (1939), George Sidney's *Bathing Beauty* (1944) and King Vidor's *Duel in the Sun* (1946) earned more money than the eight biggest Italian hits. Mario Pellicani, a Communist journalist, noted melancholically: 'Can we overlook the fact that 90 per cent of the films projected in Italy are American?' His was a slightly excessive, but not

In the 1950s, newsstands such as this one were filled with movie magazines read primarily by Italian women who imitated the stars the publications displayed

entirely baseless estimation, for in 1956 – a good year for Italian studios – Hollywood earned 60 per cent of the profits in Italy while only 30 per cent went to the domestic products shot at Cinecittà.

Picture houses were then fuller than in any other time before or thereafter. In 1950, the Italians went to the cinema, on an average, thirty times a year; it was the third highest rate in the Western world after America and Britain. That year, attendance topped 400 million tickets and, as we have seen, it reached its peak in 1955. The country counted one movie theatre per 11,000 inhabitants before the war, but this rose to one per 6,000 by 1950. Firmly backed by the Christian Democrats, Catholics established some 3,000 parish cinemas and, anxious to overcome the Communists, projected the most popular pictures – Westerns and comedies that the anti-US extreme left was not anxious to project. At that time, picture houses became central to social life – all the more so since there were few places where both sexes and all ages were admitted. On Sundays, *mamme*, dragging their children along with the elderly and their cousins, spent the whole afternoon in the local theatre, seeing a short feature or documentary newsreel and a feature film, the latter interrupted by a long intermission during

In De Santis's *Riso amaro* (1949), the fact that Silvana reads movie magazines reflects her rejection of solid proletarian values for false, American worth

which the children raised a terrible racket. In his novel *Una vita violenta* (1955), Pier Paolo Pasolini remembered this era with nostalgia:

> The film theatre was decorated with posters that gleamed in the sun. In front of it was a bar and, around it, some twenty youths. The balcony was overcrowded, people had to stand, packed like sardines, in the smell of sweat. A small baby was crying while his father had fallen asleep due to the heat.

This reminiscence was confirmed by the novelist Leonardo Sciascia in *Gli zii di Sicilia* (*The Sicilian Uncles*, 1960):

> The picture house was an old theatre, and we always went to the balcony. From there we spent hours spitting down at the stalls; the voice of the victims burst out. At the beginning of the love sequences we started breathing loudly, as though from desire – even the eldest did it.

This epoch raises a question that we cannot ignore. Italian studios produced about fifty valuable works that still appeal to film buffs, some of which have been clustered under the label of neorealism. Is this, in itself, not sufficient to explain why Italians were so fond of films? Was not neorealism a roaring success all over the world? This point has to be clarified. It is usually admitted that, starting in 1945 with the projection of Rossellini's *Roma città aperta*, neorealism declined quickly after the failure of De Sica's *Umberto D.*, and that some forty films (0.8 % of the Italian films produced at the time) may be gathered into this group. The word itself surfaced late: in 1949, *Bianco e nero*, the Italian cinema monthly, reviewing Giuseppe De Santis's *Riso amaro*, a work that would later be considered a typical neorealist movie, denounced 'the so-called Italian neorealism'. Fame came slowly, first abroad, and only later as an echo in Italy. Only twelve of the neorealist works released – among them Rossellini's *Roma città aperta* and De Sica's *Ladri di biciclette*, were successful, while eighteen failed even though they should have enticed many spectators, either because of their

Female spectators dressed like the *mondine* of *Riso amaro*, underscoring the impact of neorealism's influence even on popular fashion

unusual narrative rhythm, as in the case of De Santis's *Caccia tragica* (*Tragic Hunt*, 1948) or because of their religious theme in the case of Rossellini's *Francesco giullare di dio* (*The Flowers of St Francis*, 1950), a poetical evocation of the much revered St Francis of Assisi.

Italian critics were generally favourably disposed towards the pictures now considered neorealist. Two extremely popular magazines, *La domenica del Corriere* and *Tempo*, did their best to rescue De Sica's *Sciuscià* from disaster. *Tempo* declared (23 March 1947) that this masterpiece was 'one of the strongest cries of despair of the century, intelligent and audacious'. Yet audiences did not pay much attention to the opinions of journalists. The Italian hits were first and foremost epics, in the wake of a half-century-old tradition, the most striking successes being, in the late 1940s, Giorgio Walter Chili's *I dieci comandamenti* (*Ten Commandments*, 1945, not to be confused with Cecil B. DeMille's 1955 epic blockbuster); Alessandro Blasetti's *Fabiola*, and L'Herbier's *Gli ultimi giorni di Pompei* (1950), whose common feature was that, as they deal with religious matters, they were promoted by the Church. In the 1950s, the most favoured genres were comedies and melodramas that some have called 'pink' or 'rosy' neorealism – neorealism without deadly conflicts and

with a happy ending. Significantly, the main characters of these films were lower middle-class or working-class people, modest contractors, craftsmen and clerks, all intent on improving their situation and climbing up the social ladder. On the screen, Italy was relentlessly moving: characters swapped the train first for a motorbike, then for a car, and everyone was fascinated by the possession of consumer goods. In short, the mainstream cinema represented a revitalised nation, individualist but loyal to family links and in the process of becoming more affluent – announcing thus what would be called, in the late 1950s and early 1960s, the so-called economic 'miracle'. This was by no means a 'miracle', but was rather an economic growth made easier by international economic conditions, state policies, and especially by the hard work of 2 million countrymen who had emigrated to find work in factories in the urban areas.

DECLINE OR TRANSFORMATION?

Then, at the beginning of the 'miracle,' the number of cinemagoers began to diminish. The blame was put on television. When broadcasting began, on 3 January 1954, many assumed that, once offered pictures at home, potential spectators would stop going to the cinema. We see now that the evolution of both media was not so straightforward: they were in competition but, at the same time, complemented and influenced each other. Italians were not immediately converted to television during its early years, because television sets cost the equivalent of the annual income of a country doctor and so were too expensive for the majority of the population. On the other hand, the decline in cinema attendance was not catastrophic. Compared to the previous peak, the drop from 1957 onwards looked great, but the takings of the mid-1950s had been exceptional, and if we work out the average of the figures over two decades, we come to the conclusion that television did not kill the cinema. Adopting colour film and CinemaScope, the studios produced quality works that were more attractive than the old-fashioned, black-and-white movies rented by television because they were cheap, while exhibitors advertised the much-admired American pictures that were not yet available to the small screen.

After World War I, families had formed the bulk of the audience. In the 1960s, the extended family, including nearby relatives, disintegrated. The young's migration to the cities provoked the closure of most rural and parish theatres. On the other hand, those on good salaries who had settled in the outer suburbs were quick to take their Vespa scooter or Cinquecento (the inexpensive car owned by the majority of people) to visit the city centre to see a film. The postwar generation was very different from the previous ones. In 1947, the school-leaving age had been raised to fourteen, while vocational training courses were developed. Those who were between twenty and thirty years of age were much more learned than their fathers. In two decades, 1 million Italians with professional training and 500 thousand holders of a GCSE were recruited for jobs in the service industry. These people were not content with patiently receiving what was on display. They wanted to debate social issues and were accustomed to reading the new literary genre, the impressionist film chronicles written by famous novelists such as Alberto Moravia.

Actively sponsored by the state, Italian producers improved the quality of their movies. A discerning age group was thus sensible to films based on an intelligent script and shot with much care. Italian films equalled the American ones at the box office in the early 1960s and topped them (47 to 41 per cent) in 1965. Yet, the setback to US productions did not mean that US influence was receding. Hollywood's strategy had changed because shooting in a country where wages were customarily lower was highly profitable. Two categories of 'Italian' pictures – epics set in the classical period and spaghetti Westerns – shot thanks to American money by international teams with international stars – sold particularly well in the peninsula and abroad.

The postwar generation did not scorn these films, but it was much more interested in original Italian productions, for instance, Fellini's *La dolce vita* which made more money than any previous Italian film; Visconti's *Rocco e i suoi fratelli* and Dino Risi's *Il sorpasso*. Young people, who felt exploited by their bosses and by their elderly relatives, approved of the harsh satire aimed at the ruling class and at the hypocritical morals these people championed. Not surprisingly it was this same age group that played a leading role in the tumultuous upheavals that began in France and Italy in 1968.

SENSATIONAL AND EXPENSIVE, THE TWENTY-FIRST-CENTURY CINEMA

Up to the end of the 1960s, cinema attendance decreased slowly. The diminution speeded up in the 1970s so that, in the early 1980s, it had reached 200 million spectators; this figure was reduced to only

1 million in the mid-1990s – one eighth of the level in the peak years. Part of the decline was due to the sociopolitical situation: 1968 signalled the beginning of troubled times. After several months of social unrest, the more dramatic *anni di piombo* ('years of lead') of Italian terrorism began: kidnappings and assassinations spread fear in urban areas and prevented many from frequenting public places; this had an effect on cinema attendance.

But the decline in the number of moviegoers had deeper causes. The number of people leaving villages and small towns led to the closure of country cinemas. It was not by chance that this began in the islands and in the southern regions, places where this exodus was rife. Settling in suburban areas deprived of bars, picture houses or dancing halls, often isolated among other newcomers, these people usually bought a TV set. Having had to purchase a car on credit to drive to work and the requisite domestic appliances, they tried to reduce other spending. Since exhibitors had doubled their admission charges to compensate for loss of revenue, many spectators gave up going to the movies. Money was not the only parameter. New activities became popular, requiring more participation and initiative than film watching. Totocalcio, a lottery based upon betting on soccer matches, turned into a national craze that also increased the interest in soccer. *La domenica sportiva* (a popular Sunday-afternoon sports programme), did not initially appeal to the public on its launch in 1954, but gradually built up a following, from less than 1 million spectators in 1960 to 5 million in 1970, with these millions remaining at home on Sunday afternoon (previously the most popular time to visit the cinema in Italy), thus impacting attendance figures. The same decade witnessed the expansion of tourism; the boom in the building trade along the coasts reflected a transformation of cultural models and provided yet another way to spend one's income. Year after year, distractions that required time, mobility and personal involvement eroded cinema attendance. There was no sudden drop, but rather a gradual evolution contrasting with the brutal fall observed in other European countries (50 per cent in three years in the UK). In this respect, Italy was an exception in a continent that was deserting cinemas.

Not only the public but also the very nature of theatres and programmes changed. Small exhibitors sold their premises to larger companies that concentrated the viewing facilities in the sixteen main urban areas and built multiplex theatres consisting of one large auditorium and a series of smaller studios, all arranged around a single projection room, to economise on staff. These multiscreen sites were located in shopping malls equipped with parking lots and a variety of stores, bars and recreational facilities so that people, instead of choosing the film they wanted to watch in advance, decided on the spur of the moment to see what was available. Multiplex theatres were managed in a business-like manner. Big international companies monopolised them in order to reduce film-rental costs and to receive better terms for screen advertising. They selected a limited number of pictures, mostly American blockbusters with spectacular special effects, computer-generated and manipulated images, films likely to overwhelm spectators with emotion in large halls fitted with Dolby sound. In order to compensate for the increased cost of furniture and equipment, exhibitors charged higher prices. Going to the cinema became an expensive form of entertainment, not within the reach of every budget. From that point on, there was little difference between Italian programmes and those projected in other European countries.

During the fifteen years between 1955 and 1970, Italian cinema was considered one of the best in the world and a model for young film-makers. Most Italians held the same view and were highly proud of 'their' films. This was not usual. Previously, audiences were fond of actors who were not 'exportable' because, in their films, the quality of which mattered little, what counted was an amusing text relying on linguistic puns and cultural situations that were incomprehensible to foreigners. Many equated cinema with America, and Hollywood standards served as a gauge when praising or more often critiquing national productions. Neorealism, acclaimed abroad, was not appreciated in the peninsula before it faded. The encounter between a remarkable series of cinematic masterpieces and a lively, competent public was an impressive but not mysterious occurrence. Film-makers, technicians, producers and spectators had gone through the same difficulties (war, reconstruction) and shared the same longing for some kind of social change; the films had the public they deserved and vice versa. Such an exceptional conjunction did not last. Most Italians defected to other forms of entertainment, such as soccer, pop music, television or the Internet, with the result that the golden age of Italian cinema only lasted a very brief period despite its enormous influence on the art of the cinema all over the world.

FURTHER READING

Aprà, Adriano et al. (eds), *Storia del cinema italiano* (Rome/Venice: Marsilio, 2001–10).

Bernardini, Aldo, *Cinema muto italiano. Vol. 1: Ambiente, spettacoli e spettatori* (Rome: Laterza, 1980).

Brunetta, Gian Piero, *Storia del cinema italiano* (Rome: Editori Riuniti, 1993).

——, *Il cinema italiano contemporaneo* (Rome: Laterza, 2007).

Corsi, Barbara, *Per qualche dollaro in meno. Storia economica del cinema italiano* (Rome: Editori Riuniti, 2001).

Gundle, Stephen, *Between Hollywood and Moscow: The Italian Communists and the Challenge of Mass Culture, 1941–1993* (Durham, NC: Duke University Press, 2000).

Manzoli, Giacomo and Guglielmo Pescatore (eds), *L'arte del risparmio: stile e tecnologia. Il cinema a bassocosto in Italia negli anni Sessanta* (Rome: Carocci, 2005).

Quaglietti, Lorenzo, *Storia economica-politica del cinema italiano, 1945–1980* (Rome: Editori Riuniti, 1980).

Sorlin, Pierre, *Gli Italiani al cinema* (Mantua: Tre Lune, 2009).

PART FIVE

An Age of Crisis, Transition and Consolidation

Introduction

Peter Bondanella

In retrospect, Italian cinema probably reached its high-water mark around the mid-1970s or early 1980s. Thus, the last three decades or so in Italian film history have witnessed several changes. Numerous key figures of the postwar era, particularly some of the best-known directors, have passed away. In addition to a diminishing number of renowned auteurs, the important role genre or so-called 'B' films played earlier in the industry's industrial punch has greatly decreased: very few of the films made in Italy in the last few decades belong to the recognisable generic forms discussed in the previous section of this anthology except for the *commedia all'italiana*. One specific variant of Italian film comedy popular of late, the Christmas film (the *cinepanettone*), has become so vital to the economic health of the industry that it deserves Alan O'Leary's close attention in this section. On the other hand, new developments in Italian film themes during this period have led to increased focus upon certain historical themes: the Italian Holocaust experience (analysed by Millicent Marcus); the Mafia, the Camorra or other similar organised criminal activities (discussed by Dana Renga); and the greatest threat to Italian society in the postwar period, Italian terrorism on the right and on the left (considered by Giancarlo Lombardi). The number of such films has increased to such a degree, and their success at the box office at home and abroad has been impressive enough in recent years, that it may well be time to look at these thematic preoccupations as film genres in their own right.

This part also includes a discussion by Catherine O'Rawe of masculinity in contemporary Italian films, focusing upon a new generation of young male stars and the nature of their particular audience appeal; as well as a treatment by Flavia Laviosa of contemporary female directors with entirely different sociological and feminist perspectives than those espoused by the older generation of female directors. To offer insight into the specific procedures typical of Italian scriptwriting (and its sometimes quite different character from that in Hollywood films), Gianfranco Angelucci discusses his collaboration with Federico Fellini and provides concrete examples of how he contributed to the script for Fellini's penultimate film, *Intervista*.

29 Scriptwriting, Italian Style

Scriptwriting for Fellini

Gianfranco Angelucci

The team of scriptwriters around Fellini was an imposing one: Tullio Pinelli, Ennio Flaiano and then Brunello Rondi beginning with *La strada* in 1954. They were the names that appeared on Fellini's credits until *Giulietta degli spiriti* (*Juliet of the Spirits*, 1965). Then Bernardino Zapponi joined Fellini for *Toby Dammit* (*Toby Dammit*, 1968), *Fellini Satyricon*, *Roma* (*Fellini's Roma*, 1972), *Il Casanova di Federico Fellini* (*Fellini's Casanova*, 1976), *La città delle donne* (*City of Women*, 1980) and *Ginger e Fred*. Tonino Guerra also appeared meanwhile for *Amarcord* and then for *E la nave va* (*And the Ship Sails On*, 1983). Finally, I arrived with *Intervista*, Fellini's penultimate film, a work that triumphed at the Moscow and Cannes Film Festivals.

It was Federico who wanted me to share the film's paternity with him: 'This time you are getting credit as well,' he told me unexpectedly during the shooting. I remember exactly the moment and the position in which Fellini was seated on his director's chair with his name printed on the back, as well as the sign of affection that he showed to me with his warm hand on my hair and the sudden note of seriousness that he assumed as he communicated his decision to me, as well as the hurried tone with which he sought to dispel any sense of embarrassment, as he rose impulsively to give instructions to Tonino Delli Colli, the director of photography, who was finishing up adjusting the illumination for the scene to be shot. I felt as if I had received the flat blade of the sword that a king might use to make one a knight on my forehead and shoulders. I did not expect this, or perhaps I did but it was an effort to really believe it. It was an incredible privilege: in the future my name would be associated with Fellini, and I would be remembered for having written a film with him and would find myself in the company of that pantheon of writers who had preceded me and that I had admired when reading the film credits, sunken in the seat of a provincial cinema theatre as a young boy. How could I have imagined all this after I had arrived as a university student with my thesis under my arm and had met Fellini for the first time in one of the most luxurious hotels in Rome on the Via del Corso to ask him for an interview?

FELLINI'S METHOD

My first work as an assistant scriptwriter was on *Roma*. My assignment was to investigate a possible film location from the perspective of a journalist, to 'go and write a report'. You look around, stick your nose into things, ask questions, enter homes, mingle with people and form your own opinion and seek to translate it as honestly as possible to the person reading the report. Composing a professional journalistic report in this way was a habit he acquired when he worked alongside Rossellini. At the beginning of an idea – any idea at all – it was first necessary to conduct a preliminary inquiry and to directly derive information: from people's behaviour, their faces, their slang, what the locations looked like. This was designed to capture the less obvious aspects of the argument that had been selected. The second step was to outline a story on the typewriter without too many literary flourishes, simply describing what had been observed. Fellini suggested 'a description like a police inspector or a notary might make', for he believed that any director should be obliged to first pass through the profession of journalist to acquire the discipline for synthesis and for writing that was clean, clear and comprehensible to everyone. For Fellini, films were born in this fashion. *La strada*, Moraldo Rossi, Fellini's first assistant scriptwriter has recounted, came into existence from endless wanderings around Via Cassia to the north of Rome and around the zones of Viterbo, Bagnoregio and Civita Castellana.[1] These were locations Fellini had already used for *I vitelloni*. *Il bidone* required months of hanging around with *bidonisti*, organised swindlers who lived off cheating people. On *Le notti di Cabiria*, Pier Paolo Pasolini collaborated: he knew the capital city's periphery as well as its lower-class populace, inside out and he was capable (as a man from Friuli and a skilful philologist) of treating with great fidelity popular conversations, expressions, phrases and Romanesque cadences of speech, as he had demonstrated in his first novels *Ragazzi di vita* (*The Ragazzi*, 1955) and *Una vita violenta*.

THE INVESTIGATIONS

The first job Fellini assigned to me on *Roma* was to investigate the world of the young demonstrators of the 1970s in order to learn more about their attitude to sex. This material then became part of a volume published on the screenplay and was also eventually incorporated into the sequences of Piazza di Spagna and Villa Borghese.[2] It was also the first time I received any recompense from the hands of the producer, Elio Scardamaglia – an amount that seemed to me quite excessive! For *Il Casanova di Fellini*, I was tasked with interviewing the Latin lovers of the Riviera Romagnola (Rimini, Riccione) and the playboys of the capital, supposedly the modern successors to the great Venetian lover. This material also formed part of a book.[3] Thereafter, I explored the world of crime news, for weeks spending time every night with the editors of the Roman daily newspaper *Il Tempo*. I became part of the team that drove an Alfa Romeo at breakneck speed through the streets of Rome, often reaching the scene of a crime before the police did. Fellini delighted in reading my descriptions of the facial details, the clothes, the tics of each character treated in my reports. The next step was a lengthy interview with a police inspector, a kind of Serpico from Calabria who drove around on a Kawasaki motorcycle wearing a bandana, looking like a hippy, and whose beat included the Piazza di Spagna area, where he investigated the drug scene there at great risk to himself.[4]

Thereafter, I worked on the film *Intervista*, initially entitled *Un regista a Cinecittà* (*A Director at Cinecittà*). Fellini asked me to collect information about this famous film studio, and an illustrated volume of the results was published in Italian, English and French, serving as the departure point for the development of the screenplay.[5] In much the same way, before Fellini's death, we were working on some film subjects that Fellini had postponed during his last years. The first concerned Venice (*Venezia*): we had assimilated pages

Gianfranco Angelucci plays the part of a director shooting a television spot at Cinecittà in Fellini's *Intervista* (1987)

and pages of information, flipping through narratives and memoirs of gifted writers about Venice (Carlo Della Corte, Toni Cibotto, Alberto Ongaro). Another project in progress was provisionally entitled *L'attore* (*The Actor*), since Fellini wanted to recount his own relationship with those precious and indispensable creatures that physically incarnated his fantasies. The story was to start from an empty theatre, a deserted stage where a talk show was supposed to take place. Little by little the characters would wander slowly in. The first would be Marcello Mastroianni, soaked to the skin because he arrived at the train station of the little town where the theatre was located very late at night and was unable to find a taxi. He finally entered the empty theatre and had the impression of crossing the frontier of an unknown dimension. No doubt this scene was an echo of the director's imagination in *Il viaggio di G. Mastorna* (*The Journey of G. Mastorna*) that Fellini never succeeded in shooting. Only after Marcello (Fellini's *alter ego*) climbs on the stage and begins to recite a sort of monologue, do the other invited guests begin to materialise, as if at a celebration; and these guests are the actors Fellini always had by his side, from Giulietta Masina to Roberto Benigni and Paolo Villaggio. These last two actors appeared together in Fellini's last film, *La voce della luna* (*The Voice of the Moon*, 1990). Together the two comedians would have given life to a sequence taken from Collodi's *Pinocchio*.

In this final period of his life, Fellini followed his desire to tell stories about his own profession – the actors, the director, the producer – enriching each chapter with his fantasies and personal memories and dealing with sophisticated problems of film language: how the mind transforms abstract images – both for the person who gives birth to these images and for those who watch them; the magic of represention; the illusionism of lighting; the fascination with painting that he had never abandoned. 'When they no longer allow me to make films,' he would declare, 'I shall become a *madonnaro* on the sidewalks.' A *madonnaro* is a street artist who reproduces with coloured chalk the paintings of the great masters, particularly portraits of the Madonna, on public sidewalks.

When he suffered an ischaemia to the brain in 1993, in spite of being confined to bed and partly paralysed, Fellini was already nursing a film project on his own condition as a paraplegic: he asked me to collate all the facts about his hospital stay, and he had his room fitted out like an office, not only to respond to the letters that arrived from all parts of the world but to nail down the ideas we were assembling. From the many notes taken together during the long months of his convalescence, first in Rimini, then in Ferrara, and finally at the Polyclinic Hospital in Rome, I composed the novel *Federico F.* after his death.[6]

FELLINI'S RELATIONSHIP WITH HIS SCRIPTWRITERS

Fellini did not always hold group meetings with his scriptwriters: perhaps he had endured too many of such meetings devoted to films that interested him very little at the beginning of his career. Nevertheless, he spoke about his beginnings as a kind of golden age when, together with Tullio Pinelli, he collaborated with famous directors who had become important before the war. Fellini liked to relive this beginning of his cinematic apprenticeship when everything seemed to resolve itself into a carefree game where the commitment was minimal and the gain was maximised. In the many years that we worked with each other, I never heard him speak of the script in terms of hard work. Rather, he tended to diminish or to reduce drastically the time that he dedicated to a script, considering it the fruit of an automatic kind of writing that derived spontaneously from an idea. And Tullio Pinelli, his most frequent collaborator, always confirmed Fellini's view of scriptwriting: in spite of all Pinelli knew about what unfolded in the scenes of a script, the final film always uncovered a surprise. As he remarked to me once, 'when I finally sat down to watch the projection, it seemed as if I was looking at nothing that I had written, for Fellini's films took life on the set, and that moment was his original moment of creativity that he shared with nobody else'.[7] Fellini's method remained unchanged throughout his career: he entrusted various sequences to his collaborators to develop, and each one proceeded separately. Then these outlines ran together on his desk, as he intervened,

erased, changed the order of things, glued together inserts and added suggestions seated before his Olivetti Lettera 32 typewriter.

A PROFESSIONAL SCRIPTWRITER

Naturally, during my cinematic career I did not write solely for Fellini. I also wrote for myself, subsequently directing various films (documentaries, a feature film, television commercials) with colleagues of my own generation, as well as with other famous figures in the cinema, such as Fellini scriptwriter Ennio Flaiano.

With Flaiano, I prepared numerous episodes for a television series, outlined the required material, and then in the mornings we would meet at his house or sometimes in a residence on Via Tevere where he lodged at the beginning of the 1970s. A famous and beloved writer who had won Italy's most important literary prize, the Premio Strega, with his first novel *Tempo di uccidere* (1947), Flaiano was witty, sharp-tongued and extremely cultured, as well as very hasty in his work. When I arrived with my writing, he placed himself before a typewriter – he owned one of those huge electric IBMs with a roller ball – and he rapidly typed and retyped the text, inserting by hand additions filled with his inimitable sense of irony and with that sulphuric vein of his that invented such amusing remarks as 'we think we are marrying our fiancée and instead we marry our wives'. I enjoyed myself a great deal in his company, and since I was much younger, at the end of the morning, he always took me to lunch before taking his leave. He liked to talk and I liked listening to him. The scriptwriters of the older generation, in comparison to their successors, were almost all real storytellers, fascinating narrators, something that is rarely encountered today. These days in the cinema, it seems that everyone takes himself far too seriously and lacks a sense of playfulness. Perhaps this is the reason – at least in Italy – for the cinema's progressive decline. Zavattini is famously reported as saying that the Italian cinema began to decline when its creators stopped using public transport! When Luciano Vincenzoni, the inventor of extraordinary stories that formed the basis of such films as Mario Monicelli's *La grande guerra*, Guy Hamilton's *I due nemici* (*The Best of Enemies*, 1961) and Pietro Germi's *Sedotta e abbandonata* (*Seduced and Abandoned*, 1964), discovered he did not have a lire in his pocket, he forced his way into the office of producer Dino De Laurentiis, obtaining ten minutes of his time, and two hours later he had the producer completely seduced by his stories and determined to put him immediately under contract! Rodolfo Sonego, scriptwriter for many films starring Alberto Sordi, was a real treasure trove of stories inspired by his turbulent and adventurous life, some of which he recounted in *Una vita difficile* (*A Difficult Life*, 1961), the masterpiece by Dino Risi, and for whose biggest commercial success he also wrote the script: *Il sorpasso*. Ruggero Maccari was an irresistible humorist and together with Ettore Scola – not only a great scriptwriter but eventually an even greater director – the two men scripted practically half of the successful films in the *commedia all'italiana* genre; the other half were the fruit of the fantasy of Age (Agenore Incrocci) and Furio Scarpelli.

We are speaking here of hundreds of films, many masterpieces, from a commercial cinema, yet a cinema full of good taste, intelligence and a satirical spirit; a cinema capable of X-raying the Italian society it treated. Many scriptwriters came from journalism and from weekly humour magazines where they had practised developing a spare style replete with witty remarks and brilliant dialogue. These were individuals born, for the most part, between 1920 and 1930, who contributed their talent to the greatest season of Italian cinema. Talent of this standard and in such a quantity was not seen again, even though there are still many good scriptwriters. Some of them worked in pairs or in a group, but even when various hands were at work in the process, usually a single person took care of the definite version, and if that individual had great talent, you could see it in the film's style. Most scriptwriters preferred isolation to reach the right concentration when they wrote: the corrections, adjustments and comparisons came later. I always worked better alone, after the ritualistic discussions ended and in my screenplays, I preferred to follow this method.

With Fellini, I carried out the assignments he gave me: he passed me a scene and I developed it, or I sketched out extemporaneous dialogues directly on the set or one day before the next day's shooting. On other occasions, we wrote simultaneously in different rooms but within earshot of each other in Fellini's office on Corso d'Italia in Rome. When I finished a page, I would bring it to him and he would work on it. But sometimes the opposite took place: every contribution was welcome. And every script, as far as I know, was ultimately checked by Tullio Pinelli, the master scriptwriter, who had worked with Fellini from the time of *Lo sceicco bianco*.

THEN MY TURN ARRIVED

This occurred in 1986 when Fellini decided to shoot a film dedicated to Cinecittà. His intention was to return to a formula with which he had happily experimented in *Block-notes di un regista* (*Fellini: A Director's Notebook*), produced in 1969 by the American Peter Goldfarb for television. In that earlier film, Fellini, playing himself, described the evolution of *Il viaggio di G. Mastorna*[8] and *Fellini Satyricon*, explaining how one story flowed into the other and recounting some of his own personal vicissitudes. In this new project, he intended to develop a kind of personal diary, to compose a declaration of love to the cinema by making, as he continued to repeat, a film in the making (*un film in diretta*): that is, to show the work in the very moment when it was created. Thus he wished to remove every literary artificiality from the cinema. He assigned me to write a *soggetto* treating the film studios on Via Tuscolana, agreeing that from that point we would rough out a script about Fellini's relationship with the sound stages, the lighting, the scenography, make-up, actors and the costumes – in short, the usual magic of the cinema. The enterprise effectively took off from my treatment, a kind of reportage on the reality that surrounded us every day at the studio: the topography of the place, its organisation, its characters and the secret life of Cinecittà. It would take too much space to publish the entire account, but I believe it would be useful to examine some parts of it here, material that has never previously appeared in print. The reader is invited to compare this early version of the film in progress to better understand how such ideas were transformed by Fellini's fantasy by comparing the following narrative with the final product, *Intervista*, available on DVD.

A PORTION OF THE ORIGINAL TREATMENT OF *INTERVISTA*, PREVIOUSLY UNPUBLISHED

'Surrounded by a thick, high wall, its rectangular buildings set well apart from each other among pines, flower beds and tree-lined paths, a quiet place where you can hear only the muffled roar of the traffic in the distance and birdsong overhead, at first sight Cinecittà could conceivably appear to be a hospital or a rather grand nursing home. To begin with, it is the setting that creates this image, but once you have passed through the gates and entered the compound, closer inspection makes the whole idea even more feasible. Some of its buildings are low and glass-fronted: they have been built using man-made materials, plastic, ABS, anodised aluminium, in rather gentle pastel shades of china blue and sea green. They are elongated edifices, rather like outpatients' departments or research laboratories; and from them, appropriately enough, emerge distinguished-looking men in white coats and half-moon spectacles, white-haired, their faces pink and reassuring, or thin and reflective, with a measured, relaxed bearing and a confident gait, talking to each other in muted voices as befits the quiet around them. The building they are leaving is the developing and printing department (directly to the left as you enter the enclosed area of Cinecittà) beneath the shade of age-old pine trees, together with lush oleander and pittosporum bushes.

For the women it is different, because their long coats are pink, with a small white collar, sometimes worn unbuttoned at the top for added flair. They go past in a hurry, often wearing Scandinavian-style clogs, or, like Signora Maria, they go about their business gliding elegantly up and down the moving walkways of the section. They look less like nurses than luxury attendants. The modern prefabricated department of developing and printing is so peaceful, quiet and unobtrusive, (there is nobody on the door, no noise, no groups chatting or standing around), that once past the first courtyard of the penitentiary, the Cinefonico building promises some fun and a bit of a hullabaloo. There is always an air of cheerfulness, there, for no particular reason, a light-headed feeling of lizards basking in the sun. If the sun is shining, there will be somebody sitting on the steps or half stretched out on the travertine slabs to either side. The atmosphere in this section is exactly what you find in those parts of buildings in a hospital which were put up before the others: no matter how many restorations and new coats of paint, you can never relate them to the most recent extensions. That is how the people who work there treat the place; they too have the air of old soldiers recruited at the first draft, and occupy the rooms in the same way that one would wear an old pair of slippers.

The Cinefonico is right next to the bar, or the store as it is called in barracks and prisons. Here, the peaceful nursing home suddenly comes to life; it would be closer to the truth to say it fills with people, because a quick glance discovers no real sign of actual liveliness or dynamism, but rather a lingering about, the way fish do in a fountain, a gentle floating around and opening of mouths with no other aim in mind. It is especially when the bar is closed and so no longer looks like a bar at all, that the disorientated wandering, the casual

formation of groups that follows no known logic, brings very much to mind the scene in the garden of a convalescent home. There is a seemingly endless amount of time to be filled, and nothing to fill it with but meals, very infrequent medical inspections and protracted therapy sessions, a difficult stretch of time you can do nothing to help pass except by taking it steady, like treading with slow and thoughtful steps along the seabed.

The overall effect of this group of individuals in pyjamas – or so they appear if you continue to regard them in this particular light – or in dressing gowns with their shoes and socks on, has something aquatic about it. The same effect occurs when the groups break up, much as fish do, only to regroup almost unchanged a bit nearer or farther away, according to the currents perhaps, or the insects on the surface which they can only reach by darting up as quick as a flash. Here the impression of lunacy becomes more tangible because if the imagination pictures individuals in pyjamas, the reality goes way beyond that. The groups along these avenues, some standing still, others moving, are likely to be wearing fantastic costumes which give a more detailed indication of the type of mental disturbance involved: you can see Admiral Lord Nelson, one of Savonarola's monks, the scruffy soldier at the head of an invincible army carrying a wooden sword like children do, a seventeenth-century prostitute, and a female rock singer in tights, often mingling with ordinary patients dressed in checked shirts and fustian breeches.

Meanwhile the hospital as a whole carries on its normal, mysterious life as before. Other people in coats are seen strolling along the avenues, or suddenly appearing round the corner of a large building, shouting something. Sometimes, because the site is so large, people use bicycles, tricycles or wheelbarrows to get about. Recently, they have also introduced forklift trucks, those small mechanical tractors that are used to lift weights and clear obstacles. Of the objects they carry best it is better to say nothing: it would appear that the disturbed inmates here devote all their energies to building the most crazy toys, particularly when it comes to judging proportions. There are skittles as high as three-storey apartment blocks, castles with spires on top, oases with palm trees, entire Parthenons, the Nike of Samothrace, the treasure chest of Drake the Pirate, a galleon flying the skull and crossbones, and even a pig's trotter as high and as large as Rome's main railway station.

The materials are never particularly valuable –
clearly, these people are only playing at what they are
doing – but the results are often stunning. This is one
of the reasons why, as the therapy is so obviously
beneficial, but without over-indulging the patients' egos
too much, two words have been put up in elegant, fairly
large lettering on a pair of machine shops, set back a
bit and less conspicuous than the other buildings:
MODELLING and SCULPTURE.

On the strength of this message, whoever is shut in
there to work feels reassured by the nobility of the
category of their efforts, and can comfortably leave the
present famous landmarks in order to explore in art:
the Greece of Phidias and Praxiteles, the Florence of the
Medici. Outside the workshops, in fact, you can find a
bit of everything, especially statues which are usually
very large but some also life-size, standing up,
stretched out, on their backs in the field, and heaped
one on top of the other. And inside the workshops,
which derive their light from the skylights in the roof,
the work is clearly fast and furious, using stucco and
plaster of Paris, but also plastic casts, molds and mock-
ups. When demand is heavy, that is to say, when there
are a very large number of patients wanting to work,
then some are assigned to projects which involve
building entire villages, one or other of the hills to
either end of the grounds being chosen as the site. To
look at the results, you would think they were genuine
works of architecture, complete with roads, colonnades,
shops, house fronts, dry-stone walls, belvederes,
piazzas, fountains and bell towers. Whole teams are
employed on these building programmes and each
individual has his job to do: painting, stucco work,
decorating and repairing.

After the restaurant, a visit to the bar. The universe
that is created here is also vaguely segregated, prison-
like, modelled round movements and actions that are
always the same and can thus be seen as maniacally
defensive distinguishing features. As a result, the bar is
packed, taken literally by storm every time it opens,
and every time it closes, when the patrons have to
dolefully tear themselves away. The bar represents the
harbour, the crossroads, the gateway to the Orient, a
meeting point and a point of diaspora, a place for
hiring people, a rendezvous, a sounding board for
information of every sort, a labyrinthine bazaar trading
in people, objects and services. At the bar is where the
telephones are and where money flows, and in fact it is
the only place anywhere in the establishment where it
is possible to spend and purchase, where money

Fellini and Angelucci on the set of a documentary Angelucci
shot about Fellini's *Casanova* (1976)

circulates as it does in the outside world, where contact
with that world becomes real, concrete and less illusory
and clouded than in any other corner of the enclosure.

At Cinecittà, they sell everything, even specialising in
certain lines. There are those who sell casual clothes,
like Vinicio, and other boutique fashions; leatherwear is
a separate activity, with belts and bags; and then there
are perfumes of any brand or provenance; for designer
articles, you only have to ask. You know who to go to
for wristwatches and bracelets, who handles gold and
precious stones; there is a choice of smokers'
accessories; if it isn't in stock, they can order it for you.
A radio? A portable television? How much do you want
to spend, when do you want it for? This sort of trading
is not even worth mentioning, since it can be found in
any enclosed institution, like some downmarket
complement to the consumerism in the outside world, a
picturesque and also slightly wretched re-offering of the
styles and status symbols which are given recognition
in that society beyond the walls. What you would not
be expecting, on the other hand, is another kind of
produce, so unlikely, in fact, that it gives the enclosed
world of Cinecittà a fable-like quality. There is a hole in
the wall of the enclosure, near the swimming pool
through this narrow opening, if you call him, a certain

A caricature drawing of Angelucci by Fellini; Fellini often employed such sketches to create his film characters

Nello will appear, a country bumpkin, ugly as a face on a tarot card, carrying little baskets of eggs which are still warm and pigeons, guinea-fowl, spring chickens, ducks and turkeys which have all been well fed.

It seems almost idyllic, an acre of Arcadia evoking the spirit of Virgil's nature poetry which is by no means alien to the district. The large number of meadows, fields and green spaces foster the bucolic air and are conducive to contact with rural life. Nature here is spontaneously generous, as you can discover just by looking down on the ground, and if you know how to recognise tasty rocket salad in the field or plain wild chicory, you can gather whole bundles of them here. Some of the sound technicians are particularly keen on this relaxing hobby, while others concentrate instead on mushrooms, pine seeds and poplar saplings, picking and collecting in abundance. Some pick up pine cones and pine seeds by the sackfuls; others go looking for snails when the flower beds are sodden after heavy showers of warm rain. And there are others for whom nature's spontaneity is still not enough; so they get what they want by creating little gardens, or, even more imaginatively, cultivating fruit trees. Where, though? Anywhere, of course: this kind of manual work and the contact with the earth, fruits and seeds symbolise in themselves the acquiring of health, equilibrium and a

road to salvation. A man who comes from the land knows by instinct where to find the very stuff of the universe, and when he is troubled, he goes back to the bosom of the earth, to its refuge and slow heartbeat.

If, particularly in the summer, you go past the building where the movieolas are, you may suddenly hear piercing screams and yells shattering the quiet. You can never be sure if it is the film editors doing the screaming or their editing equipment, on which they wind and unwind out miles and miles of story, sometimes beautiful stories, imprisoned by magic in a transparent roll and a magnetic tape. The film editors see themselves as their custodians, all are dreamily touched by their tragedy; almost all of these editors bear a grievous wound, their faces set in pained sympathy with destinies to whose secrets they alone hold the key. It is the kind of work pathologists and surgeons do, this cutting-up, which perhaps allows no room for merriment or chaos, and which, it seems, the hospital here cannot do without. Closeted in their cubbyholes with capricious, tyrannical directors, whose flights of fancy they are obliged to stitch together endlessly, the editors experience fascination and outrage while avoiding any personal judgment, suspending their own critical faculty altogether. One of these film editors is nicknamed 'Roly-poly' because he has a natural tendency to pudginess; some time ago, with a resigned though also gratified expression on his face, he showed off to his colleagues the love bites that a woman producer had given him in the privacy of the editing suite.

At one time the security men used to be called patrolmen and they did their rounds on bicycles. They were ex-police officers or ex-military police, extremely trustworthy, always on hand, and never showy or exhibitionistic. They used to wear shapeless leather coats almost to their knees, in which they were protected against everything; draughts, wind, snow, fog and rain their faces furrowed by very deep lines, weather-beaten like the bark of trees; their strong, gnarled hands gripping their handlebars, purple in winter from the cold, and inevitably unsuited to precision jobs requiring manual dexterity. They had generous-looking, clear, trustworthy eyes like large dogs have. And indeed the dogs at Cinecittà, who had found a safe haven and resided here, used to follow this patrol on its leisurely circuits like a pack of hounds behind their leader, obediently but also protectively. This pack took their pace from the unhurried pedalling motion of the patrol, and went wagging their tails, with no discipline in the ranks, along the tree-lined avenues, circling the studios, sniffing the air, barking if some danger signal took them by surprise in their daily routine of surveillance.

These days the security men are trained on rifle ranges, to be ready for anything. They tour the avenues of Cinecittà on high-powered Hondas, communicate via walkie-talkie sets, get quickly out of their small cars that are covered in white and blue stickers, patrol the site with fraught efficiency, men of few words, their minds on something else, indifferent to the big dogs trying with little success to keep up with them.

The wind blows along the avenues at Cinecittà. It is the Roman sirocco, a humid, aromatic wind. It has reached this far after crossing the centre of Rome, sweeping through houses and courtyards, swirling among the granite ruins, piazzas, obelisks and arches, billowing into vast cathedrals fragrant with incense, ruffling the tops of trees and houses, spreading through the dormitory towns in the suburbs, and so into the countryside beyond, past sheep cotes and the crumbling remains of tombs, aqueducts, mausoleums, towers, finally colliding with the barrier of hills and entwining itself round its own currents inside the walls of this strange sleeping prison. Here it plunders the avenues in a rush of air, and the litter and drink cans and pine needles are picked up by the wind, the pine cones are sent rolling, the bushes bending from the force of it, the high branches of the pines and the dark shoulders of the cypresses leaning sideways, as it whistles through the porches and moans along the long studio corridors, tearing material from scaffolding in fierce gusts which set black plastic sacks flapping noisily. And the dogs, with their noses in the air, smell everything that the wind brings with it, stretching their necks to its scents, blinking their eyes and twitching their nostrils all the time. Who knows what they are picking up on the breeze?

This is the time for ghosts. They say there *are* some at Cinecittà, that they can be heard in the administration block, on the other side of the vast meadow facing the entrance, the sort of building that looks as though it has been assembled from a child's construction kit, box-houses in coloured wood put together in a rather uninspired way, with building-block simplicity.

Phantoms. The place allows them in, and welcomes them. And why should they not be there? Nadia talks about these things. She is a gentle-mannered little lady,

all dressed in white, from her coat, which has a vaguely military look to it, to her light wool dress with the little round collar and dropped waist, her fishnet stockings also white, and cream-coloured shoes of soft leather. To look at her, it is hard to judge her age, with make-up on her porcelain-like face, and her hair, which is thirties-style, in blond ringlets as perfect and neat as a doll's wig. She was running some old Italian newsreels through the movieola when, there on the faded screen she saw, with the aid of a powerful lamp, more ghosts appear: these were real spectres, images of the dead, famous women film stars, distinguished actors, politicians of the fascist regime, producers, set designers, scene painters, who were no longer living. A long strip of film was actually entitled 'The Ghosts of Cinecittà' and, using an ingenious dissolving technique in which figures emerge from paintings or walk through walls and doors, it told the comic story of two ghosts who happen to find themselves included quite by chance in the production of a film. And why exactly is Nadia, a graceful, innocent ghost herself, the sentinel of this crossroads, and guardian of these shadows? It is here, Fellini tells us, in this department that Cinecittà keeps a sense of its own past, the memories of itself; and are not the Muses or art itself daughters of Mnemosyne and Jupiter? [end of unpublished material]

THE LEAVE-TAKING

There were other projects that awaited us after this one, which was finally entitled *Intervista* and won quite a few festival prizes. *Venezia* was perhaps the most beautiful subject among the numerous ones that Fellini pursued and that we wrote together. This was perhaps something like a new *dolce vita* brought up to date, where the narrative concerns an older film director who agrees to leave his home in the US to shoot a film on Venice. His real motive was the hope of re-encountering a magnificent woman he had loved in his youth. The story ought to be translated into English, since it was articulate, well constructed and rich with ideas and inventions, truly a splendid final project. A *dolce vita*, as I said, but one narrated at an age in which life is usually less sweet but has nevertheless not yet lost all its sweetness, nor its mysteries or its inexhaustible curiosity that renders life precious. I was beginning to develop the *soggetto* into a script when Federico suddenly died on the last day of October 1993.

NOTES

1. For contemporary accounts of the creation of *La strada*, including Rossi's essay 'Fellini and the Phantom Horse', see Peter Bondanella and Manuela Gieri (eds), *La Strada: Federico Fellini, Director* (New Brunswick, NJ: Rutgers University Press, 1987); see also Moraldo Rossi, *Sogna Federico Sogna: Fellini, quell mio unico perfido amico* (Recco: Le Mani, 2011).

2. Federico Fellini, *'Roma' di Federico Fellini*, ed. Bernardino Zapponi (Bologna: Cappelli, 1972).

3. Liliana Betti and Gianfranco Angelucci (eds), *Casanova rendez-vous con Federico Fellini* (Milan: Bompiani, 1975).

4. The policeman's name was Nicola Longo, and a brief outline of this never-shot film may be found in *'Discorsetto Introduttivo*: un inedito di Federico Fellini', *Caffè Michelangelo* vol. 9 no. 1 (2044), p. 18 (including a photograph of Longo on his motorcycle with Fellini riding behind him in 1981, both without helmets!).

5. Gianfranco Angelucci (ed.), *Un regista a Cinecittà* (Milan: Mondadori, 1988).

6. Gianfranco Angelucci (ed.), *Federico F.* (New York: Bordighera Press, 2008); or *Federico F.* (Rome: Avagliano Editore, 2000).

7. Pinelli's assessment was made to the author in a private conversation shortly before his death (the original Italian: 'Quando finalmente mi sedevo per assistere alla proiezione, mi sembrava di non vedere nulla di ciò che avevo scritto, perché i film di Fellini prendevano vita sul set, e questa era la sua creazione originale non condivisibile con nessun altro.')

8. For the Italian script, see Ermanno Cavazzoni (ed.), *Il viaggio di G. Mastorna* (Macerata: Quodlibet, 2008).

FURTHER READING

Aldouby, Hava, *Federico Fellini: Painting in Film, Painting on Film* (Toronto: University of Toronto Press, 2013).

Angelucci, Gianfranco, *Segreti e bugie di Federico Fellini: Il racconto dal vivo del più grande regista del '900. Misteri, illusioni e verità inconfessabili* (Cosenza: Luigi Pellegrini Editore, 2013).

Bondanella, Peter, *The Cinema of Federico Fellini*, Preface by Federico Fellini (Princeton, NJ: Princeton University Press, 1992).

Gili, Jean A., *Fellini: Le magicien du réel* (Paris: Gallimard, 2009).

Pacchioni, Federico, *Inspiring Fellini: Literary Collaborations behind the Scenes* (Toronto: University of Toronto Press, 2014).

Perryman, Marcus (ed. and trans.), *The Journey of G. Mastorna: The Film Fellini Didn't Make*, Preface by Peter Bondanella (Oxford: Berghahn Books, 2013).

28 Modern Mob Movies

Twenty Years of Gangsters on the Italian Screen

Dana Renga

Young Spartans went to war with the feats of Achilles and Hector in their heads, but around here you go to kill and be killed thinking of *Scarface*, *Goodfellas*, *Donnie Brasco*, and *The Godfather* [...]. There's no real difference between movie audiences in the land of the Camorra and elsewhere. Cinematographic references everywhere create mythologies of imitation. If elsewhere you can be like *Scarface* and secretly identify with him, here you can *be* Scarface, but you have to be him all of the way.[1]

The Italian Mafia is an ongoing problem; it has pervaded almost every facet of cultural life, and has left thousands of victims in its wake. A regular look at Italian newspapers reveals stories of corruption, clan wars, homicides and drug busts, all Mafia-related. The Mafia is endemic to Italy, and has killed tens of thousands of people; most are members of the organisation, but victims also include anti-Mafia activists, judges, police officers, collaborators of justice and bystanders. In short, the Mafia's extensive reach into and disruption of Italian society qualify it as a form of domestic terrorism. Moreover, unlike most other national traumas of the twentieth and twenty-first centuries, the Mafia has no end point. And if it has no end, how does one properly mourn and overcome it? The breadth of recent Italian feature films, documentaries and made-for-television movies and miniseries on the Mafia might suggest that Italy has begun the process of working through that is essential to come to terms with trauma. However, and with few exceptions, newer Italian Mafia movies are made in the realist mode and smooth over Mafia-related trauma so as to focus on stories that are both pleasurable and familiar. Many biopics conclude with the celebration of the life and death of an anti-Mafia crusader and suggest that the country is populated with heroes

ready to combat evil at all costs, while films that focus on women in or around the organisation sublimate their subversive potential into sentimental love stories. Much recent Mafia cinema puts forth a fantasy of a nation united against Mafia villainy and disavows trauma creation and subsequent national mourning.

Matteo Garrone's internationally acclaimed hit *Gomorra* (*Gomorrah*, 2008) on the Camorra, the Mafia of Naples and the region of Campania, signalled a new direction in Italian Mafia movies, both in terms of generic approach and style. Its rough exposé of the Camorra's violent underworld departs from Roberto Saviano's bestselling book in its almost anthropological gaze at mob life. Unlike Saviano's overt work of denunciation or other films that treat the Mafia of Campania, such as Antonio and Andrea Frazzis' *Certi bambini* (*A Children's Story*, 2004) or Vincenzo Marra's *Vento di terra* (*Wind of the Earth*, 2004), Garrone's film is almost entirely without explicit judgment. Garrone lived on site in Scampia for three months before he commenced filming. He examined the inner workings of Camorra clans from within their own homes, cast *camorristi* both as extras and in more central roles, and turned to them for advice on how to properly film a drug deal. Two of the film's most memorable characters are Marco (Marco Macor) and Ciro (Ciro Petrone), teenage renegades who attempt to emulate Al Pacino's Scarface and Raffaele Cutolo, protagonist of Giuseppe Tornatore's *Il camorrista* (*The Professor*, 1986). Indeed, the film highlights the Mafioso's very real obsession with on-screen mobsters and his penchant for all-out violence while laying bare the metacinematic and heterogeneous nature of Mafia movies at large.

As a whole, Italian films that represent the country's various Mafias resist a unified generic characterisation. For example, although Mafia cinema from the 1960s and 1970s by Francesco Rosi, Elio Petri and Damiano Damiani

'The world is ours!' Film citation to *Scarface* (1983) (both Hawks and De Palma) in Garrone's *Gomorra* (2008)

is commonly classified under the rubric of engaged or political cinema, several films by these directors share affinities with the Western, the Gothic film and the film noir. Recent Mafia cinema is also far from homogeneous, and is increasingly indebted to traditional film models such as melodrama, the film noir, the political thriller, the woman's film and the biopic. This chapter looks at the evolution of mobster cinema over the last twenty years, and pays particular attention to films made since 2000 that conform to the traditional logic of desire that dominates the classical cinema. To what extent, might we ask, can dominant film forms translate the national trauma of Italian Mafia?

THE 1990s: PLAYING WITH GENRE

While honeymooning in the eponymous city, the characters in Francesco Rosi's political thriller *Dimenticare Palermo* (*The Palermo Connection*, 1990) visit Palazzo Gangi, the celebrated setting for the ballroom scene in Luchino Visconti's *Il gattopardo*, what could be called the mother of all Italian Mafia movies. As the couple begins to dance, the sound of Verdi's 'Waltz in F Major' floods the screen and the camera leaves the pair to reveal, in a sweeping long take, the opulence of the grand ballroom before settling on an image of a leopard

on the tile floor. This scene is an obvious homage to the waltz danced by Prince Don Fabrizio and Angelica (Claudia Cardinale) in Visconti's film, a moment that points to the tactic of *transformismo* at work in the Italian political scene post-Unification, which has generally favoured the Mafia. 'If we want things to stay as they are, things will have to change,' says Tancredi (Alain Delon) in Visconti's film, an ideology that is at the heart of *Dimenticare Palermo*, in which Sicily and Sicilians are depicted as trapped in the past and governed by the codes of vendetta and *omertà* (silence before the law). Indeed, while searching for his roots in Palermo, New York politician Carmine Bonavia (James Belushi) experiences a city in ruins populated by clichéd figures such as prostitutes, fishmongers and women in black who contribute to stereotypes of southern Italy as backwards and indolent, a representation that Roberta Torre consciously exploits in her Mafia musical *Tano da morire* (*To Die for Tano*, 1997), a garish exposé of the life, death and afterlife of low-ranking Palermitan Mafioso Tano Guarrasi. Both films reveal that *dimenticare*, 'forgetting', Mafia-dominated Palermo is by no means easy.

Two films by Marco Risi released around the same time as Rosi's film portray a quite different Palermo.

In *Ragazzi fuori* (*Boys on the Outside*, 1990), a follow-up to his *Mery per sempre* (*Forever Mary*, 1989), the city is claustrophobic and centreless, and is inhabited by marginalised young men who are far from 'reformed' (the earlier film took place in a juvenile penitentiary). Characters try to get by through working on the black market or in prostitution, as does the transsexual Mery of the first film's title. While Roberto Benigni's Mafia comedy *Johnny Stecchino* (*Johnny Stecchino*, 1991) implies that the theft of bananas is Palermo's most dangerous crime, Risi's film shows otherwise through its graphic depiction of rape, prostitution, battery and murder. *Ragazzi fuori* suggests that Sicilian youth culture is doomed and that organised crime steps in where the state fails the individual.

Following the murders of anti-Mafia prosecutors Giovanni Falcone and Paolo Borsellino in 1992, the general focus of films about the Mafia shifted from its players to its victims. Mafia biopics in the 1990s clearly position the spectator on the side of the (eventually) fallen and memorialised hero. Films like Giuseppe Ferrara's *Giovanni Falcone* (*Giovanni Falcone*, 1993), Ricky Tognazzi's *La scorta* (*La Scorta* aka *The Escort*, 1993), Alessandro di Robilant's *Il giudice ragazzino* (*The Boy Judge*, 1994) and Michele Placido's *Un eroe borghese* (*A Bourgeois Hero*, 1995) are loosely based on the true stories of various anti-Mafia crusaders – judges, lawyers, bodyguards – who battle the Mafia and pay with their lives. In Tognazzi's film, the main character is a judge who is cast as a Christ figure whose followers, the men of his escort, would willingly sacrifice themselves to serve him and advance the battle against the Mafia. As such, *La scorta* implies that the Mafia can be defeated.

The episode 'Due sequestri' ('Two Kidnappings') from Paolo and Vittorio Taviani's film *Tu ridi* (*You Laugh*, 1998) is much more ambiguous in its depiction of the Manichean power relations at work in the films mentioned above. In juxtaposing the stories of two kidnappings, the first of the elderly doctor Ballarò (Turi Ferro) by a group of Brigands at the turn of the century and the second, 100 years later, of a young child named Vincenzo (Steve Spedicato) loosely based on that of Giuseppe di Matteo by his father's Mafia clan, the Taviani brothers demonstrate how much the Cosa Nostra has evolved and the extremes to which it will go to protect itself. While Ballarò dies a natural death in the Sicilian mountains surrounded by children, Vincenzo is murdered, and his body is dissolved in acid so as to punish his father, who betrayed the Mafia and turned

state's evidence. However, the film works somewhat to humanise his killer and problematises the good guy–bad guy dynamic of other contemporary films.

Most Mafia movies made during the 1990s focus on the Sicilian Cosa Nostra, the Mafia that has historically received the most media attention in Italy and abroad. Two notable exceptions are Antonio Capuano's *Pianese Nunzio, 14 anni a Maggio* (*Sacred Silence* aka *Pianese Nunzio, Fourteen in May*, 1996) and Alessandro Piva's critically acclaimed low-budget dark comedy *LaCapaGira* (*TheHeadisSpinning*, 1999). The former film takes place in Camorra-occupied neighbourhoods of Naples, and tells the story of a local priest who is both an anti-Mafia crusader and a homosexual involved in a relationship with thirteen-year-old Nunzio Pianese (Emanuele Gargiulo). Capuano's film, loosely based on real events, destabilises the viewer who is wont to identify with the film's hero. Indeed, the film demonstrates how the Camorra uses Father Borelli's paedophilia as a weapon to silence the priest and halt his anti-Mafia activity. Instead, *LaCapaGira* is set in the south-eastern port town of Bari and follows a group of petty criminals who we assume are loosely associated with the Sacra Corona Unita, the Mafia of the region of Puglia, as they attempt to track down a misplaced shipment of cocaine. The film, which is shot almost exclusively in the local dialect of Bari, is dialogue-driven and narrative is minimised to focus on the local underworld subculture whose economy, it is suggested, will continue to develop and thrive without intervention from the authorities.

THE NEW MILLENNIUM: THE ANTI-MAFIA MARTYR BIOPIC

The new millennium has witnessed a proliferation of Mafia movies that tell the 'true stories' of anti-Mafia martyrs. Marco Tullio Giordana's *I cento passi* (*One Hundred Steps* aka *The Hundred Steps*) and Pasquale Scimeca's *Placido Rizzotto* (*Placido Rizzotto*), both from 2000, focus on two men who fought the Mafia from within. These films readily establish a binary dichotomy of good over evil; i.e., real heroes Peppino Impastato and Placido Rizzotto fight for freedom and justice while real Mafia bad guys Gaetano Badalamenti, Michele Navarra and Luciano Leggio come off as quintessential villains. Millicent Marcus explores the various functions of commemoration at play in both films. In particular, she points out the memorialist impulse at work therein and concludes that each represents 'cinematic tomb inscriptions' that memorialise two forgotten martyrs.[2]

In addition, these films are shown in schools and civic organisations throughout Italy; they are used as pedagogical tools to raise consciousness with regard to the anti-Mafia movement; and they appear to inaugurate a new millennium of awareness of and protest against the Mafia in Italy. Similar dynamics play out in other films such as Roberto Faenza's *Alla luce del sole* (*In the Light of the Sun*, 2005) and Marco Risi's *Fortapàsc* (*Fort Apache*, 2009), where members of the Mafia are depicted as ruthless, violent and corrupt. For example, Faenza's film, which narrates the life of Father Giuseppe Puglisi, who was murdered by the Mafia on his fifty-sixth birthday, opens on a disturbing scene in which young Mafia neophytes feed kittens to dogs soon to be entered in dogfights and thus establishes the Mafia as diabolical.

In most of these films, the male protagonist is constructed as the viewer's ego ideal. In *I cento passi*, we embark on a journey of discovery with the protagonist, Peppino (Luigi Lo Cascio) and are meant to identify with him, to feel his anger and frustration as the Mafia exploits his native town, to share in his tenacity during his heroic battle, to express horror at his gruesome execution and to shed a collective tear during the popular protest that acted as his memorial. Indeed, an analogous process of identification plays out in the films by Scimeca, Faenza and Risi. Upon closer examination of the sexual dynamics at play in these films, however, such a straightforward reading falls apart. For example, in the case of *I cento passi*, the staging of Peppino's homosexuality is ambivalent and evasive in the extreme. In the film, his difference is erased in order to solidify viewer identification and assure narrative closure. Ultimately, Giordana's film suggests the impossibility of desiring differently in a Mafia context, and Peppino's death resolves his non-conformity.

Stefano Incerti's *L'uomo di vetro* (*The Man of Glass*, 2007) tells the story of Leonardo Vitale, the first Mafia turncoat or *pentito* and deviates from other Mafia biopics in that the lead character is insane and his heroism (his speaking out against his Mafia family, which eventually costs him his life) is ambiguous. Indeed, Incerti's film stands out from its contemporaries in both its depiction of an unconventional hero and innovative imbrication of religion, sacrifice, psychosis and sexuality in a Mafia context.

DOCUMENTING THE MAFIA

During much of the 1980s and early 1990s in Sicily, one Mafia-related death took place every three days. After the high-profile murders of several soon to be 'excellent cadavers', such as Falcone, Borsellino and General Carlo Alberto della Chiesa, and a series of deadly bomb attacks in Florence, Milan and Rome in 1993, Cosa Nostra decided to become less visible to minimise its media presence and to return to business as usual. The Mafia was working to become 'invisible', as is implied in the title of Stefano Maria Bianchi and Alberto Nerazzini's documentary *La mafia è bianca* (*The Mafia Is White*, 2005), which investigates the organisation's infiltration into regional politics and the health-care system. 'If the Mafia is [...] white, how can I see it?' asks the film's narrator. A series of documentaries made in the mid-2000s about the Sicilian Mafia, such as Marco Turco's *In un altro paese* (*Excellent Cadavers*, 2005), Marco Amenta's *Il fantasma di Corleone* (*The Ghost of Corleone*, 2006) and Ruggero Gabbai's *Io ricordo* (*I Remember*, 2008), returns to the assassinations of Falcone and Borsellino to render visible the Mafia's bloody past and, in the case of the first two films, its thriving present.

The docufiction *Io ricordo* pays particular attention to the Falcone case, and includes interviews with several Italians who lost family members and friends to the Mafia or survived its violence. The film is targeted at schoolchildren, and one of the film's main narrative threads involves a father who explains to his son that he is named Giovanni to honour Falcone's memory, and concludes on a hopeful note: a group of about forty children wearing shirts with the names of different people who lost their lives to the Mafia pronounce the names of the victims they honour. The credits are preceded by a script that implies that Mafia power is in decline and affirms that 'it is a new generation, one that recognises itself in the fundamental principles of the Constitution'. Thus, *Io ricordo* espouses a post-Mafia mentality that is unpersuasive considering the present-day power and reach of Cosa Nostra.

As a whole, documentaries on the Camorra and the 'Ndrangheta (the Mafia of the south-western region of Calabria) take a much less optimistic stance. Just some years ago, accounts of Mafia violence in Naples went largely unnoticed internationally. The Naples today that is imagined in several documentaries that investigate the Camorra and the eco-Mafia, such as Esmeralda Calabria and Andrea D'Ambrosio's *Biùtiful cauntri* (*Beautiful Country*, 2007) and Santiago Stelley's *Toxic: Napoli* (*Toxic: Naples*, 2009), recalls Palermo during the 1980s. Enrico Caria's satirical docufiction *Vedi Napoli e poi muori* (*See Naples and Die*, 2006) is made in the style of Michael Moore's investigative cinema and depicts contemporary Campania as grotesque and beyond salvation. Stereotypical images of Neapolitan pizza, beaches, traditional desserts and thriving marketplaces are juxtaposed with scenes of the garbage crisis, corpses in the streets and troops occupying the region's cities, all of which offer a bitter commentary on 'post-Renaissance' Naples.

Considering its strength and influence, surprisingly few feature films have been made on the 'Ndrangheta. Francesco Sbano's *Uomini d'onore* (*Men of Honor*, 2006) and Ruben H. Oliva's *La santa, il viaggio nella 'ndrangheta sconosciuta* (*The Saint, Journey into the Unknown 'Ndrangheta*, 2007) are two recent documentaries that disclose the history, structure, international influence, familial codes and commercial interests of, paradoxically, Italy's least visible yet most powerful and internationally active Mafia. Sbano's film is particularly chilling as it includes interviews with a current high-ranking boss, a Mafioso in hiding and another active in Germany, who readily explain Mafia ethos and reveal their undying loyalty to an organisation which is on its way to being completely integrated into legal business and politics. Indeed, the film closes on an image of the boss framed in front of the ocean, his face and voice obscured, as he reveals that he would give his life for the society because 'being a man of honor is the best thing in the world', before cutting to images from an initiation ceremony. The finale emphasises that with the 'Ndrangheta, there is no end in sight.

POLITICAL FILMS

Nanni Moretti's *Il caimano* and Paolo Sorrentino's *Il divo: La spettacolare vita di Giulio Andreotti* (*Il Divo* aka *The Deity*, 2008) are often brought up in tandem as engaged or political films that offer ironic critiques of several time Prime Ministers Silvio Berlusconi and Giulio Andreotti, two of the most powerful and controversial political figures of the last fifty years. Both have been

accused and tried several times of Mafia collusion, but never ultimately found guilty. Moretti's film concludes with a film within a film (also dubbed *Il caimano*) of one of Berlusconi's trials where the director himself plays the Prime Minister, who is found guilty of corruption charges. However, final images of an apocalyptic scene at the courthouse following a protest against the tribunal's decision foregrounds the ex-Premier's fascinating pull over the Italian people. In showing us four different Berlusconis, the postmodern *Il caimano* unveils Italian politics as a series of representations that adapt to the times, as has the Mafia. *Il divo* also investigates the abuses of power and the collusion between the Mafia and politics by telling Andreotti's story around the years of the *tangentopoli* or 'bribesville' scandals in the 1990s. Sorrentino's 'rock opera', as he frequently calls it, includes intricate visual effects such as dream sequences and surreal moments – as, for example, when Andreotti (Toni Servillo) 'confesses' his crimes to his wife or engages in the alleged 'kiss' with boss of bosses Totò Riina (Enzo Rai).

The imbrication between the Mafia and politics is clear when a skateboard that rolls through the halls of the Senate and takes flight is followed by an abrupt cut to the explosion that killed Falcone (Elio De Capitani) in his car (a skateboard was used to place the bomb in a pipe under the highway). As in Moretti's film, narrative action culminates in a trial scene where, we learn in the credits, Andreotti is found innocent. To be sure, both films present Italy's traumatic history as a self-conscious pastiche, as a wound that is by no means healed.

THE MAFIA NOIR

One of the key tenets of film noir is a lack of narrative resolution whereby the hero comes to terms with his past misdeeds, realises that he is a valued member of his family and community and envisions a future ripe with promise. Thus, the film noir illustrates the

The rumoured kiss of Mafia boss Riina (Enzo Rai) and Giulio Andreotti (Toni Servillo) in Sorrentino's *Il divo* (2008)

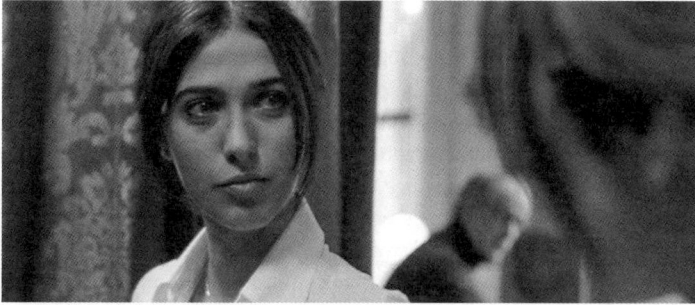

Titta (Toni Servillo) begins to understand the consequences of love in Sorrentino's *Le conseguenze dell'amore* (2004)

impossibility of moving beyond past traumatic injury. Fundamentally, the noir protagonist is incapable of escaping his true demon: himself. Hence, the noir endlessly rehearses, yet fails to resolve, traumatic experience. Read this way, the noir can be considered the genre *par excellence* for representing the Italian Mafia in that it is a seemingly unending wound to the nation.

Paolo Sorrentino's *Le conseguenze dell'amore* (*The Consequences of Love*, 2004) and Michele Placido's *Romanzo criminale* (*Romanzo Criminale*, 2005), depict male characters who never face up to their histories, and cannot settle down into normative lifestyles. The first film centres on Titta Di Girolamo (Toni Servillo), a former investment banker who lost 220 billion euros of Cosa Nostra money in a venture gone awry and as punishment is exiled to Switzerland to work as an errand boy for the Mafia. Placido's film recounts the exploits of members of the notorious Rome-based criminal syndicate, the Banda della Magliana, during the 1970s and early 1980s. Both films feature a femme fatale, Sofia (Olivia Magnani) in the first and Patrizia (Anna Mouglalis) in the second and, as is typical in noir, these women are projections of male fantasy. The femme fatale is both a symptom of male anxiety and a source of fascination for the protagonist, who eventually either gives into her or chooses to repudiate her. Both Sofia and Patrizia are empty vessels; Sofia is a construct who mediates Titta's relationship with the symbolic Mafia father, while Patrizia literally mediates complicated relationships between the state (one of her lovers is Police Commissioner Scialoja [Stefan Accorsi]) and the mob (another lover is the gangster Dandi [Claudio Santamaria]).

In both films, women are distractions that carry dire repercussions for those who fall victim to their allure. In the end, Sofia is gravely injured in a car crash and expunged from the story, while Patrizia's narrative ends ambiguously after Dandi's murder. And although all male protagonists connected with the mob meet violent ends, the Mafia remains intact in both films.

THE GREEK TRAGEDY

Antonio Capuano's decadent *Luna rossa* (*Red Moon*, 2001) is loosely based on Aeschylus' *Oresteia* and takes the form of a Greek tragedy. The film depicts the decline of the Cammarano family, a powerful Camorra clan whose members live together in an isolated and claustrophobic villa/bunker and spend much of their time committing murder and engaging in a variety of sexual exploits. This postmodern film is episodic and is characterised by intense theatrical dialogue, a vibrant palate, an edgy indie soundtrack and *engagés* themes of bodily mutilation, incest, parricide and matricide. *Luna rossa* centres upon family conflicts and hyperbolises the perverse family dynamics at work in the Mafia. Ultimately, young Oreste (Domenico Balsamo) collaborates with the authorities (the film is told in an elaborate flashback that begins and ends with Oreste's testimony), but not before sleeping with his sister Orsola (Antonia Truppo) (inspired by Electra) and avenging the death of his father Amerigo (Toni Servillo) by murdering his mother. Although it is suggested that the family is wiped out, another quickly steps in to usurp its power position.

THE MELODRAMA AND THE WOMAN'S FILM

Most recent Italian Mafia cinema in part follows the generic conventions of melodrama, and focuses on familial conflicts and recounts stormy romances (and the same can be said for recent Italian cinema at large). While Italy's various Mafias are in the foreground of many of these films, like in the biopics discussed above, narrative hinges on the private emotional world of the films' characters, as is the case with Claudio Fragasso's *Milano Palermo – Il ritorno* (*Milan Palermo – The Return*, 2007) and Andrea Porporati's *Il dolce e l'amaro* (*The Sweet and the Bitter*, 2007), which both conclude when the hero (a police officer in the first and a reformed Mafioso in the second) finds love and recognises that he is a valued member of his family and community.

In addition, most television series that revolve around the mob have a melodramatic thrust. This is certainly the case of the final seasons of the long-running hit *La piovra* (*The Octopus*, 1984–2001), where overt critiques of the Mafia are subordinated to sentimental concerns. Also, Giuseppe Ferrara's *Donne di mafia* (*Mafia Women*, 2001) focuses on the passions and contentions of a group of women married to the mob and Marco Risi's *L'ultimo padrino* (*The Last Godfather*, 2008) narrates the beliefs, health concerns and quirks of boss of bosses Bernardo Provenzano (Michele Placido) during the months leading up to his arrest.

Laura Mulvey argues that in the melodrama centred upon a male protagonist, narrative frictions are generally resolved in the service of affirming patriarchy. When a woman looks excessively, however, reconciliation is more challenging, and is frequently impossible.[3] This is certainly the case of Roberta Torre's *Angela* (*Angela*, 2002), Edoardo Winspeare's *Galantuomini* (*Brave Men*, 2008) and Marco Amenta's *La siciliana ribelle* (*The Sicilian Girl*, 2009). The first two tell the stories of Angela Spina (Donatella Finocchiaro) and Lucia Rizzo (Donatella Finocchiaro), women inside the criminal system, while the latter focuses on a historical figure, the *pentita* and eventual suicide Rita Atria (Veronica D'Agostino). All three films can be classified as 'woman's films' as they privilege a female point of view, are concerned with female desire and appeal to a female viewer. Moreover, the films depict women who are somewhat 'emancipated' in the Mafia context: Angela works for her husband as a Cosa Nostra drug runner; Lucia is a mob boss of a small clan of the Sacra Corona Unita; and Rita rebels against the Mafia and turns state's evidence. However, because their stories are recounted following the generic expectations of the woman's film, it follows that they must pay dearly for their emancipation. After engaging in an affair with her husband's godson, Angela is exiled from both her family and her Mafia family and the film closes on an image of her as, it is suggested, she perennially waits for her lover's return.

Lucia is both brutally raped in front of her young son and explicitly analogised to Eve, a comparison that suggests that she is responsible for the fall from grace of the entire sub-region of Salento. Finally, Amenta's film rewrites Rita's story to depict her quest for justice as unambiguous (Atria's actual diary entries bespeak her as someone both inside and outside of Mafia culture). In Amenta's rendition, Rita's odyssey is complete when she commits suicide and sacrifices herself in the name of justice.

Davide Barletti's *Fine pena mai: Paradiso perduto* (*Life Sentence*, 2007) and Claudio Cupellini's *Una vita tranquilla* (*A Quiet Life*, 2010) can be classified as male melodramas as they focus on male emotion and excess and demonstrate a crisis of masculinity as a result of an outside force that upsets familial life. *Fine pena mai* recounts the story of real-life mobster Antonio Perrone (Claudio Santamaria), a member of the Sacra Corona Unita sentenced to forty-nine years in prison. The film takes the form of a long flashback during which the protagonist reads a letter written to his wife to explain himself in the hopes that she might one day forgive him for leaving her and their son alone. In its depiction of sympathetic Mafiosos addicted to the fast-paced gangster lifestyle, Barletti's film is indebted to Martin Scorsese's *Goodfellas* (1990), yet departs from the mob classic in that the hero refuses to betray his co-conspirators. Instead, *Una vita tranquilla* is an Oedipal drama that looks at the complicated relationship between Rosario Russo (Toni Servillo), an ex-Camorrista hitman who abandoned his family to save himself, and his son Diego (Marco D'Amore) who has tracked him down in Germany. *Una vita tranquilla* is about the Mafia, and deals with the Camorra, the eco-Mafia, hired guns and men on the run. But it is mainly interested in the Oedipal traumas of abandonment, parricide and filicide inherent in the father–son relationship. The film insists that, in a Mafia context, there is no escaping or getting over the past, even though Rosario claims to have 'repented' for his sins. Ultimately, *Una vita tranquilla* maintains that Italy at large does not acknowledge the trauma of Mafia perpetrators.

Melodrama engages everyday scenarios while staging age-old battles between good and evil that ultimately find narrative closure and thus reassure the audience. 'In melodrama,' E. Ann Kaplan writes, 'the spectator is introduced to trauma through a film's themes and techniques, but the film ends with a comforting closure or cure. Such mainstream works posit trauma […] as a discrete past event, locatable, representable and curable.' The Mafia is an integral concern of Italian national cinema, and is a versatile subject with which to tell stories of heroism, romance and family drama. In the films discussed in this essay, the Mafia looms large. In most of them, however, pleasurable narrative forms – such as the biopic, film noir, melodrama and the woman's film – reassure the viewer who ultimately believes 'she is safe and that all is well in her world'.[4] That is, until she opens a local newspaper.

NOTES

1. Roberto Saviano, *Gomorrah: A Personal Journey into the Violent International Empire of Naples' Organized Crime System*, trans. Virginia Jewiss (New York: Farrar, Straus and Giroux, 2006), pp. 256–7.

2. Millicent Marcus, 'In Memoriam: The Neorealist Legacy in the Contemporary Anti-Mafia Film', in Laura E. Rorato and Kristi M. Wilson (eds), *Italian Neorealism and Global Cinema* (Detroit, MI: Wayne State University Press, 2007), p. 292.

3. Laura Mulvey, 'Afterthoughts on "Visual Pleasure and Narrative Cinema" Inspired by King Vidor's *Duel in the Sun* (1946)', in *Visual and Other Pleasures* (Bloomington: Indiana University Press, 1989), p. 37.

4. E. Ann Kaplan, 'Melodrama, Cinema and Trauma', *Screen* vol. 42 no. 2 (2001), pp. 204, 203.

FURTHER READING

Albano, Vittorio, *La Mafia nel cinema italiano da 'In Nome della legge' a 'Placido Rizzotto'* (Manduria: Barbieri, 2003).

Angrisani, Silvia and Guido Bonsaver, 'That's Camorra', *Sight and Sound* (November 2008), pp. 18–22.

Babini, Luana, 'The Mafia: New Cinematic Perspectives', in William Hope (ed.), *Italian Cinema: New Directions* (Oxford: Berg, 2005), pp. 229–50.

Bondanella, Peter, *Hollywood Italians. Dagos, Palookas, Romeos, Wise Guys and Sopranos* (New York: Continuum, 2004).

Bonsaver, Guido, 'Charismatic Criminals', *Sight and Sound* (November 2008), p. 22.

De Stefano, George, *An Offer We Can't Refuse: The Mafia in the Mind of America* (New York: Faber and Faber, 2006).

Dickie, John, *Cosa Nostra: A History of the Sicilian Mafia* (New York: Palgrave Macmillan, 2004).

——, *Blood Brotherhoods: The Rise of the Italian Mafias* (London: Sceptre, 2011).

Lupo, Salvatore, *History of the Mafia*, trans. Antony Shugar (New York: Columbia University Press, 2009).

Marcus, Millicent, 'In Memoriam: The Neorealist Legacy in the Contemporary Anti-Mafia Film', in Laura E. Rorato and Kristi M. Wilson (eds), *Italian Neorealism and Global Cinema* (Detroit, MI: Wayne State University Press, 2007), pp. 290–306.

O'Healy, Áine, 'Anthropological Anxieties: Roberta Torre's Critique of Mafia Violence', in Flavia Laviosa (ed.), *Visions of Struggle in Women's Filmmaking in the Mediterranean* (New York: Palgrave Macmillan, 2010), pp. 83–101.

Renga, Dana (ed.), *Mafia Movies: A Reader* (Toronto: University of Toronto Press, 2011).

——, *Unfinished Business: Screening the Italian Mafia in the New Millennium* (Toronto: University of Toronto Press, 2013).

Small, Pauline, 'No Way Out: Set Design in Mafia Films', *Italian Studies* (March 2011), pp. 112–27.

29 Screening Terrorism

Cinematic Portrayals of the Italian Armed Struggle

Giancarlo Lombardi

The strong symbolic connection between film and the memory of Italian political terrorism is underscored by the fact that, to this day, Italians remember the seventeen years that witnessed the insurgence of left-wing and right-wing terrorist attacks (1968–85) as *anni di piombo* (the 'years of lead'), the Italian title of Margarethe Von Trotta's *Die Bleierne Zeit* (*Marianne and Juliane*, 1981). Following the narrative of this German film, Italian directors often repeated Von Trotta's account of recent historical events associated with Italian terrorism set against the intimate description of devastating family relations resulting from these historical circumstances.

Italian cinema has tackled its own similar recent history by separating the two essential components of Von Trotta's film, thus producing what I consider to be two parallel emplotments of the past: on the one hand, it has retold some of the key events in this season of terror (the Moro kidnapping, bombings in Bologna and Brescia, Guido Rossa's murder), while on the other, it has portrayed fictional Italian terrorists, centring on their rapport with families, friends and significant others. My analysis of the cinema of Italian terrorism will differentiate between these two groups of films, locating the threads common to both of them.[1]

REMAKING HISTORY

Much like the Kennedy assassination, to which it has been likened, the kidnap and murder of Aldo Moro in 1978 has been defined as a locus of national trauma. The archive footage of the newsreels announcing the abduction of the president of the Christian Democratic Party and the eventual recovery of his body has been inserted so often into recent Italian cinema that several scholars have come to consider it a fetishistic metonym for the 'spectacular happenings' of the 1970s.[2]

The three movies that focus directly on the Moro affair borrow from three very different genres. Giuseppe Ferrara's *Il caso Moro* (*The Moro Case*, 1988) belongs to the tradition of investigative cinema or *cinema d'inchiesta* which harks back to the cinematography of Francesco Rosi, Elio Petri and Citto Maselli. Renzo Martinelli's *Piazza delle cinque lune* (*Piazza of the Five Moons*, 2003) colours basic characteristics of that same genre with the most typical features of the action thriller. Marco Bellocchio's *Buongiorno, notte* is, instead, an auteurial revisitation of the events suffused with profound oneiric overtones. Against these three movies, we should juxtapose the ghostly presence of Aldo Moro continually evoked in Paolo Sorrentino's noir biopic of Giulio Andreotti, *Il divo*, and the portrayal of the role played by the Banda della Magliana, a criminal gang indirectly involved in the aborted recovery of the statesman, in Michele Placido's cinematic version of *Romanzo criminale*, based on Giancarlo De Cataldo's bestselling novel.

The cinematic portrayal of Aldo Moro has long been associated with the chameleonic performances of Gian Maria Volonté, first in Elio Petri's *Todo modo*, and later in *Il caso Moro*. Filmed two years before the abduction of the statesman, *Todo modo* depicted Moro as a corrupt politician who controlled the fate of the entire country. Behind the tragic overtones associated with Volonté's performance, in *Il caso Moro*, his later portrayal of Moro as victim inevitably recalls his earlier representation of Moro as victimiser. Thus, although Volonté's recreation of the dead statesman is the centrepiece in Ferrara's meticulous historical reconstruction of the Moro kidnapping, it inevitably subverts its intended elegiac overtones by calling to mind Moro's controversial past as the Christian Democrat manipulator who once proclaimed that his own party would never withstand public scrutiny.

Il caso Moro presents the chain of events that led to the murder of Aldo Moro with the strict factual adherence proper to the docudrama. Unfolded, the narrative shifts its focus constantly from the 'people's prison', where the hostage is being held and questioned, to the Moro household, where his family struggles against the stubborn resistance of governmental forces refusing to negotiate for his release. Government officials are portrayed with the same cryptic stuffiness once reserved by Volonté for Aldo Moro in *Todo modo*: their indictment, at the end of the movie, is absolute. Ferrara's valiant effort to present the events in the most objective fashion is forcefully undermined by his insistence that the cast impersonate the originals so closely that they actually appear as mere caricatures.

The twenty-fifth anniversary of Moro's abduction and murder witnessed the release of two strikingly different films on the affair. *Piazza delle cinque lune* was an investigative thriller that elected to retell the story from the perspective of a retired judge called back to action when presented with new evidence indicating that the Red Brigades (BR) had conducted the Moro abduction following the joint orders of the Italian and US secret services. Based on the findings of Sergio Flamigni, head of the Commissione Moro from 1980–3, Martinelli's film employed cinematic conventions that would cater to younger viewers thirsty for action-packed narratives. His desire to mix instruction and entertainment fell short as recent history was drowned in generic clichés that deprived it of verisimilitude.

Commissioned by Raicinema to commemorate the statesman's death, Bellocchio's *Buongiorno, notte* takes great liberties in recounting the fifty-five days leading up to the assassination. This is the only time that the cinematic perspective adopted is that of a member of the BR: Chiara (Maya Sansa), the woman who was to be known as 'jailor'of the 'people's prison'. Bellocchio's film shows the events from the sole perspective of the terrorists, choosing as a vantage point the only terrorist who seems to be questioning the validity of the attack. The director emphasises the subjective narrative stance by portraying the terrorist's dreams and reveries, often

showing the hostage through the keyhole from which she routinely gains access to him. The film's oneiric quality derives from the frequent inserts of black-and-white film footage borrowed from Russian newsreels and Italian neorealist cinema, effectively revealing the ideological conditionings of left-wing terrorists. The final montage of the parallel sequences of two opposite resolutions of the Moro kidnapping – one real and the other invented – arguably constitutes Bellocchio's most original contribution to the cinematic repositioning of the affair. Images of Moro being led out of the apartment to be executed in the trunk of the car where he would later be found, are literally framed by shots that imagine, instead, a positive ending to the abduction, showing the hostage walking freely out of his prison while his captors are fast asleep because Chiara drugged them at dinner. The joyful fast pace of Aldo Moro walking downhill at dawn, with the Palazzo delle Esposizioni looming in the distant background, is there to remind viewers that, upon his physical death, the statesman's image was resurrected into that of a martyr, at the twofold expense of a terrorist organisation that lost all popular support and of his fellow politicians who sacrificed his life to safeguard their status. The Palazzo delle Esposizioni, mixing echoes of ancient Rome through its Coliseum-like windows with not-so-distant memories of the fascist era that blessed its construction, powerfully evokes the political martyrdom experienced by Aldo Moro.

The idea of Moro (Roberto Herlitzka) as a sacrificial scapegoat returns through his haunting presence in *Il divo*, in which he appears as a ghost to remind Giulio Andreotti (Toni Servillo) of his least absolvable sins. Andreotti himself declares that, of all the turmoil experienced in his many years in politics, the death of Aldo Moro remains the most traumatic event. In a powerful exchange with his wife, Andreotti admits to his responsibility for some of the darkest moments in recent Italian history, yet he claims that such actions were necessary for the well-being of the country:

Andreotti, with Moro (Paolo Grazioso) in Andreotti's bathroom behind him, from Sorrentino's *Il divo* (2008)

Libano is stabbed in the 'Vespasiano' in Placido's *Romanzo criminale* (2005)

In *Romanzo criminale*, Freddo walks among the ruins of Bologna's train station

The direct or indirect responsibility for all the carnage in Italy from 1969 to 1984, that left precisely 236 dead and 817 injured. To all the families of the victims I say that I confess. I confess that it was my fault, my most grievous fault. I'll say it, even if it's pointless. Havoc used to destabilise the country to provoke terror to isolate the extremist parties and strengthen the centre ones like the Christian Democrats has been described as the 'tension strategy'. It would be more correct to say 'survival strategy'. Roberto, Michele, Giorgio, Carlo Alberto, Giovanni, Mino, dear Aldo, by vocation or necessity, all confirmed lovers of the truth. All bombs ready to explode that were defused into silence (translation from DVD subtitle).[3]

And just as Sorrentino shows Andreotti's wife always at his side, he often chooses to place Aldo Moro right behind him as a figment of the politician's imagination (or guilty conscience), dressed in gym clothes that forcefully declare Moro's depoliticised status, or appearing in the most unexpected places and constantly speaking with the hieratic tone of his letters from captivity.

It is Moro's spectral presence that stands most strikingly in contrast to all the other protagonists of Sorrentino's film, whose caricature features symbolically as *masks of power*. The adoption of the fast narrative pace of the contemporary Hollywood noir *à la* Tarantino enables Sorrentino to reveal recent Italian history, highlighting its most dysfunctional qualities.[4]

The influence of Quentin Tarantino's directorial style in tone, narrative pace and episodic quality is also evident in Placido's *Romanzo criminale*. The director here chooses to contract significantly the events narrated by Giancarlo De Cataldo in the eponymous fictional account of the story of the Banda della Magliana, the criminal gang that controlled Rome's drug and prostitution rings throughout the 1970s. Placido's most original contribution rests in frequent metaphorical

juxtapositions between two Romes, that of the recent past and Ancient Rome. The three leaders of the gang are vividly envisioned as a triumvirate, with one of them, Libano (Pierfrancesco Favino) often calling himself the Emperor of Rome. In this light, Libano's death by stabbing as he exits a public bathroom, called by Romans a Vespasiano, is particularly striking.

Another member of the triumvirate, Freddo (Kim Rossi Stuart), dies like Caesar at the hands of one his former allies, yet unlike the Roman Emperor, he is killed on the steps of a church. Of the three leaders, only Freddo invites viewer empathy, effectively reinforced by his desire not to come into contact with the Mafia or the Italian secret service, or to be involved in matters pertaining to the Moro kidnapping: the gang has been asked by a local mobster to identify the location of the hostage, only to be told eventually that no one has any real interest in saving Moro. Freddo's characterisation is particularly effective in one of the film's most controversial sequences, where in order to portray his disbelief at the devastation following the explosion of a bomb in the Bologna railway station, images of Kim Rossi Stuart are superimposed on archival footage of the bombing. Despite the cold-heartedness evoked by his nickname, Freddo is the sole gang leader whose emotional ties and reactions are likely to foster viewer sympathy.

Italian film has never truly been able to tackle directly the most traumatic event in recent Italian history: the Bologna bombing of 1980. This tragic event has thus been portrayed either through cinematic indirection, or as a distant narrative end point (or starting point) – mentioned but not shown. The only account of the broken lives of the many victims of a terrorist attack whose perpetrators have yet to be fully identified, Massimo Martelli's *Per non dimenticare* (*Lest We Forget*, 1992), limits its focus to the choral voice of those who can no longer speak and its group portrayal of the random targets of the bombing at the Bologna railway station is particularly powerful because of its brief intensity. Heading a large cast of stars who graciously appeared in cameo roles, Giuseppe Cederna plays the nameless survivor of the massacre, a man who escaped the bombing because he had left the waiting room shortly before the explosion in order to buy a pack of cigarettes. Through his eyes, viewers revisit the very last minutes in the lives of the many people who died, yet Martelli employs cinematic indirection in his resolve not to show the explosion nor the devastation that ensued. Of each character's fleeting on-screen portrayal, the viewer is left with a mere sketch, powerfully anticipated diegetically by the presence, among the cast of characters, of a sketch artist who quickly draws the face of a woman sitting across from him, and later tells a stranger sitting next to him that any face in the crowd hides a story that can never truly be known. Like his sketch artist, Martelli draws quick sketches of a crowd paying particular attention to the fact that, because of the brutal interruption of their lives, their stories will never truly be known in their entirety.

Luciano Ligabue's second feature film, *Dazeroadieci* (*From Zero to Ten*, 2002) tells the story of a group of forty-somethings who decide to travel back to the resort where they used to vacation during their teenage years. They have not returned since 1980, when their trip was brutally interrupted by the death of one of their closest friends who was among the victims in Bologna. Their trip is an attempt to complete that last journey and to pay homage to the memory of their youth. Their encounters with past lovers, friends and acquaintances are coloured by nostalgia and curiosity: their conversations always lead to questions meant to assess, in pseudo-statistical terms, the extent to which their post-adolescent dreams have been fulfilled. In light of the dramatic event that acts as its backdrop, *Dazeroadieci* is a film that confronts Italian viewers in a most direct fashion, asking them to reflect on the impact that the *anni di piombo* had on their lives.

Just as Ligabue waits until the end of his movie to refer to the traumatic event that once interrupted his characters' trip, Massimo Natale shows Bologna's railway station only in the opening and closing sequences of *L'estate di Martino* (*Martino's Summer*, 2010). Dedicated to the victims of the mass slaughter, Natale's film mixes fairytale elements with traditional *bildungsroman* features to tell a story of generational struggles, sibling rivalry and ideological strife. Set on the southern shores of Italy, in an area adjacent to a NATO base, *L'estate di Martino* portrays the coming of

age of a local adolescent who, upon his encounter with an American officer (played by Treat Williams), the cinematic symbol of post-Vietnam pacifism, questions his father's Communist ideology and, while learning the philosophy of surfing, acquires the inner strength to challenge his older brother, whose girlfriend he eventually steals. The entire diegesis is literally framed by the Bologna bombing, portrayed as a wave crashing on the shore when the film, as the station's clock reaches the time of the explosion, suddenly cuts to the Ionian Sea. As the film reaches its dramatic climax, viewers discover that the short opening sequence in the station is reprised as Martino's new girlfriend sits in the waiting room shortly before the bomb explodes. Martelli's *Per non dimenticare* is suddenly referenced when the young woman takes a photo of a couple opposite her kissing. In his movie, Natale combines the lessons of Martelli and Ligabue, as his characters experience a coming of age through the brutal, traumatic interruption brought about by the terrorist attack.

In recent years, two films have offered historically accurate revisitations of episodes of the *anni di piombo* that had never been previously discussed. In both films, the detailed portrayal of the events serves a clear didactic purpose, since each movie acts as a cautionary tale. Giuseppe Ferrara returns to address terrorism in *Guido che sfidò le Brigate Rosse* (*Guido Who Challenged the Red Brigades*, 2007) and, just as he did in *Il caso Moro*, he asks his performers to mold themselves after the historical figures they are playing. Ferrara identifies Guido Rossa (Massimo Ghini), a union representative killed by the Brigate Rosse in 1979, as the true unsung hero of the *anni di piombo*. His uniqueness is signified by his passion for mountain climbing: long before his sacrifice is mentioned, a voiceover opens the diegesis presenting Rossa as one of the greatest *alpinisti* of the *dopoguerra*. The film opens and ends on the same black-and-white images of a man climbing a mountain. In the opening sequence, a handwritten letter penned by Guido is visually superimposed: in it, Guido announces his intention to abandon mountain climbing because he feels the necessity to return to the ground and embrace different challenges.

This last part is spoken over images of a man, presumably a factory worker, bending over fire, and quickly leads to the opening credits. There is no question that Ferrara has chosen to depict Guido as a modern-day Prometheus, a titanic champion of mankind and a mythic figure for socialist engagement

In Ferrara's *Guido che sfidò le Brigate Rosse* (2007), the mountain climber and the letter are superimposed

since the times of Karl Marx. Ferrara's choice never to show, either in the opening or in the final sequence, Guido reaching the top of the mountain, is a clear reminder of the ineffectiveness of his heroic gestures. Guido dies because he is alone in denouncing the identity of the BR infiltrators in his factory and, upon his death, his family is given a medal, while the BR responsible for his murder ascends to the Executive Council of the organisation. Ferrara's profound pessimism is strongly underscored by the epigraph appearing on the screen shortly before the final credits: 'We owe to terrorism 419 homicides and a decisive contribution to the shift to the right of the entire country' (author's translation). Here, Ferrara is no longer speaking just about the past, but about its legacy: this is where the film reaches its bleakest conclusions, drawing a line between left-wing terrorism, the *strategy of tension* which enabled it during the last two decades of the First Republic, and the political climate of a Second Republic that still bore its imprint.

While Giuseppe Ferrara divides his diegesis between the portrayal of his Promethean hero and that of the BR cell which eventually murdered him, Renato De Maria focuses his entire narrative, much as Marco Bellocchio did, on the actions of a terrorist organisation in *La prima linea* (*The Front Line*, 2009). For the first time, a film tackles the historical reconstruction of an organisation that was not the Brigate Rosse. Prima Linea had a shorter lifespan but an extremely violent trajectory. De Maria's film has a dual plot, following the history of the organisation while tracing the love affair between its two leaders, Susanna Ronconi (Giovanna Mezzogiorno) and Sergio Segio (Riccardo Scamarcio). The entire narrative is told in retrospect through Segio's perspective, as a confession behind bars occurring long after his apprehension. The film shifts continuously from past to present, often depicting in alternate montage different moments in the past, thus making for a very difficult viewer experience. Despite its romantic subplot, *La prima linea* is a film that demands thought rather than emotion from its viewers: it is photographed in extremely cold colours, which facilitate viewer detachment and critical reflection, and its screenplay has the barren simplicity of an Antonioni film. Riccardo Scamarcio and Giovanna Mezzogiorno deliver their lines in a hushed tone, often with coldness

Sergio's admission of guilt in *La prima linea* (2009)

and detachment: when Scamarcio speaks to the camera, at the very end of the movie, such detachment is finally motivated by the words of acknowledgment of the pointlessness of his criminal enterprise: 'My responsibilities are judicial, political and moral. I assume all three of them' (author's translation).

It is another character, however, who utters the words that reach deeper into the ideological core of De Maria's film: an old friend of the protagonist who, unlike Segio, never made the fatal leap to join the armed struggle. His are the words that motivate the strange linguistic choice of calling the movie La prima linea rather than Prima linea, the name of the organisation. The last time he meets Segio, his friend attempts to convince him to abandon clandestinity and leave the armed struggle behind, reminding him that 'you are the first row of a procession that no longer exists' (subtitle translation). In the title of his movie, De Maria thus seeks to evoke the deluded state which led most terrorist groups to believe that their actions had large popular backing. What is clearly illustrated, instead, is the profound solitude of these men and women, a solitude they cannot escape even as they seek solace in a relationship with a fellow terrorist.

SNAKES IN THE GRASS

While the Brigate Rosse and its ilk terrorised Italy, cinema often portrayed their devastating presence without referring to specific events, which were still too close and too real to be historicised in any way. The intensity of the escalating violence was such that the entire country practically felt at war with internal, invisible forces: the concept of terrorism as civil war was indeed at the very heart of the rationalisations offered by the former leaders of the Brigate Rosse in their prison memoirs. It is no surprise, then, that several films chose to focus on the devastating effects on the families of those who had joined the armed struggle.

As Alan O'Leary noted, films such as Dino Risi's Caro papà (Dear Papa, 1979), Bernardo Bertolucci's La tragedia di un uomo ridicolo (The Tragedy of a Ridiculous Man, 1981) and Gianni Amelio's Colpire al cuore (Blow to the Heart, 1982) portray terrorism as an Oedipal struggle, placing generational conflict at the very heart of the cinematic diegesis.[5] And while Risi and Bertolucci elect for a more traditional restaging of the struggle by the unsurprising final revelation that a son has betrayed his father, joining a terrorist organisation and choosing his own parent as a target (Risi has the father kneecapped by

his own son, while Bertolucci shows us a son staging his own kidnapping), Gianni Amelio goes in the opposite direction, telling the story of a father who became an evil role model, a cattivo maestro. Although unique in its portrayal of a father who is a sympathiser with a terrorist organisation, and for this reason is eventually brought to justice by his own conservative son, Amelio's film shares significant parallelisms with Giuseppe Bertolucci's Segreti segreti, which opted for an all-female cast to talk about terrorism from yet another 'familial' perspective. Common to both films is the exclusive concentration on terrorists and their sympathisers: virtually no mention is made of their victims. While Amelio kills his terrorist early in the film, shifting the focus to a more indirect representation of the issue, Giuseppe Bertolucci follows his militant for a longer period, depicting her attacks as well as her eventual imprisonment. In both films, the protagonist is portrayed especially in relation to his or her family. In close connection to the portrayal of the terrorist as family member stands the theme of the delazione (informing), bearing its unspoken yet direct reference to the phenomenon of turning informer and collaborating with the law. It is the figure of the terrorist as penitent that assumes peculiar characteristics when analysed, in these films, with respect to the two social networks to which s/he belongs: family of origin and terrorist organisation. Colpire al cuore tells the story of the Oedipal rivalry between an Italian academic and his teenage son. The former is a sympathiser and possibly an active member of a terrorist organisation, while the latter is a law-abiding conservative who does not hesitate to report his father to the police when he realises that he might be aiding and abetting a young terrorist, to whom both father and son are obviously attracted. Segreti segreti, instead, chooses an opposite path, focusing on several dysfunctional pairings of mothers and daughters, likening terrorism to a family affair, a struggle between bad mothers and disobeying children, and thus stressing the idea of terrorism as civil war. The tale of a terrorist who shoots a judge in Venice, and then returns home where she witnesses (and causes) her mother's suicide soon before being arrested, Segreti segreti is a complex film where several stories are tightly interwoven in an opaque narrative. The elliptical and non-linear narrative inhibits its immediate communicability; formal incommunicability is replicated, at a thematic level, through the familial and societal disintegration that play such a powerful role in the symbolic economy of the film. Like Amelio, Giuseppe Bertolucci returns constantly to the idea of terrorism as civil war. The same internal rift poignantly represented by the image of the family torn apart is further expressed by the environment in which a large part of the movie takes place: post-earthquake Irpinia, whose ruins often form the object of Bertolucci's lingering camera. The broken walls of many a house thus witness another disruption coming from 'inside', this time from the very ground on which we all stand. Terrorism, with its devastation, is thus compared to an earthquake that has shaken Italy to its very core, causing death in equally unforeseeable and shattering fashion.

In the mid-1990s, long after the *anni di piombo* have come to an end, cinema returns incessantly to this subject as Parliament and the national media begin discussion of the possibility of granting *indulto* (state pardon) to the imprisoned terrorists. All the films released in this decade participate in this discourse, humanising the figure of the imprisoned terrorist and foregrounding their victims or their surviving relatives, since they were the most vocal opponents of the *indulto* itself. Thus, Mimmo Calopresti's *La seconda volta* (*The Second Time*, 1995), Franco Bernini's *Le mani forti* (*Strong Hands*, 1996) and Marco Turco's *Vite in sospeso* (*Belleville*, 1996) all choose to portray terrorism by giving (in)direct voice to its victims. Signs of their time, these films offer a more palatable image of the terrorist, who is thus shown to be worthier of state pardon. What is particularly effective, in this process of demystification of the terrorist, is the fact that none of these terrorists is ever portrayed 'in active duty'. Indeed, these terrorists are all immortalised in a neutralised state of captivity. In full reflection of the current debate, several of these films stage a new encounter between victim and victimiser, or between the victimiser and a representative of the world s/he once tried to subvert. *La seconda volta* begins as Alberto Sajevo (Nanni Moretti) accidentally meets the young terrorist who was once jailed for shooting him; *Le mani forti* opens on the psychotherapy session between a secret agent and the sister of one of the victims of the attack he once directed; Wilma Labate's *La mia generazione* (*My Generation*, 1996) stages the encounter between a

terrorist and the *carabiniere* who should induce him to collaborate with justice; and *Vite in sospeso* narrates the meeting between a terrorist in exile and his estranged brother, who is trying to understand the reasons for his choices. In all four films, the terrorist is asked to account for his or her past, and thus revisit that past as part of a process of partial redemption.

The decade that follows produces Marco Tullio Giordana's *La meglio gioventù* (*The Best of Youth*, 2003), probably the most nuanced portrayal of a terrorist, bridging the divide I have drawn in my reconstruction of the cinema of terrorism. The six-hour film, originally meant for television, makes precise historical references to significant events of the last four decades: the Florence Flood of 1966; the student revolts of 1968; the explosive autumn of 1969; the ecological poisoning of Seveso in 1976; the advent of democratic psychiatry and the closing of state mental institutions in 1978; and the murder of Falcone and Borsellino in 1992. Yet, no mention is ever made of the two watershed events in the history of the *anni di piombo*, the Moro affair and the bombing of the Bologna railway station. Although the Brigate Rosse is never spoken of, an unnamed terrorist organisation is prominent in the narrative. Giordana's sumptuous fresco of a generation that spent itself with unbridled generosity, that glorious youth that gave its best years to make a better world for those who followed, happens to include a young woman who made a drastic choice in the name of ideals she believed to be imperative. The vivid portrayal of the descent into clandestinity of Giulia (Sonia Bergamasco), who abandons her family in order to join the armed struggle, lies at the very heart of the movie. Her subsequent incarceration, organised by a loving husband who prefers her safe behind bars, and her distant reappearance in the life of a daughter she hardly knew, constitute only one of the many narrative strands in Giordana's film, yet it remains particularly evocative because it brings back the portrayal of the terrorist in Italian cinema to its most creative nucleus. Following in the footsteps of *Colpire al cuore* and *Segreti segreti*, it interprets Italian political terrorism as a highly dysfunctional *family affair*.

NOTES

1. Alan O'Leary follows a similar path in his monograph, *Tragedia all'italiana: Italian Cinema and Italian Terrorisms, 1970–2010* (Oxford: Peter Lang, 2011), where he dedicates entire chapters to the Moro affair and to *stragismo*, followed by individual chapters on patriarchy, gender and memory in the cinema of terrorism.

2. Alan O'Leary, 'Dead Man Walking: The Aldo Moro Kidnap and Palimpsest History in *Buongiorno, notte*', *New Cinemas* vol. 6 no. 1 (2008), pp. 33–45; Catherine O'Rawe, 'More More Moro: Music and Montage in *Romanzo criminale*', *The Italianist* no. 29 (2009), pp. 214–26; Ruth Glynn, 'Moro as Figure of Speech: The Displaced Confessions of the Women of the Brigate Rosse', in Ruth Glynn and Giancarlo Lombardi (eds), *Remembering Aldo Moro: The Cultural Legacy of the 1978 Kidnapping and Murder* (Oxford: Legenda, 2012), pp. 78–95.

3. What follows are a list of the important events to which this statement refers, with names keyed in italics to the list of people Andreotti mentions: *Roberto* Calvi (1920–82), president of the Banco Ambrosiano, a private bank with close ties to the Vatican, was found hanging from Blackfriars Bridge in London shortly after being indicted for the financial fall of his bank. Although initially deemed a suicide, Calvi's death has long been considered a political homicide. *Michele* Sindona (1920–86), freemason, finance mogul, closely involved with the Mafia in Italy and the US, was imprisoned in the US for fraudulent bankruptcy. He was poisoned in jail in Italy, where he had been sentenced to life imprisonment for the murder of *Giorgio* Ambrosoli (1933–79), an Italian lawyer, who had been charged by the Bank of Italy to investigate and liquidate the assets of the Banca Privata Italiana, originally managed by Sindona. *Carlo Alberto* Dalla Chiesa (1920–82), Carabinieri General, was the leader of the anti-terrorism task force which disbanded the Brigate Rosse. During his 100 days as prefect of Palermo, he waged war against the Mafia and its political protectors: as a consequence, he was brutally murdered, together with his wife. *Giovanni* Falcone (1939–92), the judge who headed the 'Pool Anti-Mafia', led the Maxi-trial of Palermo in 1987 after the arrest of Tommaso Buscetta, the first mobster to collaborate with justice. He was slaughtered, along with his bodyguards, possibly as a consequence of his investigations into the Mafia ties of prominent politicians close to Andreotti. *Mino* Pecorelli (1928–79), director of *Osservatore Politico*, was a political journalist who exposed, in his libellous magazine, corrupt politicians of his time. Despite his close ties to the secret service, he was found dead shortly after having declaring his inside knowledge of mysteries surrounding the assassination of *Aldo* Moro (1916–78).

4. See Nicoletta Marini Maio, 'A Spectre Is Haunting Italy: The Double "Emplotment" of the Moro Affair', in Ruth Glynn, Giancarlo Lombardi and Alan O'Leary (eds), *Terrorism Italian Style: Representations of Political Violence in Contemporary Italian Cinema* (London: IGRS Books, 2012), pp. 157–74.

4. O'Leary, *Tragedia all'italiana*, p. 20.

FURTHER READING

Antonello, Pierpaolo and Alan O'Leary (eds), *Imagining Terrorism: The Rhetoric and Representation of Political Violence in Italy, 1969–2009* (Oxford: Legenda, 2009).

Caviglia, Francesco and Leonardo Cecchini, 'A Quest for Dialogism: Looking Back at Italian Political Violence in the 70s', in Torben Vestergaard (ed.), *Constructing History, Society and Politics in Discourse: Multimodal Approaches* (Aalborg: Aalborg University Press, 2009), pp. 127–49.

Fantoni Minella, Maurizio, *Non riconciliati: politica e società nel cinema italiano dal neorealismo a oggi* (Turin: UTET, 2004).

Glynn, Ruth and Giancarlo Lombardi (eds), *Remembering Aldo Moro: The Cultural Legacy of the 1978 Kidnapping and Murder* (Oxford: Legenda, 2012).

Glynn, Ruth, Giancarlo Lombardi and Alan O'Leary (eds), *Terrorism Italian Style: Representations of Political Violence in Contemporary Italian Cinema* (London: IGRS Books, 2012).

Lombardi, Giancarlo, 'Unforgiven: Revisiting Political Terrorism in *La seconda volta*', *Italica* vol. 77 no. 2 (2000), pp. 199–213.

Lombardi, Giancarlo, 'La passione secondo Marco Bellocchio: gli ultimi giorni di Aldo Moro', *Annali d'italianistica* no. 25 (2007), pp. 397–408.

O'Leary, Alan, *Tragedia all'italiana: Italian Cinema and Italian Terrorisms, 1970–2010* (Oxford: Peter Lang, 2011).

O'Leary, Alan, 'Dead Man Walking: The Aldo Moro Kidnap and Palimpsest History in *Buongiorno, notte*', *New Cinemas* vol. 6 no. 1 (2008), pp. 33–45.

Uva, Christian (ed.), *Schermi di piombo: il terrorismo nel cinema italiano* (Soveria Mannelli: Rubbettino, 2007).

30 Italian Cinema and Holocaust Memory

Millicent Marcus

During his time in Auschwitz, Primo Levi had a recurrent nightmare which he described as follows: he has returned home, and is now surrounded by family and friends to whom he recounts his ordeal of hunger, lice, the hard bed, the Kapò who boxes him in the nose and sends him to the washroom because he is bleeding. At a certain point, Levi realises that his listeners are not following him, that indeed they are indifferent, talking among themselves as if he were not there. His sister gets up and leaves the room without uttering a word.

Alas, Levi's nightmare turned out to be prophetic of the way in which Italians would react to the searing documents issuing from the hand of this Holocaust survivor. And indeed, the film industry would be no exception to this pattern of cultural reticence concerning the plight of the nation's Jewish populace under the Racial Laws of 1938 and the subsequent Nazi occupation which led to the genocide of 8,529 members of Italy's 'oldest minority'.[1] A survey of Italian feature films and made-for-television miniseries fully devoted to fascist anti-Semitism and/or the Nazi campaign to exterminate European Jewry yields only sixteen examples over the fifty-year period between the end of World War II and the mid-1990s. A pair of films made during that time devotes single episodes to the Shoah – *Dov'è la libertà?* (*Where Is Freedom?*, 1952) by Roberto Rossellini; and *Tutti a casa* by Luigi Comencini – while two others – Liliana Cavani's *Il portiere di notte* and Lina Wertmüller's *Pasqualino Settebellezze* – feature non-Jewish protagonists and hence sidestep the issue of genocide. Such scant cinematic coverage of the Holocaust is especially surprising, in view of the fact that the Italian film tradition, consecrated by neorealism, had served as the primary vehicle for confronting the country's most painful and blameworthy failings, and for claiming collective responsibility for them. The persecution of Italy's Jews, unfortunately, constitutes a lapse in this cinematic custom of national self-mirroring, and the scarcity of Holocaust-related films over the second half of the twentieth century testifies to what I call the 'weak memory' of this historical episode. Historian Niccolò Zapponi, for example, finds it significant that the inaugural film of neorealism, *Roma città aperta*, 'avoided venturing into the most wretched, and least "open" area of the city: the Ghetto'.[2] Film critic Paolo Finn writes that, in fifty years of Italian cinema, there has been 'a decidedly limited production of works regarding this subject', a subject which constitutes 'one of the most despicable and dramatic of our history, never adequately reconsidered'.[3] Fascist anti-Semitism and the fate of the Jews under the Nazi occupation of Italy is 'an absolutely unpalatable theme for mass audiences … a theme that would have raised unresolved questions about our embarrassing recent past'.[4]

The relatively few film-makers who took up the challenge of Holocaust representation worked at a decided disadvantage compared to those who treated themes more suitable to the cultural climate of the postwar years. Aside from the obvious fact that there was little demand for such subject matter, those who undertook to tell the story of Italy's Jews under fascism and the Nazi occupation found themselves without a tradition or discourse within which they could locate their own work. The few films to emerge on the topic never coalesced into a coherent corpus whose shared subject matter would have established the basis for an ongoing cinematic conversation. With a pair of conspicuous exceptions – Gillo Pontecorvo's *Kapò*; and Vittorio De Sica's *Il giardino dei Finzi–Contini* (*The Garden of the Finzi-Continis*, 1970) – this obscure body of work had no impact on the flow of Italian film history, and as a result, created no continuous tradition, no genealogy, no cumulative discourse, no representational traces. In other words, these films did not talk to each other.[5] It is as if each film-maker who embarked on a Holocaust narrative had to do so from scratch, without a precedent to draw upon, to elaborate and complicate, to react against polemically or to rewrite parodically. This means that the body of Italian Holocaust films was an amorphous and incoherent one, where individual works did not hark back to a linear genealogy but instead to a variety of isolated cinematic ancestries. Due to such discontinuity, the minor films which emerged within this cinematic corpus did not gain the kind of visibility that a coherent body of films would have conferred even upon its less acclaimed examples. Consider, for contrast, the vast and uneven welter of films dedicated to the representation of fascism, or the corpus of films which assume the trappings of the *commedia all'italiana* or *cinema politico* genres, in order to register social criticism, with varying degrees of success.

Without such a representational memory, the Holocaust films to surface in this postwar period have more in common with concurrent cinematic production than with previous Italian works on the subject. Thus what I would call the 'second-wave films' (1960–6) share with other works of the time a tendency toward melodramatically tinged sentimental romance, while the mid-1970s auteurist production flirts with the sexual brinksmanship of that transgressive period. In the Italian Holocaust filmography of 1945–90, stylistic and thematic patterns indeed arise, but they do so more as a result of the surrounding Italian cinematic context than out of any conscious attempt on the part of film-makers to situate their work within a specific discourse on Italian Holocaust representation.[6]

There is one film – Luigi Comencini's *Tutti a casa* – within this sparse and inchoate body of work whose remarkable self-consciousness about its testimonial

task warrants close critical attention. Importantly, the film both announces the need to bear witness, while at the same time revealing itself to be woefully inadequate to the task, given that only two episodes within its picaresque plot are dedicated to the Shoah. Its soldier-protagonists, Innocenzi (Alberto Sordi) and Ceccarelli (Serge Reggiani), wander aimlessly about the country when the Italian army is disbanded in the aftermath of the Armistice with the Allies on 8 September 1943. During one scene, the men watch as a transport train leaves a flurry of notes in its wake, and a young girl, dressed in white, purposefully and carefully collects the scattered pieces of paper from the tracks. While the child is filmed realistically and takes her place among the many other flesh-and-blood characters who arbitrarily stray into the path of this picaresque journey, her angelic whiteness and her gesture of supreme, almost superhuman compassion confer upon her a profoundly emblematic status with respect to the film's literal level. In gathering these scraps of paper that would otherwise be carried off by the winds of oblivion, she is the receiver of witness, the custodian of memory, the answer to the victims' plea that their testimony be heard. But her youth is a highly ambiguous signifier. On the one hand, it is the guarantor of that innocence (and here the pun on the surname of the film's protagonist is deliberate) which makes her the perfect vehicle of Holocaust truth. On the other hand, because she is a child, and by definition helpless within the greater scheme of things, this collector of messages is unable to act upon them in any effectual way. Together with her youth, this little girl's solitude serves as a powerful indictment of the adult world's collective acquiescence and indifference to atrocity.

The figure of the compassionate young gatherer of messages also has strategic importance for what we

In Luigi Comencini's *Tutti a casa* (1960), a young girl gathers the notes left behind by the deportees in a train bound for Auschwitz

Such films as Vittorio De Sica's *Il giardino dei Finzi–Contini* (1970) represent the exception in a period characterised by scant cinematic treatment of the Shoah

might call the 'representational history' of the Holocaust. Although this segment of *Tutti a casa* is extremely brief, it is rich with potential for a fuller rendering of the Italian Jewish plight, suggesting an infinite number of possible narratives that could spin off from this particular moment in the plot. Each of the many notes that drop along the tracks of the deportation train could be a Holocaust text in its own right, containing the nucleus of a story that could be fully developed to tell its own unique and vivid account of a life heading toward extinction. In the young girl who collects and receives these messages, Comencini is acknowledging the enormity of this history's representational challenge – to memorialise its victims properly, to fashion public narratives capable of transmitting the richness of these private lives and the tragic injustice of their loss. The meagre footage, and the elliptical treatment of the Jewish plight in this scene of *Tutti a casa* is symptomatic of the general diffidence toward Holocaust subject matter demonstrated by film-makers working in the period from 1945 to the 1990s.

All this was to change quite dramatically with the release of Roberto Benigni's *La vita è bella* and Francesco Rosi's *La tregua* (*The Truce*, 1997) as Italian screens finally began to accommodate the powerful testimonial impulse that arose in the last years of the millennium.[7] Between the years 1997 and 2011, twelve works,

including feature films and television miniseries, have been produced on the subject. Such statistics speak eloquently of the shift from weak memory to the recovered memory of our contemporary cultural climate. In addition to these two key films, this period has seen the emergence of the following films to treat the Shoah: Andrea and Antonio Frazzi's *Il cielo cade* (*The Sky Is Falling*, 2000); Ricky Tognazzi's *Canone inverso* (*Making Love*, 2000); Ettore Scola's *Concorrenza sleale* (*Unfair Competition*, 2001); Ferzan Özpetek's *La finestra di fronte* (*Facing Windows*, 2003); Massimo Piesco and Giorgio Molteni's *Il servo ungherese* (*The Hungarian Servant*, 2004); Carlo Lizzani's *Hotel Meina* (2007); and made-for-television films by Fabrizio Costa, *Senza confini* (*Without Borders*, 2001); Alberto Negrin's *Perlasca: Un eroe italiano* (*Perlasca: An Italian Hero*, 2002); Leone Pompucci's *La fuga degli innocenti* (*The Flight of the Innocents*, 2004); and Pasquale Squitieri's *Il giorno della Shoah* (*The Day of the Shoah*, 2009).

This outpouring of films on fascist anti-Semitism and the Final Solution did not occur in a vacuum, however. Such a shift in production is a sign of what Fabio Girelli-Carasi and Giacomo Lichtner have greeted as the belated emergence of a Jewish discourse in the Italy of today.[8] At the institutional level, this recent public impulse to memorialise the plight of Italian Jewry has taken several conspicuous forms, including legislation approved in 2000 to establish 'Il Giorno della

With the emergence of two high-profile filmic representations of the Holocaust in 1997 – Benigni's *La vita è bella*, illustrated here; and Rosi's *La tregua* – Italian cinema signals a shift from the 'weak memory' of the first five postwar decades, to the 'recovered memory' of our contemporary cultural moment

Memoria' every year on 27 January, the day of the liberation of Auschwitz; and a law passed in 2003 mandating the foundation of a Museo Nazionale della Shoah in Ferrara.

How do we account for this surge of interest in the Holocoaust after so many years of relative silence? Using Fabio Girelli-Carasi's terms, why would a Jewish discourse arise at this particular historical juncture? The most obvious answer is generational. With the passing of those who directly lived the experience, either as survivors, perpetrators or bystanders, we are fast approaching the era of what could be called, at best 'second-hand' memory, and hence the urgent need to bear witness and to transmit the testimony to future generations. But another factor not to be discounted is the convergence of this testimonial impulse with the end of the Cold War, whose ideological polarisation had prevented any serious engagement with Holocaust history. Left–Right oppositional thought during the Cold War years had created a stranglehold on the historiography of World War II, making it impossible to revisit the Italian Jewish plight with any degree of critical distance. It should come as no surprise that the Right would have been be loathe to resurrect one of fascism's most deplorable chapters, but the Left's stake in avoiding the issues of the Racial Laws, and the subsequent genocidal campaign is less obvious. Such avoidance may have stemmed from to the need to protect a certain understanding of World War II history that privileged anti-fascism as the foundation on which the progressive movement of postwar Italian politics based its claim to legitimacy. Any emplotment of the wartime past that threatened the resistance master narrative – and the plight of Italian Jewry certainly qualifies as such a threat – would have to be overlooked in order to maintain the prestige and authority of the foundational account. With the fall of

the Berlin Wall in 1989, the collapse of the Soviet Union in l991 and the subsequent demise of the Italian Communist Party, the Left–Right stranglehold on past historiography could relax and the other stories, or indeed, the stories of 'the other', could at last be told. In terms of the Shoah, it was as if the floodgates had finally been opened, and the belated work of confronting this anguished episode in Italian national history could finally begin. Significantly, historian Niccolò Zapponi connects this development to what he calls a 'global change in culture' motivated by

> the ever more widespread drive toward rethinking the 'fascist' event from the *Jewish* point of view, towards closing a period during which it has been remembered mainly from the point of view of militant anti-fascism. A thorough examination of this question would entail establishing in what way, during the past two decades (approximately), the whole of the Western world has rethought its identity with respect to the Nazi massacres.[9]

In this important formulation, Zapponi acknowledges the need for a comparative and indeed international approach to the question – an approach which exceeds the scope of my current, narrowly focused essay, but whose challenge, it is to be hoped, will be taken up by other scholars in global dimensions.

Another important factor in explaining the current impulse to revisit the plight of the Jews under fascist and Nazi rule has been the influx of Third World immigrants, prompting Italians to reconsider their relationships to the 'other in our midst' and acknowledge the extremes to which intolerance may lead. A striking example of the link between the plight of racial minorities in contemporary Italy, and that of the Jews under the Nazi-fascist regime, may be found in Ettore Scola's short fiction film, '43–'97 (43–97, 1997). Encoded in the film's title is its dual temporal focus, starting with the Nazi evacuation of the Roman ghetto on 16 October 1943, and ending with the persecution of Third World immigrants to Italy in the late 1990s. The passage of time between the film's two terminal years is marked by a montage of film clips, from World War II newsreels, to *Roma città aperta*, De Sica's *Ladri di biciclette*, Mario Monicelli's *I soliti ignoti*, Dino Risi's *Il sorpasso*, Luchino Visconti's *Il gattopardo*, Federico Fellini's *Amarcord*, Scola's own *Una giornata particolare* (*A Special Day*, 1977), Massimo Troisi's *Ricomincio da tre* (*I'm Starting from Three*, 1981), Giuseppe Tornatore's *Nuovo Cinema Paradiso*, Nanni Moretti's *Palombella rossa* (*Red Lob*, 1989), Gianni Amelio's *Ladri di bambini* and Francesco Rosi's *La tregua*. This montage is shown on the screen in the movie theatre *within* the film, for it is here that a young escapee from the ghetto round-up in 1943 seeks refuge from his Nazi persecutors. At the end of the montage, the lights go up to reveal that in place of the boy escapee of 1943, there sits a white-haired gentleman who cleans his glasses. We have transitioned to colour, but there is an acoustic throwback to the 1940s segment in the sound of footsteps echoing on the cobblestones and the return of the hurried piano music that had accompanied the Nazi chase. At this point, an adolescent of African descent runs panting into the theatre and sits one row behind our aged protagonist. Recognising his younger self in this desperate fugitive, the Jewish gentleman bestows upon him a knowing smile – one of understanding and consolation. And now, both of them sink down into their seats as the lights go down and the credits for Scola's film scroll down the screen-within-the-screen.

Guiding Scola's selection of films to be included in this montage is a variety of factors, including the most obvious one of personal taste. Among the clips are a series of ground-breaking films within the history of postwar Italian cinema, as well as those which represent an array of genres – neorealism, *commedia all'italiana*, *cinema politico* – and auteurs. Many of the clips include child protagonists, and most foreground both their own spectacular nature, and internalised responses to their uses of cinematic spectacle.

At its most obvious, '43–'97 is about the link between the past and the present of racial intolerance, about the urgent need to revisit Holocaust history now, lest the logic of persecution visit itself upon the new Italian 'other' of Third World immigrants. As Scola

wrote concerning the discovery 'that one is considered "different" by birth and by race. It happened in the past to Jews and blacks and today it is happening to immigrants and *extracomunitari* [those outside the European Union.]'[10] On the metacinematic level, the film is a complex study of the relationship between off-screen historical context and on-screen cinematic representation – in other words, the film asks us what it means to seek sanctuary in a movie theatre. Cynically understood, such a turning away from the cobblestone streets suggests that cinema is a place of denial, escape or withdrawal from the arena of necessary historical action. But the relationship that Scola posits between the montage on the screen-within-the-screen and the frame story of the two minority fugitives from persecution is far more complex and nuanced. By embedding a panorama of Italian film chronicle within a narrative of searing historical allusiveness, Scola is confronting one of the largest and most abstract of theoretical issues: the connection between the film medium and its referent in the life of the country or, in specifically semiotic terms, he is exploring the link between cinematic signifier and historic signified. In the Italian case, Scola has always been a proponent of the particularly close ties between film and national history. 'The specificity of Italian cinema', he claimed in a 2004 interview, 'as opposed to the cinemas of France or Germany, is that it is so thoroughly intertwined with reality that it scans *la vicenda Italia* [the Italian case]. Our cinema has always been social chronicle.'[11]

Scola's montage of clips from 1943–97 forms a kind of para-history – one which at every point asks us to question the way in which what is happening outside the theatre is mirrored, critiqued, transformed, transcended, overlooked and sanitised on screen. Perhaps more than a para-history, the montage creates a simulacrum of history – each clip has the power to conjure up and signify the moment of its making – *Roma città aperta* is equated with the struggles of the Roman Resistance, *Il sorpasso* is the Italy of 'Il boom economico', *Palombella rossa* heralds the waning of the Italian Left, and so forth. In his choice of clips, then, Scola has selected cinematic signifiers which not only represent, but have actually come to replace in the public mind, the historical and cultural signifieds that produced them. This blurring of the distinction between the cinematic medium and its external referents is made explicit in the confusion of levels between Scola's 'outer film' – the story of the Jewish escapee from the ghetto round-up – and the montage we see on the screen-within-the-screen. Such a collapsing of levels occurs when the closing credits for Scola's outer film are projected on the screen-within-the screen, so that the boundaries between outside and inside, container and contained, break down. The implications for us in the viewing audience are not hard to see. When the elderly gentleman turns around to acknowledge the young victim of persecution within his own audience, it is as if the film were turning to us and asking us to confront the social injustices in our midst.

In this way, the cinema's status as sanctuary can be defended against charges of escapist withdrawal from the cobblestone streets of the historical arena. It is the cinema's commitment to monitor, critique, and engage in the progress of *la vicenda Italia* that can provide the impetus to corrective action. The refuge offered by the movie theatre points to the ultimate power of the medium to intervene in the off-screen world, to bring about a condition of enlightenment and social desire which will render obsolete the very rescue operation that the film performs for the protagonists in the years 1943 and 1997.

It is significant that Scola's plea for the Utopian potential of cinema should pivot on the issue of Holocaust representation. By bracketing his short film with an allusion to the round-up of Roman Jewry on 16 October 1943 and Rosi's cinematic treatment of the Shoah in 1997, Scola foregrounds the process by which this repressed history has belatedly become the subject of cinematic representation. In his decision to frame the film with a Holocaust narrative, but to embed within it a micro-history of Italian cinema, Scola is constructing a 'representational parable' – an instructive tale about the medium's need to take on this repressed chapter of the past history of World War II. Such a strategy vindicates both the specificity and the greater applicability of the Italian Holocaust case. While '43–'97 asserts the uniqueness of this particular 'recovered memory', it also insists on the cinema's responsibility to challenge all such instances of public unwillingness to face disquieting truths, past or present.

If the recent spate of films emerging from Italy is any indication, then it seems that the 'weak' Holocaust memory of the last century has given way to something far stronger and more profound in the new millennium and that, as far as the Italian cinema is concerned, Primo Levi's nightmare about the unlistened-to story of the Shoah has finally been overcome.

NOTES

1. This essay represents a synthesis, and updating, of the material included in my book, *Italian Film in the Shadow of Auschwitz* (Toronto: University of Toronto Press, 2007). A version of the essay was published in Italian under the title 'Il cinema come specchio della memoria', in *Storia della Shoah in Italia* (Turin: UTET, 2010), pp. 419–33.
2. Niccolò Zapponi, 'Fascism in Italian Historiography, 1986–93: A Fading National Identity', *Journal of Contemporary History* no. 29 (October 1994), p. 565.
3. See Finn's review of Ettore Scola's *Concorrenza sleale* in *Cinemasessanta* no. 4 (March–April 2001), pp 21– 2.
4. Ibid., p. 22.
5. For this argument, I am deeply indebted to Liana Fargion Picciotta, who shared her insights with me in a conversation at the Centro di Documentazione Ebraica Contemporanea in Milan on 15 July 2004.
6. For a list of films produced in Italy on the plight of Jews during fascism and the Nazi occupation, see the Appendix to this essay. Synopses and interpretations of these films can be found in my book, *Italian Film in the Shadow of Auschwitz*.
7. For a more cautious view of the 'break-through' status of these two films, in comparison to the French case, see Giacomo Lichtner, *Film and the Shoah in France and Italy* (London: Vallentine Mitchell, 2008), p. 219.
8. See Fabio Girelli-Carasi, 'Italian-Jewish Memoirs and the Discourse of Identity', in Stanislao G. Pugliese (ed.), *The Most Ancient of Minorities* (Westport, CT: Greenwood Press, 2002), pp. 191–9; and Lichtner, *Film and the Shoah in France and Italy*, pp. 5–6.
9. Zapponi, 'Fascism in Italian Historiography', p. 550
10. Ettore Scola, *Concorrenza sleale* (Turin: Lindau, 2001), p. 5 (author's translation).
11. See the interview with Maria Pia Fusco, 'Scola: Uno specchio per i giovani', *La repubblica* (16 July 2004), p. 45 (author's translation).

FURTHER READING

Galluccio, Fabio, *I Lager in Italia: La memoria sepolta nei duecento luoghi di deportazione fascisti* (Civezzano: Non luoghi, 2003).

Girelli-Carasi, Fabio, 'Italian-Jewish Memoirs and the Discourse of Identity', in Stanislao G. Pugliese (ed.), *The Most Ancient of Minorities* (Westport, CT: Greenwood Press, 2002), pp. 191–9.

Insdorf, Annette, *Indelible Shadows: Film and the Holocaust* (Cambridge: Cambridge University Press, 2002).

Lichtner, Giacomo, *Film and the Shoah in France and Italy* (London: Vallentine Mitchell, 2008).

Marcus, Millicent, *After Fellini: National Cinema in the Postmodern Age* (Baltimore, MD: Johns Hopkins University Press, 2002).

——, *Italian Film in the Shadow of Auschwitz* (Toronto: University of Toronto Press, 2007).

Picchietti, Virginia, 'A Semiotics of Judaism: Representations of Judaism and the Jewish Experience in Italian Cinema, 1992–2004', *Italica* no. 83 (2006), pp. 563–82.

Zapponi, Niccolò, 'Fascism in Italian Historiography, 1986–93: A Fading National Identity', *Journal of Contemporary History* no. 29 (October 1994), pp. 547–68.

Zimmerman, Joshua (ed.), *Jews in Italy under Fascist and Nazi Rule 1922–1945* (New York: Cambridge University Press, 2005).

Zuccotti, Susan, *The Italians and the Holocaust: Persecution, Rescue, and Survival* (Lincoln: University of Nebraska Press, 1996).

APPENDIX
Weak Memory 1945–90

L'ebreo errante (*The Wandering Jew*, 1947) Goffredo Alessandrini

Il grido della terra (*The Cry of the Land*, 1948) Duilio Coletti

Il monastero di Santa Chiara (*The Monastery of St Clare*, 1949) Mario Segui

Dov'è la libertà? (*Where Is Freedom?*, 1952, one sequence) Roberto Rossellini

Tutti a casa (*Everybody Home*, 1960, two sequences) Luigi Comencini

Kapò (*Kapò*, 1960), Gillo Pontecorvo

L'oro di Roma (*The Gold of Rome*, 1961) Carlo Lizzani

Vaghe stelle dell'Orsa (*Sandra*, 1965) Luchino Visconti

Andremo in città (*We'll Go to the City*, 1966) Nelo Risi

Il giardino dei Finzi–Contini (*The Garden of the Finzi–Continis*, 1970) Vittorio De Sica

Diario di un italiano (*Diary of an Italian*, 1971) Sergio Capogna

Il portiere di notte (*The Night Porter*, 1974, genocide underplayed) Liliana Cavani

Pasqualino Settebellezze (*Seven Beauties*, 1976, genocide underplayed) Lina Wertmüller

La linea del fiume (*The Line of the River*, 1976) Aldo Scavarda

L'ebreo fascista (*The Fascist Jew*, 1980) Francesco Molé

Storia d'amore e d'amicizia (*Story of Love and Friendship*, 1982) Franco Rossi

La Storia (*History*, 1987) Luigi Comencini

Gli occhiali d'oro (*The Golden Spectacles*, 1987) Giuliano Montaldo

Jona che visse nella balena (*Jonah Who Lived in the Whale*, 1993) Roberto Faenza

18.000 giorni fa (*18,000 Days Ago*, 1994) Gabriella Gabrielli

Recovered Memory 1997–the present

La vita è bella (*Life Is Beautiful*, 1997) Roberto Benigni

La tregua (*The Truce*, 1997) Francesco Rosi

Canone inverso (*Making Love*, 2000) Ricky Tognazzi

Il cielo cade (*The Sky Is Falling*, 2000) Andrea and Antonio Frazzi

Concorrenza sleale (*Unfair Competition*, 2001) Ettore Scola

Senza confini (*Without Borders*, 2001) Fabrizio Costa

Perlasca: Un eroe italiano (*Perlasca: An Italian Hero*, 2002) Alberto Negrin

La finestra di fronte (*Facing Windows*, 2003) Ferzan Özpetek

Il servo ungherese (*The Hungarian Servant*, 2004) Massimo Piesco and Giorgio Molteni

La fuga degli innocenti (*The Flight of the Innocents*, 2004) Leone Pompucci

Hotel Meina (*Hotel Meina*, 2007) Carlo Lizzani

Il giorno della Shoah (*The Day of the Shoah*, 2009) Pasquale Squitieri

The *Cinepanettone**

Alan O'Leary

> Above all else, comedy is an invitation to belong.
> Andy Medhurst[1]

The *cinepanettoni* ('film-Christmas-cakes') are a series of farcical Italian comedies, one or two of which were released annually in time for the Christmas holidays (see Appendix). The number of Italians who attended the annual *cinepanettone* as part of their ritual celebrations of the season has meant that the films were regularly among the most popular of the year. The name, *cinepanettone*, is of course a derogatory one, and suggests the films are a matter of mere consumption, a cultural over-indulgence when the spectator is already full, akin to the slice of *panettone* ingested after a substantial Christmas meal.[2] The *filone* (the Italian term for a cycle of similar films) remains almost unstudied, even as it and its audiences are regularly deplored. One critic writes of the *cinepanettone* as 'an embarrassing Italian phenomenon [that] causes indignation at its every appearance to a good part of society and which has become synonymous with superficiality, with banality, with vulgarity'.[3] Others speak of 'a product which captures thousands (or better, millions) of spectators who never go to the cinema except for once a year in order to savour their *cinepanettone*'. The same writers continue: 'Stupefied by the alimentary and sentimental excesses of the Christmas period the consumer absorbs more readily.'[4] Notwithstanding this critical disdain, the lack of attention to the *filone* is remarkable given its success, which reached a peak in the first decade of the new century.

My purpose here is to give an account of the *cinepanettone*, and to claim for it the status of 'Italian national cinema'. To argue as much is to challenge the conventional idea that Italian national cinema is comprised of realist and auteurist works that have been appreciated outside Italy itself. It is also to refuse the idea

that Italian national cinema is best conceived of as a kind of diplomatic project intended to represent the 'best' of the country's cinematic culture at an international level. Given the contested quality and status of the *filone*, it may seem a paradoxical gesture, but it is an essential one, to place the *cinepanettone* not at the margins but at the centre of discourse about Italian cinema.

ITALIAN NATIONAL CINEMA

National cultures have traditionally served as a way of demarcating academic areas of interest and, at least in the Anglophone academy, film studies have taken a foothold in departments of modern languages. Italianist cinema scholars therefore have a stake in retaining the national as a category of description, especially as the status of cinema studies was initially precarious within what were traditionally schools of literature, linguistics and history.[5] It was institutionally imperative to assert a canon of individual film texts of undoubted aesthetic or ethical appeal, a canon (by analogy with the received litany of literary greats) that had 'made Italy' – indeed, that had 'made Italians'. In a context such as this, the study of genre cinema was almost unthinkable, and what emerged was a teaching and research syllabus that ignored most of the 'popular' in the sense of commercially successful within Italy itself. Italian cinema came to mean neorealism and the great auteurs, and the legacy of this approach is still with us today.

This legacy manifests itself in scholarship that defines its role in edifying and paternalistic terms, and that deals exclusively with the Italian cinema (however defined) that the scholars believe should be known and admired rather than the range of films that have actually been produced and watched. This is often accompanied by a reflectionist model which sees a putative 'best' cinema as the 'mirror' of the Italian nation. In the Anglophone academy, this approach takes the form of a diplomatic project to celebrate those texts that resound the glory of Italy, and the work of many writers on Italian film is conceived precisely in terms of proselytising for an Italian national culture.

Such a nationalistic cinema history has come in for criticism from within Italian cinema studies itself, from political and other perspectives. While areas of the discipline remain conservative, some have made the move from an essentialising model, in which the national cinema is seen as a direct reflection or expression of the national culture, to a constructivist model, in which the cinema is seen to be one of the means through which the 'imagined community' of the nation is posited and pictured. Some refuse the national cinema paradigm altogether, whether because it elides cultural discontinuities and the experience of, say, Italy's minorities and incoming migrants, or because cinema is itself a transnational phenomenon, drawing themes, technologies, personnel and funding from across borders, and with designs on an international market.

I deploy the concept of national cinema here for strategic reasons, in order to put the experience and taste of a despised popular audience at the centre of our concerns. Some have argued that comedy ought to be considered as Italy's quintessential national mode, based both on its commercial popularity and on its ability to 'touch on themes very close and particular to the culture'.[6] Although I necessarily devote much of my space here to a descriptive account of the *cinepanettoni*, I believe we should give equal attention to the context of their consumption as to the content of the films. In other words, the *cinepanettone* can be argued to be Italy's national cinema because of its consumption within Italy itself and its adoption as part of annual holiday ritual, something demonstrated by the longevity and scale of its success within Italy itself. The divisive character of the films' success is, ironically, another reason we can speak of them as Italian national cinema: the fact that they are as deplored as they are enjoyed suggests the *cinepanettoni* are engaged in a contested subtending of national identity.

THE *CINEPANETTONE*

The word *cinepanettone* itself seems to have been coined in the early 2000s as a journalistic term to refer to the variation of the 'film di Natale' (Christmas film) formula created by director Neri Parenti with his young co-scriptwriters Fausto Brizzi and Marco Martani, generational comedies featuring diverse forms of

humour to appeal to a wide audience. Most of the *cinepanettoni* since 2000 are set in foreign (for Italians) locations and have titles with the form *Natale+preposition+location*, even if the 'Christmas' aspect has often been assumed rather than elaborated, and they tend frankly to reveal that they were shot in late summer and early autumn. The films usually feature a parallel (and sometimes tripled) plot, centred, until 2005's *Natale a Miami* (*Christmas in Miami* by Neri Parenti), around the comic actors Massimo Boldi and Christian De Sica, opposing regional (Milan and Rome, respectively), physical and ideological types. Often the most entertaining and anticipated moments in the films are those in which the Boldi and De Sica characters finally meet, typically in a confined space like a changing room or shower, and engage in a pseudo-formal and heavily accented exchange of dialogue, sometimes followed with a shared mini-adventure (in *Natale a Miami*, for example, they evade a serial killer straight from Central Casting; in Parenti's *Natale sul Nilo* [*Christmas on the Nile*, 2002], they get stranded in the desert and risk decapitation by an implausible Bedouin).

Boldi, who defected from producer Filmauro to produce a rival and less successful series of films, has been a loss to the *filone* since 2006: his corpulence allowed him to exemplify the 'grotesque body' like that described by Bakhtin in his work on Rabelais and carnival:

> The stress is laid on those parts of the body that are open to the outside world, that is, the parts through which the world enters the body or emerges from it, or through which the body itself goes out to meet the world. This means that the emphasis is on the apertures or the convexities, or on various ramifications and offshoots: the open mouth, the genital organs, the breasts, the phallus, the potbelly, the nose.[7]

Massimo Boldi's 'grotesque body' in *A Natale mi sposo* (*I'm Getting Married at Christmas*, 2010)

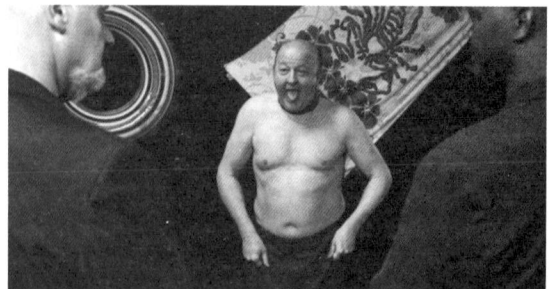

Gestural energy: Christian De Sica in *Natale a Beverly Hills* (*Christmas in Beverly Hills*, 2009)

One of the paradoxes of the films' reception is that they are associated with the recruitment of the starlet of the day from television and advertising (these have included Anna Falchi, Elisabetta Canalis, Michelle Hunziker and Belén Rodríguez) and with the exploitation of the appeal of her body. Consequently, the films are frequently deplored for their sexism; but the body most often shown nude in the films is Boldi's, which – flabby, sweaty, sometimes incontinent – is the opposite of the toned and tanned perfection of the starlet physique and a parodic counterpart to it.

Boldi's body is also opposed to that of his erstwhile partner Christian De Sica. The latter typically performs a gestural and mobile physicality that relies on precision of timing and explosive energy; a physicality that is at once hypermasculine and verging on camp, and is careless of social convention. Such a persona has its roots in the theatrical farce and in the *commedia dell'arte*, a form, like the *cinepanettone*, founded on regional stereotypes and variations on stock scenarios. Aficionados of the *cinepanettone* regret the demise of the Boldi–De Sica odd couple, seen at its greatest commercial success in 2002, when *Natale sul Nilo* took well over 28 million euros at the Italian box office. Recent entries have done less well: Parenti's *Natale in Sud Africa* (*Christmas in South Africa*, 2010) accrued a relatively disappointing (though still substantial in Italian terms) 18.5 million euros, and the producers decided, perhaps unwisely, to return to an older formula for the 2011 entry, Parenti's *Vacanze di Natale a Cortina* (*Christmas Vacation in Cortina*), which reprises the Italian mountain location and ensemble structure of Carlo Vanzina's *Vacanze di Natale* (*Christmas Vacation*, 1983) and earned 11.7 million euros.

If the term *cinepanettone* was originally coined to refer to the films of the 2000s, the category has nonetheless come to include a dozen more films released for or before Christmas. It is applied retrospectively to the aforementioned *Vacanze di Natale*, an ensemble comedy, directed by Carlo Vanzina and written by him with his brother Enrico, set over Christmas and New Year in the exclusive ski resort of Cortina d'Ampezzo. This inaugural film of the *filone* is closely modelled on *Vacanze d'inverno* (*Winter Vacation*), a 1959 film of social mores and class awkwardness directed by Camillo Mastrocinque and starring Alberto Sordi and Vittorio De Sica (father to Christian); as such it demonstrates that the *cinepanettone* has roots deep in the Italian cinema tradition. *Vacanze di Natale* is also a winter and contemporary version of another ensemble piece, *Sapore di mare* (*Time for Loving*), released in February of the same year, again by the Vanzina brothers and featuring an almost identical cast to their Christmas film. *Sapore di mare*, a summer beach comedy of manners and desires set in a generic early 1960s, is itself a tribute to Italian *commedie balneari* (seaside comedies) of those years, and employs a jukebox-compiled soundtrack of period songs.[8] *Vacanze di Natale*, too, employs a compiled soundtrack, this time of no fewer than seventeen chart songs (Italian and otherwise) from recent months, and these are perceived by fans to be essential to the impact of the film.[9] (Recent chart hits continue to be a feature of the *cinepanettone*, though fewer are used because of the prohibitive cost of rights.) After a hiatus, *Vacanze di Natale* generated several follow-ups or variations: *Vacanze di Natale '90* (*Christmas Vacation '90*, 1990), *Vacanze di Natale '91* (*Christmas Vacation '91*, 1991), both directed by Enrico Oldoini; Parenti's *Vacanze di Natale '95* (*Christmas Vacation '95*, 1995), Carlo Vanzina's *Vacanze di Natale 2000* (*Christmas Vacation 2000*, 1999), and, as mentioned above, *Vacanze di Natale a Cortina*, the most recent release at the time of writing.[10]

The *Natale+preposition+location* films of Neri Parenti and the variations on *Vacanze di Natale* do not exhaust the *filone* of the *cinepanettone*. Another pair within the series accentuates the satire of male homosociality and behaviour (always a theme): *Paparazzi* (*Paparazzi*, 1998) and *Bodyguards – Guardie del corpo* (*Body Guards*, 2000),

Michelle Hunziker and Fabio De Luigi and a shocking interruption in *Natale in crociera* (2007)

directed by Neri Parenti, are episodic films which focus on 'topical' professions as a means to allow a group of male protagonists to interact with each other, often in a slapstick idiom, while permitting the display of celebrity faces and bodies both female and male. The episodic construction of these two films also relates *Paparazzi* and *Bodyguards* to the portmanteau cinepanettoni *Anni 90* (*The Nineties*, 1992) and *Anni 90 – Parte II* (*The Nineties: Part 2*, 1993), both directed by Enrico Oldoini and concerned with a satire of contemporary mores filtered through allusions to media culture (one episode alludes to adverts concerned with AIDS and safe sexual practice).

A further pair of films is comprised of the metacinematic exercises undertaken by the fraternal partnership of Carlo and Enrico Vanzina in *A spasso nel tempo* (*Adrift in Time*, 1996) and *A spasso nel tempo l'avventura continua* (*Adrift in Time: The Adventure Continues*, 1997), farcical elaborations of the *Back to the Future* films (1985, 1989, 1990) which riff on schoolbook history and on film and television culture. The Vanzinas' *S.P.Q.R. 2000 e ½ anni fa* (*S. P. Q. R.: 2,000 and a Half Years Ago*, 1994) is also a metacinematic exercise replete with allusions to films like *Spartacus* and the various Ben-Hurs. The film is a satire of political corruption and the 'Mani pulite' (Clean Hands) investigations into the kickback system in public life relocated to the classical Roman period.

What links all these films, and what makes them *cinepanettoni*, are primarily the release date (they are marketed as 'il vostro film di Natale', 'your Christmas film'); the presence of certain actors (especially Boldi and De Sica, alone or apart); and the register of farcical comedy. It is important to distinguish the different strains within the broader cycle because a common and inaccurate complaint about the *cinepanettoni* is that they are 'sempre uguali' (always the same). It is true that many will reprise popular gags and situations from earlier films, and certain stereotypes, themes (social

class, infidelity, the instability of gender categories and sexualities) or sources of humour (dialect and *doubles entendres*, sexual embarrassment) will recur. It is likewise true that the *cinepanettone* is a conservative genre in formal and, in certain respects, in ideological terms. But the *cinepanettoni* vary, both between and *within* the films: they are also hybrid texts which may feature, for example, thriller and travelogue elements in order to appeal to a variegated public.

One striking example is a scene from Parenti's *Natale in crociera* (*Christmas on a Cruise*, 2007) with Fabio De Luigi and Michelle Hunziker as the stock figures of *inetto* (bungling man) and spirited blonde. Having narrowly escaped death when their car has plunged over a cliff somewhere in the Caribbean, they reach a bar where they intend to telephone for help. Instead they witness the aftermath of a bloody shootout staged with an efficiency that is unexpected and shocking in this comic context.

The interruption by another genre of the light-hearted story indicates the internal differentiation of the audience for the film in the theatre itself. In other words, different aspects of the films are addressed to different groups in the cinema audience, an audience whose ages might range from five to ninety-five and which will be composed of all classes and genders. Scriptwriter Marco Martani has described how even the comedy is carefully calibrated in the films to appeal to distinct groups,[11] so that (in theory at least) laughter is sequentially generated from each segment of the audience, and the contagious effect in the context of cinema viewing is such that the laughter will tend to become universal and continuous. This phenomenon of multiple address leads to difficulty in the critical assessment of the *filone* because the evaluative criteria employed are often inappropriate, based on an idea of the text as a coherent and unitary object, whereas the *cinepanettone* is a centrifugal form intended for the fluctuating attention of its diverse publics.

CULTURAL EMBARRASSMENT

The publics for the *cinepanettone* may be diverse, but in critical discourse they are regularly homogenised and seen as a cultural embarrassment, as in the examples quoted at the beginning of this chapter. This is confirmed by responses to an online questionnaire that I have designed and circulated about the *cinepanettone*,[12] in which respondents were asked if they believed there was a typical spectator for the *cinepanettone* (roughly half believed there was) and, if so, to provide a description of that person. Judging by the tone of the responses, a translated sample of which I provide below, take-up has been skewed to those with a low opinion of the *filone*. The expression 'l'italiano medio' (the average Italian) occurs frequently, sometimes linked to social class or status:

- An average Italian of low intelligence and irony.
- The average Italian, that is, low/average culture.

The *cinepanettone* has often been seen as, at once, symptom and cause of the success of Silvio Berlusconi and the Italian Right in the past two decades. Descriptions of the spectator make this link and also assert his gender.

- Typical Berlusconi type.
- The boors, the *nouveaux riches* and the Berlusconi types.
- The ignorant Italian, the stupid Italian and the right-wing Italian (more than 50 per cent).
- A person without culture, who doesn't read and doesn't keep himself informed, doesn't go to the cinema regularly and doesn't know the history of cinema, probably a supporter of the centre Right, bigoted and tasteless and with an extremely short attention span and low capacity for concentration.
- Male chauvinist and vulgar.
- A pig of a man who likes to see tits and ass all over the place [...] and who amuses himself with vulgarities and phrases in dialect and who masturbates while he thinks about the latest slag who has acted in the film.

It appears unlikely, given the success of the *cinepanettone* and its address to a variegated audience that includes families and persons of all ages and both sexes, that its spectator can be so confidently characterised or gendered. The *cinepanettone*, it seems, represents not only an aesthetic problem, but also a cultural one: it is the wrong sort of film watched by the wrong sort of spectator. Perhaps such material as

quoted above is to be expected in the anonymous responses to an online questionnaire, but the sentiments expressed are really not so far from those of authoritative commentators. Speaking retrospectively of the 1980s, the decade in which the *cinepanettone* was born, the great historian of Italian cinema Gian Piero Brunetta writes as follows:

> In fact, the cinema of the Vanzinas, of Neri Parenti, of Enrico Oldoini, can be adduced as the most salient emblem of a decade which, at least in its presiding images, was characterised by a need to laugh, a renunciation of thought, a celebration of appearance; by cynicism and rampant ambition, by a considerable lowering of the quotient of comic intelligence, by a conviction of the perfect permeability between cinema and television.[13]

Note the slippage here between the historian's low view of the quality of the films and his low view of the quality of their audience, possessed of a heedless 'need to laugh', guilty of a 'renunciation of thought'. In referring to the cinema of the Vanzinas, Neri Parenti and Enrico Oldoini, Brunetta is, of course, taking about the three directors most associated with the *cinepanettone*, and his characterisation of the audience for the *filone* as uncritical and thoughtless has become ubiquitous among those in possession of, or aspiring to, cultural capital.

In order to challenge, as I believe we must, the dismissive consensus on the *cinepanettone* and its audiences, I would like to return to Bakhtin's notion of the carnivalesque, already mentioned above. In Bakhtin's celebratory account, carnival was a period in which the whole community participated in the inversion of hierarchies and the suspension of normal codes of behaviour, something which involved the indulgence of appetites and all the pleasures and needs of the body. The *cinepanettone* evidently lends itself to analysis in carnivalesque terms, associated as it is with a festive suspension of quotidian norms and priorities. The intuition of the anonymous critic who coined the term *cinepanettone* to indicate that the films are part of the excess and over-indulgence of the Christmas period was fundamentally sound: the publics for the *cinepanettone* are diverse, but they are united in a national ritual of eating, drinking and going to the cinema, where they laugh along with (participate in) 'a popular cultural discourse set in opposition to official languages of morality and control':[14] precisely the kind of languages spoken by the authoritative critics and respondents to the questionnaire, above.

These same critics and respondents might object that, far from providing a transgressive escape from the norms and regulation of contemporary Italian society, the *cinepanettone* is a celebration of the worst excesses of Italian political and mediatic culture, as exemplified in the carnivalesque antics of the paradigmatic jester king, former Prime Minister Silvio Berlusconi. On this reading, the *cinepanettone* is simply the unguarded version of the demagogy and ideology of a grotesque ruling class: a transgression – in its supposed sexism, xenophobia and homophobia – only of politeness, and a validation of prejudice and oppression rather than their subversion. It has become, in other words, the 'official' feast of the ruling order which, like the ecclesiastic, feudal or state feasts to which Bakhtin saw carnival as being opposed, '[sanctions] the existing order of things and [reinforces] it'.[15]

Bakhtin himself offers a possible answer to this objection. He argues that carnival and other 'forms of protocol and ritual based on laughter' offered an 'extrapolitical' dimension: 'They belong to an entirely different sphere.'[16] Such an assertion goes against academic doctrine: as undergraduates we are already taught that no form of representation escapes ideology and imbrication with power; but this truism is vapid if it stops us from accounting for the pleasures offered by a form. And the pleasurable politics of the *cinepanettone* are similar to those identified by Medhurst in his defence of the reactionary content of some English stand-up comedy: 'a politics of defence not attack, of refusal not uprising, of embracing your own, of consolidation against condescension'.[17] That is to say, in its carnivalesque celebration of socially inappropriate behaviour and values, the *cinepanettone* also offers, precisely, a sense of community, even of home. Laughing, writes Medhurst, you *feel at home*:

> It's all about belonging, and the comic text or practitioner can call on a variety of devices in proffering the invitation. Belonging is why most television comedies have laugh tracks, why narrative film comedies will fade or cut or leave visual pauses when they think a great line has just been delivered and thereby reassure the audience that this is the right time to laugh, why stand-up comedians are filmed in theatres or studios with audiences present and why there are frequent cuts away from the comic to the convulsed consumers, why there are few more

> rapturous communal experiences than being in an audience rocking and hooting at the same gag, and why there are fewer finer pleasures in life than a group of old friends remembering and cementing their bonds through helpless, heedless laughter.[18]

The ritual consumption of the *cinepanettone* perhaps offers precisely this: a feeling of home, as the spectator enjoys the antics of his or her fellow Italians abroad. The *cinepanettone* constitutes Italian national cinema because of its consumption almost exclusively within Italy itself and its adoption as part of annual holiday ritual, something demonstrated by the longevity and scale of its intranational success. That success has faded, but the *cinepanettone* remains a perfect illustration of the process, constructive and contested, of imagining the national community. For many, the *cinepanettoni* are a shared celebration, an assertion of community; for others, of course, the very idea these films could speak of or for 'us' is appalling. But the *cinepanettone* has been the Italian national comic genre *par excellence*.

APPENDIX
The *Cinepanettoni*

The entries have the year of release, title, director, Italian production companies and, where appropriate, the presence of Massimo Boldi (MB) and/or Christian De Sica (CDS), the two actors most closely associated with the *cinepanettone*. Titles have been translated where they have not already been in the text.

1983   *Vacanze di Natale*. Carlo Vanzina. Filmauro. (CDS)
1984   *Vacanze in America* (*Vacation in America*). Carlo Vanzina. C. G. [Cecchi Gori] Silver Film. (CDS)
1990   *Vacanze di Natale '90*. Enrico Oldoini. Filmauro. (MB/CDS)
1991   *Vacanze di Natale '91*. Enrico Oldoini. Filmauro. (MB/CDS)
1992   *Anni 90*. Enrico Oldoini. Filmauro. (MB/CDS)
1993   *Anni 90 – Parte II*. Enrico Oldoini. Filmauro. (MB/CDS)
1994   *S.P.Q.R. 2000 e ½ anni fa*. Carlo Vanzina. Filmauro. (MB/CDS)
1995   *Vacanze di Natale '95*. Neri Parenti. Filmauro. (MB/CDS)
1996   *A spasso nel tempo*. Carlo Vanzina. Filmauro. (MB/CDS)
1997   *A spasso nel tempo l'avventura continua*. Carlo Vanzina. Filmauro. (MB/CDS)
1998   *Paparazzi*. Neri Parenti. Filmauro. (MB/CDS)
1999   *Vacanze di Natale 2000*. Carlo Vanzina. Filmauro. (MB/CDS)

2000 *Bodyguards – Guardie del corpo*. Neri Parenti. Filmauro. (MB/CDS)

2001 *Merry Christmas*. Neri Parenti. Filmauro. (MB/CDS)

2002 *Natale sul Nilo*. Neri Parenti. Filmauro. (MB/CDS)

2003 *Natale in India (Christmas in India)*. Neri Parenti. Filmauro. (MB/CDS)

2004 *Christmas in Love*. Neri Parenti. Filmauro. (MB/CDS)

2005 *Natale a Miami*. Neri Parenti. Filmauro. (MB/CDS)

2006 *Natale a New York (Christmas in New York)*. Neri Parenti. Filmauro. (CDS)

2006 *Olè*. Carlo Vanzina. Medusa. (MB)

2007 *Natale in crociera*. Neri Parenti. Filmauro. (CDS)

2007 *Matrimonio alle Bahamas (Wedding in the Bahamas)*. Claudio Risi. Mari Film/Medusa. (MB)

2008 *Natale a Rio (Christmas in Rio)*. Neri Parenti. Filmauro. (CDS)

2008 *La fidanzata di papà (Daddy's Fiancée)*. Enrico Oldoini. Mari Film/Medusa. (MB)

2009 *Natale a Beverly Hills*. Neri Parenti. Filmauro. (CDS)

2010 *Natale in Sud Africa*. Neri Parenti. Filmauro. (CDS)

2010 *A Natale mi sposo (I'm Getting Married at Christmas)*. Paolo Costella. Mari Film/Medusa. (MB)

2011 *Vacanze di Natale a Cortina*. Neri Parenti. Filmauro. (CDS)

[2011 *Matrimonio a Parigi (Wedding in Paris)*. Claudio Risi. Mari Film/Medusa. (MB)]

The Boldi films of 2007, 2008 and 2010 were released in November to avoid competition with the Filmauro *cinepanettone*, released in mid-December. The last entry is in brackets because it was released in October and so cannot be considered a *cinepanettone*, even if it reprises elements and actors from previous films and despite the presence of its producer/star Massimo Boldi.

NOTES

*   My thanks to Catherine O'Rawe for reading a draft of this chapter and for allowing me to use some material we have worked on together.

1. Andy Medhurst, *A National Joke: Popular Comedy and English Cultural Identities* (New York: Routledge, 2007), p. 19.

2. The *panettone* is a sweet seasonal desert found all over Italy but identified traditionally with the city of Milan and containing candied fruit and raisins; it is often served with sweet sparkling wine.

3. Giorgio Simonelli, *Cinema a Natale: da Renoir ai Vanzina* (Novara: Interlinea, 2008), p. 185 (author's translation).

4. Gianluigi Negri and Robert S. Tanzi, *Natale al cinema: da 'La vita è meravigliosa' a 'A Christmas Carol'* (Alessandria: Falsopiano, 2009), pp. 190, 191 (author's translation).

5. Millicent Marcus, 'A Coming-of-Age Story: Some Thoughts on the Rise of Italian Film Studies in the United States', *Thinking Italian Film*, special edition of *Italian Studies* vol. 63 no. 2 (2008), pp. 266–9 (p. 267).

6. Francesco Casetti and Severino Salvemini, *È tutto un altro film: più coraggio e più idee per il cinema italiano* (Milan: Egea, 2007), p. 25 (author's translation).

7. Mikhail Bakhtin, *Rabelais and His World* (Bloomington: Indiana University Press, 1984), p. 26.

8. 'Sapore di mare' is the title of a sensual beach song, not in the film, by Gino Paoli from 1963.

9. See the testimony on fan website, available at http://www.vacanzedinatale.it/vdn2.htm; accessed 6 March 2012. Click on 'Il film' and then 'Presentazione'.

10. The production company Filmauro has announced a rethink of its production strategies and declared the 2012 entry to be the last of its *cinepanettoni*. See the ANSA report available at http://tinyurl.com/6raynp2; accessed 29 August 2011.

11. Interview with author and Luca Peretti of Yale University.

12. The Italian-language questionnaire will have closed by the time of publication but was available at https://www.survey.leeds.ac.uk/cinepanettone/. Of the 297 respondents, 268, at the time of writing, have identified themselves as Italian.

13. Gian Piero Brunetta, *Il cinema italiano da 'La dolce vita' a 'Centochiodi'* (Rome: Laterza, 2007), p. 608.

14. I borrow here the carnivalesque terms of Medhurst's description of English music-hall comedy in *A National Joke*, p. 68.

15. Bakhtin, *Rabelais and His World*, p. 9.

16. Ibid., pp. 5, 6, 7.

17. Medhurst, *A National Joke*, p. 69.

18. Ibid., p. 20.

32 Stars and Masculinity in Contemporary Italian Cinema

Catherine O'Rawe

Male stars have received surprisingly little critical attention in Italian film studies: while much work has been done on the female stars of postwar Italy (the so-called *maggiorate fisiche*) and their relation to changing conceptions of national identity, male stars have, as yet, been rather neglected.[1] Yet the last decade has seen a flourishing of male stars in significant film roles, whereas the position of female stars in Italy remains less certain. In 2005, Michele Placido's *Romanzo criminale* showcased a new generation of stars (Kim Rossi Stuart, Riccardo Scamarcio, Pierfrancesco Favino, Elio Germano, Claudio Santamaria) along with the more established Stefano Accorsi. Although most of the above-named had been working steadily for years prior to *Romanzo criminale*, the ensemble nature of that film was instrumental in foregrounding many of the features of current mainstream Italian cinema production: its emphasis on homosocial bonding, its turning towards the past, particularly the contested years of the *anni di piombo*, and its use of strong male performers, often working together repeatedly.

Some of the genres that make up the mainstream of Italian cinema (the teen film, the popular comedy, the male melodrama, and the films of 'middlebrow *impegno*' that revisit the recent Italian past) interact interestingly with the star personae and performance styles of the actors who dominate these genres. On-screen configurations of masculinity might also, importantly, relate to those off screen, bearing in mind how, as Peberdy states: 'onscreen performances [...] not only reflect the cultural moment in which they are situated but also feed back into the discourse, becoming part of the mediated process through which understandings of gendered identity are situated'.[2] I will first take as a case study the star image and performance style of former teen heartthrob turned serious actor Riccardo Scamarcio, before looking more generally at the landscape of male stardom in contemporary Italian cinema, and examining the recurring representation of the homosocial bond and male melodrama across genres as varied as popular comedy and middlebrow *impegno*.

Kim Rossi Stuart, Claudio Santamaria and Pierfrancesco Favino in *Romanzo criminale* (2005)

RICCARDO SCAMARCIO AND THE TEEN FILM

The renaissance since the mid-2000s of popular Italian comedy has had as one of its most popular *filoni* the teen comedy, of which the initial figurehead was undoubtedly Riccardo Scamarcio.[3] He shot to stardom in adaptations of two Federico Moccia novels, Luca Lucini's *Tre metri sopra il cielo* (*Three Steps over Heaven*, 2004) and Luis Prieto's *Ho voglia di te* (*I Want You*, 2007), films that addressed the cult audiences of those novels as well as bringing in a more mainstream audience. Scamarcio's role as the troubled rebel Step involves a brooding machismo that belies an emotionality that manifests itself around the women in his life and his best friend. The films have received little critical attention, and the few discussions of Scamarcio that have taken place have focused on his star image and on the heartthrob status the films accorded him. However, in terms of Scamarcio's performance, and the film's framing of him, there is much of interest, as both films present us with a 'star introduction': a sequence with no dialogue, an emphasis on the physicality of Step, and which finished with an impenetrable gaze by him into the camera, demonstrating the importance of his eyes and of the star close-up, both in securing Scamarcio's appeal and in determining his acting choices.

The star framing is accentuated in *Ho voglia di te* by the sound of paparazzi-style camera clicking by a photographer later revealed to be Step's love interest, Gin (Laura Chiatti), who has been stalking him and creating her own fan album. The diegetic acknowledgment of a Step/Scamarcio fandom points to the critical emphasis on his image and persona, and explains also why performance analysis is a lacuna in relation to the teen film (as it is, not incidentally, in relation to most Italian film). Nevertheless, Scamarcio is often called upon in these films to be silent, to gaze at other characters, with reaction coming mainly from the use of his eyes (the lowering of his eyelashes is a common action) and slight facial movement, such as swallowing. This underacting has led Scamarcio to be overlooked as an actor, although this neglect can also be linked to the genre that made him famous.

The teen film has never enjoyed critical favour, and the target of opprobrium has often been its (presumed) young female fanbase. As Nash and Lahti note, in relation to Leonardo Di Caprio's stardom post-*Titanic*: 'the proximity to both feminized iconography and to female consumers carries with it certain degrading

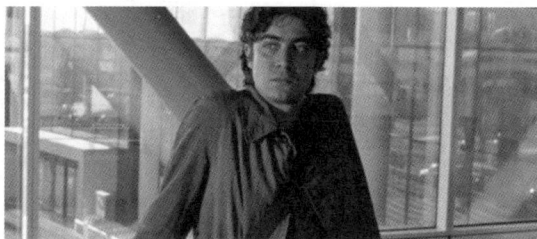

Riccardo Scamarcio as Step in *Ho voglia di te* (2007)

connotations for male stars'.[4] Scamarcio's subsequent career in middlebrow films by respected directors such as Daniele Luchetti, Costa-Gavras, and Ferzan Özpetek, among others, is still marked by a perceived desire for legitimacy, as evidenced by his disavowal of his own beauty and star image, both via interviews and even by means of self-parody in a romcom like Lucini's *L'uomo perfetto* (*The Perfect Man*, 2007), and a constant questioning by interviewers as to his feelings about his earlier films and his younger fans. This tension became most acute when Scamarcio played Sergio Segio, the former leader of the armed group Prima Linea in Renato De Maria's *La prima linea*; critics were worried that Scamarcio's impressionable fans would get the wrong idea about the extra-parliamentary violence of the 1970s, and even victims' groups, who were consulted during the film's funding process, expressed anxiety about a possible glamorisation of terrorism.[5]

MIDDLEBROW *IMPEGNO* AND HOMOSOCIAL BONDING

La prima linea is only one of a wave of recent films revisiting the traumatic experiences of the nation during the 1970s and 1980s, the so-called *anni di piombo*, or 'years of lead', which were marked by popular unrest and extra-parliamentary violence. In such films, events like the Moro affair or the bombing of Bologna train station in 1980 have been woven into melodramatic plots centred on family life or homosocial/fraternal bonds: successful examples of this type of film include *Romanzo criminale*, *La meglio gioventù*, *I cento passi*, Michele Placido's *Vallanzasca – Gli angeli del male* (*Angels of Evil* aka *Angel of Evil*, 2010) and his *Il grande sogno* (*The Big Dream*, 2009) and Daniele Luchetti's *Mio fratello è figlio unico* (*My Brother Is an Only Child*, 2007). These films are anchored by impressive central performances by the group of charismatic male actors who now dominate current Italian cinema: Scamarcio, Germano, Rossi Stuart, Favino, Santamaria and Luigi Lo Cascio.

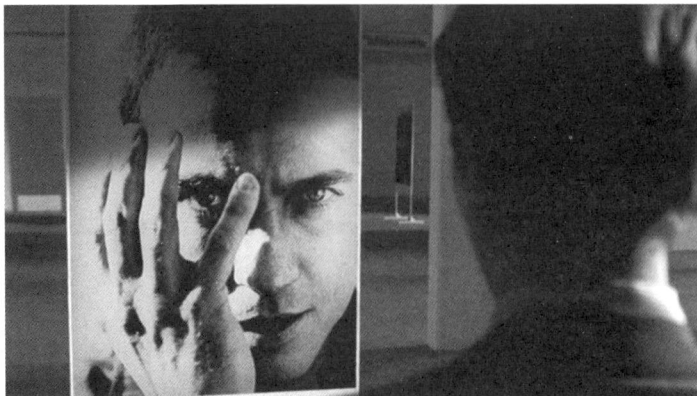

The homosocial bond runs through many of these films of what I term 'middlebrow *impegno*', that is, films that work with star casts, melodramatic or sentimental plots, and an address to a mainstream viewer to construct narratives that thematise political commitment, often in a homosocial key. In *La meglio gioventù* and *Mio fratello è figlio unico*, the bond is fraternal: in both films the struggle between politically polarised brothers, a struggle that stands in for the political conflict of post-68 Italian society as a whole, ends with the expulsion of the dangerously radical brother from the family, and thus from the Italian body politic as a whole. The choice of the exceptionally attractive Alessio Boni as Matteo in *La meglio gioventù* and Riccardo Scamarcio as Manrico in *Mio fratello è figlio unico*, underscores the troubling fascination of the 'other' brother, even as both films end with the re-establishment of political moderation. The 'haunting' by the dead brother that also marks each film's ending, points to the difficult resolution of the trauma of Italy's *anni di piombo*. These films also feature contrasting performance styles from the lead male pair: in *La meglio gioventù*, Boni is repressed and inscrutable as Matteo, significantly being recognised after his death from a photograph of his dead body in which he covers his face with his hand.

His character's reticence is linked to his struggle with his sexuality, and indeed almost the only moment in the film when Matteo is physically expressive is when he deliberately engages in some out-of-control and absurd dancing to defuse the awkwardness of dancing with a girl. In contrast, Lo Cascio is open and naturalistic. In *Mio fratello è figlio unico*, the physical presence of Scamarcio and Germano is contrasted: Accio draws attention to his awkwardness with a clumsy dance to impress his brother's girlfriend, while

Manrico is seen 'performing' during his political orations, displaying his charisma, and eliding the character's charisma with that of Scamarcio.

In other films, such as *Il grande sogno*, *Romanzo criminale* and *Vallanzasca*, the homosocial bond is that of a male friendship group or rivalry. Again, the films enact an uncertain affection between men that goes hand-in-hand with the marginalisation of female characters – though while in *Romanzo criminale* and *Il grande sogno* women are a token to be passed between rival men, in *Vallanzasca*, the pretext that female characters exist to serve is unmasked startlingly, when the conflict between Rossi Stuart's protagonist and his arch-enemy Francis Turatello (played by Francesco Scianna) is ended by a symbolic marriage between the two. The schematic nature of female characterisation is exemplified in *Romanzo criminale*'s use of the female stereotypes proper to the gangster film, in which women's roles are as girlfriend or whore. The sharing of the prostitute Patrizia by gangster Dandi and cop Scialoja (played by an almost unrecognisable Stefano Accorsi, a long way from his heartthrob days) is, however, interestingly used as a metaphor for the complicity between the Banda della Magliana and the Italian state, and it is fair to say that in many of these retro films male characterisation is ambivalent, with both cops and anti-heroes portrayed as equivocal.

PERFORMING MEN

It is instructive to examine the performance modes on display in some of these films: a biopic like *Vallanzasca* (an account of the criminal career in the 1970s of Renato Vallanzasca) obviously privileges the mode of 'impersonation', in which 'the real personality of the actor should disappear into the part'.[6] Impersonation, as opposed to the mode of personification, in which the actor plays a version of him or herself, 'serves to grade positively the standing of the actor among peers'.[7] Although the film was surrounded by polemics about its perceived glamorisation of criminality, it is interesting to note that it puts the suffering male body on display in a striking fashion. Vallanzasca is tortured, literally, beaten and bloodied, and the film, through Rossi Stuart's committed performance, stages this corporeal authenticity. The emphasis in the film, as with the television programme *Romanzo criminale: la serie* on lingering beatings and close-ups of wounded men, recalls Steve Neale's description of the violence in Anthony Mann's films:

> in a heterosexual and patriarchal society, the male body cannot be marked explicitly as the erotic object of another male look: that look must be motivated in some other way, its erotic component repressed. The mutilation and sadism so often involved in Mann's films are marks both of the repression involved and of a means by which the male body may be disqualified, so to speak, as an object of erotic contemplation and desire.[8]

I cento passi also privileges impersonation – Luigi Lo Cascio has to enter the role of anti-Mafia activist Peppino Impastato, and also to perform as Peppino in a final home video-style montage that then collides with a series of archive photos of the 'real' Peppino in a way that is both memorialising and slightly uncanny. The sequence reminds us of the fictional status of the film, and that the naturalism of Lo Cascio's performance is no less a performance for all its supposed authenticity. This naturalism is of course in stark contrast to a biopic like Sorrentino's *Il divo*, in which the mannered nature of Toni Servillo's acting is not intended as an impersonation, but has a distancing effect, reminding us of the unknowability of Giulio Andreotti. Similarly, in *Il caimano*, Nanni Moretti enacts the difficulty of impersonating Silvio Berlusconi, in which three different actors, including Moretti himself, attempt the portrayal.

The most contentious impersonation is undoubtedly that of Riccardo Scamarcio as Sergio Segio in *La prima linea*. Scamarcio's performance is characterised by a notable lack of affect, especially in the straight-to-camera monologues that open and close the film.

Riccardo Scamarcio as Sergio Segio and Giovanna Mezzogiorno as Susanna Ronconi in *La prima linea* (2009)

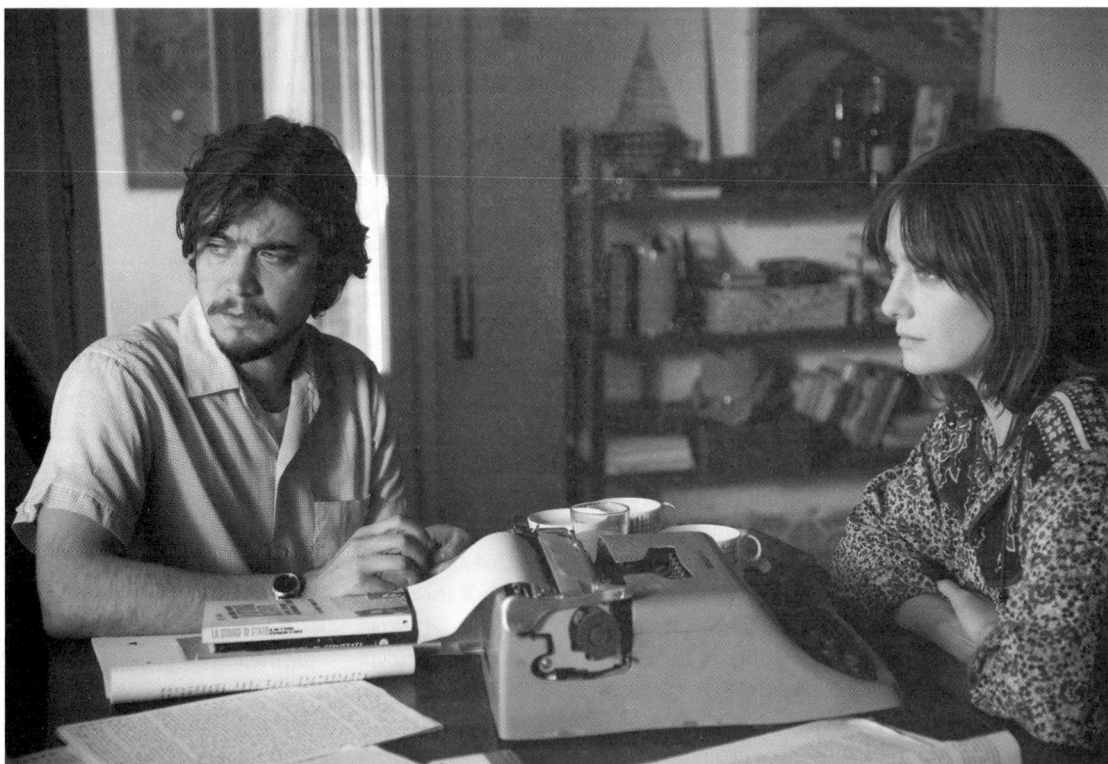

This lack of affect is part of the film-makers' avowed attempt to distance the audience from the character following the polemics that accompanied the film's production. The physical change that Scamarcio undergoes – his famous blue eyes partly obscured by strong eyebrows and a moustache hiding his upper lip – involves a deliberate negation of star persona. As King notes, this kind of physical transformation 'frees the actor […] insofar as it suppressed what in non-actors would be regarded as the authenticating markers of their personality'.[9]

The return to the 1970s enables us to ask particular questions about the success of these films: first, we can locate them in relation to what Alan O'Leary has described as 'tainted heritage': 'heritage or nostalgia films where the commodification of the past is of a piece with the public elaboration of a traumatic history'.[10] So Italy's dark recent past 'is now as much of an object of tourist desire, and therefore an exportable commodity, as its beautiful scenery and beni culturali'.[11] We can also ask questions about the kind of nostalgic reversion to a 70s masculinity that is on view here. The success, for example, of the TV series of Romanzo criminale (2008–10), produced by Cattleya for Sky Italia, has made cult stars of actors Vinicio Marchioni, Alessandro Roja and Francesco Montanari, and is even more violent and sexually explicit than the film, might allow us to wonder about the relationship between the representation of such unreconstructed vernacular masculinity and a contemporary Italian culture marked by the hypermasculine performance of berlusconismo. We might, for instance, wonder about the return to a 1970s that is, notably, depicted with virtually no reference to one of the key elements of social change of the period, feminism.

MEN, MELODRAMA AND COMEDY

The emphasis on the homosocial bond is not specific to these retro dramas; it runs through much of Italian production, across different genres, and in contemporary popular cinema we see a particular attention to male anxiety about gender roles. In fact, it can be argued that many of the films under discussion in this chapter are 'male melodramas' to use the term Mary Wood applied to political thrillers of the 1970s.[12] We can see this male melodrama in many current films that showcase anxieties about paternity. In Luca Lucini's romantic comedy Solo un padre (Just a Father, 2008) Luca Argentero plays a single father left to bring up his daughter when his wife dies suddenly in

childbirth, while in dramas such as Kim Rossi Stuart's Anche libero va bene (Along the Ridge, 2006), Daniele Luchetti's La nostra vita (Our Life, 2010) and Antonello Grimaldi's Caos calmo (Quiet Chaos, 2008), the male protagonist is similarly left bereft by the death or departure of his wife and has to struggle to negotiate a new role as primary carer.

In La nostra vita, the performance of Elio Germano as the grief-stricken Claudio won him the Cannes Best Actor Award, and cemented his reputation as a heavy-weight actor. The scene where he leads the congregation at his wife's funeral in a rendition of Vasco Rossi's 'Anima fragile' stunningly externalises the character's anguish and the use of the music of a populist icon such as Rossi brings together working-class masculinity and affect in a striking fashion. The ending of the film, with Germano and his two little sons in bed in a kind of ecstatic homosocial paradise suggests the possibilities inherent in a world without women, a world full of fun and male bonding. Caos calmo portrays a similar playful dynamic between Nanni Moretti's widowed character, Pietro, and his brother, and it is certainly fair to say that Italian cinema tends to exclude playfulness from its obsessive accounts of heterosexual relationships. A less high-profile, but still very interesting representation of male emotionality and grieving is Maria Sole Tognazzi's L'uomo che ama (The Man Who Loves, 2008), which uses the alpha male persona of Pierfranceso Favino only to undercut it: his character, Roberto, spends much of the film weeping, brooding and longing for his ex-girlfriend, and the film's novelty is in the fact that it puts male emotionality so shamelessly on display and inverts the typical conventions of melodrama. Here, it is the man who desires, although the film suggests that he is somewhat emasculated by his employment as a pharmacist in a shop, working as a subordinate to an elderly female employer.

In Italian comedy, which tends to revolve around rigid stereotypes of gender difference, male bonding is often portrayed as a blissful, if temporary, respite from the controlling nature of girlfriends or wives. Successful films such as Fausto Brizzi's Femmine contro maschi (Women against Men, 2011); Gabriele Muccino's Baciami ancora (Kiss Me Again, 2010); and Federico Moccia's Scusa ma ti voglio sposare (Sorry but I Want to Marry You, 2010), show male late thirty-something protagonists moving in together or commiserating over failing relationships in a reversion to adolescent behaviour. Men's hobbies and passions are seen as threatening to heterosexual coupledom: in Femmine *contro maschi* the ardent Juventus fan Piero (Emilio Solfrizzi) loses his memory and is convinced by his wife that he hates football. In nearly all cases, a compromise is reached, which involves the male protagonist re-committing to the relationship (in the case of *Femmine contro maschi*, the compromise involves Piero agreeing to wash himself regularly, thus setting the bar impressively low for married happiness) but it is never clear how much of his life with his male peer group he will be allowed to hang on to, and true relationship equality is rarely considered.

The tendency for Italian popular comedy to replay over and over the tensions of the bourgeois couple is nothing new, nor is the focus on the white, male, middle-class protagonist, the *italiano medio*, and the heteronormative address of these films (even a comedy like Umberto Carteni's *Diverso da chi* (*Different from Whom?*, 2009), which stars Luca Argentero as a gay politician, ends up being a romantic triangle with a female character). Stars such as Argentero (who began his career on television with the programme *Grande Fratello* (*Big Brother*), and now works with directors such as Placido and Özpetek) and Raoul Bova, are capable of bridging different types of audience. Bova, in particular, has developed a significant career in recent years, moving between TV series (*La piovra* [*The Octopus*, [1995–8]; *Ultimo* [*Ultimo*, 1998–2004]; and *Intelligence – Servizi e segreti* [*Intelligence – Services and Secrets*, 2009]; and middlebrow socially engaged dramas (*Io l'altro* [*I, the Other*, 2006]; *La nostra vita*; *Attacco allo stato* [*Political Target*, 2006–]); teen-addressed comedies such as *Scusa ma ti chiamo amore* (*Sorry but I Love You*, 2008); to *Scusa ma ti voglio sposare*, and the popular films by Paolo Genovese – *Immaturi* (*The Immature*, 2011) and *Immaturi: Il viaggio* (*The Immature: The Journey*, 2012). The last two films, based around a group of late thirty-somethings reunited years on from the high school *maturità*, follow current Italian comedic trends for ensemble comedy, whose appeal depends upon a range of comic figures and recognisable types, rather than on a single star performer.

The popular *filone* that has used this ensemble format most effectively and over a long period is the despised *cinepanettone*, or Christmas comedy, films which, since the mid-1980s, have dominated the Christmas box office in Italy. Although the films are often slammed by critics for their exploitation of the female body and their use of TV showgirls and starlets in leading roles, this is also the Italian film cycle that most explicitly puts male anxiety on display. Alan O'Leary has written of the 'unruly star body' of the

corpulent Massimo Boldi in films such as *Natale sul Nilo*, who for years made a very effective comic pairing with Christian De Sica, whose parodic and excessive performance of hypermasculinity is always on the verge of stumbling into same-sex encounters. De Sica is undoubtedly the star and anchor of these films, and the ostensiveness of his performance style, its over-the-topness and distance from naturalistic verisimilitude, creates absurd comedy but also has the potential to expose gender faultlines. Again, the comic types are familiar and long-standing in Italian cinema. There is the 'nice guy' or *italiano medio* played by Fabio De Luigi in three films by Neri Parenti: *Natale a New York*, *Natale in crociera* and *Natale a Rio*. He is a figure of audience identification, and the only male to whom the possibility of a conventional heterosexual romance is conceded. The *italiano medio*, who also has characteristics of the comic *inetto*, or romantically inept man, is a figure familiar from the *commedia all'italiana* genre, and from the films of Leonardo Pieraccioni, yet the hugely popular nature of the *cinepanettone* until very recently suggests that the films are tapping into some familiar gender stereotypes in Italy.

CONCLUSION

It is clear that much work remains to be done in interrogating screen constructions of Italian masculinity. Instead of regarding it as natural and unquestioned we need to open it up to questioning, especially around issues of male beauty (objectification and its disavowal), and the dominance of certain performance modes. In terms of the broader context in which star performances are embedded, it would be useful to examine the role of migrant or non-white actors, who are consistently marginalised from a cinematic imaginary that privileges the obsessive revisiting of the homosocial basis of Italian society. Finally across so many of these genres and styles, we see a preoccupation with a masculinity that appears to be in crisis, constantly renegotiating its own position in relation to women, the family and history. If it is the case, as Tania Modleski has asserted, that 'male power is actually consolidated through cycles of crisis and resolution, whereby men ultimately deal with the threat of *female* power by incorporating it', it may be that these recurring narratives of crisis are actually reasserting the centrality of hegemonic masculinity.[13] What is beyond doubt, however, is that male stars, and male stories, are finding a large and interested audience in Italy.

NOTES

1. On male stars, see Jacqueline Reich, *Beyond the Latin Lover: Marcello Mastroianni, Masculinity, and Italian Cinema* (Bloomington: Indiana University Press, 2004); Marina Pellanda, *Gian Maria Volonté* (Palermo: L'Epos, 2006). On female stars and Italian national identity, see Stephen Gundle, *Bellissima: Feminine Beauty and the Idea of Italy* (New Haven, CT: Yale University Press, 2007); Stephen Gundle, 'Sophia Loren, Italian Icon', *Historical Journal of Film, Radio and Television* vol. 15 no. 3 (1995), pp. 367–86; Réka Buckley, 'National Body: Gina Lollobrigida and the Cult of the Star in the 1950s', *Historical Journal of Film, Radio and Television* vol. 20 no. 4 (2000), pp. 52–67.
2. Donna Peberdy, *Masculinity and Film Performance* (London: Palgrave, 2011), p. 170.
3. 'Il *teen movie* costituisc[e] uno dei fili principali su cui si regge l'attuale tessuto dell'industria cinematografica italiana', cited in Christian Uva, 'Nuovo cinema Italia: per una mappa della produzione contemporanea, tra tendenze, formule e linguaggi', *The Italianist* no. 29 (2009), pp. 306–24 (p. 315).
4. Melanie Nash and Martti Lahti, '"Almost Ashamed to Say I Am One of Those Girls": Titanic, Leonardo Di Caprio, and the Paradoxes of Girls' Fandoms', in Kevin Sandler and Gaylyn Studlar (eds), *Titanic: Anatomy of a Blockbuster* (New Brunswick, NJ: Rutgers University Press, 1999), pp. 64–88 (p. 71).
5. Scamarcio is not alone in striving for legitimacy following a career in teen-oriented films: Silvio Muccino, who found fame in Gabriele Muccino's *Come te nessuno mai* (*But Forever in My Mind*, 1999), has moved into directing and producing, having co-written several of his films) and Nicolas Vaporidis (the *Notte prima degli esami* series) has turned his attention to producing.
6. Barry King, 'Articulating Stardom', *Screen* vol. 26 no. 5 (1985), p. 251.
7. Ibid. Kim Rossi Stuart also constructs an impressive impersonation in *Piano, solo* (Ricardo Milani: *Piano, Solo*, 2007), a biopic of jazz pianist Luca Flores.
8. Steve Neale, 'Masculinity as Spectacle: Reflections on Men and Mainstream Cinema', *Screen* vol. 24 no. 6 (1983), pp. 2–17 (p. 8). Neale is paraphrasing Paul Willemen's argument about Mann.
9. King, 'Articulating Stardom', p. 31.
10. Alan O'Leary, *Tragedia all'italiana: Italian Cinema and Italian Terrorisms 1970–2010* (London: Peter Lang, 2011), p. 24.
11. Ibid.
12. Mary Wood, *Italian Cinema* (Oxford: Berg, 2005), p. 189.
13. Tania Modleski, *Feminism without Women* (London: Routledge, 1991), p. 7.

FURTHER READING

Bellassai, Sandro, *La mascolinità contemporanea* (Rome: Carocci, 2004).

Dell'Agnese, Elena and Elisabetta Ruspini (eds), *Mascolinità all'italiana: costruzioni, narrazioni, mutamenti* (Turin: UTET, 2007).

Gundle, Stephen, 'Stars and Stardom in the Study of Italian Cinema', *Italian Studies* vol. 63 no. 2 (2008), pp. 261–6.

Günsberg, Maggie, *Italian Cinema: Gender and Genre* (Basingstoke: Palgrave, 2005).

Hipkins, Danielle, 'Why Italian Film Studies Need a Second Take on Gender', *Italian Studies* vol. 63 no. 2 (2008), pp. 213–34.

Landy, Marcia, *Stardom Italian Style* (Bloomington: Indiana University Press, 2007).

O'Leary, Alan, 'The Phenomenology of the *Cinepanettone*', *Italian Studies* vol. 66 no. 3 (2011), pp. 431–3.

——, *Tragedia all'italiana: Italian Film and Italian Terrorisms 1970–2010* (Oxford: Legenda, 2011).

—— and Catherine O'Rawe, 'Contemporary Italian Filmgoers and Their Critics', in Karina Aveyard and Albert Moran (eds), *Watching Films: New Perspectives on Movie-Going, Exhibition and Reception* (Bristol: Intellect, 2013), pp. 351–68.

O'Rawe, Catherine 'Brothers in Arms: Middebrow *Impegno* and Homosocial Relations in the Cinema of Petraglia and Rulli', in Danielle Hipkins (ed.), *Intellectual Communities and Partnerships in Italy and Europe* (London: Peter Lang, 2012), pp. 149–67.

33 Women behind the Camera

New Horizons in Contemporary Cinema

Flavia Laviosa

The publication of *Off Screen: Women and Film in Italy* in 1988 and *The Women's Companion to International Film* in 1990 marked the beginning of an international interest in Italian women film-makers. Ten years later, *Dizionario delle registe: L'altra metà del cinema*, the first and laudable attempt to produce a comprehensive and detailed volume on Italian women directors, informed international academia of the remarkable number of women operating in the film industry and the impressive quality of their work. More recently, three additional publications – *Glass Ceiling. Oltre il soffitto di vetro. Professionalità femminili nel cinema italiano*; *Lost Diva Found Woman. Female Representations in New Italian Cinema and National Television from 1995 to 2005*; and *I Morandini delle donne. 60 anni di cinema italiano al femminile* – further document and recognise the vast contribution made by women (actresses, directors, screenwriters, producers and costume designers) to the history of Italian cinema.

The complex and variegated galaxy of contemporary Italian cinema includes multiple generations of women film-makers all engaged in exploring new genres and hybridised aesthetics. Although working in a hostile climate of economic austerity, talented, energetic, innovative voices and creative forces take various directions and continue to gain international recognition. Furthermore, it is worth noting that the number of films directed by women has doubled in the past ten years, and the amount of short films has tripled since 1993.[1] This chapter strives to evaluate the continued and rising visibility of women directors whose works contribute to a multifaceted definition of Italian cinema and represent a rich and vital artistic component within the obstacles and contradictions that regulate the Italian national context. More specifically, this chapter considers three generations of directors – Rossella Schillaci, Emanuela Piovano and

Giovanna Gagliardo – and their most recent films – the documentary *Altra Europa* (*Other Europe*, 2011); the feature film *Le stelle inquiete* (*Simone and Gustave*, 2010); and the documentary *Vittime* (*Victims*, 2009) are examined. These film-makers have been selected, from among the myriad women directors currently active in the Italian cinemascape, for being representative of distinctively unique cinematic styles, for their varied choices of contemporary and historical themes, and for their commitment to cinema as a militant art form.

Rossella Schillaci earned a master's degree in visual anthropology and documentary direction from the University of Manchester in England. She worked in India where she participated in the EU-India Documentary Initiative, shooting *Living beyond Borders* (2004), which was broadcast on Indian national TV. She is a prolific and dynamic film-maker who has directed an impressive series of documentaries: *Ascuntami* (*Listen to Me*, 2000); *L'Euro soffia su Stromboli* (*Euro Blows over Stromboli*, 2001); *Quannu veni l'acqua?* (*When Is the Water Coming?*, 2003), *Pratica e maestria* (*Practice and Mastery*, 2005); *Vjesh/Canto* (*Singing*, 2007); *La fiuma. Incontri sul Po e dintorni* (*She-River*, 2008); *Only the Sea Is Missing* (2009); *Shukri, a New Life* (2010); and *Altra Europa*. Schillaci has also produced and directed documentaries for RAI and Mediaset.

In *Altra Europa*,[2] Schillaci gives a truthfully dramatic, uncompromisingly honest and unequivocally real answer to the questions: what happens to African migrants once granted political refugee status in Italy; which challenges will they need to face; and what are their prospects for a decent livelihood in the country? The director is witness to an episode that occurred in her neighbourhood in Turin which made the headlines in the Italian news. On 13 October 2008, the abandoned San Paolo clinic, in Corso Peschiera in the city centre, was occupied by more than 200 political refugees from

Somalia, Ethiopia, Eritrea and Sudan, who did not have housing after spending their first months in Italy in refugee camps. The director represents the dramaturgy of the real, offering a captivating visual statement of the inhumane and degrading living conditions of these people in Turin. In the unused five-storey building, now inhabited by an African community, there is only one tap with running water on each floor, with eighty people per floor; there is electricity, but no heating. The documentary follows the new 'guests' over a period of one year, as they endure a brutally cold winter and an oppressively hot summer, candidly capturing their daily struggles in the ramshackle building. All the occupants of the former clinic have faced major adversities and have travelled under dangerous conditions to arrive in Italy, hoping to start a new life. Contrary to their expectations, they find themselves captured in a form of 'suspended' life, limited in their actions, living in unhealthy and unsafe conditions, with uncertain prospects of work, inadequate or no source of income, and completely isolated from the rest of the city.

Schillaci focuses upon three characters – Shukri from Somalia, Khaled from Eritrea and Ali from Sudan – with the intention of telling their stories of precarious lives and defeated dreams. The first half of *Altra Europa* lingers on the biographical details – telling of how the central characters escaped war and managed to reach Italy, and follows them in their daily struggles marked by their courage and determination to survive and provide for the families they have left behind. In their uncertain search for a 'better future', they find assistance in humanitarian groups and volunteers who bring food to the clinic and help them learn practical job skills. Episodes of private moments in the clinic and of the day-by-day pursuit for work are linked by the recurrent voiceover from *Titanic*,[3] the radio programme

Shukri, a political refugee from Somalia, in *Altra Europa* (2011)

established and conducted by a group of refugees, which gives updates on what happens in the occupied clinic, in Turin and other regions of Italy and Europe. In the second half, which has a faster narrative tempo and more syncopated editing, the film presents the refugees' rallies in the streets of Turin, the protests by the Italian citizens, the chaotic meetings and controversial debates with the city council authorities and prefecture officials, the arguments among the refugees, and the general confusion and tension. The film predictably ends with a sense of helpless uncertainty for the future, as the inevitable evacuation and the transfer of over 300 refugees to the renovated Alessandro Lamarmora armoury, where they are kept under military surveillance, put an end to the occupation of the clinic.

Schillaci's film is striking due to its poetic grace even in the scenes denouncing the refugees' subhuman living conditions. The empathetic presence of the camera in the crowded bedrooms in the male and female quarters, in the shared washing facilities, during communal meals and lively parties with African music and dance, as well as in the quiet moments of rest, silent prayer or solitary despair, dramatically conveys the people's irreconcilable emotional misplacement both as political refugees and jobless migrants. The film is structured around rhythmic transitions from the 'solo' voices of Shukri, Khaled, Ali and others, consistently driven by the dramaturgic forces of melancholy and nostalgia, to the narrative tension of the collective uprising and polyphonic relentless resistance.

With an intimate and compassionate filming style, Schillaci presents the contemporary global history of an Italy dealing with new pressing immigration policies and confronted with socioeconomic changes in the fabric of its cities and communities. *Altra Europa* is the expression of film-making in a contemporary urban 'ghetto'. A closed clinic that turns into a 'guesthouse', the headquarters of condoned segregation hosting human misery, exposed, neglected and marginalised, which represents the testimony of national shame and ironically is located in the heart of the historical and industrial capital, Turin, on the eve of the pompous celebrations of the 150th anniversary of the unification of Italy.

With the African refugees' personal experience as the epicentre of this docu-tragedy, the film restructures the discourse of realism in a type of cinema engaged in representing the complex and unambiguous truth about unwanted foreign migrants. *Altra Europa* bears the historical responsibility of documenting the ostracism and rejection of a civil society and the inefficient and delayed intervention of institutions, while it also has the duty of showing the socio-ethic ignominy of a European nation. This narrative gives an unsettling and spinning trajectory to the events, dramatically leading to a conclusive sense of promising hope for some and inevitable tragic defeat for others. The film ends with the dramatic remark – 'it is not worth the trouble to come to Italy' – pronounced by one of the refugees as he eventually leaves the clinic. Schillaci's work can be considered the ultimate cinematic eyewitness of the unfolding history of immigration in contemporary Italy, as well as a form of social resistance and political activism.

Emanuela Piovano is an author, director, producer and more recently distributor, who graduated with a university degree in film history and criticism. She worked for several years for Paolo Gobetti's Archivio Nazionale Cinematografico della Resistenza, RAI and the film journal *Il nuovo spettatore*. Piovano started her career as the producer of *Processo a Caterina Ross* (*The Trial of Caterina Ross*, 1982) by Gabriella Rosaleva. She founded Camera Woman in 1984 and produced and directed the documentaries *D'amore lo sguardo* (*The Gaze of Love*, women directors in Turin, 1984); *Il corpo, il gesto, le donne, il cinema* (*Body, Gesture, Women, Cinema*, 1986); *Senza fissa dimora* (*Without a Steady Home*, 1987); *Camera Oscura* (*Camera Obscura*, 1988); *Milonga de la nina* (*Child's Milonga*, a study of photographer Marilaide Ghigliano, 1988); and *Epistolario Immaginario* (*Imaginary Letters*, video-letters from prison, 1988). In 1988 she founded her own production company Kitchen Film[4] and Sunny Side. Together with Anna Gasco and Tiziana Pellerano, she also directed the documentary *Le rose blu* (*Blue Roses*, 1989) about the fire that destroyed the Vallette women's prison in Turin and killed eleven inmates on 3 June 1989. She directed the docu-fiction *L'aria in testa* (*Air in the Head*, 1992), the RAI programme *Parole incrociate* (*Crosswords*, 1995), and *La grande dea madre* (*The Great Goddess Mother*, 1996). Her feature debut, *Le complici* (*The Accomplices*, 1998), was the adaptation of Maria Rosa Cutrufelli's eponymous novel. This was followed by the romantic drama *Amoufù* (*Foolish Love*, 2003). Piovano's most recent film is the drama *Le stelle inquiete* (*Simone and Gustave*, 2010).

Le stelle inquiete[5] is the first feature film made about the French philosopher Simone Weil (1909–43), following the documentary *Je suis Simone (la condition*

Le stelle inquiete (2010): Simone Weil and Gustave Thibon freely riding bicycles in his vineyard

ouvrière)[6] (*I Am Simone. The Condition of the Working Class*, 2009) by Fabrizio Ferraro. Rossellini's *Europa '51* borrowed circumstances from Weil's life, but, as Bazin points out, 'without in fact being able to recapture the strength of her thinking'.[7] Liliana Cavani and Italo Moscati also hoped to direct a film about this major intellectual figure, and their *Lettere dall'interno* (1974) was the first screenplay for a biopicture about Weil that was never produced.

Weil was born to Jewish parents and spent most of her short life in pursuit of knowledge; she was politically active and studied mysticism. *Le stelle inquiete* is not a biopicture, but it is specifically about a little-known fragment of Weil's life, the summer months of 1941 when, in July, she was forced to leave German-occupied Paris to avoid anti-Semitic persecution. She moved to St Marcel, near Marseilles, in the Ardèche region of southern France, where she was a guest at the vineyard owned by the philosopher-farmer Gustave Thibon and his wife Yvette. Before leaving for New York in 1942, where she spent the following nine months, Weil gave Gustave her journals, from which he extracted and edited her religious thoughts, which he titled *La pesanteur et la grâce* and published in 1947. In

1943, Weil moved to London where she died of tuberculosis, leaving her writings to Gustave, who edited and published them posthumously.

Piovano gives an intimate portrait of Weil, choosing to present her feminine side and private relations, in the broad context of her social activism, political theories and philosophical thought. The director explains that she

> was interested in the story of this revolutionary of utmost integrity who always sacrificed her body and who for the first time discovers what it is to be a woman (as can be read in the letters written to her best friend Simone Pétrement).[8]

The director follows Simone in her experience of work and life on a farm, where she chooses to live in an abandoned shed, to sleep on a bed of corncobs and eat only a few potatoes. However, Piovano does not idealise Weil; on the contrary, she reveals the difficult traits of her rigid and intractable character.

Le stelle inquiete conjugates the art of cinema with history, poetry, mysticism, philosophy and social activism. As World War II unfolds in the background, Gustave (Fabrizio Rizzolo), Simone (Lara Guirao) and Yvette (Isabella Tabarini) live safely removed from war and devastation. The three establish a rare and precious intimate relationship of attraction, complicity and jealousy. The months spent at the vineyard represent a crucial chapter in Weil's life. As she familiarises herself with working conditions on the farm, she engages in extended philosophical conversations and exchanges of views with the Catholic, royalist and spiritualist Gustave. Inevitably a burning intellectual passion for new ideas ignites their encounters, leading, as Piovano suggests, to an intense love story between opposite minds and connected souls. The film is interspersed with philosophical and poetic citations from Weil's writings, while episodes of daily routine on the farm are punctuated by radio announcements of war events in northern France. The recurrent juxtapositions of these intertexts weave the emotional narrative and build up the political tension of the film. The Italian title of the film, as Piovano explains, 'can be read in two distinct and complementary ways: "le stelle inquiete" referring to Simone's and Gustave's souls as restless stars, and also "le stelle (in)quiete" in reference to the protagonists as stars living a quiet and happy interlude of their lives'.[9]

Giovanna Gagliardo started her career as a journalist and specifically as editor of the Roman branch of the newspaper *Il Giorno*. Later, she contributed for many years to the culture page of *Il Messaggero*, and in the 1980s, she contributed to the cultural pages of *La Repubblica* and *L'Espresso*. At the same time, she began to work as a screenplay writer for the RAI television series *La vita è un romanzo* based on news items. In cinema, she started as scriptwriter and screenwriter of *L'amica* (*The Friend*, 1969) by Alberto Lattuada. In the 1970s, she worked as collaborator and assistant to the director Miklós Jancsó, and wrote the screenplays of all the Hungarian director's Italian films. Her debut film as director was *Maternale* (*Mother and Daughter*, 1978), followed by the RAI film *Il sogno dell'altro* (*The Other's Dream*, 1980); the feature film *Via degli specchi* (*Mirrors Street*, 1982); the documentary *Passi della memoria* (*Memory's Steps*, 1985); the film *Caldo soffocante* (*Stifling Heat*, 1990); and the documentaries *Il mito di Cinecittà* (*The Myth of Cinecittà*, 1991), *Viva l'Italia* (*Long Live Italy*, 1994) and *Che colpa abbiamo noi* (*It's No Fault of Ours*, 1997). Her most recent documentaries are *Bellissime Parte prima. Il Novecento dalla parte di 'Lei'* (*Beautiful-Part One. The Twentieth Century on Her Side*, 2004) and *Bellissime Parte seconda. Dal 1960 ad oggi dalla parte di 'Lei'* (*Simply Beautiful-Parte Two Since 1960 till Today on Her Side*, 2006), which trace the history of Italian women in the twentieth century; *L'abito di domani* (*The Dress for the Future*, 2009), which tells the sociocultural and economic history of Italy through fashion; and *Vittime*, which revisits the years of terrorism in Italy through the stories of victims' families. Her most recent film is *20 Anni* (*20 Years*, 2012), a docu-fiction which starts on the night of the fall of the Berlin Wall in 1989 and ends in September 2008 with the collapse of Lehman Brothers.[10] Gagliardo's extraordinary research and cinematographic editing, as demonstrated in her recent historical documentaries, can be considered a theoretical manifesto for the creative re-use of archival footage for a counter-history of Italy.

On 9 May 2009, President Giorgio Napolitano held a ceremony[11] at the Quirinal Palace to commemorate the Giorno della Memoria (Day of Memory)[12] dedicated to the victims of national and international terrorism. The documentary *Vittime*[13] opened the ceremony. The film was also screened in Rome on 10 December 2009 to honour the fortieth anniversary of the Piazza Fontana massacre in Milan.

Vittime covers a period of thirty years of Italian history arranged in reverse chronology, starting on 2 March 2003 – the day of the assassination of the

The bombing of Piazza Fontana in Giovanna Gagliardo's *Vittime* (2009)

railway police officer Emanuele Petri in Castiglion Fiorentino – and ending on 12 December 1969, with the Piazza Fontana bombing at the Banca Nazionale dell'Agricoltura in Milan. The documentary opens with images taken from newsreels of the state funerals of the victims of various massacres, from Piazza Fontana through to the funeral of Emanuele Petri. Gagliardo's voiceover comments on the images, as she lists the dates of the massacres, the large number of attacks and the troubling statistics of the dead and wounded.[14] This was, she concludes, 'A true war in time of peace.' *Vittime* reopens the historical and national wounds of the dark years of the terrorist attacks and explores the abyss of the 1970s and 1980s through immersion in the silent and silenced pain of the innocents that were caught in this perverse revolution. Without ideological overtones, or political commentary, the director presents the private drama that marked an entire nation, thus reflecting on this collective mourning in order to prevent it fading into oblivion. The director is committed to addressing the human pain and loss, so she assembles personal stories of what happened to people and their families and retells history specifically from their point of view – going beyond the trials, street protests, political speeches, commemorative ceremonies, debates and investigations. While Gagliardo chooses Milan, Genoa, Turin, Bologna and Brescia because they were the sites of the worst bloodsheds by left- and right-wing terrorist organisations, she also selects the less well-known stories of citizens targeted for the uniforms they wore, or their ideas or professions: journalists, university professors, judges, industrial managers, police officers as well as many ordinary citizens.[15]

Vittime is the expression of cinema-history and an example of cinema documenting political violence. Gagliardo takes on the moral and civil responsibility of remembering death in the streets, squares and trains of a nation devastated by the fury of escalating violence. A medley of faces, photos, memories of family members are skilfully edited with the newspapers headlines and images from the RAI archive. The visual support of television broadcasts from those years have a strong evocative force, as they give each victim or survivor the dramatic effect of historical immortality. Gagliardo recomposes the facts, gives voice to the faces of a national tragedy which has never really healed, thus offering a history 'parallel' to the official account of terrorist violence as broadcast by the media, examined in the trials, and eventually archived by the state.

Gagliardo develops the dramaturgy of the real by using only the news of the day, as announced on television, leaving out investigations and documentaries that followed the events. The episodes of violence in *Vittime* follow a complex chronological succession. The director chooses to go forwards and backwards in time because everything started in Piazza Fontana, and she ends her film precisely where she began it. Gagliardo develops the film's narrative around three cardinal moments: the ground zero of Piazza della Loggia, Brescia in 1974; the Bologna railway station in 1980; and Piazza Fontana, Milan in 1969. Marked by this unorthodox chronological presentation and characterised by a dynamic sequence of urban spaces struck by the massacres, the narrative pace of *Vittime* is strengthened by an emotional crescendo involving the viewer in the memory of the private and national drama. Presenting three terrorist attacks out of strict chronological order with a focus upon three target cities creates a disquieting group of interrelated national tragedies. The many protagonists of each independent chapter of *Vittime* are tied together by the appearance of a girl with a camera, the essence of a young generation charged with the responsibility of passing on history.

The poetic lines of Francesco De Gregori's song, 'Tutto più chiaro che qui' (1992), open the documentary. The instrumental version is the soundtrack to the film, while it changes in different musical arrangements for each story and each transition between stories. The images that conclude the film are from archival footage of the funeral of the Piazza Fontana victims. By reconnecting the end to the opening of the film, Gagliardo indicates the circular nature of death, meant to express both a complete circuit of past stories and a threatening cycle of repeated events *ad infinitum*. The words of the priest, asking for immediate justice for the innocent victims as he celebrates the funeral mass, sound strident when heard at the end of the film, soon after Roberto Prina, a survivor of the Piazza Fontana explosion, bitterly remarks that the culprits have never been identified. While connecting personal memories and emotions with the national tragedies, Gagliardo succeeds in assembling a volume of testimonies of universal value. Her attention to the tragedy of the dead, the trauma of the survivors and the inconsolable pain of the families acts as counterpoint to the gravity of documented truth, the useless loss of life, the moral breakdown of the Italian judiciary system and the civil defeat of a weakened nation.

Schillaci, Piovano and Gagliardo explore aesthetics and address themes that interweave private spheres with public events, explore contemporary realities, re-examine intellectual figures and revisit historical wounds, while producing a montage of artistic documents and provocative testimonies. This is the art of film-making that can ultimately give reality its rich qualities and complexity. The range and quality of their diverse works offer great promise for the future of women behind the camera in contemporary twenty-first-century Italy.

NOTES

1. Emanuela Mascherini, *Glass Ceiling. Oltre il soffitto di vetro. Professionalità femminili nel cinema italiano* (Città di Castello: Edimond, 2009), p. 117.
2. The film was awarded the RAI Film Prize at the 12th RAI International Film Festival, London 2011; and the prize for best documentary at the Salina Doc Fest 2011, ITALIA.DOC section.
3. Named after the 1941 ship as a metaphor for the many cargos of humanity shipwrecked in the Mediterranean.
4. In honour of The Kitchen, the non-profit multidisciplinary art-and-performance space in the Chelsea neighbourhood in Manhattan, where Piovano's first production, *The Trial of Caterina Ross*, was screened in 1984.
5. The film was awarded prizes in 2011 at the following festivals: I've Seen Films – Spazio Donna and Globi d'Oro.
6. Shot in Paris at Île Seguin, the former site of the Renault car factory, which has been turned into an island of art and science, the documentary covers the months of Weil's work in three different factories between 4 December 1934 and 23 August 1935.

7. André Bazin, *Bazin at Work: Major Essays and Reviews from the Forties and Fifties* (New York: Routledge, 1997), p. 138.
8. Silvana Silvestri,'La filosofa e il vignaiolo', *Alias* (8 January, 2011), p. 10.
9. Personal conversation with Emanuela Piovano, 17 January 2011.
10. Email correspondence with Giovanna Gagliardo, 27 December 2011.
11. This event coincided with the anniversary of the assassination of Aldo Moro on 9 May 1978.
12. This remembrance was instituted with Law no. 56 on 4 May 2007.
13. The film was produced under the auspices of the Associazione Italiana Vittime del Terrorismo.
14. Between 1969 and the end of the 1980s, during the so-called *anni di piombo*, Italy experienced 12,770 episodes of terrorist violence, eight massacres and numerous attacks that killed 342, wounded 5,390 and left 1,500 people permanently injured. In 1979 alone, the country suffered 2,200 attacks, of which 215 were by leftist terrorist groups and fifty-five by subversive right-wing organisations.
15. See the essay by Giancarlo Lombardi on 'Screening Terrorism' in this anthology.

FURTHER READING

Bieberstein, Rada, *Lost Diva Found Woman. Female Representations in New Italian Cinema and National Television from 1995 to 2005* (Marburg: Schüren, 2009).

Bruno, Giuliana and Maria Nadotti, *Off Screen: Women and Film in Italy* (London: Routledge, 1988).

Cavani, Liliana and Italo Moscati, *Lettere dall'interno. Racconto per un film su Simone Weil* (Turin: Einaudi, 1974).

Kuhn, Annette and Susannah Radstone (eds), *The Women's Companion to International Film* (London: Virago Press, 1990).

Mascherini, Emanuela, *Glass Ceiling. Oltre il soffitto di vetro. Professionalità femminili nel cinema italiano* (Città di Castello: Edimond, 2009).

Morandini, Morando Sr and Morando Morandini Jr, *I Morandini delle donne. 60 anni di italiano al femminile* (Pavona di Albano Laziale: Edizioni Iacobelli, 2010).

Sossi, Tiziano, *Dizionario delle registe. L'altra metà del cinema* (Rome: Gremese, 2000).

PART SIX

New Directions in Critical Approaches to Italian Cinema

Introduction

Peter Bondanella

This final section considers new critical approaches in writing on Italian cinema, unusual figures in Italian film history, the impact of Italian film upon other national cinemas and various methodologies employed to analyse Italian cinema. Laura Rascaroli raises the question of whether or not the very concept of a national cinema remains useful. Post-colonial theory informs Àine O'Healy's treatment of the impact of foreign immigration upon what may well be most accurately described today as Italy's 'transnational' cinema. Mary Wood applies genre theory to director Mario Bava, perhaps the most talented of all of Italy's so-called 'B' directors and the individual who has become a cult figure in recent decades with works in a wide variety of fields (science fiction, thrillers, horror films, pepla). Her discussion raises the question of whether or not it is useful to 'promote' a talented genre director to the status of auteur? Fabio Vighi shows how psychoanalytic theory can be a useful tool in studying Italian films. Peter Bondanella analyses not Fellini's cinema but how the maestro's works have influenced other directors in a variety of ways. And finally, Gian Piero Brunetta considers both the past of Italian film history's scholarship and possible new directions for this rapidly changing body of knowledge. A detailed bibliography concludes the book offering a more substantial list of references than those contained in the brief 'Further Reading' sections after individual essays.

34 Italian Cinema in the Post-national Age

Laura Rascaroli

The roots of the astonishing transformations of the global market economy and the world's geopolitical settlement that have dominated the daily news reports of the late 2000s go back to at least the momentous year 1989, when the fall of the Berlin Wall both encapsulated and catalysed the profound mutations that would lead to a complete restructuring of European and global geopolitics. Within an utterly changed ideological, political, geographical, economic, social and cultural framework, Europe has been placed under extreme pressures, which have been reshaping the ideas, borders and institutions of the continent, as well as of the individual nations within it. Within this new scenario, Italy itself has witnessed vast changes and has come to be seen as crucial to the evolution of the recession in Europe – and, thus, to the survival of the European Union itself and of the common currency.

As one of the several terms that have become current in the 1990s in an attempt to conceptualise some of these transformations, 'post-nationalism' is productive insofar as it captures the idea of the progressive reduction of the prominence of the nation state, especially in terms of levels of sovereignty and autarky, vis-à-vis the growth in importance of supranational, global and often geographically unanchored capitals, markets, institutions and powers. The term 'transnationalism' similarly emerges from theories of globalisation and late capitalism to describe phenomena linked to flexible accumulation and time–space compression, which are associated with the weakening of the importance of nation states and of the increasing mobility of monetary capital on the global markets.

The post-national and transnational labels are now widely utilised to describe the societies of the twenty-first century, and have also been frequently applied to the cultural sphere. With regards to cinema, the introduction of these terms arguably responded to and simultaneously produced the crisis of well-established critical paradigms, first and foremost that of national cinema. Such a traditional template for the study of film now appears quite unsuitable to account for the present multiplication of intercultural cinematic imaginations – for instance, in Europe, those represented by *cinéma beur* (the cinema of French subjects of Maghrebi descent), by British-Asian cinema, and by the many émigré, hyphenated, cosmopolitan and diasporic directors of today. It is equally unsuitable to describe a cinema that is less frequently the product of one nation, but that is much more often the result of international co-production and even of supranational systems of production and distribution – for instance, the European programmes Eurimages of the Council of Europe and MEDIA of the European Union which, introduced in 1988 and 1991 respectively, 'marked a new beginning for Europeanism', as suggested by Luisa Rivi.[1]

Thus, post-national and transnational cinema become germane expressions that help us to define and encapsulate a range of phenomena, both economic and cultural: the increased hybridism of the films produced in Europe today; the peculiarities of multinational co-production and of EU and Council of Europe funding for both production and distribution; the crisis of the national film industries;[2] the internationalisation of markets; and the effects of new technology and of geographically unanchored platforms for the distribution and consumption of films (Internet). While not entirely unambiguous, these concepts offer new metaphors to define European cinemas and explore their mutating industrial contexts and artistic practices. Other emerging terms and critical frameworks attempt to account for the ways in which film is today increasingly migrating from the traditional cinema theatre to new environments and screens, a phenomenon triggered by the change from the analogue to the digital image, and from old forms of consumption to others that respond to novel technological panoramas.

Asking the question – what is Italian cinema in the post-national age? – raises issues about work, authorship, industry, export and reception within the broad parameters of European cinema and of the discipline of film studies. This chapter examines the question of what labels such as post-national and transnational add to 'Italian cinema' as an object of study and how Italian cinema presently comments on those labels. It will also reflect on what contemporary Italian films can say about post-national Italy, as well as about Europe and its cinema today.

THE NEW INDUSTRIAL CONTEXT AND THE EXPORT OF ITALIAN FILMS

The Italian film industry is currently undergoing profound transformations, which depend on both internal and external factors. The economic support traditionally provided by the Ministry of Culture (Ministero per i Beni e le Attività Culturali) has only apparently increased in 2008, with the introduction of fiscal incentives (tax credit and tax shelter), which have been gradually implemented since April 2010.[3] These are additional to incentives that were already put in place by Law 28/2004, also known as both 'Legge Urbani' and 'Legge Cinema', and first applied in 2006. As in the past, public funds are assigned to products deemed of 'cultural value' (and it is a point of interest that European programmes support small- and medium-sized entrepreneurs rather than single films). The expression 'cultural value' is in inverted commas here not least because of its ambiguity; remarking how the Legge Urbani has not solved the perceived problems of Italian cinema, Simone Isola wonders how Eduardo Tartaglia's comedy *La valigia sul letto (The Suitcase on the Bed*, 2010), for instance, could be deemed a film of national and cultural interest.[4] A much-publicised component of the selection process for public financing is a reference system of points assigned to authors, directors and actors who have already received prizes or achieved commercial success. Introduced to guarantee transparency and meritocracy, the system has proved inadequate, insofar as it has not succeeded in preventing politics to affecting the panels' choices.[5] Furthermore, it means that only the same small number of subjects has access to the funds, and that it is harder to debut today. This situation is generating a diaspora of young Italian

talent travelling abroad to seek opportunities. While this may ultimately result in a perverse form of internationalisation of Italian cinema, it is not out of line with the mobilisation of professionals that is one of the features of a transnational Europe.

Contrary to the impression created by the new incentives, public investment in Italian cinema has severely and progressively decreased since the introduction of the Legge Urbani. In 2011, the funds assigned to the FUS (Fondo Unico per lo Spettacolo) were less than one-third of those in 1986.[6] Furthermore, films now receive funding for only 50 per cent of the total cost (as opposed to 90–100 per cent as in the past), and on the condition that they secure matching funding. Thus, the Italian film industry is under pressure to adapt to the new rules introduced by the Legge Urbani and to develop new and more modern marketing strategies. Within a context of shrinking state support, as well as of significant growth in production costs, Italian producers are forced to look elsewhere, mainly at presales of distribution rights and, in much smaller proportions, at private capital or product placement. Product placement in particular, which became legal in 2004, has not guaranteed significant income for Italian cinema, in a context in which television attracts most spectators and, consequently, most advertising. One of the effects of this situation is the increased importance of distributors, who negotiate the transfer of rights, both theatrical and non-theatrical. Non-theatrical presales in the Italian context mean predominantly one thing: home video and television.[7] And television, in an Italy in which the market has been dominated by a duopoly since the mid-1980s, identifies with two subjects only: Mediaset/Medusa Film and RAI Cinema/01 Distribution (which are also big players in the home-video market). Consequently, the financial, systemic, political and stylistic influence of television on contemporary Italian cinema cannot be overemphasised:

> It is [Rai and Mediaset] that decide whether a film gets made or not. This unavoidably leads to an expressive and thematic flattening; stories that are not appropriate for the televisual and general public are shunned, in a bid to avoid the risk of the 18 certification, which precludes TV screening.[8]

Aside from the impact on themes and style, there are other and more severe shortcomings; for instance, Rai-produced Italian cinema, paradoxically, is not screened on TV. In the whole of 2009, eight Italian films were shown on RaiUno during prime time, two on RaiDue and seven on RaiTre.[9] Italian producers agree that state TV is remiss in not promoting Italian cinema adequately. According to official discourse, this is because it has no audience left, having already been exploited on other markets (home video, Internet and pay TV). As producer Caterina D'Amico opines, however, '[t]he truth is that cinema on TV doesn't work well because regular appointments, an adequate promotional support and quality programming are all missing'.[10] In the absence of an appropriate strategy for the promotion of Italian cinema, the limitations of the national system of production and distribution become even more evident; television dominates the market, but has decided not to invest properly in the product.

Thus, the current financial difficulties of Italian producers are explained by factors such as 'the contraction of public resources, the saturation of the internal market and its domination by a few, strong subjects that influence the commercial dynamics along the entire chain of non-theatrical distribution'.[11] Given that the increase in cost of film production (corresponding to an average gap of 15–20 per cent of the industrial cost) cannot be absorbed by the national market alone, it becomes clear that the true frontier of expansion for Italian cinema is constituted by the sales of rights on foreign markets. These currently account for only a small fraction of the total economic value of Italian cinema. Today, however, there is no state funding to support Italian exporters.[12] At a European level, it is the MEDIA programme of the European Union that, since its inception in 1991, has offered support through four subsequent schemes; the most recent one, which covers the period 2007–13, has seen an investment of 755 million euros. In Italy, only one society, Adriana Chiesa Enterprises, has received funding from the programme thus far, in a context dominated by France, Germany, Scandinavian countries and the UK. This may be explained by the objective of the programme itself, which is at odds with the peculiar situation of Italian exporters: 'MEDIA schemes […] tend to favour those societies that have in their catalogue a number of recent non-national European films that are theatrically distributed in as many territories as possible.'[13] This, however, is extremely rare in Italy, where exporters mainly deal in 'non-recent' (i.e., post-theatrical) national films, aiming at international sales on the home video and TV markets.[14] For these reasons, Italian distributors are simply not competitive in regard to European funding.

While professionals of the sector recognise that Italian films need to travel more in order for the national industry to thrive, it is apparent that certain almost impervious obstacles need to be overcome first. Within the home markets of European nations, all invariably dominated by Hollywood blockbusters and by indigenous cinema, the niche open to the films of other nations is small and the competition is severe. The problem, indeed, is not uniquely Italian, but is, rather, European. In 2005, Wendy Everett noted that:

> the market share of European films in EU cinemas has fallen steadily from approximately 60% in the mid-1960s, a period now widely characterised as the golden age of European cinema, to a mere 23%, in other words, less than a quarter, in 2000. Once again, at the heart of this problem is the fact that on average, in 2000, European films secured only 26% of their already meagre box-office takings from sources outside their country of origin. With a few well-known exceptions, therefore, it appears that European films do not travel well.[15]

Recent data do induce some optimism with regards to the crisis experienced by European cinemas since the 1980s; and a renewed presence of Italian films on the international scene has been guaranteed since the year 2000 by the attention and prizes received at key international festivals. Yet, Italian export is well below the average European numbers; according to the Osservatorio Internazionale Roberto Rossellini sull'Audiovisivo e Multimedialità (OIAM), the combined export of Italian cinema and TV fiction in 2008 produced 20 million euros, compared to 100 million in France and 600 in Great Britain.[16] But what Italian cinema travels abroad?

ANICA's recent study of the export of Italian films in Europe, which considers the 379 films that, over the period 2006–8, were produced entirely in Italy or co-produced with foreign societies, concludes that no obvious correspondence exists between success at the national box office and the ability of Italian films to 'travel well'. In other words, the most profitable national production, from *cinepanettoni* to lowbrow comedies, very rarely finds an international outlet, in spite of achieving box-office success at home.[17] The only Italian cinema that crosses the borders can be described as art-house and authorial, and is almost invariably introduced to the international arena through participation in important film festivals, through screenings at the specialised professional markets that are attached to some such festivals, or via co-production with foreign societies (which is in itself an index of a film's ability to attract foreign investment form the start).

In order to substantiate these claims, it is useful to compare the results of the internal box office and of the most successful films on the international market. In 2008, for instance, the national box office was topped by the *cinepanettone* produced by Filmauro, entitled *Natale a Rio*, a rather extraordinary performance in a market dominated by US blockbusters; followed in fifth position by *Grande, grosso e … Verdone* (*Great, Big and Verdone*), also a Filmauro production; in sixth by *Scusa ma ti chiamo amore* (*Sorry, If I Love You*); in tenth by *Gomorra*; in twelfth by *Il cosmo sul comò* (*The Cosmos on the Dresser*); in nineteenth by *L'allenatore nel pallone 2* (*The Soccer Coach 2*); and in twentieth by *Parlami d'amore* (*Talk to Me about Love*).[18] The Italian films enjoying the greatest distribution abroad in the same year were, in decreasing order of success: *Come Dio comanda* (*As God Commands*); *Il divo*; *Gomorra*; *Caos calmo*; *Pranzo di ferragosto* (*Mid-August Lunch*); *Caravaggio*; and *Scusa ma ti chiamo amore*.[19] As can be seen, only *Gomorra* and *Scusa ma ti chiamo amore* figure in both lists (and do so in reverse order of success). While *Gomorra*, Matteo Garrone's austere adaptation of Roberto Saviano's book on the Neapolitan *camorra*, is an exception in terms of internal box office (which is dominated by farces and comedies by or with established comedians such as Christian De Sica, Carlo Verdone, the trio Aldo, Giovanni & Giacomo, and Lino Banfi – all of which are Italian productions that were only distributed nationally), Federico Moccia's romantic comedy *Scusa ma ti chiamo amore* equally stands out in the group of the champions of Italian export, which is dominated by the auteur dramas of directors whose work is regularly screened at international festivals, such as Paolo Sorrentino, Matteo Garrone, Gabriele Salvatores and Nanni Moretti, protagonist of *Caos calmo*. The list also includes a comedy by a first-time director, *Pranzo di ferragosto*, on which I will say more below; and a TV biopic, a 2007 international co-production photographed by Vittorio Storaro, Angelo Longoni's *Caravaggio*, which was screened at several film festivals and film markets, and which enjoyed some international theatrical and DVD distribution. Very similar patterns and comparable results are yielded by the analysis of the data available for the entire first decade of the twenty-first century.

The type of cinema capable of travelling abroad constitutes a significant fraction (between 40 and 55 per cent) of the national production; but because it is not a standardised product, it cannot guarantee continuity in terms of export. Plus, as is suggested by the above examination of the current state of the Italian industry, it is not adequately supported, marketed and promoted. However, as Everett argues in her article on European cinema, the solution is hardly the standardisation of the production in the direction of the most successful popular cinema – precisely because, as already noted, the national lowbrow comedy does not travel well and, often, does not travel at all.

TRAVELLING FILMS

These data can have multiple interpretations; one is that, in order to travel well and, thus, to thrive, more Italian cinema needs to become more international, to be better able to appeal to non-Italian audiences. In 2010, on the occasion of the 67th Venice Film Festival, at which Italian films were much applauded but received no prizes, jury member and Academy Award-winning director Gabriele Salvatores asked himself why Italian films are no longer as able to cross borders, in particular 'emotional' ones, as in the past, and remarked: 'Perhaps it is so because directors had found a universal way to tell stories, perhaps because, beside stories, there was also the invention of a style, and the effort to communicate with the audience.' Mario Martone, who was in the competition with his noteworthy re-reading of the Italian *Risorgimento*, *Noi credevamo* (*We Believed*, 2010), a film perhaps not that accessible to foreign audiences, polemically responded by highlighting how, in the 1970s, efforts were made to 'translate' the complexity of Italian films, and mentioned Roberto Rossellini who, as a jury member at Cannes, succeeded in obtaining the Golden Palm for the Tavianis' *Padre padrone*.[20]

At given moments in its history, Italian cinema was highly successful abroad. This happened at least twice

Domenico (Luigi Lo Cascio) in the closing sequence of *Noi credevamo* (2010)

As this newspaper advertisement attests, Italian films were extremely popular abroad during the silent period; one import, *Cabiria*, leads to another, Carmine Gallone's *La donna nuda* (*The Naked Truth*, 1914)

A Fellini retrospective in Paris underscores the continuing appeal of Italy's greatest auteurs abroad

with particularly significant results. The first time was in the silent cinema period, during which Italy had a leading international role and successfully exported both epic films like Enrico Guazzoni's *Quo vadis?* (1912, with nine months on Broadway); Mario Caserini and Eleuterio Rodolfi's *Gli ultimi giorni di Pompei* (1913); and Giovanni Pastrone's *Cabiria*, which screened for six months in Paris and almost a year in New York; and popular diva-driven melodramas such as Caserini's *Ma l'amor mio non muore*; or Pastrone's *Il fuoco*.[21] The second transnational phase of Italian cinema, inaugurated by the season of postwar neorealist films that won acclaim and prizes all over the world,[22] was in the 1950s and 60s, and is often referred to as a golden age, driven by world-famous auteurs, including Rossellini, Fellini, Visconti and Antonioni. In this era in particular, Italy left a profound mark on world cinema.

It is quite significant that most of the best recent celebrations of Italian cinema have taken place abroad.[23] In 2009, three great international events were

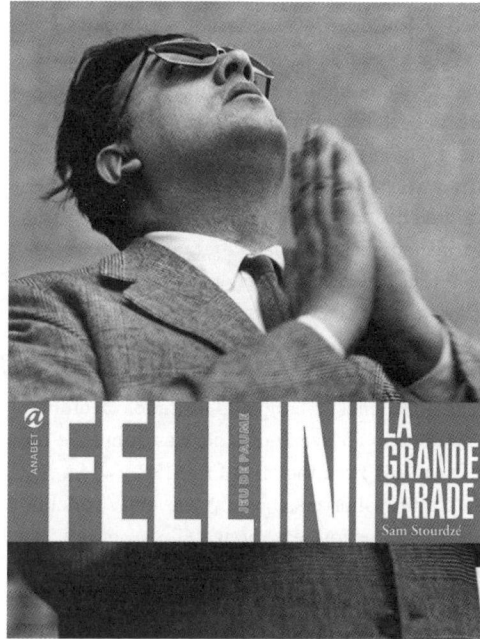

devoted to Italian directors. Paris honoured Federico Fellini with *Tutto Fellini!*, a screening of his entire oeuvre organised by the Cinémathèque française and accompanied by the exhibition *Fellini, la Grande Parade*, held for three months at the Jeu de Paume Museum.

Lyon's Lumière Film Festival celebrated Sergio Leone twenty years after his death with a complete retrospective programme of his restored films entitled *Il était une fois Sergio Leone*. Finally, New York's Lincoln Centre screened no less than forty postwar Italian films under the title *Life Lessons: Italian Neorealism and the Birth of Modern Cinema*. In 2010, the Austrian Film Museum in Vienna presented a major season devoted to *Dino Risi and the Commedia all'italiana*, comprising thirty-four films (including thirteen by Dino Risi), following another major retrospective on Italian cinema of the 1960s at the Museum in 2009. These events, some of which were accompanied by lectures or by the release of publications and new digital editions of the films, indicate that not only Italy's art film but also its genre cinema of the golden age are regarded as a world patrimony, whose centrality to ideas of modern cinema is widely recognised and celebrated internationally. They furthermore suggest that foreign markets should be able to welcome contemporary Italian production of all types, and not only authorial and director-driven cinema.

Indeed, in the 1950s, 60s and 70s, the films of De Sica, Rossellini, Fellini, Visconti, Antonioni, and of the subsequent generation of auteurs (among whom Pasolini and Bertolucci are prominent for international fame) were well received beyond the national borders and indeed were often international productions starring foreign actors or filmed abroad.[24] The international success of Italian cinema in those decades extended to include generic production – most famously the spaghetti Western, but also the horror movie.[25] But it is on the international success of the *commedia all'italiana* that I wish to pause here. This genre, one of the most fecund and profitable sectors of Italian production for over a decade, was popular abroad, especially from the end of the 1960s, winning many international prizes, including several Academy Award nominations for Best Foreign Film. A prominent example is the film that inaugurated the genre, Mario Monicelli's *I soliti ignoti*, which was nominated for an Academy Award, was remade as *Crackers* by Louis Malle in 1984 and, with the title *Big Deal*, became a Broadway musical by Bob Fosse in 1986. While the *commedia all'italiana* no longer exists, the corresponding phenomenon of the contemporary middlebrow comedy – represented by such directors as Cristina Comencini, Gabriele Muccino, Ferzan Özpetek and Paolo Virzì – does not travel as well. Is it lacking in quality? Or is it too Italian and thus not 'translatable'?

While exporting Italian film remains problematic, there are counter examples, which, given the context, are all the more significant. Although nobody today seems to match the constitutive cosmopolitanism of auteurs such as Rossellini, Antonioni, Visconti and Bertolucci, some Italian directors are moving beyond the national borders. A noteworthy example is Paolo Sorrentino with his *This Must Be the Place* (2011), an Italian, French and Irish co-production that was filmed in Italy, the US and Ireland, starring a truly international cast that includes Sean Penn and Frances McDormand, and featuring a North American plot and characters. While Sorrentino's example is rather unique, it is representative of the fact that Italian cinema is looking again, and with ambition, at international markets. A co-production like *This Must Be the Place* is, of course, made to travel. In the context of the present reflection, it seems useful to examine examples of films that have travelled well while being more decidedly 'made in Italy'. I wish to consider three here: Gianni Di Gregorio's *Pranzo di Ferragosto*; Luca Guadagnino's *Io sono l'amore* (*I Am Love*, 2009); and

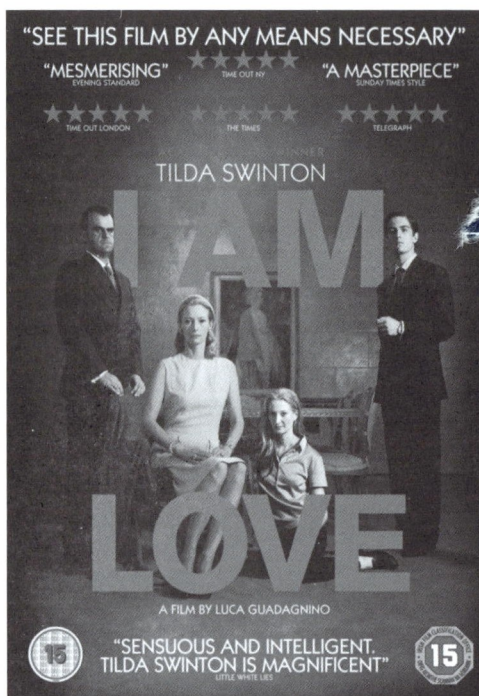

Tilda Swinton very much assisted the foreign reception of Luca Guadagnino's *Io sono l'amore* (2009)

Michelangelo Frammartino's *Le quattro volte* (*Le Quattro Volte*, 2010). Only Frammartino's film was a co-production, with Italian, German and Swiss money; it was filmed in Calabria with a non-professional cast. Guadagnino's film, whose mainly Italian cast is complemented by international star Tilda Swinton, had an estimated budget of $10 million and was filmed in Italy and London. Di Gregorio's film, which had the much more modest budget of 500,000 euros, was entirely shot in Rome with predominantly non-professional actors.[26]

Io sono l'amore signals its international credentials from the start by the presence of Tilda Swinton in the cast and as a producer. It was screened at Sundance, Venice and Toronto. The last festival, while not having a traditional film market, attracts producers and distributors from all over the world, and provides the opportunity to test the North American appreciation for non-English-language European films. Indeed, Guadagnino's film was quickly sold in North America, and was nominated at the 68th Golden Globe Awards for Best Foreign Film.

Le quattro volte was also successful on the international market, perhaps unexpectedly for a film that is almost completely silent, employs non-

Michelangelo Frammartino's *Le quattro volte* (2010) was a surprise success on the world market, given its extremely simple production

professional actors and a diaphanous fictional storyline barely disguising a poetic documentary on rural Calabria. It premiered at Cannes and was then shown at festivals in Europe, North and South America and Japan, including Toronto, New York, São Paulo and Tokyo. *Pranzo di ferragosto* is, however, the most surprising of my three examples. While both Guadagnino's and Frammartino's films are instances of innovative and stylish auteur cinema, *Pranzo di ferragosto* (the debut of an unknown director born in 1949 and active mainly as a screenwriter since the mid-1980s) is what one would be tempted to define as, although certainly not derogatively, a small film, as well as a regional comedy that relies on a cast of idiosyncratic but sympathetic characters. A low-budget production, *Pranzo di ferragosto*, which won the prize for Best First Film at Venice, was then screened at a string of international festivals in Brazil, the US, Japan and Europe, and sold very well both in Europe and in North and South America.

These three films represent different cinematic traditions, thus demonstrating that the international market is able to absorb diverse expressions of contemporary 'made in Italy' fare. *Io sono l'amore* is lavishly filmed; with nods to both Pasolini (with a storyline that is similar to *Teorema*) and Visconti's sumptuous melodrama, and exhibiting an international flair, it puts itself forward as an heir to Italian auteur cinema. With the attention it gives to the everyday, to ethnography, to the ordinary folk, to the interface of fiction and documentary, and even to a pantheistic spiritual dimension, *Le quattro volte* is closer to both Rossellini and to Zavattini. While displaying a strong

regionalist inspiration, it is a work that, combining minimalism and intellectual rigour, is simultaneously embedded in Italian tradition and locale and informed by a gaze and breadth of international ambition. *Pranzo di ferragosto* derives from the tradition of regionalist comedy, but also resonates with some Fellinian traits, especially through its eccentric characters; the protagonist, to an extent, may even remind spectators of the maestro's own *vitelloni*.

In a context in which, as a consequence of a progressively post-national, transnational and globalised socioeconomic environment, Italian cinema must look beyond the national borders for its survival and development, the international success enjoyed by a regional comedy, a stylish melodrama and a lyrical non-fiction film indicates that quality Italian cinema of all genres and types is potentially able to succeed abroad, and would do so more frequently if properly supported. The past mobility of Italian genres such as spaghetti Westerns, horrors and *commedia all'italiana* suggests that even the contemporary middlebrow comedy, which constitutes a not irrelevant section of the national product, should do better abroad than it currently does. Indeed, the above analysis suggests that, in the Salvatores vs Martone dispute, it is the opinion voiced by the latter that points us in the right direction. The problem is not so much one of quality or untranslatability; new marketing strategies and new support for the distribution and promotion of Italian cinema are needed. Italian exporters, in particular, must be encouraged to become more effective at securing European funding.

ideological and economic entity, but rather rethinks and reframes it. As Susan Hayward has argued, the critical approach of recent scholarship not only undermines the concept of national cinema, but also

> carves out spaces that allow us to *revalue* [it]. It makes it possible to reterritorialise the nation (to rewrite Paul Virilio, echoing Deleuze perhaps) not as bounded, demarcated, and distinctive, but as one in which boundaries constantly crisscross both haphazardly and *unhaphazardly*.[34]

Looking at contemporary Italian cinema from a post-national perspective allows us to draw comparisons between past and present cosmopolitan dimensions of Italian film, as well as to discuss the interfaces between the artistic, aesthetic, economic and industrial spheres as something which exceeds national borders and implies a series of boundary crossings. Italian productions have always functioned within networks of economic and cultural relationships; today, they do so in particular within a late-capitalist, post-national and post-industrial European context. Such a context is increasingly shaped by concerns and dynamics that are supranational and transnational, and often Europeanist. The application of post-national and transnational perspectives does change Italian cinema as an object of study, because it places it in broader and more permeable economic and cultural contexts. It also shows that Italian cinema helps us define and understand what a post-national and transnational film is in Europe today, in a context in which the interconnectedness of economies and policies and the new practices of international co-production and European-funded production and distribution are heavily shaping the nature of the film industries of single European nations.

NOTES

1. Luisa Rivi, *European Cinema after 1989: Cultural Identity and Transnational Production* (New York: Palgrave Macmillan, 2007), p. 53.
2. Dimitris Eleftheriotis, 'Cultural Difference and Exchange: A Future for European Film', *Screen* vol. 41 no. 1 (Spring 2000), p. 93.
3. Francesca Medolago Albani, Francesca Palleschi and Federica D'Urso, *I quaderni dell'ANICA, n. 5. L'export di cinema italiano*, p. 16. Available at www.anica.it/online/attachments/081_quaderno5.pdf; accessed 20 December 2011. All translations from Italian are mine.
4. Simone Isola, 'CineGomorra', in Simone Isola (ed.), *Cinegomorra. Luci e ombre sul nuovo cinema italiano* (Rome: Sovera, 2010), p. 24.
5. Ibid., p. 23.
6. Ibid., p. 27.
7. On the internal market, the theatrical 'window' accounts today for only about one-fourth of the total film's income; the subsequent 'windows' include home video, pay per view, video on demand, television, pay TV, web. The complete process lasts an average of six–seven years (Albani et al., *I quaderni dell'ANICA*, pp. 18–20).
8. Isola, 'CineGomorra', p. 22.
9. Ibid., p. 23.
10. Quoted in ibid.
11. Albani, Palleschi and D'Urso, *I quaderni dell'ANICA*, p. 20.
12. Some funds for the export of films of cultural interest were made available by the 'Legge Urbani', until money ran out in 2009. Some very modest support also comes from MISE (Ministero dello Sviluppo Economico) and ICE (Istituto Nazionale per il Commercio Estero).
13. Albani, Palleschi and D'Urso, *I quaderni dell'ANICA*, p. 47.
14. A MEDIA 'Selective Funding' also exists for groupings of distributors from different EU countries who wish to distribute recent non-national European films, for a maximum of 150,000 euros. In the period 2006–8, for instance, European distributors obtained 'selective' support for ten Italian films, which thus enjoyed theatrical distribution in other countries (predominantly, France, the Netherlands and Belgium). In the same period, fourteen Italian films benefited from Eurimages funds for distribution made available to countries, such as Albania, Bosnia Herzegovina, Serbia, Macedonia and Turkey, which cannot access MEDIA funding (Albani, Palleschi and D'Urso, *I quaderni dell'ANICA*, p. 53).
15. Wendy Everett, 'Images on the Move: Reframing the Cinemas of Europe', *Screen* vol. 46 no. 1 (Spring 2005), p. 99.
16. Available online at http://www.iamo-observatory.org/rassegna-stampa-presentazione; accessed 20 December 2011. The Osservatorio's activities have been suspended since funding was not received by the Regione Lazio in 2010.
17. It suffices to look at the internal box-office data for the year 2011, which was particularly successful for Italian cinema: the top film, Checco Zalone's comedy *Che bella giornata* (*What a Beautiful Day*), grossed a staggering 43.5 million euros, just a little less than James Cameron's *Titanic* (1997); it was followed by the last chapter of the *Harry Potter* saga, and by two more Italian comedies, Paolo Genovese's *Immaturi* and Albanese's *Qualunquemente* (*Whatsoeverly*, 2010).

18. All the other titles in the top twenty were US blockbusters. Ufficio Studi ANICA (ed.), *Il cinema italiano in numeri: anno solare 2008. La conferma.* Available at http://www.anica.it/online/attachments/006_dati.cinema.2008.pdf; accessed 20 December 2011.

19. Albani, Palleschi and D'Urso, *I quaderni dell'ANICA*, p. 85.

20. Quoted in Isola, 'CineGomorra', p. 12. The connection between winning prizes at international festivals and the ability of films to travel abroad has been established in the previous section of this essay.

21. See Aldo Bernardini and Vittorio Martinelli, *Cinema muto italiano. I film degli anni d'oro: 1911–1914*, Vol. 2 (Turin: Nuova ERI, 1994).

22. On the transnationalism of the neorealist style, see Saverio Giovacchini and Robert Sklar (eds), *Global Neorealism: The Transnational History of a Film Style* (Jackson: University Press of Mississippi, 2011).

23. Lorenzo Codelli, 'Italy', in Ian Haydn Smith (ed.), *International Film Guide 2010: The Definitive Annual Review of World Cinema* (London: Wallflower Press, 2010), p. 203.

24. On the transnationalism of Italian and European art cinema in the 1950s and 1960s, especially, see Mark Betz, *Beyond the Subtitle: Remapping European Art Cinema* (Minneapolis: University of Minnesota Press, 2009).

25. Stefano Baschiera and Francesco Di Chiara, 'Once Upon a Time in Italy: Transnational Features of Genre Production, 1960s–1970s', *Film International* vol. 8 no. 6 (2011), pp. 30–9.

26. Budget information is drawn from Internet Movie Database. Available at http://www.imdb.com; accessed 20 December 2011.

27. Dimitris Eleftheriotis, *Cinematic Journeys: Film and Movement* (Edinburgh: Edinburgh University Press, 2010), p. 189.

28. Derek Duncan, 'Stairway to Heaven: Ferzan Özpetek and the Revision of Italy', *New Cinemas: Journal of Contemporary Film* vol. 3 no. 2 (September 2005), pp. 101–13.

29. Diego Dalla Via, 'Immigrazione', in Gianni Canova and Luisella Farinotti (eds), *Atlante del cinema italiano. Corpi, paesaggi, figure del contemporaneo* (Milan: Garzanti, 2011), p. 238.

30. As, for instance, Derek Duncan has argued of *Saimir* in 'Italy's Postcolonial Cinema and Its Histories of Representation', *Italian Studies* no. 63 (2008), pp. 195–211.

31. Abigail Keating, 'All Roads Lead to Piazza Vittorio: Transnational Spaces in Agostino Ferrente's Documusical', *Studies in Documentary Film* vol. 5 nos 2–3 (August 2011), pp. 197–210.

32. Áine O'Healy, 'Mediterranean Passages: Abjection and Belonging in Contemporary Italian Cinema', *California Italian Studies Journal* vol. 1 no. 1 (2010), p. 17. Available at http://escholarship.org/uc/item/2qh5d59c; accessed 20 December 2011.

33. Dalla Via, 'Immigrazione', p. 258. See also Roy Menarini, 'La trama senza storia: il cinema contemporaneo italiano e il difficile rapporto con il presente', in Ugo Volli (ed.), *La Cultura Italiana, Vol. IX, Musica, Spettacolo, fotografia, design* (Turin: UTET, 2009), pp. 410–29.

34. Susan Hayward, 'Framing National Cinemas', in Mette Hjort and Scott MacKenzie (eds), *Cinema and Nation* (London and New York: Routledge, 2000), p. 93.

FURTHER READING

Betz, Mark, *Beyond the Subtitle: Remapping European Art Cinema* (Minneapolis: University of Minnesota Press, 2009).

Duncan, Derek, 'Stairway to Heaven: Ferzan Özpetek and the Revision of Italy', *New Cinemas: Journal of Contemporary Film* vol. 3 no. 2 (September 2005), pp. 101–13.

——, 'Italy's Postcolonial Cinema and Its Histories of Representation', *Italian Studies* vol. 63 no. 2 (Autumn 2008), pp. 195–211.

Eleftheriotis, Dimitris, 'Cultural Difference and Exchange: A Future for European Film', *Screen* vol. 41 no. 1 (Spring 2000), pp. 92–101.

——, *Cinematic Journeys: Film and Movement* (Edinburgh: Edinburgh University Press, 2010).

Everett, Wendy, 'Images on the Move: Reframing the Cinemas of Europe', *Screen* vol. 46 no. 1 (Spring 2005), pp. 97–105.

Giovacchini, Saverio and Robert Sklar (eds), *Global Neorealism: The Transnational History of a Film Style* (Jackson: University Press of Mississippi, 2011).

Hjort, Mette and MacKenzie, Scott (eds), *Cinema and Nation* (London and New York: Routledge, 2000).

Isola, Simone (ed.), *Cinegomorra. Luci e ombre sul nuovo cinema Italiano* (Rome: Sovera, 2010).

O'Healy, Áine, 'Mediterranean Passages: Abjection and Belonging in Contemporary Italian Cinema', *California Italian Studies Journal* vol. 1 no. 1 (2010). Available at http://escholarship.org/uc/item/2qh5d59c; accessed 20 December 2011.

Rivi, Luisa, *European Cinema after 1989: Cultural Identity and Transnational Production* (New York: Palgrave Macmillan, 2007).

35 Post-colonial Theory and Italy's 'Multicultural' Cinema

Áine O'Healy

The attempt to bring contemporary Italian cinema and post-colonial studies into dialogue with each other is a project that immediately raises definitional and methodological questions. What do we mean by post-colonial theory? How does the discourse of the post-colonial apply to the increasingly transnational, transcultural dimensions of Italian society? How can the insights of post-colonial critics facilitate an analysis of many recent Italian films seeking to address these phenomena by focusing on immigrant characters or on transnational themes and narrative trajectories? And how do issues of identity, difference and authorship come to bear on an analysis of this kind? This chapter will address these questions in order to lay the ground for a post-colonial consideration of the growing number of Italian films that register in diverse ways the country's transformation from a nation of emigrants to the home of millions of foreign-born residents.

Like other theoretical trends generally classed as post-structural, post-colonial discourse came to prominence in the English-speaking world in the 1980s in the wake of Edward Said's *Orientalism* (1978) and subsequent studies by Gayatry Spivak, Homi Bhabha and others. Earlier publications by writers from the Francophone world, such as Frantz Fanon, Aimé Césaire and Edouard Glissant, which reflected the experience of French colonialism and called for new ways of thinking about race, culture and identity, soon found resonance in Anglophone post-colonial writing. There has been much debate regarding what properly constitutes post-colonialism, but it has always been clear that it embraces much more than simply an investigation of the interactions between European nations and the populations they had once colonised. Although most of its early English-speaking practitioners were trained in literary studies, all prominent contributors to the field

have shown an openness to interdisciplinary influences, adapting to their needs the insights of diverse Western theorists from Michel Foucault to Jacques Derrida and Jacques Lacan, while remaining attentive to the hitherto marginalised or silenced voices of thinkers from non-hegemonic cultures. The importance of Said's identification of orientalism as a discourse cannot be underestimated. Working from a Foucauldian understanding of the discursive construction of political power arrangements, Said showed how taken-for-granted understandings of racial and cultural hierarchies are created and consolidated over time through language, insidiously bolstering hegemonic interests and authority in the process. Other key terms and insights emerged in subsequent work by other post-colonial theorists, including those of subalternity, counter-discourse, hybridity, mimicry, ambivalence and double consciousness, all of which have provided potent deconstructive tools for cultural analysis.

Over the years, post-colonial criticism has transformed traditional understandings of subjectivity and identity, of culture, geography, history and international politics. In an essay first published in 1992, Bhabha argued the merits of bringing a post-colonial perspective to bear on the analysis of discourses of cultural difference and marginality in the contemporary West.[1] For Bhabha, this perspective unsettles the traditional approach that places the Third World and the First World in binary opposition to each other. It deconstructs and redraws boundaries and borders, overhauls traditional notions of culture, substitutes the concept of hybridity for that of cultural purity, and lays bare the hybrid location of all cultures in the current, globalised arena. In recent years, many scholars have broadened the scope of the field, productively applying the heterogeneous discourse of post-colonial studies to a broad variety of cultural texts in diverse national and transnational contexts.

Italian scholars have nonetheless been relatively slow to embrace the analytical force of post-colonial theory. Their reluctance may be related to a widespread Italian tendency to disavow or downplay the realities of the nation's own colonial exploits and a related failure to accept the relevance of a post-colonial perspective for an analysis of Italian culture. This general resistance to post-colonial studies in Italy has been misguided on two counts: in its denial of the influence of Italy's colonial legacy on cultural practices in Italy today; and in its narrow understanding of what post-colonial discourse actually encompasses. Nonetheless, just as new studies by Anglophone writers were calling into question the ongoing relevance of post-colonial discourse in the neoliberal era, replacing it with other terms and emphases, such as migration studies, transnationalism and globalisation, several Italian scholars began to acknowledge the validity of a post-colonial approach, arguing that contemporary Italy – along with Europe as a whole – is without question a post-colonial space. Far from suggesting that all traces of colonial domination and the manifestations of material and epistemic violence that accompany it have been superseded (a connotation that several commentators have attributed to the signifier 'post'), these scholars seek to identify the forms that neo-imperial hegemony has taken on in the global era, stressing continuities with the apparatuses of colonial domination. Sandro Mezzarda and Federico Rohola, for example, argue that the 'metaborder' between the metropolis and its respective colonies that characterised the colonial era has by now yielded to an altered geographical disposition, wherein the mechanisms of domination and subordination inherited from colonialism are being reproduced within the space of Europe itself.[2] Fully implicated in the neoliberal/neocolonial regime of global capitalism (or 'Empire', to use the term proposed by Michael Hardt and Antonio Negri),[3] today's Europe is conceptualised as a space whose boundaries are more elusive than the sharp dichotomies imposed by historical colonialism but whose modalities of exclusion and marginalisation are no less insidious.

Although Miguel Mellino has identified a general unwillingness among Italian academics, even among those few scholars who acknowledge the validity of post-colonial discourse when applied to the Anglophone world, to trace connections 'between the problems and approaches developed within post-

colonial studies and the specific history of Italy, its cultural dialectics and struggles and internal politics',[4] it should be acknowledged that a small number of literary scholars working at Italian universities have been engaged in the analysis of Italian literature from a post-colonial perspective for more than a decade. Though their work is still considered outside the mainstream of academic discourse in Italy, these scholars have productively applied the post-colonial critique of essentialism, exoticism and orientalism to the interpretation of texts by canonical Italian writers, while also paying attention to the voices of writers from Italy's former colonies and to the growing body of literature produced in Italian by immigrant, diasporic and post-colonial writers. There has not yet been a comparable surge of interest in articulating a post-colonial critique of contemporary Italian cinema.

In the scant body of work investigating elements of the 'post-colonial' in contemporary Italian cinema, the focus of critical attention has generally been placed on an analysis of the visual or narrative construction of racial difference in Italy's so-called cinema of migration, tracing the continuities of this discourse with patterns of representation established during the colonial era. Taking a sociological approach, an insightful article by Antonella D'Arma looks at the evolving figure of the black woman in Italian cinema over the past several decades.[5] Beginning with a brief review of films from the 1970s and 1980s – and particularly those starring the Eritrean-born actress Zeudi Araya – D'Arma notes that the dominant image of the black woman during that period coincided with the colonial-era icon of the 'beautiful native woman', now reconstructed as a modern femme fatale. Exotic, mysterious and sexually irresistible, this distinctive figure emerges in cinematic representation primarily as the seductress of white men. For D'Arma, these representations suggest that the stereotypes derived from colonialism still permeated the collective imaginary years after the end of the colonial era, 'reinforcing new manifestations of racism and fears vis-à-vis the Other, perceived as [a] threat to [Italian] identity'. More varied and ambivalent are the images of African women that have emerged since 1990, that is, since the onset of mass immigration to Italy. Basing her survey on a sample of twenty Italian films produced between 1990 and 2003, D'Arma provides a striking catalogue of the stereotypes inhabited by black women migrants in Italian cinema in recent years, the majority of which are constructed as prostitutes, in a pattern that suggests an 'atemporal colonial reality that subsists even today in the Italian collective imaginary'. Although D'Arma is perceptive in her identification of the stereotype, she does not explain its functioning at a symbolic level. In this context, Bhabha's theorisation of colonial discourse is particularly useful.

Extrapolating from the insights of Fanon, Bhabha argues that the ideological construction of otherness established by colonialism is grounded in the concept of 'fixity'.[6] This fixity is the 'sign of cultural/historical/racial difference' and its principal strategy is the stereotype, that is, a 'form of knowledge and identification that vacillates between what is always "in place", already known, and something that must be anxiously repeated'; ambivalence is integral to the structure of colonial discourse and ensures the stereotype's 'repeatability in changing historical and discursive conjunctures, [informing] its strategies of individuation and marginalization'. For Bhabha, the reality effect produced by representations that have consolidated into stereotypes cannot be countered by images that are more authentic, in the sense of being more mimetically faithful to an underlying, pre-given reality. Nor can they simply be replaced by anti-realist representations. Bhabha thus proposes moving beyond the attempt to characterise images simply as positive or negative, which implies a 'prior political normativity' and depends on 'processes of subjectification made possible (and plausible) through stereotypical discourse'. Far from advocating the deconstruction of colonial discourse in order to reveal its ideological misrepresentations and thus to 'subject its representations to a normalising judgement', Bhabha believes that it is crucial to understand this discourse as a 'regime of truth' and to discern within it the 'productivity of colonial power'.

One of the products of the colonial 'regime of truth', Bhabha argues, is the 'recognition' of racial difference, a recognition achieved principally through the construction of 'skin, as a signifier of discrimination'. The repetitious insistence on skin, or what Fanon called the epidermal schema, is imbricated in the process of discrimination. Suppressing the awareness of the *production* of racial difference, discrimination presents itself as 'natural', based on the 'evidence of the visible', or on colour 'as the cultural/political sign of inferiority or degeneracy, skin as its natural "identity"'. Bhabha's understanding of the 'stereotype-as-suture' places an emphasis on the ambivalence of colonial authority and its orders of identification. Drawing on Freud's theory of fetishism, he argues that the

stereotype is a fetishistic mode of representation. It is thus both narcissistic and aggressive, allowing the subject to embrace simultaneously two contradictory beliefs. This process of splitting has specific consequences, since 'the recognition and disavowal of "difference" is always disturbed by the question of its representation or construction'. Moreover, the fiction imposed by the colonising subject is always threatened by the potential return of the look of the other.

I bring these arguments into play in order to examine two Italian films released in recent years where we observe a self-conscious attempt to grapple with the increasingly interracial, transnational aspects of contemporary Italian society, a decidedly post-colonial and still incipiently 'multicultural' space. First, let us consider Cristina Comencini's *Bianco e nero* (*Black and White*, 2008), whose very title pointedly draws attention to the issue of epidermal difference. Rather than attempting to assess whether the film is progressive or racist, whether its depiction of non-European characters is positive or negative, I am interested in the productive enactments of racial difference that it offers throughout. Inspired by Stanley Kramer's *Guess Who's Coming to Dinner?* (1963), this crowd-pleasing romantic comedy unfolds in a middle-class Roman environment, where all the characters, black and white, enjoy a significant level of economic comfort. There are no allusions to clandestine immigration, trafficking in women or the many other problems highlighted in most of Italy's so-called cinema of migration. Despite its circumscribed social setting, the film's self-reflexive consideration of race and racism is certainly worthy of scrutiny.

Bianco e nero takes a rather conventional tale of adulterous love, where two married people are swept away by a mutual infatuation that threatens to wreck their dull but stable marriages, and adds racial difference to the mix. The lovers – Nadine (Aïssa Maïga), a Senegalese embassy employee, and Carlo (Fabio Volo), a computer technician – are drawn to each other not only by physical attraction but also by a shared reluctance to embrace the humanitarian zeal that inspires their respective spouses, who both work for a benevolent organisation catering to Africans. Despite its contrived plot, awkward juxtapositions and self-conscious dialogue, *Bianco e nero* makes a deliberate effort to explore the processes of fetishism and disavowal at work in racial differentiation and their implications for the consolidation of a 'multicultural' social landscape.

Nella vita non è tutto bianco o nero...esistono le sfumature.

un film di
CRISTINA COMENCINI

BIANCO e NERO

FABIO VOLO   AMBRA ANGIOLINI   AÏSSA MAÏGA   ERIQ EBOUANEY
ANNA BONAIUTO   FRANCO BRANCIAROLI   TERESA SAPONANGELO e con KATIA RICCIARELLI

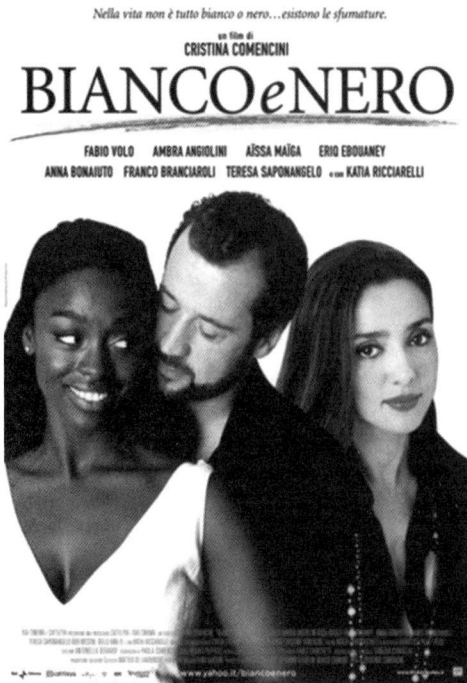

The poster advertising Comencini's *Bianco e nero* (2008) appeals to Italian consumers with the image of a biracial triangle

The poster used to advertise *Bianco e nero* appeals to Italian consumers in broadly conventional terms with the image of a biracial triangle composed of two popular television personalities (Fabio Volo and Ambra Angiolini) and the alluring black actress Aïssa Maïga, who, though well known in France, is unfamiliar to Italian audiences.

In this context Maïga's image immediately evokes the iconic Black Venus, a figure deployed with varying connotations in literary, political and visual texts throughout Italy's colonial history, and recycled, as D'Arma's study suggests, in popular Italian films of the 1970s and 1980s. One of the challenges of the film is, in fact, to invest this exotic figure with a credible sense of subjectivity, a project it only partially manages to accomplish.

Though *Bianco e nero* strives to pay equal attention to Carlo and Nadine, it is nonetheless articulated primarily as a story of (white) male maturation, focusing on the rather infantile, self-centred Carlo and his personal transformation through an encounter with a world he had never known before. In his first scene, he feigns illness in order to deflect his wife's invitation to accompany her to a fundraiser for an African charity. As she leaves the room, however, his gaze is drawn to a

book that bears the title *Africa* and privileges the image of a nude black woman on its cover. A close-up of this image is immediately followed by a shot of Carlo seated at the fundraiser, suggesting that it was the lure embodied in the 'tasteful' ethnographic photograph that finally persuaded him to attend. Yet, unable to bear the vision of poverty and deprivation evoked by the speaker, he escapes to an adjoining courtyard. It is in this context that he seems to conjure out of the darkness the apparition of Nadine – his own imagined Africa.

The beautiful Nadine thus enters the *mise en scène* through Carlo's gaze as an almost magical materialisation of his unspoken desire. Nonetheless, the film allows her an immediate assertion of defiant subjectivity, as she challenges his assumed preconceptions. Approaching Carlo, she provocatively invites him to acknowledge that she is black, flaunting the politically incorrect term 'negra' instead of the more acceptable 'nera', and drawing attention to visibility as the principal signifying component in racial differentiation. This visibility, as Bhabha has shown, is not 'given' by nature but must be repeatedly acknowledged and performed. Yet, even as she flamboyantly invokes her blackness, Nadine resists its global associations, expressing her intolerance for the images of African misery perpetrated by the charitable organisation that is directed, it turns out, by her own husband with the assistance of Carlo's wife.

Bianco e nero alludes at several junctures to constructions of racial difference in the cultural experiences of everyday life in contemporary Italy, invoking examples from children's literature and toys to Internet porn, ethnographic photography, cinema, humanitarian promotional material and imported artefacts. In the process, it suggests the competing effects of these articulations on the characters' lives and relationships. It also gestures to the ways in which children, despite the well-meaning efforts of supposedly enlightened parents, absorb the dominant discourses on race.

Crucially, an important scene in the film points to the concealed racism embodied in the enactment of political correctness and multicultural tolerance. This focus emerges in the course of a sequence at a children's birthday hosted by Carlo's bourgeois parents-in-law. During the party Nadine's eight-year-old daughter, who has been forbidden by her educated black parents to possess a white Barbie doll, manages to steal the lavish Barbie Bride presented to Carlo's

Carlo, Nadine and her husband in
Comencini's *Bianco e Nero* (2008)

daughter by her grandmother. Following the
announcement of the doll's disappearance, a search is
undertaken and the 'culprit' is exposed, much to the
satisfaction of the obviously bigoted mother-in-law, who
quickly restores the stolen gift to her grandchild. Carlo's
benevolent wife, however, intervenes by grabbing the
doll from her daughter's grasp and returning it to the
other child, insisting that she keep it. It is at this
moment that Carlo's daughter, outraged at the injustice
inherent in her mother's desire to project multicultural
largesse, begins to weep, loudly protesting that the
other child is being allowed to keep the stolen object
simply because she is black. The girl's protest makes a
memorable impact in the overall texture of the film, not
simply for its comic effect, but because it constitutes a
rare attempt to expose the forced benevolence and
residual racism at the heart of efforts to impose a
perception of multicultural equality where none exists.

Much as *Bianco e nero* attempts to endow Nadine
with the capacity to resist the objectification of
the stereotype, there is a static element in its
representation of her resistance. It is as though the film
cannot fully imagine the kind of interstitial space she
inhabits and the varied forms of subversion and protest
that it might enable, focusing instead on her (almost
perfect) mimicry of Western bourgeois mannerisms. To
its credit, however, the narrative does not impose an
artificial happy ending and remains undecided about
the ongoing viability of the relationship between the
besotted pair. In the final sequence, as Carlo and
Nadine embrace each other anew after a period of
separation, the fierce hostility of their children can be
heard in the off-screen space. Although Carlo asserts
that the children, despite their antagonism, are simply
going to have to get used to things the way they are,
there is little in the story to suggest that the path
ahead will be an easy or even practicable one.

Claudio Noce's debut feature *Good Morning, Aman*
(*Good Morning, Aman*, 2009) provides a much bleaker
vision of Italy's changing demographic profile, along
with the racism and exclusions that have accompanied
this shift. Furthermore, the film explicitly constructs
the contemporary social landscape through the
perspective of a hybrid figure who is neither fully
African (having lived in Italy for almost all his life) nor
fully Italian (since his interlocutors refuse to accept
him as such). This character is the twenty-year old,
Somali-born Aman (Said Sabrie) who moved to Rome at
the age of four and lives in a sprawling public housing
complex to the south of the city. As a Somali, he is one
of the few characters in contemporary Italian cinema
explicitly designated as hailing from the former Italian
East Africa. Speaking Italian with a marked Roman
accent, he is nonetheless interpellated by Italians
throughout the film as an abject outsider. Since the
narration is focalised entirely through his subjectivity,
it articulates a perception of the world that is linked to
his liminal position, offering challenges to the viewer
that I propose to unpack with recourse to Bhabha's
theorisation of the 'unhomely'.

In the face of humiliations large and small, Aman
cultivates the apparently unachievable fantasy of
abandoning Italy and moving to Canada, where his
purported brother, the real-life Somali-born rap star
K'nann, has achieved fame and fortune, and perhaps
more importantly, has asserted his voice. In the early
part of the film, Aman experiences various losses – he
is fired from his job by his racist manager; he loses his
closest Somali friend, Said (Amin Nur), who moves to
London to work; and he is abandoned by the attractive
Italian woman he had pursued for weeks. The element
that takes over his life as everything else crumbles
around him is his growing friendship with Teodoro
(Valerio Mastandrea), a reclusive ex-boxer who, though

Teodoro and Aman in Noce's *Good Morning, Aman* (2009)

unabashedly racist, begins to regale the young man with generous gifts of cash. Only near the end of the film does Teodoro's motive emerge. Abandoned by his wife and child as the result of killing a young Senegalese migrant in an act of drunken folly three years earlier, he somehow imagines that by building a friendship with another black youth, as a sort of fetishistic replacement for the dead migrant, he will convince his family to allow him back into their lives.

The central preoccupation of *Good Morning, Aman* is the unlivability of Aman's racialised status in a social environment that refuses to confront the ongoing legacy of colonial racism. The film conveys his mounting restlessness, frustration and sense of exclusion through the abundant use of hand-held camera, elliptical editing, extreme close-ups and the virtual absence of establishing shots. These stylistic choices allow the viewer limited access to the characters' motivations, and create ontological confusion when counterfactual elements or diegetically unmarked fantasies are intercut with the ongoing progression of the narrative.

Though much of the film is implicitly engaged with the issue of voice, or rather, with the marginalised subject's access to speech, this concern emerges only interstitially through the disjunctive articulation of Aman's subjectivity. Affecting a cool demeanour, the young man seems for the most part unwilling or unable to say what he thinks or feels. When he eventually opens up enough to relate to Teodoro a terrible scene of violence purportedly experienced by his family in Mogadishu, the Italian replies with sarcasm, effectively negating Aman's attempt to initiate a more challenging level of communication between the two of them. The only moment of decisive opposition that he is able to muster occurs near the end of the film, when, having finally confronted the duplicitous Teodoro, now hospitalised

as the result of self-injury, he appears to walk out of his life for good.

After Said's departure for London, phonecalls between Aman and his friend are heard at intervals on the soundtrack, most of them probably imagined. In the course of these calls, Aman offers upbeat reports on his life, all of which are counter to fact. Infusing the narrative with uncertainty, the contrast between the events shown on the image track and the information conveyed in the voiceover bulletins is the first clue to the film's investment in the register of the uncanny, or the 'unhomely', as it is described by Bhabha. The sense of uncanniness generated through recourse to elliptical narration increases steadily throughout the film, as the viewer struggles to make sense of the conflicting scenarios that simultaneously occupy Aman's perceptual frame. Bhabha's analysis of the articulation of the liminal space of marginality in post-colonial cultural production revolves around the concept of unhomeliness, which draws not only on Freud's *unheimlich* (usually translated as the 'uncanny') but also on the reformulation of that concept by Julia Kristeva in her analysis of racism and nationalism.[7] Kristeva understands the *unheimlich* not in terms of an external other but rather in terms of the 'other within', the 'stranger to ourselves', and argues that the anxiety experienced by the subject (in this case, the subject-as-citizen) vis-à-vis what cannot be symbolically represented in and by the self is projected outward onto foreigners and others who occupy the social margins. Bhabha also appears to draw on Kristeva's perception of a positive element in the stranger's liminality, attributing to the alien or marginalised subject a freedom from the burden of historical representation taken on by those who feel they have to defend the integrity of the nation. In his landmark essay, 'The World and the Home', he demonstrates this kind of discursive freedom or subversion in the work of writers from diasporic, post-colonial or other marginalised groups by focusing on their textual articulation of the unhomely.[8]

Using examples from novels by Toni Morrison and Nadine Gordimer, Bhabha shows how these texts reveal the fault lines characterising the effort to represent the effects of human displacement as well as the social and political consequences of migrations and cultural relocations.[9] His investigation of the trope of locality focuses on those disruptive textual moments in which the equation of home and identity is thrown into crisis through the expression of the

Saharan journey in Dagmawi Yimer's *Come un uomo sulla terra* (2010)

uncanny. In the context of post-colonial subjectivity, the unhomely – emerging as a phantom shadow of what is familiar – points to the impossibility of identifying the status of the self with conventional notions of habitation. In this way, political and private spaces are no longer perceived as distinct, nor are public history and personal memory. In short, for Bhabha, 'the unhomely moment relates the traumatic ambivalences of a personal, psychic history to the wider disjunctions of political existence'.[10]

Bhabha's concept of the unhomely might be deployed in a slightly different way for an analysis of the spectral irruption of the post-colonial in scenes from other contemporary Italian films, which similarly gesture toward the issue of Italy's unresolved colonial legacy, such as the eerie sequence in Mohsen Melliti's *Io l'altro* (I, the Other, 2006) featuring the accidental recovery of a drowned Somali woman whose body has resurfaced in the waters of the Mediterranean. A scene inflected by a comparable sense of the uncanny occurs in Emanuele Crialese's *Terraferma* (Dry Land, 2011), where the young Sicilian protagonist, taking a midnight boat trip around an island presumed to be Lampedusa, is suddenly confronted by a host of flailing black bodies emerging from the water like aliens rising from the deep. Clinging to his boat, they struggle desperately to climb on board, while the Sicilian violently pushes all of them back into the sea, as though warding off the undead. Rather than pointing explicitly to the history of Italian colonial conquest, these poignantly 'unhomely' moments evoke symbolically both the repression of colonial memory and its refusal to stay entirely buried.

Unlike contemporary Italian literature, which includes a sizeable body of work by writers affiliated

with various colonial diasporas or who occupy marginal positions as immigrants within the national space, mainstream Italian cinema has not yet been significantly marked by the direct contribution of migrant or 'post-colonial' film-makers. Isolated initiatives have nonetheless emerged, particularly in the field of independent documentary film-making. Of these, the most striking example is the work of Ethiopian-born Dagmawi Yimer, who has co-directed three noteworthy documentaries – *Come un uomo sulla terra* (Like a Man on Earth, 2010), *C.A.R.A. Italia* (C.A.R.A. Italy, 2010) and *Soltanto il mare* (Only the Sea, 2011) – on the difficult migration of asylum seekers from the Horn of Africa to Italy, and their treatment at the hands of Libyan, Italian and EU authorities.

In the most recent of these films, Dagmawi Yimer turns his enquiring gaze back at Italian citizens, and specifically at the people of Lampedusa, inviting them to express their opinions on immigration and on the Italian scene more generally. Here we get a sense of the kinds of unhomely truths the emergence of such 'post-colonial' interventions within the wider field of mainstream Italian film-making might ultimately reveal.

NOTES

1. Homi K. Bhabha, 'Postcolonial Criticism', in Stephen Greenblatt and Giles Gunn (eds), *Redrawing the Boundaries: The Transformation of English and American Literary Studies* (New York: MLA, 1992), pp. 437–65.
2. Sandro Mezzarda and Fderico Rohola, 'The Postcolonial Condition: A Few Notes on the Quality of Historical Time in the Global Present', *Postcolonial Text* vol. 2 no. 1 (2006). Online.
3. Michael Hardt and Antonio Negri, *Empire* (Cambridge, MA: Harvard University Press, 2006).
4. Miguel Mellino, 'Italy and Postcolonial Studies: A Difficult Encounter', *Interventions* vol. 8 no. 3 (2006), p. 463.
5. Antonella D'Arma, 'Lo stereotipo della donna nera nel cinema italiano, ' *Studi emigrazione* no. 169 (2008), pp. 59–71. Subsequent citations from this source are found on pp. 63 and 67. For further analyses of 'post-colonial' discourses in contemporary Italian cinema, see Duncan, O'Healy and Zambenedetti, all published outside Italy. Similar studies of earlier films from the Italian canon have also emerged in recent years.
6. Homi K. Bhabha, *The Location of Culture* (London: Routledge, 1994), p. 66; subsequent citations in the next two paragraphs from this book are found on pp. 67, 79 and 80.

7. Julia Kristeva, *Strangers to Ourselves*, trans. Leon S. Roudiez (New York: Columbia University Press, 1991).

8. Homi K. Bhabha, 'The World and the Home', in Anne McClintock, Aamir Mufti and Ella Shohat (eds), *Dangerous Liaisons: Gender, Nation and Postcolonial Perspectives* (Minneapolis: Minnesota University Press, 1997), pp. 141–53.

9. Ibid., p. 141.

10. Ibid., p. 143.

FURTHER READING

Césaire, Aimé, *Discours sur le colonialisme* (Paris: Présence Africaine, 1955).

Duncan, Derek, 'Kledi Kadiu: Italian National Cinema and Postcolonial Stardom', in Robert Clarke (ed.), *Celebrity Colonialism: Fame, Power and Representation in Colonial and Postcolonial Cultures* (Newcastle: Cambridge Scholars Publications, 2009), pp. 225–38.

——, 'Italy's Postcolonial Cinema and Its Histories of Representation', *Italian Studies* vol. 63 no. 2 (2008), pp. 195–211.

Fanon, Frantz, *The Wretched of the Earth*, trans. Richard Philcox (New York: Grove Press, 2004).

——, *Black Skin, White Masks*, trans. Richard Philcox (New York: Grove Press, 2008).

Glissant, Edouard, *Le Discours antillais* (Paris: Seuil, 1981).

Lombardi, Diop, Cristina Romeo and Caterina Romeo (eds), *Postcolonial Italy: Challenging National Homogenity* (New York: Palgrave Macmillan, 2012).

O'Healy, Áine, '"[Non] è una Somala": Deconstructing African Femininity in Italian Film', *The Italianist* vol. 29 no. 2 (2009), pp. 175–98.

Spivak, Gayatri Chakravorty, *In Other Worlds: Essays in Cultural Politics* (London: Routledge, 1987).

——, 'Can the Subaltern Speak?', in Cary Nelson and Lawrence Grossberg (eds), *Marxism and the Interpretation of Culture* (Urbana: University of Illinois Press, 1988), pp. 271–313.

Zambenedetti, Alberto, 'Multiculturalism in New Italian Cinema: The Impact of Migration, Diaspora, and the Post-colonial on Italy's Self-representation', in Michela Ardizzoni and Chiara Ferrari (eds), *Beyond Monopoly: Globalization and Contemporary Italian Media* (Lanham, MD: Lexington Books, 2010), pp. 245–68.

Mary P. Wood

Mario Bava had a long career as a cinematographer and film director from 1939 until 1979. He worked entirely in the mid- to low-budget, popular genre sector of the Italian film industry and his work thus fell victim to the pervasive critical snobbery which assigned value mainly to films displaying a realist aesthetic and serious themes. Bava is celebrated as a horror film director, but his output includes mythological films, *Ercole al centro della terra* and the 'Polifemo' episode of Franco Rossi's *L'Odissea* (*The Odyssey*, 1968); Viking adventures *Gli invasori* (*Fury of the Vikings* aka *Erik the Conqueror* aka *The Invaders*, 1961) and *I coltelli del vendicatore* (*Knives of the Avenger* aka *Massacre of the Vikings*, 1966); comedy, *Le meraviglie di Aladino* (*Wonders of Aladdin*, 1961), *Le spie vengono dal semifreddo* (*Dr. Goldfoot and the Girl Bombs*, 1966); three Westerns, *La strada per Forte Alamo* (*Arizona Bill* aka *Road to Fort Alamo*, 1965), *Ringo del Nebraska* (*Dollars of Nebraska*, 1965) and *Roy Colt & Winchester Jack* (*Roy Colt and Winchester Jack*, 1969); science fiction, *Terrore nello spazio* (*Planet of the Vampires* aka *The Demon Planet*, 1965); a comic-book adaptation, *Diabolik* (*Danger: Diabolik*, 1968); a sex film, *Quante volte quella notte* (*Four Times That Night*, 1969); a kidnap road movie, *Cani arrabiati* (*Rabid Dogs*, 1974, completed 1995); and a television adaptation of Prosper Mérimée's *La venere d'Ille* (1978). In addition, he was frequently employed (mostly uncredited) to complete, supervise or rescue other films, most notably Riccardo Freda's *I vampiri* and *Caltiki – il mostro immortale*, Jacques Tourneur's *La battaglia di Maratona*, and the Italian version of Raoul Walsh's *Esther and the King*.

Bava's horror films are as difficult to categorise neatly as the popular genre films above as they incorporate elements from more than one genre, often displaying Gothic, thriller, *giallo* and comedy traits, sometimes all at once.[1] Mario Bava's career therefore provides a prime opportunity to explore what makes

Italian film genres different from their Anglo-Saxon counterparts and how cultural value is assigned. Plenty of other Italian film-makers made cheap genre films, but few were regarded as highly by their peers and employers as Mario Bava was then, or have their entire back catalogues available on DVD and cult status among a new constituency now.

GENRE OR *FILONE*?

A study of Mario Bava's career throws into sharp relief the difficulties of applying Anglo-Saxon film genre theory to the Italian case, in the first instance because the Italian film industry, post-1945, was not structured around studios on the American model. Chris Wagstaff defines a *filone* as a formula film, but this definition fails to take into account the dynamism and inventiveness which characterise their evolution.[2] A *filone* is a strand of similar films, rather than a genre. Italian producers were adept at spotting new trends, keeping an eye open for signs of successful subjects, names, themes and stars, quickly rushing similar films into production, until public interest was seen to wane and new variants had to be tried. The oscillation between repetition and development became characteristic of the Italian film industry. Within the Spaghetti Western genre there exist many *filoni*, such as those involving the characters Django or Satana, and the mythological peplum genre fragmented into *filoni* involving heroes from various epochs, sometimes present in the same film. High-budget films relied on quick exploitation in the *prima visione* circuits (city-centre cinemas), while low-budget genre films, turned out in considerable numbers, could make their returns more slowly in a couple of years in suburban, then provincial and rural cinemas, church halls and seasonal venues in this period. This long chain explains the overlapping of *filoni* as the tail end of peplum epics would be present in the market at the same time as the spaghetti Western was developing.

Bava's Viking films provide evidence that the mythological genre did not have stable identities and borders and, despite working in many *filoni*, his films exhibit narrative continuities and repetitions from film to film – a baroque style privileging spectacular visual and graphic organisation and use of colour; the use and re-use of sets such as the monumental fireplace of *I vampiri*, *La maschera del demonio*, *La frusta e il corpo* (*The Whip and the Flesh/Night Is the Phantom*, 1963), the plastic rocks, inherited from mythological films, of *Terrore nello spazio*, and locations.

Auteurist directors also made genre films but the basic calculation made by Mario Bava's producers was that his films would not qualify for 'quality' designation and the state subvention which would only arrive two years after release. For producer, distributor and exhibitor, economic rather than critical recognition was the primary basis for evaluating Bava's type of cinema, but he should not be regarded as inferior to his overtly auteurist contemporaries. Bava's career in the 1960s and 70s has to be explained in the context of the Italian and international film industries.

NAVIGATING THE SEA OF GENRES

Mario Bava's career was shaped by his artisan origins as director of photography and by Italian cinema's use of genres and *filoni* as a survival mechanism. As Pauline Small has identified, producers, stars and those taking artistic and technical roles were essentially freelance workers, hired on an *ad hoc* basis in the postwar period.[3] This did not change as the film industry gradually modernised, becoming professionalised but not less precarious. Bava was an attractive proposition: he was experienced and therefore worked extremely fast, and his artistic and craft skills meant that his films often had the look of those with much larger budgets. His films could be released and distributed quickly, and the producers for whom he worked had both national and international contacts.

When Freda and Bava made *I vampiri*, Italy did not have a Gothic horror tradition. Box office was poor and did not spawn a *filone* until the success of Hammer's *Dracula* (Terence Fisher, 1958). *La maschera del demonio* added to the Hammer template a monstrous female killer in the sensual English actress Barbara Steele (who played the roles of both Asa and Katia), and anxieties over female autonomy. The film had modest success in Italy, was banned in the UK, and a slightly different

version was sold to American International Pictures in the US, where it was very successful. It is worth reflecting at this point on the significance of these elements.

From the 1950s, Italian popular films designed for export frequently included foreign actors in their casts, or Italian actors, scriptwriters, cinematographers and directors who adopted American-sounding names. The danger for Bava in the 1960s was that content viewed as perverse (such as the sadistic murder of the witch, Asa, the threatened vampirising by her father of Katia, and the taking over of Katia's body by Asa in *La maschera del demonio*) might cause a film to be banned and deprived of release in a lucrative territory such as the UK. On the other hand, such content was part of a film's appeal in many overseas markets and is a factor in Bava's contemporary cult reputation. Not only would Bava make slightly different versions of his films for different territories but, in order to suck the last revenue from their purchase, distributors and exhibitors would often rename and repackage the film in a double bill, accounting for multiple titles. The power of a producer to impose subjects, actors and sets is confirmed by Bava, who rarely turned down a proposed project.[4]

The *filone* phenomenon explains Bava's slowness to follow *La maschera del demonio* with another horror production. The generic practices deriving from a crowded market, a fragmented production sector cautiously trying to identify the next trend and the use and re-use of successful earlier traits encouraged Bava and his producers to rework existing hits, sets and locations, but interject his own visual flair and expertise in colour cinematography, pushing at the boundaries of these genres and *filoni* projects.

By 1960, the mythological genre was fragmenting into sub-*filoni*, with producers testing the limits, until the phenomenal success of Sergio Leone's *Per un pugno di dollari* hastened the migration of Italian actors from

Inventive visual organisation in Bava's *Ercole al centro della terra* (1958)

the mythological to the spaghetti Western. Budgets were kept low as films had to jostle for distribution space. Bava's two 1961 films – the Viking epic *Gli invasori* for Galatea, and *Ercole al centro della terra* for SPA Cinematografica – show how the above constraints were managed. The latter, filmed in delirious colour, incorporated plot elements from classical traditions, body builder Reg Park as Hercules,[5] comedy and coded sexual references, but also Christopher Lee (a Hammer stalwart) as the villain, Lycos, scheming to take over the realm of Hercules' love interest, Princess Deianira (Leonora Ruffo), who unleashes the vampires that test Hercules' prowess at the end.

The fast-paced Viking epic, on the other hand, follows the mythological story template of two brothers separated when young now leading conflicts on opposite sides, unaware of their relationship, but is much closer to the template set by Richard Fleischer's *The Vikings* (1958) than Bava's later *I coltelli del vendicatore*, which incorporates traits of *Shane* (1953), the spaghetti Western (knives take the place of guns, conflicts take place in Viking 'saloons'), and the supernatural (the witch who foretells the death of the evil Hagen [Fausto Tozzi]). Bava's added twist is that none of the characters represents a convincing evolution of representations of masculinity, both Hagen and Rurik (Cameron Mitchell) being tainted by violence and cruelty. There is much galloping over sand dunes, along riverbeds and beaches (Bava's favourite location at Tor Caldara near Anzio) as male heroes undertake quests defining their masculinity by action, in opposition to the passivity exhibited by the females.

Bava returned to horror in 1963 with *La ragazza che sapeva troppo* and three European co-productions, *La frusta e il corpo*, *I tre volti della paura* (*Black Sabboth*, 1963) and *Sei donne per l'assassino*. *Ragazza* initiated the *giallo filone*, featuring an active, modern heroine, Nora Davis (Leticia Román), using her knowledge of detective fiction to solve a murder only she believes happened. Her investigation leads her into danger. Use of low- and high-angle framings and the velvety black-and-white photography, which contributed to the atmosphere of *Maschera*, emphasise the baroque curlicues of the Spanish Steps, the ironwork screens which trap Nora in the apartment loaned by her aunt's friend, Laura (revealed as the murderer and played by Valentina Cortese), and the menace of the empty rooms to which Nora is lured, the disturbing visual organisation being characteristic of Bava's neo-baroque aesthetic. Here, the

oscillation between contemporary and Gothic worlds expresses both a desire to consolidate a new *filone* advance, and the outward indication of inner fear and unease.

Hedging his horror bets, the three stories of *I tre volti della paura* include a contemporary *giallo* set in a claustrophobic apartment; an episode inspired by French nineteenth-century horror thrillers; and a nod to the European Gothic tradition in the 'I Wurdalak' episode (a wurdalak is a kind of vampire). Bava manages to inject a lesbian relationship, black leather gloves and three murders into the *giallo*, the suggestion of paedophilia and incest in the grandfather's (Boris Karloff) vampiristic pursuit of his young grandson, and his sons and daughters-in-law in 'I Wurdalak', and showcases his special effects and predilection for spectacle and visual excess in the use of saturated colour and labyrinthine ruins. The mixture of uncertainty and the supernatural is typical of Italian horror, but a perverse excitement at being whipped is added to the monstrous female protagonist template in *La frusta e il corpo*, which re-uses the heavy pillars and claustrophobic crypts familiar from the Gothic *filone*, spatial and narrative ambiguity (is Kurt [Christopher Lee] dead or a figment of Nevenka's [Daliah Lavi] tortured imagination?) and saturated blue, yellow, green and violet.

Sei donne per l'assassino returns to the *giallo* and a glamorous contemporary world opened up by the 1960s economic boom. It is an investigation of serial murders committed in a fashion house, a location licensing attention on the bodies, clothing (or not) of beautiful young women, who are then killed in sadistic and graphic fashion. Bava adds his usual delight in colour effects which heighten the emotional impact of his characters' fear and terror, and the revelation that the killer is a woman. The sheer number of murders and

The beauty of pain in Bava's *La frusta e il corpo* (1963)

the pace of the killing spree from the opening sequences augment the *giallo* template.

The films made between 1964 and 1966 illustrate the process of genre and *filoni* development, experimentation and influence. Prompted by Leone's success, Bava interrupted his horror run with two Westerns, *La strada per Forte Alamo* (under the name John M. Old) and *Ringo del Nebraska*. Bava was denied directorial credits on the latter as it was an Italy–Spain co-production, necessitating Antonio Román's name on the credits. Both have conventional Western plots of the outsider who takes on the bad guys, restores order and rides off. Bava's Westerns are usually ignored by his fanbase and *Roy Colt e Winchester Jack* is no exception. Produced by Mario Bregni for Produzione Atlas Cinematografica, it has been damned as irredeemably mediocre by Pezzotta for its marshalling of every spaghetti Western cliché[6] but its irony and playfulness show how fast spaghetti Western *filoni* were developing. Producer/distributor P.A.C. epitomises the Italian approach to genre. Contemporaneously, it produced Bava's *Cinque bambole per la luna d'agosto* (*Five Dolls for an August Moon*, 1970) and low-budget Westerns, gradually moving into the nunsploitation *filone* of 1970s Italian soft porn. Bava's Westerns lack the stylisation of Leone's films, but share close-ups of grotesque faces and graphic violence, to which Bava adds colour effects to divert attention from the studio floor, and tight editing in landscape long shots to conceal the limitations of his locations.

Terrore nello spazio, produced by Fulvio Lucisano for Italian International Pictures, is distinguished by visual invention in the depiction of the spaceship Argos and the mysterious planet on which it is forced to land. It had modest success in the US. Characterisation is minimal and, since the crew wear identical spacesuits, only Captain Mark (Barry Sullivan) and his red-haired female assistant Sanya (Norma Bengell) are easily differentiated. Use of models in exterior shots of the landing, and the beautifully realised circular features of another wrecked spacecraft containing the skeletons of enormous alien beings show Bava's invention and visual acuity. Faced with a very low budget, Bava's aliens are conveniently non-corporeal; they take over the bodies of the hapless crew and speak through them, the ultimate in vampiristic control.[7] The vampires take over Mark and Sanya who, in a final twist, are also revealed to be aliens.

Fulvio Lucisano also produced the formulaic spy comedy, *Le spie vengono dal semifreddo*, starring well-known comics, Franco and Ciccio, and Vincent Price as Dr Goldfoot, using a host of gold-clad young women as the girl bombs in his plans for world domination. The film illustrates why Italian comedies do not travel, with the two comics gurning to camera, and Vincent Price seemingly acting in a different film. The sexist treatment of the girls reduces them to typical 1960s 'birds' but the film was predictably successful at the Italian box office.

Bava's 1966 *Operazione paura* (*Kill Baby, Kill*, 1966) returned to the Gothic *filone*, with an outsider, Dr Esway (Giacomo Rossi-Stuart), visiting an isolated village and investigating the strange deaths of the villagers, driven to kill themselves in horrendous ways after being visited by a giggling, white-clad ghost child, Melanie (played in the film by a young boy wearing a wig, named Valerio Valeri). The plot is complex, again mixing horror, the supernatural and a murderous older woman, Baroness Graps (Giovanna Galeti), who has conjured up the ghost to exact revenge on the villagers who she blames for Melanie's death. This film's lower than usual budget is not evident from the *mise en scène*. High-angle shots of the castle's corridor, lit by sconces grasped by male arms, crypt, never-ending circular staircase, and the baroque rooms of the baroness, misty exteriors bathed in yellow light, all evoke an atmosphere of threat from supernatural forces. The film is also admired for Bava's innovative camerawork, particularly in the scene where Esway races through eight identical rooms, realising that there is a figure in front of him, catching up with himself in the logic of a nightmare.

By 1967, the mass audience had moved to television and suburban cinemas were rebranded to show erotic or specialised cult films, aimed predominantly at the male audience. Dino De Laurentiis offered Bava a large budget to film *Diabolik*, based on the criminal hero of cult comics sold in Italian news kiosks. The interior of Diabolik's (John Philip Law) underground hideaway is particularly spectacular, littered with the accoutrements of extreme wealth – the sports cars, the 'modern' technology, his enormous bed, filled with stolen banknotes on which he makes love to his girlfriend Eva (Marisa Mel).

Diabolik is now fêted for its filmic translation of cartoon form. The DVD extras show how Bava understood that comics were able to create the illusion of great depth and movement by the use of depth of field, as in the cavern sequences, and by breaking up the frame into boxes, or screens within the screen. Although Bava tones down the cruelty and darkness of

the source material, visual fragmentation and excess mirror the iconoclasm represented by the figure of Diabolik. He operates at the very boundaries of society, mocking materialism and state institutions, a source of his appeal to the contemporary audience.

Following *Diabolik*'s release, De Laurentiis engaged Bava to film the o 'Polyphemus' episode of the TV series, *L'Odissea*. Backview shots of the one-eyed giant, Polyphemus (Bekin Fehmiu), smashing his human victims' bodies against the rocks preparatory to tearing off their limbs and eating them alternate with close-ups of their rescuers' horrified reactions. Bava avoids criticism for the inclusion of inappropriately cruel content in a children's programme by abstaining from shots of dismemberment or cannibalism, while prompting his young viewers' imagination to fill in the details.

Bava's output between 1970 and 1977 has been characterised as his decadent period. His last Western had generated 263 million lire at the box office, but the phenomenal success (1,229,940,000 lire) of Dario Argento's *giallo*, *L'uccello dalle piume di cristallo* revitalised production. In the next four years, Bava made five *gialli*, returning to the Gothic *filone* with *Gli orrori del castello di Norimberga* (*Baron Blood* aka *The Torture Chamber of Baron Blood* aka *The Thirst of Baron Blood*, 1972), and a sex film, *Quante volte quella notte*. All of these display the template identified earlier – repetition of successful plots, themes and visual styles from previous films. The ramping-up of the horrific and supernatural events and the graphic display of brutal deaths vary the template, together with greater display of glamorous and

luxurious interiors already present in *Sei donne* and *Diabolik*. *Il rosso segno della follia* (*Hatchet for the Honeymoon* aka *Blood Brides*, 1970) uses the setting of a wedding fashion house as motivation for the gruesome murders of brides, Bava's playfulness and sense of irony surfacing in the quotation from his 'I Wurdalak' to mask a victim's screams. *Cinque bambole per la luna d'agosto* uses Agatha Christie's *Ten Little Indians* plot (1939), multiple gruesome murders and the presence of Edwige Fenech, a central figure in Sergio Martino's more sexually explicit *gialli* of this period.

In *Reazione a catena* aka *Ecologia del delitto* (*Bay of Blood* aka *Bloodbath* aka *Twitch of the Death Nerve* aka *Carnage* aka *Last House on the Left Part 2*, 1971), Bava set himself the task of creating thirteen different depictions of violent death. In the first scene, the elderly, wheelchair-bound countess meets a violent death by hanging as the noose is dropped over her head by her husband, and her wheelchair is kicked away, leaving her body twitching at the window. Seconds later, her husband has his throat cut. Gradually greed emerges as the motivation of most of the characters as they scheme and murder in order to benefit from developing the bay into a resort. As Kim Newman has perceptively observed, 'The difference between art and commerce might be judged by the fact that, in Antonioni, the solution to the mystery is important but unknowable, while in the mainstream *giallo*, it is negligible but has to be gone into.'[8]

The spectacle of death is more important. None of the characters is likeable, although one has some sympathy for the hapless Scandinavian hippy whose

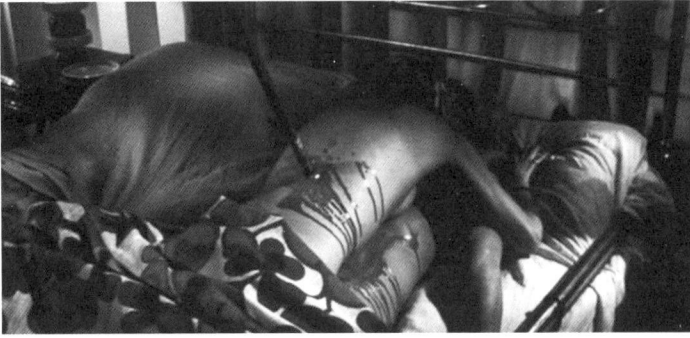

Excessive desire and excessive murder in *Reazione a catena* (1971)

only crime is to remove her clothes, dive into the bay and accidentally discover the count's rotting body. There seems to be no suggestion of punishment for sexual activity (typical of the *Friday the* 13th slasher-film franchises, which this film inspired), merely the idea that these hippies were in the wrong place at the wrong time – plot taking second place to titillation in the murder of the couple at the point of orgasm, heralded by noisy breathing and a spear appearing through the mattress.

An ecological subplot warns against disturbing the balance of nature, eliciting shots of the calm waters of the bay. Bava adds to the *filone* multiple perpetrators and an increasingly frenetic use of the zoom and reverse zoom for economic rather than aesthetic reasons, avoiding changes to lighting and camera set-ups and hire of tracks, to indicate characters talking to each other.

Bava's last films were held to be embarrassing, condemned by their low budgets to quoting murder set pieces, lighting and black gloves from his earlier films. Gothic plots from *La maschera del demonio* surface in *Castello*, hints of perversion in *Schock* aka *Schock (Transfer-Suspense-Hypnos)* (*Shock* aka *Beyond the Door II*, 1977) and extended chase sequences from *Operazione paura*. The plot points of *Lisa e il diavolo* aka *La casa dell'esorcismo* (*Lisa and the Devil* aka *The House of Exorcism*, 1974) are difficult to grasp, perhaps due to the low-budget/no-budget constraints Bava had to overcome, and his furious use of the zoom. Fans, on the other hand, admire the film precisely for the 'authenticity' of its solutions to production difficulties.

THE ROLE OF TRANSGRESSION
Joe Dante has given a vivid account of seeking out Italian horror films in drive-ins and grindhouse cinemas.[9] Not only did Italian film-makers and producers move into films with sexual or horrific content to counter competition from the US, but strong

links between Italian producers and US distributors led to US financial participation in Italian genre production. Transgression, explored through characters and social situations, was an attractive commercial option. *La maschera del demonio*, for example, starts with a hooded executioner branding the back of the beautiful witch, Asa, as she curses her executioners. A shot of the mask alternates with her point of view of the spikes in its interior, a huge mallet nails the mask of the demon to her face, enhanced sound and the oozing of blood from beneath the mask delivering the gore, death and horror so often mentioned by appreciative, male fans on IMDb.

Similarly, Asa's desiring gaze at Katia as she prepares to take over her body in order to restore her own shattered beauty displays more than a hint of transgressive sex.

Bava's films are not valued for their tastefulness, rounded characterisations and plots but precisely for what John Corner terms the 'bad popular', 'the popular as shaped within the terms of the market'.[10] At the time of their release, these films resonated with audiences experiencing enormous social change – US materialism threatening traditional values, increasing female autonomy at home and work, sexual freedom, threats to the environment – but their 'bad popular' status has enabled their absorption into the aftermarket of cult exploitation on the Internet. The eclecticism of the niche film genres covered by the Italian cult magazine *Nocturne* demonstrates how contemporary audiences distinguish themselves by acquiring knowledge and understanding of the production context of their chosen film directors or *filoni*. *Nocturne* devoted issue 24 to Mario Bava, re-released *Gli orrori del castello di Norimberga* and *Cani arrabiati* on DVD and confirmed Bava's influence on Japanese horror. The DVD extras and published contributions of Tim Lucas also feed desires for countercultural expertise.

The mask of Satan is nailed to Asa's face in *La maschera del demonio* (1960)

PROFESSIONALISM AND THE ROLE OF *TRUCCHI*

Bava's professionalism and competencies included full understanding of the economic imperatives in his niche of the film industry. Cine-literate Internet fans are interested in Bava's *trucchi* (tricks) – how he achieved the effects of instant ageing on an actor's face and the illusion of a large-scale naval battle, his inventiveness in fashioning special effects out of a pile of tripe (*Caltiki*), in-camera trickery, use of colour filters and gels – and value DVD extras which include interviews with Bava and his collaborators. In the age of computer-generated images, special effects and cheap, high-quality, sensitive cameras, Bava's films suggest the creative possibilities open to those who appreciate and seek to emulate a more individualistic, autonomous and local mode of production, contrasting starkly with the push towards homogeneity characteristic of globalised media. Professional expertise in 'bad popular' cinema is regarded as a mark of superior authenticity.

CONCLUSION

Mario Bava built his career in popular genres entirely by absorbing the practices of his sector of the film industry, revealing the complex process by which film-makers create *filoni*. Creativity in the use of cinematic means at their disposal, a stance of transgressiveness and signalling possession of the skills necessary to overcome difficulties are the rules, and the source of Bava's authority. *Filoni* traits regarded as postmodern – ambiguity, extreme horror and violence, lack of explanation of narrative context or the supernatural, visual excess – destabilise accepted notions of value and resist incorporation into Anglo-Saxon genre theory, indicating that a paradigm shift, an adjustment to our understanding of the relationship of a film to its audiences, is necessary.

NOTES

1. The term *giallo* entered popular vocabulary in 1929 when the publisher, Mondadori, launched detective fiction in yellow covers. The word is widely used for stories with any mystery element and for Italian film thrillers. For detailed discussions of the major popular film genres – the *giallo*, Italian horror film, the peplum and the spaghetti Western, see the chapters in this anthology by Mikel Koven, Jon Solomon and Flavia Brizio-Slov.

2. Chris Wagstaff, 'Cinema', in David Forgacs and Robert
   Lumley (eds), *Italian Cultural Studies: An Introduction*
   (Oxford: Oxford University Press, 1996), p. 224.

3. Pauline Small, *Sophia Loren: Moulding the Star* (Bristol:
   Intellect, 2009), pp. 20–1.

4. Ornella Volta, 'Entretien avec Mario Bava', *Positif* no. 138
   (1972), pp. 45–6.

5. The muscular heroes of popular cinema reflected the
   popularity of body-building in the 1960s.

6. Alberto Pezzotta, *Mario Bava* (Milan: Il Castoro, 1995),
   p. 67.

7. Interestingly, when Bava's vampires leave their graves
   in this film, and in the finale of *Ercole al centro della terra*,
   they leave the same trails of slime as the monsters
   of *Alien*.

8. Kim Newman, 'Thirty Years in Another Town: The
   History of Italian Exploitation', *Monthly Film Bulletin*
   (January 1986), p. 24.

9. Films were often shown in a mangled condition,
   generations of projectionists having assembled their
   own archive of titillating frames and sequences.

10. John Corner, 'Public Knowledge and Popular Culture:
    Spaces and Tensions', *Media, Culture and Society* vol. 31
    no. 1 (2009), p. 144.

FURTHER READING

Acerbo, Gabriele and Roberto Pisoni (eds), *Kill Baby Kill!*
    Il cinema di Mario Bava (Rome: UnMondoAparte, 2007).

Allmer, Patricia, Emily Brick and David Huxley (eds),
    European Nightmares: Horror Cinema in Europe since 1945
    (London: Wallflower Press, 2012).

Günsberg, Maggie, *Italian Cinema: Gender and Genre*
    (Basingstoke: Palgrave Macmillan, 2005).

Hills, Matt, *Fan Cultures* (London: Routledge, 2002).

Hollows, Joanne, 'The Masculinity of Cult', in Mark
    Jancovich, Antonio Lázaro Reboll, Julian Stringer and
    Andy Willis (eds), *Defining Cult Movies: The Cultural Politics
    of Oppositional Taste* (Manchester: Manchester University
    Press, 2003).

Hunt, Leon, 'A (Sadistic) Night at the *Opera*. Notes on the
    Italian Horror Film', in Ken Gelder (ed.), *The Horror
    Reader* (London: Routledge, 2000).

Lucas, Tim, *Mario Bava: All the Colors of the Dark*,
    Introduction by Martin Scorsese, Foreword by Riccardo
    Freda (Cincinnati, OH: Video Watchdog, 2007).

Ndalianis, Angela, *Neo-Baroque Aesthetics and Contemporary
    Entertainment* (Cambridge, MA: MIT Press, 2004).

Newman, Kim, 'Thirty Years in Another Town: The History
    of Italian Exploitation', *Monthly Film Bulletin* (January
    1986), pp. 20–4.

Sconce, Jeffrey, 'Trashing, the Academy: Taste, Excess, and
    an Emerging Politics of Cinematic Style', *Screen* vol. 36
    no. 4 (Winter 1995), pp. 371–93.

Wood, Mary P., *Italian Cinema* (Oxford: Berg, 2005).

37 The Unwanted Guest

Some Remarks on Italian Cinema's Love Affair with Psychoanalysis

Fabio Vighi

Cinema is identical to life, because each one of us has a virtual and invisible camera which follows us from when we are born to when we die[1]

What better psychoanalytic insight than Pasolini's above quotation? When he claimed that there is no difference between cinema and reality *because reality itself is inherently cinematic*, Pasolini was making, perhaps unconsciously, the strongest case in support of the relevance of psychoanalysis for the study of cinema. On 22 December 2007, a brief piece appeared in the Italian daily *La Repubblica* sporting the intriguing title: 'Sparisce con l'amante, rispunta nel film con De Sica' ('Disappeared with lover, reappears on a De Sica film'). It told the story of a forty-five-year-old Italian man who had left his wife and two children, vanishing with his lover and 5,000 euros taken from the till of the little supermarket he co-owned with his wife. It was a great surprise when, for a few yet decisive seconds, he was spotted, with his lover, in the background of a shot of the *cinepanettone Natale in Crociera*,[2] starring Christian De Sica (Vittorio's son). Immediately recognised by friends and family, it became apparent that he had accidentally entered a shot on a real cruise ship. To add insult to injury, the film plot happened to be strikingly similar to the unfortunate man's vicissitudes: a husband sends wife and son away on holiday in order to be alone with his lover, yet unexpectedly runs into them on a cruise ship. This extraordinary event confirms, in a speculative way, that our reality itself, since it is the result of a series of narrative strategies and struggles, is identical with film in its fictional configuration. In Pasolini's terms, what happened to the unfortunate man caught on film was that his virtual camera suddenly materialised. The psychoanalytic lesson to draw from this story is not only that we are always followed by a virtual camera

(the one that 'projects' us into reality), but more crucially, that the gaze of this camera turns us all into actors (whether we want it or not) and correspond to the traumatic gaze of the unconscious, whose logic we will never comprehend. This is the ultimate reason why psychoanalysis and film are intimately connected: the complex edifice we call reality rests on virtual (or fictional) foundations, the most real of which is the unconscious. The symbolic fabric of film, which is identical to the symbolic fabric of reality, is supported by a gaze that embodies all we have to 'ignore', i.e. repress or disavow, in order to connect with reality. Both reality and film are, strictly speaking, the result of the same act of repression, whereby a certain knowledge is relegated into the unconscious.

Before looking at two types of psychoanalytic interventions in film, a brief overview of my understanding of a 'psychoanalysis of cinema' is in order. What a psychoanalysis of cinema should attempt to do is a very simple thing, which certainly does not hinge on the application of psychoanalytic concepts to the medium in question. To put it bluntly, it should try to make cinema 'come alive' by forsaking the point of view of the external observer who merely effects a 'transfer of knowledge' from one field (psychoanalysis) to the other (cinema). A psychoanalysis of cinema should wrest film from its role of (often embalmed) object of cultural/historical analysis in order to allow it to vindicate its full ontological status. It is time to show that *reality imitates cinema*, and not the other way around: the alleged gap between the real and the cinematic, on account of which we study film as a cultural product, is always-already internal to, even constitutive of, reality itself. Film fictions are ontological. In the Freudo–Lacanian tradition, any openness *beyond* the fictional domain can only be conceived as a fall into the void, negativity pure and simple. Recall the finale of Peter Weir's *The Truman Show* (1998): On the run, Truman literally bumps against the fictional boundary of his gigantic stage; then he finds a little door and joins the 'real world'. Does this passage not reproduce the most basic ruse of ideology, reiterating the belief in the proverbial 'authentic reality' beyond the curtain of fictions? A more enlightening ending would have shown us Truman 'falling off' the stage and into a bottomless abyss. The difference between fictions and reality is nothing but a crack within the fictional. Film hosts the potential to reveal reality both as an intimately symbolic construct, and as the traumatic surplus of meaning that accompanies our entrance into the fabric of the world.

GETTING THERE AT CLOSING TIME: NOTES ON MISSED ENCOUNTERS WITH PSYCHOANALYSIS

At first glance, Italian cinema seems to offer particularly inviting cases for a psychoanalytic critique of film. For the purpose of this enquiry, let us quickly survey a small number of internationally renowned Italian directors who have consciously integrated psychoanalytic notions in their film narratives – Pier Paolo Pasolini, Bernardo Bertolucci, Federico Fellini, Marco Bellocchio and Nanni Moretti – and whose filmographies entitle us to argue that Italian film and psychoanalysis are indeed capable of fruitful interconnections.

Pasolini's and Bertolucci's indebtedness to Freudian culture is at the heart of their respective works, despite often manifesting itself where less directly called into question. Pasolini's *Edipo re*, for instance, though as explicitly Freudian as any film can get, is considerably less appealing to a psychoanalytic ear than such works as *Accattone*, *Mamma Roma* and *La ricotta*, which are pervaded by a truly symptomatic over-identification with the object-cause of desire (namely the Roman sub-proletariat *qua* point of exclusion of the symbolic/ideological order) despite not being overtly psychoanalytic in their inspiration. It is mainly on account of such excessive (symptomatic) attachment that these works, though purposely constructed as coherent narrative films, appear oddly fragmented. More generally, the 'post-Roma' phase of Pasolini's cinema, although more heavily influenced by Freudian theory, is less prone to unravel the dialectical overlaps between conscious filmic organisation and unconscious surplus of sense that typifies the films of the previous phase. *Accattone*, Pasolini's debut feature, especially testifies to an unwitting yet all the more powerful denouement of

the psychoanalytic potential of cinema by the way it relates to its historical context. Here, one should turn around the standard strategy of historicising film, which defines film as the product of given socio-ideologico-economic determinants: with *Accattone*, on the contrary, film tells us something that remained largely invisible in its context, namely the disturbing, even shocking presence of a 'pre-modern' sub-proletariat at the heart of Italy's economic boom. The psychoanalytic point made by *Accattone*, then, is that history itself is always the product of the dialectical relationship between the represented and what exceeds representation. To historicise *Accattone*, one needs to radically *historicise history*, conceding that a given sociohistorical context (Italy during the economic miracle) is by definition supplemented, or 'stained,' by its excluded, thus antagonistic, 'part of no part', a surplus that cannot be integrated into the ideological order.

As for Fellini, a similar kind of analysis applies, insofar as his self-confessed indebtedness to some of Jung's most popular theories should be taken with the proverbial pinch of salt. As I have argued elsewhere,[3] the overlap between Fellini's cinema and psychoanalysis is best epitomised by Fellini's concern with femininity, and especially with the process of sublimation, which is central to his work as a whole. The breathtakingly creative and imaginative wealth of Fellini's cinema hinges crucially on an at least partly disavowed stratagem whereby woman is elevated to the status of impossible (sublime) object of desire. It is the impossibility of reaching the object of desire that triggers endless (implicitly cinematic) fantasies in connection with such an elusive object. In *Amarcord*, one of Fellini's most popular works, despite the director's claims about its strong anti-fascist inspiration, it is clear that the central character remains Woman (Gradisca [Magali Noël]; the big-bosomed tobacconist; Volpina [Josiane Tanzilli], the town nymphomaniac; the midget nun; even the naked statues the kids dance around).

Furthermore, the reference to fascism, i.e. to the law, is functional (just like the sublimation of woman) to the proliferation of fantasies of transgression. Despite their obvious differences, at a basic structural level Pasolini's and Fellini's cinemas obey laws of self-displacement that are homologous in as much as they hinge on the repetition of the same sublimating gesture: narrative development is structured around the missed encounter with the object-cause of desire qua either sub-proletarian male (Pasolini) or woman (Fellini).

In Fellini's *Amarcord* (1973),
Gradisca – the object of desire –
watches a film while being watched
as if in a film

With Marco Bellocchio, we have an even closer connection between film and psychoanalysis. At a certain stage of his career, Bellocchio started borrowing explicitly from his psychoanalyst Massimo Fagioli's largely anti-Freudian theories. Films like *Diavolo in corpo* (*Devil in the Flesh*, 1986), *La condanna* (*The Conviction*, 1991) and *Il sogno della farfalla* (*The Butterfly's Dream*, 1994) were made in collaboration with Fagioli. Critics by and large regarded these works to be mere applications of Fagioli's theories, which are built around what he calls *immagini interiori*, images representing healthy, non-traumatic unconscious drives. If we recall that Freud's rejection of the cinema had originated in his scepticism toward the figurative rendering of the unconscious, it becomes apparent that the central tenet of Fagioli's theories could not be more remote from the Freudian tradition. Even a more recent film like *Buongiorno, notte*, a controversial account of Aldo Moro's kidnapping and assassination, displays signs of Fagioli's influence, particularly in the staging of the alliance between the unconscious and Chiara's desire to free the influential politician. Chiara's compulsive

gaze through the peep-hole of Moro's makeshift cell finds its fulfilment in her dream of Moro's escape.

The dreamed sequence corresponds to the release of unconscious libidinal energy materialising in the staging of Moro's liberation and subsequent stroll through Rome's suburb. As emphasised by the serene musical commentary from Schubert, this vision of a freed Aldo Moro echoes Fagioli's notion of the *inconscio mare calmo*, the idea that the drives (here, Chiara's unconscious wish) are fundamentally positive. Precisely as a deliberate application of a specific psychoanalytic axiom, however, this representation speaks for the film's *failed* encounter with psychoanalysis, for one should look for the unconscious where it is not supposed to be. In Bellocchio's treatment of Moro, the unproblematic representation of Moro's liberation acquires a resonance that it is not meant to have, one which is reminiscent of the logic articulated in Freud's *Totem and Taboo* (1913). The social order is first disturbed by the kidnapping of the Father (Moro); Chiara, however, is stricken with guilt and dreams to put the Father back in his place, thus banning the notion of

In Bellocchio's *Buongiorno, notte*
Chiara's desirous gaze will put the
'Father' (Moro) back into his place

parricide and establishing a degree of socio-symbolic balance. Paradoxically, this entails Bellocchio, the subversive Italian director *par excellence*, using the unconscious to generate the opposite of subversion, namely a semblance of order. Along these lines, the point unwittingly made by the film is that rebelliousness always relies on the figure of the Father/Master, who has to be seen occupying its proper place, as suggested by Chiara's dream. In Lacanian terms, Bellocchio's position here would seem to coincide with that of the hysteric, since the staging of Moro's freedom appears to be an unconscious strategy aimed at regaining the precious figure of a Master who can (potentially) be criticised at leisure, thus justifying the role of the rebel. All this seems to confirm the gist of Lacan's infamous address to the students during May 68: 'What you aspire to as revolutionaries is a Master. You will have one!'[4]

In the case of Nanni Moretti, his films reflect an insisted reference to psychoanalysis as indicative of a certain fixation that, as such, would seem to remain at least partially unconscious. I suggest that, rather than representing psychoanalytic knowledge transferred onto film, such fixation actually threatens to distort Moretti's auteurial attempts at encoding given significations. In the guise of a symptomatic formation that just will not go away, the narrative use of psychoanalysis, as it were, catches Moretti unaware, thus becoming a symptom, a disconnected kernel of knowledge of his relationship with film-making. An intriguing instance of such a short-circuit between intention and effect can be observed in *La stanza del figlio* (*The Son's Room*, 2001). Giovanni Sermonti, a psychoanalyst played by Moretti, is taught an existential lesson when his son dies in a scuba-diving

accident. He learns, painfully, not only that knowledge is impotent vis-à-vis chance; but also, more significantly, that his own psychoanalytic wisdom effectively overlaps with a traumatic loss (of knowledge) that is presented as ontological, coincidental with the very condition of 'being in the world'. The psychoanalyst, then, is taught the ultimate psychoanalytic lesson: he is reminded that, as he himself realises in a key scene of the film, things are 'cracked' despite all our well-meaning attempts at creating the opposite impression, i.e. that our reality (like Giovanni's family microcosm) is balanced, orderly and meaningful.

What *La stanza del figlio* stages is the classic Freudian clash between the pleasure principle (our innate tendency to minimise conflicts and tensions to achieve balance) and the domain of drives situated *beyond* the pleasure principle. It is drive, not chance, that antagonises the pleasure principle here, for Andrea's (Giuseppe Sanfelice) death is connoted as intimately related to his own death-drive (which, as Lacan told us, should not be understood merely as a suicidal tendency but rather as an 'excess of life', a surplus of desire that cannot simply be channelled into the conservative dimension of fantasy). The ambiguity about *La stanza del figlio* concerns precisely the role of the father/psychoanalyst: while the film seems (at least implicitly) to denounce the fundamental lack of knowledge that beleaguers psychoanalysis, at the same time this insight coincides with the strongest psychoanalytic claim, since the theory and practice of psychoanalysis (at least in the Freudo–Lacanian tradition) is built on an ontology of lack.

As a whole, Italian cinema has always been receptive of psychoanalytic ideas. The most appropriate

In Moretti's *La stanza del figlio* (2001), the psychoanalyst confronts the impotence of knowledge

way to appreciate psychoanalysis's relation to Italian cinema, however, is precisely by *not* looking for the deliberate deployment of psychoanalytic notions. Psychoanalytic knowledge applied to film is not necessarily conducive to a fertile understanding of cinema's allegiance with psychoanalysis. More often than not, the contrary is true: film's ignorance of psychoanalysis leads to the proliferation of symptoms. Understanding cinema through psychoanalysis, then, involves locating specific forms of cinematic knowledge whose excessive and seemingly nonsensical role within a given narrative actually stands for the disavowed core of that narrative. It is through failure that interpretation succeeds, since the target of the analysis is the kernel of non-sense that demarcates the unconscious: 'The fact that I have said that the effect of interpretation is to isolate in the subject a kernel, a *kern*, to use Freud's own term, of *non-sense*, does not mean that interpretation is in itself nonsense'.[5] Freud claimed that all dreams are about sex (unconscious libido) apart from dreams whose text is explicitly sexual. Something similar should be said about cinema's relation to psychoanalysis: as a 'knowledge that does not know itself', the unconscious of film can only be conceived of as a kernel of displaced meaning whose presence is independent of any conscious signification a given film might be entrusted to attain.

BEYOND CONTEXT: TOWARD A SYMPTOMATIC READING OF ITALIAN CINEMA

At the end of Vittorio De Sica's comedy *Il boom* (*Il Boom*, 1963), we are presented with an exemplary illustration of the basic psychoanalytic insight into the price one has to pay to enter the socio-symbolic order of sense. A typical product of the Italian economic miracle, Giovanni Alberti (Alberto Sordi) is a building contractor determined to live above his means. He is married to Silvia (Gianna Maria Canale), a beautiful middle-class woman who consorts with an elite of successful businessmen and enjoys the *dolce vita*. Right from the start, Giovanni is shown to be ravaged by debts. All his supposed friends know about his precarious situation, and yet nobody is prepared to help him. When even his wife discovers the truth, she leaves him point blank, plunging him into a state of despair. The chance encounter with the cynical wife of a powerful businessman, however, comes to his rescue. She offers to redeem all his debts in exchange for nothing less than his left eye, which would replace her husband's fake one. The grotesque situation perfectly epitomises

De Sica's caustic criticism of the general climate of inordinate economic growth of the period. As a classic example of Italian comedy with elements of social criticism, *Il boom* lends itself to be read contextually, precisely as a light-hearted yet mordant denunciation of the cynical and selfish social mood characteristic of a decisive stage in postwar Italian history. The most substantial part of this criticism would seem to be directed against the Sordi character, who, typically, distinguishes himself by a mixture of incorrigible frivolity and pathetic resourcefulness. However, such criticism is at least partially mitigated by the awareness that this character's desire to live the high life is caused less by social ambition than by his love for his wife. Ultimately, it is for the sake of his marriage that he consents to selling his eye.

If we were to stop at this type of analysis, which typically historicises the filmic narrative by regarding it as a reflection of sociocultural determinants, we would miss the crucial dimension that exceeds context, projecting us into the psychoanalytic dialectic of norm and excess, conscious and unconscious. As we have seen in *Accattone*, what the historicist approach forsakes is the unconscious kernel that a film qua symbolic construct necessarily produces. Even more patently than *Accattone*, *Il boom* unwittingly generates a surplus of meaning that allows one to reach beyond the historicist reading. For what is the significance of the central incident of the loss of the eye, which epitomises the grotesque dimension of the Italian economic miracle, if not that it represents to perfection the elementary Lacanian notion of 'symbolic castration'? While on a conscious narrative level, the film makes a mockery of the specific, historically given identity (the 'new type of Italian' produced by the boom), on another, unconscious level, it provides an insight into the act that allows a given subjectivity to form itself. The entire theoretical edifice of Freudo-Lacanian psychoanalysis is constructed upon the idea that entrance in the universe of sense (language in its socialising function) is correlative to a loss (of enjoyment) that takes place the very moment we say 'I', thus forming an identity, becoming (desiring) subjects. Lacan's formulation is very precise: '*jouissance* has to be refused in order to be attained on the inverse scale of the Law of desire'.[6] Ultimately, film itself as a social medium is castrated, self-alienated and therefore has to do with the law of desire: to come into being it must 'become language', thus generating desire along with its attendant fantasies. The childlike hyperactivity

In Risi's *Il sorpasso* (1962), Roberto
finally becomes like Bruno,
seconds before his tragic death

of the Sordi character in *Il boom* can thus be seen in a
new light, namely as correlative to the pre-subjective
stage where the identity of the ego is not yet fully
formed. In fact, the *commedia all'italiana* as a whole
owes much of its charm to this representation of the
subject before 'symbolic castration'.

Similarly, in Dino Risi's much-celebrated *Il sorpasso*,
the final death of Roberto Mariani can be read as
corresponding to the moment Bruno Cortona – another
'larger than life', immature and excessive male of the
commedia all'italiana – enters the symbolic order by
eschewing the 'surplus enjoyment' (Lacan's *plus de jouir*)
of his previous existential trajectory. Roberto dies the
very moment he becomes like Bruno, that is to say
when he finally manages to abandon his burdensome
reflexive attitude and begins to enjoy life without
worrying about the consequences of his actions. He
dies, then, as Bruno's double, and it can be surmised
that only such a traumatic loss can allow Bruno to
become an individual. The intuition, not consciously
developed by Risi, is that when Roberto endorses
Bruno's recklessly hedonistic enjoyment and dies, Bruno
witnesses, as if in a mirror, the loss of his own 'surplus
enjoyment', and for the first time faces the prospect of
socialisation, of assuming responsibility for his actions.
After all, that the two characters are 'two sides of the
same coin' is apparent also from a contextual reading:
rather than two opposite subject-positions in 1960s
Italy, they are 'identical' insofar as they stand for two
complementary sides of the economic miracle, namely
a (future) member of the ruling class (Roberto, a law
student) and a consumer (Bruno).

It would be interesting to pursue a socially critical
reading of the *commedia all'italiana* by exploring its
unconscious addressing of the psychoanalytic theme of
subjectivation: what many of these films actually

critique is the regressive aspect inherent in capitalist
dynamics of economic growth, in as much as these
dynamics create the illusion that full (pre-symbolic)
enjoyment can be achieved. If this is the case, then, the
tragic dimension so often inscribed in these comedies
plays a fundamental role in dispelling such illusion,
reminding us that capitalist dynamics are correlative to
a highly efficient symbolic order.

I began by endorsing Pasolini's seemingly
paradoxical claim that life and cinema are identical.
The significance of a psychoanalytically grounded
understanding of cinema resides in illuminating the
reasons and consequences of such a claim. Filtered
through psychoanalysis, cinema has a chance to
unravel the dynamics that regulate our immersion in
the socio-symbolic order, that is to say in reality as we
know it. Cinema shows us what always-already takes
place in our relationship with the world, but tends to
remain invisible to us. It works as a magnifying lens,
giving us the opportunity to focus on the disavowed
mechanisms that regulate the emergence of meaning,
insofar as meaning is sustained by our investments in
fantasy and desire, as well as by our expectations of
enjoyment. We should fully endorse the radical
psychoanalytic thesis that *ordinary reality itself is a
medium* – it is the medium, the screen, through which
we keep destructive (unconscious) drives at a safe
distance. Psychoanalysis tells us that every
symbolisation of reality, i.e. every attempt we make to
create meanings, is correlative to the production of an
enigmatic surplus of sense, which in turn threatens to
make our world inconsistent. When we say that cinema
is identical to reality, we mean that it reproduces the
elementary dynamics concerning the negotiation of
sense that are already inbuilt in the way we relate to
reality. It is this understanding of psychoanalysis that

film theory should pursue. A radical film theory always begins by acknowledging that filmic images deal with reality rather than with its pale imitation – not, however, because of their power to transcend the fictional domain, but because the fabric of reality is fictional. Symbolic representation is the mode and condition of existence of reality itself, inclusive of its relation to what is unrepresentable. As a form of thought, then, cinema always thinks the real, since it is inextricably entangled with existence; conversely, reality can only be thought of as an intrinsically cinematic form of appearance.

The most prolific way in which psychoanalysis has been appropriated by film theory is via the notion of spectatorship, which first appeared within the 'structuralist Marxism' of the 1970s and 80s. A number of spectatorship or apparatus theories have emerged in rapid succession since the publication, in the mid-70s, of such texts as Christian Metz's *The Imaginary Signifier* and Laura Mulvey's 'Visual Pleasure and Narrative Cinema'. In relation to Italian cinema, film theorists have by and large used psychoanalysis to explore spectatorship issues.[7] This chapter argues that there is a more cogent way to conceptualise a 'psychoanalysis of film'. As a rule, spectatorship theories investigate the audience's imaginary identifications with film, neglecting what I see as the central psychoanalytic issue at stake: the analysis of how film negotiates its own symbolic efficacy, irrespective of spectators' appropriations. It is not just a matter of emphasising how audiences are resistant to being categorised around normative lines of class, gender or ethnicity. Rather, we should insist on a radically self-reflexive point: film itself as a narrative construct produces a surplus of sense that escapes conscious narrative strategies. With regard to Italian cinema, I have highlighted what I regard as two paradigmatic aspects of its connection with psychoanalysis. On the one hand, there is the Italian directors' recurrent use of psychoanalytic knowledge, which, however, often misses the key psychoanalytic insight into how knowledge itself is constitutively split between its conscious and unconscious sides. On the other hand, I have suggested how psychoanalytic film theory could reorient itself via a symptomatic reading of Italian cinema. The *commedia all'italiana* offers a particularly fertile ground for this type of analysis precisely because it tends to enjoy, rather than reflect upon, the symptoms it produces.

NOTES

1. Pier Paolo Pasolini, 'Ora tutto è chiaro, voluto, non imposto dal destino', *Cineforum* no. 68 (October 1967), p. 609 (author's translation).

2. *Cinepanettone* refers to the bawdy Italian comedies released at Christmas. The word is a pun on the name of the popular Milanese Christmas cake, the *panettone*. See the chapter by Alan O'Leary on this topic in this anthology.

3. See Fabio Vighi, *Sexual Difference in European Cinema: The Curse of Enjoyment* (Basingstoke: Palgrave Macmillan, 2009), pp. 17–26, 47–56 and 85–90.

4. Jacques Lacan, *The Seminar. Book XVII. The Other Side of Psychoanalysis* (New York: W. W. Norton, 2006), p. 207.

5. Jacques Lacan, *The Seminar. Book XI. The Four Fundamental Concepts of Psychoanalysis* (New York: W. W. Norton, 1998), p. 250.

6. Jacques Lacan, *Écrits* (New York: W. W. Norton, 2007), p. 700.

7. For recent works see, among others, Vincent Rocchio's *Cinema of Anxiety: A Psychoanalysis of Italian Neorealism* (Austin: University of Texas Press, 1999); Angelo Restivo's *The Cinema of Economic Miracles: Visuality and Modernization in the Italian Art Film* (Durham, NC: Duke University Press, 2002); Domietta Torlasco's *The Time of the Crime* (Palo Alto, CA: Stanford University Press, 2008); and Luana Ciavola's *Revolutionary Desire in Italian Cinema* (Leicester: Troubadour Press, 2011).

38 Fellini and Contemporary International Cinema

Peter Bondanella

Fellini's work is like a treasure chest. You open it up and there, right in front of your eyes, a world of wonders springs up ... ancient wonders, new ones, provincial wonders and universal ones, real wonders and fantastic ones, and great masters are like lighthouses to guide us into that harbor.[1]

Martin Scorsese

I am not supposed to like Fellini. Antonioni I should like better. Pasolini I should respect more. And I suspect perhaps I do. But I would still rather watch a Fellini film, and I know why – I do so for the factor of sheer enjoyment.[2]

Peter Greenaway

No other Italian director achieved the international recognition Federico Fellini enjoyed during much of his long career, even though his commercial popularity diminished between his last box-office smash hit in 1973 (*Amarcord*) and his death in 1993. Fellini's critical reputation suffered to some degree because of his virtual identification with the idea of the director as superstar when academic scholarship moved beyond enthusiasm for the auteur approach in the late twentieth century. Nevertheless, film critics on the *Sight and Sound* polls ranked 8½ as one of the top ten greatest films ever made four times: in 1972 (fourth place); in 1982 (fifth place); in 2002 (ninth place); and in 2012 (tenth place). *Sight and Sound* polls among actual film-makers (not critics) published in 1992, 2002 and 2012 ranked 8½ respectively the second, third and fourth greatest film ever made, with *La strada* coming in fourth in 1992. In the 2002 poll, critics ranked Fellini the seventh best director, while film directors considered him the second best director in the history of the cinema.

Such exercises tell us more about changing fads than about artistic originality, but they do suggest that

many critics found 8½ extraordinary and quite a few directors felt the same way about *La strada*. Fellini criticism amounts to an enormous mass of material in many languages and most of it focuses on close examinations of Fellini's films and not Fellini's impact on international cinema, the subject of this essay. Fellini's influence ranges from simple citations of important sequences to actual adaptations and it extends beyond feature films to the realms of popular advertising and musical theatre.

Many directors reference Fellini in a variety of surprising places, often without any particular link to Fellinian themes or style. For example, Joel Schumacher's *Falling Down* (1993) features Michael Douglas as a character identified only by his licence plate – D-Fens – alluding to his work in the defence industry. Like so many other angry white males in the early 1990s, D-Fens is deemed 'redundant' after giving many years of faithful service to his employer. In a recreation of the brilliant traffic jam that opens Fellini's 8½, D-Fens goes on a violent rampage in a Korean grocery store, confronts Latino gang members, meets a neo-Nazi gun-shop owner, and finally loses all his control when some fast-food employees inform him breakfast is no longer served, as he has unfortunately taken the era's familiar fast-food slogan too literally ('Have it your way!). In *Falling Down*, a traffic jam leads to a psychological reaction far more troubling than a film director's failure to complete a science-fiction film, but Schumacher's clever citation of Fellini in an unexpected location reveals how a popular commercial film can find inspiration in what is certainly the archetypal metacinematic work in all of film history.

Schumacher's radical distance from Fellini's original may be contrasted to Fellini's presence in Ettore Scola's *C'eravamo tanto amati* – a metacinematic reconstruction of postwar Italian social and economic history through a progression of scenes embodying different film styles from neorealism to the 1970s. Scola uses Fellini's filming of the famous Trevi Fountain sequence from *La dolce vita* as a historical marker for Italy's artistic heritage in the 1960s during the golden age of Italian cinema. Anita Ekberg's famous dip in the Trevi stands as the symbol of an entire era of European auteur film-making. In Scola's film, Fellini appears as himself, a living icon and the film director most closely identified with self-referential cinema. This is a move beyond a simple citation toward a more complex reference that is itself self-referential, since Scola's own use of Fellini forms part of a metacinematic history of postwar Italian film-making.

Italian film-makers Lina Wertmüller and Giuseppe Tornatore adapt references to specific key sequences in Fellini films for very different thematic and stylistic purposes. Wertmüller's first feature film – *I basilischi* – is a free adaptation of Fellini's portrait of provincial loafers in *I vitelloni*, except that Wertmüller's point of view is a feminist one. Her intimate knowledge of key sequences in 8½ comes as no surprise, since she worked on the set of this film, uncredited as a third assistant director.

In *Pasqualino Settebellezze* – Wertmüller's disturbing masterpiece that earned her an Oscar nomination for Best Director – the sequence from Fellini's *Roma* recreating the Jovinelli variety theatre in fascist Rome inspires the equally grotesque portrait of Pasqualino's obese sister in a variety show singing a vulgar song attacking foreign sanctions against Italian aggression in Africa. This is a direct citation and a basic imitation. But a more complex and imaginative imitation of a sequence from the same film, the steam-bath sequence in 8½, plus touches inspired by Dante's *Inferno*, gives birth to her most chilling image of the Holocaust – the concentration-camp assembly ground and the prisoners enshrouded in mist, waiting to die.

Tornatore's nostalgic hymn of love to the cinema, *Nuovo Cinema Paradiso*, like *Pasqualino Settebellezze*, revisits the Jovinelli variety from *Roma* to depict the chaotic and raucous atmosphere of a provincial movie house, filled with the same kind of idle, male loafers in *I vitelloni*: in fact, Giancaldo recalls Fellini's fictional Rimini, and Tornatore fills it with the same unusual, expressive faces sprinkled throughout Fellini's films. The film's plot is a variant on the coming-of-age theme we recognise from the progression in Fellini's career from

Lina Wertmüller's imitation of Fellini's variety theatre sequence from *Roma* (1972) in *Pasqualino Settebellezze* (1975)

I vitelloni to *La dolce vita* and concluding with 8½: a young Salvatore (Salvatore Cascio) falls in love with the cinema through his friendship with the local projectionist, and eventually leaves Giancaldo and goes to Rome to win fame and fortune as a film director. Fellini, however, rarely cites other films or other directors: his primary sources are almost always his inventive dream fantasies colourfully illustrated in his dream notebooks as he grew older.[3] Tornatore's justly celebrated conclusion to *Nuovo Cinema Paradiso* – the screening of a collection of passionate kisses cut from films Salvatore saw as a child because his projectionist mentor was forced to obey the censorship of the local parish priest – is the kind of *cinéphile* homage Fellini would never have employed. Tornatore's casting of comic actors identified with Fellini 's films – Pupella Maggio, the neurotic mother of *Amarcord*; and Leopoldo Trieste, the hapless husband of *Lo sceicco bianco* and the dreamer-poet of *I vitelloni* – consciously play on their Fellinian screen antecedents, and their performances are enriched by our memory of them.

If *Nuovo Cinema Paradiso* shows a particular kind of mood, sentimentality or feeling learned from an encounter with Fellini, Tornatore's *L'uomo delle stelle* (*The Star Maker*, 1995) relies on memories of early Fellini films to portray a confidence man – a figure Fellini made famous with Broderick Crawford's performance as Augusto in *Il bidone*. Tornatore's Joe Morelli (Sergio Castellitto) travels all over Sicily, cheating gullible people with a fake screen test that will never lead to a part in the movies. The con-artist's strange caravan filled with cameras and microphones directly recalls the equally odd caravan pulled by a US motorcycle Zampanò drives in *La strada*. Tornatore's screen tests are clearly indebted in part to those of 8½, and the ordinary people desperate for self-expression in the movies recall grotesque faces from such works as *Fellini Satyricon*, *Roma* and *Amarcord*, but most especially the crowds of odd people with unusual expressions and mannerisms gathered outside Fellini's casting office in *Block-notes di un regista*. Tornatore considers his encounter with Fellini's works a constant point of reference and, when encountering a perplexing aesthetic or technical problem, he says he would ask: 'What would Fellini do if he were here?', a similar question to the one Fellini always asked himself when shooting his early films: 'what would Roberto [Rossellini] do?'[4]

No two directors could be more different in personality, artistic vision and temperament than Peter Greenaway and Fellini. Yet Greenaway describes Fellini as a formative influence upon his career. He calls *The Belly of an Architect* (1987) a product of spending months as a student wandering around Rome, 'an excuse to be in a Rome that Fellini had made cinematic, and to try to remake some of that magic for myself'. He says a scene from *Giulietta degli spiriti* inspired the conclusion to a subsequent *son et lumière* event he organised in the Piazza del Popolo about Pope Sixtus V's attempts to resurrect the obelisks of Rome there. Early sequences in *Fellini Satyricon* – the many static tableaux of outlandish characters or situations shot by a camera moving through the *insulae* or tall apartment complexes of the Roman Suburra in the ancient city – have surely influenced similar key scenes in Greenaway's *The Cook, the Thief, His Wife and Her Lover* (1989). And finally, Greenaway admits that his *Eight and a Half Women* (1999) was a failed homage to 8½ but one that he does not regret:

> to visually quote Fellini within a film is to demand high standards of the covering material, and we could not come up with the goods … I think of it as a small genuflection in the right direction, and acknowledgement of all the pleasure and nourishment given to me by Fellini.

As Scorsese remarks, Fellini represents for these very different directors a treasure chest of motifs, styles and ideas that they can adapt for very different artistic purposes, a cinematic idiom flexible enough to express all sorts of different things. Leopoldo Trieste's memorable performance as a self-important, egotistic and ignorant but amusing provincial husband in Fellini's *Lo sceicco bianco* must certainly have been in Francis Ford Coppola's mind when he cast Trieste in *The Godfather II* (1974) as Signor Roberto, the Italian landlord in Little Italy who wants to throw an old lady out of her apartment until a young godfather (Robert De Niro) persuades him to do otherwise. His admiration for other Italian directors also moved Coppola to cast Gastone Moschin as the Mafioso Fanucci in the same film, thanks to his memorable performance in Bertolucci's *Il conformista*. Decades later (1999), Coppola returned to *Lo sceicco bianco* for inspiration when he was engaged by Illy, Italy's most prestigious espresso company, famous for its generous patronage to contemporary artists and designers, to direct a commercial for their coffee. Illy also produced espresso cups honouring Fellini's *Ginger e Fred* around the time that film was released. Coppola's spot, 'Extra ordinaria', is a wonderful homage to the beginning of Fellini's career, with a recreation of the key sequence in Fellini's original – the magical appearance of the the White Sheik, an actor played by Alberto Sordi who represents a tawdry version of Valentino's more heroic sheik from the silent film era in the Italian *fumetti* magazines of the 1950s.[5] Fellini meant the original scene in *Lo sceicco bianco* to represent a humorous wink at a famous Fragonard painting, *The Swing*: in that picture, a man hiding behind a bush spies upon a woman on a swing, her skirts billowing out to allow him a good look; in Fellini's film, it is a woman who observes her film idol high up on the swing above her. The spot is shot in sepia with a filter, as if to underscore the fact that it forms part of Coppola's own memory of the original Fellinian source. Coppola's young girl goes to a nearby bar with her White Sheik and they share an Illy espresso before the magic spell of movie fandom dissolves and the young lady's affections return to her handsome soldier boyfriend. Coppola's heroine not only retains her virtue, but her choice of Illy coffee underscores her good taste as well.

Coppola's film-director children – Sofia and Romano – inherited an interest in Fellini. In *Lost in Translation* (2003), Sofia Coppola employs the same Trevi Fountain scene recreated in Scola's metacinematic history of postwar Italy for an entirely different purpose. Screened on television in a Japanese hotel room, the Trevi Fountain sequence now functions as a clue to the emotions of the film's protagonist. The interrupted embrace of Marcello Mastroianni and Anita Ekberg in the magic waters of the Trevi (the water actually stops running suddenly as the two characters stand in it) mirrors Bill Murray's alienation and loneliness. In an interview given in 2009 to Milan's *Corriere della sera*, Sofia Coppola announced she was planning a film treating one of her childhood visits to Italy with her more famous father that would, she explained, be heavily indebted to Fellini's *Toby Dammit*.[6] Presumably Toby's (Terence Stamp) visit to Rome to shoot a 'Catholic' Western and his disgraceful performance at a film awards presentation (he is completely stoned at the time) would have served as a means of recreating her own astonishment and bewilderment upon encountering the land of her ancestors. But what emerged in 2010 as *Somewhere* seems not to have followed this original stylistic direction, even though the film won an important prize at the Venice Film Festival voted upon by a jury headed by Quentin Tarantino (the director's former boyfriend). Nevertheless, the sequence in *Somewhere* dedicated to an Italian television awards show[7] reflects the influence of the most memorable

sequence in *Toby Dammit*: in both *Toby Dammit* and *Somewhere*, celebrity brings little comfort or satisfaction.

The first feature film shot by director Romano Coppola – *CQ* (*CQ*, 2001) – did not fare well commercially after its initial showing at Cannes. It owes a debt not only to Roger Vadim's *Barbarella* (1968) but also to Bava's *Diabolik*, made in the same year – a fact underlined by the roles John Philip Law plays in *CQ* that recall his work for both Vadim and Bava. *CQ* is a campy spoof on the cheesy kinds of special effects employed in such films (the delight of cult aficionados today), but Fellini's influence also lurks behind the scenes: several frenetic press conferences complete with annoying paparazzi are lifted almost verbatim from those in both *La dolce vita* and *8½*. And the plot is exactly that of *8½*: how to bring another confusing film to a successful conclusion. In Coppola's case, the film in question is a science-fiction film just as in Fellini's template – *Codename: Dragonfly* – and the conclusion is not the magical finale of Fellini's dramatisation of artistic creativity before the audience's eyes as in *8½* but, instead, a climactic chase scene. Aspiring film-maker Paul Ballard (Jeremy Davies) plays Coppola's *alter ego* (parallel to Fellini's *alter ego* director figure, Guido Anselmi, played by Marcello Mastroianni), and he takes over the reins of the film after veteran director Andrezej (Gérard Depardieu) resigns in anger from the project and even tries to steal the rushes to sabotage its completion. Paul turns what might have resulted in a disaster into a resounding Hollywood conclusion with the dramatic car chase (quite unlike the finale of Fellini's *8½*), but of course the purpose of Coppola's film is to satirise various styles of camp film-making, rather than produce a precise adaptation of an art-house classic.

Fellini was always fascinated by commercial advertising, from his early journalistic career in the prewar period until he made television spots himself for a series of important Italian companies (Campari soda; Barilla pasta; and the Banco di Roma).[8] These commercials are all perfect examples of pure cinema, informed by Fellini's oneiric experiences and his subversive sense of humour. Advertising frequently appears in many of his films (particularly in *Ginger e Fred* and *Intervista*). Thus, it is not at all surprising that his own celebration of paparazzi and the power of the mass media (especially fan magazines and advertising), *La dolce vita*, has been referenced in at least two outstanding commercials. In 2006, one of the most extraordinary television commercials ever made in Italy promoted Peroni Nastro Azzurro light beer ('bionda' or blond beer, as the Italians call it).[9] It featured top South African model Landi Swanepoel and Ruben Quesada (stand-ins for Anita Ekberg and Marcello Mastroianni) with the real Anita Ekberg as a consultant. The commercial enjoyed a large budget and featured the perfect soundtrack – not a Nino Rota song but – 'Baby, It's You', a Burt Bacharach song popularised by the Shirelles. The commercial exists in both a black-and-white and a colourised version and in various lengths: segments included the appearance of the famous helicopter with Quesada waving at bikini-clad women next to a neon sign with huge capital letters spelling PERONI; the arrival of Swanepoel at the Rome airport in a prop plane from the 1960s with the usual frenetic attack of paparazzi photographers; dancing among the ruins of the Baths of Caracalla; and most importantly, a dip into the actual Trevi Fountain by the two actors (the Peroni company was given extraordinary permission to do so, whereas much of the rest of the commercial was shot outside Italy).

The Peroni spot represents a successful linkage between a well-known Italian product (Peroni light beer) and a cultural icon (Fellini's *La dolce vita*) and is also one of the sexiest commercials ever produced. Less interesting visually but equally reflective of Fellini's role as contemporary pop icon is a commercial for a line of Longines women's watches called *La Dolce Vita* collection. While not as extravagant as the Peroni ad, it employs three top media personalities – actress Kate Winslet; Taiwanese model/actress Lin Chi-ling; and Indian model/actress Aishwarya Rai – plus Nino Rota's famous theme song from Fellini's *Amarcord*. The spot connects what the Longines website calls 'the easy-going Italian way of life – la dolce vita – in the shape of a watch' with the world of Fellini's films.[10] In the ad, the three stars check their Longines watches, run away from the *paparazzi* Fellini invented – Winslet walks through the city streets; Chi-ling drives off in a vintage Alfa-Romeo Giulietta convertible like the one in *La dolce vita*; and Rai leaves in a limo – and they all meet up again in the city centre after a quick view of major Roman monuments. The Longines spot relies upon star power, while the Peroni ad exploits fantasy and artistic ingenuity, but both commercials underscore Fellini's lasting influence upon popular culture.

Terry Gilliam describes *The Wholly Family* (2011) on his website as a 'filmette' because of its brief length (twenty minutes). It is thus neither a traditional feature film nor an ad. Filmed on location in Naples and sponsored by the Garofalo Pasta Company, it is actually not really even a commercial since pasta figures prominently in an imaginary meal during the film but there is really no actual active promotion of a specific brand of pasta, in contrast to the short spots hawking beer or watches. *The Wholly Family* certainly owes a debt to Fellini's love affair with clowns, especially in his 'mockumentary' treatment *I clowns*.[11] Gilliam is on record as expressing his great admiration for Fellini: both began as cartoonists before moving to movies. Gilliam shot *The Adventures of Baron Munchausen* (1988), the film many consider his greatest achievement, primarily at Rome's Cinecittà while Fellini still maintained an office there, and he worked with a host of Fellini's collaborators (Dante Ferretti, Francesca Lo Schiavo, Gabriella Pescucci, Giuseppe Rotunno and others) on costumes, photography, set and production design. As Gilliam's film suffered many of the same commercial and critical vicissitudes as Fellini's masterpiece *Casanova*, the two would certainly have had much to discuss. The major portion of *The Wholly Family* consists of the representation of a young boy's bad dream, filled with chaotic and comic but somewhat menacing and authoritarian Neapolitan clowns (Pulcinellas, the figure associated with Naples in the *commedia dell'arte*). Fellini's *I clowns* begins with a similar dream about clowns where Fellini, as a young child, appears dressed as Little Nemo, the American cartoon character associated with dreamlike and extravagant figurative drawings by Winsor McCay, one of the greatest cartoonists of all times and a figure both Fellini and Gilliam admired. In 2011, after the completion of *The Wholly Family*, Rimini's Fondazione Federico Fellini recognised Gilliam's affinity to Fellini's artistic style by giving him the Premio Federico Fellini, the same award Scorsese received a few years earlier.

Citations by many diverse directors, as well as the referencing of Fellini in commercial advertising, all show Fellini's impact on popular culture and contemporary international cinema. Lack of space here prevents a treatment of all the restaurants, cafés and nightspots all over the world named after Fellini, his film titles, or his film characters, but a simple Internet search lists hundreds of such references – a testament to Fellini's impact upon the popular imagination everywhere.

MARTIN SCORSESE AND FELLINI: A COMPLEX RELATIONSHIP

The relationship between Martin Scorsese and Fellini begins in Scorsese's youth when he discovered Fellini's early films on local television stations screening postwar Italian films for the ethic Italian-American community in New York City. *Il mio viaggio in Italia* (*My Voyage to Italy*), first screened at the Venice Film Festival in 1999, describes his reaction to them and to Fellini. Years later, Scorsese would support a digital restoration of *La dolce vita* – part of his larger project to encourage film restoration of the world's cinematic heritage – and he also received the Premio Fondazione Fellini in 2005 from Rimini's Fondazione Federico Fellini as a tribute to his love for Fellini's cinema. Up to this point, we have focused upon how various film-makers have cited Fellini by what is a sometimes radical reworking of a particular sequence, stylistic nuance or character from Fellini that may well depart quite radically from the original in theme and style. Scorsese's use of Fellini in his work, while not constituting an actual remake of any individual Fellini classic, shows an ingenious understanding of how one can learn many different things from the Maestro.

One of Scorsese's first student pictures at the New York University Film School (*It's Not Just You, Murray!*, 1964) features a parody of the concluding circular dance in 8½, one of the most moving cinematic images of all time. It was one of the first of many nods by the world's directors to this key Fellini film. And Fellini guides Scorsese's hand and eye in certain sequences of his breakthrough film – *Mean Streets* (1973). Scorsese lifts the manner in which he introduces his central characters directly from Fellini's introduction of his loafers in *I vitelloni*.

Both films could be termed coming-of-age films, tales about groups of young, usually immature men (one group in New York's Little Italy, the other in the Adriatic coastal town of Rimini, Fellini's birthplace). In *Mean Streets*, Scorsese replaces the opening beauty contest of *I vitelloni* with the annual San Gennaro Festival in New York: each character is introduced quickly and skilfully by a single action defining his character (or lack of it): Tony (David Proval) throws a drug addict out of his bar; Michael (Richard Romanus), the eternal loser, buys inexpensive Japanese lens covers, thinking they are expensive, high-quality German camera lenses; Johnny Boy (Robert De Niro) blows up a post-office box with a firecracker for no apparent reason; and Charlie (Harvey Keitel) confesses himself in church. The first sequence of the film presents a black screen while Scorsese himself (and not the character Charlie) delivers an important voiceover that sums up the plot. Later, Scorsese intervenes once again as if his voice were Charlie's voice and makes a cameo appearance at the violent ending of the film.

Scorsese's voiceovers are clearly inspired by those of *I vitelloni*, especially the last voiceover in the Italian original. Scorsese may well have been inspired by the conclusion to *I vitelloni*, where one of Fellini's loafers named Moraldo (usually taken by film critics as a stand-in for Fellini himself) leaves his *vitelloni* friends behind for the big city of Rome. It is Fellini himself, and not the actor dubbing Moraldo's dialogue elsewhere, who pronounces the final dialogue of *I vitelloni*, just as Scorsese's voice replaces his actor's voice at a key moment on the soundtrack of *Mean Streets*. Such personal interventions, typical of auteur cinema and made famous by Hitchcock's many cameo appearances were also inspired by similar Fellini appearances in his 'mockumentaries', such as *Block-notes di un regista* and *Roma*, works screened in New York and on television shortly before Scorsese made *Mean Streets*. Because of the seminal influence of Scorsese's first important film, subsequent Hollywood 'coming-of-age' films – one thinks immediately of *American Graffiti* (1973) by George Lucas; Philip Kaufman's *The Wanderers* (1979); or Barry Levinson's *Diner* (1982) – indirectly also point to Fellini's indirect influence upon the American cinema of the era. Scorsese has also noted that years after *Mean Streets*, he returned to the imitation of Fellini's voiceover and his presentation of his protagonists in

Fellini's brutish Zampanò in *La strada* (1954) inspires Scorsese's depiction of the abusive and inarticulate Jake La Motta (Robert De Niro) in *Raging Bull* (1980)

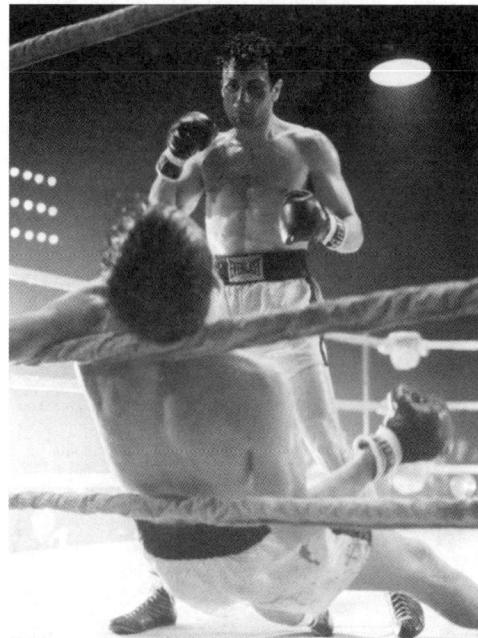

I vitelloni when introducing the major characters in
Goodfellas.

By Scorsese's own admission, *La strada* played a
key role in his work.[12] Il Matto or The Fool, played by
Richard Basehart, helped him to conceive Johnny Boy,
one of Robert De Niro's first important acting
assignments. In Il Matto's case, his practical jokes lead
to his death in a scuffle with Zampanò. Like Il Matto,
Johnny Boy is a joker whose practical jokes always go
just a bit too far, leading him from the realm of the
comic into the threshold of the tragic.

Scorsese identifies the brutish and inarticulate
Zampanò (perhaps Anthony Quinn's greatest role) as
the model for the equally brutish and inarticulate Jake
La Motta in *Raging Bull* (1980): both characters are
unable to express their feelings until their abusive
character flaws destroy the objects of their love, turning
them into pathetic, alienated and tragic figures.

Besides his creative assimilation of cinematic
lessons from Fellini and his assistance in promoting
and preserving Fellini's artistic heritage, Scorsese has
not been afraid to defend Fellini and the foreign art-
house film in general from philistine detractors. In
1991, Anheuser Busch ran a commercial for Bud Dry
beer that began with the question, 'Why Are Foreign
Films So Foreign?' It featured a sad clown speaking in
Italian, asking 'Why ask why?' in a setting that recalled
scenes by the ocean in films by both Fellini and Ingmar
Bergman.[13] After identifying asking questions with
foreign art films, some young males head for the store,
buy Bud Dry and return home to see a Hollywood
action film filled with explosions and the usual car
chases. The commercial's message is shockingly clear:
Fellini and his ilk are foreign, complex and boring; red-
blooded American males prefer non-intellectual action
films and do not ask questions. Several years later,
Fellini's death was the occasion for a negative letter to
the *New York Times* editor complaining that foreign art
films were both 'difficult' and 'foreign' (with specific

reference to Fellini). Martin Scorsese wrote an
indignant and eloquent reply that referenced the
earlier beer commercial to argue that philistine
discourse in both the ad and the letter reflected an
intolerance of difference in America and could easily
lead to unfortunate consequences in American
thinking about the rest of the world's culture.[14]

FELLINI ADAPTATIONS

Because film directors have consistently ranked Fellini
quite high in the pantheon of the history of the
cinema, it is not surprising that many of them have
turned to more than mere citations of characters,
themes or key sequences in Fellini's films and have
attempted virtual remakes as well. Book-length
treatment of this topic would be required to do the
subject justice, and therefore this chapter will only
attempt an outline of these adaptations. They can be
grouped around two different categories: the smallest
group – Fellini originals turned into Hollywood
musicals – on the one hand; and a more diverse and
larger group, filmed imitations of Fellini's masterpiece,
8½, on the other (one of which is a musical in the first
group). The three musicals in question are two
outstanding films by Bob Fosse: *Sweet Charity* (1969),
based on *Le notti di Cabiria*; and *All That Jazz* (1979),
more loosely based on its original, 8½; the third less
successful film, Rob Marshall's *Nine* (2009) was, like
Sweet Charity, originally a hit musical show on
Broadway based on 8½ that was turned into a
Hollywood film. *Nine* features an all-star cast but never
really measures up to the challenge of dramatising in
musical theatre (filmed or otherwise) the moment of
artistic creativity at the end of Fellini's original. In fact,
Nine's director figure – Guido Contini – actually gives up
on his film and only returns to film-making several
years later, as all the women in his life are assembled
mechanically in a finale that fails precisely because it
views these women more as physical, sexual presences

Bob Fosse's *Sweet Charity* (1969)
and its dance number in the Pompei
Club recalls a similar nightclub in
Le notti di Cabiria (1957)

than as artistic muses, figments of directorial fantasy who stimulate his artistic creativity.

Sweet Charity, in contrast, manages to capture the energy and sentimentality of Fellini's Oscar-winning depiction of plucky prostitute Cabiria, played by his wife Giulietta Masina following her equally famous performance as Gelsomina in La strada, who deals in sex to make a living but wants desperately to fall in love. Fosse's film profits from superb music by Neil Simon and Cy Coleman and absolutely brilliant choreography by Fosse. It comes as close as possible to recreating all of the positive aspects of Fellini's original, comparable to Woody Allen's achievement in Stardust Memories (1980, to be discussed subsequently). It was a justifiable hit and launched a number of famous songs: 'Big Spender'; 'I Love to Cry at Weddings'; 'There's Gotta Be Something Better Than This'; and Charity's theme song 'If My Friends Could See Me Now'. The dance routine in the Pompei Club, where Charity meets a famous actor, represents one of the most brilliant virtuoso performances of scenography and choreography in the history of the American musical.

In All That Jazz, Fosse replaces Guido Anselmi, the film director of 8½ who cannot complete a science-fiction film, with a semi-autobiographical character named Joe Gideon (Roy Schneider) inspired by Fosse's own efforts to edit a film dedicated to comic Lenny Bruce while simultaneously staging the Broadway musical Chicago. The resulting stress leads to Gideon's heart attack, and as he is about to die, the film turns into a spectacular variety show (one of Fellini's favourite themes). Both Sweet Charity and All That Jazz succeed in employing dance and music to recreate Fellini's celebration of artistic fantasy. But All That Jazz goes far beyond the earlier film, employing four different dance interpretations of Gideon's life that may

well have been inspired by Fosse's understanding of the important screentest scenes in 8½. Two exciting dance numbers highlight Fosse's source of artistic creativity: sex and death (or the attempt to thwart death through art). The first number concerns an airline named AirErotica, and it is one of the great creations in Hollywood musical history. The second is an equally extravagant celebration of artistry over death entitled the 'Big Exit' danced to the famous Broadway tune 'Bye Bye Love' but sung now as 'Bye Bye Life'. Here, everything in Gideon's (and Fosse's) life comes together in an auditorium around an operating table: the rhythm of the music mimics the heartbeat of the dying patient, while the dancers wear leotards with arteries painted on them. If the conclusion to 8½ underscores the celebration of the role of artistic creativity in life, Fosse's 'Big Exit' celebrates the triumph of art over death, another subject favoured by Fellini; he had planned a film about the afterlife he was never able to shoot, Il viaggio di G. Mastorna. Perhaps the most obvious homage to Fellini in All That Jazz is Fosse's choice of Giuseppe Rotunno as his director of photography, one of Fellini's most trusted collaborators, who shot the musical with a colour style reminiscent of that he created with Fellini on several occasions.

There are a number of non-musical feature films that are adaptations or remakes of 8½: Paul Mazursky's Alex in Wonderland (1970); Rainer Werner Fassbinder's Warnung vor einer heiligen Nutte (Beware of a Holy Whore, 1971); François Truffaut's La Nuit américaine (Day for Night, 1973); Woody Allen's Stardust Memories; and Spike Jonze's Adaptation (2002). Mazursky, Fassbinder and Truffaut all produce films worthy of discussion, which obviously owe something to Fellini's template, like Godard's Le mépris (Contempt, 1963), a film that appeared in the same year as 8½ and was also shot primarily at Rome's

Bob Fosse's musical tribute to Fellini's 8½ (1963) and its ending in All That Jazz (1979)

Sharon Stone blows Bates (Woody Allen) a kiss in his *Stardust Memories* (1980)

Cinecittà. Superficial similarities between 8½ and these three films stand out: they dramatise the tensions on a film set; they concentrate upon drama 'behind the scenes'; they reflect quite naturally the thematic or ideological concerns of very different directors. But unlike the adaptations made by Bob Fosse, Woody Allen and Spike Jonze, they are not primarily about artistic creativity, and because of this, we shall limit our discussion here to *Stardust Memories* and *Adaptation*.

Stardust Memories, like *Sweet Charity*, is a true remake of a Fellini original, not a radical adaptation of a Fellini original, like *All That Jazz* or *Adaptation*. Allen himself plays a film director named Sandy Bates who makes comic films but wants to turn to 'serious' work. It would be foolish to expect a director with the cerebral comic style of Woody Allen to produce a remake matching the exuberance and energy of Fosse's depiction of creativity through choreography. While Fosse employs Giuseppe Rotunno to effect a Fellinian visual style in colour, Allen hires veteran director of cinematography Gordon Willis to fill his film with images reminiscent of the exquisite black-and-white photography of Otello Martelli in *La dolce vita* or Gianni di Venzano in 8½. As one of Bates's actors declares when asked whether one of Bates's films was an homage to *The House of Wax* (1954), 'An homage? Not exactly. We just stole the idea outright.' Fosse and Allen basically stole the idea behind *Sweet Charity* and *Stardust Memories* outright, but they did something original and different in the process that added something new and fresh to the original templates.

In Allen's opening sequences, Sandy Bates experiences a version of Fellini's famous traffic jam as a metaphor for artistic blockage (the same sequence Joel Schumacher employs in *Falling Down*): in a train compartment rather than a car, Bates stares at his strangely silent, depressed and unhappy companions and then gazes across the tracks to see another, completely different train full of happy people heading in another direction (a young Sharon Stone, in her film debut, blows Bates a kiss). Suddenly we realise that we have just watched a scene from one of Bates's tragic films. Elsewhere, Allen brilliantly copies one of Fellini's trademarks: using the frame to produce a feeling of entrapment within the subjectivity of his protagonist (particularly during press conferences and question-and-answer sessions), where faces impinge upon Bates's filmic space, asking inane questions about art and his personal life and creating a sense of claustrophobia. Like Fellini's director, Bates has trouble dealing with the women in his life, and like Guido, Bates worries about the influence his producers will have over his creativity. He wants to end his film at a garbage dump, while his producers demand a Hollywood happy ending in 'jazz heaven'. Toward the end of the film, Bates finally tells one of the women in his life that he has invented a new ending for his film: everyone in his life is on a happy train – ironically, a finale close to the alternate ending Fellini actually rejected in 8½ when he selected, instead, the magic circus carousel symbolising artistic creativity. Bates and his girlfriend depart, and we learn that this train is the happy train we saw at the opening of the film. An audience claps and we realise we have been returned to an auditorium filled with film buffs watching a Sandy Bates movie. The women in Bates's life are now revealed to be different actresses in his films, and we finally learn that most of what has transpired in the course of the narrative has been a film within a film.

Fellini's stroke of genius in 8½, like Pirandello's in *Sei personaggi in cerca di un autore* (*Six Characters in Search of an Author*, 1921), was to make a film about the impossibility of making another film, just as Pirandello's theatrical masterpiece was the dramatisation of the impossibility of creating another dramatic performance. The visualisation of that impossibility created an entirely new kind of metatheatre in Pirandello and an entirely new kind of metafilm about artistic creativity in Fellini. The extrovert Fellini ends 8½ with a breathtaking celebration, a festive moment that carries the audience away by its daring simplicity and visualises the very moment of artistic creativity in subjectivity. The director figure Guido regresses to a child who marches with a group of clown musicians and then disappears from view, leaving only the primordial source of the cinema's power – light – before the screen fades to black with the film's credits. The introvert and intellectual Allen concludes his remake of 8½ with Sandy Bates alone in the theatre after his audience has left, staring at the empty screen; the camera fades to black, leaving only the house lights on the ceiling, giving the illusion of stars in the sky.

Like Woody Allen, Spike Jonze recognised that Fellini's originality offered other film directors a template for metacinema, self-reflexive discourse on the very nature of creativity in the movies. Fosse was inspired by Fellini's efforts to dramatise his ideas about choreography and musical comedy; Allen employed a Fellinian discourse to analyse his own neurotic preoccupations; and Jonze's *Adaptation*, with a first-rate script by Charlie Kaufman, moves the Fellinian discourse about film-making and artistic creativity forward by focusing not on the film director but on the scriptwriter. The idea of 'adaptation' in the film is a term with many meanings: it refers not only to turning a book into a script, but also to the Darwinian process of how flowers (in this case, orchids) adapt to survive; more importantly, adaptation also means how the heart adapts to passion. While 8½ was about the impossibility of completing a film and the film completed visualised that impossibility, Kaufman's script concerns the impossibility of turning a book called *The Orchid Thief* by

The festive ending of Fellini's *8½* (1963) that celebrates artistic creativity

Susan Orlean into a script. To complicate matters, Kaufman creates a fictional twin brother (Donald) who idolises script guru Robert McKee (a real person and the author of a 'how to do it' guide called *Story: Substance, Structure, Style and the Principles of Scriptwriting* [1997]). Nicolas Cage plays both the actual scriptwriter for *Adaptation*, the real Charlie Kaufman, and his brother Donald (the fictional antagonist of the fictional Charlie).

As luck would have it, Charlie's attempt to script something real and authentic fails, while Donald's philistine desire to land a huge contract for a horror film succeeds; Donald taunts his brother with this significant reference:

> McKee says we all have to realize we write in a genre, so we must find originality within that genre. Did you know that there hasn't been a new genre since Fellini invented the mockumentary? … My genre's thriller, what's yours?

Donald's reference to Fellini's invention alludes to those Fellini films that appear to relate aspects of the director's life but are actually fictitious constructions or pseudo-documentaries – 'mockumentaries'. This list would include not only semi-biographical works such as *I vitelloni* but also *La dolce vita*, *8½*, *Block-notes di un regista*; *I clowns*, *Roma* and *Intervista*. An extremely complicated and intricate film, *Adaptation* not only imitates but advances the self-reflexive, Fellinian discourse on metacinema. It is probable that future treatments of artistic creativity in the cinema will rely upon the self-reflexive, metacinematic discourse with which Fellini has been identified. Creating the foundation for an entire cinematographic genre – a 'mockumentary' to adopt the definition employed by *Adaptation* – represents a significant achievement in the history of Italian cinema, and with various Fellini-related projects planned in the near future,[15] there seems every reason to believe that Fellini's influence will continue to remain an important factor in the exportation of Italian cinematic culture abroad.

NOTES

1. Author's transcription from Carmen Piccini's documentary, *The Magic of Fellini*. The full text of Scorsese's discussion of Fellini may be found in his introduction to the Criterion DVD of *La Strada* and is printed in both English and Italian in Martin Scorsese, 'About *La Strada*', in Giuseppe Ricci (ed.), *La memoria di Federico Fellini sullo schermo del cinema mondiale* (Rimini: Fondazione Federico Fellini, 2003), pp. 58–61.

2. For Peter Greenaway's own discussion of his debts to Fellini, see his essay 'Magic Realism before Magic Realism', in Ricci, *La memoria di Federico Fellini*, pp. 164–6. Citations from Greenaway in this chapter come from this essay.

3. There are important exceptions to this rule of thumb. The hand of a giant Anita Ekberg who picks up Doctor Mazzuolo (Peppino De Filippo) in the episode entitled 'Le tentazioni del Dottor Antonio' ('The Temptations of Doctor Antonio') in the episode film *Boccaccio '70* (1962) is clearly a comic reference to the hand of the gorilla picking up Fay Wray in *King Kong* (1933) by Merian C. Cooper and Ernest B. Schoedsack. Another rare citation is much less obvious: Fellini borrows the ghostly apparition of a young girl holding a ball from Mario Bava's *Operazione paura* to create a portrait of the devil as a young girl whose bouncing ball brings about the death of his protagonist in *Toby Dammit*, one episode of an episodic film entitled *Histoires extraordinaires* (*Spirits of the Dead*, 1968) based on four tales by Edgar Allan Poe. Bava's figure probably also influenced the apparitions of two young females, sporting a bouncing ball in Stanley Kubrick's *The Shining* (1980). Needless to say, if this is the case, both Kubrick and Fellini appreciated Bava's work long before he became a popular cult figure among international audiences, as he is today.

4. Author's transcription from Carmen Piccini's documentary, *The Magic of Fellini*.

5. *Fumetti* were pulp magazines with the traditional bubbles of American cartoons filled with dialogue (called *fumetti* or little puffs of smoke in Italian) but with black-and-white photographs replacing the drawings of cartoon magazines.

6. Available at http://archiviostorico.corriere.it/2009/agosto/26/Sofia_Coppola_mio_nuovo_film_co_9_0908260 48.shtml; accessed 18 August 2012.

7. The awards in question ('*telegatti*' or golden cats, the word *telegatto* being derived from two Italian words for *televisione* [tv] and *gatto* [cat]) are given out for various Italian and international television programmes. Coppola gives a cameo role during the awards ceremony to Italian director Maurizio Nichetti, best known for his film *Ladri di saponetti* (*The Icicle Thief*, 1989) and for his work with Italian television.

8. For a discussion of Fellini and commercials, see Peter Bondanella, 'Fellini e la Grande Tentatrice – Breve istoria: dai maccheroncini Pop, alla Pasta Barilla al Banco di Roma', in Paolo Fabbri (ed.), *Lo schermo 'manifesto': Le misteriose pubblicità di Federico Fellini* (Rimini: Guaraldi, 2002), pp. 21–47; or more recently

Frank Burke, 'Fellini's Commercials: Biting the Hand That Feeds', *The Italianist* vol. 31 no. 2 (2011), pp. 205–42.

9. The Peroni commercial is available at http://www.youtube.com/watch?v=rYnuzTd16OY&feature=youtube_gdata_player; accessed 18 August 2012.

10. The Longines commercial may be found on YouTube at: http://www.youtube.com/watch?v=GWIs5TVdSD4&feature=youtube_gdata_player as well as the official Longines site at http://www.longines.com/watches/longines-dolcevita; both accessed 18 August 2012.

11. *The Wholly Family* may be streamed five times for a very minimal charge from the director's own website: http://terrygilliamweb.com; accessed 20 August 2012. Gilliam contributes a very lengthy assessment of Fellini in Carmen Piccini's documentary, *The Magic of Fellini*, also available on YouTube at: http://m.youtube.com/watch?gl=US&hl=en&client=mv-google&v=534CiHJd_eo&fulldescription=1; accessed 23 August 2012.

12. For Scorsese's discussion of Fellini, I am indebted to two long television interviews by Charlie Rose available on YouTube at: http://www.youtube.com/watch?v=5SNpgW0PWrM and http://www.youtube.com/watch?v=4pIpd72ix_E.

13. The beer commercial can be viewed at http://www.cynephile.com/2011/11/why-do-foreign-films-have-to-be-so-foreign/; accessed 18 August 2012. Scorsese's 1993 letter may be found in the *New York Times* archive for 25 November 1993: http://www.cynephile.com/2011/11/why-make-fellini-the-scapegoat-for-new-cultural-intolerance-letter-to-the-new-york-times-25-nov-1993/.

14. In contrast to the infamous beer spot, Wachovia Bank (now Wells Fargo) sponsored another commercial referencing Fellini that was almost in direct contrast to the philistine content of the Bud Dry spot. It opened with a question: 'What can a bank learn from a foreign film?' and then proceeded to tell its audience (another similar spot asked what could a bank learn from a Harley-Davidson motorcycle!). The single film clip chosen to represent foreign films as a group was the celebrated harem sequence from Fellini's 8½. Citing Fellini as the archetypal art-film director was the focus of both the beer and the bank ads: only the conclusions were different.

15. Fellini continues to attract the interest of film-makers. *The Journey of G. Mastorna* was his final and perhaps greatest dream. Producer Demian Kusturiza and Robin Wood Pictures, a film production company based in the UK, have recently announced plans to make a feature-length motion picture loosely based on Fellini's treatment for *The Journey of G. Mastorna*. Ermanno Cavazzoni – author of the screenplay for Fellini's last film, *La voce della luna* (*The Voice of the Moon*, 1990) – is currently working on the script. A film entitled *Deragliamenti* (*Derailments*) by experimental director Chelsea McMullan, premiered at the 2011 Toronto Film Festival, briefly examined this unrealised film and Milo Manara's graphic novel based on the script. Other Fellini-related projects are in the works. In November 2012, an experimental documentary produced by Kiné, directed by Luca Magi, and scripted by Antonio Bigini, entitled *Anita*, was screened at the Torino Film Festival. It is inspired by Fellini's unrealised treatment of *Viaggio con Anita* (*A Journey with Anita*), a translation of which may be found in John C. Stubbs (ed. and trans.), 'Moraldo in the City' & 'A Journey with Anita' (Urbana: University of Illinois Press, 1983). A film based on what happened when Fellini supposedly disappeared for two days before the 1957 Oscar ceremonies, *Fellini Black and White*, has been announced by producer Henry Bromell, starring Brazilian actor Walter Moura as Fellini. See Paul Harris's article in the *Manchester Guardian*, available at http://www.guardian.co.uk/film/2012/may/12/frederico-fellini-los-angeles-mystery; accessed 24 August 2012. Another possible project is a loose second remake of *Le notti di Cabiria* tentatively called *The Days of Mary*, starring Juliette Lewis as a young woman working as a prostitute in Reno, Nevada. Available at http://www.variety.com/article/VR1118053627; accessed 24 August 2012.

FURTHER READING

Fabbri, Paolo (ed.), *Lo schermo 'manifesto': Le misteriose pubblicità di Federico Fellini* (Rimini: Guaraldi, 2002). Originally published in Paolo Fabbri and Mario Guaraldi (eds), *Mistici & Miraggi: Mystfest 1997* (Milan: Mondadori, 1997).

Pettigrew, Damian, *Fellini: I'm a Born Liar* DVD (Firstlook, 2002).

Piccini, Carmen, *The Magic of Fellini* DVD (Image Entertainment, 2002).

Ricci, Giuseppe (ed.), *La memoria di Federico Fellini sullo schermo del cinema mondiale: Atti del Convegno internazionale di studi (Rimini, 7–9 novembre 2003)* (Rimini: Fondazione Federico Fellini, 2003).

Scorsese, Martin, Video Introduction, *La strada* DVD (Criterion, 2003).

39 The Heritage of the Past and New Frontiers for the History of Italian Cinema

Gian Piero Brunetta

In recent years, thanks to the confluence of many favourable factors, numerous perspectives have altered, the quantity of information has increased in geometric proportions, the bibliographic frame of reference has changed thanks to not a few important international contributions, and the need to observe and measure any phenomenon in the Italian cinema from a comparative point of view and in the light of the possibility of controlling at first hand our sources – filmic and non-filmic – has progressively matured. These sources have been rendered ever more accessible thanks to our informational systems and to the most open and far-sighted policies of film libraries and of both public and private institutions. Anyone who intends to undertake a new comprehensive work, either individually or collectively, can today review its cinematic sources with a 360-degree gaze and measure its range in a way that no scholar in the past could equal. The emotions that such a vision communicates have to me seemed on various occasions in recent years very similar to those of King Cyrus of Persia, when he stood before his troops on the eve of the battle against Croesus, just as Xenophon described it in *The Expedition of Cyrus*. Year after year I have observed with enthusiasm and a sense of involvement the multiplication of analytical research; the discovery, restoration and restitution to new public life of hundreds of films presumed lost; the growth of a new generation of scholars both in Italy and abroad; and the certainly slow but irreversible development of a different historiographical consciousness even in scholars who have been absorbed for years by purely theoretical pursuits. And just as film theory has produced results of less significance in respect to previous decades and has turned inward upon itself, mobilising ponderous armaments and warriors to produce almost imperceptible methodological and intellectual changes on the international scale, in like manner more modest

cooperative works – in part positivistic in nature – have allowed us to advance in numerous directions, to open extremely fruitful pathways and to set into sharper focus fuzzy shadow zones and unwritten chapters of different national histories.

Thus, the history of Italian cinema has become history on the grand scale, a history that has changed the course of world cinema that is to be studied in its individuality but also must be observed inside a field of international forces with which it was confronted from its very first infantile steps. Generously endowed with bonafide geniuses from the start and with characters that have traced out a path along all its hundred years of history, from its very beginnings, Italian cinema has, in its wide range and profundity, influenced the publics of world cinema, leading them along at least four major paths:

1   toward the valorisation and circulation of an immense historical-cultural patrimony of the past that it can still offer as a legacy to the Western world;
2   toward the confirmation of cinema as the product of talent and artistic affirmation linked to the world and the style of an author;
3   toward the collection and export of artistic and artisanal forms of knowledge inherited from the workshops of the Italian Renaissance, the kinds of knowledge revitalised by the movie camera;
4   toward the exploration of the visible and of the possibility of recounting everyone's stories, transferring onto the screen the tradition of oral narrative, creating a universal language capable of transmitting in the simplest and most direct manner the range of sentiments and means of representation, uncovering new channels of storytelling and conferring the role of modern bard of infinite collective epics upon the movie camera.

In other words, to greatly simplify and name some of the figures in this picture, we may say that Italian cinema has traversed history, from the conquest of the world, displaying the banners of the troops led by Julius Caesar, Hercules and Maciste; it has exhibited the glorious bodies of female stars who became known as Francesca Bertini, Lyda Borelli, Alida Valli, Anna Magnani, Silvana Mangano, Gina Lollobrigida, Sophia Loren, Silvana Pampanini, Claudia Cardinale and Ornella Muti, and are accompanied by the masculine forms we recognise as Massimo Girotti to Amedeo Nazzari to Gino Cervi, Vittorio De Sica, Marcello Mastroianni and Vittorio Gassman. Italian cinema may follow the paths opened by Rossellini and Zavattini–De Sica. Or it may select innovative directors such as Fellini and Antonioni as the polar stars of new modes of narration. And at the very moment when the cinema of the great masters seems to be faltering, it may even export technicians, directors of photography, set designers, costume designers, composers and other creative personalities with unmistakable signatures who have modified the very fabric and structure of cinema produced outside Italy.

Besides this, well aware of its own productive weakness, from the second half of the 1940s, Italian cinema has sought to compensate for this weakness, assembling a continental team, hypothesising the birth of a truly European cinema, and has developed for some years the utopian dream of a 'single European front for the cinema' that could act as a shield against Hollywood's massive invasion, initiating co-production agreements that in both the medium and long term have resulted in some positive reversals of the relationship of the forces in its confrontations with the hegemony of American cinema. In the space of little more than a decade, this unequal struggle from the standpoint of the means of production was transformed into a victorious action, thanks to the risk-taking capacity and the far-sighted thinking of some producers, and Italian cinema was able to export not only its masterpieces but hundreds of titles belonging to popular genres, from melodrama to the mythological film to the Western, thanks to the support of its European partners, who participated during the 1950s in these co-production adventures.

Today the work of a film historian has been significantly facilitated by the circulation of texts, by opportunities to meet, by new ideas and the results of this research, and by the opportunity to screen and watch works restored to their original condition. Only

twenty-five to thirty years ago, working on silent cinema or on the 1920s presented difficulties not inferior to climbing up a steep mountain. After 1970, the cinematic patrimony of the silent cinema, given up as definitively and irreparably lost, has re-emerged in the most diverse and unexpected (but nevertheless predictable) places, and today a gigantic quantity of filmic and extra filmic materials has been located and partly restored and conserved in cinematheques, archives and private collections around the world. The cinematheques have begun to make public their lists of collections that are organised homogeneously and capable of being analysed in their specificity and in their relationships with the entire system of world cinema. Today, we know the titles of many Italian silent films preserved in the cinematheques belonging to the FIAF,[1] and many lacunae in films considered irretrievable have been partially filled in. A good cinematic philology has also been developed and its international capital is situated in Italy, specifically Bologna. To the historiography of memory and of action by the critics, frequently near-sighted and little prepared to accept anything new, to the praiseworthy historical *bricolage* of researchers throughout Italy, whose passion has camouflaged and made up for the lack of economic support and organic projects of medium and long term sustained by some academic institution, one can now substitute a more systematic and detached system of work, carried out by a direct re-examination of all our sources and on the comparison of our own cinematic resources with those of other countries.

My own work over the course of some decades does not conceal the pleasure of research and the pioneer-like joy of archival discoveries and of the multiplicity of sources in Italy and abroad, as well as the sense of exhilarating adventure in exploring themes that have never previously entered our critical and historical horizons and in the surveying of the characteristics and complexities of our territory. The simple job of updating bibliography in the game of the selection of texts and the recomposition of a broader picture still remains a source of pleasure, just as the desire to recognise the usefulness of contributions that seem minimal in appearance or almost invisible and impossible to locate. In my circumnavigations in the history of Italian and world cinema, I have often had Ulysses by my side. In reality, I have been seated for many hours, practically tied down to a chair or a couch, seated in front of a moviola or a movie screen, spread out like sails to gather up the light of the look of hundreds of

spectators or often only set up for my own use in order
to seek to gather the sirens' song of Italian silent
cinema; in Ulysses' company, I have advanced to the
discoveries of the mysteries and the enchantments of
Circe's many islands and real and true treasure islands
not included in any known map or in the current film
guides. Ulysses has been my guide and spiritual father,
an ideal helmsman and model voyager. He has taught
me the pleasure of moving toward unknown spaces
and unexplored territories; the taste for risk and for
dirtying my hands in the lowest and often muddiest
depths of criticism or of genre films; he has
transmitted to me some of the genes indispensable to
a researcher, who aspires, even in the midst of all
uncertainty that accompanies him or the inferiority
complex that he never ceases to feel in comparison to
historians, to bestow a historical authority upon his
work and to affirm the right of the historian of the
cinema to full legitimisation in the field of studies of
contemporary history. These genes could determine, for
example, persistence and determination in following
an objective once established; pliability, curiosity, rigor,
elasticity and openness in understanding and changing
one's tools during the course of one's work; respect for
the existing critical roadmaps and for the work of
others; and the taste for transgression and for the
undisciplined contamination of disciplinary knowledge.
Thus, well aware of the limits of a work realised by a
single individual, who has not enjoyed any financial
support for his research, my Storia del cinema italiano,[2]
greatly enlarged, has been republished at the same
time as the troubled publication of the Storia del cinema
italiano in quindici volumi has appeared, a project
conceived and promoted by Lino Miccichè[3] and the
Centro Sperimentale di Cinematografia with the
support of the Ministry of Entertainment. This project
was a work conceived at the end of the 1990s – entirely
the product of 'Made in Italy' academics and entrusted
to the care of some fifteen scholars and critics selected
from different backgrounds and intellectual formations
(both academics and non-academics). The editors
were not guided by historical titles and common
methodologies, and constrained to work with a system
of historical periodisation that in many cases is very
unconvincing. And so, if in every volume, one finds
original contributions and a useful documentation, the
reading of the introductory essays generates in some
cases a considerable sense of bewilderment.

The development of historical research on cinema,
in these last two decades, has experienced a

Malthusian growth, one more rapid percentage-wise
than the world demographic increase. Cinema in
general and Italy's cinema in particular still represent
objects and territories that must and can be discovered,
enumerated and assessed in a systematic manner. It is
an object in its hybrid state, still only in part 'visible',
for which many coordinates must still be fixed,
recognised and catalogued in terms of its morphology,
its lexicon and its dynamics in the short and long term.
The quality of a historical work and the importance of
its contribution must always be linked to awareness of
its precarious nature, its uncertainty and its constant
perfectibility as a result of its being part of a work in
progress on which many have participated and will
participate. The usefulness of a methodology may be
recognised also by its capacity to adapt itself to
problems that arise only after a confrontation with the
object of study, as well as by its ability to acknowledge
any assistance received along the way.

To do the history of cinema today also means, in my
opinion, to know how to devise research projects that
explore both known terrain and unexplored galaxies,
understanding how to make up for the limits and the
ingenuousness of traditional criticism, as well as the
inaccuracy and dilettantism of much of the work done
in recent years, with much more solid intellectual tools,
with multiple skills and, at the same time, succeeding
in combining a high degree of specialisation with
absolute curiosity and openness when confronted with
the object of study. Taboos, closed mindedness,
expulsions and prejudicial refusals advance neither
research nor knowledge.

In the era of computers and data banks, work that I
have conducted over many long years in solitude, using
traditional systems of indexing and memorisation,
seems anachronistic and capable of being surpassed
by a more rational organisation of research and by a
more functional distribution of tasks to competent
researchers. In a future that I hope is near, one may
be able to proceed to the rigorous and systematic
constitution of our intellectual tools and inventories
for research in common, to the cataloguing of sources,
and to an immediacy of consultation and reproduction.
For now it is sufficient to know how to recognise the
virtual nature of our research and to move with the
conviction that the material which has emerged and
which is known is still a minimal part of what still
remains. I do not wish to have recourse to paradoxes,
but I believe it is possible to sustain with absolute
assurance the argument that the work of a historian of

cinema turns out in many cases to be even more difficult and unusual than, for example, that of the paleontologist studying the civilisation of the Camuni people in the Valtellina valley some 60,000 years ago. To rephrase a remark in Pasolini's *Il fiore di mille e una notte* (*Arabian Nights*, 1974), I believe that for a historian of the cinema, historical truth today consists not so much in his or her ability to produce *One History* but rather in his or her awareness that *many histories* exist and that being aware of them brings to light a new and unpredictable network of relationships. Fernand Braudel, at any rate, already said this: 'History can be conceived today only in an "nth" dimension.'

THE HERITAGE OF THE PAST

I shall never tire of repeating and recognising this fact. It was necessary to depart once again from a humble and absolutely necessary work of collection and verification of data in order to be able to create a common and trustworthy fabric for anyone who might wish to undertake any type of full-scale historical work that might evaluate a quantity of elements that precede the contact with the true and proper film text but that might help, at the same time, to define the characteristics of its context in the most trustworthy way possible. To not have understood the usefulness of some kinds of work – like that of Aldo Berdinini, for instance – and now having adequately supported and encouraged it, seems to me one of the many sins of blindness and cultural short-sightedness typical of the generations that have nevertheless produced the history of Italian criticism and theory in the postwar period. I am thinking of Guido Aristarco and other luminaries of Italian cultural history like him who never really acquired a capacity for observing and studying their subject in a historical sense and with the instruments of a historian. Aristarco's work is not the work of a historian, nor did it ever become so even in the writings of his last years, because Aristarco himself was a *subject* of history who privileged the important work of the so-called 'militant criticism' that was capable of having an immediate influence and was always ready to exercise its activity in relation to an immediate result. Even though he took part in and was even the winner (along with Luigi Chiarini and Giuseppe Sala) of the first competition for an Italian university chair in the History of the Cinema, even being one of the founding fathers, Aristarco only contributed in a very modest manner to the growth and the diffusion of his subject matter from the

historical perspective. He had many pioneering merits, he was an admirable 'armed critic', a man who loved open conflict and who, with his review, *Cinema Nuovo*, weaned and encouraged more than a generation of critics, but, they did not contribute to the growth of a scientific community nor a mature society capable of welcoming and creating a multiplicity of voices, critical tendencies and methodologies that were distinct and pointed in different directions. In order to escape from this phase in which no historical work could be born it was first necessary that the critic should cancel himself out as a subject capable of investing such a strong charge of emotional or ideological passion as to deaden his visual faculties and to produce an inability to respect the object of study and to analyse it in its specificity. In fact, any historical work on Italian cinema from its beginnings to the 1980s should have recourse to Bernardini. Thanks to this kind of analytic definition of the entire Italian film territory that was begun by Francesco Savio with the publication of his fundamental map of the sound film during the fascist period (*Ma l'amore no*, 1975) and then by Vittorio Martinelli and finally by Bernardini, with his project of a complete, census-like description of the entire territory – documentaries included – it soon became evident that a good historical work of filmography could be carried on even in the absence of film sources and that print documents themselves could help to outline a quantity of reliable and useful information for the classification and identification of all the individual film works.

For the generations that in the 1970s and 1980s followed the siren calls of semiotic or psychoanalytical theoreticians, historical work seemed clearly and for a long period like a sheepish, tiresome, completely unrewarding task, incapable of exploiting properly the winds and currents favourable to an eventual academic legitimisation of the field. Then, many things slowly began to change. Naturally, the work of filmographic reconstruction and micro history is to be considered necessary to the extent that it can augment research of a broader methodological and problematic scope. An increasingly closer interaction between those who work on the gathering of data, without preoccupying themselves with theory, and those who seek to employ interpretive categories to coordinate the various elements of research within a broader view, is indispensable. But, besides the usefulness and the modification of a general attitude, one must still speak of how necessary the progressive acquisition of a philological mentality is, one that is even now non-existent or avoided by the criticism of the past like the plague. This philological mentality must be distributed in equal measure between the task of gathering data and that of the recuperation and analysis of film texts: here, too, the mixture of technicians and scholars has been shown of late to constitute an incentive to growth and not an obstacle that dissipates our energies.

On many occasions, I have asked myself if one of the necessary qualities for the definition of a good historian of the cinema might not be linked more to one's capacity for contributing, with all the means at one's disposal, to the physical survival and to the revitalisation of cinematic works that are in the process of disappearing forever. It is precisely the merit of this kind of philological, technical and historiographic *bricolage*, as well as the passionate adventure of various individuals scattered throughout the world (and often not belonging to any regular institution, operating in perfect solitude for decades) that hundreds, thousands of works given up as lost have been saved and restored to their original condition. Citing some concrete examples, it is sufficient to recall the case of Italian silent cinema: from the beginnings of the 1980s when 5 per cent of the works (no more than 500 out of 10,000 titles produced), the figure has now reached almost 25 per cent of the total. 'There are no minor works, in my opinion, I want everything to be saved', Martin Scorsese recently declared in *The Future of the Movies*, establishing himself as the voice of a growing consciousness of the problems involved with conservation and restoration. A single film history, organised teleologically by a single historian endowed with monolithic certainties and the discovery of a select number of authors and masterpieces, no longer exists, but there are one, two, ten, hundreds and thousands of histories that may join together without ever reaching absolute and linear coherence: a thousand and one objects of study, a thousand and one itineraries to reach a thousand and one narratives. In this phase of heuristic conjunction between factors favourable to research (a moment almost in counterpoint to crises both of production and of consumption), there is room for everyone and there is no longer anybody capable of imposing a single dominant model and of polarising and directing research toward his or her own concept of history. In reality, there exists a very pragmatic method of verifying the originality and the traction of historical research: its usefulness as a starting point and its

practical utilisation by the international community of scholars and researchers.

The heredity of the past and the extreme mobility of the present, the diffusion of the perspective of the specialist but one not isolated from concrete problems, allow us to look with justified optimism at possible worlds and at the future projection of conservation and historical as well as theoretical research. 'We are dreamers', remarks a character in a story by Ursula Le Guin, 'and worlds will endure as long as our desire endures.' It is legitimate to hope at this point, in the full knowledge of the difficulties, the objective limits and the complexities of the problems that historians of future generations must confront, that the new paths of research will develop along the paths opened by our desires and our capacity to believe in the realisation of our dreams.

NOTES

1. Fédération International des Archives du Film (The International Federation of Film Archives), located in Paris.
2. To date, eight of the fifteen volumes have been published. See the bibliography to this book for details (translator's note).
3. Lino Micciché, the critic and scholar who helped found the Pesaro Film Festival and who had important roles at the Venice Biennale and the Centro Sperimentale. He was the author of numerous books and articles on Italian cinema and for many years taught at the Dipartimento di Comunicazione e Spettacolo at Rome's Università Tre (translator's note).

Select Bibliography on Italian Cinema

REFERENCE

Di Giammatteo, Fernaldo, *Dizionario del cinema italiano: Dall'inizio del secolo a oggi i film che hanno segnato la storia del nostro cinema* (Rome: Editori Riuniti, 1995).

Filmlexicon degli autori e delle opere (9 vols) (Rome: Edizioni di Bianco e Nero, 1958, 1974).

Grant, Barry Keith (ed.), *Schirmer Encyclopedia of Film* (4 vols) (Detroit, MI: Thomson Gale, 2007).

Hughes, Howard, *Cinema Italiano: The Complete Guide from Classics to Cult* (London: I. B. Tauris, 2011).

Lancia, Enrico, *Dizionario del cinema italiano. I film. Dal 1900 al 2000* (Rome: Gremese, 2002).

——, and Roberto Poppi (eds), *Dizionario del cinema italiano. Gli attori A–L and Gli attori M–Z* (2 vols) (Rome: Gremese, 2003).

Mereghetti, Paolo, *Dizionario dei Film* (Milan: Baldini & Castoldi, 1995 and subsequent editions).

Moliterno, Gino (ed.), *Historical Dictionary of Italian Cinema* (Lanham, MD: Scarecrow Press, 2008).

Nowell-Smith, Geoffrey with James Hay and Gianni Volpi, *The Companion to Italian Cinema* (London: Cassell, 1996).

Schedario cinematografico (8 vols) (Rome: Centro dello spettacolo e della communicazione sociale, 1972).

Stewart, John, *Italian Film: A Who's Who* (Jefferson, NC: McFarland, 1994).

BACKGROUNDS

Baranski, Zygmunt G. and Rebecca West (eds), *The Cambridge Companion to Modern Italian Culture* (Cambridge: Cambridge University Press, 2001).

Barzini, Luigi, *The Italians* (New York: Atheneum, 1964).

Bethemont, Jacques and Jean Pelletier, *Italy: A Geographical Introduction* (London: Longman, 1983).

Bondanella, Peter and Julia Conaway Bondanella (eds-in-chief), *Dictionary of Italian Literature*, 2nd rev. edn (Westport, CT: Greenwood Press, 1996).

—— and Andrea Ciccarelli (eds), *The Cambridge Companion to the Modern Italian Novel* (Cambridge: Cambridge University Press, 2003).

Brand, Peter and Lino Pertile (ed.), *The Cambridge History of Italian Literature* (Cambridge: Cambridge University Press, 1996).

Cannistraro, Philip V. (ed.), *Historical Dictionary of Fascist Italy* (Westport, CT: Greenwood Press, 1982).

Coppa, Frank J. (ed.), *Dictionary of Modern Italian History* (Westport, CT: Greenwood Press, 1985).

Forgacs, David and Robert Lumley (eds), *Italian Cultural Studies: An Introduction* (Oxford: Oxford University Press, 1996).

—— and Stephen Gundle, *Mass Culture and Italian Society, 1936–1954. From Fascism to the Cold War* (Bloomington: Indiana University Press, 2007).

Ginsborg, Paul, *A History of Contemporary Italy: Society and Politics 1943–1988* (London: Penguin, 1990).

——, *Italy and Its Discontents. Family, Civil Society, State: 1980–2001* (New York: Palgrave Macmillan, 2003).

Heiney, Donald, *America in Modern Italian Literature* (New Brunswick, NJ: Rutgers University Press, 1964).

Jeannet, Angela and Louise Barnett (eds and trans.), *New World Journeys: Contemporary Italian Writers and the Experience of America* (Westport, CT: Greenwood Press, 1977).

Jones, Tobias, *The Dark Heart of Italy* (New York: Farrar, Straus and Giroux, 2005).

Kogan, Norman, *A Political History of Italy: The Postwar Years* (New York: Praeger, 1983).

Mack Smith, Denis, *Italy: A Modern History* (Ann Arbor: University of Michigan Press, 1969; rev. edn 1998).

——, *Mussolini* (New York: Knopf, 1982).

Marrone, Gaetana and Paolo Puppa (eds), *Encyclopedia of Italian Literary Studies* (2 vols) (New York: Routledge, 2007).

Moliterno, Gino (ed.), *Encyclopedia of Contemporary Italian Culture* (London: Routledge, 2000).

Spotts, Frederic and Theodore Wieser, *Italy: A Difficult Democracy – A Survey of Italian Politics* (Cambridge: Cambridge University Press, 1986).

White, Jonathan, *Italy: The Enduring Culture* (New York: Ungar, 2001).

ITALIAN CINEMA HISTORIES
Comprehensive Studies

Bertellini, Giorgio (ed.), *The Cinema of Italy* (London: Wallflower Press, 2004).

Bertetto, Paolo (ed.), *Storia del cinema italiano: uno squardo d'insieme* (Venice: Marsilio, 2011).

Bondanella, Peter, *A History of Italian Cinema* (New York and London: Continuum, 2009).

—— (ed), *The Italian Cinema Book* (London: BFI/Palgrave Macmillan, 2013).

——, *Italian Cinema: From Neorealism to the Present*, 1st edn (New York: Frederick Ungar, 1983; 2nd rev. edn, 1990; 3rd rev. edn (New York and London: Continuum, 2001).

Brunetta, Gian Piero, *Buio in sala: cent'anni di passioni dello spettatore cinematografico* (Venice: Marsilio, 1989).

——, *Cent'anni di cinema italiano: 1. Dalle origini alla seconda guerra mondiale* (Rome: Laterza, 2003).

——, *Cent'anni di cinema italiano: 2. Dal 1945 ai giorni nostri* (Rome: Laterza, 2003).

——, *Guida alla storia del cinema italiano 1905–2003* (Turin: Einaudi, 2003); English edn, *The History of Italian Cinema 1905–2003*, trans. Jeremy Parzen (Princeton, NJ: Princeton University Press, 2009).

——, *Storia del cinema italiano 1895–1945* (Rome: Editori Riuniti, 1979).

——, *Storia del cinema italiano dal 1945 agli anni ottanta* (Rome: Editori Riuniti, 1982).

——, *Storia del cinema italiano* (4 vols) (Rome: Editori Riuniti, 1993).

Vol. I. *Il cinema muto 1895–1929.*

Vol. II. *Il cinema del regime 1929–1945.*

Vol. III. *Dal neorealismo al miracolo economico 1945–1959.*

Vol. IV. *Dal miracolo economico agli anni novanta 1960–1993.*

Celli, Carlo and Margo Cottino-Jones, *A New Guide to Italian Cinema* (New York: Palgrave Macmillan, 2007).

Di Giammatteo, Fernaldo, *Storia del cinema* (Venice: Marsilio, 2005).

Forshaw, Barry, *Italian Cinema: Art House to Exploitation* (London: Pocket Essentials, 2006).

Giacovelli, Enrico, *Un secolo di cinema italiano 1900–1999* (2 vols) (Turin: Lindau, 2002).

Landy, Marcia, *Italian Film: The National Tradition* (New York: Cambridge University Press, 2000).

Leprohon, Pierre, *The Italian Cinema*, trans. Roger Greaves and Oliver Stallybrass (London: Secker & Warburg, 1972); rev. edn of original French edn (Paris: Éditions Séghers, 1966).

Liehm, Mira, *Passion and Defiance: Film in Italy from 1942 to the Present* (Berkeley: University of California Press, 1984).

Lizzani, Carlo, *Il cinema italiano, 1895–1979* (2 vols) (Rome: Editori Riuniti, 1979); 2nd edn published as *Il cinema italiano dalle origini agli anni ottanta* (Rome: Editori Riuniti, 1982).

Sorlin, Pierre, *Italian National Cinema 1896–1996* (London: Routledge, 1996).

Wood, Mary P., *Italian Cinema* (Oxford: Berg, 2005).

The Silent Era

Alovisio, Silvio, *Voci del silenzio: La sceneggiatura nel cinema muto italiano* (Milan: Il Castoro, 2005).

Barbina, Alfredo (ed.), *Sperduti nel buio* (Turin: Nuova ERI, 1987).

Bernardini, Aldo, *Cinema italiano delle origini: Gli ambulanti* (Gemona: La Cineteca del Friuli, 2001).

——, *Cinema muto italiano: ambiente, spettacoli e spettatori 1896/1904* (Bari: Laterza, 1980).

——, *Cinema muto italiano: arte, divismo e mercato 1910–1914* (Rome: Laterza, 1982).

——, *Cinema muto italiano: I film 'dal vero' 1895–1914* (Gemona: La Cineteca del Friuli, 2002).

——, *Cinema muto italiano: industria e organizzazione dello spettacolo 1905–1909* (Rome: Laterza, 1981).

—— and Flavia De Lucis (eds), *C'era il cinema: L'Italia al cinema tra Otto e Novecento (Reggio Emilio 1986–1915)* (Modena: Edizioni Panini, 1983).

Bertellini, Giorgio, *Italy in Early American Cinema: Race, Language, and the Picturesque* (Bloomington: Indiana University Press, 2009).

—— (ed.), *Italian Silent Cinema: A Reader* (New Barnet: John Libbey, 2013).

Brunetta, Gian Piero, *Il cinema muto italiano* (Rome: Laterza, 2008).

——, *Il viaggio dell'icononauta dalla camera oscura di Leonardo alla luce dei Lumière* (Venice: Marsilio, 2009).

Bruno, Giuliana, *Streetwalking on a Ruined Map: Cultural Theory and the City Films of Elvira Notari* (Princeton, NJ: Princeton University Press, 1993).

Dalle Vacche, Angela, *Diva: Defiance and Passion in Early Italian Cinema* (Austin: University of Texas Press, 2008).

Flint, R. W. (ed. and trans.), *Marinetti: Selected Writings* (New York: Noonday Press, 1972).

Kirby, Michael, *Futurist Performances* (New York: Dutton, 1971; rpt New York: PAJ Publications, 1986).

Martinelli, Vittorio (ed.), *Il cinema muto italiano: i film degli anni venti/1921–1922, Bianco e nero* vol. 42 nos 1–3 (1981).

——, *Il cinema muto italiano: i film degli anni venti/1923–1931, Bianco e nero* vol. 42 nos 4–6 (1981).

——, *Il cinema muto italiano: i film del dopoguerra/1919, Bianco e nero* vol. 41 nos 1–3 (1980).

——, *Il cinema muto italiano: i film del dopoguerra/1920, Bianco e nero* vol. 41 nos 4–6 (1980).

——, *Le dive del silenzio* (Bologna: Le Mani, 2001).

Minici, Carlo Alberto Zotti (ed.), *Il Mondo Nuovo: Le meraviglie della visione dal '700 alla nascita del cinema* (Bassano del Grappa: Mazzotto, 1988).

Raffaelli, Sergio, *L'Italiano nel cinema muto* (Florence: Cesati Editore, 2003).

Redi, Riccardo, *Ti parlerò … d'amore: cinema italiano fra muto e sonoro* (Turin: Edizioni ERI, 1986).

—— (ed.), *Cinema italiano muto 1905–1916* (Rome: CNC Edizioni, n.d).

Scaglione, Massimo, *Le dive del ventennio* (Turin: Lindau, 2003).

Syrimis, Michael, *The Great Black Spider on Its Knock-kneed Tripod: Reflections of Cinema in Early Twentieth-century Italy* (Toronto: University of Toronto Press, 2012).

Tosi, Virgilio, *Il cinema prima del cinema* (Milan: Il Castoro, 2007), original edn (1984); English edn, *Cinema before Cinema: The Origins of Scientific Cinematography*, trans. Sergio Angelini (London: British Universities Film & Video Council, 2005).

Troianelli, Enza, *Elvira Notari: pioniera del cinema napoletano (1895–1946)* (Rome/Naples: Euroma–La Goliardica, 1989).

Verdone, Mario, *Cinema e letteratura del futurismo* (Rome: Edizioni di Bianco e Nero, 1968).

—— (ed.), *Poemi e scenari cinematografici d'avanguardia* (Rome: Officina Edizioni, 1975).

Sound and the Fascist Era

Aprà, Adriano and Patrizia Pistagnesi (eds), *The Fabulous Thirties: Italian Cinema 1929–1944* (Milan: Electa, 1979).

Argentieri, Mino, *L'occhio del regime* (Rome: Bulzoni, 2003).

Ben-Ghiat, Ruth, *La cultura fascista* (Bologna: Il Mulino, 2004); English edn, *Fascist Modernities: Italy, 1922–1945* (Berkeley: University of California Press, 2004).

Bernagozzi, Giampaolo, *Il mito dell'immagine* (Bologna: Editrice CLUEB, 1983).

Brancalini, Romano, *Celebri e dannati – Osvaldo Valenti e Luisa Freda: storia e tragedia di due divi del regime* (Milan: Longanesi, 1985).

Brunetta, Gian Piero, *Cinema italiano tra le due guerre: fascismo e politica cinematografica* (Milan: Mursia, 1975).

Caldiron, Orio (ed.), *Storia del cinema italiano. Vol. 5: 1934–1939* (Venice: Marsilio, 2006).

Carabba, Claudio, *Il cinema del ventennio nero* (Florence: Vallecchi, 1974).

Cardillo, Massimo, *Il duce in moviola: politica e divismo nei cinegiornali e documentari 'Luce'* (Bari: Edizioni Dedalo, 1983).

Casadio, Gianfranco, *Il grigio e il nero: spettacolo e propaganda nel cinema italiano degli anni Trenta (1931–1943)* (Ravenna: Longo, 1991).

——, Ernest G. Laura and Filippo Cristiano, *Telefoni bianchi: realtà e finzione nella società e nel cinema italiano degli anni Quaranta* (Ravenna: Longo, 1991).

Falasca-Zamponi, Simonetta, *Fascist Spectacles: The Aesthetics of Power in Mussolini's Italy* (Berkeley: University of California Press, 1997).

Fogu, Claudio, *The Historic Imaginary: Politics of History in Fascist Italy* (Toronto: University of Toronto Press, 2003).

Gili, Jean A., *L'Italie de Mussolini et son cinéma* (Paris: Henri Veyrier, 1985).

——, *Stato fascista e cinematografia: repressione e promozione* (Rome: Bulzoni, 1981).

Hay, James, *Popular Film Culture in Fascist Italy: The Passing of the Rex* (Bloomington: Indiana University Press, 1987).

Landy, Marcia, *Fascism in Film: The Italian Commercial Cinema, 1931–1943* (Princeton, NJ: Princeton University Press, 1986).

——, *The Folklore of Consensus: Theatricality in the Italian Cinema, 1930–1943* (Albany: State University of New York Press, 1998).

Laura, Ernesto G., *L'immagine bugiarda: mass-media e spettacolo nella Repubblica di Salò (1943–1945)* (Rome: ANCCI, 1987).

—— (ed.), *Storia del cinema italiano. Vol. 6: 1940–1944* (Venice: Marsilio, 2010).

Mancini, Elaine, *Struggles of the Italian Film Industry during Fascism, 1930–1935* (Ann Arbor: UMI Research Press, 1985).

Mida, Massimo and Lorenzo Quaglietti (eds), *Dai telefoni bianchi al neorealismo* (Rome: Laterza, 1980).

Nuovi materiali sul cinema italiano 1929–1943 (2 vols) (Ancona: Mostra sul cinema italiano, 1976).

Redi, Riccardo (ed.), *Cinema italiano sotto il fascismo* (Venice: Marsilio, 1979).

—— (ed.), *Cinema scritto: il catalogo delle riviste italiane di cinema: 1907–1944* (Rome: Associazione italiana per le ricerche di storia del cinema, 1992).

—— and Claudio Camerini (eds), *Cinecittà 1: industria e mercato nel cinema italiano tra le due guerre* (Venice: Marsilio, 1985).

Reich, Jacqueline and Piero Garofalo (eds), *Re-viewing Fascism: Italian Cinema 1922–1943* (Bloomington: Indiana University Press, 2002).

Ricci, Steven, *Cinema & Fascism: Italian Film and Society, 1922–1943* (Berkeley: University of California Press, 2008).

Savio, Francesco, *Ma l'amore no: realismo, formalismo, propaganda e telefoni bianchi nel cinema italiano di regime 1930–1943* (Milan: Sonzogno, 1975).

Short, R. K. M. (ed.), *Film & Radio Propaganda in World War II* (Knoxville: University of Tennessee Press, 1983).

Stone, Marla, *The Patron State: Culture & Politics in Fascist Italy* (Princeton, NJ: Princeton University Press, 1998).

Zagarrio, Vito, *Cinema e fascismo: film, modelli, immaginari* (Venice: Marsilio, 2004).

Neorealism and Its Heritage

Aprà, Adriano and Claudio Carabba (eds), *Neorealismo d'appendice – per un dibattito sul cinema popolare: il caso Matarazzo* (Florence: Guaraldi Editore, 1976).

Aristarco, Guido, *Antologia di 'Cinema nuovo' 1952–1958* (Florence: Guaraldi Editore, 1975).

——, *Sciolti dal giuramento: il dibattito critico-ideologico sul cinema negli anni Cinquanta* (Bari: Edizioni Dedalo, 1981).

Armes, Roy, *Patterns of Realism: A Study of Italian Neo-Realism* (Cranbury, NJ: A. S. Barnes, 1971).

Barattoni, Luca, *Italian Post-Neorealist Cinema* (Edinburgh: University of Edinburgh Press, 2012).

Bernagozzi, Giampaolo, *Il cinema corto: il documentario nella vita italiana 1945–1980* (Florence: La Casa Usher, 1980).

Bernardi, Sandro (ed.), *Storia del cinema italiano. Vol. 9 : 1954–1959* (Venice: Marsilio, 2004).

Bondanella, Peter, 'From Italian Neorealism to the Golden Age of Cinecittà', in Elizabeth Ezra (ed.), *European Cinema* (Oxford: Oxford University Press, 2004).

——, 'Italian Neorealism', in Linda Badley, R. Barton Palmer and Steven Jay Schneider (eds), *Traditions in World Cinema* (Edinburgh: University of Edinburgh Press, 2006).

Brizio-Skov, Flavia, *Popular Italian Cinema: Culture and Politics in a Postwar Society* (London: I. B. Tauris, 2011).

Canova, Gianni (ed.), *Storia del cinema italiano. Vol. 11: 1965–1969* (Venice: Marsilio, 2002).

Canziani, Alfonso and Cristina Bragaglia, *La stagione neorealista* (Bologna: Cooperativa Libraria Universitaria Editrice, 1976).

Casadio, Gianfranco, *Adultere, fedifranghe, innocenti: la donna del neorealismo popolare nel cinema italiano degli anni Cinquanta* (Ravenna: Longo, 1991).

Celant, Germano (ed.), *The Italian Metamorphosis, 1943–1968* (New York: Guggenheim Museum, 1994; also available in a CD-ROM of the same title).

Coleman, Donatella Spinelli, *Filming the Nation: Jung, Film, Neo-realism and Italian National Identity* (London: Routledge, 2011).

Cosulich, Callisto (ed.), *Storia del cinema italiano. Vol. 7: 1945–1948* (Venice: Marsilio, 2003).

Craig, Siobhan, *Cinema after Fascism: The Shattered Screen* (London: Palgrave Macmillan, 2010).

D'Ardino, Laurent Scotto, *La Revue 'Cinéma' et le néo-realisme italien* (Vincennes: Presses Universitaires de Vincennes, 1969).

Debreczeni, François and Heinz Steinberg (eds), *Le néorealisme italien: bilan de la critique* (Paris: Études Cinématographiques, nos 32–5, 1964).

De Giusti, Luciano (ed.), *Storia del cinema italiano. Vol. 8: 1949–1954* (Venice: Marsilio, 2003).

Deluca, Giovanna, *Il punto di vista dell'infanzia nel cinema italiano e francese: revisioni* (Naples: Liguori Editore, 2009).

De Vicenti, Giorgio (ed.), *Storia del cinema italiano. Vol. 10: 1960–1964* (Venice: Marsilio, 2002).

Falaschi, Giovanni (ed.), *Realtà e retorica: la letteratura del neorealismo italiano* (Florence: G. D'Anna, 1977).

Faldini, Franca and Goffredo Fofi (eds), *L'avventurosa storia del cinema italiano raccontata dai suoi protagonisti 1935–1959* (Milan: Feltrinelli, 1979).

——, *L'avventurosa storia del cinema italiano raccontata dai suoi protagonisti 1960–1969* (Milan: Feltrinelli, 1981).

Fanara, Giulia, *Pensare il neorealismo* (Rome: Lithos, 2000).

Farassino, Alberto (ed.), *Neorealismo: cinema italiano 1945–1949* (Turin: EDI, 1989).

Ferrero, Adelio, Giovanna Grignaffini and Leonardo Quaresima, *Il cinema italiano degli anni '60* (Florence: Guaraldi Editore, 1977).

Gairdoni, Laura (ed.), *Mario Serandrei–Gli scritti: 'Giorni di Gloria'–un film* (Rome: I Quaderni di Bianco e Nero, 1997).

Giovacchini, Severio and Robert Sklar (eds), *Global Neorealism: The Transnational History of a Film Style* (Jackson: University Press of Mississippi, 2011).

Günsberg, Maggie, *Italian Cinema: Gender and Genre* (New York: Palgrave Macmillan, 2005).

Haaland, Torunn, *Italian Neorealist Cinema* (Edinburgh: Edinburgh University Press, 2012).

Kolker, Robert Phillip, *The Altering Eye: Contemporary International Cinema* (New York: Oxford University Press, 1983).

Marcus, Millicent, *Italian Film in the Light of Neorealism* (Princeton, NJ: Princeton University Press, 1986).

Materiali sul cinema italiano degli anni '50 (Pesaro: Mostra Internationale del Nuovo Cinema, 1978).

Miccichè, Lino (ed.), *Il neorealismo cinematografico italiano* (Venice: Marsilio, 1975).

Minghelli, Giuliana, *Landscape and Memory in Post-fascist Italian Film* (London: Routledge, 2013).

Morreale, Emiliano (ed.), *Lo schermo di carta: Storia e storie del cineromanzi* (Milan: Il Castoro, 2007, includes DVD of 1950s cartoon versions of films that were extremely popular in the period).

Nowell-Smith, Geoffrey, *Making Waves: New Cinemas of the 1960s* (New York and London: Continuum, 2007).

O'Leary, Alan and Catherine O'Rawe, 'Against Realism: On a "Certain Tendency" in Italian Film Criticism', *Journal of Modern Italian Studies* vol. 16 no. 1 (2011), pp. 107–28.

Olivieri, Angelo, *L'imperatore in platea: i grandi del cinema italiano dal 'Marc'Aurelio' allo schermo* (Bari: Edizioni Dedalo, 1986).

Overbey, David (ed.), *Springtime in Italy: A Reader in Neorealism* (Hamden, CT: Archon Books, 1979).

Pellizzari, Lorenzo (ed.), *Cineromanzo: il cinema italiano 1945–1953* (Milan: Longanesi, 1978).

Pintus, Pietro, *Storia e film: trent'anni di cinema italiano (1945–1975)* (Rome: Bulzoni, 1980).

Prédal, René (ed), *Le néoréalisme italien*, special issue of *CinémAction* no. 70 (1994).

Re, Lucia, *Calvino and the Age of Neorealism: Fables of Estrangement* (Stanford, CA: Stanford University Press, 1990).

——, 'Neorealist Narrative: Experience and Experiment', in Peter Bondanella and Andrea Ciccarelli (eds), *The Cambridge Companion to the Italian Novel* (Cambridge: Cambridge University Press, 2003).

Restivo, Angelo, *The Cinema of Economic Miracles: Visuality and Modernization in the Italian Art Film (Post-Contemporary Interventions)* (Durham, NC: Duke University Press, 2002).

Rocchio, Vincent F., *Cinema of Anxiety: A Psychoanalysis of Italian Neorealism* (Austin: University of Texas Press, 1999).

Rossitti, Marco, *Il film a episodi in Italia tra gli anni cinquanta e settanta* (Bologna: Hybris, 2005).

Ruberto, Laura and Kristi Wilson (eds), *Italian Neorealism and Global Realism* (Detroit, MI: Wayne State University Press, 2007).

Schoonover, Karl, *Brutal Vision: The Neorealist Body in Postwar Italian Culture* (Minneapolis: University of Minnesota Press, 2012).

Shiel, Mark, *Italian Neorealism: Rebuilding the Cinematic City* (London: Wallflower Press, 2006).

Sitney, P. Adams, *Vital Crises in Italian Cinema: Iconography, Stylistics, Politics* (Austin: University of Texas Press, 1995).

Steinmatsky, Noa, *Italian Locations: Reinhabiting the Past in Postwar Cinema* (Minneapolis: University of Minnesota Press, 2008).

Tinazzi, Giorgio (ed.), *Il cinema italiano degli anni '50* (Venice: Marsilio, 1979).

—— and Marina Zancan (eds), *Cinema e letteratura del neorealismo* (Venice: Marsilio, 1983).

Torriglia, Anna Maria, *Broken Time, Fragmented Space: A Cultural Map for Postwar Italy* (Toronto: University of Toronto Press, 2002).

Venti anni di cinema italiano nei saggi di ventotto autori (Rome: Sindacato nazionale giornalisti cinematografici italiani editore, 1965).

Vitzizzai, Elisabetta Chicco (ed.), *Il neorealismo: antifascismo e popolo nella letteratura dagli anni trenta agli anni cinquanta* (Turin: Paravia, 1977).

Wagstaff, Christopher, *Italian Neorealist Cinema: An Aesthetic Approach* (Toronto: University of Toronto Press, 2008).

Williams, Christopher (ed.), *Realism and the Cinema: A Reader* (London: Routledge & Kegan Paul, 1980).

The Golden Age of Italian Cinema

Bayman, Louis and Sergio Rigoletto (eds), *Popular Italian Cinema* (Basingstoke: Palgrave Macmillan, 2013).

D'Arcangelo, Maresa and Giovanni M. Rossi (eds), *1975/1985: gli anni maledetti del cinema italiano* (Florence: Mediateca Regionale Toscana, 1986).

Attolini, Vito, *Sotto il segno del film (cinema italiano 1968/1976)* (Bari: Mario Adda Editore, 1983).

Borra, Antonello and Cristina Pausini, *Italian through Film: A Text for Italian Courses* (New Haven, CT: Yale University Press, 2004).

Brunetta, Gian Piero, *Il cinema contemporaneo da 'La dolce vita' a 'Centochiodi'* (Rome: Laterza, 2007).

De Bernardinis, Flavio (ed.), *Storia del cinema italiano. Vol. 12: 1970–1976* (Venice: Marsilio, 2009).

Dyer, Richard and Ginette Vincendeau, *Popular European Cinema* (London: Routledge, 1992).

Eleftheriotis, Dimitris, *Popular Cinemas of Europe: Studies of Texts, Contexts and Frameworks* (New York: Continuum, 2001).

Faldini, Franca and Goffredo Fofi (eds), *Il cinema italiano d'oggi 1970–1984 raccontato dai suoi protagonisti* (Milan: Mondadori, 1984).

Gieri, Manuela, *Contemporary Italian Filmmaking: Strategies of Subversion – Pirandello, Fellini, Scola, and the Directors of the New Generation* (Toronto: University of Toronto Press, 1995).

Kovács, András Bálint, *Screening Modernism: European Art Cinema, 1950–1980* (Chicago, IL: University of Chicago Press, 2008).

Miccichè, Lino (ed.), *Cinema italiano degli anni '70: cronache 1969–78* (Venice: Marsilio, 1980).

——, *Il cinema italiano degli anni '60* (Venice: Marsilio, 1975).

Montini, Franco (ed.), *Una generazione in cinema: esordi ed esordienti italiani 1975–1988* (Venice: Marsilio, 1988).

Morabito, Mimmo (ed.), *Nostri autori prossimo venturi* (Florence: Mediateca Regionale Toscana, 1987).

Pirro, Ugo, *Soltanto un nome nei titoli di testa: i felici anni Sessanta del cinema italiano* (Turin: Einaudi, 1998).

Vannini, Andrea (ed.), *1975/1985: le strane occasioni del cinema italiano–i registi e i film* (Florence: Mediateca Regionale Toscana, 1987).

Vighi, Fabio, *Traumatic Encounters in Italian Film: Locating the Cinematic Unconscious* (Bristol: Intellect, 2006).

Witcombe, Roger T., *The New Italian Cinema* (New York: Oxford University Press, 1982).

Zagarrio, Vito, *Cinema italiano anni novanta* (Venice: Marsilio, 1998; 2nd edn, 2001).

—— (ed.), *Storia del cinema italiano. Vol. 13: 1977–1985* (Venice: Marsilio, 2005).

From the End of the Twentieth Century to the New Millennium

Bullaro, Grace Russo (ed.), *From Terrone to Extracomunitario: New Manifestations of Racism in Contemporary Italian Cinema* (Leicester: Troubadour, 2010).

Cristiano, Anthony, *Contemporary Italian Cinema: Images of Italy at the Turn of the Century* (Toronto: Polypus Press, 2008).

Ferrero Regis, Tiziana, *Recent Italian Cinema: Spaces Contexts Experiences* (Leicester: Troubadour, 2009).

Hope, William (ed.), *Italian Cinema: New Directions* (Oxford: Peter Lang, 2005).

—— (ed.), *Italian Film Directors in the New Millennium* (Cambridge: Cambridge Scholars Press, 2010).

Macchitella, Carlo, *Nuovo cinema italia: Autori, industria, mercato – conversazione con Marianna Rizzini* (Venice: Marsilio, 2003).

Marcus, Millicent, *After Fellini: National Cinema in the Postmodern Age* (Baltimore, MD: Johns Hopkins University Press, 2002).

Marlow-Mann, Alex, *The New Neapolitan Cinema* (Edinburgh: University of Edinburgh Press, 2013).

Marrone, Gaetana, 'The New Italian Cinema', in Elizabeth Ezra (ed.), *European Cinema* (Oxford: Oxford University Press, 2004).

—— (ed.), *Annali d'Italianistica* no. 17 (1999). Special issue dedicated to 'New Landscapes in Contemporary Italian Cinema'.

Martini, Giulio and Guglielmina Morelli (eds), *Patchwork due: geografia del nuovo cinema italiano* (Milan: Il Castoro, 1997).

Montini, Franco (ed.), *Il cinema italiano nel Terzo Millennio: I protagonisti della rinascita* (Turin: Lindau, 2002).

Sesti, Mario, *Nuovo cinema italiano: gli autori, i film, le idee* (Rome: Edizioni Theoria, 1994).

Tornatore, Giuseppe, *Nuovo cinema paradiso* (Palermo: Sellerio, 1990).

Zagarrio, Vito (ed.), *La meglio gioventù: Nuovo cinema italiano 2005–2006* (Venice: Marsilio, 2006).

THEMES AND GENRES
Italian Cinema and the Other Arts

Attolini, Vito, *Dal romanzo al set: cinema italiano dalle origini ad oggi* (Bari: Edizioni Dedalo, 1988).

Bayman, Louis, *The Operatic and the Everyday in Postwar Italian Film Melodrama* (Edinburgh: Edinburgh University Press, 2013).

Bragaglia, Cristina, *Il piacere del racconto: narrativa italiana e cinema (1895–1990)* (Florence: La Nuova Italia, 1993).

Brunetta, Gian Piero (ed.), *Letteratura e cinema* (Bologna: Zanichelli, 1976).

Càllari, Francesco, *Pirandello e il cinema* (Venice: Marsilio, 1991).

Campari, Roberto, *Il fantasma del bello: iconologia del cinema italiano* (Venice: Marsilio, 1994).

Caputo, Roland, 'Literary Cineastes: The Italian Novel and the Cinema', in Peter Bondanella and Andrea Ciccarelli (eds), *The Cambridge Companion to the Italian Novel* (Cambridge: Cambridge University Press, 2003).

Casadio, Gianfranco, *Opera e cinema* (Ravenna: Longo, 1995).

Costa, Antonio, *Cinema e pittura* (Turin: UTET, 1991).

——, *Immagine di un'immagine: cinema e letteratura* (Turin: UTET, 1993).

——, *Il cinema e le arti visive* (Turin: Einaudi, 2004).

Dalle Vacche, Angela, *Cinema and Painting: How Art Is Used in Film* (Austin: University of Texas Press, 1996).

D'Avack, Massino, *Cinema e letteratura* (Rome: CanEsi, 1964).

De Pau, Daniela and Georgina Torello (eds), *Watching Pages, Reading Pictures: Cinema and Modern Literature in Italy* (Newcastle upon Tyne: Cambridge Scholars Press, 2008).

Fumagalli, Armando, *I vestiti nuovi del narratore: L'adattamento cinematografico da letteratura a cinema* (Milan: Il Castoro, 2004).

Galluzzi, Francesco, *Il cinema dei pittore: Le arti e il cinema italiano 1940–1980* (Milan: Skira, 2007).

Gambacorti, Irene, *Storie di cinema e letteratura: Verga, Gozzano, D'Annunzio* (Florence: Società Editrice Fiorentina, 2003).

Geduld, Harry (ed.), *Authors on Film* (Bloomington: Indiana University Press, 1972).

Guidorizzi, Ernesto, *La narrativa italiana e il cinema* (Florence: Sansoni, 1973).

Horton, Andrew S. and Joan Magretta (eds), *Modern European Filmmakers and the Art of Adaptation* (New York: Frederick Ungar, 1981).

Iannucci, Amilcare A. (ed.), *Dante, Cinema & Television* (Toronto: University of Toronto Press, 2004).

Lauretta, Enzo (ed.), *Pirandello e il cinema* (Agrigento: Atti del Centro Nazionale di Studi Pirandelliani, 1978).

Marcus, Millicent, *Filmmaking by the Book: Italian Cinema and Literary Adaptation* (Baltimore, MD: Johns Hopkins University Press, 1993).

McDougal, Stuart Y. (ed.), *Made into Movies: From Literature to Film* (New York: Holt, Rinehart & Winston, 1985).

Nichols, Nina Davinci and Jana O'Keefe Bazzoni, *Pirandello & Film* (Lincoln: University of Nebraska Press, 1995).

Pellizzari, Lorenzo (ed.), *L'avventura di uno spettatore: Italo Calvino e il cinema* (Bergamo: Pierluigi Lubrina Editore, 1990).

Pirandello, Luigi, *Shoot! The Notebooks of Serafino Gubbio, Cinematograph Operator*, trans. C. K. Scott Moncrieff (Chicago, IL: University of Chicago Press, 2006).

Testa, Carlo, *Italian Cinema and Modern European Literatures: 1945–2000* (Westport, CT: Praeger, 2002).

——, *Masters of Two Arts: Re-creation of European Literatures in Italian Cinema* (Toronto: University of Toronto Press, 2002).

Vannini, Andrea (ed.), *Vasco Pratolini e il cinema* (Florence: Edizioni La Bottega del Cinema, 1987).

Welle, John, 'The Cinema of History: Film in Italian Poetry of the 1960s and 1970s', in John Butcher and Mario Moroni (eds), *From Eugenio Montale to Amelia Rosselli: Italian Poetry in the Sixties and Seventies* (Leicester: Troubadour, 2004).

——, 'Dante in the Cinematic Mode: A Historical Survey of Dante Movies', in Mark Musa (ed.), *Dante's Inferno: The Indiana Critical Edition* (Bloomington: Indiana University Press, 1995).

——, '*Dante's Inferno* of 1911 and the Origins of Italian Film Culture', in Amilcare A. Iannucci (ed.), *Dante, Cinema & Television* (Toronto: University of Toronto Press, 2004).

Sex, Gender and Censorship in Italian Cinema

Argentieri, Mino, *La censura nel cinema italiano* (Rome: Editori Riuniti, 1974).

Baldi, Alfredo, *Schermi proibiti: La censura in Italia 1947–1988* (Venice: Marsilio, 2003).

——, *Lo squardo punito: Film censurati 1947–1962* (Rome: Bulzoni, 1994).

Baragli, Enrico, S. J., *Cinema cattolico: documenti della S. Sede sul cinema* (Rome: Città Nuova Editrice, 1965).

Boarini, Vittorio (ed.), *Erotismo, eversione, merce* (Bologna: Cappelli, 1974).

Bruno, Giuliana, and Maria Nadotti (eds), *Offscreen: Women & Film in Italy* (London: Routledge, 1988).

Bruscolini, Elisabetta (ed.), *Diveantidive del cinema italiano* (Venice: Marsilio, 2002).

Carrano, Patrizia, *Malafemmina: la donna nel cinema italiano* (Florence: Guaraldi Editore, 1977).

Cestaro, Gary, *Queer Italia: Same-Sex Desire in Italian Literature and Film* (New York: Palgrave Macmillan, 2004).

Cottino-Jones, Margo, *Women, Desire, and Power in Italian Cinema* (New York: Palgrave Macmillan, 2010).

Curti, Roberto and Tommaso La Selva, *Sex and Violence: percorsi nel cinema estremo* (Turin: Lindau, 2003).

Fantuzzi, Virgilio, *Cinema sacro e profano* (Rome: Edizioni 'La civiltà cattolica', 1983).

Gaudino, Luigi, *Cinema alla sbarra: Trent'anni di avventure e sventure giudiziarie del cinema italiano* (Udine: Forum Edizioni, 2007).

Giovannini, Fabio and Antonio Tentori, *Porn'Italia: il cinema erotico italiano* (Viterbo: Nuovi Equilibri, 2004).

Grazzini, Giovanni, *Eva dopo Eva: la donna nel cinema italiano dagli anni Sessanta a oggi* (Rome: Laterza, 1980).

Griffiths, Robin (ed.), *Queer Cinema in Europe* (Bristol: Intellect, 2008).

Grossini, Giancarlo, *120 film di Sodoma: analisi del cinema pornografico* (Bari: Edizioni Dedalo, 1982).

Gundle, Stephen, *Bellissima: Feminine Beauty and the Idea of Italy* (New Haven, CT: Yale University Press, 2007).

Jeffries, Giovanna Miceli, *Feminine Feminists: Cultural Practices in Italy* (Minneapolis: University of Minnesota Press, 1994).

Laviosa, Flavia (ed.), *Visions of Struggle: Women's Filmmaking in the Mediterranean* (New York: Palgrave Macmillan, 2010).

Masi, Stefano and Enrico Lancia, *Italian Movie Goddesses: Over 80 of the Greatest Women in the Italian Cinema* (Rome: Gremese, 1997).

Massaro, Gianni, *L'occhio impuro: cinema, censura e moralizzatori nell'Italia degli Anni Settanta* (Milan: Sugar, 1976).

Mellen, Joan, *Women and Their Sexuality in the New Film* (New York: Horizon Press, 1973).

O'Rawe, Catherine, *The Femme Fatale: Images, Histories, Contexts* (New York: Palgrave Macmillan, 2010).

Pastore, Sergio, *Proibitissimo: la censura nel tempo* (Naples: Adriano Gallina Editore, 1980).

Petrilli, Susan and David Buchbinder (eds), *Masculinities: Identità maschili e appartenenze culturali* (Milan: Mimesis, 2009).

Rigoletto, Sergio, *Masculinity and Italian Cinema: Sexual Politics, Social Conflict and Male Crisis in the 1970s* (Edinburgh: Edinburgh University Press, 2014).

Turroni, Giuseppe, *Viaggio nel corpo: la commedia erotica nel cinema italiano* (Milan: Moizzi Editore, 1979).

Tyler, Parker, *Screening the Sexes: Homosexuality in the Movies* (New York: Doubleday, 1973).

Vighi, Fabio, *Sexual Difference in European Cinema: The Curse of Enjoyment* (New York: Palgrave Macmillan, 2009).

Italian Film Comedy

Aprà, Adriano and Patrizia Pistagnesi (eds), *Comedy, Italian Style 1950–1980* (Turin: Edizioni RAI, 1986).

Argentieri, Mino (ed.), *Risate di regime: la commedia italiana 1930–1944* (Venice: Marsilio, 1991).

——, *Commedia sexy all'italiana* (Milan: Mediane, 2007).

D'Amico, Masolino, *La commedia all'italiana: il cinema comico in Italia dal 1945 al 1975* (Milan: Mondadori, 1985).

Giacovelli, Enrico, *La commedia all'italiana: La storia, i luoghi, gli autori, gli attori, i film* (Rome: Gremese, 1995).

Gili, Jean A., *Arrivano i mostri: i volti della commedia italiana* (Bologna: Cappelli, 1980).

——, *La comédie italienne* (Paris: Henri Veyrier, 1983).

Giordano, Michele, *La commedia erotica italiana: vent'anni di cinema sexy 'Made in Italy'* (Rome: Gremese, 2002).

Lanzoni, Rémi Fournier, *Comedy Italian Style: The Golden Age of Italian Film Comedies* (New York: Continuum, 2008).

Laura, Ernesto G., *Comedy Italian Style* (Rome: ANICA, n. d.).

——, *Italian History Comedy Style* (Rome: ANICA, n. d.).

Salizzato, Claver and Vito Zagarrio (eds), *Effetto commedia: teoria, generi, paesaggi della commedia cinematografica* (Rome: Di Giacomo Editore, 1985).

Serceau, Michel (ed.), *La comédie italienne de Don Camillo à Berlusconi*, CinémAction no. 42 (1987).

Trionfera, Claudio (ed.), *Age & Scarpelli in Commedia* (Rome: Di Giacomo Editore, 1990).

Political and Historical Themes or Film Genres (Including Mob Movies and Depictions of Terrorism)

Antonella, Paolo and Alan O'Leary, *Imagining Terrorism: The Rhetoric and Representation of Political Violence in Italy, 1969–2006* (Oxford: Legenda, 2010).

Bertelli, Sergio, *Corsari del tempo: quando il cinema inventa la storia (guida pratica per registi distratti)* (Florence: Edizioni Ponte alle Grazie, 1994).

Bolton, Lucy and Christina Siggers Manson (eds), *Italy on Screen: Italian Identity in the National Imaginary and International Symbolic* (London: Peter Lang, 2010).

Bondanella, Peter, *Hollywood Italians: Dagos, Palookas, Romeos, Wise Guys, and Sopranos* (New York and London: Continuum, 2004).

Bouchard, Norma, *Risorgimento in Modern Italian Culture: Revisiting the Nineteenth-Century Past in History, Narrative, and Cinema* (Madison, NJ: Fairleigh Dickinson University Press, 2005).

Brunetta, Gian Piero et al. (eds), *La cinepresa e la storia: fascismo, antifascismo, guerra e resistenza nel cinema italiano* (Milan: Edizioni scolastiche Bruno Mondadori, 1985).

Brunetta, Gian Piero and Jean A. Gili (eds), *L'ora d'Africa del cinema italiano 1911–1989* (Trent: LaGrafica-Mori, 1990).

Carotti, Carlo, *Alla ricerca del paradiso: l'operaio nel cinema italiano – 1945–1990* (Genoa: Graphos, 1992).

Casadio, Gianfranco, *La guerra al cinema. Volume 1* (Ravenna: Longo, 1997).

——, *La guerra al cinema. Volume 2* (Ravenna: Longo, 1998).

Casella, Paola, *Hollywood Italian: Gli italiani nell'America di celluloide* (Milan: Baldini & Castoldi, 1998).

Clarke, David B. (ed.), *The Cinematic City* (London: Routledge, 1997).

Dalle Vacche, Angela, *The Body in the Mirror: Shapes of History in Italian Cinema* (Princeton, NJ: Princeton University Press, 1992).

De Carmine, Roberta, *Italy Meets Africa: Colonial Discourses in Italian Cinema* (New York: Peter Lang, 2011).

Fontanelli, Mario (ed.), *Emilia-Romagna, terra di cineasti: antologia di testi, interviste e saggi critici* (Parma: Grafiche STEP, 1990).

Freda, Riccardo, *Divoratori di celluloide: 50 anni di memorie cinematografiche e non* (Rome: Il Formichiere, 1981).

Gili, Jean A. (ed.), *Fascisme et résistance dans le cinéma italien (1922–1968)* (Paris: Études Cinématographiques nos 82–3, 1970).

Gori, Gianfranco (ed.), *Passato ridotto: gli anni del dibattito su cinema e storia* (Florence: La Casa Usher, 1982).

——, *La storia al cinema: ricostruzione del passato, interpretazione del presente* (Rome: Bulzoni, 1994).

Greene, Shelleen, *Equivocal Subjects: Between Italy and Africa – Constructions of Racial and National Identity in the Italian Cinema* (London and New York: Continuum, 2012).

Gundle, Stephen and Lucia Rinaldi (eds), *Assassinations and Murder in Modern Italy: Transformations in Society and Culture* (New York: Palgrave Macmillan, 2007).

Hipkins, Danielle and Gill Plain (eds), *War-Torn Tales: Literature, Film and Gender in the Aftermath of World War II* (Oxford: Peter Lang, 2007).

Landy, Marcia, *Cinematic Uses of the Past* (Minneapolis: University of Minnesota Press, 1996).

——, *Film, Politics, and Gramsci* (Minneapolis: University of Minnesota Press, 1994).

Lichtner, Giacomo, *Film and the Shoah in France and Italy* (London: Vallentine Mitchell, 2008).

Marcus, Millicent, *Italian Film in the Shadow of Auschwitz* (Toronto: University of Toronto Press, 2007).

Michalczyk, John J., *The Italian Political Filmmakers* (Rutherford, NJ: Fairleigh Dickinson University Press, 1986).

O'Leary, Alan, *Tragedia all'italiana: Cinema and Italian Terrorisms, 1970–2008* (Oxford: Peter Lang, 2009).

Picchietti, Virginia, 'A Semiotics of Judaism: Representations of Judaism and the Jewish Experience in Italian Cinema, 1992–2004', Italica no. 83 (2006), pp. 563–82.

Ravetto, Kriss, *The Unmasking of Fascist Aesthetics* (Minneapolis: University of Minnesota Press, 2001).

Renga, Dana, *Mob Movies: A Reader* (2nd rev. edn) (Toronto: University of Toronto Press, 2011).

——, *Unfinished Business: Screening the Italian Mafia in the New Millennium* (Toronto: University of Toronto Press, 2013).

Rosenstone, Robert A. (ed.), *Revisioning History: Film and the Construction of a New Past* (Princeton, NJ: Princeton University Press, 1995).

Sorlin, Pierre, *European Cinemas, European Societies 1939–1990* (New York: Routledge, 1991).

——, *The Film in History: Restaging the Past* (Oxford: Basil Blackwell, 1980) (Italian films on the Risorgimento and the Resistance).

Zanotto, Piero and Fiorello Zangrando, *L'Italia di cartone* (Padua: Livia Editrice, 1973) (a history of Italian animation).

The 'B' Movies
The Peplum or 'Sword-and-Sandal' Epics

Bondanella, Peter, *The Eternal City: Roman Images in the Modern World* (Chapel Hill: University of North Carolina Press, 1987; rpt 2009).

Burke, Frank, *The Italian Sword-and-Sandal Epic* (Edinburgh: Edinburgh University Press, 2013).

Cammarota, Domenico, *Il cinema peplum* (Rome: Fanucci Editore, 1987).

Casadio, Gianfranco, *I mitici eroi: il cinema 'peplum' nel cinema italiano dall'avvento del sonoro ad oggi (1930–1993)* (Ravenna: Longo, 2007).

Cornelius, Michael G. (ed.), *Of Muscles and Men: Essays on the Sword and Sandal Film* (Jefferson, NC and London: McFarland, 2011).

Elley, Derek, *The Epic Film: Myth and History* (London: Routledge & Kegan Paul, 1984).

Farassino, Alberto and Tatti Sanguineti (eds), *Gli uomini forti* (Milan: Mazzotta, 1983).

Giordano, Michele, *Giganti buoni: Da Ercole a Piedone (e oltre) – il mito dell'uomo forte nel cinema italiano* (Rome: Gremese, 1998).

Joshel, Sandra R., Margaret Malamud and Donald T. McGuire, Jr (eds), *Projections: Ancient Rome in Modern Popular Culture* (Baltimore, MD: Johns Hopkins University Press, 2001).

Lucanio, Patrick, *With Fire and Sword: Italian Spectacles on American Screens 1958–1968* (Metuchen, NJ: Scarecrow Press, 1994).

Malamud, Margaret, *Ancient Rome and Modern America* (Chichester: John Wiley, 2009).

Schenk, Irbert, 'The Cinematic Support to National(istic) Mythology: The Italian Peplum 1910–1930', in Natascha Gentz and Stefan Kramer (eds), *Globalization, Cultural Identities, and Media Representations* (Albany: State University of New York Press, 2006), pp. 153–68.

Solomon, Jon, *The Ancient World in the Cinema* (Cranbury, NJ: A. S. Barnes, 1978); rev. and expanded edn (New Haven, CT: Yale University Press, 2001).

Winkler, Martin M. (ed.), *Classical Myth & Culture in the Cinema* (Oxford and New York: Oxford University Press, 2001).

——, *Gladiator: Film and History* (Oxford: Blackwell, 2004).

Wyke, Maria, 'Herculean Muscle! The Classicizing Rhetoric of Body Building', in James L. Porter (ed.), *Constructions of the Classical Body* (Ann Arbor: University of Michigan Press, 2002), pp. 355–79.

——, 'Italian Cinema and History', in Valentina Vitali and Paul Willemen (eds) *Theorising National Cinema* (London: BFI, 2006).

——, *Projecting the Past: Ancient Rome, Cinema and History* (New York: Routledge, 1997).

The Spaghetti Western

Beatrice, Luca, *Al cuore, Ramon, al cuore: La leggenda del Western all'italiana* (Florence: Tarab, 1996).

Casadio, Gianfranco, *Se sei vivo, spara! Storie di pistoleri, banditi e bounty killers nel western all'italiana (1942–1998)* (Ravenna: Longo, 2004).

Cawelti, John G., *The Six-Gun Mystique* (Bowling Green, OH: Bowling Green Popular Press, 1970).

Cox, Alex, *10,000 Ways to Die: A Director's Take on the Spaghetti Western* (Harpenden: Kamera Books, 2009).

Ferrini, Franco (ed.), *L'antiwestern e il caso Leone* (Rome: Bianco e Nero, 1971).

Fisher, Austin, *Radical Frontiers in the Spaghetti Western: Politics, Violence and Popular Italian Cinema* (London: I. B. Tauris, 2013).

Frayling, Christopher, *Once Upon a Time in Italy: The Westerns of Sergio Leone* (New York: Abrams, 2005).

——, *Sergio Leone: Something to Do with Death* (London: Faber and Faber, 2000).

——, *Spaghetti Westerns: Cowboys and Europeans from Karl May to Sergio Leone* (London: Routledge & Kegan Paul, 1981); rev. edn (London: I. B. Tauris, 2006).

Giusti, Marco, *Dizionario del western all' Italiana* (Milan: Mondadori, 2007).

Grant, Kevin, *Any Gun Can Play: The Essential Guide to Euro-Westerns* (Godalming: FAB Press, 2011).

Hughes, Howard, *Once Upon a Time in the Italian West: The Filmgoers' Guide to Spaghetti Westerns* (London: I. B. Tauris, 2004).

——, *Spaghetti Westerns* (Harpenden: Oldcastle Books, 2010).

Morricone Western (Milan: Mediane, 2006).

Moscati, Massimo, *Western all'italiana: guida ai 407 film, ai registi, agli attori* (Milan: Pan Editrice, 1978).

Nachbar, Jack (ed.), *Focus on the Western* (Englewood Cliffs, NJ: Prentice-Hall, 1974).

Pezzotta, Alberto, *Il western italiano* (Milan: Il Castoro, 2012).

Roth, Lane, *Film Semiotics, Metz, and Leone's Trilogy* (New York: Garland, 1983).

Staig, Laurence and Tony Williams, *Italian Western: The Opera of Violence* (London: Lorrimer, 1975).

Weisser, Thomas, *Spaghetti Westerns – the Good, the Bad and the Violent: A Comprehensive, Illustrated Filmography of 558 Eurowesterns and Their Personnel, 1961–1977* (Jefferson, NC: McFarland, 1992).

The Spaghetti Horror Films and Exploitation Films

Allmer, Patricia, Emily Brick and David Huxley (eds), *European Nightmares: Horror Cinema in Europe since 1945* (New York: Columbia University Press, 2012).

Balun, Chas, *Beyond Horror Holocaust: A Deeper Shade of Red* (Key West, FL: Fantasma Books, 2003).

Fenton, Harvey et al. (eds), *Cannibal Holocaust and the Savage Cinema of Ruggero Deodato* (London: FAB Press, 1999).

Grainger, Julian, *Cannibal Holocaust: The Savage Cinema of Ruggero Deodato* (London: FAB Press, 2011).

Harper, Jim, *Italian Horror* (Baltimore, MD: Luminary Press, 2005).

——, *Legacy of Blood: A Comprehensive Guide to Slasher Movies* (Manchester: Headpress/Critical Vision, 2004).

Landis, John, *Monsters in the Movies* (London: DK Books, 2011).

Lupi, Gordiano, *Cannibal: Il cinema selvaggio di Ruggero Deodato* (Rome: Profondo Rosso, 2003).

McCallum, Lawrence, *Italian Horror Films of the 1960s: A Critical Catalog of 62 Chillers* (Jefferson, NC: McFarland, 2002).

Magilow, Daniel H., Kristin T. Vander Lugt and Elizabeth Bridges (eds), *The Nazi Image in Low-Brow Cinema and Culture* (New York and London: Continuum, 2011).

Manti, Davide, *Ca(u)se perturbanti: Architetture horror dentro e fuori lo schermo – Fonti, figure, temi* (Turin: Lindau, 2003).

Martin, John, *Cannibal: The Most Disgusting Consumer Guide Ever!* (Liskeard: Straycat Publishers, 2007).

Mathijs, Ernest and Xavier Mendik (eds), *Alternative Europe: Eurotrash and Exploitation Cinema since 1945* (London: Wallflower Press, 2004).

Morsiani, Albert (ed.), *Rosso italiano (1977/1987): dieci anni di horror con Argenti, Bava, Fulci e … gli altri* (Modena: Avofilm, 1988).

Palmerini, Luca M. and Gaetano Mistretta, *Spaghetti Nightmares: Italian Fantasy-Horrors as Seen through the Eyes of Their Protagonists* (Key West, FL: Fantasma Books, 1996).

Paul, Louis et al., *Italian Horror Film Directors* (Jefferson, NC: McFarland, 2005).

Rhodes, Gary D. (ed.), *Horror at the Drive-in: Essays in Popular Americana* (Jefferson, NC: McFarland, 2003).

Schneider, Stephen Jay, *100 European Horror Films* (London: BFI, 2008).

—— and Tony Williams (eds), *Horror International* (Detroit, MI: Wayne State University Press, 2005).

Shipka, Danny (ed.), *Perverse Titillation: The Exploitation Cinema of Italy, Spain and France, 1960–1980* (Jefferson, NC: McFarland, 2011).

Slater, Jay (ed.), *Eaten Alive! Italian Cannibal and Zombie Movies* (London: Plexus, 2002).

Stine, Scott Aaron, *The Gorehound's Guide to Splatter Films of the 1980s* (Jefferson, NC: McFarland, 2003).

Tohill, Cathal and Pete Tombs, *Immoral Tales: European Sex and Horror Movies 1956–1984* (New York: St Martin's Griffin, 1995).

The Italian *Giallo* or Mystery Thriller

Boyd, David and B. Barton Palmer (eds), *After Hitchcock: Influence, Imitation, and Intertextuality* (Austin: University of Texas Press, 2006).

Crovi, Luca, *Tutti i colori del giallo: il giallo italiano da De Marchi a Scerbanenco a Camilleri* (Venice: Marsilio, 2002).

Forlai, Luigi and Augusto Bruni, *Detective thriller e noir: Teoria e tecnica della narrazione* (Rome: Dino Audino Editore, 2003).

Giuffrida, Sergio and Riccardo Mazzoni (eds), *Giallo: poliziesco, thriller e detective story* (Milan: Leonardo Arte, 1999).

Koven, Mikel J., *La Dolce Morte: Vernacular Cinema and the Italian Giallo Film* (Lanham, MD: Scarecrow Press, 2006).

Navarro, Antonio José (ed.), *El giallo italiano: La oscuridad y la sangre* (Madrid: Nuer Ediciones, 2001).

Olney, Ian, *Euro Horror: Classical Horror Cinema in Contemporary American Culture* (Bloomington: Indiana University Press, 2012).

Rea, Luca, *I colori del buoi: Il cinema thrilling italiano dal 1930 al 1979* (Florence: Igor Molino Editore, 1999).

Smith, Adrian Luther, *Blood & Black Lace: The Definitive Guide to Italian Sex and Horror Movies* (Liskeard: Straycat Publishers, 2000).

——, *The Delirium Guide to Italian Exploitation Cinema 1975–1979* (London: Media Publications, 1997).

Williams, Linda Ruth, *The Erotic Thriller in Contemporary Cinema* (Bloomington: Indiana University Press, 2005).

The Italian *Poliziesco* Film

Attori a mano armata: The Main Actors of the Most Violent Season of the Italian Cinema (Milan: Mediane, 2007).

Casadio, Gianfranco, *Col cuore in gola. Assassini, ladri e poliziotti nel cinema italiano dal 1930 ad oggi* (Ravenna: Longo, 2002).

Curti, Roberto, *Italia odia: il cinema poliziesco italiano* (Turin: Lindau, 2006).

——, *Italian Cinema Filmography, 1868–1980* (Jefferson, NC: McFarland, 2013).

Magni, Daniele and Silvio Giobbio, *Cinici, infami e violenti: Guida ai film poliezieschi italiani anni '70* (Milan: Bloodbuster, 2005).

Nerenberg, Ellen, *Murder Made in Italy: Homicide, Media, and Contemporary Italian Culture* (Bloomington: Indiana University Press, 2012).

Padovani, Gisella and Rita Verderame (eds), *L'almanacco del delitto: I racconti polizieschi del 'Cerchio Verde'* (Palermo: Selleria Editore, 1996).

Tomas Milian: The Tough Bandit, The Rough Cop, and the Filthy Rat in Italian Cinema/Il bandito, lo sbirro e Er Monnezza (Milan: Mediane, 2007).

Torlasco, Domiata, *The Time of the Crime: Phenomenology, Psychoanalysis, Italian Film* (Palo Alto, CA: Stanford University Press, 2008) (not specifically on the Italian crime film but on five major works by Antonioni, Bertolucci, Cavani, and Pasolini considered as detective films).

Rome in the Cinema

Bondanella, Peter, *The Eternal City: Roman Images in the Modern World* (Chapel Hill: University of North Carolina Press, 1987; rpt 2009).

Bruscolini, Elisabetta, *Rome in Cinema between Fiction and Reality* (Rome: Fondazione Scuola Nazionale di Cinema, 2001).

Di Biagi, Flaminio, *Il cinema a Roma: Guida alla storia e ai luoghi del cinema nella capitale* (Rome: Palombi Editore, 2003).

Solomon, Jon, *The Ancient World in the Cinema* (Cranbury, NJ: A. S. Barnes, 1978); rev. and expanded edn (New Haven, CT: Yale University Press, 2001).

Wrigley, Richard (ed.), *Cinematic Rome* (Leicester: Troubadour, 2008).

ACTORS AND ACTRESSES

Alberico, Giulia, *Il corpo gentile: Conservazione con Massimo Girotti* (Rome: Luca Sossella Editore, 2003).

Bernardini, Aldo, *Nino Manfredi* (Rome: Gremese, 1999).

—— and Claudio G. Fava, *Ugo Tognazzi* (Rome: Gremese, 1978); 2nd edn (1985).

Bertolino, Marco and Ettore Ridola, *Franco Franchi e Ciccio Ingrassia* (Rome: Gremese, 2003).

——, *Bud Spencer & Terence Hill* (Rome: Gremese, 2002).

Buratti, Fabrizio, *Fantozzi: Una maschera italiana* (Turin: Lindau, 2003).

Caldiron, Orio, *Totò* (Rome: Gremese, 1980).

—— (ed.), *'Totò a colori' di Steno: Il film, il personaggio, il mito* (Rome: Edizioni Interculturali Federazione Circoli di Cinema Italia, 2003).

Cammarota, Domenico, *Il cinema di Totò* (Rome: Fanucci Editore, 1986).

Caputo, Marcello Gagliani (ed.), *Altrimenti ci arrabbiamo: Il cinema di Bud Spenser e Terence Hill* (Milan: Bloodbuster).

Carano, Patrizia, *La Magnani* (Milan: Rizzoli, 1986) (Preface by Federico Fellini); rpt (Turin: Lindau, 2004).

Causo, Massimo (ed.), *Tognazzi: L'alterego del cinema italiano* (Nardò: BESA, n. d.).

Degiovanni, Bernard, *Vittorio Gassman* (Paris: Éditions PAC, 1980).

De Berto, Raffaele, *Un secolo di cinema a Milano* (Milan: Il Castoro, 1996).

Della Casa, Stefano and Franco Pinto (eds), *Torino città del cinema* (Milan: Il Castoro, 2001).

Delli Colli, Laura, *Monica Vitti* (Rome: Gremese, 1987).

Deriu, Fabrizio, *Gian Maria Volonté: il lavoro d'attore* (Rome: Bulzoni, 1997).

Detassis, Piera and Mario Sesti (eds), *Bellissimi – generazioni di attori a confronto: "L'ultima onda" del cinema italiano e la grande tradizione del dopoguerra* (Ancona: Il Lavoro Editoriale, 1987).

Diva italiana: An Exclusive Collection of Rare Photos (Milan: Mediane, 2005).

Divo italiano: An Exclusive Collection of Rare Photos of the Italian Movie Stars (Milan: Mediane, 2006).

Fabrizi, Aldo, *Ciavéte fatto caso?* ed. Mario Giusto (Milan: Mondadori, 2004).

Faldini, Franca and Goffredo Fofi, *Totò: l'uomo e la maschera* (Milan: Felltrinelli, 1977); *Totò*, 2nd rev. edn (Naples: Tullio Pironti Editore, 1987).

——, *Totò: Storia di un buffone serissimo* (Milan: Mondadori, 2004).

Fava, Claudio G., *Alberto Sordi* (Rome: Gremese, 1979).

—— and Matilde Hochkofler, *Marcello Mastroianni* (Rome: Gremese, 1980).

Fofi, Goffredo, *Alberto Sordi: L'Italia in bianco e nero* (Milan: Mondadori, 2004).

Francione, Fabio and Lorenzo Pellizzari (eds), *Ugo Tognazzi regista* (Alessandria: Edizioni Falsopiano, 2002).

Gambetti, Giacomo, *Vittorio Gassman* (Rome: Gremese, 1982).

Gassman, Vittorio, *Un grande avvenire dietro le spalle: vita, amori e miracoli di un mattatore narrati da lui stesso* (Milan: Longanesi, 1981).

Gelley, Ora, *Stardom and the Aesthetics of Neorealism: Ingrid Bergman in Rossellini's Italy* (London: Routledge, 2012).

Guback, Thomas A., *The International Film Industry: Western Europe and America since 1945* (Bloomington: Indiana University Press, 1994).

Gubitosi, Giuseppe, *Amadeo Nazzari* (Bologna: Il Mulino, 1998).

Harris, Warren G., *Sophia Loren: A Biography* (New York: Simon & Schuster, 1998).

Hochkofler, Matilde, *Anna Magnani* (Rome: Gremese, 1984).

——, *Anna Magnani: Lo spettacolo della vita* (Rome: Bulzoni, 2005).

Kezich, Tullio, *Giulietta Masina* (Bologna: Cappelli, 1991).

Landy, Marsha, *Stardom, Italian Style: Screen Performance and Personality in Italian Cinema* (Bloomington: Indiana University Press, 2008).

Laura, Ernesto G., *Alida Valli* (Rome: Gremese, 1979).

Lupi, Gordiano, *Tomas Milian, il trucido e lo sbirro* (Rome: Profondo Rosso, 2004).

Masi, Stefano, *Roberto Benigni* (Rome: Gremese, 1999).

—— and Enrico Lancia, *Italian Movie Goddesses* (Rome: Gremese, 1997).

——, *Sophia Loren* (Rome: Gremese, 1985).

Mingozzi, Gianfranco (ed.), *Francesca Bertini* (Bologna: Le Mani, 2003).

Montini, Franco and Piero Spila (eds), *Gian Maria Volonté: Un attore contro* (Milan: Rizzoli, 2004).

Moscati, Italo, *Anna Magnani: Vita, amori e carriera di un'attrice che guarda dritto negli occhi* (Rome: Ediesse, 2003).

——, *Gioco perverso: La vera storia di Osvaldo Valenti e Luisa Ferida, tra Cinecittà e guerra civile* (Turin: Lindau, 2007).

——, *Sophia Loren: La storia dell'ultima diva* (Turin: Lindau, 2005).

Navarro, Giorgio and Fabio Zanello, *Tomas Milian: Er cubbano de Roma* (Florence: Igor Molino Editore, 1999).

Pistagnesi, Patrizia (ed.), *Anna Magnani* (Milan: Fabbri Editore, 1988).

Ponzi, Maurizio, *Gina Lollobrigida* (Rome: Gremese, 1982).

Pruzzo, Piero and Enrico Lancia, *Amadeo Nazzari* (Rome: Gremese, 1983).

Reich, Jacqueline, *Beyond the Latin Lover: Marcello Mastroianni, Masculinity, and Italian Cinema* (Bloomington: Indiana University Press, 2004).

Small, Pauline, *Sophia Loren: Moulding the Star* (Bristol: Intellect, 2009).

Tatò, Francesco (ed.), *The Stuff Dreams Are Made Of: The Films of Marcello Mastroianni* (Rome: Marchesi Garfiche Editoriali, 1998).

Tognazzi, Ugo, *L'abbuffone: Storie da ridere e ricette da morire* (Cava de' Tirreni: Avagliano Editore, 2004).

THE ITALIAN FILM INDUSTRY: INSTITUTIONS, PUBLICS, ECONOMICS

Abruzzese, Alberto and Carlo Macchitella (eds), *Cinemitalia 2005: Sogni, industria, tecnologia, mercato* (Venice: Marsilio, 2005).

Alloway, Lawrence, *The Venice Biennale 1895–1968: From Salon to Goldfish Bowl* (Greenwich, CT: New York Graphic Society, 1968).

Aprà, Adriano, Giuseppe Ghigi and Patrizia Pistagnesi (eds), *Cinquant'anni di cinema a Venezia* (Venice: Edizioni RAI, 1982).

Barlozzetti, Guido et al. (eds), *Modi di produzione del cinema italiano: La Titanus* (Rome: Di Giacomo Editore, 1985).

Bernardini, Aldo and Vittorio Martinelli (eds), *Titanus: la storia e tutti i film di una grande casa di produzione* (Milan: Coliseum Editore, 1986).

Bizzari, Libero, *Il cinema italiano: industria, mercato, pubblico* (Rome: Edizioni Gulliver, 1987).

—— and Liberto Solaroli, *L'industria cinematografica italiana* (Florence: Parenti Editore, 1958).

Brunetta, Gian Piero (ed.), *Identità italiana e identità europea nel cinema italiano* (Turin: Edizioni della Fondanzione Giovanni Agnelli, 1996).

Campari, Roberto, *Hollywood–Cinecittà: il racconto che cambia* (Milan: Feltrinelli, 1980).

Casetti, Franco (ed.), *La cineteca italiana: una storia milanese* (Milan: Il Castoro, 2005).

Chiarini, Luigi, *Un leone e altri animali: cinema e contestazione alla Mostra di Venezia 1968* (Milan: Sugar Editore, 1969) (Preface by Jean Renoir).

Contaldo, Francesco and Franco Fanelli, *L'affare cinema: multinazionali, produttori, e politici nella crisi del cinema italiano* (Milan: Feltrinelli, 1979).

Corsi, Barbara, *Con qualche dollar in meno: storia economica del cinema italiano* (Rome: Editori Riuniti, 2001).

Del Buono, Oreste and Lietta Tornabuoni (eds), *Era Cinecittà: vita, morte e miracoli di una fabbrica di film* (Milan: Bompiani, 1979).

Della Fornace, Luciana, *Il film in Italia dalla ideazione alla proiezione: strutture e processi dell'industria cinematografica* (Rome: Bulzoni, 1978).

Di Monte, Ezio et al. (eds), *La città del cinema (produzione e lavoro nel cinema italiano 1930/1970)* (Rome: Editrice R. Napoleone, 1979).

Farassino, Alberto and Tatti Sanguineti, *Lux Film: Esthétique et système d'un studio italien* (Locarno: Éditions du Festival international du Film de Locarno, 1984); Italian edn (Milan: Il Castoro, 2000).

Franchi, Mariagrazia and Elena Mosconi, *Spettatori: forme di consumo e pubblici del cinema italiano 1930–1960* (Venice: Marsilio, 2002).

Freddi, Luigi, *Il cinema* (2 vols) (Rome: L'Arnia, 1949); rpt (Rome: Gremese, 1994).

Gili, Jean A. and Aldo Tassone (eds), *Parigi–Roma: 50 anni di coproduzioni italo-francesi* (Milan: Editrice Il Castoro, 1995).

Grassi, Giovanna (ed.), *L'altro schermo: libro bianco sui cineclub, le sale d'essai e i punti di diffusione cinematografica alternativa* (Venice: Marsilio, 1978).

Huaco, George A., *The Sociology of Film Art* (New York: Basic Books, 1965).

Ivaldi, Nedo, *La prima volta a Venezia: mezzo secolo di Mostra del cinema nei ricordi della critica* (Padua: Edizioni Studio Tesi, 1982).

Kaufman, Hank and Gene Lerner, *Hollywood sul Tevere* (Milan: Sperling & Kupfer Editori, 1982).

Kezich, Tullio and Alessandria Levantesi, *Dino. DeLaurentiis, la vita e i film* (Turin: Feltrinelli, 2001). English edn, *Dino : The Life and the Films of Dino De Laurentiis*, trans. James Marcus (New York: Miramax Books, 2004).

Laura, Ernesto G. (ed.), *Tutti i film di Venezia 1932–1984* (2 vols) (Venice: La Biennale, 1985).

Magrelli, Enrico (ed.), *Sull'industria cinematografica italiana* (Venice: Marsilio, 1986).

Mariotti, Franco (ed.), *Cinecittà tra cronaca e storia 1937–1989* (2 vols) (Rome: Presidenza del Consiglio dei Ministri, 1989).

Monicelli, Mino (ed.), *Cinema italiano: ma cos'è questa crisi?* (Bari: Laterza, 1979).

Nowell-Smith, Geoffrey and Steven Ricci (eds), *Hollywood & Europe: Economics, Culture, National Identity 1945–95* (London: BFI, 1998).

Quaglietti, Lorenzo, *Storia economico-politica del cinema italiano 1945–1980* (Rome: Editori Riuniti, 1980).

Redi, Riccardo, *La Cines: Storia di una casa di produzione italiana* (Rome: CNC Edizioni, 1991).

—— and Claudio Camerini (eds), *Cinecittà 1: industria e mercato nel cinema italiano tra le due guerre* (Venice: Marsilio, 1985).

Repetto, Monica and Carlo Tagliabue (eds), *La vita è bella? Il cinema italiano alla fine degli anni Novanta e il suo pubblico* (Milan: Il Castoro, 2000).

Rocca, Carmelo, *Le leggi del cinema: Il contesto italiano nelle politiche comunitarie* (Rome: Editore Franco Angeli, 2003).

Savio, Francesco, *Cinecittà anni trenta: parlano 116 protagonisti del secondo cinema italiano (1930–1943)* (3 vols) (Rome: Bulzoni, 1979).

Sorlin, Pierre, *Sociologia del cinema*, trans. Luca Baldini (Milan: Garzanti, 1979).

Viganò, Dario, *Un cinema ogni campanile: chiesa e cinema nella diocesi di Milano* (Milan: Il Castoro, 1997).

Vivere il cinema: cinquant'anni del Centro Sperimentale di Cinematografia (Rome: Presidenza del Consiglio dei Ministri, 1987).

Zagarrio, Vito (ed.), *Dietro lo schermo: ragionamenti sui modi di produzione cinematografici in Italia* (Venice: Marsilio, 1988).

FILM THEORY AND FILM CRITICISM
Film Theory

Aristarco, Guido, *Il dissolvimento della ragione: discorso sul cinema* (Milan: Feltrinelli, 1965).

——, *Il mito dell'attore: come l'industria della star produce il sex symbol* (Bari: Edizioni Dedalo, 1983).

——, *Marx, le cinéma et la critique du film* (Paris: Études cinématographiques, nos 88–92, 1972).

——, *Storia delle teoriche del film* (Turin: Einaudi, 1951).

Barbaro, Umberto, *L'arte dell'attore* (Rome: Bianco e Nero Editore, 1950) (written in collaboration with Luigi Chiarini).

——, *Film: soggetto e sceneggiatura* (Rome: Edizioni Bianco e Nero, 1939).

——, *Il film e il risarcimento marxista dell'arte* (Rome: Editori Riuniti, 1974).

——, *Neorealismo e realismo*, ed. Gian Piero Brunetta (2 vols) (Rome: Editori Riuniti, 1976).

Bazin, André, *Bazin at Work: Major Essays & Reviews from the Forties & Fifties*, ed. Bert Cardullo, trans. Alain Piette and Bert Cardullo (New York: Routledge, 1977) (contains essays on Italian cinema not included in the volume *What Is Cinema? Vol. II* below).

——, *Qu'est-ce que le cinéma? Vol. IV. Une esthétique de la Réalité: le néo-réalisme* (Paris: Éditions du Cerf, 1962).

——, *What Is Cinema? Vol. II.* Berkeley (University of California Press, 1971) (contains many of the essays in the French edition).

Bettetini, Gianfranco, *L'indice del realismo* (Milan: Bompiani, 1971).

——, *The Language and Technique of the Film* (The Hague: Mouton, 1973).

Bondanella, Peter, 'Writing Italian Film History: A First-Person Account', *Italian Studies* vol. 67 no.2 (July 2012), pp. 252–66.

Bruno, Edoardo (ed.), *Teorie e prassi del cinema in Italia 1950–1970* (Milan: Mazzotta Editore, 1972).

——, *Teorie del realismo* (Rome: Bulzoni, 1977).

Brunetta, Gian Piero, *Buio in sala: cent'anni di passioni dello spettatore cinematografico* (Venice: Marsilio, 1989).

Casetti, Francesco, *Dentro lo squardo: il film e il suo spettatore* (Milan: Bompiani, 1986).

——, *Teorie del cinema 1945–1990* (Milan: Bompiani, 1993); *Theories of Cinema, 1945–1995*, trans. Francesca Chiostri and Elizabeth Gard Bartolini-Salimbeni with Thomas Kelso, rev. English edn (Austin: University of Texas Press, 1999).

Chiarini, Luigi, *Cinema e film: storia e problemi* (Rome: Bulzoni, 1972).

——, *Cinema quinto potere* (Bari: Laterza, 1954).

——, *Il film nella battaglia delle idee* (Rome: Fratelli Bocca, 1954).

De Lauretis, Teresa, 'Semiotics, Theory and Social Practice: A Critical History of Italian Semiotics', *Cine-Tracts* vol. 2 no. 1 (1978), pp. 1–14.

Eco, Umberto, 'On the Contribution of Film to Semiotics', *Quarterly Review of Film Studies* vol. 2 no. 1 (1977), pp. 1–14.

——, 'Towards a Semiotic Inquiry into the Television Message', *Working Papers in Cultural Studies* no. 3 (1972), pp. 103–22.

Gambetti, Giacomo, *Zavattini mago e tecnico* (Rome: Ente dello spettacolo Editore, 1986).

Micciché, Lino, *Filmologia e filologia: Studi sul cinema* (Venice: Marsilio, 2002).

O'Leary, Alan and Catherine O'Rawe, special issue of *Italian Studies Thinking Italian Film* vol. 63 no. 2 (2008).

——, 'Against Realism: On a "Certain Tendency" in Italian Film Criticism', *Journal of Modern Italian Studies* vol. 16 no.1 (2011), pp. 107–28.

Pasinetti, Francesco, *L'arte del cinematografo: articoli e saggi teorici* (Venice: Marsilio, 1980).

Pasolini, Pier Paolo, 'The Catholic Irrationalism of Fellini', *Film Criticism* vol. 9 no. 1 (1984), pp. 63–73; rpt Peter Bondanella and Cristina Degli-Esposti (eds), *Perspectives on Federico Fellini* (New York: G. K. Hall/Macmillan, 1993), pp. 101–9.

——, 'The Cinema of Poetry', *Cahiers du Cinéma in English* no. 6 (1966), pp. 34–43.

——, 'Cinematic and Literary Stylistic Features', *Film Culture* no. 24 (1962), pp. 42–3.

——, *Empirismo eretico* (Milan: Garzanti, 1972); *Heretical Empiricism*, ed. Louise K. Barnett , trans. Ben Lawton and Louise K. Barnett (Bloomington: Indiana University Press, 1988); 2nd rev. edn (Washington: New Academia Publishing, 2005).

——, 'The Pesaro Papers', *Cinim* no. 3 (1969), pp. 6–11.

——, 'Pier Paolo Pasolini: An Epical-Religious View of the World', *Film Quarterly* no. 18 (1965), pp. 31–45.

——, 'The Scenario as a Structure Designed to Become Another Structure', *Wide Angle* vol. 2 no.1 (1978), pp. 40–7.

Piazza, Roberta, *The Discourse of Italian Cinema and Beyond: Let Cinema Speak* (London and New York: Continuum, 2012).

Italian Film Criticism (Exclusive of History or Theory)

Aristarco, Guido, *Neorealismo e nuova critica cinematografica: cinematografia e vita nazionale negli anni quaranta e cinquanta: tra rotture e tradizioni* (Florence: Nuova Guaraldi Editrice, 1980).

Bianca, Pividori (ed.), *Critica italiana primo tempo: 1926–1934* (Rome: Studi monografici di Bianco e Nero, 1973).

Bolzoni, Francesco (ed.), *Critici e autori: complici e/o avversari?* (Venice: Marsilio, 1976).

Bondanella, Peter, 'New Directions in Teaching Film in Italian Studies Programs', *Italica* no. 83 (2006), pp. 7–21.

——, 'Recent Work on Italian Cinema', *Journal of Modern Italian Studies* vol. 1 no 1 (1995), pp. 101–24.

Brunetta, Gian Piero, *Gli intellettuali italiani e il cinema* (Milan: Bruno Mondadori, 2004).

——, *Umberto Barbaro e l'idea del neorealismo (1930–1943)* (Padua: Liviana Editrice, 1969).

d'Amico, Massolino, *Persone speciali* (Turin: Nino Aragno Editore, 2003).

De Marchi, Bruno (ed.), *La critica cinematografica in Italia: rilievi sul campo* (Venice: Marsilio, 1977).

De Santis, Giuseppe, *Verso il neorealismo: un critico cinematografico degli anni quaranta*, ed. Callisto Cosulich (Rome: Bulzoni, 1982).

Farassino, Alberto, *Scritti strabici: Cinema, 1975–1988*, ed. Tatti Sanquineti (Milan: Baldini Castoldi Dalai Editore, 2004).

Flaiano, Ennio, *Lettere d'amore al cinema* (Milan: Rizzoli, 1978).

——, *Un film alla settimana*, ed. Tullio Kezich (Rome: Bulzoni, 1988).

Fofi, Goffredo, *Capire con il cinema* (Milan: Feltrinelli, 1977).

——, *Il cinema italiano: servi e padroni* (Milan: Feltrinelli, 1971).

Furno, Mariella and Renzo Renzi (eds), *Il neorealismo nel fascismo: Giuseppe De Santis e la critica cinematografica 1941–1943* (Bologna: Edizioni della Tipografia Compositori, 1984).

Grazzini, Giovanni, *Il cinemondo: dieci anni di film, 1976–1986* (11 vols) (Rome: Laterza, 1987).

Hiller, Jim (ed.), *Cahiers du Cinéma – The 1950s: Neo-Realism, Hollywood, New Wave* (Cambridge, MA: Harvard University Press, 1985) (articles by Bazin, Ayfre, Rivette, Rohmer, Truffaut and others on Italian cinema).

Kezich, Tullio, *Il cento film: un anno al cinema 1977–1978* (Milan: Edizioni Il Formichiere, 1978).

——, *Il dolce cinema* (Milan: Bompiani, 1978).

——, *Il filmottanta: cinque anni al cinema 1982–1986* (Milan: Mondadori, 1986).

——, *Il millefilm: dieci anni al cinema 1967–1977* (2 vols) (Milan: Edizioni Il Formichiere, 1978).

——, *Il nuovissimo millefilm: cinque anni al cinema 1977–1982* (Milan: Mondadori, 1983).

Moravia, Alberto, *Al cinema: centoquarantotto film d'autore* (Milan: Bompiani, 1975).

Renzi, Renzo, *Il fascismo involontario e altri scritti* (Bologna: Cappelli, 1975).

——, *La sala buia: diario di un disamore* (Bologna: Cappelli, 1978).

——, *Da Starace ad Antonioni: diario critico di un ex balilla* (Padua: Marsilio, 1964).

Torri, Bruno (ed.), *Nuovo cinema (1965–2005): Scritti in onore di Lino Micciché* (Venice: Marsilio, 2005).

COLLECTIONS OF INTERVIEWS WITH DIRECTORS

Garibaldi, Andrea, Roberto Giannarelli and Guido Giusti (eds), *Qui comincia l'avventura del signor ...: Dall'anonimato al successo ventitre protagonisti del cinema italiano raccontano* (Florence: La Casa Usher, 1984).

Geduld, Harry (ed.), *Film Makers on Film Making* (Bloomington: Indiana University Press, 1967).

Georgakas, Dan and Lenny Rubenstein (ed.), *The Cinéaste Interviews on the Art and Politics of the Cinema* (Chicago, IL: Lake View Press, 1983) (interviews with Bertolucci, Petri, Pontecorvo, Rosi, Rossellini and Wertmüller).

Gili, Jean A. (ed.), *Le cinéma italien* (Paris: Union Générale d'Éditions, 1978).

——, *Italian Filmmakers – Self Portraits: A Selection of Interviews* (New York: Gremese, 1998).

Samuels, Charles Thomas (ed.), *Encountering Directors* (New York: Putnam's, 1972) (interviews with Antonioni, Fellini, De Sica).

Tassone, Aldo (ed.), *Parla il cinema italiano* (2 vols) (Milan: Edizioni il Formichiere, 1979–80) (the most complete series of in-depth interviews with Italian directors).

ITALIAN DIRECTORS
Gianni Amelio

Amelio, Gianni, *Lamerica: film e storia del film*, ed. Piera Detassis (Turin: Einaudi, 1994).

——, *Il vizio del cinema: Vedere, amare, fare un film* (Turin: Einaudi, 2004).

——, Sandro Petraglia, and Stefano Rulli, *Le chiavi di casa* (Venice: Marsilio, 2004).

——, Monica Repetto and Carlo Tagliabue (eds), *La vita è bella? Il cinema italiano alla fine degli anni Novanta e il suo pubblico* (Milan: Il Castoro, 2000).

Crowdus, Gary and Richard Porton, 'Beyond Neorealism: Preserving a Cinema of Social Conscience – An Interview with Gianni Amelio', *Cinéaste* vol. 21 no. 4 (1995), pp. 6–13.

Domenico, Scalzo, *Gianni Amelio: un posto al cinema* (Turin: Lindau, 2001).

Martini, Emanuela, *Gianni Amelio* (Milan: Il Castoro, 2006).

—— (ed.), *Gianni Amelio: le regole e il gioco* (Turin: Lindau, 1999).

Vitti, Antonio. *The Films of Gianni Amelio: The Search for a Cinema of Social Conscience, True to His Roots* (Pesaro: Metauro Edizioni, 2009).

Michelangelo Antonioni

Achilli, Alberto, Alberto Boschi and Gianfranco Casadio (eds), *La sonorità del visibile: immagini, suoni e musica nel cinema di Michelangelo Antonioni* (Ravenna: Longo, 2000).

Antonioni, Michelangelo, *'L'Avventura': A Film by Michelangelo Antonioni*, ed. George Amberg (New York: Grove Press, 1969).

——, *Blow-Up* (New York: Frederick Ungar Publishers, 1971).

——, *Chung Kuo Cina*, ed. Lorenzo Cucco (Turin: Einaudi, 1974).

——, *Comincio a capire* (Catania: Girasole Edizioni, 2000).

——, *Il deserto rosso*, ed. Carlo Di Carlo (Bologna: Cappelli, 1978).

——, *'L'eclisse' di Michelangelo Antonioni*, ed. John Francis Lane (Bologna: Cappelli, 1962).

——, *Identificazione di una donna*, ed. Aldo Tassone (Turin: Einaudi, 1983).

——, *I film nel cassetto*, eds Carlo di Carlo and Giorgio Tinazzi (Venice: Marsilio, 1995).

——, *Unfinished Business: Screenplays, Scenarios, and Ideas*, English version, Carlo di Carlo and Giorgio Tinazzi, trans. Andrew Taylor (New York: Marsilio, 1998).

——, *Il mistero di Oberwald*, ed. Gianni Massironi (Turin: Edizioni RAI, 1981).

——, *The Passenger*, eds Mark Peploe, Peter Wollen and Michelangelo Antonioni (New York: Grove Press, 1975).

——, *Il primo Antonioni*, ed. Carlo Di Carlo (Bologna: Cappelli, 1973) (Italian scripts for *Gente del Po, N. U., L'amorosa menzogna, Superstizione, I vinti, La signora senza camelie* and *Cronaca di un amore*).

——, *Professione: reporter*, ed. Carlo Di Carlo (Bologna: Cappelli, 1975).

——, *Screenplays of Michelangelo Antonioni* (New York: Orion Press, 1963) (English scripts for *L'avventura, Il grido, La notte* and *L'eclisse*).

——, *Sei film* (Turin: Einaudi, 1964) (*Le amiche, Il grido, L'avventura, La notte, L'eclisse, Il deserto rosso* plus a Preface by Antonioni).

——, *Tecnicamente dolce*, ed. Aldo Tassone (Turin: Einaudi, 1976).

——, *That Bowling Alley on the Tiber: Tales of a Director*, trans. William Arrowsmith (New York: Oxford University Press, 1986).

——, *'Zabriskie Point' di Michelangelo Antonioni* (Bologna: Cappelli, 1970).

Arrowsmith, William, *Antonioni: A Critical Study* (New York: Oxford University Press, 1995).

Bauer, Mattias and Rada Bieberstein (eds), *Michelangelo Antonioni: Bild-Projection-Wirklichkeit* (Munich: Edition text+kritik, 2013).

Biarese, Cesare and Aldo Tassone, *I film di Michelangelo Antonioni* (Rome: Gremese, 1985).

Brunette, Peter, *The Films of Michelangelo Antonioni* (New York: Cambridge University Press, 1998).

Cameron, Ian and Robin Wood, *Antonioni* (London: Studio Vista, 1968).

Chatman, Seymour, *Antonioni or, The Surface of the World* (Berkeley: University of California Press, 1985).

Di Carlo, Carlo, *Il cinema di Michelangelo Antonioni* (Milan: Il Castoro, 2002).

——, *Les images d'Antonioni* (Rome: Cinecittà International, 1988).

Di Carlo, Carlo (ed.), *Cher Antonioni* (Rome: Ente Autonomo di Gestione per il Cinema, 1988).

——, *Michelangelo Antonioni* (Rome: Edizioni di Bianco e Nero, 1964).

—— (ed.), *Michelangelo Antonioni 1942–1965* (Rome: Ente Autonomo di Gestione per il Cinema, 1988).

Estève, Michele (ed.), *Michelangelo Antonioni: l'homme et l'objet* (Paris: Études Cinématographiques nos 36–7, 1964).

Huss, Roy (ed.), *Focus on 'Blow-Up'* (Englewood Cliffs, NJ: Prentice-Hall, 1971).

Leprohoun, Pierre, *Michelangelo Antonioni*, 4th edn (Paris: Éditions Séghers, 1969).

——, *Michelangelo Antonioni: An Introduction*, trans. Scott Sullivan (New York: Simon and Schuster, 1963) [translation of an early version of the original French edition].

Lyons, Robert J., *Michelangelo Antonioni's Neo-realism: A World View* (New York: Arno Press, 1976).

Mancini, Michele and Giuseppe Perrella (eds), *Architetture della visione/Architecture in Vision* (2 vols) (Rome: Coneditor, 1985).

Michelangelo Antonioni: identificazione di un autore (2 vols) (Parma: Pratiche, 1983, 1985).

Moore, Kevin Z., 'Eclipsing the Commonplace: The Logic of Alienation in Antonioni', *Film Quarterly* vol. 48 no. 4 (1995), pp. 22–34.

Nowell-Smith, Geoffrey, '*L'avventura*' (Bloomington: Indiana University Press, 1998).

Perry, Ted and Raymond Prieto, *Michelangelo Antonioni: A Guide to References and Resources* (Boston, MA: G. K. Hall, 1986).

Pomerance, Murray, *Michelangelo Red Antonioni Blue: Eight Reflections on Cinema* (Berkeley: University of California Press, 2011).

Orsini, Maria (ed.), *Michelangelo Antonioni: I film e la critica 1943–1995: un'antologia* (Rome: Bulzoni, 2002).

Ranieri, Nicola, *Amor vacui: il cinema di Michelangelo Antonioni* (Milan: Metis, 1990).

Rascaroli, Laura and John David Rhodes (eds), *Antonioni: Centenary Essays* (London: BFI/Palgrave Macmillan, 2011).

Renzi, Renzo, *Album Antonioni: une biographie impossible* (Rome: Cinecittà International, 1990).

Tinazzi, Giorgio, *Michelangelo Antonioni* (Milan: Il Castoro, 2002).

—— (ed), *Michelangelo Antonioni: Écrits 1936/1985* (Rome: Cinecittà International, 1988).

Trebbi, Fernando, *Il testo e lo squardo: antitesi, circolarità, incrociamento in 'Professione: reporter': saggio su Michelangelo Antonioni* (Bologna: Pàtron Editore, 1976).

Vitella, Federico, *Michelangelo Antonioni: L'avventura* (Turin: Lindau, 2010).

Wenders, Wim, *My Time with Antonioni: The Diary of an Extraordinary Experience*, trans. Michael Hofmann (London: Faber and Faber, 2000).

Zumbo, Saverio, *Al di là delle immagini: Michelangelo Antonioni* (Alessandria: Edizioni Falsopiano, 2002).

Dario Argento

Carluccio, Giulia, Giacomo Manzoli and Roy Menarini (eds), *L'eccesso della visione: il cinema di Dario Argento* (Turin: Lindau, 2003).

Cozzi, Luigi (ed.), *Giallo Argento: Tutto il cinema di Dario Argento* (Rome: Mondo Ignoto, 2001); rev. edn of *Dario Argento: il suo cinema, i suoi personaggi, i suoi miti* (Rome: Fanucci Editori, 1991).

Dario Argento (Milan: Mediane, 2007).

Della Casa, S. (ed.), *Dario Argento, il brivido della critica* (Turin: Testo & Immagine, 1996).

Gallant, C. (ed.), *Art of Darkness: The Cinema of Dario Argento* (London: FAB Press, 2001).

Giovanni, Fabio, *Dario Argento: il brivido, il sangue, il thrilling* (Bari: Edizioni Dedalo, 1986).

Jones, Alan, *Profondo Argento: The Man, the Myths & the Magic* (London: FAB Press, 2004).

McDonagh, Maitland, *Broken Mirrors, Broken Minds: The Dark Dreams of Dario Argento* (London: Sun Tavern Fields, 1991).

Pugliese, Roberto, *Dario Argento* (Milan: Il Castoro, 1996).

Pupi Avati

Avati, Pupi, *Il cuore altrove e altre storie* (Rome: Gremese, 2002).

Maraldi, Antonio (ed.), *Pupi Avati: cinema e televisione* (Gambettola: Centro Cinema Città di Cesena, 1980).

Romano, Paolo and Roberto Tirapelle (eds), *Il cinema di Pupi Avati* (Verona: Sequenze, 1987).

Sarno, Antonello, *Pupi Avati* (Milan: Il Castoro, 1993).

Mario Bava

Cozzo, Luigi, *Mario Bava: I mille volti della paura* (Rome: Mondo Ignoto [Profondo Rosso], 2001).

Howarth, Troy, *The Haunted World of Mario Bava* (London: FAB Press, 2002).

Lucas, Tim, *Mario Bava: All the Colors of the Dark* (Introduction by Martin Scorsese. Foreword by Riccardo Freda) (Cincinatti, OH: Video Watchdog, 2007).

Pezzotta, Alberto, *Mario Bava* (Milan: Il Castoro, 1997).

Marco Bellocchio

Aprà, Adriano (ed.), *Marco Bellocchio: Il cinema e i film* (Venice: Marsilio, 2005).

Arvat, Massimo, *Marco Bellocchio* (Turin: Quaderni del Museo Nazionale del Cinema, 1992).

Bandirali, Luca and Stefano D'Amadio, '*Buongiorno, notte*': *Le ragioni e le immagini* (Lecce: Argo, 2004).

Bellocchio, Marco, *China Is Near*, ed. Tommaso Chiaretti (New York: Orion Press, 1969).

——, *Marcia trionfale*, ed. Anna Maria Tatò (Turin: Einaudi, 1976).

——, '*Nel nome del padre*' *di Marco Bellocchio*, ed. Goffredo Fofi (Bologna: Cappelli, 1971).

——, '*I pugni in tasca*': *un film di Marco Bellocchio*, ed. G. Gambetti (Milan: Garzanti, 1967).

——, *Salto nel vuoto*, eds Alberto Barbera, Gianni Volpi and Massimo Fagioli (Milan: Feltrinelli, 1981).

Bernardi, Sandro, *Marco Bellocchio* (Milan: Il Castoro, 1998).

Brook, Clodagh J., *Marco Bellocchio: The Cinematic I in the Political Sphere* (Toronto: University of Toronto Press, 2010).

Ceretto, Luisa and Giancarlo Zappoli, *Le forme della ribellione: Il cinema di Marco Bellocchio* (Turin: Lindau, 2004).

Lodato, Nuccio, *Marco Bellocchio* (Milan: Moizzi Editore, 1977).

Ventura, Francesco, *Il cinema e il caso Moro* (Recco: Le Mani-Microart'S, 2008).

Roberto Benigni

Benigni, Roberto, *Io un po' Pinocchio: Roberto Benigni racconta il suo film tra le pagine del romanzo di Collodi* (Florence: Giunti, 2002).

—— and Vincenzo Cerami, *Life Is Beautiful (La Vita È Bella): A Screenplay*, trans. Lisa Taruschio (New York: Hyperion, 1998).

Borsatti, Cristina, *Roberto Benigni* (Milan: Il Castoro, 2002).

Bullaro, Grace Russo (ed.), *Beyond 'Life Is Beautiful': Comedy and Tragedy in the Cinema of Roberto Benigni* (Leicester: Troubadour, 2005).

Celli, Carlo, *The Divine Comic: The Cinema of Roberto Benigni* (Blue Summit, PA: Scarecrow Press, 2001).

Denby, David, 'In the Eye of the Beholder: Another Look at Roberto Benigni's Holocaust Fantasy', *New Yorker* (15 March 1999), pp. 96–9.

Masi, Stefano, *Roberto Benigni Superstar* (Rome: Gremese, 1999).

Bernardo Bertolucci

Alley, Robert, *Last Tango in Paris* (New York: Dell, 1972).

Behr, Edward, *The Last Emperor* (London: Futura, 1987).

Bernardo Bertolucci (Milan: Mediane, 2007).

Bertolucci, Bernardo, *Bernardo Bertolucci's 'Last Tango in Paris'* (New York: Delta, 1973) (includes essays by Pauline Kael and Norman Mailer).

——, Franco Arcalli and Giuseppe Bertolucci, *Novecento: atto primo* and *Novecento: atto secondo* (2 vols) (Turin: Einaudi, 1973).

——, *Ultimo tango a Parigi* (Turin: Einaudi, 1973).

Burgoyne, Robert, *Bertolucci's '1900'* (Detroit, MI: Wayne State University Press, 1991).

Carroll, Kent E. (ed.), *Closeup: 'Last Tango in Paris'* (New York: Grove Press, 1973).

Casetti, Francesco, *Bernardo Bertolucci* (Florence: La Nuova Italia, 1978).

Costa, Francesco, *Bernardo Bertolucci* (Rome: Dino Audino Editore, 1993).

Di Giovanni, Norman Thomas, *1900* (New York: Dell, 1976).

Estève, Michel (ed.), *Bernardo Bertolucci* (Paris: Études Cinématographiques, nos 122–6, 1979).

Gérard, Fabien S., *Ombres jaunes: journal de tournage 'Le dernier empereur' de Bernardo Bertolucci* (Paris: Cahiers du Cinéma, 1987).

——, T. Jefferson Kline and Bruce Sklarew (eds), *Bernardo Bertolucci: Interviews* (Oxford: University Press of Mississippi, 2000).

Halligan, Benjamin, *'La Luna'* (Trowbridge: Flicks Books, 2001).

Kline, T. Jefferson, *Bertolucci's Dream Loom: A Psychoanalytic Study of Cinema* (Amherst: University of Massachusetts Press, 1987).

Kolker, Robert Phillip, *Bernardo Bertolucci* (New York: Oxford University Press, 1985).

Loshitzky, Yosefa, *The Radical Faces of Godard and Bertolucci* (Detroit, MI: Wayne State University Press, 1994).

Prono, Franco, *Bernardo Bertolucci: 'Il conformista'* (Turin: Edizioni Lindau, 1998).

Sklarew, Bruce et al. (eds), *Bertolucci's 'The Last Emperor': Multiple Takes* (Detroit, MI: Wayne State University Press, 1998).

Socci, Stefano, *Bernardo Bertolucci* (Milan: Il Castoro, 2003).

Thompson, David, *Last Tango in Paris* (London: BFI, 1998).

Tonetti, Claretta Micheletti, *Bernardo Bertolucci* (New York: Twayne, 1995).

Ungari, Enzo and Donald Ranvaud (eds), *Scene madri di Bernardo Bertolucci* (2nd rev. edn) (Milan: Ubulibri, 1987).

Wagstaff, Chris, *Il conformista (The Conformist)* (London: BFI/Palgrave Macmillan, 2012).

Giuseppe Bertolucci

Giraldi, Massimo, *Giuseppe Bertolucci* (Milan: Il Castoro, 2000).

Alessandro Blasetti

Aprà, Adriano and Riccardo Redi (eds), *'Sole': soggetto, sceneggiatura, note per la realizzazione* (Rome: Di Giacomo Editore, 1985).

Blasetti, Alessandro, *Il cinema che ho vissuto*, ed. Franco Prono (Bari: Edizioni Dedalo, 1982).

——, *Scritti sul cinema*, ed. Adriano Aprà (Venice: Marsilio, 1982).

Gori, Alessandro, *Alessandro Blasetti* (Milan: Il Castoro, 1984).

Salizzato, Claver and Vito Zagarrio (eds), *'La corono di ferro': un modo di produzione italiano* (Rome: Di Giacomo Editore, 1985).

Verdone, Luca, *I film di Alessandro Blasetti* (Rome: Gremese, 1989).

Mauro Bolognini

Brancati, Vitaliano, *Bell'Antonio*, trans. Stanley Hochmann (New York: Frederick Ungar Publishers, 1978).

di Montezemola, Vittorio Cordero (ed.), *Bolognini* (Rome: Istituto Poligrafico dello Stato, 1977).

Franco Brusati

Occhipinti, Andrea (ed.), *Un castello disincantato: film e scritti di Franco Brusati* (Milan: Il Castoro, 2003).

Mimmo Calopresti

Sesti, Mario, *Mimmo Calopresti* (Alessandria: Edizioni Falsopiano, 2003).

Mario Camerini

Germani, Sergio Grmek, *Mario Camerini* (Milan: Il Castoro, 1980).

Renato Castellani

Castellani, Renato, *'Giulietta e Romeo' di Renato Castellani*, ed. Stelio Martini (Bologna: Cappelli, 1956).

——, *Quattro soggetti* (Rome: Centro Cattolico Cinematografico, 1983).

Trasatti, Sergio, *Renato Castellani* (Milan: Il Castoro, 1984).

Enzo G. Castellari

Lupi, Gordiano and Fabio Zanello (eds), *Il citadino si ribella: il cinema di Enzo G. Castellari* (Rome: Profondo Rosso, 2006).

Liliana Cavani

Buscemi, Francesco, *Invito al cinema di Liliana Cavani* (Milan: Mursia, 1996).

Cavani, Liliana, *'Milarepa' di Liliana Cavani*, ed. Italo Moscati (Bologna: Cappelli, 1974).

——, *Il portiere di notte* (Turin: Einaudi, 1975).

—— and Enrico Medioli, *Oltre la porta* (Turin: Einaudi, 1982).

—— and Italo Moscati, *Lettere dall'interno: Racconto per un film su Simone Weil* (Turin: Einaudi, 1974).

Marone, Gaetana, *The Gaze and the Labyrinth: The Cinema of Liliana Cavani* (Princeton, NJ: Princeton University Press, 2000).

Tallarigo, Paola and Luca Gasparini (eds), *Lo squardo libero: il cinema di Liliana Cavani* (Florence: La Casa Usher, 1990).

Tiso, Ciriaco, *Liliana Cavani* (Milan: Il Castoro, 1975).

Daniele Ciprì and Franco Maresco

Monreale, Emiliano, *Ciprì e Maresco* (Alessandria: Edizioni Falsopiano, 2003).

Luigi Comencini

Aprà, Adriano (ed.), *Luigi Comencini: Il cinema e i film* (Venice: Marsilio, 2007).

Comencini, Luigi, *Al cinema con cuore 1938–1974*, ed. Adriano Aprà (Milan: Il Castoro, 2007).

——, *Luigi Comencini: Infanzia, vocazione, esperienza di un regista* (Milan: Baldini & Castoldi, 1999).

——, *'Tutti a Casa': Un film di Dino De Laurentiis* (Rome: Salvatore Sciascia Editore, 1960).

Gili, Jean A., *Luigi Comencini* (Paris: Edilig, 1981).

——, *Luigi Comencini* (Rome: Gremese, 2005).

Gosetti, Giorgio, *Luigi Comencini* (Milan: Il Castoro, 1988).

Pirro, Ugo and Luigi Comencini, *Delitto d'amore* (Milan: Vangelista Editore, 1974).

Trionfera, Claudio, *Italian Directors: Luigi Comencini* (Rome: ANICA, n.d.).

Vittorio Cottafavi

Rondolino, Gianni, *Vittorio Cottafavi: cinema e televisione* (Bologna: Cappelli, 1980).

Ruggero Deodato

Fenton, Harvey *et al.* (eds), *Cannibal Holocaust and the Savage Cinema of Ruggero Deodato* (London: FAB Press, 1999).

Giuseppe De Santis

Camerino, Vincenzo (ed.), *Il cinema di Giuseppe De Santis* (Lecce: Elle Edizioni, 1982).

Cinema & Cinema vol. 9 no. 30 (1982) (special De Santis issue).

De Santis, Giuseppe, *'Riso amaro': un film diretto da Giuseppe De Santis*, ed. Carlo Lizzani (Rome: Officina Edizioni, 1978).

——, *Verso il neorealismo: un critico cinematografico degli anni quaranta*, ed. Callisto Cosulich (Rome: Bulzoni, 1982).

Farassino, Alberto, *Giuseppe De Santis* (Milan: Moizzi Editore, 1978).

Masi, Stefano, *Giuseppe De Santis* (Milan: Il Castoro, 1982).

Parisi, Antonio, *Il cinema di Giuseppe De Santis tra passione e ideologia* (Rome: Cadmo Editore, 1983).

Vitti, Antonio, *Giuseppe De Santis and Postwar Italian Cinema* (Toronto: University of Toronto Press, 1996).

Vittorio De Seta

De Seta, Vittorio, *'Un uomo a metà' di Vittorio De Seta: analisi di un film in costruzione*, ed. Filippo De Sanctis (Bologna: Cappelli, 1966).

Vittorio De Sica

Agel, Henri, *Vittorio De Sica* (Paris: Éditions Universitaires, 1964).

Alonge, G., *Vittorio De Sica: Ladri di biciclette* (Turin: Edizioni Lindau, 1998).

Bartolini, Luigi, *Bicycle Thieves*, trans. C. J. Richards (New York: Macmillan, 1950).

Bolzoni, Francesco, *Quando De Sica era Mister Brown* (Turin: Edizioni ERI, 1985).

Bruni, Davide, *Vittorio De Sica: 'Sciuscià'* (Turin: Lindau, 2007).

Caldiron, Orio (ed.), *Vittorio De Sica. Bianco e Nero* vol. 36 nos 9–12 (1975) (special De Sica issue with bibliography).

Cassarini, Maria Carla, *'Miracolo a Milano' di Vittorio De Sica: Storia e preistoria di un film* (Genoa: Le Mani, 2000).

Curle, Howard and Stephen Snyder (eds), *Vittorio De Sica: Contemporary Perspectives* (Toronto: University of Toronto Press, 2000).

Darretta, John, *Vittorio De Sica: A Guide to References and Resources* (Boston, MA: G. K. Hall, 1983).

De Santi, Gualtiero, *Vittorio De Sica* (Milan: Il Castoro, 2003).

De Sica, Vittorio, *The Bicycle Thief* (New York: Simon and Schuster, 1968).

——, *Lettere dal set*, eds Emi De Sica and Giancarlo Governi (Milan: Sugar Edizioni, 1987).

——, *Miracle in Milan* (Baltimore, MD: Penguin, 1969).

Gordon, Robert S. C., *Bicycle Thieves* (London: BFI/Palgrave Macmillan, 2008).

Leprohon, Pierre, *Vittorio De Sica* (Paris: Éditions Séghers, 1966).

Mercader, Maria, *La mia vita con Vittorio De Sica* (Milan: Mondadori, 1978).

Micciché, Lino (ed.), *De Sica: autore, regista, attore* (Venice: Marsilio, 1993).

—— (ed.), *'Sciuscià' di Vittorio De Sica: letture, documenti, testimonianze* (Rome: Centro Sperimentale di Cinematagrafia, 1994).

Mollica, Vincenzo (ed.), *Le canzoni di Vittorio De Sica: antologia storica* (Montepulciano: Editori del Grifo, 1990) (includes a book, two cassettes, and a compact disk).

Moscati, Italo, *Vittorio De Sica: Vitalità, passione e talento in un'Italia dolceamara* (Rome: Ediesse, 2004).

Pecori, Franco, *Vittorio De Sica* (Florence: La Nuova Italia, 1980).

Fernando Di Leo

Pulici, Davide, *Fernando Di Leo* (Milan: Nocturno Libri, 2001).

Luciano Emmer

Moneti, Guglielmo, *Luciano Emmer* (Milan: Il Castoro, 1992).

Roberto Faenza

Faenza, Roberto (ed.), *'Sostiene Pereira': filmbook* (Milan: Il Castoro, 1995).

Federico Fellini

Agel, Geneviève, *Les chemins de Fellini* (Paris: Éditions du Cerf, 1956).

Aldouby, Hava, *Federico Fellini: Painting in Film, Painting on Film* (Toronto: University of Toronto Press, 2013).

Alpert, Hollis, *Fellini: A Life* (New York: Atheneum, 1986).

Angelucci, Gianfranco (ed.), *Federico Fellini da Rimini a Roma 1937–1947: Atti del convegno di studi e testimonianze Rimini, 31 ottobre 1997* (Rimini: Pietroneno Capitani Editore, 1998).

——, *'La dolce vita': un film di Federico Fellini* (Rome: Editalia, 1989).

——, *Gli ultimi sogni di Fellini* (Rimini: Pietroneno Capitani Editore, 1997).

——, *Segreti e bugie di Federico Fellini: Il racconto dal vivo del più grande regista del '900. Misteri, illusioni e verità inconfessabili* (Cosenza: Luigi Pellegrini Editone, 2013).

Antonelli, Lamberto and Gabriele Paolini (eds), *Attalo e Fellini al 'Marc'Aurelio': Scritti e disegni* (Rome: Napoleone, 1995).

Arpa, Padre Angelo, *'La dolce vita': Cronaca di una Passione* (Naples: Parresía, 1996).

——, *Fellini: persona e personaggio* (Naples: Parresía, 1996).

Bachman, Gideon, 'A Guest in My Own Dreams: An Interview with Federico Fellini', *Film Quarterly* vol. 47 no. 3 (1994), pp. 2–15.

Baxter, John, *Fellini* (New York: St Martin's Press, 1993).

Benderson, Albert E., *Critical Approaches to Federico Fellini's '8½'* (New York: Arno Press, 1974).

Benevelli, Elio, *Analisi di una messa in scena: Freud e Lacan nel 'Casanova' di Fellini* (Bari: Dedali Libri, 1979).

Benzi, Luigi 'Titta', *Patachédi: Gli amarcord di una vita all'insegna della grande amicizia con Federico Fellini* (Rimini: Guaraldi Editore, 1995).

Bertozzi, Marco (ed.), *biblioFellini, Vol. I* (Rimini: Fondazione Federico Fellini, 2002).

——, *biblioFellini, Vol. II* (Rimini: Fondazione Federico Fellini, 2003).

——, *biblioFellini, Vol. III* (Rimini: Fondazione Federico Fellini, 2004).

Betti, Liliana, *Fellini: An Intimate Portrait*, trans. Joachim Neugroschel (Boston, MA: Little, Brown, 1979).

——, *Io e Fellini (Ma sei sicuro che non si siano gli indiani?)* (Milan: Archinto, 2000).

—— (ed.), *Federico A. C.: disegni per il 'Satyricon' di Federico Fellini* (Milan: Edizioni Libri, 1970).

—— and Gianfranco Angelucci (eds), *Casanova rendez-vous con Federico Fellini* (Milan: Bompiani, 1975).

—— and Oreste Del Buono (eds), *Federcord: disegni per 'Amarcord' di Federico Fellini* (Milan: Edizioni Libri, 1974).

Bìspurri, Ennio, *Federico Fellini: il sentimento latino della vita* (Rome: Editrice Il Ventaglio, 1981).

——, *Interpretare Fellini* (Rimini: Guaraldi Editore, 2003).

Boarini, Vittorio (ed.), *Il mio Fellini, Vol. 1* (Rimini: Fondazione Federico Fellini, 2006).

——, *Il mio Fellini, Vol. 2* (Rimini: Fondazione Federico Fellini, 2007).

Boledi, Luigi and Raffaele De Berti (eds), *'Luci del Varietà': pagine scelte* (Milan: Il Castoro, 1999).

Bondanella, Peter, 'Fellini', in Paolo Bertetto (ed.), *Action!: How Great Filmmakers Direct Actors* (Rome: Fondazione Cinema per Roma, 2007), pp. 225–31.

——, '"Amarcord": Fellini and Politics', *Cinéaste* vol. 19 no.1 (1992), pp. 36–43.

——, 'Beyond Neorealism: Calvino, Fellini and Fantasy', *Michigan Romance Studies* no. 16 (1996), pp. 103–20.

——, *The Cinema of Federico Fellini* ('Foreword' by Federico Fellini) (Princeton, NJ: Princeton University Press, 1992), Italian edn with a new Preface by the author, *Il cinema di Federico Fellini* (Rimini: Guaraldi Editore, 1994).

——, *The Films of Federico Fellini* (New York: Cambridge University Press, 2002).

——, 'Introduzione a *La famiglia* e *Happy Country*/An Introduction to *La famiglia* and *Happy Country*', *Federico Amarcord: Rivista di studi felliniani* vol. 6 nos 1–2 (2006), pp. 9–14.

——, 'La presenza di Federico Fellini nel cinema contemporaneo/Federico Fellini's Presence in the Contemporary Cinema', in *La memoria di Federico Fellini sullo schermo del cinema mondiale* (Rimini: Fondazione Federico Fellini, 2004), rpt as 'La presenza di Fellini nel cinema contemporaneo: Considerazioni preliminari/Federico Fellini's Presence in the Contemporary Cinema: Some Tentative Observations', *Federico Amarcord: Rivista di studi felliniani* vol. 7 nos 1–2 (2007), pp. 35–60.

——, '"La strada" e il cinema di poesia: dal soggetto al film/ "La Strada" and the Cinema of Poetry: From Soggetto to Film', *Fellini Amarcord: Rivista di studi felliniani* vol. 4 nos 2–3 (2004), pp. 7–18.

——, '"La strada": Soggetto di Tullio Pinelli e Federico Fellini', *Fellini Amarcord: Rivista di studi felliniani* vol. 4 nos 2–3 (2004), pp. 21–48.

—— (ed.), *Federico Fellini: Essays in Criticism* (New York: Oxford University Press, 1978).

—— and Cristina Degli-Esposti (eds), *Perspectives on Federico Fellini* (New York: G. K. Hall/Macmillan, 1993).

—— and Federico Pacchioni (eds and trans.), *La Famiglia/The Family and Happy Country (Paese felice). Federico Amarcord: Rivista di studi felliniani* vol. 6 nos 1–2 (2006), pp. 31–150.

Borin, Fabrizio, *Federico Fellini* (Rome: Gremese, 1999); English version *Federico Fellini: A Sentimental Journey into the Illusion and Reality of a Genius* (Rome: Gremese, 1999).

Boyer, Deena, *The Two Hundred Days of '8½'* (New York: Garland, 1978).

Budgen, Suzanne, *Fellini* (London: BFI, 1966).

Burke, Frank, *Federico Fellini: 'Variety Lights' to 'La Dolce Vita'* (Boston, MA: Twayne, 1984).

——, *Fellini's Films: From Postwar to Postmodern* (New York: Twayne, 1996).

——, 'Fellini's Commercials: Biting the Hand That Feeds', *The Italianist* vol. 31 no. 2 (2011), pp. 205–42.

—— and Marguerite R. Waller (eds), *Federico Fellini: Contemporary Perspectives* (Toronto: University of Toronto Press, 2002),

CD-Roms: *Federico Fellini* (Rome: Progetti Museali Editori/ENEL, 1995).

Cardullo, Bert (ed.), *Federico Fellini: Interviews (Conversations with Filmmakers Series)* (Oxford: University Press of Mississippi, 2006).

Caruso, Rossella and Giuseppe Casetti (eds), *Il amico Pasqualino: Federico Fellini 1937–1947* (Rome: Il museo del louvre, 1997).

Casanova, Alessandro, *Scritti e immaginati. I film mai realizzati di Federico Fellini* (Rimini: Guaraldi Editore, 2005).

Cavaglion, Gabriel, *Hermes, the Child and the Mother: Archetypes in Federico Fellini's Dream-Work* (New York: Nova Science Publishers, 2011).

Chandler, Charlotte, *I, Fellini* (New York: Random House, 1995). Italian edn, *Federico Fellini* (Milan: Rizzoli, 1995); French edn, *Moi, Fellini: Treize ans de confidences* (Paris: Éditions Robert Laffont, 1994).

Cianfarani, Carmine (ed.), *Federico Fellini: Leone d'Oro, Venezia 1985* (Rome: ANICA, 1985) (catalogue of Fellini retrospective at 1985 Venice Film Festival).

Ciment, Gilles (ed.), *Federico Fellini* (Paris: Éditions Rivages, 1988) (anthology of articles from *Positif*).

Cini, Roberta, *Nella città delle donne. Femminile e sogno nel cinema di Fellini* (Pisa: Edizioni del Cerro, 2008).

Cirio, Rita, *Il mestiere di regista: intervista con Federico Fellini* (Milan: Garzanti, 1994).

Collet, Jean, *La création selon Fellini* (Paris: José Corti, 1990).

Costa, Antonio, *Federico Felllini: 'La dolce vita'* (Turin: Lindau, 2010).

Costantini, Costano, *L'inferno di Fellini* (Rome: Sovera Editore, 2003).

Costello, Donald, *Fellini's Road* (Notre Dame, IN: University of Notre Dame Press, 1983).

De Benedictis, Maurizio, *Linguaggi dell'aldilà: Fellini e Pasolini* (Rome: Lithos, 2000).

De Berti, Raffaele, Elisabetta Gagetti and Fabrizio Slavazzi (eds), *Fellini-Satyricon: L'immaginario dell'antico* (Milan: Cisalpino, 2009).

de Miro, Ester and Mario Guaraldi (eds), *Fellini della memoria* (Florence: La Casa Usher, 1983) (catalogue for the 1983 Fellini retrospective at Rimini).

De Santi, Pier Marco, *I disegni di Fellini* (Rome: Laterza, 1982); rpt (2004).

—— and Raffaele Monti (eds), *Saggi e documenti sopra 'Il Casanova' di Federico Fellini* (Pisa: Quaderni dell'Istituto di storia dell'arte dell'Università di Pisa, 1978).

Di Biagi, Flaminio, *La Roma di Fellini* (Recco: Le Mani-Microart'S, 2008).

Estève, Michel (ed.), *Federico Fellini: aux sources de l'imaginaire* (Paris: Études Cinématographiques nos 127–30 (1981).

—— (ed.), *Federico Fellini: '8½'* (Paris: Études Cinématographiques nos 28–9 (1963).

Fabbri, Paolo (ed.), *Lo schermo 'manifesto': le misteriose pubblicità di Federico Fellini* (Rimini: Guaraldi Editore, 2002) (essays by Peter Bondanella, Manuela Gieri, Millicent Marcus, Cristina Degli Esposti, Marco Bertozzi and others on Fellini and the world of commercial advertising).

Fantuzzi, Virgilio, *Il vero Fellini* (Rome: Ave Editrice, 1994).

Fava, Claudio G. and Aldo Viganò, *I film di Federico Fellini* (2nd edn) (Rome: Gremese, 1987). English edn, *The Films of Federico Fellini*, trans. Shula Curto (Secaucus, NJ: Citadel Press, 1985) (translation of first Italian edition of 1981).

Federico Fellini & Dario Fo: disegni geniali (Milan: Mazzotta, 1999).

Fellini, Federico, *Block-notes di un regista* (Milan: Longanesi, 1988).

——, *Casanova*, eds Federico Fellini and Bernardino Zapponi (Turin: Einaudi, 1977).

——, *Ciò che abbiamo inventato è tutto autentico: Lettere a Tullio Pinelli* (Venice: Marsilio, 2008).

——, *La città delle donne* (Milan: Garzanti, 1980).

——, *I clowns*, ed. Renzo Renzi (Bologna: Cappelli, 1970).

——, *La Dolce Vita* (New York: Ballantine, 1961).

——, *La dolce vita* (Milan: Garzanti, 1981).

——, *Early Screenplays: 'Variety Lights' and 'The White Sheik'* (New York: Grossman, 1971).

——, *'8½': Federico Fellini, Director*, ed. Charles Affron (New Brunswick, NJ: Rutgers University Press, 1987).

——, *E la nave va*, eds Federico Fellini and Tonino Guerra (Milan: Longanesi, 1983).

——, '"La famiglia/The Family"', *Fellini Amarcord: Rivista di studi felliniani* vol. 6 nos 1–2 (October 2006), pp. 31–48 (unrealised story by Fellini and Tullio Pinelli for Pietro Germi with English translation by Peter Bondanella and Federico Pacchioni).

——, *Fare un film* (Turin: Einaudi, 1980).

——, *Fellini on Fellini*, eds Anna Keel and Christian Strich (New York: Da Capo Press, 1996). Original English edn (London: Eyre Methuen, 1976).

——, *Fellini Satyricon*, ed. Dario Zanelli (Bologna: Cappelli, 1969).

——, *Fellini's Casanova*, ed. Bernardino Zapponi (New York: Dell, 1977).

——, *Fellini's Satyricon*, ed. Dario Zanelli (New York: Ballantine, 1970).

——, *Fellini TV: 'Block-notes di un regista'/'I clowns'*, ed. Renzo Renzi (Bologna: Cappelli, 1972).

——, *'Il film "Amarcord"'*, eds Gianfranco Angelucci and Liliana Betti (Bologna: Cappelli, 1974).

——, *Ginger e Fred*, ed. Mimo Guerrini (Milan: Longanesi, 1986).

——, *Giulietta* (Genoa: Il melangolo, 1994).

——, '"Happy Country (Paese Felice)"/"Happy Country",' *Fellini Amarcord: Rivista di studi felliniani* vol. 6 no. 12 (October 2006), pp. 49–150 (unrealised script written with Tullio Pinelli for Mario Camerini based on an idea by Luigi Barzini, Jr; includes original and English translation by Peter Bondanella and Federico Pacchioni).

——, *Intervista sul cinema*, ed. Giovanni Grazzini (Rome: Laterza, 1983); rpt (2004) English edn, *Comments on Film*, trans. Joseph Henry (Fresno: Press of California State College at Fresno, 1988).

——, *Juliet of the Spirits*, ed. Tullio Kezich (New York: Orion Press, 1965).

——, *La mia Rimini* (Bologna: Cappelli, 1987). 2nd rev. edn (Rimini: Guaraldi, 2003). [English translation included as an extra to the Criterion DVD of the film].

——, *Il libro dei sogni*, eds Tullio Kezich and Vincenzo Mollica (Milan: Rizzoli, 2007) (deluxe facsimile edition and normal book edition), trans., *Fellini's Book of Dreams* (New York: Rizzoli, 2008).

——, *Il mio amico Pasqualino* (Rimini: Edizione della Fondazione Federico Fellini, 1997) (reproduction of original edition of 1942).

——, ed and trans. John C. Stubbs, 'Moraldo in the City' & 'A Journey with Anita' (Urbana: University of Illinois Press, 1983) [unrealised screenplays].

——, *Le notte di Cabiria* (Milan: Garzanti, 1981).

——, *'8½' di Federico Fellini*, ed. Camilla Cederna (Bologna: Cappelli, 1965).

——, *Il primo Fellini: 'Lo sciecco bianco', 'I vitelloni', 'La strada', 'Il bidone'*, ed. Renzo Renzi (Bologna: Cappelli, 1969).

——, *Prova d'orchestra* (Milan: Garzanti, 1980).

——, *Quattro film* (Introduction by Italo Calvino) (Turin: Einaudi, 1974).

——, *Raccontando di me: Conversazioni con Costanzo Costantini*, ed. Costanzo Costantini (Rome: Editori Riuniti, 1996). English version, *Fellini on Fellini*, ed. Costanzo Costantini, trans. Sohrab Sorooshian (London: Faber and Faber, 1995).

——, *Racconti umoristici* (Turin: Einaudi, 2004).

——, *'Roma' di Federico Fellini*, ed. Bernardino Zapponi (Bologna: Cappelli, 1972).

——, *Satyricon Politikon: le vignette tra guerra e partiti*, ed. Angelo Olivieri (Rome: Un mondo a parte, 2005) (previously unpublished political cartoons by Fellini).

——, *Lo sceicco bianco* (Milan: Garzanti, 1980).

——, *La Strada*, eds François-Regis Bastide, Juliette Caputo and Chris Marker (Paris: Éditions du Seuil, 1955).

——, *'"La strada" di Federico Fellini: transcrizione del film'. Fellini Amarcord: Rivista di studi felliniani* vol. 4 nos 2–3 (2004), pp. 47–159 (a continuity script taken from the moviola with a photograph of each individual shot of the film; Italian text).

——, *La Strada. L'Avant-Scène du Cinéma* no. 102 (April 1970), pp. 7–51.

——, *'La Strada': Federico Fellini, Director*, eds Peter Bondanella and Manuela Gieri (New Brunswick, NJ: Rutgers University Press, 1987).

——, *'La strada': sceneggiatura originale di Federico Fellini e Tullio Pinelli* (Rome: Edizioni Bianco e Nero, 1955).

——, *'"La strada": soggetto di Tullio Pinelli e Federico Fellini', Fellini Amarcord: Rivista di studi felliniani* vol. 4 nos 2–3 (2004), pp. 19–46 (the previously unpublished story for *La Strada*, including an English translation by Peter Bondanella).

——, *Three Screenplays: 'I Vitelloni', 'Il Bidone', 'The Temptations of Dr Antonio'* (New York: Grossman, 1970).

——, *Il viaggio di G. Mastorna*, ed. Ermanno Cavazzoni (Milan: Bompiani, 1995); rpt 2008 with a Preface by Vincenzo Mollica (Macerata: Quodlibet, 2008); English version, ed. and trans. Marcus Perryman, Preface by Peter Bondanella, *The Journey of G. Mastorna* (Oxford: Berghahn Books, 2013).

——, *I vitelloni e La strada* (Milan: Longanesi, 1989).

——, *La voce della luna* (Turin: Einaudi, 1990).

——, *La voce della luna*, ed. Lietta Tornabuoni (Florence: La Nuova Italia, 1990).

—— and Georges Simenon, *Carissimo Simenon – Mon cher Fellini: carteggio di Federico Fellini e Georges Simenon*, eds Claude Gauteur and Silvia Sager (Milan: Adelphi, 1998).

Fellini! (Milan: Skira, 2003) (catalogue of show of Fellini's drawings at the Guggenheim Museum in New York, October 2003–January 2004).

Fellini Amarcord: Rivista di studi felliniani (Rimini: Petroneno Capitani Editori, 2001). Official journal of the Fondazione Federico Fellini (volume I appeared in 2001).

Fellini e i suoi film nei disegni della collezione Renzi (Rimini: Fondazione Federico Fellini, 2004).

Filippini, Massimiliano and Vittorio Feroreli (eds), *Federico Fellini autore di testi: Dal 'Marc'Aurelio' a 'Luci del Varietà' (1939–1950)* (Bologna: Quaderni IBC, 1999).

Fofi, Goffredo and Gianni Volpi (eds), *Federico Fellini: l'arte della visione* (Grugliasco: Tipografia Torinese, 1993).

Fontemaggi, Alessandra and Giuseppe Ricci (eds), *Il cinema di carta: L'eredità di Fellini in mostra* (Milan: Edizioni Nuages, 2004) (catalogue of Rimini show of 2004 at the Fondazione Federico Fellini in Rimini).

Giacci, Vittorio (ed.), *La voce della luce: Federico Fellini* (Rome: Progetti Museali Editore, 1995).

Giacovelli, Enrico, *Tutti i film di Federico Fellini* (Turin: Lindau, 2002).

Gieri, Manuela, *Contemporary Italian Filmmaking: Strategies of Subversion – Pirandello, Fellini, Scola, and the Directors of the New Generation* (Toronto: University of Toronto Press, 1995).

Gili, Jean A., *Fellini: Le magicien du réel* (Paris: Gallimard, 2009).

—— (ed.), *Federico Fellini: Collection Positif* (Paris: Positif, 2009).

Gori, Gianfranco Miro (ed.), *Rimini e le cinéma: images, cinéastes, histoires* (Paris: Éditions du Centre Pompidou, 1989).

Grau, Jordi, *Fellini desde Barcelona* (Barcelona: Ambit Servicios Editoriales, 1985).

Gundle, Stephen, *Death and the Dolce Vita: The Dark Side of Rome in the 1950s* (Edinburgh: Canongate Books, 2011).

Hughes, Eileen Lanouette, *On the Set of 'Fellini Satyricon': A Behind-the-Scenes Diary* (New York: Morrow, 1971).

James, Clive, 'Mondo Fellini', *New Yorker* vol. 70 no. 5 (21 March 1994), pp. 154–65.

Kauffmann, Stanley, 'Fellini, Farewell', *New Republic* (31 January 1994), pp. 28–30.

Ketcham, Charles B., *Federico Fellini: The Search for a New Mythology* (New York: Paulist Press, 1976).

Kezich, Tullio, *Federico Fellini, la vita e i film* (Milan: Feltrinelli, 2002); English version, *Federico Fellini: His Life and Work*, trans. Minna Proctor (New York: Faber and Faber, 2006).

——, *Federico Fellini: The Films*, ed. Vittorio Boarini (New York: Rizzoli, 2010).

——, *Fellini* (Milan: Camunia Editrice, 1987).

——, *Il dolce cinema* (Milan: Bompiani, 1978).

——, *Fellini del giorno dopo con un alfabetiere felliano* (Rimini: Guaraldi Editore, 1996).

Koebner, Thomas, *Federico Fellini: Der Zauberspiegel seiner Filme* (Munich: Edition text+kritik, 2010).

Manara, Milo, *Due viaggi con Federico Fellini: Viaggio a Tulum – Il viaggio di G. Mastorna detto Fernet*, ed. Vincenzo Mollica (Milan: Oscar Mondadori, 2001).

Maraldi, Antonio (ed.), *'8½' di/de/by Federico Fellini: fotografie di/photographies de/photographs by Paul Ronald* (Rimini: Fondazione Federico Fellini, 2007).

Maroni, Oriana and Giuseppe Ricci (eds), *Libri di casa mia. La biblioteca di Federico Fellini* (Rimini: Fondazione Federico Fellini, 2008).

Miller, D. A., *8½* (London: BFI, 2008).

Mollica, Vicenzo, *Fellini: parole e disegni* (Turin: Einaudi, 2000). English version, *Fellini: Words and Drawings*, trans. Nina Marino, Introduction by Peter Bondanella (Ontario: Éditions Soeil, 2001).

—— (ed.), *Fellini sognatore: omaggio all'arte di Federico Fellini* (Florence: Editori del grifo, 1992).

—— (ed.), *Il grifo: speciale Oscar Fellini* vol. 3 no. 22 (March 1993).

—— (ed.), *Scenari: il fumetto e il cinema di Fellini* (Montepulciano: Editori del grifo, 1984).

—— (ed.), *Viaggio a Tulum: disegni di Milo Manara da un soggetto di Federico Fellini per un film da fare* (Montepulciano: Editori del grifo, 1991).

Monetti, Domenico and Giuseppe Ricci (eds), *Giulietta degli spiriti raccontato dagli Archivi Rizzoli* (Rome and Rimini: Centro Sperimentale di Cinematografia/Fondazione Federico Fellini, 2005).

Monti, Fiorella and Elisabetta Zanzi (eds), *Fellini e dintorni: Cinema e psicoanalisi* (Cesena: Il Ponte Vecchio, 1996).

Monti, Raffaele (ed.), *Bottega Fellini: 'La città della donne': progetto, lavorazione, film* (Rome: De Luca, 1981).

—— and Pier Marco De Santi (ed.), *L'invenzione consapevole: disegni e materiali di Federico Fellini per il film 'E la nave va'* (Florence: Artificio, 1984).

Moscati, Italo, *Fellini & Fellini – Da Rimini a Roma, inquilino a Cinecittà* (Rome: Ediesse, 2010).

Muniz, Andrea, *Viaggio al termine dell'Italia: Fellini politico* (Soveria Mannelli: Rubbettino Editore, 2012).

Murray, Edward, *Fellini the Artist*, 2nd edn (New York: Frederick Ungar Publisher, 1985).

Olivieri, Angelo, *Fellini Satyricon Politikon: Le vignette tra 'guerra' e 'partiti'* (Rome: Un mondo a parte, 2005).

Pacchioni, Federico, *Inspiring Fellini: Literary Collaboration behind the Scenes* (Toronto: University of Toronto Press, 2014).

Panicelli, Ida, *Fellini: Costumes and Fashion* (Milan and New York: Charta, 1996).

Pecori, Franco, *Federico Fellini* (Florence: La Nuova Italia, 1974).

Perry, Ted, *Filmguide to '8½'* (Bloomington: Indiana University Press, 1975).

Pettigrew, Damian, *Fellini: I'm a Born Liar* (Documentary film on DVD (2002).

——, *I'm a Born Liar: A Fellini Lexicon* (New York: Abrams, 2003).

——, *Federico Fellini: Sono un gran bugiardo: l'ultima confessione del Maestro raccolta da Damian Pettigrew* (Rome: Eleu, 2003).

Piccini, Carmen, *The Magic of Fellini* (documentary film on DVD) (2002) Distributed by Image Entertainment.

Pieri, Françoise, *Federico Fellini conteur et humoriste 1939–1942* (Perpignan: Collection Institut Jean Vigo, 2000).

Pinelli, Tullio, *'Le notti di Cabiria' con un'intervista di Maricla Boggio* (Nardò: BESA, n.d.).

Pinkus, Karen, *The Montesi Scandal: The Death of Wilma Montesi and the Birth of the Paparazzi in Fellini's Rome* (Chicago, IL: University of Chicago Press, 2003).

Prats, A. J., *The Autonomous Image: Cinematic Narration & Humanism* (Lexington: University Press of Kentucky, 1981).

Price, Barbara Anne and Theodore Price, *Federico Fellini: An Annotated International Bibliography* (Metuchen, NJ: Scarecrow Press, 1978).

Provenzano, Roberto C., *Invito al cinema di Fellini* (Milan: Mursia, 1995).

Real Dreams: Into the Dark with Federico Fellini (BBC documentary film) (1987).

Rhodie, Sam, *Fellini Lexicon* (London: BFI, 2002).

Ricci, Giuseppe (ed.), *Gli attori di Fellini: Giulietta 50 anni dopo 'La strada'* (Rimini: Fondazione Federico Fellini, 2005).

——, *Federico in Costume* (Rimini: Fondazione Federico Fellini, 2003).

—— and Marco Bertozzi (eds), *Il corpo, gli interni, la città nell'opera grafica di Federico Fellini* (Rimini: Fondazione Federico Fellini, 2002).

Romarcord Fellini 1993–2003 (Milan: Skira, 2003) (catalogue of an exhibit held in Rome and Paris in 2003–4).

Rondi, Brunello, *Il cinema di Fellini* (Rome: Edizioni di Bianco e Nero, 1965).

Rosenthal, Stuart, *The Cinema of Federico Fellini* (New York: A. S. Barnes, 1976).

Rossi, Moraldo, *Sogna, Federico, sogna: Fellini, quel mio unico perfido amico* (Reco: Le Mani, 2011).

—— and Tatti Sanguineti, *Fellini & Rossi: il sesto vitellone* (Bologna: Le Mani, 2001).

Salachas, Gilbert, *Federico Fellini: An Investigation into His Films and Philosophy*, trans. Rosalie Siegel (New York: Crown, 1969).

Sanguineti, Tatti (ed.), *Voci del varietà/Federico delle voci: I direttori di doppiaggio di Fellini* (Rimini: Fondazione Federico Fellini, 2004).

Sciannameo, Franco, *Nino Rota, Federico Fellini, and the Making of an Italian Cinematic Folk Opera 'Amarcord'* (Lewiston, NY: Edwin Mellen Press, 2005).

Scolari, Giovanni, *L'Italia di Fellini* (Cantalupo in Sabina: Edizioni Sabinae, 2008).

Secchiaroli, Tazio, *Federico Fellini*, ed. Giovanni Bertelli (Milan: Rizzoli, 2003).

——, *G. Mastorna opera incompiuta* (Palermo: Sellerio, 2000).

Sesti, Mario and Andrea Crozzoli (eds), *'8½': Il viaggio di Fellini – fotografie di Gideon Bachmann* (Pordenone: Cinemazero, 2003).

Solmi, Angelo, *Fellini* (London: Merlin Press, 1967).

Stourdzé, Sam (ed.), *Fellini: Dall'Italia alla luna* (Bologna: Edizioni Cineteca di Bologna, 2010); *Fellini. La Grande Parade* (Paris: Éditions Anabet, 2009).

Strich, Christian (ed.), *Fellini's Faces* (New York: Holt, Rinehart & Winston, 1982).

——, *Fellini's Films: The Four Hundred Most Memorable Stills from Federico Fellini's Fifteen and a Half Films* (New York: Putnam's, 1977).

Stubbs, John C., *Federico Fellini: A Guide to References and Resources* (Boston, MA: G. K. Hall, 1978).

——, *Federico Fellini as Auteur: Seven Aspects of His Films* (Carbondale: Southern Illinois University Press, 2006).

Tutto Fellini (Rome: Cinecittà International, 1994).

Tutto Fellini su CD-ROM (Rome: Editoria Elettronica Editel/Ente dello spettacolo, 1994).

Van Order, M. Thomas, *Listening to Fellini: Music and Meaning in Black and White* (Madison, NJ: Fairleigh Dickinson University Press, 2009).

Verdone, Mario, *Federico Fellini* (Milan: Il Castoro, 2006).

Zanelli, Dario, *L'inferno immaginario di Federico Fellini: cose dette da F. F. a proposito de 'Il Viaggio di G. Mastorna'* (Ravenna: Guaraldi Editore, 1995).

——, *Nel mondo di Federico* (Preface by Federico Fellini) (Turin: Nuova Edizioni ERI RAI, 1987).

Zanetti, Mauro Aprile, *La natura morta de 'La dolce vita': Un misterioso Morandi nella rete dello sguardo di Fellini* (New York: Edition Bloc-Notes, 2008).

Zanzotto, Andrea, *Filò: per il 'Casanova' di Fellini* (Milan: Mondadori, 1988); English version, *Peasants Wake for Fellini's 'Casanova' and Other Poems*, eds and trans. John P. Welle and Ruth Feldman (Urbana: University of Illinois Press, 1997).

Zapponi, Bernardino, *Il mio Fellini* (Venice: Marsilio, 1995).

Marco Ferreri

Accialini, Fulvio and Lucia Coluccelli, *Marco Ferreri* (Milan: Edizioni il Formichiere, 1979).

Ferreri, Marco, *Chiedo asilo*, ed. Maurizio Grande (Milan: Feltrinelli, 1980).

——, *L'ultima donna*, ed. Anna Maria Tatò (Turin: Einaudi, 1976).

Grande, Maurizio, *Marco Ferreri* (Florence: La Nuova Italia, 1974).

Standola, Alberto, *Marco Ferreri* (Milan: Il Castoro, 2004).

Lucio Fulci

Albiero, Paolo and Giacomo Cacciatore, *Il terrorista dei generi. Tutto il cinema di Lucio Fulci* (Rome: Un mondo a parte, 2004).

Bruschini, Antonio and Antonio Tentori, *Lucio Fulci: Il poeta della crudeltà* (Rome: Mondo Ignoto/Profondo Rosso, 2004).

Chianese, As and Gordiano Lupi, *Filmare la morte: il cinema horror e thriller di Lucio Fulci* (Piombino: Edizioni Il Foglio, 2006).

Gomarasca, Manlio, *L'opera al nero: il cinema di Lucio Fulci* (Milan: Nocturno, 2003).

Romagnoli, Michele, *L'occhio al testimone: il cinema di Lucio Fulci* (Rome: Granata Press, 1992).

Thrower, Stephen, *Beyond Terror: The Films of Lucio Fulci* (New York: FAB Press, 1999).

Matteo Garrone

De Santis, Pierpaolo, Domenico Monetti and Luca Pallanch, *Non solo Gomorra: Tutto il cinema di Matteo Garrone* (Cantalupo in Sabina: Edizioni Sabinae, 2008).

Augusto Genina

Costa, Antonio, *I leoni di Schneider: Percorsi intertestuali nel cinema ritrovato* (Rome: Bulzoni, 2002).

Germani, Sergio G. and Vittorio Martinelli (eds), *Il cinema di Augusto Genina* (Paisan di Prato: Edizioni Biblioteca dell'Immagine, 1989).

Pietro Germi

Aprà, Adriano et al. (eds), *Pietro Germi, ritratto di un regista all'antico* (Parma: Pratiche Editrice, 1989).

Caldiron, Orio, *Pietro Germi, la frontiera e la legge* (Rome: Bulzoni, 2004).

Germi, Pietro, *'L'uomo di paglia' di Pietro Germi*, ed. Fausto Montesanti (Bologna: Cappelli, 1958).

Giacovelli, Enrico, *Pietro Germi* (Milan: Il Castoro, 1997).

Sesti, Mario, *Pietro Germi: The Latin Lover* (Milan: Olivares, 1999).

——, *Tutto il cinema di Pietro Germi* (Milan: Baldini & Castoldi, 1997).

Marco Tullio Giordana

Erico-Reiter, Rosa, *'I cento passi': Marco Tullio Giordana* (Perugia: Guerra Edizioni, 2007).

Maraldi, Antonio and Angelo Turetta (eds), *'I cento passi': un film di Marco Tullio Giordana* (Florence: Edizioni Il Ponte Vecchio, 2005).

Petraglia, Sandro and Stefano Rulli, *'La meglio gioventù': un film di Marco Tullio Giordana* (Rome: RAI ERI, 2004).

Alberto Lattuada

Boledi, Luigi and Raffaele De Berti (eds), *'Luci del Varietà': pagine scelte* (Milan: Il Castoro, 1999).

Bruno, Edoardo, *Italian Directors: Alberto Lattuada* (Rome: ANICA, n.d.).

Camerini, Claudio, *Alberto Lattuada* (Milan: Il Castoro, 1982).

Cosulich, Callisto, *I film di Alberto Lattuada* (Rome: Gremese, 1985).

Lattuada, Alberto, *'La steppa' di Alberto Lattuada*, ed. Franco Calderoni (Bologna: Cappelli, 1962).

Oldoini, Enrico, *A proposito di 'Così come sei': dall'idea al film* (Bologna: Cappelli, 1978).

Turroni, Giuseppe, *Alberto Lattuada* (Milan: Moizzi Editore, 1977).

Villa, Federica, *Botteghe di scrittura per il cinema italiano: Intorno a 'Il bandito' di Alberto Lattuada* (Venice: Marsilio, 2002).

Umberto Lenzi

Gomarasca, Manlio, *Umberto Lenzi* (Milan: Nocturno Libri, 2001).

Sergio Leone

Cèbe, Gilles, *Sergio Leone* (Paris: Henri Veyrier, 1983).

Cumbow, Robert C., *Once Upon a Time: The Films of Sergio Leone* (Metuchen, NJ: Scarecrow Press, 1987).

De Fornari, Oreste, *Sergio Leone* (Milan: Moizzi Editore, 1977).

——, *Sergio Leone: The Great Italian Dream of Legendary America* (New York: Gremese, 1997).

——, *Tutti i film di Sergio Leone* (Milan: Ubulibri, 1984).

Di Claudio, Gianni, *Directed by Sergio Leone* (Chieti: Libreria Universitaria Editrice, 1990).

Donati, Roberto, *Sergio Leone: America e nostalgia* (Alessandria: Edizioni Falsopiano, 2004).

Fawell, John, *The Art of Sergio Leone's 'Once Upon a Time in the West': A Critical Appreciation* (Jefferson, NC: McFarland, 2005).

Frayling, Christopher, *Once Upon a Time in Italy: The Westerns of Sergio Leone* (New York: Abrams, 2005).

——, *Sergio Leone: Something to Do with Death* (London: Faber and Faber, 2000).

——, *Spaghetti Westerns: Cowboys and Europeans from Karl May to Sergio Leone* (London: Routledge & Kegan Paul, 1981).

Gabutti, Diego, *C'era una volta in America* (Milan: Rizzoli, 1984).

Garofalo, Marcello, *Tutto il cinema di Sergio Leone* (Milan: Baldini Castoldi Dalai, 1999).

Leone, Sergio, *'C'era una volta in America': un film di Sergio Leone – Photographic Memoirs*, ed. Marcello Garofalo (Rome: Editalia, 1988).

——, *Per un pugno di dollari*, ed. Luca Verdone (Bologna: Cappelli, 1979).

Martin, Adrian, *Once Upon a Time in America* (London: BFI, 1998).

Meyer, David N., 'Once Upon a Time, an Epic Was Shorn of Grandeur', *New York Times* (14 February 1999), p. 26, Arts Section.

Minnini, Francesco, *Sergio Leone* (Milan: Il Castoro, 2007).

Moscati, Italo, *Sergio Leone: Quando il cinema era grande* (Turin: Lindau, 2007).

Roth, Lane, *Film Semiotics, Metz, and Leone's Trilogy* (New York: Garland, 1983).

Saccutelli, Gianluca, *C'era una volta Sergio Leone* (Porto Sant'Elpidio: Ottava Musa Edizioni, 1999).

Smith, Paul, *Clint Eastwood: A Cultural Production* (Minneapolis: University of Minnesota Press, 1993).

Carlo Lizzani

De Santi, Gualtiero, *Carlo Lizzani* (Rome: Gremese, 2001).

Lizzani, Carlo, *Il cinema italiano, 1895–1979* (2 vols) (Rome: Editori Riuniti, 1979); 2nd edn, published as *Il cinema italiano dalle origini agli anni ottanta* (Rome: Editori Riuniti, 1982).

——, *'Fontamara' dal romanzo di Ignazio Silone* (Turin: Edizioni ERI, 1980).

——, *'L'oro di Roma' di Carlo Lizzani*, ed. Giovanni Vento (Bologna: Cappelli, 1961).

——, *'Il processo di Verona' di Carlo Lizzani*, ed. Antonio Savignano (Bologna: Cappelli, 1963).

Luigi Magni

Montini, Franco and Piero Spila (eds), *Il mondo di Luigi Magni* (Rome: RAI ERI, 2000).

Mario Martone

Ranucci, Georgette and Stefanella Ughi (eds), *Mario Martone* (Rome: Dino Audino Editore, 1995).

Franco Mastelli

Parigi, Stefania, *Franco Mastelli* (Milan: Il Castoro, 1992).

Raffaele Matarazzo

Prudenzi, Angela, *Raffaele Matarazzo* (Milan: Il Castoro, 1991).

Mattoli, Mario

Della Casa, Stefano, *Mario Mattoli* (Milan: Il Castoro, 1990).

Mario Monicelli

Borghini, Fabrizio, *Mario Monicelli: cinquantanni di cinema* (Pisa: Edizioni Master, 1985).

Della Casa, Stefano, *Mario Monicelli* (Milan: Il Castoro, 1982).

Mario Monicelli (Milan: Mediane, 2007).

Mondadori, Sebastiano (ed.), *La commedia umana: Conversazioni con Mario Monicelli* (Milan: Il saggiatore, 2005).

Monicelli, Mario, *L'arte della commedia*, ed. Lorenzo Codelli (Bari: Edizioni Dedalo, 1986).

——, *'I compagni' di Mario Monicelli*, ed. Pio Baldelli (Bologna: Cappelli, 1963).

Giuliano Montaldo

Miles, Keith and David Butler, *Marco Polo* (New York: Dell, 1982).

Montaldo, Giuliano and Vincenzo Labella, *'Marco Polo': come nasce un film* (Turin: Edizioni RAI, 1980).

Nanni Moretti

Coco, Giuseppe, *Nanni Moretti: cinema come diario* (Milan: Bruno Mondadori, 2006).

De Bernardinis, Flavio, *Nanni Moretti* (Milan: Il Castoro, 2006).

Giovannini, Memmo, Enrico Magrelli and Mario Sesti, *Nanni Moretti* (Naples: Edizioni scientifiche italiane, 1986).

Mascia, Gianfranco (ed.), *Qualcosa di sinistra: Intervista a Nanni Moretti* (Genoa: Frilli, 2002).

Mazierska, Ewa and Laura Rascaroli, *The Cinema of Nanni Moretti: Dreams and Diaries* (New York: Columbia University Press and Wallflower Press, 2004); rpt, *Il cinema di Nanni Moretti: Sogni & diari* (Rome: Gremese, 2006).

Menarini, Roy, *Nanni Moretti: 'Bianca'* (Turin: Lindau, 2007).

Ranucci, Georgette and Stefanella Ughi, *Nanni Moretti* (Rome: Dino Audino Editore, 2001).

Villa, Federica, *Nanni Moretti: 'Caro diario'* (Turin: Lindau, 2007).

Maurizio Nichetti

Orto, Nuccio, *Maurizio Nichetti: un comico, un autore* (Chieti: Métis, 1990).

Pistoia, Marco, *Maurizio Nichetti* (Milan: Il Castoro, 1997).

Ermanno Olmi

Allegretti, Elisa and Giancarlo Giraud (eds), *Ermanno Olmi: L'esperienza d'Ipotesi Cinema* (Genoa: Le Mani, 2001).

Aprà, Adriano (ed.), *Il cinema di Ermanno Olmi* (Parma: Incontri Cinematografici Monticelli Terme–Parma, 1979).

Dillon, Jeanne, *Ermanno Olmi* (Milan: Il Castoro, 1986).

Olmi, Ermanno, *L'albero degli zoccoli*, ed. Giacomo Gambetti (Turin: Edizioni RAI, 1980).

——, 'E venne un uomo': un film di Ermanno Olmi, eds Giacomo Gambetti and Claudio Sorgi (Milan: Garzanti, 1965).

Tabanelli, Giorgio, Ermanno Olmi: nascita del documentario poetico (Rome: Bulzoni, 1987).

Pier Paolo Pasolini

Bertini, Antonio, Teoria e tecnica del film in Pasolini (Rome: Bulzoni, 1979).

Bandeau, Agnès, Pasolini, Chaucer and Boccaccio: Two Medieval Texts and Their Translation to Film (Jefferson, NC: McFarland, 2006).

Boccaccio, Giovanni, The Decameron: A Norton Critical Edition, eds and trans. Mark Musa and Peter Bondanella (New York: Norton, 1977) (includes essay on Boccaccio and Pasolini's Decameron by Ben Lawton and all novelle adapted by Pasolini).

De Benedictis, Maurizio, Linguaggi dell'aldilà: Fellini e Pasolini (Rome: Lithos, 2000).

De Giusti, Luciano, I film di Pier Paolo Pasolini (Rome: Gremese, 1983).

Duflot, Jean (ed.), Entretiens avec Pier Paolo Pasolini (Paris: Éditions Pierre Belfond, 1970).

Estève, Michel (ed.), Pier Paolo Pasolini: un 'cinéma de poésie' (Paris: Études Cinématographiques nos 112–14, 1977).

——, Pier Paolo Pasolini: le mythe et le sacré (Paris: Études Cinématographiques nos 109–11, 1976).

Ferrero, Adelio, Il cinema di Pier Paolo Pasolini (Venice: Marsilio, 2005).

Fusillo, Massimo, La Grecia secondo Pasolini (Florence: La Nuova Italia, 1996).

Gervais, Marc, Pier Paolo Pasolini (Paris: Éditions Séghers, 1973).

Gordon, Robert S. C., Pasolini: Forms of Subjectivity (New York: Oxford University Press, 1996).

Green, Naomi, The Cinema of Heresy (Princeton, NJ: Princeton University Press, 1991).

Indiana, Gary, Salò or The 120 Days of Sodom (London: BFI, 2000).

Luzi, Alfredo and Luigi Martellini (eds), Pier Paolo Pasolini (Urbino: Argalia Editore, 1973).

Manzoli, Giacomo, La voce e il silenzio nel cinema di Pier Paolo Pasolini (Bologna: Pendragon, 2001).

Maggi, Armando, The Resurrection of the Body: Pier Paolo Pasolini from Saint Paul to Sade (Chicago, IL: University of Chicago Press, 2008).

Moscati, Italo, Pasolini passione: Vita senza fine di un artista trasparente (Rome: Ediesse, 2005).

Murri, Serafino, Pier Paolo Pasolini (Milan: Il Castoro, 2000).

Pasolini, Pier Paolo, 'Edipo re': un film di Pier Paolo Pasolini (Milan: Garzanti, 1967).

——, Heretical Empiricism, ed. Louise K. Barnett and trans. Ben Lawton and Louise K. Barnett (Bloomington: Indiana University Press, 1988); rpt (Washington: New Academia Publishing, 2005) (with a new translation of Pasolini's 'Repudiation of the Trilogy of Life').

——, 'Medea': un film di Pier Paolo Pasolini (Milan: Garzanti, 1970).

——, Oedipus Rex, trans. John Matthews (New York: Frederick Ungar, 1971).

——, Poems, trans. Norman MacAfee (New York: Vintage, 1982).

——, The Ragazzi, trans. Emile Capouya (New York: Grove Press, 1968).

——, Teorema (Milan: Garzanti, 1968).

——, Trilogia della vita, ed. Giorgio Gattei (Milan: Mondadori, 1987).

——, Uccellacci e uccellini (Milan: Garzanti, 1975).

——, Il vangelo secondo matteo (Milan: Garzanti, 1964).

——, A Violent Life, trans. William Weaver (London: Jonathan Cape, 1968).

Passannanti, Erminia, Il Corpo & il Potere: 'Salò o le 120 Giornate di Sodoma' di Pier Paolo Pasolini (Leicester: Troubadour, 2004).

Petraglia, Sandro, Pier Paolo Pasolini (Florence: La Nuova Italia, 1974).

Pier Paolo Pasolini (Milan: Mediane, 2007).

Pier Paolo Pasolini: A Future Life (Rome: Fondazione Pier Paolo Pasolini, 1989).

Quintavalle, Uberto Paolo, Giornate di Sodoma: ritratto di Pasolini e del suo ultimo film (Milan: Sugar, 1976).

Rhodes, John David, Stupendous, Miserable City: Pasolini's Rome (Minneapolis: University of Minnesota Press, 2007).

Rohdie, Sam, The Passion of Pier Paolo Pasolini (Bloomington: Indiana University Press, 1995).

Rumble, Patrick, Allegories of Contamination: Pier Paolo Pasolini's 'Trilogy of Life' (Toronto: University of Toronto Press, 1966).

—— and Bart Testa (eds), Pier Paolo Pasolini: Contemporary Perspectives (Toronto: University of Toronto Press, 1994).

Ryan-Scheutz, Colleen, Sex, the Self, and the Sacred: Women in the Cinema of Pier Paolo Pasolini (Toronto: University of Toronto Press, 2007).

Salvini, Laura, I frantumi del tutto. Ipotesi e letture dell'ultimo progetto cinematografico di Pier Paolo Pasolini: 'Porno-teo-kolossal' (Bologna: CLUEB, 2004).

Schwartz, Barth David, Pasolini Requiem (New York: Pantheon, 1992).

Siciliano, Enzo, Vita di Pasolini (Milan: Mondadori, 2005).

——, Pasolini: A Biography, trans. John Shepley (New York: Random House, 1982).

Snyder, Stephen, Pier Paolo Pasolini (Boston: Twayne, 1980).

Stack, Oswald (ed.), Pasolini on Pasolini (Bloomington: Indiana University Press, 1970).

Viano, Maurizio, A Certain Realism: Making Use of Pasolini's Film Theory and Practice (Berkeley: University of California Press, 1993).

Villani, Simone, Il Decameron allo specchio: Il film di Pasolini come saggio sull'opera di Boccaccio (Rome: Donzelli, 2004).

Willemen, Paul (ed.), Pier Paolo Pasolini (London: BFI, 1977).

Giovanni Pastrone

Alovisio, Silvio and Alberto Barbera (eds), Cabiria & Cabiria (Milan: Il Castoro, 2006) (Introduction by Martin Scorsese).

Berretto, Paolo and Gianni Dondolino (eds), 'Cabiria' e il suo tempo (Milan: Il Castoro, 1998).

Radicati, Roberto and Ruggero Rossi (eds), *'Cabiria': visione storica del III secono a. c.* (Turin: Museo Nazionale del Cinema, 1977).

Usai, Paolo Cherchi, *Giovanni Pastrone* (Milan: Il Castoro, 1986).

Elio Petri

Bacci, Federico, Nicola Guarneri and Stefano Leone (eds), *Elio Petri, appunti su un autore* (Milan: Feltrinelli, 2005 [includes DVD]).

Gili, Jean A. (ed.), *Elio Petri* (Nice: Faculté des Lettres et Sciences Humaines, 1974).

Rossi, Alfredo, *Elio Petri* (Milan: Il Castoro, 1979).

Antonio Pietrangeli

Maraldi, Antonio, *Antonio Pietrangeli* (Milan: Il Castoro, 1992).

Martini, G., G. Morelli and G. Zappoli, *Un'invisibile presenza: Il cinema di Antonio Pietrangeli* (Milan: Il Castoro, 1998).

Gillo Pontecorvo

Bignardi, Irene, *Memorie estorte a uno smemorato: vita di Gillo Pontecorvo* (Milan: Feltrinelli, 1999).

Celli, Carlo, *Gillo Pontecorvo: From Resistance to Terrorism* (Lanham, MD: Scarecrow Press, 2005).

Ghirelli, Massimo, *Gillo Pontecorvo* (Milan: Il Castoro. 1979).

Mellen, Joan, *Filmguide to 'The Battle of Algiers'* (Bloomington: Indiana University Press, 1973).

Pontecorvo, Gillo, *Gillo Pontecorvo's 'The Battle of Algiers'*, ed. Piernico Solinas (New York: Scribner's, 1973).

——, *'Giovanna': storia di un film e del suo restauro*, ed. Antonio Medici, 2nd edn (Rome: Ediesse, 2010).

Dino Risi

Bellumori, Cinzia, *Dino Risi* (Rome: ANICA, n.d.).

D'Agostini, Paolo, *Dino Risi* (Milan: Il Castoro, 1995).

Miccichè, Lino (ed.), *'Una vita difficile' di Dino Risi: Risate amare nel lungo dopoguerra* (Venice: Marsilio, 2000).

Risi, Dino, *I miei mostri* (Milan: Mondadori, 2004).

Viganò, Aldo, *Dino Risi* (Milan: Moizzi Editore, 1977).

Francesco Rosi

Bolzoni, Francesco, *I film di Francesco Rosi* (Rome: Gremese, 1986).

Gili, Jean A. (ed.), *Francesco Rosi: Cinéma et pouvoir* (Paris: Éditions du Cerf, 1976).

Mancino, Anton Giulio and Sandro Zambetti, *Francesco Rosi* (Milan: Il Castoro, 1998).

Rosi, Francesco, *Salvatore Giuliano*, ed. Tullio Kezich (Rome: Edizioni FA, 1961).

——, *'Uomini contro' di Francesco Rosi*, ed. Callisto Cosulich (Bologna: Cappelli, 1970).

—— and Eugenio Scalfari (eds), *'Il caso Mattei': un corsaro al servizio della repubblica* (Bologna: Cappelli, 1972).

Testa, Carlo (ed.), *Poet of Civic Courage: The Films of Francesco Rosi* (Westport, CT: Praeger, 1996).

Roberto Rossellini

Aprà, Adriano (ed.), *Roma città aperta di Roberto Rossellini* (Rome: Comune di Roma Assessorato alla cultura, 1994).

——, *Rosselliniana: bibliografia internationale, dossier 'Paisà'* (Rome: Di Giacomo Editore, 1987) (contains a complete international Rossellini bibliography).

——, *Rossellini India 1957* (Rome: Cinecittà International, 1991).

Baldelli, Pio, *Roberto Rossellini: i suoi film (1936–1972) e la filmografia completa* (Rome: Edizioni Samonà e Savelli, 1972).

Bondanella, Peter, *The Films of Roberto Rossellini* (New York: Cambridge University Press, 1993).

Brunette, Peter, *Roberto Rossellini* (New York: Oxford University Press, 1987).

Bruni, David, *Roberto Rossellini 'Roma città aperta'* (Turin: Lindau, 2006).

Bruno, Edoardo, *Rossellini Bergman: Europe Six* (Rome: Cinecittà Estero, 1990).

—— (ed.), *R. R. Roberto Rossellini* (Rome: Bulzoni, 1979).

De Marchis Rossellini, Marcella, *Un matrimonio riuscito* (Milan: Il Castoro, 1996).

Di Giammatteo, Fernaldo, *Roberto Rossellini* (Florence: La Nuova Italia, 1990).

Forgacs, David, *Rome Open City* (London: BFI, 2000).

——, Sarah Lutton and Geoffrey Nowell-Smith (eds), *Roberto Rossellini: Magician of the Real* (Bloomington: Indiana University Press, 2001).

Gallagher, Tag, *The Adventures of Roberto Rossellini: His Life and Films* (New York: Da Capo Press, 1998).

Gelley, Ora, *Stardom and the Aesthetics of Neorealism: Ingrid Bergman in Rossellini's Italy* (London: Routledge, 2012).

Gottlieb, Sidney (ed.), *Rossellini's 'Open City'* (New York: Cambridge University Press, 2003).

Guarner, José Luis, *Roberto Rossellini*, trans. Elisabeth Cameron (New York: Praeger, 1970).

Johnson, William Bruce, *Miracles and Sacrilege: Roberto Rossellini, the Church, and Film Censorship in Hollywood* (Toronto: University of Toronto Press, 2008).

Masi, Stefano and Enrico Lancia, *I film di Roberto Rossellini* (Rome: Gremese, 1987).

Michelone, Guido, *Invito al cinema di Rossellini* (Milan: Mursia, 1996).

Parigi, Stefano (ed.), *'Paisà': Analisi del film* (Venice: Marsilio, 2005).

Ranvaud, Dan (ed.), *Roberto Rossellini* (London: BFI Dossier no. 8, 1981).

Roberto Rossellini (Rome: Ente autonomo di gestione per il cinema, 1987) (catalogue for retrospective at Houston, Texas).

Roncoroni, Stefano, *La storia di 'Roma città aperta'* (Bologna: Le Mani e Cineteca, 2006).

Rondolino, Gianni, *Roberto Rossellini* (Milan: Il Castoro, 1977).

——, *Roberto Rossellini* (Turin: UTET, 1989).

Rossellini, Isabella, *In the Name of the Father, the Daughters, and the Holy Spirits: Remembering Roberto Rossellini* (Munich: Schirmer-Mosel, 2006).

Rossellini, Roberto, *Era notte a Roma*, ed. Renzo Renzi (Bologna: Cappelli, 1960).

——, *Il mio metodo*, ed. Adriano Aprà (Venice: Marsilio, 1987).

——, *My Method: Writings & Interviews*, ed. Adriano Aprà (New York: Marsilio, 1992).

——, *Quasi un'autobiografia*, ed. Stefano Roncoroni (Milan: Mondadori, 1987), French edn, *Fragments d'une autobiographie* (Paris: Éditions Ramsay, 1987).

——, *La trilogia della guerra*, ed. Stefano Roncoroni (Bologna: Cappelli, 1972).

——, *The War Trilogy*, ed. Stefano Roncoroni (New York: Grossman, 1973).

Serceau, Michel, *Roberto Rossellini* (Paris: Éditions du Cerf, 1986).

Trasatti, Sergio, *Rossellini e la televisione* (Rome: La Rassegna Editrice, 1978).

—— (ed.), *CD-ROM: Roberto Rossellini su CD-ROM* (Rome: Editoria Elettronica Editel, 1994).

Verdone, Mario, *Roberto Rossellini* (Paris: Éditions Séghers, 1963).

Walter Ruttman

Camerini, Claudio (ed.), *'Acciaio': un film degli anni trenta* (Turin: Nuova Ediziioni ERI, 1990).

Gabriele Salvatores

Ammaniti, Niccolò, *I'm Not Scared*, trans. Jonathan Hunt (Edinburgh: Canongate Books, 2003).

Grassi, Raffaella, *Territori di fuga: il cinema di Gabriele Salvatores* (Alessandria: Edizioni Falsopiano, 1997).

Malvasi, Luca, *Gabriele Salvatores* (Milan: Il Castoro, 2005).

Merkel, Flavio, *Gabriele Salvatores* (Rome: Dino Audino Editore, 1993).

Ettore Scola

Bertini, Antonio, *Ettore Scola: Il cinema e io – Conversazione con Antonio Bertini* (Rome: Officina Edizioni Cinecittà Internazional, 1996).

Bíspuri, Ennio, *Ettore Scola, un umanista nel cinema italiano* (Rome: Bulzoni, 2006).

Bondanella, Peter, 'La comédie "métacinématographique" d'Ettore Scola', in Michel Serceau (ed.), *La comédie italienne de Don Camillo à Berlusconi. CinémAction* no. 42 (1987), pp. 91–9.

De Santi, Pier Marco and Rossano Vittori, *I film di Ettore Scola* (Rome: Gremese, 1987).

Ellero, Roberto, *Ettore Scola* (Milan: Il Castoro, 1996).

Gieri, Manuela, *Contemporary Italian Filmmaking: Strategies of Subversion – Pirandello, Fellini, Scola, and the Directors of the New Generation* (Toronto: University of Toronto Press, 1995).

Hedges, Inez, 'Forms of Representation in *La Nuit de Varennes*', in *Breaking the Frame: Film Language and the Experience of Limits* (Bloomington: Indiana University Press, 1991).

Kezich, Tullio and Alessandra Levantesi (eds), *'Una giornata particolare': un film di Ettore Scola – incontrarsi e dirsi addio nella Roma del '38* (Rome: Edizioni Lindau, 2003).

Koebner, Thomas and Fabienne Liptay (eds), *Ettore Scola* (Munich: Edition text+kritik, 2010).

Marinucci, Vincio, *Ettore Scola* (Rome: ANICA, n. d.).

Scola, Ettore, *Una giornata particolare* (Milan: Longanesi, 1977).

Zagarrio, Vito (ed.), *Trevico–Cinecittà: L'avventuroso viaggio di Ettore Scola* (Venice: Marsilio, 2002).

Mario Soldati

Malavasi, Luca, *Mario Soldati* (Milan: Il Castoro, 2006).

Silvio Soldini

Colombo, Silvia, *Il cinema di Silvio Soldini* (Alesssandria: Edizioni Falsopiano, 2002).

Luciano, Bernadette, *The Cinema of Silvio Soldini: Dream–Image–Voyage* (Leicester: Troubadour, 2008).

Paolo and Vittorio Taviani

Accialini, Fulvio and Lucia Coluccelli, *Paolo e Vittorio Taviani* (Milan: Il Castoro, 1979).

Aristarco, Guido, *Sotto il segno dello scorpione: il cinema dei fratelli Taviani* (Florence: Casa Editrice G. D'Anna, 1977).

Cooperativa Nuovi Quaderni (eds), *Cinema e utopia: i fratelli Taviani, ovvero il significato dell'esagerazione* (Parma: Nuovi Quaderni, 1974).

De Poli, Marco, *Paolo e Vittorio Taviani* (Milan: Moizzi Editore, 1977).

De Santi, Pier Marco, *I film di Paolo e Vittorio Taviani* (Rome: Gremese, 1988).

Ferrucci, Riccardo (ed.), *La bottega Taviani: un viaggio nel cinema da San Miniato a Hollywood* (Florence: La Casa Usher, 1987).

——, *Paolo and Vittorio Taviani: Poetry of the Italian Landscape* (New York: Gremese, 1996).

Ledda, Gavino, *Padre Padrone: The Education of a Shepherd*, trans. George Salmanazar (New York: Urizen Books, 1979).

Orto, Nuccio, *La notte dei desideri: il cinema dei fratelli Taviani* (Palermo: Sellerio Editore, 1987).

Paolo & Vittorio Taviani: Leone d'Oro, Venezia 1986 (Rome: ANICA, 1986) (catalogue of the Taviani retrospective at the 1986 Venice Film Festival).

Taviani, Paolo and Vittorio, *Padre padrone* (Bologna: Cappelli,1977).

——, *San Michele aveva un gallo – Allonsanfan* (Bologna: Cappelli, 1974).

——, *Sotto il segno dello Scorpione – Il prato* (Turin: ERI, 1981).

——, with the collaboration of Tonino Guerra, *Good Morning, Babylon* (London: Faber and Faber, 1987).

Giuseppe Tornatore

Hope, William, *The Films of Giuseppe Tornatore* (Leicester: Troubador, 2001).

Massimo Troisi

Giusti, Marco (ed.), *Massimo Troisi: Il mondo intero proprio – pensieri e battute* (Milan: Mondadori, 2004).

Skármeta, Antonio, *The Postman*, trans. Katherine Silver (New York: Hyperion, 1993).

Troisi, Massimo and Anna Pavignano, *Ricomincio da tre: sceneggiatura dal film* (Milan: Feltrinelli, 1981).

Tonino Valerii

La Selva, Tonino, *Tonino Valerii* (Milan: Nocturno Libri, 2000).

Paolo Virzì

Virzì, Paolo and Francesco Bruni, *Caterina va in città* (Venice: Marsilio, 2003).

—— and Francesco Piccolo, *My Name Is Tanino* (Rome: Arcana Fiction, 2002).

Luchino Visconti

Bacon, Henry, *Visconti: Explorations of Beauty and Decay* (Cambridge: Cambridge University Press, 1998).

Baldelli, Pio, *Luchino Visconti* (Milan: Mazzotta Editore, 1973; rev. edn, 1982).

Bencivenni, Alessandro, *Luchino Visconti* (Milan: Il Castoro, 1999).

Bruni, David and Veronica Pravadelli (eds), *Studi viscontiani* (Venice: Marsilio, 1997).

de Carvalho, Caterina d'Amico (ed.), *Viscontiana: Luchino Visconti e il melodrama verdiano* (Milan: Mazzotta, 2001).

De Giusti, Luciano, *I film di Luchino Visconti* (Rome: Gremese, 1985).

Di Giammatteo, Fernaldo and Aldo Bernardini (eds), *La controversia Visconti* (Rome: Ateneo, 1976).

Estève, Michel (ed.), *Luchino Visconti: L'histoire et l'esthétique* (Paris: Études Cinématographiques nos 26–7, 1963).

Ferrera, Giuseppe, *Luchino Visconti* (Paris: Éditions Séghers, 1970).

Ferrero, Adelio (ed.), *Visconti: il cinema* (Modena: Stampa Cooptip, 1977).

Mancini, Elaine, *Luchino Visconti: A Guide to References and Resources* (Boston, MA: G. K. Hall, 1986).

Miccichè, Lino, *Luchino Visconti: Un profilo critico* (Venice: Marsilio, 1996).

—— (ed.), *'Il Gattopardo'* (Naples: Electa, 1996).

——, *'La terra trema' di Luchino Visconti: analisi di un capolavoro* (Turin: Centro Sperimentale di Cinematografia, 1994).

Nowell-Smith, Geoffrey, *Luchino Visconti*. London: BFI, 2003).

Partridge, Colin, *'Senso': Visconti's Film and Boito's Novel* (Lewiston, NY: Edwin Mellen Press, 1991).

Pravadelli, Veronica (ed.), *Il cinema di Luchino Visconti* (Rome: Biblioteca di Bianco e Nero, 2000).

——, *Visconti a Volterra: La genesi di 'Vaghe stelle dell'Orsa … '* (Turin: Edizioni Lindau, 2000).

Renzi, Renzo and Caterina d'Amico de Carvalho (eds), *Visconti: il mio teatro* (2 vols) (Bologna: Cappelli, 1979).

Rohdie, Sam, *Rocco and His Brothers* (Bloomington: Indiana University Press, 1993).

Rondolini, Gianni, *Luchino Visconti* (Turin: UTET, 1981).

Schifano, Laurence, *Luchino Visconti: Les feux de la passion* (Paris: Perrin, 1987); *Luchino Visconti: The Flames of Passion*, trans. William S. Byron (London: Collins, 1990).

Servadio, Gaia, *Luchino Visconti: A Biography* (New York: Franklin Watts, 1983).

Stirling, Monica, *A Screen of Time: A Study of Luchino Visconti* (New York: Harcourt Brace Jovanovich, 1979).

Tonetti, Claretta, *Luchino Visconti* (Boston, MA: Twayne, 1983).

Tramontana, Gaetano, *Invito al cinema di Luchino Visconti* (Milan: Mursia, 2003).

Villien, Bruno, *Visconti* (Barcelona: Calmann-Lévy, 1986) (in French).

Visconti, Luchino, *Bellissima*, ed. Enzo Ungari (Bologna: Cappelli, 1977).

——, *Boccaccio '70* (eds), Carlo Di Carlo and Gaio Fratini (Bologna: Cappelli, 1962).

——, *'La caduta degli dei (Götterdämmerung)' di Luchino Visconti*, ed. Renzo Renzi (Bologna: Cappelli, 1969).

——, *Il film 'Il gattopardo' e la regia di Luchino Visconti*, ed. Renzo Renzi (Bologna: Cappelli, 1963).

——, *Gruppo di famiglia in un interno*, ed. Renzo Renzi (Bologna: Cappelli, 1975).

——, *'Ludwig' di Luchino Visconti*, ed. Renzo Renzi (Bologna: Cappelli, 1973).

——, *'Morte a Venezia' di Luchino Visconti*, ed. Renzo Renzi (Bologna: Cappelli, 1971).

——, *'Le notti bianche' di Luchino Visconti*, ed. Renzo Renzi (Bologna: Cappelli, 1957).

——, *Ossessione*, ed. Enzo Ungari (Bologna: Cappelli, 1977).

——, Michelangelo Antonioni and Antonio Pietrangeli, *Il processo di Maria Tarnowska: la sceneggiatura di un film mai realizzato*, ed. Gianno Rondolino (Milan: Il Castoro, 2006).

——, *'Rocco e i suoi fratelli' di Luchino Visconti*, eds Guido Aristarco and Gaetano Carancini (Bologna: Cappelli, 1960).

——, *'Senso' di Luchino Visconti*, ed. G. B. Cavallaro (Bologna: Cappelli, 1955).

——, *La terra trema*, ed. Enzo Ungari (Bologna: Cappelli, 1977).

——, *Three Screenplays: 'White Nights', 'Rocco and His Brothers', 'The Job'*, trans. Judith Green (New York: Orion Press, 1970).

——, *Two Screenplays: 'La Terra Trema', 'Senso'*, trans. Judith Green (New York: Orion Press, 1970).

——, *Vaghe stelle dell'orsa*, ed. Renzo Renzi (Bologna: Cappelli, 1965).

—— and Suso Cecchi d'Amico, *Alla ricerca del tempo perduto* (Milan: Mondadori, 1986).

Lina Wertmüller

Bullaro, Grace Russo, *Man in Disorder: The Cinema of Lina Wertmüller in the 1970s* (Leicester: Troubadour, 2007).

Cerulo, Maria Pia et al. (eds), *Lina Wertmüller: il grottesco e il barocco in cinema* (Assisi: ANCCI, 1993).

Ferlita, Ernest and John R. May, *The Parables of Lina Wertmüller* (New York: Paulist Press, 1977).

Prats, A. J., *The Autonomous Image: Cinematic Narration & Humanism* (Lexington: University Press of Kentucky, 1981).

Wertmüller, Lina, *The Head of Alvise* (New York: Morrow, 1982).

——, *The Screenplays of Lina Wertmüller*, trans. Steven Wagner (New York: Quadrangle, 1977).

Luigi Zampa

Zampa, Luigi, *Il prima giro di manovella: il romanzo sull'ambiente del cinema* (Rome: Trevi Editore, 1980).

Franco Zeffirelli

Zeffirelli, Franco, *Il mio Gesù* (Milan: Sperling & Kupfer, 1977).

——, *Zeffirelli: An Autobiography* (New York: Weidenfeld & Nicolson, 1986).

Valerio Zurlini

Martini, Giacomo (ed.), *Valerio Zurlini: una regione piena di cinema* (Regione Emilia-Romagna/Cinecittà Holding, n. d.) (Retrospective of Zurlini's cinema with essays in Italian and English translations).

Minotti, Gianluca, *Valerio Zurlini* (Milan: Il Castoro, 2001).

ITALIAN CAMERAMEN, SCRIPTWRITERS, MUSICIANS AND SPECIAL-EFFECTS TECHNICIANS

Amidei, Sergio, *Soggetti cinematografici*, ed. Lorenzo Codelli (Gorizia: Comune di Gorizia, 1985) (collection of unrealised scripts).

Bernardini, Aldo and Jean A. Gili (eds), *Cesare Zavattini* (Paris: Éditions du Centre Pompidou, 1990).

Bertelli, Gian Carlo and Pier Marco De Santi (eds), *Omaggio a Flaiano* (Pisa: Giardini, 1987).

Borin, Fabrizio (ed.), *La filmografia di Nino Rota* (Città di Castello: Olschki, 1999).

Cecchi d'Amico, Suso, *Storie di cinema (e d'altro)*, ed. Margherita d'Amico (Milan: Bompiani, 2002).

De Leonardis, Giancarlo, *Le mani nei capelli: il mestiere del parrucchiere nel cinema* (Pomezia: Wella Peliti, 2004).

De Santi, Pier Marco, *La musica di Nino Rota* (Rome: Laterza, 1983).

—— (ed.), *Omaggio a Nino Rota* (Pisa: Assessorato per gli Istituti Culturali del Comune di Pistoia, 1981).

Dyer, Richard, *Nino Rota: Music, Film and Feeling* (London: BFI/Palgrave Macmillan, 2010).

Flaiano, Ennio, *Un film alla settimana*, ed. Tullio Kezich (Rome: Bulzoni, 1988).

Gasparra, Enrico (ed.), *Storaro: Scrivere con la luce* (Rome: Electa, 2001).

Giacomini, Stefania, *Alla scoperta del set: Con venti personaggi che il cinema lo fanno* (Rome: RAI ERI, 2004).

Lombardi, Francesco (ed.), *Fra cinema e musica del Novecento: Il caso Nino Rota* (Città di Castello: Olschki, 2000).

Masi, Stefano, *Costumisti e scenografi del cinema italiano: volume primo* (L'Aquila: La Lanterna Magica, 1989) (analysis of major Italian set and costume designers).

——, *Nel buio della moviola: introduzione alla storia del montaggio* (L'Aquila: La Lanterna Magica, 1985) (analysis of Italian editing and interviews with such master editors as Ruggero Mastroianni, Nino Barbagli and Leo Catozzo).

——, *Storie della luce* (L'Aquila: La Lanterna Magica, 1985) (analysis of Italian cameramen, including Tonnino delli Colli, Gianni di Venanzo, Otello Martelli, Giuseppe Rotunno and Vittorio Storaro).

Parigi, Stefania, *Fisiologia dell'immagine: Il pensiero di Cesare Zavattini* (Turin: Lindau, 2006).

Pellizzari, Lorenzo (ed.), *Carlo Rambaldi e gli effetti speciali* (San Marino: AIEP Editore, 1987).

Pirro, Ugo, *Celluloid* (Milan: Rizzoli, 1983).

Praturlon, Pierluigi, *Pierluigi on Photography* (Milan: Photology, 2006).

Prédal, René, *La photo de cinéma suivi d'un dictionnaire de cent chefs opérateurs* (Paris: Éditions du Cerf, 1985) (analysis of Italian cameramen, including Tonnino delli Colli, Pasqualino De Santis, Gianni di Venanzo, Otello Martelli, Giuseppe Rotunno and Vittorio Storaro).

Storaro, Vittorio, *Scrivere con la luce/Writing with Light* (3 vols) (I. *La luce/Light*; II. *I colori/Colours*; III. *Gli elementi/The Elements*) (Milan: Electa/Accademia dell'Immagine, 2001–3).

Tonino Guerra (Rimini: Maggioli Editore).

Tonti, Aldo, *Odore di cinema* (Florence: Vallecchi Editore, 1964) (memoirs of one of Italy's most important cameramen).

Trubiano, Marisa S., *Ennio Flaiano and His Italy: Postcards from a Changing World* (Madison, NJ: Fairleigh Dickinson University Press, 2010).

Zavattini, Cesare, *Basta con i soggetti!*, ed. Roberta Mazzoni (Milan: Bompiani, 1979).

——, *Diario cinematografico*, ed. Valentina Fortichiari (Milan: Bompiani, 1979).

——, *'I misteri di Roma' di Cesare Zavattini*, ed. Francesco Bolzoni (Bologna: Cappelli, 1963).

——, *Neorealismo ecc ...*, ed. Mino Argentieri (Milan: Bompiani, 1979).

——, *Opere*, ed. Renato Barilli (Milan: Bompiani, 1974).

——, *Zavattini: Sequences from a Cinematic Life*, trans. William Weaver (Englewood Cliffs, NJ: Prentice-Hall, 1970).

Index

Note: This index concentrates on names, Italian titles (understood as film titles unless identified otherwise), film genres and movements. Whenever possible and available, biographical dates and film-release dates are also included here. English versions of Italian original titles are provided in the text. Due to the length of this index, authors of critical works in the bibliographies at the end of each essay as well as in the general bibliography are not indexed here (with the exception of important historical figures). Page numbers in *italic* refer to illustrations. *n* = endnote; *t* = table. Alphabetisation is letter-by-letter, e.g. *Al di là del bene e del male* follows Albertini and Alcover.

LIST OF ILLUSTRATIONS

While considerable effort has been made to correctly identify the copyright holders, this has not been possible in all cases. We apologise for any apparent negligence and any omissions or corrections brought to our attention will be remdied in any future editions.

La dolce vita, Riama Film/Pathé Consortium Cinéma; *Panorama de la Place Saint Marc pris d'un bateau, Venise*, Lumière; *La caduta di Troia*, Itala Film; *Assunta Spina*, Caesar Film; *Maciste all'Inferno*, Fert/Pittaluga Film; *Attrici e attori in pigiama* cover (Milan: Casa Editrice Ceschina, 1926); *I Nostri Artisti*, Leopoldo Fregoli issue (Palermo: Casa Editrice Salvatore Biondo, c. 1904); *In Penombra* magazine cover, no. 6, June 1919; *Come si possa diventare artisti cinematografici* (Firenze: Scuola Cinematografica Azzurri, 1915, 1917, 1926); *Il fuoco*, Itala Film; *Ma l'amore mio non muore*, Film Artistica Gloria; *Quo vadis?* (1913), Cines; *Cabiria*, Itala Film; *Scipione l'Africano*, Consorzio Scipione; *Maciste alpino*, Italo Film; *La signora di tutti*, Novella Film; *Gli uomini che mascalzoni!*, Cines; *La donna della montagna*, Lux Film; *Darò un milione*, Novella Film; *Un garibaldino al convento*, Cristallo Film/Industria Cinematografica Italiana; *The Decameron*, P.E.A./Les Productions Artistes Associés/Artemis Filmgesellschaft; *Last Tango in Paris*, P.E.A./Les Productions Artistes Associés; *Lion of the Desert*, Falcon International Productions; *Nettezza urbana*, I.C.E.T.; *La città si difende*, Cines; *Ladri di biciclette*, Produzione De Sica S.A.; *Germania anno zero*, Tevere Film; *L'Onorevole Angelina*, Lux Film/Ora Film; *Ossessione*, Iniziative Cinematografiche Internazional; *Sciuscià*, Cinematografica Alfa; *Paisà*, O.F.I.; *I bambini ci guardano*, Scalera Film; *Voltati Eugenio*, Intercontinental Film Company/ Les Films du Losange/Société Nouvelle des Etablissements Gaumont; *Il ladro di bambini*, © Erre Produzione/© Alia Film;

Le ragazze di Piazza di Spagna, Bellotti Film; *Scusa ma ti chiamo amore*, Checchi Gori Group/Medusa Film/Sky Italia; *Riso amaro*, Lux Film; *Pane amore e fantasia*, Titanus; *Death in Venice*, Alfa Cinematografica/P.E.C.F.; *Roman Holiday*, Paramount Pictures Corporation; *Il gattopardo*, Titanus/La Société Nouvelle Pathé-Cinema/Société Générale Cinématographique; *Quo Vadis* (1951), © Loew's Incorporated; *The Barefoot Contessa*, © Figaro Incorporated; *Roma città aperta*, Excelsa Film/CIS-Nettunia; La strada, © Ponti-De Laurentiis; *Accattone*, Cino Del Duca/Arco Film; *Le fatiche di Ercole*, O.S.C.A.R. Film/Galatea Film; *Il terrore dei barbari*, Standard Produzione; *Il colosso di Rodi*, Cineproduzioni Associate/Procusa Films/Comptoir Français de Production Cinématographiques/Cinéma Télévision International; *Cartagine in fiamme*, Lux Film/Gallone-Film/Lux Compagnie Cinématographique de France; *Messalina Venere imperatrice*, Cineproduzione Emo Bistolfi; *Il trionfo dei dieci gladiatori*, Cineproduzioni Associate/Producciones Cinematograficas Balcázar; *Mondo cane*, Cineriz di Angelo Rizzoli; *Addio Zio Tom*, Euro International Films; *Cannibal Holocaust*, F.D. Cinematografica; *Per un pugno di dollari*, Jolly Film/Constantin Film/Madrid Ocean Films; *Per qualche dollaro in più*, P.E.A./Arturo González P.C./Constantin Film; *Il buono, il brutto, il cattivo*, P.E.A.; *Django*, B.R.C. Produzione/Tecisa; *Amici miei*, Rizzoli Film; *I nuovi mostri*, Deam Films; *L'ingorgo: una storia impossibile*, Clesi Cinematografica/Gaumont International/Greenwich Film Production/Paris Filmédis/José Frade Producciones Cinematograficas/Albatros-Filmproduktion; *Le mani sulla città*, Galatea Film/Societé Cinématographique Lyre; *La battaglia di Algeri*, Igor Film/Casbah Film; *Prima della rivoluzione*, Iride Cinematografica/Cineriz Il conformista*, © Mars Film S.p.A.; *The Night Porter*, Lotar Film/Ital-Noleggio Cinematografico; *I vampiri*, Athena Cinematografica/Titanus; *La maschera del demonio*, Reteitalia/Anfri; *L'uccello dalle piume di cristallo*, © Seda Spettacoli S.p.A.; *Suspiria*, Seda Spettacoli S.p.A.; *I corpi presentano tracce di violenza carnale*, Compagnia Cinematografica Champion; *Zombi 2*, Variety Film; *Fanfan la tulipe*, Les Films Ariane/Filmsonor/Rizzoli Editore/Produzione Film Giuseppe Amato; *L'eclisse*, © Robert Hakim/© Raymond Hakim; *Rocco e i suoi fratelli*, Titanus/Les Films Marceau; *Intervista*, Ajosha Productions; *Fellini's Casanova*, © Kapustan Industries N.V.; *Gomorra*, © Fandango Produzione Cinematografica; *Il divo*, © Indigo Film/© Lucky Red/© Parco Film/© Babe Sarl/© StudioCanal/©Arte France Cinéma; *Le conseguenze dell'amore*, © Fandango Produzione Cinematografican/Indigo Film; *Romanzo criminale*, © Cattleya Films/© Crime Novel Films (UK) Ltd/Babe Sarl; *Guido che sfidò le Brigate Rosse*, Sistina Cinematografica/L'Occhio di Genova/Nuova Cooperativa Doppiaggio/Pianeta Spettacolo; *La prima linea*, Lucky Red/Les Films du Fleuve/RTBF (Télévision Belge); *Tutti a casa*, Orsay Films/Dino De Laurentiis Cinematografica; *Il giardino dei Finzi-Contini*, Documento Film/CCC Filmkunst; *La vita é bella*, Melampo Cinematografica srl; *A Natale mi sposo*, Mari Film/Medusa Film/Sky Cinema; *Natale a Beverly Hills*, Filmauro/Fast Lane Productions; *Natale in crociera*, Filmauro; *Ho voglia di te*, Cattleya Films; *La meglio gioventù*, RAI Fiction; *Altra Europa*, Azul Film; *Le stelle inquiete*, A&G/Kitchenfilm/Testukine; *Vittime*, Rai Cinema/Offside/Rai Teche/Ministerio per i Beni e le Attività Culturali; *Noi credevamo*, Palomar/Rai Cinema/Les Films d'Ici; *Io sono l'amore*, © First Sun/Mikado Film; *Le quattro volte*, © Vivo Film/© Essential Filmproduktion/© Invisible Film/© Ventura Film; *Bianco e nero*, Cattleya Films/Rai Cinema; *Good Morning, Aman*, DNA Cinematografica/Rai Cinema/Relief s.r.l./Ministerio per i Beni e le Attività Culturali; *Come un uomo sulla terra*, ZaLab; *Ercole al centro della terra*, SPA Cinematografica; *La frusta e il corpo*, Leone Film/Vox Film/Francinor/Paris International Productions; *Diabolik*, © Dino De Laurentiis Cinematografica S.p.A./Marianne Productions S.A.; *Reazione a catena*, Nuova Linea Cinematografica; *Amarcord*, © F.C. Produzioni/P.E.C.F.; *Buongiorno, notte*, © Filmalbatros/© Rai Cinema; *La stanza del figlio*, © Sacher Film; *Il sorpasso*, Fair Film/INCEI Film/Sancro Film; Pasqualino Settebellezze, Medusa Distribuzione; *Raging Bull*, © United Artists Corporation; *Sweet Charity*, Universal Pictures; *All That Jazz*, © Columbia Pictures Corporation; *Stardust Memories*, © United Artists Corporation; *8½*, Cineriz di Angelo Rizzoli/Francinex.